Just the Thing

Just the Thing

SELECTED LETTERS OF
JAMES SCHUYLER
1951–1991

REVISED ANNIVERSARY EDITION

EDITED BY WILLIAM CORBETT

Turtle Point Press : Brooklyn, New York

Just the Thing: Selected Letters of James Schuyler,
1951–1991, Revised Anniversary Edition

Requests for permission to make copies of any part of the work should be sent
to: Turtle Point Press, 208 Java Street, Fifth Floor, Brooklyn, New York 11222,
info@turtlepointpress.com

Library of Congress Control Number: 2023945279
Paperback ISBN: 978-1-885983-81-7
eBook ISBN: 978-1-885983-35-0

Design and composition by Jeff Clark
at Wilsted & Taylor Publishing Services

Frontispiece: Drawing of James Schuyler by Darragh A. Park
Cover image: Portrait of James Schuyler by Fairfield Porter © 2023
The Estate of Fairfield Porter / Artists Rights Society (ARS), New York

Cover design by Misha Beletsky

Printed in the United States of America
First Edition

Contents

Introduction

It's just the thing
to do what with? To
open letters? No, it
is just the thing, an
object, dark, fierce
and beautiful in which
the surprise is that
the surprise, once
past, is always there:
which to enjoy is
not to consume.

JAMES SCHUYLER,
"A Stone Knife"

James Schuyler's friend Kenward Elmslie, to whom "A Stone Knife" is addressed, put it succinctly: "Jimmy wrote letters for the most civilized of reasons, to inform and to entertain." Schuyler liked to provide his friends—he wrote very few business letters—with his guide to beloved Italian cities, gardening advice, recipes, and quotes from his omnivorous reading. He loved to amuse them with gossip and anecdotes drolly told, but his letters are entertaining by virtue of their tone of spoken intimacy. This came naturally to Schuyler, as did his desire to amuse himself when writing letters. He could not bear to write a dull or pretentious sentence. When he falls into pomposity he catches himself, turns on a dime, and corrects his course with a joke at his own expense.

Because of their tone, but not only because of it, Schuyler's letters are all of a piece. When I took on the project of editing these letters, a friend of

Schuyler's exclaimed to me, "Great! More Jimmy!" Yes, emphatically, more Jimmy. To those who know and love his poetry, novels, art criticism, and diary, the same man and writer is present in these letters. They have his virtues: wit, humor, intelligent observations about writing, writers, and painting expressed off-handedly, bits of brilliant description of nature and weather, and a sense of the world lived in, sharply observed, and lovingly accepted for all that it is. All of a piece but with Schuyler's voice adjusted to different friends, pitched to their particular wavelengths. And, of course, his voice changes over the years as he ages and his correspondents extend beyond his contemporaries to younger friends.

What emerges is Schuyler's self-portrait, unconsciously drawn, and a portrait of the New York art world—these letters are almost exclusively to poet and painter friends—in which he moved for forty years and from which he was often apart. This apartness helps account for the number of letters he wrote. When you live in the same city as your friends you do not, at least he did not, write letters to them. But Schuyler lived throughout the 1960s with the Fairfield Porter family in Southampton, Long Island, and, during the summers, on Great Spruce Head Island off the Maine coast. It also matters that one of his two great correspondents John Ashbery (Joe Brainard was the other) lived mostly in Paris between 1955 and 1965, years in which Schuyler was the perfect pen pal.

Schuyler wrote for a third civilized reason—to keep in touch. That his letters communicated his physical presence across space and time became evident at the memorial service held for him by The Poetry Project at New York's St. Mark's Church. Old friends Jane Freilicher and Kenneth Koch memorialized their friend by reading from his letters to them. They expected that Schuyler's voice, manner, and something of his essence could be summoned in sentences he had written forty years earlier, and they were right.

In a 1985 letter to Anne Porter, Schuyler declares, "I do not regard personal letters as literature." This attitude is precisely what makes his letters so readable today. He wrote for the here and now with never a glance over his shoulder at posterity. Schuyler knew that in the realm of letters, literature takes care of itself.

James Schuyler was born November 9, 1923, in Chicago, Illinois. His parents, Marcus and Margaret Connor Schuyler, Midwesterners by birth, lived in the suburb of Downers Grove, where Mark Schuyler ran his own small newspaper. About six years later, when Mark took a job on the *Washington Post*, the family moved to Washington, D.C. There in 1929 Schuyler's mother divorced his father. Schuyler remembered his father as a "heavy, jolly well-read man," "enchantingly wonderful" but a "compulsive gambler" whom his mother could not live with. After the divorce Schuyler saw his father—he died in 1942—a few times.

A formative influence on Schuyler was his maternal grandmother, Ella Slater Connor, who came to live with the boy and his mother after the divorce. Schuyler remembered that around the time he began grade school she took him to Washington's museums, including the Freer, the Corcoran, and, most often, the Smithsonian. She also taught him the names of birds and flowers and became the model for the grandmother in his first novel, and first published book, *Alfred and Guinevere* (1958).

In 1931 Schuyler's mother married her second husband, Fredric Ridenour, a building contractor. They lived in Washington and later in Chevy Chase, Maryland, where Schuyler (now James Ridenour), completed grade school. In 1935 the family (Schuyler now had a half-brother, Fredric) moved to Buffalo, New York, then to East Aurora, a Buffalo suburb. Here Schuyler spent his teenage years under the roof of an unsympathetic stepfather. He later described his home life as something out of "a novel by Dostoyevsky." The senior Ridenour so disliked his stepson's love of reading that as punishment he denied him a library card. Schuyler managed to get around this and during high school discovered both poetry and his desire to become a writer. He also became aware of and accepted his homosexuality.

Schuyler entered Bethany College, a small school affiliated with the Disciples of Christ, in West Virginia in 1941. He was a poor student who later claimed to have played bridge through the two and a half years before he flunked out in January 1943. In his poem "A Few Days," Schuyler remembers:

> When I told Alex Katz I
> went to college in West
> Virginia, he said in that way of his, "Nah,
> you're Harvard." Wish I
> were but I'm a lot more panhandle than I am Cambridge
> Mass.

Of the first generation of New York School Poets, only Schuyler and Barbara Guest did not attend Harvard. John Ashbery, Kenward Elmslie, Kenneth Koch, and Frank O'Hara were all there in the late 1940s, and all graduated. (Schuyler referred to them as the "Harvard Wits.") Perhaps Schuyler had little need of college. Frank O'Hara said that Schuyler alone among their friends knew grammar and punctuation like "a real writer." His letters show that others depended upon him for editorial advice.

From Bethany, Schuyler joined the Navy, and after training at the sonar school in Key West (a year later Frank O'Hara attended the same school) he sailed convoy duty in the North Atlantic. On a visit to New York City he met the poet Chester Kallman, lover of W. H. Auden. On another New York visit in 1944 Schuyler got drunk, and his ship sailed without him. The details of what followed are sketchy but, in a panic, Schuyler remained AWOL until he either turned himself in or was apprehended. During the hearing that followed, his homosexuality, declared or admitted, led to his dishonorable discharge. After this Schuyler made his way back to New York City, found a clerical job at the Voice of America, met Bill Aalto, and moved into a Greenwich Village cold-water flat with him.

Aalto, who served in the Abraham Lincoln Brigade during the Spanish Civil War and lost a hand while training American combat troops during World War II, lived with Schuyler for the next four and a half years. Apart from what Schuyler described in his poems, details of their relationship are few. In 1947 they went to Italy on $6,500 Schuyler received from the sale of an Arkansas farm that had been left to him by his paternal grandmother. Aalto had plans to write a history of guerilla warfare, and Schuyler planned to write not poetry but short stories that might, he later told an interviewer, appear in *The New Yorker*. It was in this year that Schuyler gave up the name Ridenour and resumed his "own name."

Schuyler and Aalto took an apartment in Florence where, in 1948, Auden and Kallman visited them. This led to their house-sitting Auden's villa on the island of Ischia that winter. One night Aalto, violent when drunk, attacked Schuyler, after which they broke up. These lines from "Dining Out with Doug and Frank" recall the incident:

> Bill
> Aalto, my first lover (five tumultuous
> years found Bill chasing me around
> the kitchen table — in Wystan Auden's
> house in Forio d'Ischia — with
> a carving knife. He was serious
> and so was I . . .

Auden returned to Ischia, and that April (1949), Schuyler became, briefly, his secretary. This led to an epiphany of sorts. After typing a batch of Auden's poems that would appear in *Nones*, Schuyler later remembered thinking to himself, "Well, if this is poetry, I'm certainly not going to write any myself." If he was not writing poetry at the time, at least he was thinking of doing so.

Following travels through Italy and to Paris, Schuyler returned to New York, where he and his lover, the painter Charles Heilemann, moved into Chester Kallman's apartment. Through John Hohnsbeen, then working for the art dealer Curt Valentin, Schuyler found work at the Kleemann Gallery on 57th Street, and his life in New York began.

Letters

TO JOHN HOHNSBEEN[1]

Thursday Nov. 15, 1951

121 Westchester Ave.
White Plains, N.Y.[2]

John Ducks,

I am well. How are you? It is wonderful here, etc. *Long* to see you (those pretty eyes!), to hear that dear voice saying those scandalous things. Well, well, so you scalped a British-American novelist![3] *Good* for you; go it boy! When are you leaving for the West? Have you memorized the *Bhagavad-Gita* yet? So you think Vedanta is more *us* than Catholicism, Anglo-, Roman- or otherwise? Do answer me seriously; you know if there is anything I approve of more than another it's the sexy road to Heaven. Tell me all: is it Vedanta, the Mystic Way, Huxley, Heard & Hollywood, or is it still Connecticut,[4] the dear deer, the steady lay, the unprivate walls?

I love it here; real mad fun. Especially the evening game of gin-rummy before beddy-by (9:30); the 8 p.m. cup of cocoa. Mad, and I'm learning to *box*; now that's really all I've wanted to do all my life; box: hit people for fun. Sluggo Jim, the new me. I hear you & Billy Budd[5] know a cozy gym somewhere. How nice; I'm all for it, and want you to do something: lure Charles[6] into working

1. See glossary.

2. Bloomingdale Hospital, a mental hospital that Schuyler entered on October 24 following a manic episode. He remained until January and while there wrote his first significant poem, "Salute."

3. Christopher Isherwood (1904–1986), a novelist and close friend of W.H. Auden who came to America with the poet in 1939. During World War II he made his way to Hollywood, where he lived for the rest of his life.

4. Philip Johnson (1906–1905), architect. He was the first director of the Museum of Modern Art's Architecture Department before he left in 1949 to design his Connecticut residence, Glass House, "the unprivate walls" referred to here. At the time, Hohnsbeen and Johnson were lovers.

5. Actor Chuck Nolte, then appearing in Benjamin Britten's opera *Billy Budd*.

6. Charles Heilemann, a painter and a lover of Schuyler's.

out regularly. He hates being *so paunchy* (My dear, like pillows!), and he needs physical exercise. I don't want to return to the world and find a nervous wreck on my hands. So, tip him off. I'm seeing him tomorrow and will put a *bee* in his ear.

Could you come see me? I wonder—anyway: Mondays, Fridays, 2 to 5 PM; 3 visitors a session. Sundays too, but most Sundays I assume you're in the country. Speak to Charles he co-ordinates (not very well) my visitors. Perhaps if you cried a little Mr. V's[7] heart would soften. If there are any grubby copies of artsie magazines around the gallery, bring them with you. I'm starved for art.

Remember me to Mr. V, Jane[8], Philip [Johnson][9]: to everybody. But you're my blue-eyed baby. Come see me; I'll teach you how to shoot a mean left jab.

I do miss you ducks—

All love, Jimmy

P.S. An especial big squeeze to Don Gaynor[10]—tell him to send me a view card.
P.P.S. Friday Eve: Donny[11] gave me your [ ] message. Sweet baby! How's stepmama? Still lapping up the sauce?

TO JOHN HOHNSBEEN

[129 East 17th Street, New York]

June 10, 1954

Dear John D.,

No news makes dull letters. The only good news I've heard has been David's[12] report on you, for I gather your cure won't be as severe as I'd feared it might be.[13] I don't mean to diminish the earth-shaking boredom of the San

---

7. Curt Valentin (1902–1954), German expatriate and prominent art dealer who represented the work of painter Max Beckmann. He owned the Buchholz Gallery in Manhattan where Hohnsbeen worked from 1948–54.

8. Jane Wade, Valentin's secretary.

9. All editorial interpolations are in brackets. All the words in parentheses are Schuyler's.

10. Friend of Hohnsbeen.

11. Donald Windham (1920–2010), American novelist, short-story writer, and autobiographer.

12. David Protetch (1921–1969), friend of Chester Kallman at the University of Michigan. Protetch became an MD and was Auden's and Igor Stravinsky's doctor. Auden dedicated the poem "The Art of Healing" to his memory.

13. Hohnsbeen was being treated for tuberculosis at a Bedford, New York, sanitarium.

or the endlessness of even one minute spent there, but, still, he did make us all feel better about you, even if you would doubtless like to give him a good crack. I think it's terribly healthy to want to hit your doctor, don't you?

Speaking of healthy; I was terribly startled to hear Chester[14] describe a popular song as "sick." I asked him where he'd picked that up, and he said he'd thought of it by himself. I hadn't the heart to tell him how out of date "sick" is. It made me feel so 1949, all of a sudden, as though I were just about to go to my first party on East 93rd Street[15], when my brown silk suit was new.

As a matter of fact, we had quite a pleasant evening at Chester's, night before last. Me and Arthur[16] and Alexi Haieff[17] for dinner, and Sam Barber[18] and Chuck Turner[19] for after (though they arrived in the middle), and Pete[20] managed to brighten it up by rolling in soused about 9 with two chaps off the Queen of Bermuda in tow, one young and one decidedly older. The older one brightened the conversation with some salty cockney sayings, and all went well until he seemed to decide that Alexi was his idea of breast of milk fed chicken, which, innocent lamb, he didn't realize was happening at all. So A and I whipped him off (Alexi that is) to a nice safe tough bar on 2nd Avenue where a darling colored girl was singing "Red Head", and we all stayed up too late.

Last night I had dinner with Jane F[21], who sends you her regards and well wishes. I'm always fascinated by the paintings she does after a show: there are

14. Chester Kallman (1921–1975), poet and a friend of Schuyler's from the early 1940s. Met W. H. Auden in 1939 and shortly after became his lover, a relationship that lasted over thirty years. Kallman published three books of poetry and collaborated with Auden on the libretto of *The Rake's Progress*. He is mentioned in several Schuyler poems.

15. Honhsbeen's apartment.

16. Arthur Gold (1920–1990), pianist and writer. A Canadian, Gold met the pianist Robert Fizdale (1920–1995) at Manhattan's Juilliard School in 1944, the year they formed their duo piano team Gold and Fizdale. They performed an extensive repertory until their retirement in 1982. Gold and Fizdale then co-authored biographies of Misia Sert and Sarah Bernhardt. In the summer of1953 Gold and Schuyler became lovers, a relationship that lasted for three years.

17. Alexi Haieff (1914–1994), American composer born in Russia. *The New Grove Dictionary* describes his music as "neo-classical, moving with vitality and clean crispness."

18. Samuel Barber (1910–1981), American composer.

19. Chuck Turner, composer and Samuel Barber's lover.

20. Pete Butorac, a drinking buddy of Kallman's who lived with Kallman and Auden for many years as a lodger.

21. Jane Freilicher (1924–2014), painter. Her most recent show had been February 23 to March 10, 1954, at the Tibor de Nagy Gallery. See glossary.

always a couple that are very pretty, and look as though they should have been in the show, and a couple she plainly won't finish and clearly wonders why she started, and then a couple in which it seems to me I can detect what the new work will be like, in so far as it's different from the old. There was one yesterday that didn't really "work" (vork, oh vell, you know what I mean), but all the background was so beautifully and interestingly organized. I think she has an almost natural gift for color—the gift, I mean, seems to simplify and develop naturally, naturally, without her working at it too much—but her real preoccupation is composition, of wanting to be modern and flat, and at the same time to do justice to space and depth, without making dead areas "of weight"—or whatever they're called—in her pictures. In itself I think that's rare, but most so in a woman's paintings: how loose and vaguely placed so much is in the paintings of even someone as good as Berthe Morisot[22]; and the ones who do get a kind of strength of composition seem so often to get it by dealing strictly with the surface, or a middle distance just below the surface, and end by making something very like arabesques. And so you see, I think her new pictures will be stronger, lovelier, deeper than ever.

For myself, I've been on my own almost a week, and enjoying a delicious kind of slobbiness. It won't last, but while it lasts, what bliss. It's like the lady who thought she had a screw in her navel, so the doctor gave her a screw-driver and told her to unscrew it, and her ass fell off. I imagine she felt marvelously relaxed without it. I have that one twinge about 9:30 every morning—"O Christ! I'm late! again."—then I remember and sink back into the most delicious sleep that ever was. Of course I'm full of plans, and ideas, and ambition . . . but it is lovely to have a week in town when I can take busses when they're not crowded, say, in the middle of the afternoon.

Next Wednesday we're going out to Fairfield's[23] for a few days, and the Sunday after that up to New Canaan, and then I begin to work, and to visit you. Rest well: I expect to find you looking daisy fresh, and somewhat cross. So many send you their spontaneous good wishes, Jane F and John A, Chester K and Bobby F, Hal F and John M, Grace H and All the Kids at the Cedar[24]: in a word, every one I speak to who knows you, and their name is legion.

22. Berthe Morisot (1841–1895), French impressionist painter.

23. Fairfield Porter (1907–1975), painter and art critic. The Porters lived in Southampton, New York. See glossary.

24. The Cedar Tavern, 9th Street off University Place in Greenwich Village and later at 10th Street and University Place. Painters of the abstract expressionist generation, like Franz Kline, Willem de Kooning, and Philip Guston, gathered there. In *Larry Rivers: A Memoir,*

Arthur sends you his love, and we'll soon be to see you, sooner than you think. Give my greetings to Philip.

love, Jimmy

TO FAIRFIELD PORTER

[New Canaan, Connecticut]

Bastille Day eve [1954]

Dear Fairfield,

Your letter delighted me. I think it's the wittiest one I've ever gotten.

We were in town yesterday afternoon and evening, and, after seeing a movie at the Art, I ran into Larry[25] in the Cedar, and we were all sorry to hear that your back has been bothering you. I hope the shots help.

New York seemed rather frantic and tense yesterday; I'm so glad I'm not spending the summer there.[26] I suppose one has to be out of it a while to feel its size and self-absorption, its peculiar toughness. And then Larry was hungover and silly, and there was a scene with the waiter, brought on by Gandy Brodie's[27] rudeness (whatever his problems and qualities, I think it's all right to say that as Gandy stands, and sits, he's a horrid young man).

I am so interested in what you say about "willed" and "organic"; it's a problem I find myself stuck with every day with my novel.[28] Parts of it seem to me to go along very well; unfortunately, from the beginning certain dramatic events are implied, and each time I try to go into the implied story (as opposed

---

Frank O'Hara wrote, "In the Cedar we often wrote poems while listening to the painters argue and gossip." Here Schuyler refers to John Ashbery (1927–2017), poet, see glossary; Chester Kallman; Robert Fizdale; Hal Fondren, a roommate of Frank O'Hara's at Harvard and an editor in New York City; John Bernard Myers (1914–1987), director of Tibor de Nagy Gallery; and Grace Hartigan (1922–2008), painter.

25. Larry Rivers (1923–2002), painter. Fairfield Porter painted his portrait in 1951.

26. Schuyler was spending the summer in the New Canaan, Connecticut, home, rented by Arthur Gold, of the singer and music patron Alice Esty. Esty's husband, who worked in advertising, wrote the line, "I'd walk a mile for a Camel."

27. Gandy Brodie (1924–1975), painter.

28. *Alfred and Guinevere*. Schuyler began the novel in 1953. It would not be completed and published by Harcourt, Brace until 1958. In 2000 the *New York Review of Books* reissued the novel.

to the story that gets invented page by page) I seem to lose my tone. The tone seems to me anti-melodramatic, but I have willed the characters into a melo-dramatic situation, so that while they can talk about what has happened or will or may happen, it seems almost impossible for a strongly active situation to occur. I don't know if this tells why I think organic has anything to do with it; I suppose I mean partly a quality in a work of art of completeness in itself, as delightful in art as it is in a melon, and also, a way of making art. That if, at the beginning, I had not implied events outside the story more dramatic than those I describe, I could more easily bring natural and spontaneous drama out of the story itself. So this melon of mine, I am afraid, will never thoroughly ripen. (I take consolation from the maxim of learning through doing.)

Arthur Weinstein bought a Hartl[29] oil. It looks lovely in his apartment, and I gather from John Hohnsbeen that Hartl badly needs the money. It's nice to know of an exchange that gives satisfaction in several quarters.

I can't work up any strong feeling about Connecticut; it's very bushy. On the other hand, it has pleasant semi-rural moments, and I love paddling in the un-naturally blue waters of the pool.

I don't know yet when we leave for Austria; probably the first week in August. I keep forgetting I'm going, and then when I remember, I feel thrilled. I'm afraid for me Europe will always be followed by an exclamation point. It's such a treat to go there.

Your touch-typing improves by leaps and bounds. I hope this finds you feel-ing better. Take care of yourself, and let me hear from you soon. Arthur sends affectionate greetings.

As ever, Jimmy

TO FAIRFIELD PORTER

[Venice, Italy]

Sat Oct 16 [1954]

Dear Fairfield,

I'm going to Rome, then I'm going to try to find a place near there where I can stay for two months. I've heard of a town that's not exactly in the moun-tains, but sort of in the foothills of the Abruzzi, called Anticoli Corrado, that

---

29. Arthur Weinstein was an interior decorator who had an affair with Robert Fizdale dur-ing the time Schuyler and Arthur Gold were together. Leon Hartl (1907–1992) was a painter whose landscapes, still lifes, and paintings of girls were little known then and remain so to-day. Fairfield Porter described him as "very much a painter's painter" and admired his work.

sounds likely. I think Kokoschka[30] once stayed there quite a while. Anyway, I'll try to get Bill Weaver[31] on a bus with me Monday and go look at it. Otherwise, I may settle for one of what are called the Castelli, in the Alban hills, south of Rome.

I guess I did write Frank [O'Hara] in a rather 18th century way about mountains, or rather, the Alps. Really, they're very beautiful, especially in the evening, when the light goes up the buildings, and then up the valley, and onto the tops of the mountains. But there's something very ugly, too. I think it's that there are everywhere the signs of what was the original appeal for strangers — the simplicity of the places, of the people and their life — that isn't the true tone anymore. So many ski-lifts and hospitals, hostels and hikers — they're all all right, but then the "pretty" towns, like Innsbruck, really are ugly — it's like hunting out 18th century New Canaan; it just isn't what New Canaan's about. Somehow, in France and Italy, the industrial age is a part of the country — I've never seen anything incongruous in a line of pylons striding along beside the Po, among the poplars and the great huge farm houses; but in the Austrian Alps I had the impression of the corruption and disappearance of an agricultural life that's being replaced by something more complicated and less satisfying.

I put off going to the Biennale until last week (since it was Venice itself I was most interested in). I thought Bill's[32] pictures showed up wonderfully well, and the one that belongs to you was one of the two I liked best. In a big international show his work seemed quieter and more subtle than I would have thought of it as being. His pictures contain so much. The other thing I loved at the Biennale was a big Courbet show. But I didn't find the World's Fair Merchandise Mart atmosphere of the thing very sympathetic for looking at pictures. (I rather feel that way about the Academia. I wish half the pictures were back in the churches and scuole they came from. And, with a little care, they could be.)

This letter seems all complaints and querulousness. And I've enjoyed Venice so much! Perhaps it's the evening-before-departure atmosphere — I have my nerves about going off to find another place to stay, and Arthur and Bobby are in a real tizzy. Arthur was very sick with bronchitis, and though he's well now, he has to go off and give a number of concerts next week, still feeling tired and not feeling prepared. So the coming week has real terrors for them.

30. Oskar Kokoschka (1886–1980), Austrian painter.

31. William Weaver (1923–2013), translator from the Italian then resident in Rome. In his introduction to *Open City: Seven Writers in Postwar Rome* (1999), Weaver recalls his early years in the city.

32. Willem de Kooning (1904–1998), painter. This was de Kooning's second of three appearances in the Venice Biennale.

I'll write you as soon as I'm settled. Arthur sends his best to you all, and so do I.

love, Jimmy

PS: after I finished the letter, I started straightening up my junk, and found this, so I send it, as it seems to show me in a slightly more pleasant relationship to mountains! The object is a wood fish talisman I found and Arthur bought in an antique shop in Kitzbuhl.

> *How nicely the whittle marks*
> *suit the shape of the fish.*
> *How nice that it's not painted silver,*
> *but blue, like a river,*
> *and gleams just a little,*
> *like a fish seen at night.*
> *It frowns on one side of its face*
> *and smiles on the other.*
> *How bright the air is in the morning,*
> *how smoky and strange in the evening,*
> *in the mountains where it was made.*

love, Jimmy

TO JANE FREILICHER

[Rome, Italy]

Nov 3 [1954]

Dear Jane,

It's raining. I hate what I've been writing. I've spent more money than I should, and wonder how I'll get through the weekend. I have a peculiar feeling in the ball of my right foot (sort of between a fish hook and a feather). And oh yes, Bill Weaver is coming by in an hour to take me to a cocktail party I don't want to go to, because I know the people are already offended with me for not having looked them up. And the electricity keeps going off. Otherwise, I'm fine. How are you?

The boys are in England, after a big success in Belgium, and will be there next week. Arthur was very sick in Venice, with bronchitis—he's OK now, though really too broke down to be touring.

I meant my gloom to strike a lighter note than this—maybe it's because I went to see *Waterfront*[33] last night, then read in bed Keats' last letters and all about his death. I bought myself some reading books, but it turns out the cheeriest one is a selected Mathew Arnold, who assures us in one verse that old age brings neither peace nor ease, just diminished powers, less sleep, and regret for the time when one at least imagined old age might be nice. Oi. What a camp that one is. A real lead shoe-nik.

But I like Rome, and so would you. Though that academy—what a bunch. They make an off-night forum at the artist's club[34] sound like "Socrate".[35]

I seem to be in more of a state of mind to receive a letter than to write one. What are you doing? Are you going to show this year? Does Grace continue on her fantastic course? Have any of our lads found (or for that matter, sought) gainful employment? Frank wrote me a very funny letter about an outing he took with you, Joe,[36] John [Ashbery] and Hal [Fondren]. You emerged very well, and John was caught in characteristic poses.

Now I'll climb into my fancy Dan and go laugh it up with what Bill calls some "really very chic people, and quite amusing." Help. Write.

love, Jimmy

33. *On the Waterfront* (1954), directed by Elia Kazan and starring Marlon Brando and Eva Marie Saint.

34. The Club was founded in 1948 or 1949 at sculptor Ibram Lassaw's 6th Avenue and 12th Street loft by a number of downtown artists who had hung out at the nearby Waldorf Cafeteria. Among the regulars were sculptors Philip Pavia, Landes Lewitin, and James Rosati and painters Willem de Kooning, Milton Resnick, Mercedes Matter, and Franz Kline. Until 1955 the Club put on readings, concerts, talks, and dances. By far the most lively and memorable Friday nights were given over to panels of artists, which ignited fights that organizer Pavia has described as "fantastic."

35. Cantata by the French composer Erik Satie (1866–1925).

36. Joe LeSueur (1924–2001), writer and Frank O'Hara's roommate from 1955 to 1965 in four Manhattan apartments. In 2003 Farrar, Straus and Giroux published his book *Digressions on Some Poems by Frank O'Hara*.

TO FAIRFIELD PORTER

Rome

Sunday, Nov 7 [1954]

Dear Fairfield,

I so much enjoy your letter and poems, and Katy's poems, that I want to tell you right away that I haven't delayed answering, but only got them yesterday. They followed me to the country, which I had left for Rome, then followed me back. Italians, I think, like to keep letters, just a little, and dream about them, from a feeling of perhaps romance about the United States. Whatever the reason, I could go to Anguillara, eat lunch, and be back in Rome in the space of three hours; a trip it took your letter a week to make. (The real reason, I suspect, is a feeling Italians have for the proprieties. Anyone who has mail forwarded, expects it to be delayed; so if a letter takes a few days longer than necessary, that only makes its proper nature, as "forwarded mail," that much clearer.)

May I say what I like about the poems?[37] Well, yes, of course I may. I like "The Mountain" and "To the Mainland" best—I think the first is more consistent all the way through, but my preference is for the second, as a poem that I can get further into—the difference between the beautifully suggested action of "giant slowly penetrable forests" and the act of getting up and going, thinking as one goes. The first stanza I like as much as any of your poems I've read (I mean I like it a great deal), but the second stanza doesn't seem to me quite as good as it could be. The first line of it seems to me poetical after the preceding stanza (perhaps a "higher" tone; but I don't think the poem needs it). "Float then" sounds like an inversion to me for "then you float" ("float" seems to suggest a boat at rest on the water, rather than one in a noisy motion); after the simplicity of "fresh morning" and "shining sky" I don't like "sky-white water" or "glassy top" for the surface of water. To stop this carping, all I find to complain of is in the first four lines of the second stanza (I wonder about the distribution of articles, why some nouns get them and others don't), and I think that simplifying them a little, and letting one or two qualities be implied, would solve it. There are so many pretty summer evening lines in the sestina, that I wish I liked the whole poem. I love the idea of dwelling on the gradualness of a summer evening in a series of stanzas in which the things spoken of don't change; but I think the form of the sestina, rather than strengthening this, weakens it:

37. Both poems appear in *Fairfield Porter: The Collected Poems with Selected Drawings*, edited by David Kermani and John Yau and published by the Tibor de Nagy Gallery in 1985.

the end-words are so much the action of the poem, that it's not possible to invent an action dramatic enough (considering the subject) to hold them in place and keep them from eating up the lines, as the poem goes on. Perhaps if words like yellow and withering were among the end-words, it would help. But my real wish is that the poem were not a sestina.

Now all that must give little idea that I think your poems are strong and personal, full of love of seeing and tender wisdom; but that is what I think. How fresh they would read in any of our magazines.

I never got to the mountains again. I went instead into the Campagna, to Lake Braciano, to a town where I found it too noisy to stay (the Italian motor-scooter is a great curse; as for radios). I would like to say something about the Campagna—it has a spareness you would like—but I can't bring it back to me right now.

I love Rome—well, Rome is a city, and I never quite believe in loving a city. But I find a lot here that I like. I like the flower stands here, that sell very special roses (at pretty special prices) that are very beautiful, even for roses. In the bud they are usually round and globular, or egg-shaped, with the pointed end sliced off, a little like an artichoke with its leaves cut. When they open, they open wide and flat, like a single peony. Their own quality, though, is in their color, a kind of white diluting of all the colors of Roman buildings, the earth colors for which it's hard to find names. And their scent is spicy and rich and uncloying, very like the evening here, when the light turns misty and blue, and the air turns sharp and smells strongly of fall leaves.

I like walking, too, up around the Via Veneto, the middling-modern part of the city where the big hotels are, most of which have that big but hollow look of buildings built in 1900. The neighborhood is like a squashy echo of Rome. The streets are wide and lined with well-grown elm trees, whose leaves are just now coming down.

It's getting late. I have to think about eating. I get bored with spending my evenings alone, but it seems to leave me a little more to work with the next day. Besides, the boys will be here in a week, and then I'll socialize a bit. My love to Anne and the children.

love, Jimmy

PS I think what I meant about my last letter from Venice being querulous is what you meant by a little D H Lawrencey; not my favorite tone.

TO FAIRFIELD PORTER

Dec 2 [1954]

Dear Fairfield,

I'm in Genoa (for a few days) at the Hotel Splendide et de la Ville otherwise known as the Albergo Splendido. I like writing in a hotel room. It combines a nice sort of privacy with, if not exactly "accessibility to experience," at least a feeling that "if I should cry"[38] (I don't know why these quotations are running around in my head), while none of the angel orders hear me, the chamber maid might. It's a nice room too, square in all its dimensions with a herring bone floor and damask-type wall paper of a leaden color haunted by green and pink. And then there's a great construction in which to put things, made of drawers, doors, mirrors, knobs, pulls, marble, bent wood and marquetry, which stands on little curly feet. Outside the traffic of Genoa is going down from the hills above the city to the port, and back again, past a big basin fountain whose many jets make a kind of oceanic spray that was dazzlingly lit last evening in the rain. And how it's rained since I left Rome. All up the coast, after La Spezia there were torrents dashing into the sea off the cliffs and making a wide earth colored band, like a beach of waters in the milky blue and blue-green. And the Mediterranean was quite rough, for it, meaning it was moving up and down, in a kind of broken swell.

Your last letter touched me very much. I'm glad you like my translation so much — though the poem itself is of such strength that it would be hard to mar it. Or rather, ruin it, since marring it is quite easy. I've written a couple of poems lately, but I'm not pleased with them. I have, on the other hand, written some parts of my novel that I am pleased with (written lately, I mean) and have finally a feeling of its having an end, which I shall be relieved to reach. I think one trouble with undertaking something that takes so long to accomplish is that it leaves too much time to become conscious of the work's intrinsic weaknesses — still, I think that it's almost impossible to make something that is *all* flaws.

Arthur and Bobby are playing a concert here tomorrow night, their eighth in less than two weeks. They're both exhausted and look as though they were made out of Gorgonzola cheese. Then they can take off Saturday and Sunday before they go to six concerts in one week in Brussels. As Rimbaud said, *quelle vie* (though a cloistered life would not suit either of them, really).

38. Schuyler quotes from the opening line of Rilke's *Duino Elegies*.

14

I shall be back in Rome when you get this. Please write me a line at the Villa Aurelia, Porta San Pancrazio, Rome.

Give my love to Anne and the children,

love, Jimmy

Arthur and Bobby, who just came in from a rehearsal, send their regards.

TO FAIRFIELD PORTER

[Rome, Italy]

Jan 3 1955

Dear Fairfield:

I've come back from a few beautiful days in Sicily and find your letter, with your beautiful sestina and the news which has delighted all of us so much, that three of your poems are to be in *Poetry*. It's altogether delightful, and I'm so glad that your show will be on when I get to New York, which should be about February 3rd.

Unfortunately, I'm cross-eyed tired, in a rewarding sort of way, from jaunting and sight-seeing, and am leaving late tomorrow night for Vicenza, Trento, Milano, Strasbourg and Paris (a somewhat eccentric route determined by concerts the boys are giving), and don't feel my wits are collected enough to say much about the sestina, beyond that I love it unreservedly, and admire it with as little bias as my relation to it allows. It's beautiful and I'm very touched by it. My impressions of Sicily seem to have sunk inside me like a ball of tin-foil, but I hope I'll soon have a few quiet moments in which to smooth them out and look at them. Right now what comes to mind are only very dopey things, such as that Monreale disappoints and the temples at Agrigento did not surprise, but a Laurana bust of (?) di Aragona[39] in the Palermo Pinacoteca is as beautiful as any work of art I've ever seen. Palermo has an interesting smell, composed of fish, oranges and horses, and at Agrigento I picked wild snap-dragons.

Now I have to go do before-departing things, such as buy buttons and change my address with American Express. In Paris I shall ask Kenneth to show me your sestina-letter (Did I tell you the first night Arthur & I were in Europe, we

39. Francesco Laurana (c. 1430–1502?), Dalmatian-born sculptor known for his nine female portrait busts of members of the Neapolitan royal family.

were sitting in a characteristic sidewalk cafe, and they came by? Janice is blooming in the old world, knew the metro system by heart, and seemed anxious to
launch out).

love to Anne & you & the family, Jimmy

TO KENNETH KOCH [40]

It was delicious to read you in *Poetry & Discovery*; and I liked Frank's defense
[of you] in the Fairfield Porter issue.

[New York, New York]

June 3 [1955]

Dear Ken,

I see the morning mail brought Frank a letter from you, and so I think I'll
write you one before he has a chance to read it.

Let me see. There is no news. I'm living on 60th St[41] and winding up my
novel on 49th. Every week for the last three weeks I've announced that the last
week would find it wound onto spools and out of my horny fingers. Well, perhaps next week. Then of course I'll want to send it to Larry Rivers so he can
check it for typos and grammar. Oh dear, why would I want to say a thing like
that. I love Larry, Berdie, Augusta and the boys.[42]

Joe,[43] Jane, John [Ashbery], Grace [Hartigan] and Walt [Silver] are belting
through Mexico in Joe's car. First post cards being views of the Hotel Camden,
in Camden, Ark., and of San Anton'. I long for them to come back so I can get
the history. (I suspect it would be more soothing to the nerves to drive a load of
TNT through the Rockies.)

Doubtless John has already written you that he did, after all, get a Fulbright,
for Montpellier, France? Beginning in September. Elliott Stein should be
pleased. And John's play *The Compromise*, a satire on the Northwest and a ro-

---

40. See glossary.

41. Gold and Schuyler were subletting the apartment of painter Leonid Berman (1896–
1976) and his wife, harpsichordist Sylvia Marlowe (1908–1981).

42. Larry Rivers's mother-in-law, Bertha "Berdie" Berger, first wife, Augusta, and sons,
Joseph and Steven.

43. Joe Hazan, husband of Jane Freilicher.

mance of religion, or vice versa, is the nuts. I was instantly converted into a follower of the Raven who lives in the sunset.

Frank flew up for Maureen's[44] graduation yesterday; but I have not talked to him since. I assume she looked lovely. He and Mike Goldberg[45] and Arthur and I were at Fairfield's over the long Memorial Day weekend. Pleasant though rainy. Kitty says Janice will make a lovely mother (this is based partly on the fact that Janice is beautiful) and so does Anne. Anne also says you will make a lovely father. Kitty would have said so too, except she's too sensitive to qualify a man with lovely.

John Myers is off to Lake Hopatcong (sp?) N.J. for another summer of summer theater with Herbert.[46] His courage or whatever it is makes me feel faint. Also the Tibor de N Gallery has closed forever in its present location.[47] It will seem odd not to be wandering into Moriarity's after Tuesday openings. Jane's show this year was so much her most beautiful that she didn't sell one picture. It's discouraging. On the other hand, her analysis seems to have perked her up, after a sickly fall, and she's looking gorgeous and has more or less licked that old debbil colitis. Joe Hazan is much the same. His new apartment on Bethune Street has a cute terrace, where Jane raises nasturtiums.

I seem to have lost forever the picture letter I made for you. I was crazy about the poems you sent John, "The Circus" the most. Do you like Rome? Does Janice like Rome? When is the baby scheduled?[48] When are you all coming home? Write me, old chap. My love to Janice,

yours, J.

PS Frank has seen *The Boy Friend* three times.

44. O'Hara's younger sister, Maureen.
45. Michael Goldberg (1924–2007), painter.
46. Herbert Machiz (1923–1976), theater director. Machiz directed several Artists' Theater productions and was John Bernard Myers's lover. Schuyler records Machiz's death in "A Few Days."
47. Tibor de Nagy closed its original location at 206 East 53rd Street and moved to 24 East 67th Street.
48. The Kochs' only child, Katherine "Koko" Koch.

TO FAIRFIELD PORTER

[New York, New York]

July 2 [1955]

Dear Fairfield,

Here is the new translation. Now that it's had a week to cool off, I'm not so altogether pleased as I was; or rather, I see some things I would like to make better, if I can, later. Particularly the last stanza, which is written in a way that suits Italian very well, with its marvelous vocabulary of "splendid" or Miltonic words, that sound in it so natural—though I imagine Leopardi is one of the few poets who satisfactorily tamed that part of the language; to modern ears anyway (what do you think a modern ear looks like? a Juan Gris? a Soutine?).[49] And I would like to find another word than "hides" for the beginning of the 14th line: "obscures" would translate the Italian, but I think it stretches the English usage too much; "masks" would sound right, but I don't want a metaphoric word; so I settled for "hides," but I think the long i sound spoils the effect of "blind" in the next line. Do you know a small, heavy, darkly-colored word that would suit? Do I sound terribly silly?

Would you, after all, like me to come and visit you? I think I can, as it turns out the bus fare to numerous points in Maine is (as Jane once said about the rent for her studio) piteously little. I'm afraid I've misplaced the instructive card on how to get there: is it Camden one aims for? If you would still like to have me, this is what I thought of doing: Arthur and Bobby are playing in Newport on the 13th of this month (a week from this coming Wednesday), then they think of going to Boston the next day to see the museums, which I would like to do, so I could leave from Boston that evening, and be wherever I should be in Maine the next day, Friday, July 15th. Does that make any sense in relation to getting to Great Spruce Head? I can be infinitely adaptable in my travel plans.

I hope it goes without saying that there is nothing I would more enjoy doing. When you write, I suggest you put care of Arthur Gold on the envelope: we have had some trouble with letters being forwarded to Sylvia Marlowe, and it would be a shame for yours to go back to Mt. Desert before it finally got to me (though your letter to me here did arrive in the routine way).

---

49. Juan Gris (1887–1927), Spanish painter active in Paris who originated synthetic cubism. Chaim Soutine (1893–1943), Lithuanian-born expressionist known for violent reds and powerfully distorted figures.

I'll look to hear from you, anxiously. My love to you all. Arthur sends his love, too.

love, Jimmy

PS After scandal-mongering about Grace and Walt, I feel I should add that they're trying to work things out . . .

TO BARBARA GUEST[50]

[New York, New York]

July 7 [1955]

Dear Barbara,

To begin at the end: perhaps you should move the Von Hugel (sp?) downstairs,[51] and the sets of Proust, Bronte and de Sévigné up? Perhaps, though, dreaming of Albertine at Wildfell Hall would be no improvement on the Pope.

I can't type on Frank's typewriter. My touch is much too pastoral: it's like trying to go for a canter on Pegasus.

Thank you for your just words about the translation. It's a peculiar poem, one of the hardest to translate, and perhaps shows less well taken out of its place in the "Canti." One of the hardest things about translating Leopardi is trying to keep out the whine: for me, he doesn't, though when I first read him, I thought he did. In the "Setting of the Moon" it's the third, the really didactic, stanza (the one about what old meanies the gods are) that I find impossible to bring adequately into English. In Italian it has a hard, mocking tone, rather 18th century and Parini-esque,[52] that I think brings it off.

---

50. See glossary.

51. Guest was staying at the Porters' Southampton home and using the bedroom in which the von Hügel volume was on the bookshelves. Friedrich von Hügel (1852–1925) was a wealthy German baron and Roman Catholic layman who lived in London.

52. Giuseppe Parini (1729–1799), Italian poet.

19

(When I said "just words" above, I meant also to thank you for the flattering things you said about my part in it, which agreeably exceed justice.)

Have you seen "our" *Semi-Colon*[53] yet? I have, though our publisher hasn't yet sent me a copy. I like your poem very much; it has charm, a quality one doesn't often look for or find in an American poem. It also has wit, but then, even Tate[54] can be witty, God help us. But I find it hard to find words for what it is I like best—the subtlety of the sound, so strong, light and precise, that keeps one in suspense until the end, without either slowing one up or allowing the lines to slide into one another. It's like a perfectly conceived flight of steps (with fountains, one of the things I enjoy most), say, the one Michaelangelo made for the Campodoglio, in which the regularly spaced setbacks give one the illusion, as one approaches it, of an irregularly swelling cascade over which slides a slightly rippling sheet of water.

As for my own contribution to S.-C., I wrote it a couple of summers ago in a light frame of mind one afternoon in the bookshop, and as lightly found it again and gave it to John. Now that I see it in print (complete with the traditional *Semi-Colon* misprint), it makes me rather hesitate, wonder and blush. Perhaps I should have kept it a semi-private joke (though I guess that's about the status that *Semi-Colon* bestows on one's work). Anyway, I hope it's lubricity doesn't depress you.

Your invitation is most inviting, but: Arthur is tied to New York, because he and Bobby are just beginning the enormous undertaking of recording all of Mozart's two piano and four hand music, and I, if things go as I intend they should, am going to visit Fairfield after all. I'll probably go the week after this, for about three weeks. Perhaps later in the summer?

Yes, I like the "Ricordanze" very much (in Rivers-language, I'm bugged on Leopardi), and I'd like to translate it. If and when, I'll certainly show it to you. I've wanted to send you something from my novel, but I've been hung up by the last part of it, and it seems hard to think of a part that seems at all right for *PR* [*Partisan Review*]. But before I go to Maine, I'll try.

There's suddenly a cool breeze, the first since I can scarcely remember when. For the past week or more the city has been an inferno; but Jane says I'll freeze in Maine. I prefer it.

53. Mimeographed poetry magazine published irregularly by John Bernard Myers of Tibor de Nagy Gallery. Volume, Number 4 contained Guest's poem "About" and Schuyler's "Love Before Breakfast," later reprinted in *The Home Book*.

54. Allen Tate (1899–1979), poet, novelist, and editor.

I trust by now you're taking a strong line toward the house. The first thing I did when we moved into Leonid's was take down some of the Tchelichews[55] and put up a Freilicher and a couple of Porters. Some drinks need to be cut, and a jigger of Tibor de Nagy is prime in a beaker of Durlacher.[56]

love, Jimmy

TO KENNETH KOCH

[New York, New York]

August 15 [1955]

Dear Ken,

A stay in Penobscot Bay has turned my typewriter into a rusty heap. The fogs they have there, you see. I also saw all the Porters, for a month. I loved it and there and hate here, where I've just put Frank in a cab and pointed him toward the airport, as he's going to Great Spruce Head[57] to replace me.

I loved your letters.

I'm glad you're all coming home. I'm not sure though it's fair to rob Baby Kathy of a good grounding in French. Perhaps she should stay. She could support herself modeling baby clothes in the plastic napkin ring boutique at Balenciaga.

But you're not bringing Mercedes! I was dying to meet her. I like anyone connected with the *Paris Review*.

Harcourt, Brace has my novel (called *Alfred & Guinevere*—no crax, pliz). They have had it for a month. They are waiting for a parade to come by so they can throw it out the window. But now the sweaty but smiling Irish policemen are diverting traffic, for a parade is coming. Yes, a parade! See the swirling Kelly green and white sateen skirt of the sweaty but smiling little drum majorette. How brave she is, right out there in front of all the drum and bugle corps of St. Ignatius Loyola High. For it is March, and many months have passed since Jimmy's little novel went far, far away to where only the cry of the loon and the

55. Pavel Tchelichew (1898–1957), Russian painter long resident in America. His painting *Hide and Seek* has been a crowd pleaser at the Museum of Modern Art since the 1950s.

56. Dealer Kirk Askew's Durlacher Gallery represented Berman and the estate of Pavel Tchelichew.

57. Great Spruce Head Island, Maine. Island in Maine's Penobscot Bay bought by Fairfield Porter's father James and summered on by the extended Porter family.

chittering of the spruce needles on the frozen snow troubles Great Jibjib's rest . . .

New York is hot and tiresome. But I wouldn't want to live in Boston.

Or Buffalo.

Jane is learning a trade. It's some kind of electrified typewriting and super-shorthand. I guess it depresses her, but she will be able to make pots and pots of money and go far, far away from her chalks and plasticene.

Frank has written one play, one short story, ten or more poems. I have read some of the poems but not the play or the short story. He also has a new friend he likes very much, a poet named Edward Field[58] who has been published in *Botteghe Oscure.*[59] He seems sweet and good, qualities I never found it in my heart to attribute to Larry Rivers.

John [Ashbery] is going home to Sodus [New York] next week. Then he will come back on Sept. 18 before he goes to France. Morris Golde[60] is going to give a drunken rout for him I know Baby Cathy will not want to miss.

Arthur and Bobby are recording all the two piano and four hand music of Mozart. It is a lot of work, but the works are very, very beautiful.

In Maine Anne used to say every morning, "I must write Janice and invite Kenneth and Janice and the baby to come and stay with us for weeks and weeks."

I started another novel there. But I don't like it, no, not a bit. I will start another one!

Fairfield painted many pictures. He painted a picture of me! In a yellow shirt.

Did John Myers send you the;[61] with my little old play, *Lobe Before Breakfast,* in it?

Will this reach you before the stork brings you all home in a napkin?

If I can find it, I will enclose the "Think & Grin" page from *Boy's Life,* the July issue. I tore it out for you anyway, but am a great mis-placer.

It will be good to see you when you are far, far away from France.

love to Janice, love to Baby, love,

Jimmy

58. Edward Field (b. 1924), poet.

59. Literary magazine published in Rome by Princess Marguerite Caetani who lived on via Bottege Oscure.

60. Morris Golde (1920–2001), patron of dance and music who befriended all the first generation New York School poets in the early 1950s. He described himself as "an art song junkie."

61. The name of the magazine was ; (and was sometimes spelled out as *Semi-Colon*).

TO FAIRFIELD PORTER

[New York, New York]

Wednesday [August 1955]

Dear Fairfield,

Richard[62] and I had an uneventful trip back. The bus was a "thru-way" so we didn't have to change, which was nice. The only trouble with it was that every time I fell asleep they stopped the bus and turned on the lights for a rest stop.

Arthur and Bobby are both well; nothing new has happened about Arthur's troubles. He says if it doesn't work out they will skip Europe this year, anyway.

I saw a play last night I liked quite a bit, *Morning's at Seven*, at the Cherry Lane.[63] It's a nice production—I mean the set and the acting—and the play is funny and quite "real" in a sort of low key way. It's about some people who have been living together for fifty years and are beginning to get on each others nerves a little. I always enjoy writing in which characters can only express their feelings in clichés, and there's a lot of that. I think you'd like it, and it will still be on when you come in September.

John was just here a few minutes ago. He's running around town returning books and things and muttering, in amended Firbank,[64] "such herds of wild books, such wild herds of books." He's going home on Monday, I think, and then coming back four or five days before he sails.

It's really impossible to tell you how much I liked visiting you and Anne and staying on the island. I think it would make a convincing testimony if I could show you all the letters I wrote while I was there; but that isn't very practical. Anyway, I've never enjoyed any company or place so much.

I hope before you come back you will have painted all the pictures you said you would like to paint; and some others, too: if it rains or is foggy, perhaps some more interiors? I would love it if you made a painting or a pastel of the birches one sees from the dining porch by the path to the float.

Thank you over and over and over and over and over and over and over. My love to Anne and Kitty and Jerry and *Frank* and you.

---

62. Richard Stankiewicz (1922–1983), American sculptor.
63. A revival of Paul Osborne's comedy at the historic Greenwich Village Theater.
64. Ronald Firbank (1886–1926), British novelist and a grand eccentric.

I look to see you in a couple of weeks.

love, Jimmy

PS   I enclose a note for Frank.[65]
PPS I forgot two things: Verga,[66] & my unfinished capo-lavoro. I do want the painting!

TO FAIRFIELD PORTER

New York, New York

Thursday [Fall 1955]

Dear Fairfield,

How delightful to find your handwriting in an anonymously addressed envelope, when I dismally thought all the mail was another throw-away. I shall go right away to see Calcagno, and Feeley[67] too.

But how inaccurate of you to have told Frank and Kenneth that the reason you don't call me is that it is you who always call! Wasn't it I who called you in Southampton when I heard you were back and coming into town? And I who called you the day we were moving, when you and I went downtown and you bought us the beautiful white lamp that has given us so much pleasure and illumination? And often, when it has been you who called, wasn't it because we had arranged it so beforehand—as often at my suggestion as yours—on the grounds that you would be out during the day, and I would be in? I did try to call you the week of John's party, and then gave it up because I was aware of a deliberateness in your silence. One's often tempted to test one's friends in these little ways—at least I am—but it's my experience that to do so is a challenge to the friend to show that he has the nerve and heartlessness to fail one; and most of us have. Besides, I think you exaggerate the degree of initiative you take in your friendships: I know, because I'm shy, that it often takes more initiative for me to bring myself to say yes to an invitation than it took for the inviter to issue it.

While I'm at it, I'm also rather put out by this youth and age stuff. In so far as I think of you as "older," I feel honored and benefited by your friendship; but if

---

65. Frank O'Hara was visiting the Porters.
66. Giuseppe Verga's *Little Novels of Sicily*, one of Schuyler's favorite books.
67. Lawrence Calcagno (1919–1993) and Paul Feeley (1910–1966), American painters.

it turns out that you feel odd in bestowing it, I feel snubbed. I don't, though, think of you as "older" so much as I do a friend who has had a life very different from mine (but if I must think about it, then I say that I think I'm a man over thirty, past which age one might hope to have gained the right to mingle with one's elders &/or betters). I wish I thought you dwelt a little on the virtues in your behavior: and saw that if (as I hope you do) you take pleasure in the company of Frank and Jane and Kenneth and Barbara and the rest of us, it's because your mind hasn't sealed over, that you've kept a fresh enthusiasm and curiosity, a desire to catch the contagion from young creative people and at the same time to help and instruct: equally admirable. How grateful John Button is to you for the things you said to him about his painting, and who else is there who could say them? Someone else might OK his pictures—but that's just approval; someone his own age might criticize them in a helpful way, but that would lack the validity of experience. I cannot, literally, bring to mind anyone else who would and could do it: Tom Hess[68] wouldn't; Alfred Barr[69] is too diplomatic; Larry would be jealous; John Myers is a dope . . . and so on. (I thought his paintings beautiful, and praised them as best I could; but I certainly have no painting pointers to give him!) All I mean is that it seems to me merely another instance of American self-consciousness when confronted by one's oddness, when the oddness is what makes value. Do you think your paintings would keep gaining in quality—as I think they do—if you had been one of those dreary artists who hunt for it in their twenties, find it in their thirties and then do it for the rest of their lives? Oh the acres of Kuniyoshi and Reginald Marsh:[70] I don't say their work is without merit, but I think it's mostly an achieved manner, and manner, en masse, makes for ennui. I wish instead of odd, you thought yourself as unique; you seem so to me, in relation to your brothers and sister, to other artists, to other men your age, to other members of the class of '28 (if that is the right year)—but then, they haven't had a long draught from the only spring that matters. You have.

I hope this doesn't seem impudent and fresh; which was no part of my plan. Frank[71] is not going to review anymore, and Betty Chamberlin[72] called and

68. Thomas B. Hess (1920–1978), editor of *Art News*.

69. Alfred Barr (1902–1981), first director, 1929–67, of New York City's Museum of Modern Art.

70. Yasuo Kuniyoshi (1893–1953), Japanese-born American painter, and Reginald Marsh (1898–1954), painter of New York City working-class life in the 1930s and 1940s.

71. Frank O'Hara, Fairfield Porter, and Schuyler were reviewing exhibitions for *Art News*.

72. Tom Hess's deputy at *Art News*.

asked if I'd write three sample reviews; so I shall, over the weekend. I wish you were going to be here to criticize them for me (! . . . you see?), but I shall do the best I can and keep copies to show you.

I hope soon I can come out and visit you; since you said at Morris's I knew "damn well I could." Pretty strong talk, pardner.

I'm enjoying enormously working over my book with Catherine Carver;[73] I think it will turn out one that I will like much more than the one I submitted. It seems as though every place where she puts her finger is one I had at some time thought myself might be a little pulpy or squashy.

I'll write more chattily another time, when you tell me that you've forgiven me for anything in this letter that needs forgiving. None of it means anything serious, in the light of the joy it gave me to see your face light up when you finally saw me signaling wildly from that moving cab.

My love to Anne and Kitty and yourself. I long to hear news of Jerry.

as always, Jimmy

PS Would you call me next Tuesday? I expect to be in all day.

TO FAIRFIELD PORTER

[New York, New York]

Sat. [early 1956]

Dear Fairfield,

I'm delighted that the show is painted; what a relief for you. I wish I could write you that my novel is written—though my impression is more and more that nothing is ever finished. A few parts of my book have, *for me*, the quality of inspiration, and now all I can do in the most laborious bead stringing way is try to give the rest of it a similar quality. Try to make it seem "all over and at once" as you say.

Yes, the review of Pasilis was cut: not as much as the one of Goodnough;[74] this time they only cut the premise and the conclusion! What pigs and asses' ears they are; though I think I mind a little less each time (of course I mind, I

---

73. Editor at Harcourt, Brace.

74. Felix Pasilis (1922–2008) and Robert Goodnough (1917–2010), American painters. Both reviews appear in Schuyler's *Selected Art Writings*.

always will. It's idiotic to sign what completely misrepresents what one thinks). But, it has one dim advantage for me, which is that I've always disliked seeing my own things in print, but now it will be a positive pleasure, compared to seeing these mutilated tid-bits. Your review of Cloar[75] struck me as interesting and not as cut; perhaps when I read it again (I don't have it here) I'll be aware of it. Cutting is doubtless the explanation of the jerkiness and jumpiness of a great many of the reviews. It's a shame they (*Art News*) haven't more money to spend; they could hire some caption writers with a good Madison Avenue background and be really content.

I'm glad you like the Jacob[76] ballads, though I don't quite see how one kind of French cleverness is the opposite of another kind; Jacob in his frenzy took it awfully far, in fact almost made cleverness itself his subject. But that seems to me one thing that artists are about, or are like; it isn't that they're different from the people around them, it's that they are a little more than; they isolate and exaggerate. As for French avarice, any national characteristic is both a virtue and a vice, and if avarice is a recognizable French vice, it's only the other side of the virtue of economy and husbandry: the quality after all, that makes a Norman farm as thoroughly painted, "as all over and at once" as a Vuillard.[77]

I finished *The Tragic Muse*. It's a marvelous book, but I think one of his odd ones. I wish he had made it altogether Miriam Rooth's. She's perfect, and my only complaint is that I wish he'd done her career more thoroughly, I mean one step from Paris to her first success, which James says himself is awfully quick. I don't think that quite convinces. Anyway I think the fault of the book lies in that will-to-be-Balzac James had; he would try to write about M.P.'s and diplomats, but he wasn't interested enough in them to make them real. It makes the big scene where Peter S. asks Miriam to marry him lopsided, since James so successfully skirted over dealing with Peter's work, that he seems only really interested in the theater, and one can only take it on faith that he'll have the great future as a diplomat he says he'll have. As for Ned Dormer, he only seems alive to me in relation to the women and his family—I love the scenes between him and Julia Dallow. But otherwise I don't think one's convinced that he was as

75. Carroll Cloar (1913–1993), American realist painter.

76. Max Jacob (1879–1944), French poet. John Ashbery translated sections of his masterpiece, *The Dice Cup* (1917).

77. Edouard Vuillard (1868–1940), French painter, a founder of the Nabis and a significant influence on Fairfield Porter, whom Schuyler has just quoted. Several reviews of Vuillard's work appear in Porter's *Art in Its Own Terms*.

good as James said (he doesn't say he's very good) at either painting or politics. He [James] can only think of a political life satirically, but he doesn't satirize the theaters, for all his reservations. To have the balance James wanted, there would have to be one character who was as intelligently engaged in public life as Mme. Carre is in the theater. But there isn't. I feel, though, it's beside the point, that if Ned Dormer had been an American, his choice and his sacrifice would have been much more palpable—I don't, at least, feel that Christopher Newman or Caspar Goodwood[78] suffer from the shallowness or falseness of situation that Ned D. suffers from. But the book is too full of James' marvelous perceptions for me to be so captious; what a wonderful creation Mrs. Rooth is. James was as sensitive to, as much in love with,* vulgarity as Jane Austen. They could find it on the head of a pin. As for Biddy, I give her to you as an example of what I still insist exists in fiction, an altogether "good" character who is not dull or boring. She isn't a saint, and she doesn't trust Miriam, but she is gloriously good: it's amazing how James makes one feel at the end the thoroughness with which she understands and accepts Peter. She doesn't forgive him because she was too purely in love with him for him to hurt her; she can only offer him the chance to make her happy.

(* "as much in love with": OOPS! "as fascinated by" is probably more like it.)

But this isn't the way my own small effort at fiction will ever get finished; I'd better get at it.

Why don't you give me a ring on Tuesday? I think I'm busy in the evening—I don't know; in fact, I imagine another period of hurley-burley is beginning:

Arthur [Gold] signed a lease on the apartment at 333 Central Park West today! Well, really, I'm more used to being a nomad than otherwise, so in early March I'll fold my orange crates and cart them uptown. Give my love to Anne and Kitty.

love,

Jimmy

78. Christopher Newman and Caspar Goodwood are characters in the Henry James novels *The American* and *Portrait of a Lady*, respectively.

TO JOHN BUTTON

[New York, New York]

[Spring 1956]

Dear John,

I don't know why I have to tell you this today (but I do) — perhaps it's because when I look out into the fog all I can see is the hairs on your adorable chest. I'm terribly in love with you, and have been for such a long time, ever since the first time Frank took me to your apartment. I looked around at your beautiful paintings and suddenly everything I'd ever felt about you turned into a diamond or a rose or something — anyway I went striding up and down while Frank played Poulenc[79] and felt exactly like the Ugly Duckling the day he found he was a swan. Then you came home and I didn't think I could ever look at you or speak to you again, all I could do was giggle and snort and twitch. But I've looked at you a lot since then and there isn't anybody else in the world I want to look at; or want, for that matter.

It seems to me that I've been so GOOD that I couldn't hate myself more. I don't see why I couldn't have been born a robber baron type instead of a fool.

Now I'm going down and set 57th Street on fire to keep you warm.

This is all nonsense. I love being in love with you, it makes even unhappiness seem no bigger than a pin, even at the times when I wish so violently that I could give my heart to science and be rid of it.

with all my love,

Jimmy

Please don't tell Alvin [Novak]; I don't think I could bear to meet him if I thought he knew.

TO JOHN BUTTON

[New York, New York]

May 4 [1956]

Dear John,

I've been thinking about your work, and realized that when I've gruntingly praised it to you there are other things, which are not dispraise but more criti-

79. Francis Poulenc (1899–1963), French composer and pianist.

cal, that have gone unsaid and ungrunted. I only mean things I might say, for instance, to Fairfield in talking about your work, but which, if they have any value at all, could only be of value if said to you. And of course the only possible value they could have is not that you would agree with them but that among them there might be some one thing that might make you think of something which it is impossible for me to imagine.

About your drawings: I rather question the kind of drawing paper you use: it somewhat resembles photographic paper, and its gloss tends to kill the lightness of a line made with hard graphite. When smudged, it gives a very pretty atmospheric tone, but one which seems more inherent in the paper and graphite than something put there. I find it, in a word, impersonal.

There is a line you sometimes use in your drawings which is stunning because of its speed, but which does not always tell as much as it appears to; if it's undesirable, it's because it gives a look of "finish," and a work should not look more finished than it intrinsically is (a point poor dear Grace [Hartigan] will never know about, since all she's ever painted is the husks of paintings). A deeper trouble with the speedy kind of line I mean is that one important reason for making drawings, I imagine, is not to draw a likeness of what one sees but to find out what it is one sees. And to find how economically (or richly, for that matter) one can express it.

Though this will sound petty, I even question putting carefully lettered titles on drawings; I like it in that it's witty and therefore like you, but, really, the first use of drawings is the same as that of notebooks and letters for a writer: practice and keeping your hand it: Kyriena's [Siloti] finger exercises. So if I object to titles, it's merely that it verges toward an attitude of which Gide is such a perfectly sad example, keeping your diary for the public; it might imply that one had had a preconceived idea in the back of one's mind, that when one was most private one had, to a small degree, limited one's perfect freedom. (Thank God, the nature of your gift prevents you from ever knowing about that ugsome underworld where the Cadmi and Perliniums[80] bloom and where drawings are so precious that they are elevated from works of art to *objets d'art*.)

About your paintings, I only think you might think somewhat about shadows,

80. Paul Cadmus (1904–1999) and Bernard Perlin (1918–2014), American painters, promoted by Lincoln Kirstein as "subjective realists," who liked to work in egg tempera and silverpoint. Schuyler wrote of Cadmus, "Presumably there will always be artists of remarkable skill who choose to limit themselves to the bizarre and eccentric, the anecdotal and superficial. Among them, Cadmus is a master."

what they are and what goes on in them. I notice that they are present almost not at all when you don't paint from nature, as in my *Beach*. It isn't that I don't like shadows (I adore them!) but I certainly don't like what Larry [Rivers], for instance, sometimes does about them, which is to put pure color where the light falls and slime where it doesn't. After all, if you walk out of the sunlight into a dark doorway you don't necessarily smack into a pile of shit. And it's in-observant of Fairfield to imagine that a shadow is simply a hue of the same color; a tree does not always cast a dark green shadow on a light green lawn. His way often works, but it makes some of his pictures look rule-of-thumb (and the maddening thing is that that is what he does when he re-paints in his studio).

I love the thinness with which you paint, but I think you should beware of over transparency, which will make your color look faded; or as fawning reviews say, "muted and rich."

I hope you'll be able to paint a lot this summer in natural light: if the world is a good looker, it's the sun that makes it so.

Is it possible I'm really going to have the crust to offer you this plate of rasp-ings from a stale loaf? After the infinite and inexhaustible pleasure your work gives me, what gratitude. As Jane said when I asked her about Fairfield's piece, "It's OK only of course [if] the opposite of everything I said is true too."

Let me say something larger and truer: I don't know of anyone who illustrates better than you something Proust wrote, that style in art is not a matter of study, practice, revision or of refinement of diction (means) but of vision. The intensity with which you project a painting, the degree to which you make each element in the painting exist not for itself alone but as a part of the complete revelation, will always make my scalp tingle with joy. Giorgione said that's what a painting can do, show everything at a glance—and he painted a picture of a nude from the back looking in a mirror and reflected in water to prove it and confound a sculptor.

(We hold these (belch) truths to be self-evident)

Anyway, John, you are our Delacroix and I count on you to ennoble us as we sit among the wicker plant stands of Boston fern on the sun porches of our gray pebble stucco bungalows. (In the parlor of mine there is a Tiffany glass lamp on the Mission oak refectory table under a sampler my step-aunt Sylvia embroidered of a stylized peacock on black silk.)

love,

Jimmy

TO JOHN BUTTON

Southampton, New York

Last Sat. in May, 1956

Dear John,

We had the most beautiful drive out here yesterday—we left at ten and got here[81] at four and drove (or rather rattled, bounced and shook in Larry's [Rivers] Austen station-truck-wagon-bus-car) the whole way under the most blazing blueness with the air as clear as the cold breeze; wow. Name a bush or tree you would want to see in bloom in the spring and you would have seen it, from the most gnarled and spreading old apple trees with flowers so small and few they were like an illusion caused by the reflected light, to dogwoods of a monumentality the woods never dreamt of (I love the implication of some kind of Hans Andersen story in the way the snow gets gray and coarse like unrefined salt, shrinks and disappears and then a few weeks later reappears on all the fruit trees—and each fruit tree seems another kind of snow, apple trees are the feathery, fat kind that falls all day, pear trees are the heart of the blizzard that piles up the most stunning drifts, plum trees the wet, heavy kind that sticks to the undersides of branches and eaves; and even fruit trees that bloom pink look like snow in a pink evening)—but what would Hans Andersen have to say about the Levittowns with, outside their so-pleased-with-themselves ranch-type houses artfully set catty-corner on a little unseeded plot of mud, mutation azaleas in fluorescent colors whose names could only be Tropix, Sunkist, Emba and (for the real sports) Devil Woman?

Then there are the lilacs! (Did you know that the name and the shrub come from Persia? Could anything be more right?)

Larry was so Larry-like, ranging from the most colossal grandness ("Tiepolo, Tolstoi, and me") to the most minute minginess, to implications of the most hor-rifying reputation smashing rumors, that he was completely enchanting. We stopped in Smithtown for a late Chinese lunch. Larry ordered in Mandarin, and I got this in a fortune cake: [   ] a message which I had better take in a personal way.

You can tell the boys along the Strip about Elizabeth Porter and they'll agree that she's the most. As Anne says, "It's hard to believe a person could be so small." Anne also said, "Furl [Porter's nickname], there's some white wine so do

---

81. The Porters' house in Southampton.

you think I should make them that cheese dish Jerry said you could perhaps make a chess set out of?" And Kitty now prefers spelling, when she can, to speaking, so her conversation is like "H - o - w lovely," all the time. Jenny has a semi-French cut and doesn't look a bit like herself, Ruby talks too much and Fairfield is charging around the yard with a dangerous looking spade. I adore this house, and I'm so glad I'm going to spend the summer in it. (Got to go eat lunch now.)

Lunch was asparagus on fried bread, cheese, red applesauce (which Kitty said tasted exactly the way the five and dime store smells) with sour cream, and coffee. Elegant and tasty, filling without crowding you.

Drat, death and damn; I suppose I ought to work now. Really I'd much rather go on writing endlessly to you, and then go for a walk on the beach and think of some more to tell you. And I haven't told you anything I meant to tell you, about Oliver Smith's[82] beautiful house, the marvelous things Jane Bowles[83] said (she said about *Two Serious Ladies*, "it's got a quiet reputation of its own, like Hattie Carnegie"[84]) or how I'll never recover from the sincere and beautiful compliments she paid me about the text I wrote for Paul[85]—at first I said "Oh thank you" and then it came over me who was speaking and the kind of value I place on what she says: I thought I'd have to go out and run back and forth across Brooklyn Bridge a few hundred times while I calmed down. Or anything else! Oh well. I had such a good time at Elaine's[86] party and skunk drunk or not, I haven't forgotten anything I said or heard I would want to remember. I miss you most monstrously much, and I'll be back on Tuesday afternoon: are you going to the opening at the Museum, is it possible to go? (For that matter, is there any reason to?)

I anticipate the summer, and I dread it.

love, Jimmy

82. Oliver Smith (1918–1994), Broadway set designer, producer, and director. His house was in Brooklyn Heights.

83. Jane Bowles (1917–1973), playwright, novelist, and wife of Paul Bowles. *Two Serious Ladies* (1943) was her only published novel.

84. Hattie Carnegie (1886–1956), Vienna–born fashion designer who dropped her original surname, Kanengeiser, and adopted Carnegie after Andrew Carnegie. During the 1930s and 1940s she was perhaps the best—known dress designer in America.

85. Paul Bowles (1910–1999), composer and novelist. His novel *The Sheltering Sky* was a best-seller in 1949. Schuyler wrote the words for his *A Picnic Cantata* (1954).

86. Elaine Fried de Kooning (1918–1989), painter, art critic, and wife of Willem de Kooning. She recommended Fairfield Porter to Tom Hess as a reviewer for *Art News*.

PS here's a poem Kitty[87] wrote for me half an hour after I got here:

THE LAKE

Oh, the lake and its bright flowers, trees and birds
In the morning the flowers are gently sprinkled with dew
There are rushes and there is moss under the trees
And the rushes are useful because there are carpets to make out of them
In the spring when the sun shines and gentle breezes blow
It is peaceful to walk. Oh, the lake its haunts and hiding places,
Its swans so beautiful; and pretty ducks live there too
Also at six o'clock or else one in the morning
The doe with her fawn comes, and also comes the stag.
Oh, the lake!

THE END

to Jimmy from Katherine

Oh, dear John!

[undated, June 1956]

PS 1) Don't ever apologize for your manners; you have beautiful manners, sincere, sweet and direct, the only kind worth having.

2) I love it when you show off.

3) Giving people looks is part of my prissy secretive, margarine-wouldn't-melt-in-her-cunt suburban bad manners. I do it to everybody all the time and ought to get a good crack for it.

4) If you are adolescent then Marianne Moore is Shirley Temple.

5) Who in the world is Altima Barrett anyway?

6) If you don't introduce me, it was probably because you recognized the intrinsic though invisible difficulties I put in the way of anyone who tries to introduce me to someone. Here is a conversation I had with Larry Osgood during an intermission at the Poets' Theater:[88]

Me: Is that Roger Shattuck?[89]

87. Katherine, the Porter's fourth child and eldest daughter, was seven years old at the time.

88. A Cambridge, Massachusetts, theater company that produced plays by John Ashbery, Frank O'Hara, Mary Manning, and many other poets.

89. Roger Shattuck (1923–2005), writer, translator, and teacher. Author of *The Banquet Years: The Origins of the Avant-Garde in France, 1885 to World War I.*

Larry: Yes, *isn't* he handsome.

Me: Very.

Larry: And he's *so* nice.

Me: So I've heard.

Larry: And he's such a *good* translator.

Me: Yes, I've enjoyed his Apollinaire.

Larry: Would you like to meet him?

Me: No.

7) Your description of the Porters at Putney [Vermont][90] is the funniest thing anyone has written since Congreave signed his name to *The Way of the World*.[91]

8) Bye now.

Odette de Crécy[92]

TO JOHN BUTTON [93]

[New York, New York]

Friday [June 1956]

Dear John,

It's too sad not to have had a letter from you. But the mail service between there and here is really nothing; one might as well put one's letters into bottles and float them down the coast. It seems odd that our rich country should have the worst mail service of any civilized country. No wonder the English despise us.

Our heat wave is getting (for me) a bit out of hand. My ass is going to be as rosy as a baboon's from sitting naked and sweating on the red leatherette seat of my typing chair. And a little trickle runs out of each pit down to the elbows and falls, drip drip drip onto the linoleum. While my buttermilk is reaching its summer climax. It would be fun to be out walking around in it, but it's rather hell to work in. The carbon paper sticks to everything and smears and the typing paper gets like old linen rags.

Last night I saw a French farce "in the most Gallic manner!" called *Oh! Amelia*; torture; and ²/₃rds of *The Wages of Fear*,[94] yawn. Arthur said it was like

90. The Porters' son Johnny was at school in Putney.

91. William Congreave (1670–1729), British Restoration playwright known for his comedies. *The Way of the World* appeared in 1700.

92. Odette de Crécy is a character in Proust's *Remembrance of Things Past*.

93. See glossary.

94. *The Wages of Fear* (1953), directed by Henri-Georges Clouzot (1907–1977).

a training film for truck drivers; I was too stupefied to speak. Since we came in just when Yves Montand[95] was getting out of his hammock in his jockey shorts, I felt I'd had the meat of the matter and didn't stay to see the beginning. What a mystery Clouzot's reputation is. When I think that Ted Gorey[96] saw that movie fifteen times I'm not a bit surprised.

A suitcase the boys mailed from Rome arrived today, so I now have: a new yellow sport shirt; a new sport coat; and a new summer suit. The sport coat is striped brown, like a blazer, and the suit is sort of lineny or Tropical Worsted. I don't know what the color is, Camel or Natural or maybe Dust. How I love presents and new clothes and all *that* sort of thing!

The boys and Arthur W[einstein] have also decided that we will move to France next April. They asked me if I would mind and I said I like Paris. It's true, I do. The only travel I can imagine with pleasure is seeing Italy and Sicily with you; and all those other classical pretty places (Not Helsinki so much). But that's too impalpable.

> *Dreaming a dream to prize*
> *Were to ask ghosts to rise*
> *If there are ghosts to raise*
> *Whom would you call?*

I like Beddoes.[97]

> *I'll take that fainting rose*
> *Out of his breast: t'was I, thou silken blush,*
> *That ravish't thy green family of thee.*
> *Perhaps one kiss of his lives in the gyre*
> *Of its kiss-colored leaves . . .*

But I'm probably mixing it up.

Our weekend plans are extensive: we're to go hear Alice [Esty] sing some Honegger at 3, then pick up Jerry Robbins'[98] car (he's gone to Hollywood for

95. Yves Montand (1921–1991), actor, singer, who made his name as an actor in *The Wages of Fear*.

96. Edward Gorey (1925–2000), book designer, artist, and writer. Gorey roomed with Frank O'Hara at Harvard. They joined the Poets' Theater together. Gorey wrote and / or illustrated over one hundred books.

97. Thomas Lovell Beddoes (1803–1849), British poet.

98. Jerome Robbins (1918–1998), dancer and choreographer for the ballet and the musical theater, where he is known for *West Side Story*.

the weekend), drive to Bobby's cousin Pauline's at Stamford for dinner and spend the night; go to Sylvia and Leonid's at Greenwich for lunch and swim on Saturday, then to Sam [Barber] and Chuck [Turner] at Mt Kisco for dinner at Nyack; then spend the night; then to Kyriena's[99] for the afternoon and dinner and spend the night or come back here and go to lunch with Aaron[100] Monday at Ossining. I think I'll skip the Monday lunch. Besides, Arthur W is sure to throw a monkey wrench into it; it's everything he hates (especially since Jerry's car is a convertible). It's the swimming pool that interests me most; I long for a little paddle and splash-splash.

I wonder when you are leaving and if this will reach you? Well if it doesn't, it will follow you and find you.

It will be nice to see you.

love, Jimmy

TO JOHN BUTTON

[Southampton, New York]

July 3 [1956]

We're here.[101] Wouldn't you know? It's grand. And it's green, and the sky is as much white as it is blue. It got hot and sticky in the night, then the clouds made pee pee and it cooled off. The ocean looks calm until you get right down in front of it when you realize it's rising up higher than you are and slamming hell out of the inoffending beach. I wouldn't go near it, though it was full of squealing bobbing three year olds. Southampton is so different from Easthampton. I haven't seen a sissy yet. Except in the home, of course, but we don't count. We're artists.

And I'm very unhappy. Thank God I mean to work and feel I can. I imagined all right what it would be like to go away for the summer and see you so little, but I imagined you'd be happy and paint a lot, and get in a lot of dancing, not like this. And I'm not even there to hold your hand. I feel so ineffectual, so useless.

---

99. Kyriena Siloti, daughter of the great Russian pianist. She had house or "dacha" in a park near Nyack, New York.

100. Aaron Copland (1900–1990), American composer of *Billy the Kid* (1938) and *Appalachian Spring* (1944).

101. Arthur Gold and Schuyler rented the Porters' Southampton house for the summer.

Try to work—I don't mean work, I mean paint. It isn't that it helps so very much, it's just that when your mind is engaged you can't brood with quite the intensity as when you're staring at the wall or lying on your back or washing the same cup over and over. And if you feel broody for God sake don't hang around the house. Set a match to it and go sketching or cruising or for that matter walking.

I'm glad Frank is back or about to be back. As Wystan almost says somewhere "about suffering he is never wrong, the old master . . . "[102] If it should turn out you don't want to be on 2nd Street at the end of July, couldn't you go stay at 326 E 49? There are some glorious and unpainted views from its windows, and "An Interior with Sculpture by Larry Rivers" would be charming. And when you and Frank felt like getting wet you could fall on each other's necks in floods of tears. It's often given me a deal of solace, that neck and that house.

Naturally, after the unexpected developments that followed your return, we never spoke of the serious doubts you wrote me about. They don't have to be serious, dear, all it takes is a scruple. The last thing in the world I ever want to do to you is breathe on you heavily and give you a rash. I wouldn't, in fact, so much as touch the hem of your garment without a sign. And when it comes to that kind of sign, I can only read wall size words.

Now I am going to write a short snappy novel that will sell so well it will make *Uncle Tom's Cabin* seem like a Republic Pictures production. David Selznick will die to buy it for Jennifer Jones.[103] Garbo will weep to be let out of retirement. It will introduce Mae West to mother roles and put Steve Cochran[104] in the American bed. Then Granny will take her little Marcel to Balbec so he can see that squat church he's always belching about.

I miss you dear. If I don't see you next week I'll throw myself in front of a wave and drown. Forgive all my foolishness: I love you.

Jimmy

P.S. *Write!* (*Don't* put care of F. P. on it—just the address)

---

102. Schuyler plays with the first two lines of W. H. Auden's poem "Musee des Beaux Arts," "About suffering they were never wrong, The Old Masters . . . "

103. David O. Selznick (1902–1965), Hollywood movie producer of *Gone With the Wind*, among many other movies, and husband of the actress Jennifer Jones (1919–2009).

104. Steve Cochran (1917–1965), movie actor who played bad guy and he-man roles.

TO FAIRFIELD PORTER

[Southampton, New York]

July 7 [1956]

Dear Fairfield,

After two beautiful days we had three wet cold ones. The temperature went below 60 and we were all delighted and worked hard. But today it's summer again, not warm or dry enough for the beach, but nice with a lot of Boudin[105] clouds bumping around in the blue.

All our social life has consisted of having Larry for dinner last night, as thrillingly full of his favorite subject, him, as ever. He and Howie have a show at the bookshop (a sign says Larry Rivers in huge letters and then in tiny letters, "and his guest Howard Kanovitz")[106] and Larry's picture of Joseph with his socks on and his pants off had to be taken down by popular request. In its place there is a notice that says, in effect, that due to the smallness of some, others may see the shocker by asking (as Larry said, the only thing that shocks people in paintings nowadays is a "male penis"). He had also a letter from your dealer [John Bernard Myers] who hated Paris and loved London and says he is going to be very big for Jane next year because he has been to some museums and now gets what she's after. Larry had to leave early, unfortunately, because Stevie [Rivers] and a playmate had disappeared into Riverhead where there is a carnie show with a strip tease dancer and they still weren't home by 9:30. Guess they did make it safely back to their respective hysterical mother and grandmother or we would have heard.

Everything about the house is fine (not to say beautiful and a joy). Arthur W[einstein] prowled through like a cat-detective and is already to line up a membership for you in the IDA (Interior Decorators Assoc.). My only complaint is that the stove demands so little of me.[107]

The lilies by the barn opened yesterday in the rain, and the first big daisy opened this morning. The new bed is full of beautiful delicate flowers. Although I only take my face out of the Flower encyclopedia long enough to put it in my dinner, I seem to know practically none of their names—there's sweet alyssum, and poppies, deep yellow ones and a scarlet one, but are they California, Iceland or Siberian poppies? And zinnias and bachelor buttons are in bud.

---

105. Eugéne Boudin (1824–1898), French landscape painter.

106. Howard Kanovitz (1929–2009), painter.

107. The Porters had a famously temperamental Aga stove that had to be kept lit year-round. Schuyler seems to have expected more difficulty from it.

We had a charming card from Laurence, who says he likes the chaperoning job and will be here about July 27th for three or four nights. We'll be glad to see him (though it occurs to me now that I will probably be in town then reviewing). He has such elegant handwriting.

I writing in the studio (I sound like a Chinaman)—and of the pictures you left out I particularly love the one of Jerry that's given you so much trouble. It doesn't look unfinished or incomplete to me, it has a beautiful intensity of focus, first on the face, secondly on the dishes, with everything else "There" to just the degree that what's around what one looks at *is* seen. And I love the living room, transparent as a water color and the snowy spring light.

I had a post card from John A in which he says he guesses it's definite that he'll be in France another year, though he will be here in September. I enclose the two poems he sent me I mentioned at Kenneth's. I'd like them back, and I'd like to see the ones he sent you, if you have them, and I'll return them.

Soon as I can pull myself together and wrap it, I'll send you a book I have for you. It's four poets, and I want to give it to you because I like Wyatt[108] so much, and think you might too, and because the editor's introduction is interesting. He says some simple things about scanning five beat lines that seem to make a subject I've never much grasped a lot clearer. When I send it I'll mark the passage I mean.

When circulars come, and they do, shall we just put them in the basket by the front door?

Alvin N [Novak] has decided that he and John shouldn't live together anymore, which is sad and stupid. It wouldn't surprise me though if he changed his mind later; I think in the end he is the one who would be worst off. Or benefit least, or something. Jane's comment was, "it proves again that man's inhumanity to man is equaled only by his inhumanity to himself."

The boys are going in next Tuesday to play on a TV show and will bring the lady la Rochefoucalud[109] (sp?) back with them if she can prevail on Joe [Hazan] to drive out Friday for the weekend. I hope so. I'm dying to see her.

Kenneth said they were going to visit you in August. I think Great Spruce Head is the perfect place to contain him and set him off. And he can write his Katherine Kanoe Kantos.

Every second, today simply becomes more overpoweringly beautiful. I'd like

108. Sir Thomas Wyatt (1503–1542), British poet, diplomat, and soldier credited with introducing the sonnet into English.

109. Francois De La Rochefoucauld (1613–1680), French aphorist. Schuyler is referring to Jane Freilicher.

to make an anthology of all the lines of poetry with the word blue in them, beginning with Frank's "It's the blue!" " . . . *si blew, si calme* . . . " " . . . in unending blueness . . . " (On the other hand I can't think of a drearier poem than the one of Herbert's[110] that begins so marvelously about "Sweet day, so cool, so calm, so fair . . . " (I think it is) and then points out that it won't last forever. I hate all those dusty-answer poems about how someone or something is as pretty as a peach but after a while it's going to be all awful looking. And I don't think it's Christianity that's to blame — though it might be Protestantism — Dante doesn't talk that way.)

I've been alternately reading Proust and the *Divine Comedy*. No comment. And I read *Measure for Measure* again. When you read him, there is really no one but Shakespeare; the exhilaration, the invention, the clarity, the truth. I think really I like the late comedies the most, *Measure for Measure, The Winter's Tale* and *The Tempest*. Though my special love is *As You Like It*, it's so artificial, it doesn't make the faintest pretense that its existence was obliged, was called for. Bigger works of art always seem to threaten to help one in some way or other, and therefore the fact that they exist is a part of the Social Good; *As You Like It* is just there, like the one red poppy across the lawn, pure excess of delight.

Speaking of pure excess, I've been on a diet. A few weeks ago I weighed 171, now I weigh 163, and I'm not going to think about stopping until I find out how I look and feel at 155. In fact we are all on diets, and since we've been here have broken down only once, when we stormed up Main Street at 10:30 one night and had hot fudge and butterscotch sundaes. Of course we talk about nothing but food — even to the exclusion of Europe, our one other subject — and Bobby and I read antiphonally from Sheila Hibben[111] and Tante Marie's Pastry book to an accompaniment of moans. It does seem absurd that when we open that marvelous oven great cinnamon smelling gusts don't come poring out.

My love to Anne and Katy and Elizabeth. Were you able to get someone to help with the house work?

I hope I'll hear from you soon.

love, Jimmy

Arthur and Bobby send their love.

---

110. George Herbert (1593–1633), British metaphysical poet and divine. Schuyler quotes Herbert's poem "Virtue."

111. Helia Hibben (1890–1964), American cookbook writer.

TO FAIRFIELD PORTER

[Southampton, New York]

Monday July 16 [1956]

Dear Fairfield,

The enclosed was an answer to the first of three letters I had from you but before I posted it two more came, so I thought I would tear it up and write another letter, which I haven't done. Now today I have an answer to my other letter; so it's getting too confused not to write right away even though it's hastily.

Thank you for sending John's [Ashbery] poems. What I like best about all of them, taken together at first reading, is the emerging of a new tone — one that I think is in the poem "Chaos" in his book — that might betoken some beautiful yet unwritten poems. I like "White Roses" a lot; but I have to let them sink in a little.

Reading it over, I don't mind (though I agree about it) the Ashberianness of "Poem." Repeating, even parodying, ourselves seems inevitable; but after a little time has passed, it's often hard to say which flower bloomed first, and whether one is wax. So much of art is an exercising of an achieved style — there are so many Monets I would like singly and together, without finding a special uniqueness in any of them. The uniqueness seems to me between the total work and the rest of the world. (Not that repetitions don't become boring; [Thomas] Hardy's verse affects me like that, and so though I know there are poems of his I like, I resist reading him.)

As a matter of fact, the new garden bed is very like the wallpaper in the back room, including the yellow California poppy, and a little blue flower whose name I don't know. Light and deep pink cornflowers are out too, and a little snapdragonish flower, rather like a wild flower which I think is called butter-and-eggs, only these bloom in violets, blue-pinks and light reds (on different plants, that is).

Frank[112] and John came out and stayed at Larry's for two days last week. That was fun. Frank left me a copy of a long poem called "In Memory of My Feelings" which I said I would copy and haven't yet; when I do I'll make a carbon and send it to you.

112. Frank O'Hara (1926–1966), poet. Schuyler met O'Hara at a party in John Bernard Myers's 9th Street apartment after a Larry Rivers opening at the Tibor de Nagy Gallery. O'Hara and Schuyler shared an apartment at 326 East 49th Street, on and off, from 1952 until January 1957.

I sent the silver poets or whatever it's called last week. I hope you have it by now.

I find, reading Proust a second time, the things I want to mark are very different. Perhaps the first time around one mistakes what is essentially dramatic revelation for perceptions and condensations of ideas. The rhythm of the book is very different, this time, too. I find that my memory translates vividness into length and vice versa. For instance I remembered the scene where the Princess and Duchesse de G both appear in a theater box as much longer; whereas I remembered—I can't think of an example; but often where he describes a place or person at great length, it's become as though I've seen the place or known the person, there isn't any sense of the length of time it took to make the acquaintance. Also I find I've unwoven the story quite a bit and assembled it under subjects, places and people: a biography of Charlus, an album of landscapes. The book has very little of the true dramatic sequence, the rhythm of life, at all; it doesn't begin in the middle like Homer, and bring you up to now and then into the future; or begin now, like *War and Peace*—I guess that's what makes it sometimes stifling, it's all recollection, and one knows that the "now" that comes to the end of the book is, by that time years behind the narrator. Still the last revelation is very potent.

Now it's late. I'll try to write you more consequentially soon; I have not turned in my book and I am hung-up (as they say) on a very small matter. But I won't feel good until I'm unstuck. My love to Anne and Elizabeth and Katy[113] who owes me a letter.

love, Jimmy

PS I didn't notice when it came, but Laurence's card was addressed to Mr. Frank O'Hara, Mr. Robert Gold, Mr. Arthur Fizdale. It's quite a *coup* to get all of us wrong!

113. Porter's wife, Anne (see glossary), and daughters Elizabeth and Katy.

TO JOHN BUTTON AND FRANK O'HARA

[Southampton, New York]

[Summer, 1956]

Dear "John" and "Frank,"
(Or shouldn't I call you by your camp names in a letter?)
I loved your antiphonal psalm—it was like getting a jeweler's box with a sparrow in it that had been fucked to death by John Simon[114] (now explain that to John, Frank). So I thought I'd let Schiz and Oid, the two halves of my personality, collaborate and bake you both a plate of my favorite cakes. ("Take one krater of goat piss and crumble into it enough camel dung to make a workable paste. Pat into cakes and put aside to rest. When an iridescent sheen like that in the eye of a peacock feather appears, bake the cakes in a fast oven, garnish with rabbit berries and serve hot in a napkin. These tasty morsels are the Quiffquiff spoken of so highly by Lawrence of Arabia . . . ")
My, we really are just like the Bronte sisters . . .
So you've seen some movies have you, you rats. Out here they are following up *The Catered Affair,* which I drew my tiny line at, with *Diabolique,*[115] a movie truly worthy of an exegesis in VILE.[116] If they think they're going to throw me back on my own resources they've reckoned without my lack. I'm not called the Big Void for nothing.
Now let me see if I can't get my mind out of my asshole for a moment. No, I can't.
Dear John: Have you painted your Maine picture? If not why not?
Dear Frank: I'm sorry I haven't copied your poem yet, but, you see, I've been doing an awful lot of staring . . . (I'll speak of it in detail soon; on a less spiritual occasion).
I found a sentence I like in Raymond Chandler.[117] It's spoken by one of his

---

114. John Simon (1925–2019), Yugoslavian-born book, movie, and theater critic notorious for his put-downs and negative reviews. There may have been bad blood between Simon and Schuyler. In his vitriolic review of David Lehman's 1999 book on the New York School poets, *The Last Avant-Garde,* Simon referred to Schuyler throughout as "Crazy Schuyler." Simon panned O'Hara's performance in the Poets' Theater 1956 production of John Ashbery's play *The Compromise.*

115. *The Catered Affair* (1956) starred Bette Davis; Simone Signoret starred in Henri Clouzot's thriller *Les Diaboliques* (1955).

116. *Vile* was an underground gay magazine that published purportedly true life stories.

117. Raymond Chandler (1888–1952), novelist, screenwriter, and creator of the private eye Philip Marlowe.

enormous and incredibly tough toughs (and whose gun is called a "cannon") and is as follows:

"Scramola, Jumpchay."

Could Dante do better? His toughs also call coons "smokes," a vileness I had forgotten.

Now honest, how do you two pussy-fevered bulls expect your mother to keep her mind on her tale of tiny tots when you get her all steamy and fetid? Next thing I know I'll have Guinevere slipping her mother's hairbrush up her slough . . . (now, now, dear, mustn't put human dung on your garden. Remember the Chinese!)

Well, I guess I want to finish pricking out the silhouette of my dick and am going to put lipstick on my sphincter so I can plant a nice kiss on the outside of this letter, I had better get at it before the sun sinks into Lake Agawam and goes permanently out. Tell me, is it true — as I've heard — that you've both had your teeth filed down to *fine points*? And that Frank has permanently injured his health by wearing a headache band around his—hips? And that John pitched forward in his new heels and split his chin? I do hope not.

Well, Sieve-lips and Paddle-tongue, I sure hope for all our sakes that this doesn't fall into the hands of the Feds!

Love from yo' ol' Mammy,

Jimminey Yuk-Yuk

TO JOHN BUTTON

[Southampton, New York]   *Friday afternoon*
                                          [Summer, 1956]

Dear John,

And so he got on his girl's bike and said good-bye and peddled away . . . The heavy set, thick waisted little old lady with the toil worn hands and the care worn face dabbed with a corner of his gingham apron at her corn flower blue, far sighted eyes that could nail a basket at a hundred yards. "Bye," she mumbled in her broken English. For truth to tell, she was a Polish princess who gladly, willingly, had sacrificed titles, lands, to come to our country and enjoy in the sweat of her brow the benefits of democracy in this half-forgotten little corner of Iowa. It broke her heart but it cured her piles. (To be continued in the next issue of VILE, the least magazine. Next month you won't want to miss part one

45

of Frank O'Hara's stirring study of the life and loves of Lord Byron, A Real Gone Guy—and for you men folks there'll be more of those John Button silk screen pop-ups that have created such a stir in the lavender set . . . so, don't miss VILE, the only magazine that reads the way it smells).

You know that terrible noise that made you nervous on the beach today? Well, I wasn't quite honest when I said it was jets—you see—uhm—shucks— it's just the noise my breathing makes when I'm near you.

I've been, as Henry James says somewhere, measuring the room with a rest-less foot. With two of them, in fact, sneering at the greenery, picking crabs off my arms and poisoning them with lead white, looking at your painting and sob-bing and wishing it were yesterday again, and generally wondering what keeps my head attached and why it isn't flying around the yard like a swallow at the Battle of Verdun. I love you. You adorable bundle of bliss. How was I to know that when I thought my heart was breaking it was really just opening up like an old cocoon, so the most beautiful butterflies in the world could dash out and swarm around me chanting Hawaiian love chants? (You'll admit it's not the sort of thing one would know in advance . . .)

Do you miss me? Do you love me? Are you keeping? I'm not. Not a bit.

I ought to write you seriously, I want to write you seriously, I will write you seriously, but not today. I can't. The only way I can get through today is by reliving golden moments from my recent past. If I tried to think a thought or plan a plan all the little nylon threads that are holding me together would snap.

I keep starting up from the typewriter with the general but specific intention of going in the house to pack. Whoa Dobbin. Keep your hair ribbon on, boy. It's Friday the 13th the day after the 12th, one of the great dates of history. Don't walk under any birds. You might get clobbered.

But: if you love me, everything will be all right; and I'm not just being Chris-tian Science smarmy about it. It will be all right because I want it to be and I'll make it be. I know it as certainly as I know there are rocks in my bed. So chin up, head down, and don't be afraid to use your brass knuckles in the clinches.

Now I'll slip on my truss and my leopard skin elastic stocking and trundle this up to the post office.

With all my love,

Jimmy

TO JOHN BUTTON

[Southampton, New York]

Sunday [Summer, 1956]

Dear John,

When will I be able to write the letter I want to write you? It's too much — it's as though I thought, uhm, today would be a good time to weave these tapestries[118] I've been planning, a unicorn and a lot of men and women and dogs, all on a background of mille fleurs; or as though I walked down Park Avenue and thought, now a nice sunny afternoon like this, if I really put my back into it I can get these windows washed. Or set out to make a rubbing of Rockefeller Center.

No matter what I manage to tell you, it won't be the right things — and I'll leave out all the connections — and forget that if I say *this* it won't make any sense because you don't know *that* — besides, you're not an Aztec, why should you want a bloody heart dropped in your lap? "For heaven's sake stop hacking at yourself or we'll never get to the movie —" "Get me the plumber and let's go: what's playing?" "Dick Steel in *The Big Rim.*" "I've already seen it."

There, now I've effectively prevented myself from saying anything beautiful or true or real — hah — the hell I have.

I was awfully glad I stayed up with Frank the other night after you wandered off to your trundle. He was the most marvelous devil's advocate a chap could ask for. I don't mean everything he said to me was nice, and quite a bit of it I would almost as soon not have heard, but I liked it because it turned out none of it hurt. (How that boy can identify — at one moment he would become, say, Alvin, only an Alvin who was rather like Paul Muni in *Scarface*,[119] and his voice would get all snarling and full of hate for me, because I was a threat to Alvin's home, then he'd remember what's happened since you came back from Maine, take a deep flaming drag on his fag and a big suck out of his sherry glass and send jets of blarney up into the starry night while we waited for another idea to be born. Usually it was Joey [LeSueur] who climbed out of Cassiopeia's chair and descended with the tablets of the law.) One of the few things I got to say, or needed to say, was, when he started the "but Jimmy, are you certain, are you

---

118. Schuyler refers to *The Hunt of the Unicorn* at the Cloisters in Fort Tryon Park in northern Manhattan.

119. Paul Muni (1895–1967), actor who played the lead in *Scarface* (1932), directed by Howard Hawks.

really sure, in your heart *and* in your mind . . . " and then a lot of guff about buried attachments and the-grass-is-greener—anyway what I said was, "That's no problem at all for me Frank: I love John more than I've ever loved anyone in my life." And it's that, dearest, that I hope will motivate everything I do. I don't want to do anything you wouldn't approve of or like, that isn't worthy of you. Because I know you believe in passion, and I know that you believe too in the reality of other people and their feelings. An awful lot of people don't believe in both those things.

Oh dear: I feel all gluey and silly—and what's funny is that I feel so certain I could make you happy; sex, too (that was the one thing I shut Frank up about: he just doesn't know. Why shouldn't people who're in love be cockshy and virginal? That's the way love is for people who are shy about their deep feelings. I can't tell you how strange it made me feel to walk into that room and see you all naked—it was so personal! I wanted to put my hands in my pockets and go sauntering and whistling around the room, idly kicking out the window panes . . . One thing Frank said I thought was very cute, when he was telling a story and suddenly gave a guffaw when he saw my face, which was addressed to your body like an August moon above the bosom of the sea, and said, "I *hope* I'm not inter-*rup*-ting you!"—with his eyes sparkling and snapping like hot diamonds—or possessed sapphires—)

I just got brought down to earth with a jolt—I feel like a dirigible made of solid platinum all coated with Van Dyke brown—a step is heard in my barn—I faint and try to hide your letter—the one I'm writing I mean—it suddenly seemed as big as a stove—Grace Hartigan and Mary Clyde[120] are coming over! I think when they get here I'll rush out screaming and lashing: "It's not reality that's the trap, Grace! It's you! Phew! Fish! I can't stand it. Here's some ice girls, you can shove it up and cool off: Where's the gin? Has that smoke been lapping it up again? Get the pissing hell outa my way. I'm trying to give myself to John Button and you all keep interrupting—"

Not that I don't know that you need this tottering wreck about as much as you need an 80 cup obsidian samovar. It's like offering someone who deserves all of Venice a little room (with a toilet in one corner and no shower) out behind the glass works.

I enclose a card from John, a picture of the original of Marcel's Belchbec Beach.

120. Mary (Abbott) Clyde (1921–2019), American painter who showed at Tibor de Nagy Gallery.

You'll get more of this quite, quite soon—here I'll direct a stream of fire at the page and then see if I can sign my name.

with all my love,

Jimmy

Monday

Dear John, H'lo. I'm back, battered and torn but still clinging to the mast of life. My mounting tension found itself a little physical outlet last night. I was reading in bed, started dozing and got up to take a leak before I put out the light. The hall was dark and I turned off one door too soon, stepped onto nothing and went crashing down the laundry stairs. So I just lay there whimpering and thought about Life and wondered whether I'd broken my back or just gotten a splinter up my ass. Neither it turned out, though I did scrape enough skin off my left ham to make a fine binding for a Modern Library Giant (guess I'll have to call my next book "There Are No Accidents: The Story of a Boy") and my right ankle hurts in a slight, persistent, rather preoccupying way. As a matter of fact, I've been doing quite well in the punish yourself line. Every time the stove needs coal I go with great dignity and poise into the coal bin, pick up the shovel and then slam it into the coal with such vehemence that I always bark at least one knuckle. And the night before last we had lobster. I was trying to break one of those nameless appendages lobsters have that are sort of like steel nut picks and it simply wouldn't break. A wave of will and of Charles-Atlas-like strength went through me and I snapped it and it jabbed me in the palm. But I went right on munching, happy in my ugly little victory.

Arthur and I are not getting along. At all. After the weekenders went away last evening we went for a walk and had a kind of no-fight; I mean we should have, and kind of began to, but I absolutely froze. Mostly because I don't know yet what I want to do. I know better today than I did last night. So don't be surprised if you see me soon. (It's been odd, because very soon after you and Frank left, Arthur W[einstein], Angelo[121] and a girl named Claire Rosenstein[122] appeared, so it was all a kind of socializing blank.) I feel tired and shocked and at my worst.

One thing: I don't want anything that happens between me and Arthur to be a pressure on you. Things haven't been really right between us for a long time;

---

121. Angelo Toricini (1928–2016), color and art consultant to choreographer George Balanchine, among others.

122. Remembered by Angelo Toricini as a pretty, bright, and witty young woman.

and if now it stops, instead of going on more-or-less well, it won't be easy, but it won't kill either of us. Also, if I leave Arthur I don't want you to fell that that obliges you to—well, to anything. I believe in asking for love where and from whom you want it, but I know nothing good comes of pressure and demands.

I love you,

Jimmy

TO JOHN BUTTON

[Southampton, New York]

Saturday [Summer, 1956]

Dear John,

I'm out here in the barn while the boys, Nellie, Jane, Joe, Al K., Mollie and Larry[123] are around the dining table playing 21, writing to you from whom I haven't had a personal letter in a whole week: fiend, unchained beast, monster, beautiful boy, handsome man, adorable painter.

It's just as well; when Arthur and I had our talk, finally, last evening, and I told him that I'm going back to New York, I had no reason to think I was going from him to any greater satisfaction. You didn't come into it, nor should you have; there's been a real estrangement between us for a long time. If Arthur's upset, he's also relieved. We haven't said we're breaking up, though that in effect is what it is. I feel distressed, but greater than my distress is my certainty that I'm doing the right thing.

I'm writing Frank to ask him (or rather tell him: how one takes one's friend-ships for granted—and how marvelous Frank's is in my life—an Irish emerald as big as Plymouth Rock) about staying there. Dear dusty vision of the UN Building, with the reflection of the sunset streaming down your wet face.

So far no one else knows about this (though I'm writing Frank) and I would like to do it with as much silence and grace as a loose tongue and a trick knee permit.

I don't know yet what day I will come into town—this week, I assume. My arrival doubtless will coincide with Alvin's; great.

---

123. Painters Nell Blaine (1922–1996), Jane Freilicher, Joe Hazan, Al Kresch (1922–2022), Mollie (?), and Larry Rivers.

Well, John, I hope you'll drop by the studios at Flushing while we're filming Interrupted Summer, the Marjorie Schuyler Story.[124]

Christ how it rains! I wonder if I can make it to the P.O. without drowning. I love you,

Jimmy

ps: I hope this doesn't sound cold; I'm befuddled. I don't have to ask you to imagine how difficult this is for me. I meant what I wrote you: I don't want you to feel in any way responsible: if my feeling for you has made this happen sooner than it might have, that's certainly a good thing. There's a point where one knows something should end, but you can't do it, after which you can very easily spoil something that shouldn't be spoiled. So don't write to me here, & I'll see you dear—so soon—not soon enough but soon.

Darling!

I guess you can see from that that the afternoon mail has come and brought me a letter from you. I'm the fiend and the rest of it, and you're marvelously you. Don't be cross with Frank: he was drunk and I made him keep going— and I didn't write you the thousand, thousand sweet things he said about you, and about me, and about the possibility of us. If anyone was being not nice, it was me—I wanted to hear all he had to say. He's a terror but he is our Frank.

I suppose I should tear this up and write another, but I haven't any more words. It delighted me that you signed that joint-letter "with endless love," because there are 2 lines of Wystan's that pop into my head all the time, surrounded with your radiance. Caliban says them to Ariel:

> *Elegance, art, fascination,*
> *Endlessly in love with you:*[125]

Jimmy

124. Schuyler alludes to *Interrupted Melody*, the film biography of the opera singer Marjorie Lawrence.

125. The lines are from Auden's *The Sea and the Mirror*, his commentary on Shakespeare's *The Tempest*.

TO KENNETH KOCH

[New York, New York]

Wed. [Summer, 1956]

Dear Boy,

I've been thinking—no, that's not the way to put it; I've an idea—no, that's not the way either; I've been lying on the bed and it seems to me that

        we should

          all do

            a lot

              more

                of it

(so that's how W. C. Williams gets that look)—anyway there is the question of these painters who insist we make public spectacles of ourselves. According to Button & Blaine, we're limited to 170 (one seventy) words per poet per painter (I mean the poet *including* the painter, not 170 words each); well, I started mine about John and found that after a page and a half I had hit the 600 point and hadn't even gotten to him yet. So I planned a plan which my room-mate [Frank O'Hara], once again a minion of the M.O.M.A. has given his seal to, on or of. He says he doesn't care what happens and it might as well be this way as any other.

All it is is that we each write Sentences. Isn't that simple? (Climb back out of the bay, dear, it's cold and you'll get the plate in your head all rusty.) I mean like, Sentences about Howard Kanovitz, Sentences about Mary Abbot Clyde, Sentences about John Button,[126] Curses about Herbert Machiz. . . . You know, sort of like The Cheerful Cherub: "You keep out of my way and I'll keep out of yours"; "Don't tell me how to wear hats and I won't tell you where to part your hair"; and so on. Just a lot of nice home-made sentences. Anyway, you must do it right away because while no one cares whether it ever happens it has to happen now if it's going to happen at all. That you aren't better acquainted with your chosen artist's work doesn't matter much, as it turns out that if you try to describe a teaspoon in 170 words it may turn out sounding quite a bit like Gi-

---

126. Tibor de Nagy exhibition September 25–October 13 of Abbott, Button, and Kanovitz. In the show's brochure, *Three Painters Introduced by Three Poets*, Koch writes about Abbott, Schuyler about Button ("John Button's strength is truth, his weakness beauty . . . ") and O'Hara about Kanovitz.

52

tou Knoop.[127] So let 'er rip, Big Red (and remember it's not 170 sentences they want from us, but words).

Isn't Great Spruce Head beautiful? I could go on quite a while telling you about it, but then, you are there.

J & J[128] came back from Mexico, very tan and smelling of coconut oil and a little weary. This time I think they were a little less staggered by its beauty (our Jane isn't taking any sass from anybody) and more at home. It's always hard to say whether they had a *good* time anywhere, but they did visit the gladiola center of Mexico and the cucumber center and saw lots of movies with Spanish subtitles.

The frothy New York social season keeps on draining away; tomorrow night we're going to dinner at David Noakes's[129] and Stuart Preston[130] will be there. No wonder all the ovens in New York are being converted to non-toxic natural gas.

(Larry called up just now and managed to make so many innuendoes in one and a half minutes my head feels like the merry-go-round at the end of *Strangers on a Train*).[131]

Oh. I also saw Larry briefly yestereve (ah, bitter sticky and muggy it was, the Chihuahua for all its hairlessness was a sweat) and he said he'd read your "G.W. Crossing the D." aloud to some Southampton Big-Wigs and they loved it, they broke up, they thought it was terribly funny. Isn't that cute? Anyway Larry seemed to think it was a step toward the Southampton auditorium, Broadway and too many pickles too late at night at Sardi's[132] (John Button knows a marvelous pill for indigestion that cures acidity without setting up an alkali whateveryoucallit). Anyway, it occurred to me I've never heard Larry read from any work other than his own, and I wish I had tuned him in on this little device I have that picks up what anyone is saying anywhere in the world at any time. (I had it trained on Harry's Bar in Venice at the time; pigs all of them).

127. Gitou Knoop, sculptor living in the Hamptons.

128. Jane Freilicher and Joe Hazan.

129. David Noakes, Harvard friend of John Ashbery. Schuyler dedicated the poem "Greetings from the Chateau" to Noakes.

130. Stuart Preston, art critic for *The New York Times* in the 1940s and 1950s who wrote a book about Vuillard.

131. The 1951 movie directed by Alfred Hitchcock starring Farley Granger and Robert Walker.

132. Broadway restaurant popular with the theater crowd.

I really have nothing to say that warrants a fresh page, but, two page letters are better than none.

We love Janice's [Koch] postcard. We love Janice, and we thought and talked about her a lot on her birthday, and fulminated against a social order that prevents us from expressing our sentiment in a tangible form. I would call a diamond tangible, wouldn't you? But then, alas, so are pralines.

I had lunch with my editor [Dan Wickenden] from Harcourt, Brace, and it's a shame that an unusually kind heart, gentle tongue and faulty memory prevent me from reporting the conversation to you. Anyway, they seem to like it (*Alfred & Guinevere*) enormously, and have plans for publishing it during my life time—and I don't mean I'm taking a short view of my span, either. Though when illustrations were suggested, on the grounds it would make it more "of a package," I did almost bring up my Chef Salad Marmiton. Then I thought, oh well, at least it doesn't have to be pressed into clay like the works of those poor Babylonian novelists. Think how the author of Gilgamesh must have felt—he didn't even have reprint rights. The people at Harcourt are also extremely proud of the way their books look. Since I think only books printed in France and a few subsidiary states can be looked at without experiencing one of the major disgusts, I don't really care what they do to it. After all, the origin of our art is the spoken word, isn't it, Kenneth? Ho ho ho.

We misses thou and thou moglie and thou bambinakins. I hope baby K soon gets over her xenophobia so I can rush in and smother her with kisses without getting socked in the eye. Hurry back; the telephone is as a dead thing without you.

love,

PS and do do your sentences tout-de-suitee and send me them; John Myers wrote from Venice that he doesn't want this show to lay an egg. Isn't he *cute*?

TO KENNETH KOCH

[New York, New York]

Wednesday
(perhaps August 22, 1956? chi sa)

Dear Kenneth,

I hasten into air mail to tell you how beautiful, right and true, how perfectly suitable and extremely witty I think your paragraph is about Mary Clyde. I'm glad you understand what I meant about sentences (don't ever use the word camp ("camp?") to me again unless you're wearing something a lot flouncier than you usually wear), maybe if I had said "statements" it would have been closer to what I had in mind. Anyway, what you've written has made me feel quite down-in-the-mouth about what I've written, and may permanently prevent Frank from writing anything about Howie (I just read it to him on the phone and he joins me in sincere acclaim) — the only sort of tribute worth having from us; rancorous jealousy and corroding envy.

No, but seriously, I think it's completely apt, charming and very CUTE. Except, really, it isn't cute. Tell me your secret daddy do: how *do* you manage to be charming and not cute? I can't seem to swing it.

News! New York has no news. It has plenty of movies though. I have seen *Proud and Beautiful* Michèle Morgan[133] covered with sweat in her bra and underskirt; lovely Lauren Bacall[134] weeping because she was caught in *The Cobweb* at the steering wheel of her roadster; hair miraculously envelope the face of *The Werewolf*; the drab exterior of the *Earth vs. The Flying Saucers* whose interiors could do with a little chintz; I have seen Her Serene Majesty *The Swan* and found the philosophy of Molnar[135] to resemble mine when I was in love with Helen Twelvetrees;[136] I have heard *The Foreign Intrigue Concerto* (fr. the mv. of the sm. nm.) and *A Kiss Before Dying* (fr. the mv. of the sm. nm.) and heard the word "*cochon*" and seen it translated as "you cad." Truly, why should the Gods concern themselves with mortals, who live and die like leaves? (Homer)

I have also discovered that Harcourt, Brace might as well change their tradename to Were, Wolf & Co. I'm completely enraged by the advance they're offering me, which is, as Jane once said about the rent on her studio, piteously little. After talking to this one and that one it seems indubitable that I can get it jacked up — " . . . but the people! And the noise!"[137] and if you don't know the joke of which that is the tag, you have led a very lovely life.

133. Michèle Morgan (1920–2016), French actress.

134. Lauren Bacall (1924–2014), movie actress noted for her roles opposite her husband Humphrey Bogart.

135. Ferenc Molnar (1878–1952), Hungarian playwright known for his comedies.

136. Helen Twelvetrees (1907–1958), actress in many 1930s movies whose career suddenly collapsed.

137. When asked his impression of the World War I Battle of Ypres where he had been wounded, British actor Ernest Thesiger is supposed to have said, "My dear the *noise*! And the people!"

Come back, come back, Big Sheba, and let's spend our evenings collaborating on something non-definitive and coruscating. We could call it *The Making of Americans*; or do you prefer calling it *In the American Grain*?[138] Personally, I cast my vote for *The Collected Verse Letters of Amy Lowell*.

I've been feeling very concerned lately about Toby Wing.[139] You haven't seen her up there have you? Around 1934 she was a cunning breasty little thing in jodhpurs, with hair like a drift of natural gas and the merry eyes of a bat. Frank and I send our love to Janice and Baby Kay and (now don't blush and stammer and gawk around) to you.

John Myers is rumored due *today*, and Naomi[140] will be here ever so soon. Pretty soon they'll all come winging, swinging, railing and motoring home and the terrible hiatus of the summer will seem never to have been.

John Button: "Personally, I'm *glad* it's almost the 1st of September."

Frank: "Well I'm sure I don't know what I could do about it if it wasn't."

I don't know how I have the courage to write you a letter after you used the word camp to me. I bet nobody ever answered one of Horace Walpole's letters with, "What's all this camp about Strawberry Hill?"

love,

Jimmy

PS Of course the last sentence of your piece must stay.

TO FAIRFIELD PORTER

[New York, New York]

Sunday [August 26, 1956]

Dear Fairfield,

I just had a long chin with Kenneth, who got back this morning by train since they couldn't get a plane: I was very sorry to hear that your sickness had continued, but glad that you went into Camden and got diagnosed so you know

---

138. *The Making of Americans* is a novel by Gertrude Stein; William Carlos Williams wrote the long historical essay *In the American Grain*.

139. Toby Wing (1916–2001), Hollywood actress in the 1930s who gave up a promising career for marriage.

140. Naomi Weinstein, singer and wife of playwright Arnold Weinstein.

where you're at. Myself, I am so inclined to think that whatever goes wrong with me is purely psychosomatic that it's often a relief to find out that it has a name (such as, The Common Cold), and an independent existence of which thousands of other sufferers are as aware as myself. Oh well: there isn't any consoling side I know of to being sick—do what the doctor says, rest and get well.

The swallows are coming home, the Kochs today and Naomi and Arnold [Weinstein] last night. Naomi is brown and plump, very becomingly so, though of course she says she hates it and is going to lose it right away. Arnold says he has lost weight but this is visible only to Naomi. He is very funny, cute and silly. I saw them last night at the Gruens'[141] (oops: I always remember Anne saying how she hates hearing married people or a family called, "The Blanks": she is right), where I both liked Jane Wilson's new pictures and felt disappointed that more hadn't "happened" since her show last year. One thing I liked about her show was that it made me feel something was going to happen (in her work, I mean). Though the ones I saw were altogether figurative, they still seem dependent on the "abstract-impressionist," snarled-yarn convention, which I find just now one of the less attractive common-places of New York painting.

Harcourt sent me a contract, but I haven't signed it. The terms are even less favorable for first novels, on the grounds that it's so short (and therefore the retail price will be low), and the expense of illustrating it, a scheme to which I first gave half-hearted assent, but am now flatly opposed to. My public (and sincere) reason is that the book by being non-descriptive makes a stronger appeal to the visual imagination, an appeal which illustrations would hamper. My private reason is that it's almost an absolute certainty that I would hate the work of the artist they would choose. Anyway, I wrote them that I would have to think about it, and intended to get advice from someone "more professionally experienced than myself" (I was advised not to invoke "the agent threat" yet: the whole thing is so silly, and just the way I've always found the business world to be—especially on that desolate and desecrated seashore where the monsters of the sea of art and the squatters in their jungletown regard each other with mutual distrust).

I may write an interview (did I tell you?) for the October issue with a sculptor named (oh dear) Rosack? Rosehack? Rorshack?[142] Maybe you know who I

141. John Gruen, (1926–2016), composer, photographer, and writer who wrote the memoir of the 1950s New York art world, *The Party's Over Now*, and his wife, Jane Wilson (1924–2015), painter.

142. Theodore Roszak (1907–1981), Polish-born American sculptor.

mean. Anyway Tom [Hess] asked me if I liked it and I said well enough, so he said he hated it and we'd better just give him an interview.

Here is what I wrote for the Tibor de N first show catalogue about John: do you think it's OK? I guess its pretty full-blown, but it seems to me an Introduction gives one more license than a review.

I'm going to review that show, as well. I told Tom I guessed that since I was writing an introduction somebody else ought to review it, and he said, "I don't see why." Things *are* different than they were back in B.C. days!

I hope this finds you feeling much better. My love to Anne.

love, Jimmy

TO JOHN BUTTON

[New York, New York]

Labor Day [1956]

Dear John,

I'm sorry to have to write you, rather than speak, but perhaps the fact that I do is another reason for saying what I have to say.

It's simply that I shall not make any more effort to make happen what I so profoundly wished would happen, I mean that we would be lovers. Your physical rejection of me is too wounding and continuous for me to bear it. (The serious things in life are almost always funny: you made a movement of withdrawal from me in bed this morning that so angered and hurt me that I would have gotten up and dressed and left—except I was feeling too dopey from my sleeping pill to be bothered.)

I think we are probably more physically compatible than you imagine—our ideas of privacy and respect may, however, be quite different. It is odd of you, for instance, to tease me to drink: you have seen in your own family the horrifying destructiveness of alcoholism, and you ought to respect my reasons for not drinking, whether I discuss them with you or not. To take a much smaller instance: you might have left it up to me to let Mike Goldberg know that I am "on" Miltowns;[143] I really dislike being talked over by my most casual acquaintances.

What is more serious is that I tried very hard to preserve Arthur's esteem (and Bobby's) for you when I left Southampton: and no matter how little value you

143. Miltown, a commonly prescribed tranquilizer.

58

place on it, their esteem is certainly worth more than any momentary pleasure making a quip to Angelo Torricini may have given you, or divulging affairs not your own to Rudi,[144] who told Ernst Hacker,[145] who told Arthur W., and so on. There is no end to what gossip sets in motion.

What is most serious (if true) is that you told Larry about Fairfield's private affairs. No matter what Larry may have surmised, he did not before really know anything (I got this from Jane). I don't imply at all that you were motivated by malice, but you do provide people who are malicious with weapons: would you really care to take the responsibility for what Larry is capable of saying to Anne Porter, and do you think she deserves having it said to her? (Not that her nature isn't large enough to encompass it.) And what about the obligations your friendship with Fairfield, John Ashbery and with me place on you?

I'm sorry to speak — I mean, write — so harshly and coldly to you. It's the measure of the intensity of my love for you, and of my unhappiness.

Don't be distressed by *anything* in this letter beyond its importance. In all likelihood your gossip won't cause anything so very terrible to happen; if I lecture you about gossiping, it's only in the dim hope that you may in the future be choosier about the people in whom you confide.

As for myself, I think it will be a relief for you: you can't be unaware that the only gestures of affection you make to me are when you are drunk, or when there are other people present or nearby. The meaning of that is too easily read. I still want your friendship as much as I ever did.

Jimmy

TO DAN WICKENDEN

[New York, New York]

Labor Day [1956]

Dear Dan Wickenden,
Here is the new chapter I spoke of to you. It is intended to divide the present cc: V: its place is after the entry ending, "Must remember things like that in case Alfred ever gets me into trouble." and before the entry beginning, "Betty

---

144. Rudy Burckhardt (1914–1999), Swiss-born American photographer, moviemaker, and painter.
145. Ernst Hacker (1917–1987), American painter.
146. See glossary.

and I set following Stanley and Alfred in the A.M. . . . " The balance of that chapter now becomes Chapter VII, and so on. If you are satisfied with it, please indicate its place in the manuscript, and change the numbering of the chapters that follow.

For myself, I think I am satisfied with it: it seems a good idea to have more of the boys, and to have them more directly, in the story: also, the small bit about Alfred's father was badly needed: and of course there is the original reason for writing it, that the first diary excerpt was too long.

I hope you like it.

I'm sorry, but it is impossible for me to come by this week. I will have upwards of twenty shows to see and write about in four days. Such is the dispersal of galleries and studios that simply getting to see them is a tiring labor, much less inventing the time to write sensibly about what I will have seen. For the three following weeks I have a full time job to do, then back to reviewing. My time is not my own.

I trust you'll write me about any discussion for or against illustrating or decorating the book, or about any style or artist seriously thought of. The other day I looked at *The Ponder Heart*,[147] and while its presentation is charming, its length does not seem much increased by the decorations, and my book is surely not shorter than it? My mind is still open about this, though less when it comes to actually depicting—there's a nice old fashioned word for you—any of the characters. To be conservative is often to be attractively original, and don't you like the French way of inserting a page with only a numeral on it before each chapter? And isn't the use of colored type on a title page winning?

I will let you know as soon as I can what I think about the terms of the agreement. I hope that the fact that I am taking a little [time] about it will not give the impression that I am dickering on the side with any other publisher. I am not. On the other hand, the sums of money involved are of so little use in helping me to find the time [sic] to even begin another book, that I can't sincerely say I feel pressed. One thing that did surprise me: had I submitted the book as it now is, I would understand Harcourt, Brace taking it as a one-shot fluke; but the fact that I could bring off (and think I have) so difficult a revision (as a writer you know the difficulties involved in totally changing a work to which one is altogether committed: and though my novel may be called a "light" one, no one

147. Novel by Eudora Welty (1909) with drawings by Joe Krush published by Harcourt, Brace in 1954.

takes his lightness more seriously than I), seems to me both a proof of ability and of objectivity, and an earnest that my next novel will be better, with a stronger story, bolder, more vivid and funnier. I don't mean to pride myself on an ability to lay golden eggs; but I don't see any advantage to pretending blindness to my own capabilities.

I hope you and your family enjoyed the long weekend.

I anticipate hearing from you by telephone or by letter.

Yours sincerely,

PS I'll deal with the offending word as soon as I have time.[148]

TO FAIRFIELD PORTER

[New York, New York]

Monday evening [Fall 1956]

Dear Fairfield,

Are you there? You don't seem to be here. In New York, I mean, where I heard you would be. Well, if you are there, I hope you are doing whatever the doctor says you should be doing. I'm sure it is resting and you aren't.

You probably know already that John is arriving on the Queen Elizabeth the day after tomorrow. He wants to stay with me and Frank and with you and Anne before he goes home, so I imagine he'll call you.

I started back at the Holliday[149] shop today. I thought it would seem as though I had never been away but it seems as though I have been away about seventy-five years. I managed to look into about two dozen books I've vaguely thought I wanted to read if I could ever get hold of them and discovered I don't want to read any of them (books like *Proust's Oriane*:[150] but a look at the photograph showed me his model wouldn't be nearly as interesting to read about as the *real* Duchesse de Guermantes). The people are very nice, and the fact that I can

---

148. "Nigger" was the offending word.
149. Periscope-Holliday Bookstore on East 54th Street where Schuyler worked in 1952.
150. *Proust's Oriane: A Diptych* by Princess Marthe Bibesco, translated by Edward Marsh and published in 1952.

figure out that when a lady asks for *Hong Kong Pierce* what she wants is *Shanghai Pierce*[151] gives me some sort of unwarranted prestige. Oh well.

Frank and I liked your and Kenneth's sestina very much and would have written so but thought you were leaving sooner than you did. (It took a letter of yours two days longer to reach me than one from John from Paris; that's from Sunset, not Great Spruce Head. I guess if the American postal system is going to be poor it might as well be the very worst.)

I don't know anything about my book. I have a contract but I won't sign it. I just sit and wait to hear from Harcourt, Brace, from *The New Yorker*, and from the Greatest Agent in the World, a woman said to be made of some substance more durable than a diamond.

Your piece about Jane reads beautifully, it's witty and it's amazing how many interesting things you pryed out of our clam. Personally I wish they had given the color cut a full page; but I guess the god of layout must be served. I guess it's silly to be annoyed by it (layout, I mean) but it would be amusing if one tenth the energy that goes into that nonsense were ever spent on trying once to make a really accurate color reproduction. Oh well! (again).

I had post-reviewing gloom over the weekend; I hope my review of Jane doesn't read too much like an ad for a new Hair Rinse. But I think her show will be much her best and most interesting; it's as though she had become a little simpler and more direct about everything, and at the same time the initial conception of most of the pictures seems bolder and clearer; also more imaginative, in a way that's been more or less out of her work since her first show, and I'm glad to find back (I mean the kind of spirit that was in her Leda and the football picture in her first show). Really, if my review has a blurb quality, it's on purpose: it seems to me all right if you like a show as much as I like this one just to shout and point. Especially if you haven't much room to shout in.

Arthur said something about the piano movers having forgotten to bring two bags: instead of your schlepping (sp?) them in on the train, why don't you call Larry and ask him to take them the next time he drives in? Which will doubtless be soon. After all, he's indebted to you, and Arthur W did commission a portrait from him this summer: so it won't break his wrists to do it. (The only reason I'm being sarcastic is that I'm afraid you might think it would be imposing on Larry; an idea that makes me feel quite dizzy.)

I looked at all the books in the Children's Section today but I couldn't find one worthy of Katy's attention. Something happened about the time they

151. Book about a Texas cattle baron.

started calling children's books Juveniles. I don't know what it was but it's terrible.

My love to Anne. I'll write Katy soon even if I haven't anything to say. (I'm listening to Rossini's *William Tell* but I wish it were Donizetti's *Anna Bolena*.) love,

Jimmy

TO MARGARET DAISY CONNOR
SCHUYLER RIDENOUR [152]

[New York, New York]

Nov. 20 [1956]

Dear Maney,

Thank you for the lovely birthday presents. The preserves look beautiful, and I am well into the peach. It's delicious. And the three quinces are on the table by my typewriter. They always remind me of that Chinese porcelain whosis of Dad's, The Peaches of Immortality I think it was called. And their delicate, almost "invisible" scent, well, I guess what it hauntingly reminds me of is themselves!

The ten dollar check was certainly welcome. Since last September I have been in psychoanalysis. Now that I am in it, I can see that it would have helped me a lot had I tried it sooner. Live and learn! I might have let you know sooner, but, well, maybe it's not a bad idea to try a thing out before you announce that it's the hottest thing since Rinso. Psychoanalysis, like quite a few things in life, is not exactly free. In a very real sense, "it costs as much as you think it costs." It also costs cash. So, anytime you and Dad feel you can spare a few bucks, it will be both appreciated and a help.

It was very perceptive of you (you *are* very perceptive) to know that I was feeling anxious last summer; and I knew it was altogether loving of you to say that the children would come down to drive me home for a rest. I won't labor the point, but Fred[153] is to me in some ways still Freddy. He's certainly not my baby brother any more; and he's too tall to be my little brother; but he is my younger brother, and when I come home for a visit it will be very much under my own steam.

---

152. See glossary.
153. Fredric Ridenour (1933–2019), Schuyler's half-brother.

I guess that may sound pretty dogmatic. I'm not very interested in dogmatism. I do have, however, among my qualities, a certain independence of mind, and I don't have to look any further than my own mother to find out "where I got it from." Personally, I like it.

Give my love to Dad and the kids. Tell Hilde[154] I was very pleased to get her sweet card on my birthday. And write soon.

love,

Jim

TO DAN WICKENDEN

[New York, New York]

Dec. 19 [1956]

Dear Dan,

Thank you for your unofficial note and here is one in return. (I can't speak yet about your book or *The Malefactors*:[155] I haven't received them yet. Just a beautiful photograph—how beautiful she was in her Bernhardt style; and Joyce's hands, how they remind me of Cellini's *Narcisso*[156] with its lissome and drawn-out "am-I-not-the-loveliest-of-things?" torso: which may have been psychology (after all Cellini saw a salamander in the fire so he had sharp eyes), but was also for a sound aesthetic reason: that in the place it used to occupy in the Boboli Gardens the exaggeration was necessary for the optic illusion—bound round some leaves of recollection written with a beautiful simplicity (and directness) that seem intriguing to Miss Beach's character. Or so I judge from the first three sentences. I really cannot put down Agatha Christie's *Death on the Nile* (a big scarlet Rolls Royce had just stopped in front of the local post office).

"A girl jumped out, a girl without a hat and wearing a frock that looked (but only *looked*) simple." Why scarlet? Because—it is too horrible! but then, it's only a story—it is "Linnet Ridgeway!" who gets it) to pick up *A Midsummer Night's Dream*:

---

154. Brunhilde Ridenour (1936–2021), wife of Fredric.

155. Caroline Gordon's (1895–1981) novel, based on the life of Hart Crane, published by Harcourt in 1956.

156. Benvenuto Cellini's (1500–1571) sculpture of a male youth, now in Museo Nazionale del Bargello in Florence.

THESEUS: . . . *Four happy days bring in*
Another moon; but, O, methinks how slow
This old moon wanes! She lingers my desires,
Like to a stepdame or a dowager,
Long withering out of a young man's revenue.

HIPPOLYTA: *Four days will quickly steep themselves in night:*
Four nights will quickly dream away the time;
and then the moon, like to a silver bow
new bent in heaven, shall behold the night
of our solemnities.

Why the moon? Because—it's too beautiful but then, it is a masterpiece—the whole play is moonshine.

THESEUS: *Moonshine and lion are left to bury the dead.*

(His last line before his exeunt speech) and there is Puck's last song;

Now the hungry lion roars
And the wolf behowls the moon;

(Have you ever read Forrest Reid's *Peter Waring*,[157] once called *Following Darkness,* from the most beautiful line in Puck's song: "Following darkness like a dream"? A title he changed because he thought its significance (to him) was misunderstood?)

And then there are the books I read as a happy editorial associate of *Art News*; lately, Berenson's *Seeing and Knowing*[158] (ah, B. B., so it is only you who provide the continuity in the age of figurative drought! and Roger Fry's *Transformations,*[159] dated in an interesting way but altogether provocative and chockfull of food for thought.

Why all this moonshine? Because of what happens before *A & G* begins (which, at present, Alfred explains to Mrs. Perlmaster in chapter 13): the only "really and truly" thing in the book. Now the problem turns on the word nigger: a word which is obsolete, but which is used by many people: for instance,

157. Forrest Reid (1875–1947), Irish novelist, critic, and autobiographer. *Peter Waring* appeared in 1939.
158. Bernard Berenson (1865–1959), art historian renowned for his writing on Italian Renaissance painting. He lived at the villa I Tatti outside of Florence and was known by his initials, B.B.
159. Roger Fry (1866–1934), British critic, artist and historian who championed the art of Paul Cezanne.

by many people in Washington, where our story begins (or should I say, began?). A word which will not simply offend Negroes, but particular friends, for instance, the singer Martha Flowers,[160] who lately has had the pleasure of reading a not (superficially) inaccurate portrait of herself in my old pal Truman Capote's *The Muses Are Heard*.[161] And I can imagine how many of the other members of the cast of *Porgy and Bess*[162] felt, because many of them are not just "coons," good time kids, or hopheads, or anything else: they are serious performing artists. And Martha, who has a beautiful voice and an excellent training, most of all.

Anyway, to make this too long letter a little shorter, you said in your editorial suggestions that the name Lily does suggest a colored maid; well, it is true that many Negroes are named for flowers: (Martha is named for all of them!) I think in this particular instance, it is the emotional context that makes it plain that Lily *is* a colored maid. And, if you permit the small jest (as good old Hercule Poirot might say: at least he didn't kill Linnett. Even the author of *The Murder of Roger Ackroyd* wouldn't stoop to so low a device; I hope!) I wonder if Lily Van Ameringen Auchincloss, Girl Editor, would *altogether* agree with you? Mrs. Auchincloss is a very broad minded and good humored woman, and, though not so white as the driven snow, she would not be jim-crowed south of the Mason-Dixon line, still . . .

Now what has happened (in the story) is that two white, middle class children had their first direct experience of death: a dead Negro in a park (Rock Creek Park, to be precise). There is a black thread that goes through the book, but that is a fear (an animal fear, one might say) of death; and not necessarily xenophobia. ("I like Lily but I don't love her." A., Chapter 1. Much later: "Lily wouldn't like it and mother would like it a whole lot less." Alfred, in the simplest sense, does love Lily. He is also very aware of how "the grown-ups" respond to stimuli!) At any rate, because of that, I'm trying to make the last chapter (it's well under way) a big release: like *feux-d'artifices*, and there may be some in it yet.

So much to say, and now I have to go out. Into a Christmas in New York! Well, you reviewed the book about that — as well — for the *Trib*.[163] That's another true story! that is just a story.

160. She played the role of Bess in *Porgy and Bess*.
161. Truman Capote (1924–1984), writer. *The Muses Are Heard* is Capote's 1956 account of the *Porgy and Bess* tour of Russia.
162. George Gershwin's (1898–1937) opera, first performed in 1935.
163. *New York Herald Tribune*, one of seven daily newspapers then published in New York City.

Anyway, I hope you will think about the first chapter (I am! and how) in that light. I don't think my suggestions to merely censor Alfred's speech will serve. Still, there is a way, I am certain, of excising the word nigger. (Jesperson[164] pointed out, quite a while ago, how English, more than any other language, tends to perpetuate class distinctions: and he was not speaking in a political sense, but (*apropos* Dickens) of language as a means, even a weapon to keep people of inferior station (so-called) or race, in their place.)

I somehow doubt though that Martha Flowers is going to open my first novel and be confronted by a wounding word. Well, I put it in; now I will try to think of a way to take it out. *Ars breve, vita longa,* though either way, I think it would be nice if both were as long as possible, don't you? Though Horace is not the dopiest poet who ever wrote; not quite, anyway.

I'm delighted that David and Dorothy like John Becker's verses.[165] And for you and yours at Christmas, I can only amend Puck in wishing that:

> Not a mouse
> Shall disturb your hallowed house.

> Season's Greetings,

> Sincerely,

> Jimmy

TO KENNETH AND JANICE KOCH

[New York, New York]

Wed. Dec 11 [1956]

Mes Enfants du Paradis,[166]

Gifted Kenneth, he of the beautiful Horse song in Nov. *Poetry* and of the radiant smile; gifted Janice, she of the beautiful smile speaking Middle English to the enchanted; Gifted Katherine, laughing and crashing around; and— Raoul!—already building a bright tomorrow! Little Leonardo (of Leonarda) da Koch.

Now old Doc. Schuyler, who once lived for a winter in Florence, or *Firenz,* as you doubtless call it, and very near where you live (Via Erta Canina; well

---

164. Otto Jesperson (1860–1943), Danish philologist.
165. John Becker, writer of children's books.
166. Play on director Marcel Carne's 1945 movie, *Les Enfants du Paradis.*

named) strongly recommends you move as soon as you feel like it to Rome. Of course Raoul should see the light of day where Janice feels most at home: but: Rome is nearer than Paris, less expensive, a much easier place (with contacts: friends, which Old Doc is about to provide) to find a nice apartment in: I mean a modern one, with hot and cold and all the rest, say, up near the Porta San Pancrazio, with all Rome at your feet, and Piazza Argentina mere minutes away by bus. Or on the other bank, witty Parioli. Also, I don't know who Janice's doctor was, but the sweetest, the finest, the most in Doctor is named Dr. Jona (Iona); a real family doc. who has both Italian and American degrees (which is a very good idea nowadays) because he had to come here during the Mussolini-Hitler entente. To meet him is to fall in love with him (he's so short! and kind) and he's Bill Weaver's doctor, who could tell you more if you want to know more.

Then there are my friends John and Ginny Becker (Via Botteghe Oscure 32, Palazzo Caetani) world's least stuffy couple (always excepting yourselves). If I can find it I'll enclose a batty note from Ginny. John is fun, too, but quieter, more piquant. I'm sorry I haven't their phone number, but it's doubtless in the elenico.

Through them and Bill you can meet *anyone* in Italy you want to meet. For instance, thru Bill, Pier Paolo Pasolini,[167] whose first book of poems (I forget the title) seemed very talented to me; it came out in the fall of '54. I hope you'll look at it and tell me if it's any good. He writes in Friulian dialect[168] (which is like writing in American rather than in Wystan) in Charles Orléans[169] forms; was a sort of disciple of Sandro Penna (whose work I so brilliantly satirized without having read it). Oh: the Beckers know a most interesting man, I think his name is Rissi (his wife, who is Australian or something is rather hell though beautiful & loves to give big cocktail parties) who has actually *read* E. Bishop, W. C. Williams, older and younger American poets in American and is terribly interested and makes nice movies not big ugsome movies. I haven't met him, only her, but he is also said to be the most sexually attractive man in Italy. But I forgot. I'm not writing Prof. Ashes [Ashbery]. But Rome is full of people, all aching to know you—natives and polyglots—messes and heroes, just like New York. And it's so beautiful in

167. Pier Paolo Pasolini (1922–1975), Italian Marxist poet, journalist, novelist, and movie director.

168. Region of northeast Italy.

169. Charles d'Orleans (1391–1465), French poet and prince.

the winter! And the spring comes on so soon! And if you want to go back to Tuscany for its own lovely spring, it's mere hours away by train.

Now I want Bill's address; Joey is out; Frank is out; I am not speaking (surprise, surprise) to A. G. [Arthur Gold] (to whom Uncle Kenny once said, "I think you *are* a big cross purpose"— so right in all his pronouncements;) — (well, I had to put it somewhere! the parenthesis, I mean)— though what I enjoy most is the not listening; but somebody somewhere has it! And when in Rome, Bill is indeed The Missing Link. Now this is my sensible letter: I will also enclose] my zoom letter of last Sat., written between reviews: that's over with for this month. And they're pretty good reviews too, very batty. Ditto my *Ode*, not to speak of *The Real Jean Harlow*. I decided to put chapter titles on A & G; silly ones. To make it easier for idiots like my editor, Dan Wickenden, very sweet, but who keeps suggesting I give Lily "a marked squint" "(although the name Lily does somehow suggest a colored maid)." Of course, they're all named for flowers, like Joe's maid, Mildred.

I enclose various merz-es and messages.

December in New York is one big mess. Everybody gets drunk too much: Mike Goldberg looks gray and shaky: New York looks bright and shaky; Frank, I am sorry to say, looks gray and shaky. Write him Plenty Heap big buck-up notes and postals; Xmas is depressing for some of us deracine Christians. Especially if you were brought up by a lot of ugsome Brothers and Sisters, like Frank.

Ah! how we need your steadying home in The Little Clan (Jane, the Elstir-Oriane, Joe, the Mme. Verdurin—ah how lovely The Joe Hazan story! He is learning to play chess; he enjoyed his recent nose operation; he is going to buy a house near New York and the sea! I hope it has enough bedrooms for all of us.)

And Baby Jimmy: well, he is enjoying his analysis very much thank you; betimes. How like a lover! so seldom seen! so remote, yet so near! How shy one is, so earnest to please and delight; one's little winning ways and gaucheries (is that a word? if it wasn't it is now). But that is a part of the Fred Loomis story! The Allison White Foundation! Most Progressive force in the U.S.A. Perhaps I will become heterosexual like the French! Or many-faceted, like a rose! Frank says I should take on Marisol;[170] frankly, she is just too butch. No, my type is more blond and lissom, someone not made for office work: watch out Kenneth: the gorilla boy is on the loose.

170. Marisol Escobar (1930–2016), Ecuadorian-born American sculptor known for life-size human figures carved from wood and painted.

I enclose, too, S & S's ad. for a collection of my shorter pieces. Read both sides. It is an action ad. You have to turn it over.

And now a New Year message: someone has the gift of universal sympathy: is it Frank? That Irish aristocrat, like Grace Hartigan? Is it beautiful John Ashbery, who is a genius, and therefore eliminated? Is it Delphinium here, with what Jane calls "his beautiful timorous voice"? (Watch out Jane, King Kong is ready to peel you like a new Fay Wray[171]—or is it handsome unhappy Cy Twombly I love? Whose new paintings are sheer poetry? Or G. [George] Montgomery,[172] he of the massive shoulder?) No, it is Kenneth Koch! It is always the wide-open Singers of the Body Electric the dopey editors catch onto last: so let her shoot! Like the fountains at Tivoli! What a beautiful name, Tivoli Koch. Anyway, think about *When The Sun Tries to Go On*, and all your other odes, and then write your Song of Yourself! *Le Chant du Monde!*

But if it is Paris our Janice wants to go to, then Paris it is. But Rome is more homey, and that's fun too.

I'm very serious about the Beckers: they like to have fun! Instead of a car they have a little bus so they can take the family and the dog (a sort of goofy Italian Jenny) and some friends on marvelous xxxxx xxxxxxx—oh well, so I can't spell junckets. Jukits? Jumpits? Trips. To Tivoli! wonder of fountains. To handy Lake Nemi! once sacred to Diana! and other sights and picnic grounds near and far. Ginny Becker is the life of the party: you will get on like houses. So, heroic singer, sing!

love,

Jimmy

PS: No, I will not send draft one of this letter. This is the letter I meant to write; I'm a reviewer: what a difference! Give, D. H. Walt, give! and maybe even I will learn. Inspired by heroic example of honored bardic friend. Or maybe I will send it. A hesitater! a debater! The loon is loose, but progressing! No I won't send it. I looked at it and it's boring. An editor!

William Fense Weaver, Via del Consolato 6, Rome. It's as easy to make a phone call from F. to Rome as from NY to Southampton! But you do it your way!

171. Fay Wray (1907–2004), star of *King Kong* (1933).

172. Cy Twombly (1928–2011), American painter and sculptor. Twombly lived in Manhattan off and on from 1951 until 1957 when he took up permanent residence in Italy. George Montgomery, photographer and poet based in New York.

TO KENNETH KOCH

[New York, New York]

Jan. 57

Dear *genial* Kenneth,

Here is your deliciously flattering postcard and I haven't yet written you. I am a discredit to the island of Manhattan.

Your December news made me cry. I really hate it for Janice and you to have undergone an experience like that. And that I wrote suggesting you go to Rome was based on experiences of my own that lead me to distrust any hospital in Italy except the newest and best-staffed. (My own Italian hospital experience featured (temporary) morphine refusal by laughing nuns. A pox on all their convents.)

So you've been to San Giminiano. Bravo. I never got there. I just stared at it while whirling by on various sorties elsewhere.

I take it from your letter that while Johnny Jump Up is a sneerer at statues you are not? I hope? I am a statuary lover myself and if you are too I have a few hints on how to extend your pleasure. For instance, there is Michaelangelo's passion, Jacopo della Quercia. One of his masterpieces is the tomb of Illaria del something-or-other in a church at Lucca, a must-see city whose striped churches tell the striped churches of Florence where to get off (always excepting San Miniato: isn't its interior a joy? the floor!) And at Siena there is a replica of his fountain in the piazza and the considerably weathered fragments of the original fountain are inside the palazzo comunale (Siena! most beautiful of cities? Don't miss the Duccio altarpiece and the Giovanni de Paolos in the museo del duomo. The latter *are* the spring time). But his most important work is at Bologna, dairy capital of the Emilia, Italy's swampy Wisconsin, a series of bronze panels around the door of the Cathedral (San Petronio?) that are among the masterpieces of post-Roman art. Looking, for instance, at the Expulsion, you will note the resemblance between it and Massacio's in the Carmine (you have seen them? Yes?) and wonder who influenced who, as I still wonder. Anyway, after drinking in the della Quercias you will look over your shoulder at an elaboration of Giambologna's, a fountain full of ladies with water squirting out of their tits and, behind that, the palazzo comunale in which there is a superb staircase by Bramante which is little more than a ridged ramp. It's a great deal of fun to walk up and down it. It's quite nice to go to Bologna by bus, through Prato of the silk mills (and an outdoor pulpit by Donatello) and Pistoia, up and over a singularly steep mountain (4 star view of the Val d'Arno)

71

down into Bologna! city of arcades! of leaning towers! famed for its veal! city of beautiful church facades! (do not miss the one in stucco) how fat all the people are! they eat too much! who can blame them! see them all piling into Caesarina's! Hear Caesarina shouting at them all! She is bringing out the lasagna! smell it? Uhmmmm. Can we really eat a veal steak a la Bolognese on top of all that lasagna? Well, we are damn well going to try. (Caesarina's is right down the street — the Strada Maggiore? — from world famed Pappagallo, which is an expensive tourist trap, on your right (you are walking with your back to the two leaning towers).

Now we are back in Florence, happy to have discovered the glories of Jacopo della Quercia. I assume you go constantly to the Bargello — but have you peeked into the charming Bardini on our bank? And I forget which museum has all the interesting Etruscan nick-nacks; for instance, the so-called Chimera, which is at least famous and mysterious if not very interesting or beautiful. Have the Sicilian oranges hit the fruit stands yet? They are squisito.

I think it would be very cute if you took a little trip south. For instance, you pop into a train, get out at Naples, hop on board a boat (not even stopping to look at the Roman paintings in the Museo Nazionale even though they are a revelation) eat dinner, go to sleep and in the morning there is Palermo! Sparkling in the sunshine. You take a carriage — so popular in Sicily, such a thrill for Katherine — and go galloping off to your hotel, either in downtown Palermo near the Quatro Fontane or — why not? — one of the better hotels out near the gardens ofla Favorita. It is a mere trolley ride up to Monreale, with its enchanting Moorish courtyard, its fountain, what a jewel. A mere hop skip and jump to Segesta, your first Greek experience. To Cefalu of the great mosaics. Or, if you're tired of boats, why not take the train right down the coast and cross the straits of Messina by ferry? Taormina, Syracuse. There, it is already spring. The orange and lemon trees are in fruit; the freesias are in bloom; so are the almond trees. You cannot imagine what a boost it can give you unless you have done it. Spring in Sicily. Wow. Or, if that is too far (and really, it is not; no matter how far it seems) I will not sneeze at Amalfi, "*jolie petite ville, aux maisons blanches, nichée a l'étroite embouchure de la vallée des Molini, en un paysage d'une beauté unique.*" I do not recommend the expensive Hotel Cappuccini, but rather the Luna, "*dans un ancien couvent a mi-chemin entre Amalfi et Atrani, avec cloitre pittoresque et beau jardin.*" It was a lot better than pittoresque and, was not, in '48, expensive.

On the other hand perhaps Katherine would rather roll around in the snow. Perhaps it is snowing in Bolzano?

Or perhaps she would like to go down to the straw market by the dribbling bear (if you ever get the chance to eat wild boar, don't; it is very rank) and buy an Etruscan hat? They are conical, flaring toward the brim, and exactly the same as the hats Etruscan farmers are wearing in various reliefs.

Now we come to your review. My, what a pair of pigeons. First, I think you should say what you think, simply, freely, clearly. Back up any conclusions you draw by quotations from the books themselves. About M. Moore's book:[173] remember, it comes after her collected poems, and that that contains what she thinks is the best of what she has written over a period of forty years; also, that it comes after the publication of her La Fontaine, which explains the new-style poems in funny couplets. The poem about Jock Whitney's race horse[174] was commissioned by *Flair* (remember *Flair?*); Miss M. decided *Flair* was disgusting and bought it back. Then *New Yorker* got it. It is a lousy poem, I think. But, in the last ten years or so she has become a public figure, but she remains, by nature, a private person. She is also still a member of the avant-garde: the poem about Escudero and rhythm was turned down by every magazine she sent it to. I think that particular poem is interesting because it is about a kind of (visual) metric such as she has created herself (that it is inimitable Richard Wilbur[175] has successfully proved). Also, that she is really *on* the old man's road (Wystan is just petulant about it) and she is writing like an old poet—there is a loosening, almost—by her standard—a verboseness. I don't see how any of this can be of any use to you. But I really feel that a new book by her is an occasion for praise. Sort them out, describe the differences, make some observations about them. I don't think you'll find it difficult.

Now for the "fine anglo-saxon haid" as Caroline (ugh) Gordon once said (or, "la signoria Tight" as the maid at the Villa Aurelia used to call her, while sardonically describing her little ways). It is *The Old Man's Road*[176] you are re-viewing, isn't it? I read some of it and dropped it with a little whinny of disgust. He really is a pig. Well, now let's see. First, he wrote the poems at the end (for five years, allowing for a trip back now and then) of his self-exile in "Amedica." He has the chair of poetry at Oxford, his bally old university, and when he gave his address ("Making, Knowing, Judging": have you read it? you might want to lump it in with the poems; it's been published in England for several months;

---

173. Kenneth Koch was about to review Marianne Moore's book *O, to Be a Dragon* for *Poetry Magazine*.

174. "Tom Fool in Jamaica."

175. Richard Wilbur (1921–2017), poet and translator from the French.

176. Auden's privately published "slim volume," later incorporated into *Hommage to Clio*.

I'm sure you can get it in Florence or call Bill W.[Weaver] and ask him to have that English bookshop in Via Babuina send you one; I think the two dykes who run it are the meanest things going but Bill adores them. He is a trial. But he can be sweet, entertaining and helpful if you get along with him: did you?)— as I was saying, when he gave his address he was very nervous about how he would be received; he was of course a hit. That hasn't much to do with the book, has it? Well, he has always been envious of Eliot, and if the Old Man's Road is no 4 Quartets it may be, in a nasty sort of way, his Ash Wednesday (why should the agèd beagle stretch its legs, he yawned, scratching himself with a singing bone). Also, within the year his other Ideal, Robert Graves,[177] gave him a good going over, I mean in quite a rough way, and a lot of the poems in *The Shield of Achilles*[178] are written within the dogma of Graves' *White Goddess*. Now I bet W.H.A. is good and sore at her (the W. yawn G. I mean). The poems are probably also the expression of a periodic self-disgust (another instance is the kind of mutilation that got into his collected poems: putting camp titles on serious poems; tearing apart "The Orators"; ripping choruses out of plays he had written with Isherwood; taking off dedications; editing-out the personal: "Wystan, Stephen, Christopher, all of you, think of your losses"—if that is how it went—becomes "Subjects, Objects, all of you . . . " and so on.), so you might read them thinking that every—what shall I say?—every barb he launches, every attack he makes, can find its mark in his own work. (And, of course, in his own nature and his own situation.) Now, you like his early work. Isherwood had a great deal to do with it: he criticized his poems, cut them to pieces and so on. It's all in *Lions & Shadows*. But, as the boy grew older, there wasn't anybody bright enough to keep up with him (and don't forget how long his collaboration with Isherwood lasted: they went to China together, they came to America together). And he has little faculty for self-criticism (which is a quality—if it is worth anything—one might expect a poet, an artist, to develop rather than posses innately). Also, he got a lot of his ideas from Groddeck[179] (of whom he became a friend when he lived in Berlin). He has always talked and thought from the point of view of a lay-analyst; but one who has not himself been analyzed: a tricky business. His conversion—or rather, reversion—to the Anglican church dates from his mother's death, during the war (they used to sing *Tristan and Isolde* together at the piano). Since then he has become increasingly a

177. Robert Graves (1895–1985), British poet, novelist, and scholar.
178. Published in 1955.
179. Georg Groddeck (1855–1934), psychiatrist, author of *The Book of It*.

lay-preacher (I mean real sermons in real churches), an apologist for angli-canism and quite willing to attack psychoanalysis (vide some peculiar notes called "Hic et Ille" published in *Encounter*[180] last spring) in principio, and in a way that lines him up with such thinkers as Monsignor Sheen.[181] (I assume you've already availed yourself of the British Institute's pretty good library? in the Via Tornabuoni. And while you're down there why don't you step behind the Palazzo Strozzi and buy Janice a bunch of flowers from the adorable man I hope still has a flower stall there?) Anyhow, I think you ought to lay the book out like a split cod. I think it is anti-human. If you need an incentive, I will tell you what he really thought of Frank's and John's mss. for the Yale.[182] He didn't think either of them was very good, and he chose John's *faute de mieux*. After all, he's paid to edit the thing, the poet, as you know, is not, so he has to choose someone (though I think he did let one year slip by). Anyhow, I doubt if he will do it much longer; he's bored with it. (I don't see any point, by the way, in your—or my—submitting a mss. to it. It is a fact that all that gets reviewed is 'um Auden's preface; it's like having your work preceded by a big smog bank.

Now if you can find an idea in this rumbling, you are a very clever poet. Any-how, if you want any reassurance before you send it off to Rago,[183] why don't you make carbons and let John, Frank and me see it first? We tell 'um what we think 'um. Ugh. Yes. W. H. Auden him bad Indian. Captain Kenneth him track him on snow shoes fix 'um good. Mooka[184] help 'um. Ugh. Yes.

Oh phooey. I promised myself on the last page I wouldn't run onto another page. I am tired and hungry. The city is covered with snow. I want to go see Sid Caesar.[185] Ah nertz. It's too late. And I haven't told you any news. Maybe there isn't any news.

180. Influential British magazine focusing on literature and politics, edited by Stephen Spender and Irving Kristol. After its demise it was revealed that the American Central Intel-ligence Agency provided the funds to publish *Encounter*.

181. Bishop Fulton J. Sheen, spokesman for the Catholic Church who had a brief vogue delivering his message on television in the 1950s.

182. As judge of the Yale Younger Poets Series, Auden found no manuscript worthy of the prize. He was then told that John Ashbery's *Some Trees* and a Frank O'Hara manuscript had been rejected before he got to see them. He asked to see both and awarded the prize to Ashbery.

183. Henry Rago, poet and editor of *Poetry*.

184. Character in John Ashbery's play *The Compromise*.

185. Sid Caesar (1922–2014), TV comedian and star of the popular *Your Show of Shows*.

At five p.m. New York time on New Year's eve I was sound asleep. Then I woke up and went to a New Year's eve party at Jane & Joe's. They have become New York's leading party givers. Everybody was there; Joe's parrot flew across the room and landed on Lorraine Smithberg's bun! or chignon. Gene Smithberg[186] tried to quiet her but she kept screaming she wanted to see the parrot RIGHT THERE ON A SPIT IN THE FIREPLACE NOW! John Gruen kept on dancing in his maroon tuxedo coat. The Gay Nevelsons[187] kept on drinking and dancing. Rudi [Burckhardt] was there with Edith [Schloss] who had on something funny around her neck. Tibor[188] and Roland Pease[189] were there. Roland has sold his first novel to Doubleday with a $2,500 advance I can't stand it! Doubleday has asked him to take the word fuck out of his novel (it occurs 18 times) so the book clubs will buy. Arnold kept saying he was going to drink less in the New Year while his cup ranneth over. Esther Leslie[190] looked gloomy until 2:30 a.m. when Frank decided she was the Swan Queen and threw her on the floor. They looked very happy lying there on the floor. Cy Twombly said, "Edwin Denby[191] is beautiful. He looks like a Whistler." How it made me laugh. I wonder why? Some of the boys—Joey, Georgy Montgomery, Johnny Button, Alviny Novak—went off to a boy party given by Bernard Perlin. "He called up central casting," reports Alvin, "and said send one of each." Lincoln Kirstein insulted everybody—George the most—so George fell down and then went to the Remo "because if I fell down there at least it wouldn't be in front of people I know." Others went on to the club. "Dull" reports Rudi and Jane. "No more hootch." Frank does not remember what happened after he got to the club but when George came in at 6 Frank was on the phone babbling to Don Berry in Boston! (D.B. is a married painter, a sort of juvenile delinquent Larry Rivers.)

186. Gene Smithberg, therapist, friend of Nell Blaine, and husband of Lorraine.

187. Al Gay and Susan Nevelson.

188. Tibor de Nagy (1908–1993), art dealer and gallery owner. He arrived in New York City from Hungary in 1947 and worked as a banker. He remained in banking when he founded the Tibor de Nagy Gallery in 1950. The gallery showed the work of Fairfield Porter, Jane Freilicher, Nell Blaine, Grace Hartigan, Larry Rivers, John Button, and Helen Frankenthaler, among other artists. Tibor de Nagy Editions published books of poetry by Frank O'Hara, Kenneth Koch, Barbara Guest, John Ashbery, Kenward Elsmlie, and James Schuyler.

189. Roland Pease (1921–2012). His novel *Sweet Nothing* was not bought by a book club. Pease was an editor, art collector, and close friend of Tibor de Nagy.

190. Esta Leslie, wife of painter Alfred Leslie.

191. Edwin Denby (1903–1983), poet and dance critic with whom Schuyler had a brief affair.

I can hardly wait for the first phone bill of the New Year. Then a lot of other dumb things happened.

I really must eat. Goodbye for now, Kenneth. Tell Janice to write me a letter. Yours for less Auden, love,

Jimmy

PS. It is K.K. who wins the Mystery Song Competition. "Toward a Better World" is my favorite song of '56. (As sung by Elvis Presley: what a natural that boy is. What a song-plugger. Can he ever put it across. He reminds me of The Boy *Arnold Weinstein*.)

WRITE and I will too.

P.P.S. WHA gets all those big ugly words out of the complete (or King Size) O.E.D. It reminds me of Aldous Huxley reading the *Encyclopedia Britannica* knowledge (dehydrated at that) as a substitute for experience. The vocabulary of the poems I read is decidedly Alexandrinian: I don't see how a poem can have any organic life—can make any appeal to the senses— under the weight of such words. It might be interesting to look them up in the O.E.D.—perhaps there is one at the British Institute—and find out how they got into the language: do any of them come by way of church scholiasts? A vocabulary we can do without. Anyway, reading them in the context from which WHA took them would throw light on why he took them. (The kind of words I mean didn't appear in his work until *Nones*,[192] and all of the poems in that were written after he had bought his very own O.E.D.)

TO JOHN ASHBERY

[New York, New York]

Saturday [June 22, 1957]

Dear Grace Metalious:[193]

I haven't got so much to say as would crowd a minniepostcard, but I'll go to any lengths to get one of your letters (that sounds as though you kept a lot of letters and doled them out to the needy—I know it isn't quite like that. . . .).

192. Schuyler worked briefly as Auden's secretary. In his elegy "Wystan Auden" he writes, "poems, some of which I typed / for him (they're in *Nones*)."
193. Grace Metalious (1924–1964) wrote the bestselling novel *Peyton Place* and was, for the moment, notorious.

I'm working six days a week at the museum[194] at the front desk! Along with Alvin, Johnny, Naomi and Jeanne Keyes, who often asks for you and was bemused and thrilled to hear you have a mustache (have you still?). Jimmy Merrill[195] described it as French: otherwise he spoke very well of you, and made you sound handsome as the dawn over Parc Buttes Chaumont[196] or whatever it's called. Do you think you should be photographed in it and then shave it off? Though I was recently pleasantly surprised to discover where and how one tickles . . .

Jane read me a letter of yours with some amusing Fairfieldisms in it. Yes, in a sense the group has rather fallen apart, but then, without energetic you and lazy Kenneth, there is scarcely enough to constitute a group. I certainly hope Frank and Joey enjoy his dropping in. Ha. The other evening he appeared at the museum at exactly six o'clock. (I had avoided an enterprising Poindexter[197] opening the evening before just cause I knew he was laying in wait at it) so we had dinner at the Old Colony, the first time I had set hoof in it since dear knows when. They still have the Delmonico steak for $1.65, sob. This narration is leading nowhere (what I'm really brooding about is why, every time I turn on the radio, are they playing Strauss's "Burlesk"[198] for stringed pain and orchestra). He showed me a rather dopey sestina about Greece, and then said, "It bears the same relation to my work that 'The Instruction Manual' bears to John's." It's a sequence of those that leaves me feeling like an excerpt from the Smugglers chorus in *Carmen*.

Jane and Joe have bought 16 West 11th Street—the second house from the parish house on the south side—remember? It cost a fabulous price and now they are spending another fortune literally raising the roof so Jane can have a studio. It's very pretty and sedate, though the simplest of the dwellings on that block. They also have a house for the summer at Water Mill; and Frank and Joe have the apartment at Larry's, so weekends have taken on their summer vacuum. (I work every Sunday.) Larry and Jane Wilson are both appearing on the $64,000 Challenge,[199] against a jockey who knows all about art. Larry almost got hung

194. Schuyler had begun working at the Museum of Modern Art. Frank O'Hara, John Button, and Alvin Novak were already working there.

195. James Merrill (1926–1995), poet whose Ingram Merrill Foundation made several grants to Schuyler.

196. Paris park that had mythic statues for the surrealists.

197. Manhattan art gallery founded in 1956 by Elinor Poindexter.

198. Richard Strauss (1864–1935), German composer.

199. TV quiz show on which Larry Rivers won $32,000, after which he went to the Cedar Tavern with the check and bought drinks for the house.

up on what an Archipenko[200] was made of ("metal," said foxy Larry, then coughed up the right answer, "bronze"), but tomorrow night he goes for the $32,000 question, and if he passes that, then for the big wheel. It's making them both quite nervous. Naomi and I couldn't look when Jane appeared for the first time last week—it all has something to do with the ill-concealed interest *Life* magazine takes in art lately. Don't you think they need a feature on poets and their pet apartments?

I wish you would hurry back; I'm so afraid I'll gain back all the weight I lost before you see me . . .

The other night John and I saw Judy and Mickey[201] in *Girl Crazy*. He really was the cutest boy, and made me think of you for some obscure reason.

I haven't written anything, I wish you would, though. Have you? Send it, if so. Oh. John Myers *said* he loved *A Nest of Ninnies*,[202] but prefers to suspend publication of ; to publishing it. Naturally. How is Pierre?[203] Please point out to Kenneth that he owes me a letter. Give Janice and baby all my love, and write me.

love, [long collaged list of names]

TO JOHN ASHBERY

New York, New York

August 16, 1957

Fellow Democrat:

Your last letter—what a joy. Naturally I couldn't answer it immediately. I was too bent double with mirth, and the only thing that straightened me up was

200. Alexander Archipenko (1887–1964), Russian-born sculptor who immigrated to the United States in 1928.

201. Judy Garland (1922–1969) and Mickey Rooney (1920–2014) appeared in *Girl Crazy* (1943) directed by Busby Berkeley.

202. In the summer of 1952 returning by car from Southampton, Schuyler and Ashbery began collaborating on the novel *A Nest of Ninnies*. It took them sixteen years to finish the book. One reason for this was that they did not collaborate by mail when Ashbery was in Paris. Doubleday published the novel in 1969, and W. H. Auden hailed it in the *New York Times Book Review* as "destined to be a minor classic."

203. Pierre Martory (1920–1998), French novelist, poet, and editor. Martory worked for many years as chief cultural critic for *Paris Match*, reviewing plays, concerts, and the opera.

your searingly intelligent and lovely review in *Poetry*.[204] As Furl said, "It's so—
CLEAR. You can see all the way around to a—180 DEGREE ANGLE."
Fairfield's world, you see, is really only half a world; *I* liked it because I could
see all the way around 359 degrees where I found Kim Novak smiling on the
last degree.

(You would love the advertising copy for *Jeanne Eagles*: Kim[205] is plastered
all over town in different attitudes and costumes but always the same rigid expression and all say, "This, too, was Jeanne Eagles." Is that how you spell her
name? oh well.)

It isn't clear to me, little traveler to the Lake District, whether you leave on
27th Aug or arrive on the 27th Aug. Which? Avez vous a place to stay? You are
most welcome at the 49th Street Youth Hustle, which extends its extra bed to
you (a single with pillow). As soon as I finish this letter I am going to paint the
bathroom white, so even bathing might be more of a pleasure than before. However, if you are already contracted to David Noakes or some other schmo, I will
not be more than usually annoyed. But let me know.

News? I got 500 (*not* five thousand) dollars out of the Author's League to write
a play, on the basis of Audrey Wood's[206] reading my novel (which now is scheduled for next Feb.—did you ever?). So I can pay my analyst that 200 he's been
beefing about . . . Life is quite sordid and while I would like to write a play and
become renowned I think I would rather paint my bathroom; and living room.

John Button has a new lovely friend, a modern dancer named Paul Taylor,[207]
who has not quite severed relations with his previous friend, a deaf mute, said
to be extremely nice but inclined to throw things when PT makes motions of
departure. He is of the Merce-Rauschenberg[208] world and a Virginian, like long
lovely Cy Twombly. Anyway it has made John terribly whispery and "Hello
Young Lovers."[209]

204. Ashbery reviewed Gertrude Stein's *Stanzas in Meditation* and managed to mention
Kim Novak.

205. Kim Novak (b. 1933), actress and blonde bombshell. She starred in *Jeanne Eagles*
(1957), a biography of the actress Jeanne Eagles (1894–1929), a beauty who died of a heroin
overdose.

206. Audrey Wood, agent who represented Tennessee Williams through most of his career.

207. Paul Taylor (1930–2018), dancer and choreographer. He published his autobiography,
Private Domain, in 1987.

208. Merce Cunningham (1922–2009), dancer and choreographer. Robert Rauschenberg
(1925–2008), artist who designed sets and costumes for Cunningham's dance company.

209. A song from the musical *The King and I* (music by Richard Rodgers and lyrics by
Oscar Hammerstein).

Alvin's friend, Ken, spent a week in the hospital waiting to have a corneal transplant, when the doctors decided he wasn't quite blind enough to rate getting such a costly operation free. It did seem indiscreet of him to spend all his time reading. The doctors, all the same, are beasts.

Everybody except one is in the Hampton's this summer. Grace has the gatehouse or guest house on the Ossorio[210] estate and broke with Giorgio and took up with Bob Keene,[211] whose smart book shop on Southampton's main street is well known to you. G. left but, after an evening at the 5 Spot,[212] took a cab out to East Hampton, walked in and found Grace and B. K. asleep and began beating B. K's head in. This woke him up. He, it tuns out, was a commando or something in the war so he began beating Giorgio's head in. Grace pulled them apart, in a sudden access of strength (John Myers says she has lost 15 pounds). Now peace once more reigns, though how Giorgio paid the cab fare back to New York, I can't think. They say it cost a hundred dollars.

Now there must be some cheerier news than that, though if there is, it has been carefully kept from me. Oh. I am finally going to write a long piece for *Art News*, about Leland Bell,[213] whose last show I found delectable. Like me, he is an admirer of Derain[214] (*et toi?*).

Do let me know if you would like to stay here. Tell Kenneth I am going to write him I swear it. Or if not to him then to Janice. My best to Pierre. I hope you won't be too sad about coming back, but everyone is dying to see you, such as Jane Niederhofer Freilicher Hazan, Alvin Novak Wollitz, John Button Taylor and yours truly, the merry widow.

love, Clo-Clo
(or is it Clau-Clau?)[215]

P.S. Frank and Joey are both at Larry's, both writing plays.

---

210. Alfonso Ossorio (1916–1990), artist and early collector of Jackson Pollock.

211. Georgio was George Spaventa (1918–1978), sculptor. Robert Keene owner of a bookstore in Southampton. He was Grace Hartigan's second husband.

212. Five Spot, jazz club, then on Cooper Square.

213. Leland Bell (1922–1991), painter. Schuyler's "Leland Bell Paints a Picture" appeared in the September 1958 issue of *Art News* and in his *Selected Art Writings*.

214. Andre Derain (1880–1954), French painter, one of the original Fauves.

215. Clo-Clo is a character in the French actor and director Jean-Louis Barrault's (1910–1994) comedy *Bizarre, Bizarre* (1937).

TO JOHN ASHBERY

[New York, New York]

August 12 [1958]

Dear Kid,

Yes, I did send some perms to you at 40 Rue Spontini (what sort of a house is it? attractive? plain?), what luck that my other letter got through. Perhaps one day a divine supply of energy will well up in me & I'll make other copies of them and send them to you; in the meanwhile, you will have to struggle along as best you can on your diet of Raymond Roussel.[216] He sounds nourishing.

Perhaps it was in The Lost Missive (not a bad title, huh?) that I pointed out the urgent importance of you letting Tom [Hess] know that you will not be available to review for the October issue. He is very sensitive about these things, you know. And so tell him that you will be back to review for the November issue. Then if you should find work and happiness over there, you can always write him different.

A bug in my gut, which caused me to spend several days on the potty, prevented me from seeing more than two of my nine shows for the September issue (Irving Sandler[217] must be rolling in gold). They were two stunning shows at the de Aenlle Gallery,[218] and I know you will enjoy my brief notices.

Thrill, I finished my Lee Bell paints a picture! The impossible has been accomplished! It is superbly dull! Tom has expressed no particular reaction, beyond pointing out that I got Maurice Quentin de la Tour's[219] name wrong and that the Rubens' "Horrors of War" is, or are, in the Pitti Palace and not the Prado. Oh well heck, I'm a artist, not an IBM machine.

Don't know if your Mammy sent me the money: John Button was expecting his pension check from California, which, for his own convenience, he had sent care of me, so he borrowed my mail box key and then went to Philadelphia for a week with it. I trust they are enjoying themselves together.

---

216. Raymond Roussel (1877–1933), French poet and novelist to whose work Ashbery was remained devoted. He gave one of his Harvard Norton Lectures on Roussel. It appears in *Other Traditions* (2001).

217. Irving Sandler (b. 1925), art critic and, in Frank O'Hara's phrase, *"balayeur des artistes."*

218. The show was titled *Varied Abstract* and included work by Jacques Douchez, Jose Bermudez, and Boris Lurie.

219. Maurice-Quentin de Latour (1704–1788), French painter.

I also reviewed a book for the fall *Evergreen Review*, a hot little item called *Meditations in an Emergency*.[220] I gave it the thumbs up. Don Allen[221] also asked me to review Jack Kerouac's new novel! I said sure! It is really very good though I have no notion of how to go about saying so. Perhaps I will just borrow your Gertrude Stein review and substitute suitable names. It is called, as I'm sure you are dying to know, *The Dharma Bums*.

Are you aware that Frank is this moment strolling the avenidas of Madrid? Porter[222] sent for him, he flew off to Iberia last Saturday. When I last spoke to him he was trying to open a suitcase with a stuck lock. After Madrid (this Sat. ?) he goes to Rome, then after a few days to Venice, perhaps Milan and Berlin (Sept. 1); then he may have a week to do with as he sees fit with, which should, I imagine, include Paris. If you are inclined to send him a welcome to the old Sod card, c/o the Inghilterra (via Bocca di Leone) in Rome should reach him. I imagine he will be there most of next week.

Are you sure the first sentence of your whodunit isn't swiped from the title of Julian Green's novel, *Minuit*?[223]

Now off to cash my pitiful wage check. (The whole department has been moved into the members' penthouse.)[224] You would not know the old place; it looks as though it had been decorated by the exclusive 326 East 49th Street Decorators, especially in my fine how to decorate your kitchen corner with books style.

Love,

J

220. Frank O'Hara's first book of poems.

221. Donald Allen, editor at Grove Press which published O'Hara's book and the magazine *Evergreen Review*. See glossary.

222. Porter McCray (1908–2000), O'Hara's boss at MoMA.

223. Julian Green (1900–1998). Born of American parents in Paris and reared partly in the United States, wrote most of his novels, memoirs, and voluminous diary in French. He was elected to the *Academie Francaise*.

224. A fire at MoMA caused this more.

TO JOHN ASHBERY

[New York, New York]

Sept 11, 1958

"Has love no voice?" — *The Rake's Progress*

Dear Clayhanger,[225]

A line to speed, I hope, you on your way. Are you coming back to us? I look to every post to tell me — according to my present calculations, you are leaving The Cedar-sur-Seine next Wednesday. Can it be true? Of course you will miss David Noakes' cocktail party on Monday, which someone named Goldstone is giving on Riverside Drive in honor of David's presumed passing of his orals that day: what confidence. But you'll be in time to catch about two days of Bill Weaver's felicitous company. Though he has been here more than a week, I have seen him only once. As he says, he is busy advancing his career.

There was a note on our October assignment sheets that they were longer than usual due to the absence of two staff members. Oof. What a hash I made. I am truly sorry you were not here to cover the March Gallery Opening Group and the Fleischman Gallery stunning new talent show. Nothing ready at the Brata (Gallery), unfortunately. Trying to work full time *and* review is something I would rather not think about than have to do.

I'm two-thirds through the Pasternak.[226] It is utterly crushing, since it is very beautiful and also full of the most horrendous facts. Physical suffering is really something one ought to try to avoid, I guess. There certainly was a lot of it in Russia around 1920.

Sandy Gregg[227] flew off to France yesterday, en route to his other homeland. The benighted dear for some reason decided to take a copy of the Pasternak with him; it is not quite clear to me why. Perhaps we will never see him again. Or perhaps you already have: he was going to try to find and see you, depending on when his plane got to Paris and his train left for Normandy.

Don't be frightened of 49th Street; David [Noakes] has been staying there a bit and says he has never seen it looking so clean. I took this as a tribute to Sandy's initiative rather than his own (one could scarcely expect a fellow on the eve of his orals to do much in the cleaning line).

---

225. Arnold Bennett's (1887–1931) novel published in 1910.
226. Boris Pasternak's (1890–1960) novel *Dr. Zhivago*.
227. Sandy Gregg, Ashbery's classmate at Harvard, who became a professor of Russian.

It is to odd to think of you, Frank, Joan,[228] Grace and all the Terrorists together in Paris. I hope you haven't taken a fancy to trotting about dressed up as a matelot . . . In fact, it sounds like much too dangerous a place for you to be. Come home.

I had lunch with Jane yesterday; the dear girl is her merry self. At the moment she is giving her undivided attention to the case of the 8 year old Staten Island boy who murdered his parents. "Say, what do you think about that kid?" she said. She also allowed, at the Poindexter Gallery, that one of Paul Harris' sculptures looked like a piece of dough that had got out of hand.

She reports that Kenneth is spending his last Water Mill days writing feverishly. The big pig. I knew all those drawings he was making were too good to be true.

Don Allen said he received some "very beautiful" poems from you. For the anthology,[229] I gather. New ones? Old ones? Both? Have you any novelties, and if not, hurry.

I aches to see you.

love, J.

Anna of the Five Towns[230]

TO JOHN ASHBERY

The Museum of Modern Art
New York 19   *September 17 [1958]*

Dear Americana,
(There is a new Colonial series of homes opening out Smithtown way. Your preferred model is called The Roanoke, a colonial ranch house adaptation. One of the features all the models have is genuine hand-hewn beam cathedral ceilings.)
This third letter is after a noon trip to 49th Street. There was a note and a check for ten skins from your mother: she says John is staying on for "another

---

228. Joan Mitchell (1926–1992), painter, lived and worked in New York from the 1950s until the late 1960s when she took up permanent residence in France.
229. *The New American Poetry, 1945–1960*, edited by Allen and published by Grove Press.
230. Novel by Arnold Bennett.

month or two." When *are* you coming back? Or are you going to try to make your money last longer than that, or parley a further late payment?

Guess who would like to rent the apartment for next month: Mr Merczeg[231] (I tell him I'm traveling a lot in my business. "How are things over there?" he mysteriously queried today.) There is going to be a new super coming in on the 1st, and Mr M. has to stay around New York to collect his compensation. Then he's going to Florida. I guess he won't steal the ice box or deface the Norman Bluhm.[232] (I did get him to say he would try to fix the ice box—). I hope he's tidier than David N[oakes] & friend; unless the friend intends to do a pile of picking up and sweeping. It's those tidy ones that go to pieces when they leave their own spic 'n span digs.

My department [at Museum of Modern Art] here has moved into the old Theater Guild Building. Our office is quite cute, a once lavish drawing room with three-quarter partitions put up and painted a pleasant uniform dirty egg-shell. It makes me feel vaguely Sovietized, as though we ought to be clomping around in big boots and pitching vodka glasses at the moldings.

Did you know that Bill Aalto[233] died this summer? I just learned the other day that he left me several hundred dollars in veterans insurance. I have to fill out some very complicated and depressing papers to get it. My first reaction was that I didn't want to hear about it much less collect it: but on reflection I decided money is money and you know what my needs usually are along those lines. It does seem strange to think he is gone, though.

I didn't mean to end these ramblings on quite that note, but now I have to write a letter about an old Dutch drawing set to an old French tune. I did little for the past two weeks except sort and file papers. Oi.

I trust by now you have succeeded in getting Grace out of the Peristyle. Donald[234] had a badly infected ear but is better now. He liked getting your card. My best to Pierre.

love,

The Perkins Rose People[235] J.

---

231. Mr. Merczeg was the elderly superintendent of 326 East 49th Street. When Schuyler could no longer manage the rent alone, he shared the apartment with Merczeg.

232. Norman Bluhm (1921–1999), painter. One of Frank O'Hara's closest painter friends.

233. Bill Aalto (1916–1958) Schuyler's lover from 1944 to 1949.

234. Donald Droll, an art dealer with whom Schuyler was having an affair.

235. Jackson Perkins, rose grower in Newark, New York, a few miles from Ashbery's hometown, Sodus.

TO JOHN ASHBERY

The Museum of Modern Art
New York 19   *Sept. 17, 1958*

Dear Prisoner in a Chinese Laundry,[236]
   The evening of the day I wrote the enclosed letter I found your special at home; so it is pointless to send it. On the other hand, I am not going to write a whole letter and then throw it away. No sir.
   Though sad for myself, I am really happy for you that you can stay longer where you want to be. Paris. Really, you are lucky. Did you astutely wait until the fruit was picked to ask your family for more cashola?[237] David [Noakes] told me he had written and done his bit.
   Have you finished translating the *roman policier*?[238] Who is paying you for it—an American publisher? You ought to find something short and snappy you could translate on a royalty basis, the way David did that jazz book.[239] On the other hand, if you don't need the money right now, relax . . .
   I don't know yet what I'll do about 49th Street; burning's too good for it. George Montgomery might just take it for a few months—that is, if he is going to take an apartment he knows of that won't be available until April. Anyway, I will not throw your bed, books and records to the sooty breeze.
   Do you have any notion of how long you will stay there? Or will you try for another extension when this one is up? It seems as though it would be nice for you to have a toe-hold in New York—I mean, 49th Street to come back to. If I knew when you were coming, I might try to get someone on a month to month basis . . .
   If I should give up the apartment, would it be all right to store your bed, desk, books and records? Unless someone like John Button would store them—except he is said to want to move himself.
   I wish we had finished *A Nest* and it was on somebody's autumn book list. It is fact that there is nothing else quite like it in all literature. Perhaps our own originality frightened us.
   You haven't mentioned Pierre in many a day—how is the duck? I too have

236. The humorist Jack Douglas wrote a book with this title.
237. Apples were grown and sold on the Ashbery family farm in upstate New York.
238. *The Deadlier Sex* by Genevieve Manceron.
239. David Noakes translated Andre Hodier's *Jazz: Its Evolution and Essence* (Grove Press, 1956).

sampled Equinil,[240] and pronounce it goo-delicious. In Mexico City it can be bought without a prescription; needless to say, Buttons came back heavily supplied. If the same situation obtains in Paris, I suggest you stock up before you return. So useful for those "trying days" when you don't feel quite "up to snuff."

With Frank not due back until tomorrow, the social season plods tranquilly along. I understand Joe (Le Sueur) is going to give a party for him this Saturday. It is certainly fate that caused Grace and Frank to be in Paris for the first time together: just as it caused Bill Weaver to be on one of his rare absences from Rome. It is rather like the Pasternak novel, which is a great hymn to coincidence and accident. One of the most beautiful things in it is that the hero, driving through a street in the winter, sees a candle burning on a table in a room and is deeply moved by it and thinks of a line of verse about it which turns up in one of the poems at the end of the book. In the room at the time is a woman he is later to love: it is of course impossible that they ever know of this mysterious encounter.

Yes, of course you should write Tom [Hess]. Tell him how much you love *Art News* and writing for it and dream of coming back to it, and that you're finishing your thesis. Also, if you have any ideas for an article you could write there, tell him about it. He is very article-prone; and even if he said no, it would still sound as though you were interested. Besides he would scarcely want to get rid of the co-author of "Death Paints a Picture";[241] it is terribly funny. What about a piece on Moreau, Proto-Surrealist, or (probably a better idea) a conversation with Helion?[242] I don't think that would be cutting into Schneider's territory,[243] since Tom goes abroad and talks with Giacometti.

Well, time for my bi-annual haircut. Keep your snood clean, pet.

love, Josette Day[244] J.

240. Equanil, a tranquilizer similar to Valium.
241. Ashbery collaborated with Kenneth Koch on this poem.
242. Gustave Moreau (1826–1898), French symbolist painter who taught Matisse and Rouault. Jean Helion (1904–1987), French painter who painted both abstract and representational work.
243. Pierre Schneider, *Art News* Paris correspondent.
244. Josette Day, French actress who appeared in Jean Cocteau's *Beauty and the Beast* (1946).

TO JOHN ASHBERY

[New York, New York]

Oct. 15, 1958

Dear Kewpie,

Your letter sounds so happy, and your new hospice so grand, it's obviously *wrong* for me to wish you would come back. Still . . .

My social life is fairly minimal; but then I just reviewed twenty-some shows, including Jane, Mike Goldberg, Hyde Solomon, a swatch of Davis Gallery artists, *all* of 20th century German art at World House, an alluring group at Castelli . . . and I have to do one late on Jackson Pollock (not Reginald).[245] Far from making me feel like the world's most wanted reviewer it just makes me wish I were far, far away in a truly seedy Parisian park.

Tom (Hess) told me you were coming back in November. . . . what did you write him?

You just got an invitation here in care of Frank to cordially attend an informal party from 5 to 7 on Oct. 19 at the Poets' Theater. RSVP. (I could see it was an invitation so I opened it.) The enclosed was mooning around 49th Street some little time; I hope it's not an offer of emeralds and delight provided you left last week for Bayonne.

I'm glad you have such an overt affection for Zurich, since I have rather a sneaking one. It seems to me I stayed at the Hotel Stork with a river in front and a carillon almost in bed with me, though no one else of any interest.

You did know, don't you, that Jane is having another show in November? John Myers' idea. Her pictures are lovely; John is also so mad at Helen Frankenthaler[246] that he intends to get one of Jane's paintings into every major collection. Helen left the gallery for Andre Emerich, a mysterious and I should think self-defeating move.

I have of course seen almost zero of Frank socially since he came back. He refuses to discuss Europe, for fear I suppose of giving someone a little satisfaction. Oh, I told Bill Weevey some of the things you said about Grace so big mouth told Joey so Frank said to me, "I hear John was very witty about Grace in a letter to you." When I allowed as how Bill was a squealer he said, "Oh well, *you* told John I was mad at him last spring." Honestly, Kate. Then he lectured

---

245. Reginald Pollack (1924–2001), figurative painter and printmaker.

246. Helen Frankenthaler (1928–2011), abstract painter who first exhibited at Tibor de Nagy Gallery.

me on my paranoia; I didn't just bother to enlighten him on the things you said about Grace in your letter to Kenneth, just in case there is a heaven.

Donald [Droll] had a ghastly infected ear but it's better now. We are both on poor street. Though I am finally on the permanent staff here (where's my hat? I want out), and have joined their lavish group insurance policy, which will pay *half* my analysis. You can't imagine what it means to me, you can't you can't.

One thing that did seem to give the Grafton nightingale[247] great satisfaction is his meeting with Pierre. He convinced me that P. liked him much better than he did me, which I am, of course, quite used to.

Aren't I dear.

Maybe I'll send you some perms if you'll send me *"Rain."* [248]

Fairfield's new pleasure is to call up on my phone and ask for Frank. "May I speak to Frank? I want to find out if he can come out this weekend." etc. He continues a caution, though Jane assures me that when I am not around he is charm itself. The Hazans have not changed much during your absence.

The night I reviewed Jane's show she allowed me to stay to eat, along with the Hunters, which I think put me a social category just above Bertha.[249] Bob and Anne were very cute; she is normally pregnant and he is having kittens about his orals (I believe the two events are quite likely to coincide). I also spent a hysterical evening with Kenneth lately. I have another entry for our dictionary of K. K's accepted ideas: he thinks it's very funny that the French really do think Poe is a great writer.

I'm reading *Bouvard and Pecuchet*;[250] it's the loveliest novel ever penned, and the spiritual ancestor of our own life work.

Write me again. A firmer hint, when you feel up to it, about your state-side plans will always be more than welcome. Tell Naomi to send us a view card. My best to Pierre.

Ever-thine,

Hilton Kramer[251] J.

247. Frank O'Hara's hometown was Grafton, Massachusetts.
248. A poem by Ashbery.
249. Robert Hunter was John Ashbery's Harvard roommate. He and his wife, Anne, lived at 16 West 11th Street, in the same building as Joe Hazan and Jane Freilicher. Bertha was a maid employed by Ashbery and Schuyler at 49th Street.
250. Gustave Flaubert's last published novel.
251. Hilton Kramer, then art critic for the *New York Times*.

PS new initials in Oct. *Art News*, L.L He or she is better than HDH but not IHS.[252]

Is it true Isador and David Stimer (Steiner) are a thing?[253]

FO'H and Allen de Ginsberg "made it" after the grand MOMA opening. Tsk tsk.

TO JOHN ASHBERY

[New York, New York]

Nov. 11, 1958

Dear Veterans Day Celebrant,

Thank you for your letter and greetings and clippings. I crashed the age barrier over a hearty spread at the Kochs where a laughing Janice, when I admitted to my thirty-five summers, murmured, *"Nel mezzo del camin . . . "* They gave me a bottle of Macadamia nuts, a book about China and a game called PunFun, which I refused to take home with me. (Macadamia nuts taste sort of like cashews.)

I am now living at 326 East 49th. Not living with D. is depressing and so is sharing an apartment with Mr. Merzeg. In fact, I am not sure I can stand the latter, and may spend the time until he clears out at Alvin's; I have always wanted to visit Hoboken though I would hate to live there.

Did David Noakes get a job at the Sorbonne? He said he intended to contribute half a month's rent to my Fund, partly conditioned on getting a job, and it would surely be appreciated. I have never been broker. He might even want to tack onto it $3 for long distance calls to some place I have never heard of (though they may well have been calls made by his buddy. who knows).

Mr. Merczeg has contributed to the eventual well-being of the dump by replacing the broken window, fixing the frig—it now sounds like The Spirit of St. Louis—and some of the plumbing. He is a perfectly friendly old salt but I do not really like looking at him, talking to him or the smell of his pipe.

John Myers just called me to say he is reviving *Semi-Colon* and intends to feature in its first issue the business lunch episode from *A Nest of Ninnies*. I have

---

252. LL is Lillian Lonngren, HDH is Herbert D. Hale, and IHS is Irving Sandler.

253. Isador Fromm, Gestalt analyst and follower of Fritz Perls. David Steimer, music teacher who taught Naomi Newman Weinstein and was Alice Esty's pianist.

already fantasized the scene in which Barney Rosset[254] pleads for publication rights of the completed work. Swear that we will finish it this winter—I long to get back to that tacky Florida night club. Do you think it would be all right to call the chapter, assuming we entitle the chapters, "A Distant Strand"?

When in January are you coming back?

I enclose a card from Sandy. There seems no way of letting him know that his bathrobe is safe at the apartment.

I have been too involved with my emotional life to pay much attention to anything else. The Gruens gave a party for Jane's opening. I cannot say I had a deliciously good time there; nor did anyone else, as far as I could see. Though there was plenty of chatter. Elise Asher[255] flew around me like a big gray moth because I was reviewing her show at the Grand Central Moderns.

Here is the tenth of the month (I mean the 11th) and *Art News* is not out yet. Things go from worse to worse.

Every time I mention you to Kenneth he says, "He hasn't written to me. I guess he didn't like *Lunch*." [256] Recently he announced his retirement from the stage, after a disastrous appearance at the Carl Fischer Hall with Lucille Dlugecewski (sp?!)[257] and a drummer named Al. But he is still forging a libretto for Virgil, so now Ned Rorem[258] is courting his gifts.

Janice is pregnant. She will have the baby in the spring.

I assume you know that Mike Goldberg and Patsy Southgate Mathiessen[259] got married a few weeks ago?

"Das all for now folks. My best to Pierre.

Love, Tilly[260] J.

PS: I have kicked the tranquilizer habit; for the time being, anyway. I am always prepared to resume at a moments notice.

---

254. Barney Rosset (1922–2012), founder and editor in chief of Grove Press.

255. Elise Asher (1914–2004), painter and poet married to the poet Stanley Kunitz.

256. *Lunch* was a new poem by Koch.

257. Lucille Dlugoszewski (1925–2000), composer.

258. Ned Rorem (1923–2022), composer, essayist, and keeper of a diary from the late 1940s more or less to the present day in which Schuyler is rarely mentioned.

259. Patsy Southgate (1928–1998), writer, had been married to the novelist Peter Matthiessen (1927–2014).

260. Perhaps the cartoon character Tilly the Toiler.

TO JOHN ASHBERY

[New York, New York]

Feb. 4, 1959

Dear Vic,[261]

I was just dishing you with Missus Hazan ("dishing" i.e.: that you owe each of us a letter) and decided I would send you a follow-up letter to finalize my thoughts. Also, to enclose this wonderful picture of you and Frank arranging festivities at the Closierie I found in Mary Worth; and a better than average chapter from Smilin' Jack.[262]

My life has taken a marital turn back toward the good, or D. It is wonderful how two informed, intelligent, modern people can, after all, manage to share the same apartment. So write me at 438 East 87th, huh?

Frank told so many glorious tales of your Pollock-TNAP daze that you are now an office legend, and sort of our unacknowledged (not to say unpaid) Paris representative. Just wait until they start asking you to install some of our wonderful Munch Graphics and Architecture Worth Saving shows. You'll be begging to come home.

Jane has made quite a thing out of retailing John Ashbery anecdotes she drained out of Frank a few minutes after he got off the jet. Her favorite is one in which you tell Joan Mitchell that you sexed up that *roman policier* translation by inserting sentences like, "He felt her luscious titties." I think she may even have called up Dr. Burgler[263] and told it to him. It was nice to think that for a while we were all part of one financial family, and I have a questionable fantasy of the three of us in one office under a large and flaking Barnby . . . [264]

Nellie [Blaine] is sailing (today?) on the Cris Colombo for Naples, Egypt and Greece. You will doubtless run into her in the apartment in Grenoble one fine spring day. She gave quite a cheery blow-out Saturday last: Furl explained to me why my reviews are not really about the paintings but a moral appraisal of whether the artist has certain character qualities. I explained to him why his

261. Vic of the radio soap opera *Vic and Sade*, first broadcast in 1932.

262. Ashbery and Frank O'Hara helped arrange a dinner at Closerie des Lilas restaurant after a traveling show of American art circulated in Europe at MoMA. Mary Worth was a comic strip character; Smilin' Jack, a character in the Sunday comics.

263. Jane Freilicher's psychiatrist.

264. Ralph Barnby, fictional painter in Anthony Powell's *A Dance to the Music of Time*.

Winslow Homer[265] article is a crock of shit. Fortunately, big Lee Bell was sitting next to me; but I didn't press my luck.

I recently wrote a review designed to offend all Kathe Kollwitz[266] lovers that was quite humorous. Unfortunately after it was put through the editorial meat-grinder it not only disclosed me as a simp but made no sense. So I am finally going to appear in the Letters to the Editors column as the author of a letter that begins, "Dear sirs: I understand that some admirers of Kathe Kollwitz are clamoring for my liver and lights . . . "

By the by, you *did* write dearest Tom that little note, didn't you? He called me up and I let Frank tell him, fresh from your mouth, that you were not coming back so very soon, that he knew you planned to write to him, and that you had some wonderful ideas for articles you wanted to give him the benefit of. How about "Darthea Speyer[267] Goes to an Opening?" Or a catalogue raisonne of Paris pissoirs? Or Elliott Stein Paints a Steinlen?[268] Or "My Night with Bernard Buffet's[269] Ex-Boy Friend"?—who I hear is gorgeous. But you doubt-less have lots of fertile ideas of your own—maybe a trifle on Mont St. Michel and Chartres . . .

My wonderful collection of French Drawings finally came home to roost for a few weeks at the Metropolitan. (How could you not have responded to the wonders of Boucher, Daumier and Guys?[270] I don't think you're a Francophile at all—though I agree that most of the so-called modern works could effectively be flushed down the nearest can.) There was a black-tie opening to which I squired Anita Ventura Hatofsky,[271] following a tasty repast at Josephine How-ell's[272] digs. I cut a neat figure in George Montgomery's prep school dinner jacket—the neatness is accounted for by a fairly vast black cummerbund belonging to Donald, that hid most of the uglier moments—buttoning the

265. Porter's article "Homer: American vs. Artist: A Problem in Identities" appeared in the December 1958 *Art News*.

266. Kathe Kollwitz (1867–1945), German artist best known for prints.

267. Darthea Speyer, United States cultural attache in Paris.

268. Steinlen (1859–1923), Swiss/French painter and printmaker.

269. Bernard Buffet (1928–1999), French painter.

270. French artists Francois Boucher (1703–1770), Honore Daumier (1809–1872), and Constantin Guys (1805–1892).

271. Anita Ventura Hartofsky, childhood friend of John Ashbery's who came to New York City through her friendship with Donald Droll.

272. Josephine Howell, interior decorator and friend of Donald Droll.

trousers I felt like one of those Gay Nineties heroines clinging to a bedpost while Hattie McDaniel[273] hauls at her corset laces.

Now it is time for me to go eat lunch with Donald and Alvin, who are going to Florida this weekend for a week. When asked by A. for advice on how he should behave with D. my gracious riposte was, "Keep your hands to yourself." More later.

Lincoln's Birthday

Dear Kiddie,

This is part II of a letter and I just hope I can find part I.

How did you like my "official" style? I think it compares quite favorably with the canned asparagus tip salad at a Grange lunch in Wales, N.Y. I wish I were at one right now, as I am eking (sp?) out a hangover with post-reviewing blues. I think it is criminal that you did not have the fun of doing Reg Butler's[274] show at the Matisse. Last night the inner cell went to Rudi's studio and saw some of his flicks.[275] They were very lovely, but since the curtain rose somewhere after 10, and F. and I had been polishing a bottle at John Button's since 6, they are but a dream to me.

Listen, this is the serious part: I am 99% definitely moved into D.'s [Donald Droll] (438 E. 87 'case you've forgotten; write me there): what shall I do with your things, and which things? Frank has your phonograph and some records (the total Webern, for instance; his little face did not light up when I mentioned Couperin and Rameau).[276] But there's the bed, and the chester-drawers, your books and your bricks and fold-up table: is storage all right? It shouldn't be *too* expensive. Assuming you are ever coming back, that is. I gather you wrote Kenneth that your date of return has now been upped to September (he added, "but I guess the snows of Paris will once more fall on that head before we get to see it"). Anyway, you must write me about this right away, because I may be surrendering the apt. at the end of this month, and it is now the 12th. (I do not think

273. Hattie McDaniel (1895–1952), actress best remembered as the maid to the O'Hara family in *Gone with the Wind*.

274. Reg Butler (1913–1981), British sculptor.

275. Rudy Burckhardt directed over fifty movies, some as short as two minutes, using poems by Kenneth Koch, Vincent Katz, Frank O'Hara, and others as scripts. His longer movies were often unscripted and starred his poet, painter, dancer, and musician friends.

276. Anton Webern (1883–1945), the most radical composer of the Second Viennese School. Francis Couperin (1668–1733), French composer celebrated for his harpsichord music. Jean-Philippe Rameau (1683–1764), French composer.

storing with John Button—assuming he would be willing, which I doubt—is such a good idea. For one thing, the house might fall down at any moment; for another, he is always threatening to move to a yet more undesirable spot, and I am sure that the custodianship of someone's chattels is all it would take to set him in motion—he's a big I'd love to do it for you / I'm being imposed upon queen, you know.) Anyway, since it is obvious that I am going to store your duds, I don't know why I bother mentioning it.

But write me about it anyway. I assume you want all those poorly bound French books thrown out? (Joke.)

Well, it is finally nearly five so I have only one more hapless half hour to drag through before Frank and I go to John Myers' for a drink (the thought of one sickens me). I wish I had the energy to tootle over to 49th Street to see if by chance there is a letter from you. But the possibility that there isn't depresses me too much.

Now I will go roam purposely around the halls.

Be a good tot, and my best to Pierre. Donald always wants to know when I've heard from you and gets a charge out of your letters.

Speaking of letters: what shall I do with that trunkload of pash-notes in your desk? Tie a ribbon around them and send them to Sodus?

Ever,

Sade J.

(that looks nasty: Vic and Sade, I mean, of course)

Feb. 18 Perhaps I will never mail this letter . . . Or perhaps I will mail it today. For some reason it's very scirroco here; at any rate the one Italian typist in the office left early because the wind was giving her a headache. I loved your card with its rare Philadelphia view. Did I tell you that Baby Baldwin [Donald Droll's cat] now lives with us? He has become very friendly, and prefers a tinned food called "Cadillac" to "Purr," which puts itself forward as the "Catillac" of cat food. What he really likes are raw kidneys, and staying in bed all day, which I guess he gets from me.

TO JOHN ASHBERY

[New York, New York]

April 23, 1959

Dear Brother Courage,[277]

After a 5:30 viewing of *Shanghai Express*[278] at MOMA, as we in the game call it, in the company of Frank, Waldo Rasmussen,[279] Joe LeSueur and Norman Bluhm, it was delightful to come home to 87th Street and Don [Droll] and find your threatening letter. I do apologize for not writing you daily, particularly since it is the only thing I am likely to do that would give me any pleasure. But my life has been little more than a suppressed wail from the pit of job-slavery; more of that anon (if I run out of material).

Donald is well and happy and sends you his love. He asks after you and reproaches me for not writing so often that I would be quite suspicious, except that I always seem to have more immediate and inscrutable pals on hand to fret about, such as now-thirty year old Alvin Novak. (John Button recently hit the age limit for child stars too; you haven't heard such takings-on since Mitzi Green was cast as Becky Thatcher,[280] they both act as though the most tomorrow might hold is some sort of comeback, like the one Jane Withers made in *Giant*.[281]

First things first: I can't believe you had your mystery dinner with the [Sandy] Gregg Famille and still don't know that the (Robert) Hunters are, and have been for some little while, the proud owners of a bouncing boy. Bob quite bluntly calls him, "Mr. Wonderful." On my brief viewing of the infant (I'm ashamed to say I've forgotten his name), their apartment seemed to consist of an average size bassinet surrounded by a tumultuous sea of authoritative books on baby care, nipples, changes of garment, premature teething-rings and hysterical injunctions that even if we did whisper it probably wouldn't wake up Mr. Wonderful. Nor did it; not even an unexpected call from the folks back

---

277. Play on title of Berthold Brecht's (1891–1956) play *Mother Courage*.

278. *Shanghai Express* (1932), directed by Josef von Sternberg and starring Marlene Dietrich.

279. Waldo Rasmussen, colleague of Frank O'Hara's in the MoMA International Program.

280. Mitzi Green (1920–1969), child star in early Paramount talkies. She appeared as Becky Thatcher in John Cromwell's adaptation of *Tom Sawyer* (1930).

281. Jane Withers (1926–2021), child star in the 1930s who later played Josephine the Plummer in a long-running television commercial. George Stevens directed *Giant* in 1956, starring Elizabeth Taylor, Rock Hudson, and James Dean.

at the gravestone works,[282] where the three of them are going to spend the summer. Then Bob, who passed his orals with flying colors, will assume his duties in the English department at Dartmouth. The prospect so filled Anne with terror that she actually invited me to make a trip up for tea some coming winter afternoon.

Honestly, if Furl hadn't failed the Taste (Good) test eons ago, I'd be faintly cross about his dishing us to Mme. Freilicher-Hazan. However, since she troubled to write you about it (and you are the only person who doesn't make her nervous, including chum), and was very friendly when we tea-d in the Museum Garden this week, I 'spec no serious harm has been done. He did completely flip over that opening. Well. Frankly, I have fibbed so often about how Frank and I were in a meeting and didn't get out till after 6:30, I've quite come to believe it myself. Fact is, we *were* stupefied from work, and, along with Waldo, met Donald a bit after six on the opening night, when what you aptly characterized as "frozen piss" was falling from the skies. After ruining every garment we owned flailing about on the corner in the obscure hope that a celestial cab would appear, we decided to let the Madison Avenue bus go its over-crowded way and repaired to the Berkshire for a refreshing dry martini. We might have known what sort of stores we were laying up. (Poor Jane really got a neckful: seems the announcement was misprinted, and everybody—such as there were —stayed at the gallery until eight o'clock. I gather it was one of the more trying evenings of Jane's life, including the subsequent party at Robert Dash's[283] (now a reviewer for *Art News*; though Hubert Crehan[284] makes him seem like weak tea in the *mauvais gout* department). Anyway, Furl was much meaner to Frank and to John Button (who didn't go of his own free will, and not because of any plot between us all) than to me; which I found a refreshing change. He has managed to recollect every occasion on which Frank ever broke a date or stood him up, over the last (let's not count them) years, and accused him of them in a lump. This caused Frank to fly off to the Cedar and tell Jerry (who shares—I think—Jane's old studio, the [Walter] Auerbach one, with Joe Rivers) how mean Jerry's dad had just been to him. Then at a party the Boys [Gold and Fizdale] gave more or less under duress, following Alice Esty's recent concert-debacle, Furl stalked up to Frank (which was quite a trick, since the guests were

282. Robert Hunter's family owned a tombstone works in Milbank, South Dakota.

283. Robert Dash (1931-2013), painter who shared a New York studio in the 1950s with Fairfield Porter. See glossary.

284. Hubert Crehan (1905–1980), painter and art reviewer for *Art News*.

crowding each other out the windows) and said, "I'm very anxious that Jerry go back into analysis and I just hope *you* wouldn't say or do anything to prevent it." Not, you will admit, the most charming thing to say to a guy.

As for me, he just "hoped I would see the show before it closed," to which I . . . but let's skip it. I did see it. It was very nice, though not so nice as last year, perhaps; but then, it had no double portrait of us in it.

Jane reports that, Kenneth to the contrary, Fairfield is being extremely pleasant in the country.

Donald and I have taken a house with the Kochs for the summer, outside Southampton. It is reasonably near the station—within walking distance if you have plenty of pack-mule blood in your veins—the same one the Boys had summer before last, complete with orchard and separate dwelling unit (a reformed barn) for us who like to batch it. I really never thought that Kenneth and Donald would "make" it, as they say downtown, but on a recent weekend they drove out in Josephine Howell's car together, spent the night at the Porters (when Anne showed Kenneth to Jerry's room in the family part of the dwelling, he said, "I'm frightened," to which Anne said, "You do well to be frightened.") found and rented the house and drove back, ever the best of friends. Kenneth explains it on the grounds that they come from similar backgrounds.

As for 49th Street; Mr Merzeg reigns supreme, on a month to month basis, your furniture and undisturbed books are still there, which is saving your folk a peck by not storing them. I admit I'm reluctant to break up house-keeping, on the other hand, it is quite a dump. I also recently got a letter saying the building had changed ownership, and that if I persisted in staying on after my lease expired (next fall) I would be a "stuatory [sic] tenant." Which doesn't sound very nice. We will see what tomorrow brings; it certainly won't be cash.

Frank is so busy working on a big show at the museum, writing a book about Jackson Pollock for Braziller (soon to be followed by one on Kline for the Musee de Poche),[285] that he let me write an article on "The New York Art Scene" for Darthea Speyer's widely-distributed USIS French mag. Unfortunately it was not turned over to me until the ultimate moment, when I was busy disgracing myself—as far as deadlines and hours go—both at the museum and at *Art News*, so I sent it off a week late. This has caused me some anxiety, since the Good Woman planned to pay a merry $200.

Well, well, so you and Tom [Hess] are currently locked in one another's arms.

285. George Braziller published O'Hara's monograph on Jackson Pollock in 1958. O'Hara never completed the monograph on Franz Kline.

I always knew it would be you, the quiet one, who won out. By the way, I mustn't assume any false laurels, and it was Frank who jogged him about Ashbery/Helion,[286] not me.

I can't stand this typewriter another second (all . . . the keys stick), so I will finish this tomorrow at the Musee National d'Art Moderne . . .

(P.S. Shudder. April 29, 1960) [More may have been cut off by photocopy.]

TO JOHN ASHBERY

[New York, New York]

July 24, 1959

Dear John:

Swift as a thought—

I have been getting the heat put on me for not finishing an Edwin Dickinson[287] monograph (which I was graciously allowed to do in about 30 seconds), and, when I was snarling to Dr. Frankfurter's[288] secretary about it, she said my piece was doubly important since he (Dr. F) had written (cabled?) you a "kiss-off" letter about your Artaud piece—or research, or whatever it is. Assuming you are back in Paris, and that you give a hot damn, my advice is to send the stuff (you can always make it up, if necessary: Frankfurter isn't going to check on your research) with a letter giving some reason or other why you didn't have it there by the deadline. A misunderstanding about when it was needed, or due, is always a good one. Dr. F.—I gather—has a bug up his ass about *Portfolio* incorporating *Art News Annual* coming out on time. And Tom Hess (with whom you made a *big* hit in Paris) won't be back to calm the old oaf down until next week. (I'm uncertain Tom *is* getting back then—though Joanna [Shaw] thinks he is.)

I have started many letters to you—which I'm sure you will find a great satisfaction. But I am profoundly wounded by a crack on a recent postcard about "it being big of me to send my regards to you via les Boys [Gold and Fizdale]." What an idea. As I recall it, my last telephone chat with A. G. [Arthur Gold] (I was filling in photo-order forms with my free hand at the same time) included this excerpt from a discarded Noel Coward[289] opus:

---

286. Ashbery's "Jean Helion Paints a Picture" appeared in the February 1960 *Art News*.

287. Edwin Dickinson (1891–1978), painter. Schuyler's piece on his work appeared in *Art News* and has been reprinted in his *Selected Art Writings*.

288. Alfred Frankfurter (1905–1965), editor and president of *Art News*.

289. Noel Coward (1899–1973), British playwright, actor, and singer.

A.G.: *Do you have any special messages for anyone in Paris?*
(The spirit of mischief appears and tweaks J. S. by his nez retroussé)
J.S.: *Yes! Give John my dearest love.*
A.G.: *(In an enigmatic tone which the audience is unable to interpret)*
All right

at this point Mr. Coward's typewriter was impounded.

I admit it was very vile of me to mention you to "him"—I have been getting along quite well with the boys this spring; but I haven't seen them more than I wanted to; or vice versa—but no harm was meant.

Now this is serious: Mr. Merczeg is in the Veteran's Hospital (where I went and extorted the July rent from him, a five dollar bill at a time: he does have a pension, and Vet Hospital's are free, but it sure took a lot out of mother. My analyst thought I had been very sensible. Next time I'll send him). This leads me to the surprising news that your things are still at 326 East 49th Street (except the phonograph, which Frank has, and some records: he has some and I a few others). I was there a few days ago, and your things are safe; and it has been cheaper than moving and storage plus week-end consuming trips and supervision by me. So: please let me know right away when you are coming back (the building is going to be torn down in November anyway, so I doubt if any of us will be spending any very merry holidays there again). I hear a different story (about your return) from every traveler.

I hope to go to Southampton for a month next Saturday—all of August—but if you are not going to be back in September, I would rather cope with storage before I go out than at the end of my holiday. On the other hand, if you don't get this letter in time to answer it, I will still count you number one on my best friends list.

Pierre certainly made a hit with Alvin: *no* innuendoes intended (by me or Alvin). As a matter of fact, though Alvin didn't say it, I think he had a bit too much of the inner-life of Arnie-Naomi-and-Isod souse of the border.

This is very hasty and doesn't tell anything I meant to tell; I will write you a long, long letter from the Bungle Barn, where I will be hard at work on my opus, THE BIG SNOOZE.

love, Jimmy

P.S. The point to all the gibberish about Artaud-Frankfurter is that I thought you might have gotten an upsetting letter from him—if you are firm and grand, it will suffice. When Tom's away, nobody knows what they're doing at 32 E. 57th—.

TO JOHN BUTTON

New York, New York

Wednesday 9/9/59

Dear host,

Your friend — is his name Drole? (sp?) what an odd name — told Alvin about your welcome to Nirvana auld lang syne party get together; how lovely and how nice to have news of you so soon.

Our news — the humidity is plainly trying to prove something and I wish it would stop. Trying, I mean. It got all black and blasted heathish at twilight so I whipped into my The Rains Came outfit and ran down and kicked the loiterers off the stoop; but nothing came of it so I trundled back up and cast a mighty lusterless eye on the *Great Gildersleeve*.[290] Good grief.

Then George called. From a hospital, yet. Chalk one up for science. He does hate having to stay in bed (isn't he strange?) and eagerly anticipates getting no phone calls, no visitors, no mail. Do help disabuse him on the last count with the most stunning Kolorama Super-Greeting the West can offer — I see it as a wall-size study of Ruth St. Denis[291] entertaining the International Cub Scouts by dancing her "Indian Idol" on a sequoia stump. His address is —

> George Montgomery
> Room 352
> New York Hospital
> 32 East 68th St.
> New York 21, New York

Also, he may have serum hepatitis rather than infectious. Seems he had a lot of insulin shots this summer after a near-fatal bee sting. (No camp: he faints within thirty seconds of getting stung; always has. It has a beautiful Greek name which I have forgotten — bee sting allergy, that is.)

Guess who else was in the audience last night besides Frank (in dark glasses), Stevie Rivers and Alvin (loved "Divertimento"). Porter McCray. Whoops. Frank and Porter chatted. There's no two ways about it, Frank has *savoire faire*.

John Ashbery sent me the enclosed clipping for you. The petit garcon de Baltimore is you: the clipping is from *Radar*, the picture paper Pierre Martory

290. Television program.
291. Ruth St. Denis (1878–1968), dancer and choreographer who, with her husband, the dancer Ted Shawn, founded the Denishawn dancing schools.

writes for.[292] He got bored with captions and has started using his friends' names. Ashes also says: "Yesterday Pierre almost got fired because he gave the name 'Cocksucker' to a horse that had its picture in *Radar,* and the editor in chief turns out to speak perfect English. However he managed to convince him that it was all an unfortunate mistake." Whoops again. Ashes has parlayed his stay into another extension. Guess the only way we'll ever see him is by going t'other side. I'm game. I won't go to Southampton but I will go to Paris.

I meant this only to be a note of a note—it's you who want letters from Mr. Button sir—

I cannot describe the weather; it's like living in an abandoned guppy bowl. I hope great southern waves of coolth are crushing in off the vast Pacific.

love, Jimmy

Andrea Leeds[293]

TO JOHN ASHBERY

> UPSTATER-N.Y. Gentleman lover of art, literature travel, life in all its variety Particularly fond of France
> Would appreciate interesting correspondence with those whose sophisticated taste finds life a trifle dull these days. Enquirer Box P-4756

Schuyler
c/o Button
28 East 2nd Street
NYC 3 For immediate use

Sept. 10 [1959]

292. *Radar* was a trashy imitation of the American magazine *Look.* Photographs arrived for publication without captions or explanations. In providing the captions Martory used the names of many of his American friends, including Frank O'Hara and Alvin Novak. One caption of an American sailor waving began, "American sailor John Button says goodbye to . . . "

293. Andrea Leeds (1913–1984), actress described by Ephraim Katz in *The Film Encyclopedia* as "Wholesome star of a handful of Hollywood films in the 30s."

Engel—

Your letters! I just received them. I came into town to supervise the 49th Street mess (I joyously accept the present of your comfy *lit*; would I had a place to move it to, or the money—shudder—to move it with) and for some supplementary head shrinking brought on, to be blunt, by the Beast of Grosse Point Farms' [Donald Droll] devious ways. That was no tiff. Anyone who combines maximum frigidity with total hypocrisy laced liberally with cock-teasing and deceit is not my ideal beau. Or if you prefer less trenchant language, he is a prom-trotter. However, only his ex-wife and I have ever experienced what lies under that buttery exterior, so I have not bothered trying to rally anyone to my banner. Who would believe *me*? when Donald is obviously so sweet and nice? Phoo.

Of course your art works, letters and decorative etceteras will be taken care of. Please don't worry about them. As of last week, no letter had come for you from PR [*Partisan Review*]. If I were you, I would write them a direct simple query, suggesting that perhaps the check has gone astray?

About the gaseous journal to which we contribute: did you send a statement of your expenses? A little padding is not out of order; but not too much. TBH is quite wise in the ways of Europe and New York. Between we gells, I have received a $150 advance against the $200 (including "$50 for expenses") I was promised for my Dickinson piece. Write Tom a nice letter, telling him about the exciting Harvard news, what a wonderful piece you could write for "*Portfolio* incorporating Art News Annual" on [Raymond] Roussel, and that you are hard up and would like to be paid in advance of publication. After that stern note, you might allow as how you would settle for 3/4ths or a half of what is due. (Elaine de K., FP once told me, bullied them into paying on acceptance. But let's face it, she's butch.) Anyway, Tom will be nice about it. But be sure you make it sound like you really need it now; otherwise it might just slip his mind.

I had an idea for an article you could write for AN or Portmanteau: why don't you finish off Hélion and tell TBH you want to do Magritte?[294] Surely that would be fun. Since those techniques articles are so fraught with peril, you might say you'd like to visit the old master and do an interview-article. (Why don't you just rub out Pierre Schneider? I don't see why NY need suffer the burden of two Annette Michelsons.)[295]

294. Rene Magritte (1898–1967), Belgian surrealist painter.
295. Annette Michelson (1922–2018), film historian and, later, editor of *October*.

I've heard Bob and Fizdale[296] play through the "Grand Duo," but not when they had it all worked up. It is sublime. How I envy you both.

Frank read your letters with crows of delight; he eagerly anticipates the clipping with his name in it. Please tell Pierre I will go to any lengths to get my name in *Radar*; including sending him a nice fresh tube of Stripe, should that be his desire.

Read the enclosed letter. Now you have read it. Well, after I wrote it I got one from Al [Leslie] and *The Hasty Papers* are not being assembled just yet; but soon. So: send him something yourself(I didn't change my mind to be mean, I just thought you would know best what you want to send. I assume Al is all for the way way out.)

Now I have to go sieve the shit out of the Kitty Litter used today by Man, Johnny's cat. Somehow I cannot get used to addressing him by name.

Hastily and with a great big hug—love, Bettina[297]

PS: please do send George Montgomery some funny clippings, cards and cheery *trovati*. He is in New York Hospital & hates being chained & confined (He is also *quite* sick): New York Hospital/Room H352/32 E 68/NYC21

TO KENNETH KOCH

[New York, New York]

Saturday [September 1959]

Dear Kenneth:

It was a joy to hear your voice the other day. Oh dear, that sounds like the beginning of a letter from a fervent listener behind the iron curtain. You did catch me at a uniquely bad moment, since I was writing a letter asking for a loan (a rather long term loan), and I would almost as soon have leapt out of the window (a fall of one flight, I hasten to add). It will probably go unanswered and lay the ground work for future embarrassment. Still—to get back to the phone

296. Schuyler mimics Pierre Martory who had gotten Robert Fizdale and Arthur Gold's names wrong in this way.
297. Reference uncertain.

call—I may feel glummish now, but all the same I look forward with the interest of a sometime *National Inquirer* reader to your thumb-nail sketches of life up at University Heights. (By the way when the freshmen are too much with you, there is, I believe, in the Cathedral of St. John the Divine a superb set of tapestries. Let me think what they are. Yes: the only set (in America?) woven from the great Raphael cartoons, which you have so often enjoyed on your London jaunts. I have not visited them yet myself, since St. J the D. is, in my view, one of the more repulsive achievements—an insufficient reason to avoid capolavori of such quality. For an extra hundred lire the sacristan will show you the Capadocian lead monstrance with its *curious* pagan motifs.

The last sentence is a limp parody of what I like the least in Firbank. Come on now, fess up (and *don't* tell John or Frank) doesn't Firbank ever make you feel that just when you wanted a French loaf and cheese you'd been handed a wafer with an ooze of rose-petal jam on it? And he can be so maudlin. And icky. Much as I've loved *Vainglory* and *Flower Beneath the Foot* and *Sorrow in Sunlight* (a pox on Carl Van Vechten[298] for getting F. to change the title of the American edition to *Prancing Nigger* which is much less apt). I'm just as much disaffected by Cardinal P[299]—nobody ever seems to point out quite how stale his vapid religious jokes are—and the snobby one about the actress who gets killed by a mouse-trap and as for *Santal*, oh well, I'm not really an absolute philistine and he was a great writer (I just remembered that French maid in *Vainglory* saying, "such herds of wild chairs; such wild herds of chairs!").

Segovia[300] and his guitar—good grief. Hath FM no mercy? Ah. A new rock-and-roll hit: "Life's a holiday / on Primrose Lane / oh yes / on Primrose lane / life's a holiday." Do you think our lyrics lack true simplicity? Let me see, something topical, just right for Harry Belafonte[301] to sing with a choral background in the Sert Room at the Waldorf-Astoria. Ah yes.

> *Harry: Family of Man*
> *chorus: hmmmmmmmmmm*
> *Harry: I am a mem-ber*

298. Carl Van Vechten (1880–1964), novelist and photographer who championed Firbank's work in America. He befriended and photographed many of the African Americans writers, artists, and musicians associated with the Harlem Renaissance.

299. Firbank's novel *Concerning the Eccentricities of Cardinal Pirelli* (1926).

300. Andrés Segovia (1893–1987), Spanish-born guitar virtuoso.

301. Harry Belafonte (1927–2023), African American singer, actor, and activist known for his performances of Calypso tunes.

chorus: *(pseudo spiritual light crescendo)*
Harry: *of the Famil-ly*
chorus: *(fades out)*
Harry: *(softly, like Camay soap) of Ma-an*

This Adelaine[302] song could go on indefinitely, invoking a meeting with a girl named Olga, whose eyes inclined to melt the iron curtain (they were "lit by the freedom flame") at the Moscow Trade Fair, the despair of separation and the possibility of their rejoining sponsored by the U.N. in the interests of closing the culture gap. It might be daring to introduce the word ideology; I think a humming chorus could spin it out for a good quarter of an hour.

"It's 10:55 time to perk up with high vitamin C pineapple drink" Back to WNYC. Maybe there are some bargains in the markets this week. Rutabagas ought to be in good supply along about now.

Business. On reflection, and receipt of a non-hostile and even friendly note from Donald (which was a relief, if only because we have a lot of friends in common and will doubtless, in the social round, and not too distant future, enjoy the dubious pleasure of propinquity), I do not see why you should not write him about the money for the house. Or phone him at home if you prefer. Anyway, point out simply that, originally, he was to have signed the lease with you, that I can't pay now, and . . . you take it from there. I doubt that he has the money, or could get it out of his family; on the other hand, there is not too much future in exaggerated delicacy. (By the way, no, it will not upset me; though it might be better business not to say you had asked me for permission first.)

Along with the starkly simple friendliness, Donald asked me to ask you if you could bring back his linens and blankets. I pass that along for what it is worth. D. says in his note that he has tried to get hold of you . . . ?! ?! ?! I find it hard to believe that The Burning of the Mail has become a daily rite in the unpruned orchard on Mecox Road (Bridgehampton, Long Island). In mulling over this request, you may want to bear in mind these facts: that Donald doesn't have the use of Miss Howell's car when she is in this country (which she very much is); that Esta Leslie owns a little car, and would go to any lengths for her Donald; and if she wouldn't, Alvin would, and *his* Jim has the use of a snappy convertible. It seems to me unlikely that, however you arrange to bring your own things back, you would have space for Donald's. Or maybe you will. My inter

---

302. Schuyler may be referring to the song "Adelaine's Lament" sung by the character Adelaine in Frank Loesser's 1950 musical *Guys and Dolls*.

est in restoring the fitted sheets to 438 East 87th is moderate. It verges on anarchy.

But about the money: I am serious when I say it *won't* upset me if you want to (at least) discuss it with Donald.

Tell Janice I anticipate her projected letter, and, when it comes to her letters, I'm very weak in the taking the thought for the deed department. An envelope of hand-selected stones from Cacchi (her nickname does derive from one of the Italian words for persimmon doesn't it?) would also be most welcome.

28 East 2nd [John Button's apartment] is, in many little ways, a curious apartment to stay in. Anything I open, out falls a half-consumed tube of lubricating jelly or else a crucifix. There was even one (not a crucifix) in the small leather tool kit on J.'s English bike. Many a seafaring man who accepted a ride on the handle bars must've gotten a rude surprise; though not, of course, if he had read his *Decameron*. The seven-toed cat is named Man and these cold nights has taken to bundling in my blanketed crotch. My dream life resembles Scriabin's[303] "Poem of Ecstasy," with which Your City Station is favoring me. And, while there is FM, Hi-Fi, TV, Stereo, a tape recorder with tapes, an electric hand-saw and a steam iron, there is no clothes brush or wash cloth (of the facial sort, I mean). Still, he is a dear good boy, and I had the taste to wait thirty seconds after he left before taking down the heroic nude of Jose[304] and replacing it with a more plastic and decorous work. One of Courbet's fleshier nudes would have a sobering effect.

Did you know that bums often address strangers not as Bud, or Jack, or guy or fellow or man, but as Jimmy? It lends piquancy to living just off the Bowery. It is almost impossible not to pause when someone who would send a Neapolitan beggar into a trance lurches up and says, "Lisshen, Jimmy . . . " "Don't pick on me buster. Dorothy Day's[305] got a nice little place right down the street."

And now, out into the deceptively warm looking sunlight.

come sempre,

Jimmy

303. Alexander Nikolayevich Scriabin (1872–1915), Russian composer known for his *Poem of Ecstasy: Symphony #4*, Op. 54.

304. Painting by John Button.

305. Dorothy Day (1897–1980), journalist and reformer, cofounded the Catholic Worker movement in the 1930s, which ran a soup kitchen in the Bowery.

TO DONALD ALLEN

[New York, New York]

Sunday, Sept. 20 [1959]

Dear Don:

Here, from the welter of papers I've been carrying about, are a few poems; and a copy of the play that amused Frank, and (of "historical" interest), an imaginary conversation, written after seeing Frank's first book and walking up Park Avenue with him one May evening. I may send you a few more, but there aren't any I like better than "February," "The Elizabethans Called it Dying," and "Freely Espousing."[306]

I was so interested in what Frank told me about his talk with you last Sunday. Olson[307] may well be right, and there is a real point to putting in "background" or older poets. But if you want to represent the influence of readers as systematically omnivorous as Frank, John A., Prof. Koch and, me too, well: wow. Frank sometimes tends to cast the splendid shadow of his own sensibility over the past, as well as his friends, and while a brush of his wings is delightful, it is also somewhat heady. I thought you might be interested in what I remember people as actually reading.

John Wheelwright: particularly the poems in *Rock and Shell*.[308]

Auden: like the common cold. Frank and Kenneth still profess; I grudgingly assent (though if Auden doesn't drop that word numinous pretty soon, I shall squawk).

For the greats: Williams, Moore, Stevens, Pound, Eliot. I doubt if any very direct connection can be found between Moore and anyone. I wanted to write like her, but her form is too evolved, personal and limiting. After a bout of syllable counting, to pick up D. H. Lawrence is delightful.

Eliot made the rules everybody wants to break.

Stevens and Williams both inspire greater freedom than the others, Stevens of the imagination, Williams of subject and style.

Pound I wonder about. Like Gertrude Stein, he is an inspiring idea. But a somewhat remote one. A poem like Frank's *Second Avenue* might seem influenced by the *Cantos*, but Breton is much closer to the mark.

---

306. These poems appeared in Allen's *New American Poetry* anthology and later in Schuyler's book *Freely Espousing*.

307. Charles Olson (1910–1970), poet and rector of Black Mountain College.

308. John Wheelwright (1897–1940), poet whose book *Rock and Shell* appeared in 1933.

Continental European literature is, really, the big influence: the Greats, plus Auden, seemed to fill the scene too completely—so one had to react with or against them, casting off obvious influences as best one can. In the context of American writing, poets like Jacob and Breton spelled freedom rather than surreal introversion. What people translate for their own pleasure is a clue: Frank, Holderlin and Reverdy; John A. (before he'd been to France, Jacob's prose poems; Kenneth and I have both had a go at Dante's untranslatable sonnet to Cavalcanti; I've translated Dante, Leopardi and, fruitlessly, Apollinaire and Supervielle (I like the latter's stories better than his poems). But Pasternak has meant more to us than any American poet. Even in monstrous translations his lyrics make the hair on the back of one's neck curl.

But back to Americans. The horrid appearance of the sestina in our midst (K. and Fairfield Porter used to correspond in sestinas) can be traced directly, by way of John Ashbery's passion for it, to one by Elizabeth Bishop.[309] Its title eludes me: one of the end words is coffee, and it is in her first book.

Hart Crane: very much, and perhaps for extra-poetical reasons that aren't so extra. But he has exactly what's missing in "the poetry should be written as carefully as prose" poets: sensibility and heart. Not "The Bridge," of course (not yet anyway)—I think it's impossible for anyone not to premise so overtly an "American" idea. I don't mean that I don't enjoy the poem; but there is, at bottom, the rather hick idea of America challenging Europe, when Whitman had already conquered with a kiss. But do look at "Havana Rose" in the uncollected poems, or "Moment Fugue" (I'd give the tooth of an owl to have written that), or a song like "Pastorale:

> No more violets
> And the year
> Broken into smoky panels.

What a beginning.

John and Frank not now, and Kenneth perhaps, admire or admired Laura Riding;[310] but she won't let her poems be reprinted. I have always found them rather arid going, myself.

On reflection: I don't think I'm right about Gertrude Stein. Certainly the

---

309. Elizabeth Bishop's (1911–1979) sestina "A Miracle for Breakfast" appeared in her book *North and South* (1946).

310. Laura Riding (1910–1991), poet.

Becks[311] production of *Ladies Voices* (on the same bill as Picasso's *Desire Caught by the Tail*, in which Frank and John A. appeared as a couple of dogs, night after night) in 1952 influenced me immediately and directly. To represent her by a work like *Ladies Voices* would be truer than to include almost anything of Eliot's. I like Eliot but what Parson Weems[312] was to other generations *The Waste Land* was to us: Pablum.

Also, in tracing influences—the important ones—there is this: that while John Wieners[313] by chance first got the word from Olson at a Boston reading (then later went to Black Mountain College) and put it to good use, it is an experience unlike that of any other talented poet I know. Frank studied with Ciardi;[314] but if another writer had been giving the course, Frank would have taken it. (Olson's own allegiance to Pound-Fenellosa[315] can't be generalized for others—unless you have room for all of Proust, *The Golden Bowl*, *Don Juan* (very operative on Frank and Kenneth) and Lady Murasaki. All through high school one of my sacred books was Mark Van Doren's *Anthology of World Poetry* (1928). (In which I first read poems by Thoreau; I'm not all *that* international.)

I was so delighted to hear that you asked Frank about Edwin Denby's poems; I hope you have seen *Mediterranean Cities* as well as the earlier book. His harsh prosody I find a relief.

There is a poet who died whose name escapes me:[316] Frank and John admire his work very much, and I think Frank has copies of the *QRL* with poems of his. Perhaps Frank has already mentioned him to you.

I trust we'll talk soon. I didn't mean to go on at this length, but if you can find anything for your anthology in these maunderings, so much the better.

Yours,

Jimmy

311. Julian Beck (1925–1985) and Judith Malina (1926–2015), actors and founders of the Living Theater, the best known, if not most notorious, experimental theater company of its day.

312. Parson Weems (1759–1825), American clergyman whose biography of George Washington invented the story of Washington's chopping down the cherry tree.

313. John Wieners (1934–2002), poet, who, after attending Black Mountain College and living in San Francisco, Buffalo, and New York City, returned to his native Boston.

314. While at Harvard, O'Hara took poet John Ciardi's (1916–2000) creative writing class.

315. Ezra Pound translated Ernest Fenellosa's *The Chinese Character as a Medium for Poetry*.

316. David Schubert (1913–1946), poet whose only book, *Initial A*, appeared posthumously in 1961. The poet Theodore Weiss and his wife, Renee, championed Schubert in their magazine, the *Quarterly Review of Literature*.

TO JOHN ASHBERY

[New York, New York]

October 13, 1959

Dear John,

You would scarcely recognize the old block—Turtle Bay does not seem to be invading so much as Gatsby's and The Living Room are trying to join hands. Up the street (toward 2nd Avenue) there is a new apartment house, in the recessed entrance style with outdoor planters (I noticed on another nearby planter this sign: "Owners of dogs fouling the premises will be prosecuted." rather a comedown from the old "curb your dog" whimsy), and what used to be the 1st and 49th Rikers is now The Delegate (or is it the Diplomat?) a hamburger joint of formidable appearance, sort of New York post-Edwardian-revival, with fat gold letters slinking across the glass. Were you here, I'm sure we'd be dropping in, but as it is they have yet to get a whiff of my green stuff. You will thrill to learn that not all is change, and the Beekman Towers Coffee Shop still features its characteristic smell of boiling dropped egg water. As for this dump itself, well. There was plenty of El Ropo clogging the atmosphere, but that has gone. I have also been trying to throw things out, in preperation (sic . . .) for my next move. This is an almost impossible task for me, since the discovery of one undone Chinese puzzle ball in a paper bag is food for an evening's conjecture on what plans you might have had for it. I have managed to bring myself to relinquish my collection of yellowing Agatha Christie's . . . in fact the *roman policier* gets a zero vote in my books right now; which is rather a relief, since it seemed I might never be sated and my reading would sink from depth to depth. Happily one day while reaching for the truly unreadable Margery Allingham[317] I found I had bought *A London Life* instead . . .

Your letter. If you're a bit fâché with Tom I don't blame you; he can be an awful crab. If *Portfolio* is out it is being kept a secret from me; though I doubt that it is, since I know they were working on proofs quite lately. Don't worry about your Artaud piece; it is impossible that you would not write more interestingly than [Roger] Shattuck, even when addressing yourself to such unappetizing stuff. Frankly, it is only admiration for you that could bring me to read it, since nothing I ever read by him seemed to warrant the fuss. Not even Norman Bluhm's enthusiasm for the letters from Rodez can alter that opinion. I am

---

317. Margery Allingham (1904–1966), author of Albert Campion mysteries.

mildly curious though to find out just which judge he played in *Joan of Arc*—Falconetti[318] is the only member of the cast whose identity I have ever been sure of . . .

Perhaps you could prevail on Tom to let you do Magritte on the basis of milk-starvation? Surely corrupt Belgium is flowing with same . . .

When I got your letter I was in the middle of writing Al Leslie (trying to find out just what he means by a word in a speech I quoted from his *The Chekov Cha-Cha* (or *Me, Dondi Leslie*) "cutism": cute-ism; or cut-ism—"a rage for making cuts"; or a typo for "cultism"; the context offered few clues) and told him about [John Ashbery's] *The Compromise*. Kenneth has the copy that was here among his orderly belongings, and I will try to get him to stir his stumps about it. It does seem as though you ought to be paid a little something for it. Perhaps if you sent it to Barney Rosset as a translation of the first work by a teenage motor-cyclist from Arles you would find your option was taken up.

Kenneth is correcting or has corrected the proofs of *Ko, or, A Season on Earth*[319] (the subtitle got in despite some of the most unpleasant remarks I have ever addressed to Kenneth's tin but living ear). And I have read and had read to me his opera libretto, which is lovely and hilarious, although the playing time now is just under that of *The Ring*. This has occasioned many demands for expert service on where to cut, and any rejoinder such as, "Who do you think I am? Felice Romani?"[320] only produced ample proof that Kenneth indeed does not know who Romani was. I wish you were here to deal with the dear boy, since you seem the only one who is trenchant enough to succor and control. You may recall how he took on over being the Lady Day of the 5 Spot; well, now that he is a prof at Columbia, is writing an opera with V. Thomson,[321] and has a comic epic about to hit the stands, I leave it to you to imagine the state he is in. Rather like the mother in *The Sea-Gull* "Get my muff . . . Oooh . . . why do you all torment me so? I'll never be able to perform tonight . . . squeal . . . I must! It's my art . . . the public wants me! . . . hello? Larry? . . . "

How can I be so mean?

318. Carl Dreyer (1889–1968) directed *Joan of Arc* (1928), the only movie in which the French actress Falconetti (1892–1946) appeared.

319. Grove Press published Koch's long poem.

320. Felice Romani (1788–1865), opera librettist of many of Guiseppe Verdi's libretti.

321. Koch wrote the libretto for *Angelica*, an opera set in Paris in the late 19th century with the architect and city planner Baron Haussman as its hero. In the end, composer Virgil Thomson rejected Koch's libretto.

Pierre's letter was a major enchantment. I hope you will not be like Mae West's oriental beau in *Klondike Annie*,[322] and let him correspond with "a few men friends of his own race." The thought of you so intimidated me that I signed off with a tame bye-bye.

You both went over like dirigibles (sp?) full of helium with Arthur Gold. I don't know why I should find it faintly miff-making to be in the "Yes. *Isn't he? Aren't* they?" role while he hymned your collective praises. In fact I felt quite studied when he got to the part where you are the only person at the Flore with whom one can hold a conversation. Oh well, it's a fact that it would have taken less starch out of mother had the beast of the Baldwin kept his eye on your skills several eons ago. The boys are in fine fettle, of course. I dreamt the other night that Bobby was going to marry Claire Rosenstein. Must remember to tell Dr Loomis.[323] But all he'll say is, "And what did you make of it?" *Plus ca change . . .*

You have never handed in your sealed report on the N. Weinstein R. Pollack to-do. Isn't he rather a repulsive-ola? Or have I been misinformed?

The last I heard, Kenneth was awaiting word from you about his world editorship of *Locus Solus*,[324] and gave no sign of giving up same. But, should he, I'm keenly interested . . . would it include any token fee? Hmm? It's not that I don't love art, but the prospect of spending a lot of time and postage on America's leading friends without remuneration might be disheartening. (Secretly, I don't think K believes anybody except you, he, Frank & me have anything to offer. While I am of this opinion too, of course, it seems rather limiting for a magazine.) Just how big is this revista going to be, and how seldom will it appear? If you wish I will go ahead and line up Marianne Moore for "The Brooklyn Letter." (Her reading of a poem about the Dodgers on the *Jack Paar Show* was a recent occasion for pain; although only a few could understand a word she said. The part where the announcer drew her into a commercial for a self-developing Kodak Land Camera was especially chilling.)[325]

322. *Klondike Annie* (1936), directed by Raoul Walsh.

323. Schuyler's psychiatrist at the time.

324. Little magazine founded by Harry Mathews and edited by him, Ashbery, Koch, and Schuyler.

325. Marianne Moore, a fan of the Brooklyn Dodgers baseball team, got picked up by Parr's television talk show, and later by *Life Magazine*, when the Ford Motor Company asked her to name the new car that became the Edsel. Moore played the role of a winning eccentric spinster poet. The poem about the Brooklyn Dodgers is "Hometown Piece for Messers Alston and Reece."

I have about recovered from a severe case of TV poisoning, contracted on 2nd Street. The actual possession of a set is an insomniac's torture and delight, particularly on those evenings when I found myself rushing home a little early to catch a chopped-up Laurel & Hardy or an Our Gang festival, and not winding up until the wee hours with Norma Shearer on the late-late.

There were many delights, of course, and I have forgotten the titles of most, but some special charmers (I hope I haven't written you this already), were: *New Faces of 1937* with Harriet Hilliard[326] (the opening number was "The Widow in Lace," a song well-remembered by me) and introducing Ann Miller:[327] *Three's a Family*, a wartime housing shortage comedy with Charlie Ruggles, Fay Bainter, Helen Broderick, Hattie McDaniel and others; Norma Shearer, Robert Montgomery, Mrs Patrick Campbell and—oh dear, the blond woman who had an ermine toilet seat and starred in *Murder by the Clock*[328]—in *Riptied* (oops: *Riptide*, I mean): Irving Thalberg[329] had wonderful ideas about how beautiful and glamorous beauty and glamour are. If you ever get a chance, don't miss it; the big scandal scene alone is worth it, in which Robert Montgomery, drunk as somebody in Scott Fitzgerald, tries to boyishly get from his balcony to Norma's, only to go crashing through an awning onto the ballroom terrace (everybody is on the Riviera, natch) . . . but it's too predictably lovely to describe. And, *I've Got Your Number*,[330] with Pat O'Brien and Allen Jenks as telephone repairmen, Joan Blondell as a wise-cracking switchboard girl (there's more "says who" ing and "Oh (burn yo . . ."), Glenda Farrell as a medium and Louise Beavers as her other-world control . . . "But Martha, you didn't have a southern accent before you passed over . . . " Miss Beavers, distractedly: "Well, you see, honey, ah lives on de south side ob heaven . . . "

How I am running on. The only New York fashion note of my observing is the long-expected and over-whelming triumph of the bulky-knit sweater. Really, they should be called fluffy-knits, since embracing anyone wearing one is rather like throwing your arms around a huge *pomme-soufflé*. Had I any cash, I

326. Harriet Hilliard (1919–1994), who became, after marriage, Harriet Nelson of the hit TV show *Ozzie and Harriet*, appeared in Lee Jason's movie.

327. Ann Miller (1919–2004) of burlesque, Broadway, and M.G.M. movie musical fame.

328. *Murder by the Clock* (1931), directed by Edward Sloman.

329. Irving Thalberg (1899–1936), legendary Hollywood whiz-kid, studio head, and producer on whom F. Scott Fitzgerald based his unfinished novel *The Last Tycoon*.

330. *I've Got Your Number* (1934), directed by Ray Enright.

would hasten the return of a personal vogue for hand-knit English heavies. The "Italian cut" suit continues in weird and dismal adaptations.

I don't think anyone *we* know has been to see Yves Montand (though the Hazan-Gruens doubtless made a liar of me last night). The only thing that could get me there would be a prolonged re-enactment of the hammock scene from Ted Gorey's favorite flick.

Oh. The last time I saw *him* was at dinner at the Epsteins,[331] some while ago —in the summer, that is. He had to rush away to a sordid hotel room for a private view of the uncut *Manon*[332] (Clouzot's of course). Barbara misses you: in fact, you and I seem the only members of Our Gang they have not lowered the boom on, though Jason grudgingly admits that Larry has made a good thing of painting. Barbara went so far as to ask after "old Jane." I got tiddly and referred to Jason as "another tragic American success story," to Bubsey's[333] merriment if not to his.

Well, folks, I guess that about winds up the news for tonight!

Give Pierre my love,

love,

J

Roach of Roach Hollow[334]

ps—No sign yet of R. Blaser.[335] There'd be no harm in writing a short answer to Tom's note, renewing your appeal for an advance and pointing out that you are short of cash & put out the money yourself for both articles. I assure you, it won't queer any future dealings with the egg; I think he rather likes playing the grouch who has to be asked three times before he'll hand over the car keys.

331. Jason (1928–2022) and Barbara Epstein (1928–2006). Jason was the prominent New York publisher who had an illustrious career at Random House. He is credited with launching the quality paperback, which revolutionized American publishing in the 1950s. Barbara Epstein was a founding editor of *The New York Review of Books*.

332. Clouzot's movie version of *Manon Lescaut* was released in 1949.

333. Barbara Epstein's nickname.

334. This refers to the footlocker Frank O'Hara left at 326 East 49th Street. When it was opened, cockroaches swarmed out of it.

335. Robin Blaser (1925–2009), poet. His poem "The Cup" appeared in *Locus Solus* I.

TO JOHN ASHBERY

The Museum of Modern Art
New York 19

Nov. 2, 1959 (good heavens)

Dear Glen Tetley,[336]

I wrote part one of this dullest of epistles just a week ago. It seemed too petulant to mail, but since it answers a few questions re Fart News in your sublime latest, I'll send it along anyway.

Tell Pierre bless his heart, and I'm scouring the mailbox for my very own *Radar* cover. Did you tip him off that American stripteuses are often called Billie and Jackie and Johnnie and did he act on same? I rather anticipate a white hysteria, all feathers and fur (fox).

I don't know that Kenneth's schedule *is* as heavy as he thought it would be; he says that Columbia University has a built in goofing-off system. He just completed applications for three different fellowships—A Ford Foundation grant; a teaching Fulbright in Athens (I look forward to your joint poems, written under the influence of Retsina: "The Strangler Gets Two,"), and I suppose the third is the Guggenheim fellowship, traditional with pearls. I'm sorry I was mean (if I was) about K in my last since he has 1) been sickly (his nose swelled up) and 2) V. Thomson has been a beast about his marvelous libretto. I must say for the dear boy that he gave it right back to V.T. with knobs, but I don't think that's going to get the libretto set. I told him to "think big" and try for Milhaud;[337] actually, it's impossible to think of any composer bright enough for it.

While I was feeling merciful toward the Cincinnati Song Bag,[338] you had better, all the same, write toute de suite ordering him to hand over *The Compromise* to Al oops Alfred [Leslie]. I had tried, and he laughingly allowed that he had "a batty postcard about it from Al." So, since Alfred is interested, and you want it printed, act now! You know how easily the good soul gets diverted; as who doesn't.

Yes, 326 is coming down, but at a later date—say, February. The plan is that George Hamilton Montgomery and I will move into the O'Hara digs on 9th Street, as soon as same moves into his new apartment (with Joe-ey), which will be, as you've doubtless heard, the ground floor of the [Patsy] Southgate

---

336. Glen Tetley (1926–2007), ballet dancer, choreographer, and a friend of Gold and Fizdale's.

337. Darius Milhaud (1892–1974), French composer of classical and popular music and numerous movie scores.

[Michael] Goldberg Carriage House; the upper floor being reserved for Mike's studio. It is said to be small and of an unearthly, European charm. No, the city doesn't have to find me an apartment but the landlord does have to pay me to move; which is a blessing, since I can't pay my dentist or my analyst. In general I'm feeling rather restless about it. As the other apartments become vacant, the roaches and silverfish seek hospice in friendly apartment 37. Something quite indescribable strolled across me the other night, as I was reading Hamlin Garland's A *Daughter of the Middle Border.*[339] I think it may have been she herself; at any rate there was quite a bit of leaping and screaming before I made the kill. Oh well, at least I left the bedbugs behind at Johnny's. By the time I left 28 East 2nd my bottom looked like an old pomander.

I hazard that Miss Janice is pregnant; such was my surmise after seeing her the other night in a blue knit. Kenneth had told me in early September that they were aiming for a May deadline, so they could all sail for Europe next summer, assuming one of his grants comes through. I guess that's what's called Planned Parenthood. Anyway, at the time Kenneth allowed that he was the tired commuter on the 7:17 from Southampton.

A current New York item is Earl McGrath-Stephen Spender.[340] Oof. Oh to be in Paris, strolling through the Noguchi gardens[341] . . . (are they as ugly as the photographs imply?)

Tom conned me into a few reviews for the December issue, and awarded me such plums as Louise Nevelson and Paul Brach.[342] I guess that ought to teach me. He also thinks we should all be meaner; I agree in principle but do not feel like getting socked in the eye.

I enclose a sample review of Furl's from *The Nation*[343] (the next time you write him, whenever that will be, do mention that I sent it . . . he's been very

338. Koch was a Cinncinnati, Ohio, native.

339. Hamlin Garland (1860–1940), novelist on America's Midwest. A *Daughter of the Middle Border* (1921) is one of his four autobiographical works. He figures in Schuyler's poem "Money Musk."

340. McGrath, New York gallery owner, and Sir Stephen Spender (1909–1995), British poet, editor, and man of letters. Spender would write the only major review of Schuyler's novel *What's for Dinner?* to appear in America.

341. Isamu Noguchi (1904–1988), sculptor who designed for Unesco the *Jardin Japonais* (Garden of Peace) that featured his sculptures.

342. Schuyler's reviews of sculptor Nevelson and painter Brach appear in his *Selected Art Writing*.

343. "Happenings," a review of Allen Kaprow reprinted in Porter's *Art in Its Own Terms* (Zoland Books).

friendly lately but I don't like the quizzical, ruminative look he gets now and then).

Frank, LeRoi Jones,[344] Allen Ginsberg and One Other are reading at the Living Theater tonight—a benefit for LeRoi's Totem Press which is going to publish *Second Avenue* as a pamphlet. You had better hustle up *Locus Solus*, or we are going to find Jonathan Williams[345] discovering us, like a couple of old Mina Loys[346] (I was delighted to hear Edwin, the other night, after I had bluntly hinted that I didn't think Mina was any good really, insist that she had her merit while referring to her as Myrna Loy.[347] Has any poet writing in English successfully mentioned a clown? If so, it's news to me.)

I loved your description of *Les Liaisons Dangereuses*,[348] particularly the evocation of Yvonne Thomas[349] as an archtype which indeed she is. La Belle Yvonne called this morning to invite me to dinner, but I couldn't go. I might have switched dates (one of the flesh) had she gone into detail about her guest list but she didn't so I didn't.

Speaking of the flesh, I'm sure you'll rejoice with me in my brief encounter with an editor of *Sports Illustrated*, which the editor rather resembled. Quite a dope to talk to (among his numerous acquaintances were: Dado Ruspoli; J. Wilder Green;[350] Bill Weaver; and so only—I suddenly can't imagine why that seemed discreditable—it was a matter of tone), but oo-la-la those skiing muscles, minded me of, "I don't know how I ever did without it!" And it is always enchanting to find the exception that proves the rule—I mean to meet someone who does what one usually doesn't like so well that it is indeed a pleasure. Alas, any interest in a reprise seemed largely on my side (that's what I get for not knowing Dado Ruspoli), and I am back on the bench humming "Autumn Leaves."

By the way, did you take your disk of French hits to France with you? The sleeve is there but not the songs . . .

344. LeRoi Jones (1934–2014), poet, playwright, political activist, essayist, and editor. In the late 1960s he changed his name to Amiri Baraka.

345. Jonathan Williams (1929–2008), poet and publisher of Jargon Books. Jargon published Mina Loy's *Lunar Baedecker*.

346. Mina Loy (1882–1966), poet, once married to poet/boxer Arthur Cravan.

347. Myrna Loy (1905–1993), actress known for playing Nora Charles to William Powell's Nick Charles in *The Thin Man* series of movies.

348. Novel in letters by Choderlos de Laclos published in 1782.

349. Yvonne Thomas, French abstract painter who showed in New York City.

350. Dado Ruspoli, man about Rome. J. Wilder Green, Deerfield Academy schoolmate of John Ashbery's who worked at MoMA.

I have been very telephonically chummy with Arthur Gold. Hmm. Plainly I'm running out of news so will close now.

Give Pierre my love. The next time I bump up against Wilder I'll slip him the news that you too now own a Pollock. Most of our conversations are as follows: W: "When's John coming back from Paris?" Me: "Oh, not for another year or so." W: Isn't he the lucky one. Since Wilder recently bought a duplex in the 70's, I guess you are not alone in luckiness.

By the way: don't take Porter's [McCray] hint about a permanent European representative too seriously; it *could* happen — but he dreams beautiful dreams, and many of them don't come true for years and years, if ever. Oh. How odd you should think I might mind your well considered opinion of the Paris Biennale[351] — it had all of us vomiting, though it's worth one's job to say so above a whisper, so I'll shut up now.

love, J.
Pachita Crespi[352]

TO JOHN ASHBERY

[New York, New York]

Nov. 16, 1959

Dear John,

Though I really should address this to Pierre — I think it is so perceptive of him to have grasped my essential relationship to mothers and elephants. Also, that I would put myself in bizarre danger at John Button's seemingly reasonable behest struck a chord. I'm inclined to ask the Bronx Zoo to furnish me with an elephant picture so I could send *Radar* a fictitious letter for their readers column; but that picture of Alwyn [Alvin Novak] rather alarms for Pierre's job and so I will let sleeping pachyderms lie.

Janice says Kenneth wrote you, so you doubtless know what's what downtown. K won a $100 prize from *Poetry* — it isn't called the Alice Babar Award, but it's like that. Virgil has also set four poems of his, which Alice Esty intends to belt out at her next recital.

By the way, if you should receive payment for your contribution to *Portfolio* (incorporating *Art News Annual*) let me know, please. It would surprise me less

351. Ashbery disliked the exhibition.
352. Costa Rican artist and illustrator.

than finding an eel in my bed if they just glided over the balance of my stipend. Although I had firmly resolved never to review again, greater poverty than any man deserves to know made its pinch felt, so TBH lined up a few greats for me: Louise Nevelson, Albers, a gorgeous Dubuffet[353] retrospective and Paul Brach. Ho hum. I certainly wish you had been on tap (a Braytonism)[354] for some swell editing. Oof.

Frank is beginning to complain rather loudly about not receiving your poems. Me too. Do stop fussing and send.

No, Hamlin Garland is quite terrible; except he has the virtue of being full of names, people and places. I also haven't read his fiction, particularly his socalled master works, *Rose of Dutcher's Cooley* and *Main Traveled Roads*. Perhaps the enclosed idle thought of an indolent fellow gives my Hamlin Garland views best[355] (the part about Paris I got out of a hair-rising hour spent with George Orwell's *Down & Out in Paris and London*). I have also lately read: 700 pages of Casanova's fibs (fun); Dreiser's *The Titan*—he's very different than I imagined and really quite compelling, sort of as though one's view of life were based on reading only the *Mirror* and the *Wall Street Journal*—two E. Nesbits[356] (for the simple of all ages); Carl Van Vechten's *The Blind Bow Boy* (Frank has just brought in his *Firecrackers*: Vincent is the outlet for this particular brand of dope) which is just like Dreiser since all it does is describe interiors and ladies' dresses, only elegant ones; René Grousset's history of the Chinese Empire,[357] which is funnier than you might think: all his comparisons are to figures of Roman history, so on almost any page one stumbles on phrases like, " . . . this Chinese Messalina . . . " which gives the whole an unexpectedly W. C. Fields flavor; William Dean Howells' *Indian Summer*, a gem; (now I ache to read *The Undiscovered Country*, because the title is so pretty) something called in its paperback edition *Desert Passion*, an excerpt of *Rose de sable* by Henry de Montherlant,[358] whom I figure as the French Mary McCarthy; and many more. I have also pulverized my head over your anthology of black humor, though I can't say I've done much laughing; this may be the language barrier however.

353. Jean Dubuffet (1901–1985), French painter who was influenced by the work of children and the insane.

354. Brayton Lewis, partner of Bob Vanderbilt in the Periscope-Holliday Bookstore, whose clichéd verbal mannerisms amused Schuyler and Ashbery.

355. Schuyler's poem "Money Musk."

356. Edith Nesbit (1858–1924), author of children's books.

357. *The Rise and Splendor of the Chinese Empire* (1952).

358. Henry de Montherlant (1895–1972), French novelist.

Last night I saw *Yellowstone Kelly*, a must for TV fans of such programs as *Cheyenne* and *77 Sunset Strip* (the last today's equivalent for what Raymond Chandler movies used to be — it consists of an hour of attractive people racing up and down Sunset Boulevard in convertibles to the tune of what sounds like French jazz). I can't really recommend *Yellowstone*, although it was of course uplifting to see young Edd Byrnes expire in the arms of big Clint Walker.[359]

There has been an absolute dearth of possible to look at movies. Although Saturday a few of the chosen gathered at the hut of garde-forestier-chef de Katiba, John Button, and dug *Dinner at Eight*.[360] My goodness. Jean Harlow was great, Madge Evans a dream of loveliness and Marie Dressler, supreme. Miss Dressler (Joey kept recollecting that in her day she was, "the best loved woman in Hollywood") played a kind of Maxine Elliot,[361] with a lot of furs and Pekineses and raunchy recollections. At one point Miss Harlow said, "I was reading a book the other day," and Miss Dressler almost shot out of her voluminous and totally sequined Adrian[362] gown. It was a glorious double take. Noted TV critic John Button also "caught" the moment when someone said "Daddy says he's free (hic) and over twenty-one." The little "hic" was where (*pace* J.B.) the word white was edited out. Truly, he is a keen observer. . . .

I had the horrible experience the other night of bouncing out in a hurry to meet George and clapping on the padlock, just in time to realize that my keys were within and I without. The friendly locksmith on 53rd was sitting up late trying to balance his books but declined to come to my aid; on the assumption that is was no time for me to get fussy about the streets, I guess. He did condescend to sell me a hack-saw blade for 50 cents (the price of a ~ on the machine is no cents sign); nor would he rent me a handle for it. It took me an hour and a half, and while I felt quite accomplished — I really never had sawed a big metal padlock off a door before — I was not cheered to note that not so much as a head peeked out, though I made enough noise to set all distant Pierre Boulez'[363] hairs aquiver . . . You spoke truer than ever when you mentioned the marauding

359. Television actors Edd Byrnes (who played Kookie in *77 Sunset Strip*) and Clint Walker (1927–2018) appeared in the movie *Yellowstone Kelly* (1959).

360. George Cukor directed this 1933 comedy.

361. Maxine Elliott Hicks (1905–2000), late-nineteenth/early-twentieth-century theater actress.

362. Adrian Adolph Greenburg (1903–1959), legendary Hollywood fashion costumer and designer.

363. Pierre Boulez (1926–2016), French avant-garde composer and conductor.

bedouins of 49th Street. 326 is now at least half empty, and quite sinister. Shudder. I can hardly wait to move to warm, murderous 9th Street.

A Ford Foundation Grant is something you apply for if someone or thing who is asked to recommend people recommends you; Grove Press put up Frank and Kenneth. The sum at stake is 10,000 clams. It is also too late to get in on it this year. I really haven't the heart to try to interest Richard Howard in my poetry, since my own interest is pie-pan deep. If I don't pull myself together and write something soon I am going to find myself quite unfit to live with. Oh well.

It seems to me I had some funny things to tell you, but if I did my post-birthday[364] blues (you are a dear to remember), combined with one of the glummer looking Mondays since the beginning of time, has quite driven them, out of my mind.

I enclose some film notes you won't want to miss. If read backwards in the dark they have a kind of Kaprowesque charm . . .

What a name to end a letter with! Write soon, and tell Pierre[365] he is a great writer and to hurry up and write another novel so we can all go set up light housekeeping in Ghana.

love, JS

William Fuss

PS Please give Harry Mathews my best regards.[366]

TO JOHN ASHBERY

[New York, New York]

December 18, 1959

Dear Krismas Kid,

I haven't anything in particular to write about, except to send you and Pierre great branches of visi-pruf mistletoe . . .

---

364. Schuyler's birthday was November 9.

365. Pierre Martory's well-received first novel, *Phebus ou le beau Marriage*, was published in 1953. A second novel was rejected because of its homosexual theme, and though Martory continued to write fiction, he published no more novels.

366. Harry Mathews (1920–2017), poet, novelist, co-editor of *Locus Solus*, and long-time resident in Paris. See glossary.

The great skate-key building across the street with seasonable motifs of giant red tuba-lights, which adhere up and down the facade like an invasion of Martian body crabs. There has never been anything quite like it in the history of Yule. In fact, it is so inscrutably horrible that I wish I had a color photo of it to send to you . . .

I just this minute finished reading an essay about Reverdy (in a dopey book called *Surrealism: The Road to the Absolute*)[367] which makes me feel sort of extra-temporal and French. Whatever that means. I suppose I mean that falling face down in a Parisian gutter seems somehow a superior experience to falling down in one here; a dubious proposition. Is Reverdy as good as I think he is? Quick, an answer.

Issue one of *Locus Solus* is in the works. I have pried a copy of *Bertha* out of Kenneth,[368] and a nice poem that is sort of a parody-imitation of Roussel; though I guess it is more humorous in the dear boy's overt way than the great Raymond ever permitted himself to be. Frank has also promised "Easter," which I think should have been printed some while ago (LeRoi Jones is bringing out *Second Avenue*—F O'H will soon be America's most widely printed poet)—and I can get some other things too: you wouldn't care to give the 49th Street Harriet Monroe[369] a hint as to how much space is available? Is *Locus Sodus*[370] (as Janice has dubbed it) going to be the size of a Pataphysical publication, or more like the Funk & Wagnall's Year Book? Barbara G. [Guest] will be here in a day or two & I will see what sort of glass beads she is currently hawking; and I am writing Robin B [Blaser]. Do I get to select your work and Harry's, or do you think you boys can manage that by yourselves? How come you have never sent Frank your current poems? Hmmmm? Not only do I want to see them, but the author of *Ko, or, A Season on Earth*, seems to find it the main question worthy to be addressed to me. Do give me some more concrete information about this publication; or should I write Harry direct? I trust my name as editor will be prominently displayed . . . you know what a greedy I am.

After the afternoon coffee break. Let me see. If there are any great Xmas doings in the works, they are being kept from me. This evening I am going to get tanked with Arthur Gold at Alexi Haieff's; actually, he is living in Eugene

367. Pierre Reverdy (1889–1960), French poet. *Surrealism: The Road to the Absolute* was written by Anna Balakian and published in 1959.
368. Kenneth Koch's play *Bertha*, published in 1959 by Grove Press.
369. Harriet Monroe (1860–1936), founding editor of *Poetry* (Chicago).
370. Sodus, New York, John Ashbery's hometown.

Berman's[371] apartment, said to be done in many shades of eggplant and gold. Tomorrow night Donald Droll and I (!) are having dinner at the house of someone quite boring; Sunday brings an egg-nog festivity at the Alex Katzes.[372] Somehow it all lacks the wondrous woopidoo of yesteryear. A typical instance of New York Marivaudage is the following exchange between me and Edith.[373] Edith "The Katzes are going to have a kitten." Me: "That's nothing. The Kochs are going to have a cookie."

Poor Janice is rather plagued by Katherine. Kenneth gave her a Charlie Brown doll, and Kahkie does nothing but play hospital with it, which consists of Charlie Brown having a series of miscarriages, supplemented by long explanations of how the little baby has now gone to heaven. Katherine, it seems, remembers in toto all the stories that were fed her during the Glencoe disaster. I admire women, and Janice the most.

Frank is going to Spain at the end of February, and will probably get to stay a month or more. Envy permits me no comment . . . I feel rather like Duse's[374] last words. "Why must I die in Pittsburgh?" If you could see the weather today; I'm sure Jane is lying down resting her ankles this very minute.

I don't believe I have seen any entertainments worth reporting on. I did hear the boys play Mozart with the Philharmonic, an experience too uplifting to be gone into in detail, and one which you can imagine without my help.

Oh. I have been meaning to report one piece of graffiti to you, inscribed on the walls of what Peyrefitte calls "the wooden baths" (at least in English translation) . . . in amongst all the sadie/mazie inscriptions and detailed delights and invites I found the simple declaration, MEET MISS ISRAEL OF 1958 ROOM 211.

TO JOHN ASHBERY

The Museum of Modern Art
New York 19

Dec. 30, 1959

Dear "Troubled,"
Say! You really have a poser!

Oh well, I won't try to sound like the *Daily News*. My worthless advice is:

371. Eugene Berman (1899–1972), painter and brother of Leonid Berman.
372. Alex Katz (b. 1927), the painter, and his wife, Ada. See glossary.
373. Edith Schloss Burckhardt, first wife of Rudy.
374. Elenora Duse (1859–1924), Italian actress.

write Mrs [Corinne] Hoexter explaining the original arrangement at the time Shattuck was to do the article, and then say that it had not occurred to you to undertake a long and difficult piece for $75. You certainly won't get an extra $125, but you ought to get at least $50. What I'm not sure about is whether you should mention a compromise additional fee, or see what they will offer. Perhaps you could consult the yarrow stalks. My inclination is to try to pass the buck to them; and should it come to the point of calling a spade a spade, I would certainly say that expenses were about $50 rather than $30 (unless you have already said otherwise). Anyway, make your letter to Mrs Hoexter short, startled and pained. Then wish her a Happy New Year.

About the wonderful post-war theater revival which has no more occurred in France than elsewhere: I 'spect that "they" (the horrible Dr Alfred [Frankfurter] always looms largely in *Portfolio* doings) want a variety of contributors to *Portfolio*, and not the same old contributors. It seems to me that you could write Tom [Hess] asking him if that is the case, but pointing out how uniquely qualified your passion for the theater makes you; but if it is really out of the question (due to Editorial Policy), you think that your friend is the next best qualified person to write it . . .

It has taken me until today to wring the $50 still owed me for Dickinson out of them. After writing a threatening letter several weeks ago ("I would like to be paid the balance due me as soon as possible," underscored in ink) I still had to call the ineffable Corinne. Her opening was wren-like, "And what can I do for you?" Edwin described her, with excessive objectivity, to Edith as, "A middle-aged Jewess"; what she is really like is an S.S. Van Dine[375] murder movie in which Billie Burke[376] turns out to be the killer . . .

Now I am going to trip down to Frank's office and borrow your letter and new poems.

What you said about my Hamlin Garland poem is too yum-yum for me not to memorize it . . . I will try to pull myself together and send you others. I wish that one called "Alice Fay at Ruby Foo's" had lived up to its title. Oh. *Evergreen* is rumored to have accepted a short play of mine for publication. It is about a wife who finds a bundle of letters in her husband's desk from their best friend, Egbert, who is at present her lover. The letters disclose that previous to his mar-

375. Willard Huntington Wright (1888–1939), mystery writer who created the detective Philo Vance.

376. Billie Burke (1885–1970), actress in silent movies and talkies. She played Glinda, the Good Witch, in *The Wizard of Oz*.

riage Egbert was the husband's lover . . . this tasteless confection (since the husband is named Henry, ample play is given the wife with sentences that begin, "Oh Henry . . .") is called *After Feydeau*. (Before you get all het-up, I think I may have written it before I ever lamped, *Egbert, or, The Dolls*.)[377] Its appearance in print may well signal my retirement into the nearest nunnery (and all we Dover Wilson[378] fanciers know that nunnery was Elizabethan for cat-house).

New Year's Eve holds out the strange promise of a party at Sandra Lee's, to which Jane invited me. Champagne is the promised beverage . . .

Well I could run on a little longer but I will want to get this in the last mail pick-up. I'm gathering material for *Locus Sodus*, as Janice calls it—*Bertha* and a Roussel-inspired poem from Kenneth; "Easter" and others from Frank. Can you and Harry pick your own or may I? How many pages is the mag going to be? I don't want to send over a lot of things and then have some of them not printed owing to lack of space . . .

Happy New Year! Tell Pierre I wish I were with you both on the beautiful rue Alfred Durand-Claye!

How could I forget? For even a moment. The necktie is the most beautiful I have ever seen, and I take it off only when sleeping. It's just like one of your most sumptuous enigmatic poems.

love, J
Carol Carstairs[379]

TO ADA KATZ

New York, New York

June 6 1960

Dear Ada:

HOORAY![380]

Here are some gifts and some reading.

The printers copy of my novel is the kind of artifact essentially without value, and yet which one can't quite bear to throw out. Perhaps you and Alex will be

377. A play by Ashbery.
378. John Dover Wilson (1881–1969), British Shakesperean scholar and educator.
379. Carol Carstairs, New York art gallery owner.
380. This letter was sent to New York Hospital where, two days earlier, Ada Katz gave birth to her son, Vincent.

braver than I. *The Dream of the Red Chamber*[381] is a loan from our mutual friend, Donald Droll. It is said to be overpoweringly grand. You and Alex give it the go-round and see what you think. *Redrawn by Request*[382] is, in my opinion, a hoot. If you (plural) don't like it; that's all right, too. Still, there is something about "Why Mother's Get Gray" and "The Worry Wart" that speaks deeply to my hick mid-Western soul.

The French Drawings Catalog, a book of infinite value, is presented with the compliments of the department of Circulating Exhibitions of the Museum of Modern Art, and The International Council at the Museum of Modern Art, to Mr and Mrs Alex Katz, as a token of gratitude for their permitting art to exist.

Boris Pasternak: Selected Poems, John Ashbery's rare edition. The poem to Anna Akhmatova[383] alone is enough, in the Sicilian phrase, to make a stone weep.

German Stories and Tales: Stifter's "Rock Crystal" is,[384] I guess, the most beautiful story ever written by a follower of Goethe. Marianne Moore shed tears through her finger ends translating it.

And, really, you would probably rather have a wonderful bunch of flowers or a tome I've never heard of on a subject I know nothing about—

Oh well, what matters, is that there are now three Katzes.[385] As Alex might say, "Wow! What a subject!"

love,

Jimmy

TO JOHN ASHBERY

49 South Main Street
Southampton, New York (c/o Porter)

September 3, 1960

Dear John, I thought it'd be well advised to let you know about this—no I have *not* turned my back on modern art. xxx The Rat.

381. Epic eighteenth-century Chinese novel of manners by Cao Xueqin (c. 1715–1763).

382. An anthology of cartoons published in 1955 by J. R. Williams, creator of the series *Out Our Way*.

383. Anna Akhmatova (1889–1966), Russian poet.

384. Adalbert Sifter (1805–1868), German Romantic novelist and short-story writer.

385. The Katzes' son, Vincent, was born in 1960. See glossary.

Dear Chester,

"*N'est-ce plus ma main . . . ?*"

I hope you're having a marvelous lederhosened summer, full of (I wanted to list a lot of double entendre Austrian tasties but my German spelling, you will be surprised to learn is inferior to my English).

Business first: I "and others" (it is a deep secret; the other is John Ashbery) are invisibly editing an anthology-magazine. It will go to press on Majorca in October—part of its unstated objective is a riposte at THE NEW AMERI-CAN POETRY, which has so thoroughly misrepresented so many of us—not completely, but the implications of context are rather overwhelming. Anyway, for issue one we want a cheerful, serious, international, kind of Paris–New York edited contents, and that of course means you. Have you any new poems? If not, I'd like very much to represent you by the *scena* from the *Rake's Progress*, "Has love no voice," to finish of act.[386] Two other contributions are previously published (Edwin Denby's "Mediterranean Cities"—entire: "we" may all know that book, but I know how little known his poetry is; and Anne Channing (Porter's) poems; which came out in that well known magazine *The Bonaker* (—I will tell you what a Bonaker[387] is this fall). Is there any copyright compli-cation? Is there a detachable piece from the Berlioz story? What are you work-ing on now? Well, you'll know best what's on hand. Please send what you like, up to fifteen pages—preferably less: I'm plopping in a quite short story sort of in the *Alfred & G* style; one of Frank O'H's poems is a 1952 effort called "Party Full of Friends"; George Montgomery makes a few terse utterances—and so on. I think, in general, you will approve.

Why, Saint Restituta,[388] do you send your winds over Lake Agawam each time I decide to typewrite out-doors? "*Ma sai, stupidone, che tutte le serre mi da' vento alle piacevole prate di patete . . .*" "*Patete!!!*"

When are you going to come back? Who will call who first? My tattered bull-headedness (oops—that was supposed to be tattered bullhead-dress, like those Mexican hot-chas, but let it pass)—can't wait to tell the Plaza typewriter folks what I think of this re-conditioned so called Royal portable de luxe—

I think I will contribute that paragraph to the Larry Rivers Get Well fund.

386. Kallman collaborated on this libretto with W. H. Auden. Igor Stravinsky composed the music.

387. Native of Eastern Long Island.

388. Restituta of Sora (died c. 271). Legend has is that she was brought to Sora by an an-gel. Some consider the legend "untrustworthy." In his elegy "Wystan Auden," Schuyler wrote, "On Ischia he [Auden] claimed to take / St. Restituta seriously."

Look, when you hit the States, why don't you telephone the Museum and, in a disguised voice, say you are Kurt Brown, Mr Kallman's secretary and that Mr Kallman is back? Then my so-called secretary, Mrs Berit Potoker, will leave me a note that someone whose name is either Kurt Krasner, Rock Hudson or Ansley T. Jeffington[389] called; and I will KNOW. Oh well, really, I do look forward to seeing you, and I hope the coming season (of which I shudder I had a glimpse last night: you should meet Bob Rauschenberg's pet Australian marsupial, Sweetie) won't be full of mutual acquaintances — dare I call some of them friends? — such as Merton Glasscock, Tits Galore and Merkin O'Toole looking at me askance and saying, while I am secretly trying to get the pickled onions out of my sherry toddy, "I saw Chester last night," followed by a fraught pause.

The wind has dropped. I suppose that means the fog is ready to do its stuff.

Considering its lethargic look, it can move with surprising speed. And it is only the fact that it is Saturday evening that prevents me from going into the house and calling the Plaza Typewriter folks this minute. That, and the fact that a check I gave them recently may have bounced. Thank goodness there's no mail delivery tomorrow or Monday which, ugh, is Labor Day.

I hope in all this camp you can discern that the "Occasional anthology" is a serious opus. Please send what you like prontissimo, to: John Ashbery, 35 rue de Varenne, Paris VII, France. Or to Mr. Harry Mathews, (just a sec. while I step into the barn & find Harry's address). It is: Mr. Harry Mathews,

> Le Haut du Peuil
> Lans-en-Vercors (Isere)
> France

which I believe is near Grenoble. Have you met him? He is a young writer, an ardent *Rake's Progress* fan, he and his wife and children live either at Lans-en-Vercors, on their farm, or in Paris; although they spent this summer at Wainscott (near here) visiting family.

I set my face against non-paying publications, and the profits realized from this pub. will be on a divide the profits, per page, basis. Mother will count pages but she draws the line at lines; and will only count pica if the designer appears to be fibbing — no problem here, since I am not about to visit Majorca.

If Wystan is with you, please tell him he's of course invited to contribute, too: I only hesitate because I feel that at this point there are so many demands for

389. Krasner and Hudson were movie actors. Jeffington is unknown.

his work. But if he would like to jump into the pool, the other otters would love to have him. Since I am (but don't tell John Ashbery) more or less no.1 editor of issue 1, a page of his pothooks would thrill all of us.

Oh. (The sun is now straight in my eyes—I suppose I could move my chair, but the last time I did, a batch of paper clips vanished into the lawn. Criminetties . . . all the Diefenbach[390] boys just plunged through the hedge. They are playing a game, I guess. Go away little boys or I will change you into swans—and remember, you do not have a little sister. A nephew of Anne Porter's, whom I like very much, or did when we spent a month or so together in Maine a few years ago, is convinced that Wystan once translated *The Chalk Circle in C.'s*.[391] (sic for calk: the ribbon is functioning so that I see each line only when I reach the next): I am uncertain whether Laurence M. (Bunny) Channing, Jr. hopes to produce it at Cambridge (he has a healthy contempt for—is it Bentley's very own?—hashing), or is writing a thesis or what; anyway, I have no recollection of same: has either of you? If it exists, is it available? From what I know about Bunny, if he wished to produce it, it would be for either the Poets' Theater, or some follow up to the Brattle.[392] (This is based on a conversation Anne had at another nephew's wedding last Sunday.) Anyway, Anne owns all of Auden in American editions, except the plays, and so far I haven't traced it; but I have a recollection of some translations in that magazine called——, where I first read your work in print. All that comes creeping back in the disheveled twilight (the temp. just dropped thirty degrees) is an image of a more-or-less pocket sized magazine, and some German Englished by Wystan.

I am going back to work next Tuesday, but please write me here. (And please do write, dear boy!) I intend to keep coming out here for long weekends—quite possibly until well in the summer.

There are a million things I meant to tell or ask you. Like: At Julia Gruen's birthday party yesterday (her second) Larry R. said, "Hey I heard from John Myers it was so stormy flying he says he said Hail Marys for an hour and a half! He relapsed!" For once I think I had the taste not to say anything witty, I just stared past Morton (call me Slim) Feldman[393] at the Henry Ford's distant manse and wondered.

390. The Diefenbach family lived next-door to the Porters in Southampton.
391. Bertholt Brecht's play *The Caucasian Chalk Circle*.
392. Poets' Theater in Cambridge, Massachusetts, produced plays by poets including John Ashbery, Frank O'Hara, V.R. Lang, and Mary Manning. The Brattle was a movie theater on Cambridge's Brattle Street.

What would cause Bunny a thrill I can dimly recall the great age of . . . would be if Wystan wrote a yes or no on a postcard and sent it to him. (About Brecht, I mean).

Laurence M. Channing, Jr.
Wareham, Indian Neck
Massachusetts.

Did you know that Fairfield Porter is a sort of cousin, quite close, of T. S. Eliot's? I guess that's why his older brother is named Eliot—though scarcely for T. S., who may be younger than Eliot, who is an attractive grandfather; for family reasons I mean.

Supper time. The youngest Diefenbach just pointed out that in the house I could type with the light on. How true. WRITE! love,

P.S. Dear John: I'm not cross with you anymore. xxxxx Pip.

TO HARRY MATHEWS

181 Ave A
[New York, New York]   *Sept 21 [1960]*

Dear Harry—

Yr letter of the 5th with enclosures was just re-routed to me here—I guess it's a good thing that Southampton is building a new post office. They need it—

This is really just a scribble to say that I'll write more seriously as soon as I've met some bill-paying deadlines—

Yes, I think the contents could well be in the front. Is Walter back on Majorca? I'd love to see some paper samples.

I don't think the paper band idea is practical—from my imported book selling days, the bands either arrive torn or they have to be placed on carefully; which (there) they aren't. I think the cover simply said, or looked like (below) it would be enough

Locus Solus
I

Or should we be very Frenchly classical—

393. Morton Feldman (1926–1988), American composer and essayist who was stoutly built.

I
Ashbery –
O'Hara – Poems
Denby – MCities
Schuyler – Current E.
Mathews –
Koch – Payola

I like keeping the Roussel quote for the title page. I wrote John asking him for a run-down on the contents: I don't have a list of what went off with you.

No yes or no about the "Chekov Cha-Cha" yet, but soon — (It will be yes, if I know my Al Leslie) —

Please tell John — in your frostiest tones — that he is swiftly mounting many a shit list; David Noakes & I had an acerb exchange on that subject today. Anyway he had better make with the letter.

Fairfield was here when your letter arrived, so I passed your regards on direct — And Edith B., fresh from Maine & full of delightful malice, says Rudi enjoyed seeing you so much —

Now I'll see if I can find repose in the *New York State Conservationist* — there's damn little in the paper.

Oh. You might also tell him that Tom Hess is thrilled by the news of his possible return.

New York City is ever more for fish than usual; one needs either a helicopter or very stout shoes.

Thanks for your very kind words about my Elaine de K. poem; she's really marvelous.

I hope I'll get a copy of your opus —
best,

Jimmy

TO HARRY MATHEWS

[New York, New York]

Sept 31, 1960

Dear Harry —

I enjoyed talking to you today so much — it's just after dinner: Jane Freilicher, Jane Wilson [Gruen] & her daughter, Julia — who'll be two tomorrow & can already sing "drink to me only . . . " were guests —

133

Jane Freilicher & I had a moment to talk (over my Corona) & we confessed to one another that we'd been guilty of a dreary assumption: that because you have private means & a "posh" background you *couldn't* be talented.

How silly; & to what a remarkable degree your work confirms *my* silliness. In extenuation, I can only say that in my lifetime, a fortune (on my mother's side) melted like wax brokers in the autumn sun of '29. On the Pound-Schuyler side, the great losses—of land—took place in the 19th century. So, though my friends sometimes make *me* feel that true distinction of birth is, say, Red Hook, ca. '31, it was firmly instilled in me (by the time I was five) that one was polite to servants because they couldn't help it; & to people who had more (cash, land, toys, clothes) because, by our inscrutable standards, anybody who didn't count St-Martins-in-the-Field, New York State, the first Mayor of Albany (we tended to skip the absconders, drunks & other ne'er do wells) in their patrimony was new-rich; and couldn't help it too.

How boring. It's left me in a situation where what a beard & no socks are to Allen Ginsberg, a Faberge cigarette case is to me—

Right this second I can remember a pair of topaz cuff-links in Venice (nothing flashy) about $70, an amber cigarette holder in Amsterdam (in 1947)—*very* cheap for what it was—!

Now I've told you a little about myself. Too much? I hope not. (I'm scribbling in the dining room & time is fleeting)—

Separately from this I'll send you & for J.A. more *Locus Solus* material.

Believe me, this *Locus Solus* is all going to turn out well—aesthetically, financially, anyway you slice it.

I'm sorry you & Nicky didn't get to chat with Charles Egan.[394] He *can* be bearish; but he is O so worth it. (Lord, look at this sheet!)

Do write me what you read, send me poems from time to time.

I'm glad you picked up on "The Chekov Cha-Cha": I'd gotten stale on it.

Anne Channing Porter is a *most* gifted person—her handwriting is identical with Emily Dickinson's, only Anne's is finer and stronger, and it is almost impossible to get her to part with a poem. She is the wittiest person I have ever met & a devout & unpushy Catholic.

I loved the picture of Graves[395] whomping out his Etruscan piece—the old goat sounds just like Wystan Auden.

394. Nicky was Niki de Saint-Phalle (1930–2003), French sculptor and Mathews's first wife. Charles Egan owned a New York art gallery and showed de Kooning, Guston, and Kline, among other abstract expressionist painters.

395. Robert Graves (1895–1985), British poet, novelist, and author of the *White Goddess*, who lived for many years on Majorca.

I wish you would both stop burning up your work—if you can't stand the sight of them, why not just put them in a chalk cave for the post-BOOM-aboriginals to find & marvel over?

Burning works of art, good, great, unfinished or troublesome, is best left to the crazies of the world.

all my best

Jimmy.

P.S. Please tell Nicky that everyone who met her was *boul-verse* by her beauty & charmed by her manner.

I heard she spilled a drink on an insolent non-entity—Marc (?) someone—
B R A V A

TO JOHN ASHBERY

Grace–New Haven Community Hospital
Tompkins 1   *May 15 [1961]*
Howard Ave.
New Haven, Conn.[396]

Dear John—

Well, dear boy, here I am—in the rather advanced psychiatric clinic run by Jimmy Merrill's[397] ex-analyst (which may explain how I came to afford $300 a week for mental hygiene). I had a *vile* winter, but now I feel over the hump—Today I was out of doors for the first time since March. Joy—the bliss of a warm sun and a cool breeze off the pizza parlors!

I was terribly impressed by *Locus Solus*. Harry seems to have all the qualities of a self-interested saint.

By the way I did look for that tax check—your checks are all filed in an orderly way, & I did not find it.

396. The thirty-seven-year-old Schuyler had quit his job at the Museum of Modern Art in February, and after a nervous breakdown in March Grace–New Haven Hospital. He would never again hold regular employment.

397. John Bernard Myers and Merrill arranged for Schuyler's admittance to Grace–New Haven. Merrill paid the hospital bills.

My news is zero — let's see. Yesterday I bid & made a slam (yawn) —

So the burden of writing cheery notes (long notes) is on you, now that I've regained use of my letter writing head.

Do you and Pierre continue, after your fashion? I always hope so.

Fairfield proposed me for *The Nation* art critic; but Lincoln K [Kirstein] bids for R. Rosenblum.[398] Grrr; even if I haven't met him.

Time for 8 p.m. milk & cookies —

Love to P. —

love, Jimmy

TO ROBERT DASH

[Southampton, New York][399]

August 11, 1961

Dear Bob,

Fairfield is hammering a book out to you, which made me rise from my E.M. Forster (no books like the old books) and answer your delightful letter; which made Maine feel as un-Hamptonian as it is.

On the way here I was at Ducktrap; which I recognized not by name but as a motif of yours.

I'm writing very little: I don't know when, since youth, I've felt so blocked or maybe just blah about it. Each day seems as though it will be the answer since the reply to why write? is usually, why not? Well, either it will clear up or it won't; no point in WORRYING about it . . .

Adele[400] left today, after a week and a half; she was scared at night by the woodsiness and isolation, which is so thorough it's like an insulation from danger. But she got used to it and hated going back to hot New York. Which I also hated when I was there Aug. 1 for a couple of days. I thought of visiting you, but I barely had energy to lie around the Kochs' and read mystery stories.

Your life always sounds so energized, it makes me minimize what little out

---

398. Schuyler did not get the position. Robert Rosenblum, art historian and critic.

399. Schuyler is writing from Great Spruce Head Island, where Porter took him after his discharge from Grace–New Haven Hospital. He stayed with the Porter family for eleven years.

400. Adele Honig, friend of Schuyler's who worked with him at MoMA.

put I make myself. But there is some. Your house (maybe) in the Poconos sounds cute: do you need a helpmate?

May I come and pay a visit after reviewing, around Sept. 1? Hmm?

love, Jimmy

TO HARRY MATHEWS

Southampton

Wednesday Oct 25, 61

Dear Harry,

It was awfully good to hear from you. I'm glad you're settled down after your unhappy domestic turmoil; and the news about the novel is very good indeed. I'm really impressed by Kenneth's *Locus*;[401] that is what I get to of it at his house, between bridge hands (the new rage, chez nous). A *Nest of Ninnies* never seemed as funny to me as it does in print; if John and I can get a Ninny fellowship that will allow us to finish it.

I've been soliciting for *L.S.5* — Kenneth's issue makes me feel competitive — where am I going to find a contributor like the Pillow Book?[402] Kenneth is also holding out on me (grr): he has more or less finished a long prose work — I guess you could call it a novel — and since I'm desperate for prose I want part of it. But he claims he is still working on it and can't release so much as a comma. I think he secretly believes that each new work of his is going to be serialized in *Life* magazine, with photographs of Larry Rivers standing by.

One thing I do not begin to feel is the editor's curse, the dull anxiety for New names. I'm not sure I know any, and if I did they probably wouldn't be any good. On the other hand, one worries a little about the beauty of repetition . . .

When you see Ashes [John Ashbery], would you gently point out to him that he has never acknowledged some poems I sent him? Even if they were terrible I still would like to hear about it.

I hope you forgave me for all your unanswered letters. You probably know I had a nervous breakdown last winter, and was away for some months. Though the heart of downtown New Haven seemed more like the thick of things than

401. Each editor of *Locus Solus* edited an issue.

402. *The Pillow Book of Sei Shonagon* dates from A.D. 996, with later revisions, and is one of the classics of Japanese literature.

the grassy walks one usually associates with sanatoria. It was rather fun, once they put me on happy pills and convinced me my bed was not full of pins (ugh). And I did play a deal of bridge.

I hope you will do #4; I've uncovered a bale of poems it would delight me to impose on you.

Keep well. Fairfield, Anne and the small blondes send their regards.

All my best,

Jimmy

TO JOHN ASHBERY

Of course your friend may translate & publish "Freely Espousing"; & any others, I hinted.

[Southampton, New York]

[December 1961]
Wed. night

Dear John Bunny,

It occurs to me that the best way to get a letter from you is to write one to you. John Hohnsbeen, encountered at Chester's birthday party (along with "Chris" Isherwood, Lincoln K. and other loves) reports that your best American friend is Jim Lord[403] and that you sometimes pass out in your sauced food at dinner. Well, well. John also said he loves the wonderful spaces in your poems.

Speaking of poems: while not exactly cross, Medea did not leap for joy on hearing of your rejection of two of my favorite poems. I hope you haven't used them for toilet paper, because I want you to give them to Harry for my issue of *Locus Solus*. I'll be sending others of my own, too; I'm sick and tired of being the least published poet in the Group.

My issue of *L.S.* is shaping up: will your play be ready for inclusion? What are you, and Harry, putting in? Someone in England named Anselm Hollo[404] sent me, at Harry's suggestion (please thank him for me) an interesting batch of stuff. It seems simplest to accept them all rather than be picky. They're all quite good, for that matter.

403. James Lord (1934–2013), biographer of Giacometti and author of *Picasso and Dora*.
404. Anselm Hollo (1934–2013), poet and translator from his native Finnish. Hollo came to live in America in the early 1960s.

Harold Rosenberg[405] attacked me at a party for Mary Abbot Clyde about a piece he'd done for *Locus Solus* and where was it? I said I assumed it was in your upcoming issue and (being drunk) asked him for some poems. Kenneth took me rather severely to task; maybe H. R. was drunk too and will forget. I'm having a deal of trouble getting anything out of such Grand Old Men as Barbara Guest, Kenneth Koch, Frank O'Hara and Bill Berkson.[406] Promises, nothing but promises.

Barbara Z. Epstein was at Chester's and demanded fervently for news of you. I turned her over to Hohnsbeen. Which reminds me, Ted Gorey is practically the most famous humorist in America today. Oh. And Jason [Epstein], who is now God of Random House, promised me publication if I would write a book of sketches similar to "Current Events." I have just applied for an Ingram-Merrill grant to do so. How much did you get, by the way? I asked for $4,000, throwing in a whine about the cost of psychotherapy, since three grand seemed a more probable figure. (John Gruen was practically guaranteed one last year, but the big goof asked for $10,000. He didn't get it.)

Did I tell you in my last letter that the Kochs, Kenward (sigh) Elmslie[407] and I are a regular weekly bridge foursome? Last night, Kenward, as I call the dream of my life, and I gave the Hazans their first lesson in the demon game. Kenneth had predicted that Joe's mind was not retentive enough for the game's complexities, but he took to it much more quickly than Jane, who kept saying, "Joe, I can't understand you." As you've probably heard, the house they built at Water Mill is a spring, summer and autumn gem. Joe is full of surprises. And cash.

Fairfield's show is breathtakingly lovely. He broke a gallery record by selling eleven paintings before opening. The only other show in town worth looking at is Franz Kline,[408] who in a drunken fit lately declared me his favorite person. I think he mistook me for Frank.

But let's not talk shop.

405. Harold Rosenberg (1906–1978), essayist and art critic who wrote books on Arshile Gorky and Willem de Kooning.

406. See glossary.

407. Kenward Elmslie (1929–2022), poet, librettist, and songwriter. See glossary.

408. Franz Kline (1910–1962), abstract expressionist painter famed for his black-and-white paintings. In April 1960 Schuyler wrote, "Kline, in other words and like most American artists, whatever genre they work in, suffered from respect. He seems to have taken seriously the message that art is skill, a hard thing to master and possibly even a dreary thing. It is rather like a man who wants to chop down trees but first learns how to untruss a fowl and which way the port goes round."

My head doctor (my psychiatrist I mean, not my dentist) keeps insisting I go home and visit de folks. "But it seems like a waste of time," I said. "A thing you do very little of anyway," he rejoined (he is rather like Marshall in *A Nest*). "Yes," I insisted, "but this seems like an active waste of time," which of course was just the golfball he was waiting for me to drop into the hole. They're a sinister, plotting lot. (I'm devoted to mine.) So I suppose I shall have to go. I wish I could visit the legendary scene of your birth, but I'm afraid the sight of a friend of yours would cause your mother to cry for several days. That's supposed to blackmail you into feeling guilty enough to come home. As I rather tactlessly said to John H [Hohnsbeen], "I think of Ashes every second." "And when do you think of me?" the trollop inquired.

So you're not going to Sicily with the Hazans. What a jealous nature mine is. Write!

Love to Pierre,

love, Wanda Hendrix[409]

TO FAIRFIELD PORTER

Jan. 9, 1962

Dear Fairfield,

I knew I had written a poem in the hospital, and that it wasn't a bad one, but I never could find it. Of course it's about the small painting you gave me when I went to New Haven. Now, much later than I meant to, here is a present of a poem about it.

You may be sure that John Ashbery is my best friend; I'm not.

I borrowed twenty dollars from Wystan Auden in my loss-hysteria. *Art News* has GOT to pay me!

Please show the poem to Anne and ask her if she likes it.

I miss you.

Love,

Jimmy

409. Wanda Hendrix (1928–1981), movie actress who appeared in Robert Montgomery's 1947 film noir, *Ride the Pink Horse*.

FOR FAIRFIELD PORTER

of an evening real as paint on canvas.
The kind that makes me ache to have the gift
for dusting off clichés:
not, make it new, but see it, hear it freshly.
The context (good morrow, haven't we met in this context before?)
in which, squelch, a brush lifted a load
of pigment from the thick glass palette, and, concentrated,
as though he saw neither the work in hand nor the subject,
The painter began. A rapt away look, like a woman at the theater,
who sorts laundry, makes a mental note while the stars anguish
to buy a bottle of Scuff-Coat tomorrow at Bohacks.
The painting portrays a sloppy evening in a burst of daily joy:
orange flames at left—were they bushes?—a gray-black tree,
at right, a few houses, buildings, no more than, well,
two gray strokes together, casual as a scribbled note, make a slate
roofed tower. Then there's one place where the light pink came to rest
under a faded butter-cup sky.
It's like this: the orange assertions, dark thereness
of the tree, malleable steel gray blueness of the ground; and sky;
set against, no, with, living with, existing alongside and part of,
the helter skelter of rust brown, of swift indecipherable. The day
is passing, is past: mutable and immutables, came to live
on a small oblong of stretched canvas. Blue shadowed day,
under a milk of flowers sky, you're a talisman, my Calais.

James Schuyler
Grace–New Haven Hospital
April 8, 1961

410. "A Blue Shadow Painting" is a phrase from Schuyler's poem "Money Musk." This
poem is previously unpublished.

TO JOHN ASHBERY

[Southampton, New York]

March 29, 1963

Dear John,

Help, has your Valentine's Day amnesty run out?

Worst things first—yes, your records were taken in one of the numerous thefts my pads have sustained in the past two years. Frank has had a few of your records for about the past four years, but I think mostly 19th century opera; anyway he didn't have any of your Lyre Bird discs—they are gone. I think the books are intact; but since they're in a language I don't read much, I haven't kept close track. If there are any you're especially concerned about, tell me and I'll look the next time I'm in town. I'm very sorry about the records. It happened the summer before last when I was in Maine, when they were featured in one of the better hauls, along with a portable typewriter, a highly modernistic though not very pleasing phonograph and some suits of more than historic actual worth. I was so thoroughly disencumbered that when Jerry's [Porter] apartment was entered two weeks ago it cost me merely a $7.95 traveling clock and a $1.50 birthday present for Lizzie [Porter] . . .

My praise of *The Tennis Court Oath*[411] has been so long postponed that it has congealed into a gem-like state I can't translate back into words. A truly inspiring and ennobling work. It is also funny and beautiful, the only qualities I care much about. Nor have my days gone undelighted by "Into the Dusk Charged Air" (a title I unintentionally paraphrased in a small effort called "Under a Storm Washed Sky"). I love your poetry. It doesn't pall, unlike . . .

Yes, I've been living in Southampton and presumably writing a novel. It stumbles along, though I don't feel very interested in it. In fact I might stop it and start another, if I felt a twinge of confidence that it, the other, would be any better.

On the other hand, not reviewing is a source of deep joy to me.

I pop into town now and then, for visits to the dentist and bridge table. The latter "craze" in our small set reached an attractive climax in a bridge-dinner Kenward gave last November for Jane's birthday. It seemed very Larchmont, in a way I like.

Kenward also provided a wonderful New Year trip. The foursome went in

411. John Ashbery's *The Tennis Court Oath* (Wesleyan University Press, 1962).

Joe's [Hazan] car to Kenward's house in Vermont,[412] a very cute old farm house on a hill with splendid woodsy views. We were almost snowed in by a tremendous blizzard, to my delight and Joe and Kenward's alarm; the one had to get back to his job and the other to his analyst. So we did some fearful and exciting driving—no one in Montpelier would credit that we had emerged from the mountains under such conditions.

Most of the past month I devoted to the flu and then to strep throat. This caused me to miss Edwin's "Sweet Sixty" party, a dinner at Donald's [Droll] for ninety with a new film by Red Grooms,[413] and such. I did go to another wingding there for John Button's opening (among the pictures was a big nude of his boy friend as Ganymede with a rather stuffed looking eagle, which caused Jane to murmur, "Oh, oh, adults only."). Among the people who were distinctly cool toward me were Joan Mitchell, Porter McCray and Frank; on the other hand I was awfully drunk, so their response may not be altogether inexplicable.

About the only thing I miss are the better-type films (I got good and sick of TV some time ago). The only ones I've seen and liked in an age are *Eclipse* and *Divorce Italian Style*. I hear you admired *Purple Noon*;[414] me too. Yum yum.

The art year has been rather drab.

Do you really think there is a possible way of continuing A *Nest* by mail? Would alternate pages work? I'm sure none of our fans could tell the difference (among the most ardent of whom is Rudi B.) I will if you will.

Please give Pierre a tremendous kiss for me, unless he thinks it's too fresh. Write soon and I'll send an answer winging back, I promise.

Fairfield and Anne send their love,

xxxxx, J.

Donald Meek[415]

---

412. Calais, Vermont.

413. Red Grooms (b. 1937), artist and moviemaker.

414. *Eclipse* (1962), starring Alain Delon and directed by Michelangelo Antonioni. *Divorce Italian Style* (1961), directed by Pietro Germi. *Purple Noon* (1959), starring Alain Delon, directed by René Clément, and based on Patricia Highsmith's novel *The Talented Mr. Ripley*. Delon's presence in two of these movies may explain the "Yum, yum."

415. Donald Meek (1880–1946), character actor who played the whisky drummer in John Ford's *Stagecoach* (1939).

TO JOHN ASHBERY

[Southampton, New York]

Feb. 22, 1964

Dear John,

Here are some poems I hope you'll consider inserting in your mag.[416]

I don't have any excerptable bits from that maggoty mince meat that passes for my work in progress; and I haven't the brute courage to take "The Home Book" away from lovable Ted Berrigan.[417] It had sort of vanished, but he tracked down a copy in an old coffer of Edwin's, so I feel that if it exists at all, it's owing to him.

A few of these poems ("Roof Garden"; "With F & G at L"; "Faberge") are in *Salute*[418] (I mean the Richard Floriano opus), but since I know that the circulation of that is 2 copies (Alice Esty and d'Harnoncourt)[419] I don't think that need count as prior publication? Anyway, I think "Faberge" is one of my best efforts, and if you print any I hope you'll print that.

Fairfield has been busy trotting about by jet to places like Alabama and Wisconsin, lecturing to art students. He likes it. Joe Hazan gets more giggly as the date of his retirement draws near; I'm terrified they might decide to live abroad, dealing my social life its final blow. But I guess they're chained to their real estate. I hope so.

I saw an alarming item that one or more people had been killed at the St. Mark's B****s;[420] and a following item that all such like establishments would be sternly scrutinized. However, on visiting Frumps' Haven on 28th[421] last week, all seemed much as usual. In fact, a little too much so, if anything.

This evening *Il Grido* is being screened at East Hampton: a cultural event about as staggering as a revival of *Il Pirata*[422] by the Sodus Grange. Our movie diet out here consists of James Garner comedies for us oldsters and Troy Don

416. *Art & Literature*, edited by Ashbery, Anne Dunn (see glossary), Rodrigo Moynihan, and Sonia Orwell, and published in Paris 1964–1967.

417. Ted Berrigan (1934–1983), poet and editor of C magazine.

418. Published in 1961 by Richard Floriano's Tiber Press, *Salute* was a collaboration between Schuyler and the painter Grace Hartigan.

419. Rene d'Harnoncourt (1901–1968), Alfred Barr's successor as Director of the Museum of Modern Art. *Salute* cost $250, and it was therefore a collector's item upon publication.

420. St. Mark's Baths.

421. Everard Baths.

422. *Il Grido* (1957), directed by Michelangelo Antonioni. *Il Pirata* (1827), opera by Vincenzo Bellini (1805–1835).

ahue[423] specials for the teens, who evince no interest at all in seeing him. I was so stimulated by *Charade*[424] I went to see it three times; so you see.

La Dame du Bois de B[425] is finally going to be shown in New York. It will come as the climax of a French Film Festival consisting of all the pictures that the Thalia has been showing on alternate weeks since the day it opened. A movie house called The New Yorker sometimes shows nice things (30's pictures with Joan Blondell) but never when I'm in town.

Oh. I'm sorry I didn't see you last fall. I didn't go to your reading because they make me nervous, and I was told that you were sailing the next morning. I learned the truth too late. A number of people implied that I was a mean and heartless person; but really, I'm not any more so than I ever was.

Be a sweetie and write me soon. Did you know that Ted Berrigan and Ron Padgett,[426] inspired by *A Nest*, are writing a novel? Hmm? Do you think there's any possible way we can continue by mail, and beat them to the Harper's Novel Prize? I'm willin'.

Give Pierre a big hug from me,
love, Jimmy

Robert Macaire[427]

TO JOHN ASHBERY

[Southampton, New York]

Friday [March 13, 1964]

Dear Blackie Cinders,[428]
'Course you can publish "The Home Book"; nothing would please the old goat more.

---

423. James Garner (1928–2014), movie and television actor. Troy Donahue (1936–2000), actor and, briefly, a teen heartthrob.

424. *Charade* (1963), directed by Stanley Donen and starring Cary Grant and Audrey Hepburn.

425. *Les Dames du Bois de Boulogne* (1945), directed by Robert Bresson from a script by Jean Cocteau.

426. Ron Padgett (b. 1942), poet. See glossary. Padgett and Berrigan met and became friendly in Padgett's hometown of Tulsa, Oklahoma. Berrigan, who was born in Providence, Rhode Island, was at graduate school in Tulsa.

427. Nineteenth-century French opera.

428. Blackie Cinders, a character in the comic strip *Ella Cinders*.

I don't think I've done much since I last wrote. I was in New York a couple of times, and saw a nice Mae West double-header, *Klondike Annie* and *I'm No Angel*.[429] The second is very fine, with lots of dialogue like, "Oh, so you're gettin' high hat, eh." The movie consists almost entirely of a series of first appearances for Miss West, with the cameras panning all over a concrete area or a Modern age penthouse before alighting on the chunky blonde in yet another beaded outfit. And it was a joy to see an authentic 1932 item not on TV, which is no good at nuance.

I have the impression that Fairfield is eagerly awaiting a line from you—or has one arrived I don't know about? If we have a rivalry, and doubtless we have, it's for your attentions.

I hope what you say about coming to the island isn't an idle threat; it would quite make the summer for me. Are you and Jane planning to tie it in with her lecture stint at Skowhegan?[430] Though I've seen the little lady a good deal lately, she hasn't mentioned it. But I know she likes to leave herself uncommitted in as many directions as she can.

F [Fairfield] is about to go to Philadelphia to paint a scientist who was the first to differentiate phagocytes. He is 94, and F. was told that the portrait commissioners would "like the earliest possible dead-line."

A theater group in NY is going to give an anxious public a new production of *Shopping and Waiting*. Alex is doing such decorations as it requires; my idea would be an exact replica of Scribner's book shop. Kenneth is to be on the same bill, and I hear he is making Red Grooms' life a living hell. A giant papiermâché mouse is a needed prop, and K has denounced him for making it look like a rat. The bill will be rounded out by *Billy the Kid*, which the director tells me is "a very dark play by Mike McClure."[431] I suppose a whole evening devoted to *Shopping and Waiting* is just too advanced an idea, though I rather fancy " . . . and now as it might be done by Xavier Cugat and Abbe Lane . . . "[432]

I think we are deserting Southampton for the up-coming academic year in favor of Carbondale, Illinois, home of Southern Illinois U. They want F. to be artist in residence. I've always had a sort of hankering to get to know my natal

429. Raoul Walsh's *Klondike Annie* (1936) starred Mae West and Victor McLaglen. Wesley Ruggles's *I'm No Angel* (1933) matched West with Gary Grant.

430. Art school in Skowhegan, Maine.

431. Michael McClure (1932–2020), poet and playwright. His play *The Beard* (1965) "starred" Jean Harlow and Billy the Kid.

432. Xavier Cugat (1900–1990), Latin band-leader known as "King of the Rhumbas," and Abbe Lane, actress and singer married to Cugat.

state a mite better, and the library is bound to be an improvement on the one here, whose most exciting title is something called, *I Drank the Zambesi*.[433]

Tell Emanuelle Khan[434] to take it easy; write me soon,

love,

Jimmy
Lucille Webster Gleason

PS: I seem to have a letter of Edith's, written in some May or other, on my desk, which says that Giorgio Franchetti[435] "just came back from Paris from an Ilse Getz party where everyone was stronzo except John Ashbery."

TO KENWARD ELMSLIE

[Great Spruce Head Island]

July 13 [1964]

Dear KGE,

Are you enjoying your respite from "it"?

We've had the most incredibly cool weather—and rather more fog than I care for. Still, anything to get out of the heat wave. Today I went to explore a nearby island, and got hopelessly astray in a spruce and alder tangle. Finally I saw water & found that, like somebody in a book, I had walked in a circle and was back where I had beached the canoe. Now doesn't that make you want to plunge into the wilds yourself?

It is easy to do. Let us know when you're coming, & we will meet you in Camden at the Public Dock, at the time you say. Just make it a weekday, because these trips are also used for provisioning at French & Brown, the Charles & Co. of Maine. It's also sort of an outing. So the time of arrival can be general rather than specific.

Camden is reached by the Maine Turnpike to Brunswick, then U.S. 1. I think it takes us about 5 hours of driving time from Boston, though doubtless it could be done in less.

---

433. *I Drank The Zambesi: A Naturalist's Safari in the African Mountains for a Last Glimpse of the Disappearing Wild Life* by Arthur Lovridge (1953).

434. Emanuelle Khan, a fashion designer active in New York during the 1960s and 1970s.

435. Giorgio Franchetti, Italian baron and art collector, and brother-in-law of Cy Twombly.

Or, you can fly to Bangor, and charter an itty-bitty plane which will bring you here. Frank O'Hara once came that way. The thing against it is that fog may mean spending the rest of your life in Bangor. Besides, you would probably want to stop in Brunswick to visit Bowdoin, where Hawthorne went to college, and the church in which Harriet Beecher Stowe was moved to write *Uncle T's C.*

If you come, which would be *nice*, don't forget your tennis racket.

I had a very cute letter from Joe Brainard,[436] and a packet of seeds from Jane. Joe wrote all about his *work*, which proves (if there was a doubt) that he's a real painter, since that is all they ever write about. Except, not working.

Anyway, please come & see us (you're probably skiing in Chile this minute, you sly boots). And bring Whippoorwill,[437] should you wish, though he must promise not to get into the sheep pen as a recent poodle visitor did.

xxx

love,

Jimmy

TO ROBERT DASH

[Great Spruce Head Island]

July 21, 1964

Dear Bob,

So, have you bought a house? Or lined up any likelys?

We've mostly been combing the fog out of our hair, though the last week has been better. *Very* coolish. I'm gardening quite a lot, of the foxglove, forget-me-not, Iceland poppy style—kind of Aunt Polly's garden. You must put me on to some interesting books about it. Naturally most of what I've done won't look like anything *this* year—but I 'ave 'opes for next.

I had a nice letter from Joe Brainard, who seems to get quite a bang out of striding up and down your vast studio. And a nice (though faintly querulous) and unexpected letter from Carl (Morse).

436. Joe Brainard (1942–1996), painter and writer who was soon to become Elmslie's companion. See glossary.

437. Elmslie's pet whippet, celebrated by Schuyler in "The Morning of the Poem" and in a series of paintings by Joe Brainard.

Fairfield's painting up a storm—is that news? Wonderful flower paintings, among others—a great (quality, not size) bowl of white rosa rugosa against a gold-yellow wall, and wild flowers in a blue vase on a white ground—both very elegant.

And you? *Des toiles beaux* (or is it *belles*?), I doubt not.

My stepfather [Fredric Ridenour] died about a week ago—he had had several attacks, so it was not a surprise—it was very quick, and I think, painless— he was about 70. It's made my feel serious and very mortal. And I've had a succession of memories, from my early childhood, of him, all showing his best & most admirable qualities, and they have come perfectly spontaneously. I didn't anticipate that. I'm glad he didn't die at a time when it would have made me glad. That would have been ignominious, and eventually led to overwhelming guilt feelings. He was much nicer during the last decade, because he doted so on his grandson Johnny.

I don't know yet how this will affect my mother (I don't mean emotionally)— I hope she will be able to go on living in their house. My brother Fred and his family live in the same town, which is a great blessing.[438]

Do you know exactly when you're coming back from Vermont? I don't know whether I'll visit you—the last trip up here knocked me out, and I hesitate to do any more traveling, I really hate it. Labor day also is late this year, so we'll be leaving here later than usual, probably. But don't withdraw the invitation! And do let me know your plans.

How is dear old Marley-Bones?

The new *Art & Literature* came, with me [*The Home Book*], F.P., Barbara, and gifted others in it. It is good looking, but it doesn't incite me the way C[439] does—perhaps it's its stateliness—

I have forgotten the name of the town you're near—so I'll send this to New York, and assume it will wend it's way to you.

All here are well & F (who just passed through the room) says to send his love—

xxx

&

hugs—

Jimmy

438. East Aurora, New York, a suburb of Buffalo.
439. Ted Berrigan and Ron Padgett began the mimeograph magazine C in 1964.

TO JOHN ASHBERY

[Southampton, New York]

Dec. 24, 1964

Dear John,

Gee, what a nice letter, nuggety-rich as a Butterball turkey (I assume they are featured in Sodus as they are at all super markets on Western Long Island). The one thing I'm not quite clear about is your going to Elmira: you do mean for Christmas, rather than New Year, don't you? Would it be too soon if I came on the 31st? I would like to spend as much time with you and as little with my German sister-in-law as possible. She's really very nice, and a lovely wife and mother, but her friends don't call her Brayton [Lewis] for nothing.

Speaking of mothers, I played bridge with Jane and Joe night before last. Jane propped herself up on a vast mound of cushions and said she felt and looked like a Turk. The time before when I saw them, Barbara Guest, famed lead star mother, kept exhorting them to have lots and lots of babies. "The trouble is, Barbara," Jane said, "that Joe has such a terribly low pain threshold." My trip to NYC was otherwise rather a dud. First I ran into Bob Dash at my dentist's. He had just fainted while having his teeth cleaned, and caused me a few uncalled-for palpitations over that familiar and rather insightful (you haven't met my dentist) operation. (In recent years my mouth has had such a thorough restoration that I'm planning to add a couple of ladies in mob-caps to show de tourists around.) Then I went to Scribner's, where the many eyes of Donald Gaynor fell on me. Then walking up Fifth Avenue I bumped into an old Dr Kallman satellite named Mary Valentine[440] who said, "I work in this building, what are *you* doing here?" I think it's the first time I ever had to explain why I was on Fifth Avenue, which always seems like the logical place to be. Nor did I get to *Les Parapluies du Cherbourg*, my main reason for going to town. I'm now saving it for pre-roomette viewing, so I'll have something nice to think about while the train stumbles through the night.

Well, I'd a lot rather have you handy in D.C.[441] than in distant Parree. If you do go there, I'll be happy to supply a map with key to places associated with my early years. I'm sure you'll want to pay a visit to the Valley Vista Apartments and

---

440. Dr. Kallman, Chester Kallman's father, a dentist. Mary Valentine, friend and contemporary of Chester Kallman.

441. Ashbery was considering an offer to be the art critic for *The Washington Post*.

the la Reine, not to speak of 4404 Stanford and The John Oyster School (so convenient to the Shoreham and The Wardman Park).[442] At least Washington contains the Smithsonian, most Rousselian of museums. It's a little bit of heaven to go drifting under the Spirit of St. Louis on your way to the Hall of President's Wives (Mrs Coolidge wins, hands down. Though I've never seen Bess [Truman] or Mamie [Eisenhower]). Nor is their collection of Colt revolvers to be sneezed at.

I'd love to weave in a few more strands of cellophane when next we meet. I feel I've been living in a storm-swept Florida nightclub for the last six and a half years. By the way, I think the enclosed clipping would make a lovely jacket for your next collection, which you might call *The Echeveria Basket*. Before I seal this up I'll try to root out the snippets about you from the *TLS*. I know what a joy it is to see one's name in print, especially when it's a Stanley Morison font.[443] And you'll doubtless need them in your Washington flatlet when you start work on *Un Francis Carco de nos Jours*.[444]

But $14,000! Why it's more than $1,000 a month. You'd better take it (my real reason for saying this is that I'm already emotionally oriented toward spending many afternoons with you in Whistler's Peacock Room at the Freer).[445]

I will telephone to hash over travel plans. Can we come back from Sodus in day time? It seems a fine chance to scribble and chat, and writing on the road is part of the Ninnies tradition.

Please remember me to your Mother and give her my best wishes,

love,

Jimmy
The Mesembryantheum Collector

PS It's taken all afternoon to find the *TLS* bits, thanks to the more black than comely ladies who spend each Thursday playing cache-cache in my room.

442. In 1931 Schuyler attended the John Oyster School in Washington, and in 1932 he lived at 4404 Stanford in Chevy Chase, Maryland.

443. Stanley Morison (1889–1967), typographer and graphic designer who designed the font Times New Roman in 1932 for the *London Times*.

444. Francis Carco (1886–1958), French writer of realistic fiction in the 1920s.

445. The Freer Gallery is part of the Smithsonian Institution.

TO JANE FREILICHER AND JOE HAZAN

[Great Spruce Head Island]

July 20, 1965

Dear Jane and Joe,

Greetings from Droughtsville Island. It's very peculiar here, where things that should be wet and juicy go crunch crunch underfoot. But wonderfully beautiful. The unwonted amounts of sunshine (one foggy day in three weeks; last year it was the other way round) have really made the water warm enough for swimming—in the cove, at least—and so I have. Rather nice.

I guess I'm writing to you from affection, since there's certainly no news. Fairfield has ceased to hobble and suppurate and went for his first swim today. He has also kicked the penicillin habit (as the doctor said he now can), and has been painting up quite a little storm. His niece Anina has also been batting out some wonderful F. Porter's; Fairfield says he is getting jealous. This afternoon I found him in a far meadow painting with nothing on but a big straw hat, so I guess it's safe to say he's all well.

My gardening pride was a bit assuaged when I found Canterbury Bells and foxgloves blooming here; I wish the damn things weren't biennials. But I haven't gardened at all, just written, read and slept (in quantities in reverse order). Right now I'm reading *The Lore & Language of School Children*,[446] about 500 pages of such pearls as:

> *Ladies and gentlemen*
> *Please take my advice*
> *Pull down your pants*
> *And slide on the ice*

Happy days in The Oyster School playground! (I once went to a grade school named for a Mr Oyster.)

Did Ted Berrigan do you [Jane] up brown for AN! I've been getting funny postcards from him, that seem to indicate a Westward move. And somebody told me that Our Grace [Hartigan] is giving up Maine for the Hamptons—not enough art world up here. Perhaps the Lincolnville Center folks[447] gave her the

---

446. *The Lore and Language of School Children* by Iona and Peter Opie (1959).

447. Alex and Ada Katz, painters Lois Dodd and Neil Welliver, Rudy Burckhardt and his second wife, the painter Yvonne Jacquette, and Edwin Denby summered in and around Lincolnville, Maine.

cold shoulder; or more likely they're not de Kooning enough. Has she loomed? And what about Bubsey Zimmerman Epstein, said to be summering in Sag?

Tomorrow I'm going into Camden for the afternoon—there's nothing like living on a semi-desert island to give a small town sparkle. I love loafing around the gift shops, such as The Laughing Cow, and attending the work shirt sales. There's also a sweater factory outlet for "seconds" that Katie heavily patronizes. Luckily they only have women's sweaters, for they're authentically country knitted out of scratchy twine in shades of mold and dung. Then, too, Camden is where Bob Keene played as a tad (he once showed me in a photograph where the old livery stable was—in fact, come to think of it, it is now The Laughing Cow, which gives the town what auction catalogs call "association value").

(I can hear Katie downstairs learning to type—death by hiccups.)

Katie started to go on a diet, but after a couple of wan and peckish days I found her making not one but two lemon pies.

Has Elizabeth dropped any bon mots yet? Can she swim? I'd like to hear everything she's done.

I have the feeling that all the news is at your end—why not send me a bale? Please remember me to Lourdes, and tell her Senora Porter thrives, and she and the girls go to mass every Sunday in a lobster boat.

love to you both—I mean, to you three

Jimmy

Kenneth gave the enclosed card to Kenward, who palmed it off on me—

TO JOHN ASHBERY

[Great Spruce Head Island]

Aug 7, 1965

Dear Toots and Caspar,[448]

If I read my recent Hazan Newsletter aright, this should find you, or soon find you, in Sodus. How long are you staying this side? I think I'll be in Southampton by Sept. 2 or 3—any hopes of lamping you on your way back? I hope so, though I can't say Jane held out any encouragement.

Were you at Water Mill, and did your Parisian savoir-faire bridge the social gaps? It was quite funny this June, posing for J & J, then strolling up the road

---

448. From the comic strip *Toots and Casper*.

a piece for an ingrassimento at the Boys. They seemed to make much more of an effort to charm and wine me than in other Junes. Perhaps it is to the best interest of perennial diner's-out to help the status stay quo.

I 'spose you heard about Fairfield's scary accident[449] — he's OK, though he thinks he may have gravel on the knee. So I won't terrorize you with further details. It was awfully good to get away from Southampton, where the LIRR's "Ahooey-ta-hooey" was like a dagger in my heart. Now if we can prevent him from drowning himself in the canoe all is, I think, well.

By the way, he is projecting, if he has not all ready committed, more letters to the Moynihans, about the non-arrival of issue 5 of *Art & Lit*. Once that's cleared up, I suppose he'll return to the subject of the subscription he gave his friend in Vermont. In Fairfield, the Little Magazine has met its match. Of course this is not keeping him from proceeding with an article for you on J. Cornell.[450]

Say, I was so sick last Xmas. When Harry M [Mathews] was here I laughingly told him I doubted you had believed me, and he snickered in reply, "oh well you know how John is." Hunh. But I forgive *you* if you forgive *me*. My trip home, by the by, was quite a success, and my nephew John, who is nine, seems to think I'm sort of an Ernest Thompson Seton;[451] an idea I did as much as I could to perpetuate, taking him for a nice tramp in the woods as more he-mannish than a game of catch. My mother was in much better spirits than her letters try to make me think; in fact, practically all the time I was there she was 1, on the phone, 2, dandling her grandchildren, and 3, watching TV — she is a great fan of Arlene Francis and Peter Lawford.[452] Her only complaint about me was that I wanted to go to bed so early instead of watching the late show — she said she thought it was "funny" of me. In fact, the only thing that marred my trip was going back through Rochester and not getting off.

I enclose a swatch of homespun from the Penobscot Looms[453] — tell me if you like it, and if you would like to publish it. I won't mind if you don't want to, provided you think up a good reason — a rather easy thing to do. The heroine of it is real, and so was Hamlin, and the incident in scene one is said to be historical fact. I have not, however, consulted the Paris Hill town records.

449. Porter's car collided with a train on Long Island.

450. "Joseph Cornell" appeared in *Art & Literature* in 1966 and was republished by Zoland Books in Fairfield Porter's *Art in Its Own Terms* edited by Rackstraw Downes.

451. Ernest Thompson Seton (1860–1946), outdoorsman, author of nature books, and co-founder, in 1910, of the Boy Scouts.

452. Arlene Francis (1908–2001), actress and star on television panel show *What's My Line?* Peter Lawford (1923–1984), movie actor and brother-in-law of President John F. Kennedy.

453. The play *Mollynocket* reprinted in *The Home Book* (Z Press, 1977).

Here come de mailboat. Got to scoot.
Please remember me to your mother, and do write—
love,

Craig Boland
Jimmy

TO JOHN ASHBERY

Saturday
Jan 15, 1966

Dear John,

It seems quite funny to be back in this earth-hugging dwelling. In fact, as I gaze down, or rather at, the aluminum clothes pole it seems as though I could just open the window and—crash. Frankly, I think it's rather refreshing to be able to look down into the trees as you do.

It was lovely staying with you and seeing you, and I'm sorry I was so under the weather the last couple of days. In fact, I still am but since I don't feel worse I guess it's my way of feeling better. Yesterday it was no new shoes for Brother: I hadn't realized what the end of the strike [New York City transit strike] would mean to all the women who've been saving their Christmas presents to exchange during the January sales. I got as far as Altman's,[454] where it seemed the Westchester Garden Club was reenacting the "Extirpation of the Albigensians." It was a good thing, since I went back to 36th Street and got some Jane written.

This noon (lunch for some, breakfast for others) I made the mistake of showing Fairfield Joe B's [Brainard] baby steps in art criticism. I was deep in the *Times* social notes when he suddenly flung them on the table crying, "I hate these!" It was the first time I've seen him tremble with rage in many a moon— at least, over such a trivial matter. Of course I made the mistake of a few stabs of mild defense, but he didn't stay to hear, only to shout that they were even more odious than Ted Berrigan's criticism (an opinion that was news to me) and that he especially hated "the sneakiness." As soon as the room had stopped whirling, I followed him to the studio and assured him that I had not planned to ruin his day but only done so by accident. As a matter of fact, their interest to me is in finding out what interests someone Joe's age, and not much else. Anyhow everything's OK now and we made it up by carrying a two ton mirror from

454. Department store at 34th Street and Fifth Avenue.

my room to the studio so he can paint a self-portrait. Since he has always been averse to doing this you may wonder why the change. A glance at the cover of the current *Art News*[455] explains all.

I am coming in next weekend, and will try to make a dinner date with PK,[456] and you included. That doesn't sound right: I mean, unless I hear differently, I'll assume I have a dinner date with you on Saturday and will ask PK to join us. Perhaps we could grill a chop, open a can of peas and finish off with some dietetic apricots chez toi? I'd be happy to help, and suggest a proper menu so as not to rob the Ninnies of all our attention. If you think this is a good idea, would it be nice to ask Kenward & Joe, or rather Joe & Jane—a better idea: you know how Jane loves to get out of the house, and I can't truthfully say that Joe B. always makes a small dinner "go." If this is OK, let me know.

(And if the above doesn't send you racing off to Elmira, I don't know what will.)

A sample of my devious thinking: if Jane and Joe were asked, I think PK would be less likely to say, "Guess I'd better be going too," when they rise to leave; which is usually pleasantly early. Oops: that pleasant is only in terms of my particular aspirations.

Know your skyline: the building with the thorny black pyramid on top is The New York Life Insurance Co. Bldg. It's very cute up close, with a lot of svelte 20's Gothic touches. And did you know (this is no doubt not true) that John Garfield died while fucking on G.P. West?[457] The uptown corner house, I believe. Those two facts ought to add plenty to your viewing pleasure.

The mail just came and with it, Busoni![458] I hope you will appreciate that of the three tickets I am keeping 13 for myself . . .

Say, you didn't seem very excited by the idea of wasting Feb. 18th on G&F [Gold and Fizdale], but won't you come as my guest? Fairfield, as well as Peter, may be coming. Perhaps it would help if you thought of it as going to hear [Charles] Ives'[459] 3rd symph (did you notice in today's *Times* that he was called,

---

455. This cover reproduced Paul Georges's *The Studio*, a ten-foot-high self-portrait with nude model.

456. Peter Kemeny, a friend of Schuyler's who committed suicide by throwing himself under a train at the Times Square subway station. He is remembered in the poem "Dining Out with Doug and Frank" as a "gifted and tormented / fat man.)

457. John Garfield (1913–1952), actor and native New Yorker. It is accepted folklore that Garfield died of a heart attack while "in the saddle." Ashbery was subletting an apartment on Gramercy Park.

458. Ferruccio Busoni (1866–1924), Italian-German composer.

459. Charles Ives (1874–1954), American composer.

"the Emersonian prankster"? Which I suppose makes Margaret Fuller the Norma Vincent Peel of Brook Farm).[460]

I trust you won't leave this open on the calling card table in your foyer—nor twit FP about anything in it. He's never quite recovered from hearing that I wrote you a funny letter about his sucking me at the Gay Chico. 'Nuff said. love, x J.

The Supremes

PS I was telling Anne & Katie that I'd found "The Nutcracker" quite lou-zay, which caused this exchange: Anne: "But I was taught at my mother's knee that Balanchine could do no wrong." Katie: "Who *was* your mother? Anne: "In this case, Edwin Denby."[461]

TO RON AND PAT PADGETT

Southampton, New York

Jan. 16, 1966

Dear Ron and Pat,

I was sitting here (in Fairfield's barn studio: there's a huge anti-discrimination tea party in the house I decided to eschew) writing an article about Jane Freilicher—"What! Another?"—when Inspiration, if it was she, grabbed her purse and trudged off to New York where people like Kenneth, Frank and Joe Brainard (not to speak of John Ashbery, Ted, and Marianne Moore) live leaving me with a typewriter and a sunset the color of a Walgreen's shrimp salad sandwich. What better time to write you that long postponed letter on yellow paper?

I spent last week in New York, getting the good of the transit strike. I was staying in John Ashbery's apartment, a twelfth (good grief) floor one on Gramercy Park, and it was restful to look down on the streets full of perfectly motionless cars, like a huge pop sculpture, while the phonograph played Busoni's "Indian

---

460. Margaret Fuller (1810–1850), transcendentalist writer and editor of *Dial* (1840–1842). Norma Vincent Peel, stage name of a striptease dancer punning on the Manhattan churchman and author of *The Power of Positive Thinking*, Norman Vincent Peale. Brook farm was an experimental utopian farm community of Transcendentalists, including Nathaniel Hawthorne, in West Roxbury, Massachusetts, from 1841 to 1847.

461. As America's preeminent dance critic, Denby championed George Balanchine's dances and dance company.

Fantasy." It was also fun spending an afternoon with Joe B marching about on such errands as buying a vanilla bean and a pair of ranch pants and going to see Durer and his Contemporaries at the Morgan Library (my, Germans can be, uh, plain). But getting to the Carnegie Tavern an hour late and finding dinner date and ticket fled was a pain in the ass.

I also saw "The Nutcracker" which to my surprise was an almost perfect mess. Unfortunately Allegra Kent[462] came on at the end and once again perfection was forced to go unachieved.

It seems to me there can't be any news Joe hasn't written you: there's always a letter addressed to you waiting to be mailed to you when I get to his studio. Which reminds me, I saw his Xmas present for you, which I thought was thrilling in a great big beautiful way. I also cleaned up: besides a rug, "the most beautiful postcard in the world," an illustrated copy of the Pl-t-n-c Blow,[463] he gave me a set of drawings called MY PLANTS FOR JIMMY very beautiful and just what the title implies. They're under lock and key right now, awaiting a swift trip to the framers.

The Hazans have moved into a nifty penthouse on 5th Avenue at 12th Street. In fact, it's a duplex with marble stairs which they are carpeting at vast expense, for the sake of Baby Elizabeth, who now can toddle if you give her a finger to cling to. Every evening when Daddy Joe comes home he turns on the FM, picks up baby and they do ballroom dancing, or whatever sort the music calls for. (Did you know that young Joe was a professional Hindu dancer? I mean, professional dancer of Hindu dances. He was never, to my knowledge, a professional Hindu.) Elizabeth can also say, "See?" in a very distinct way, and she likes to get plenty of applause for it.

John Ashbery I thought would languish for Paris but he doesn't. He says all the years he lived abroad he was anxiously worrying about having some day to come back to New York, and now it's off his mind. And he likes his job (in so far as one can like any job), which is largely because Tom Hess is crazy about him. They get along like houses. John also said, while gazing across his bloody Mary at the sunset, ". . . the dawn, with greasy fingers . . . " We've written another chapter of A Nest of Ninnies, and gotten them out of Florida. Fabia is now gainfully employed as a receptionist in the office where Marshall Bush and Irving Kelso also work. It takes us an awfully long time to get anything done, since some-

462. Allegra Kent, prima ballerina in Balanchine's New York City Ballet company.

463. The Platonic Blow, a pornographic poem by W. H. Auden. Ed Sanders, editor of Fuck You: A Magazine of the Arts, pirated the poem from Auden's manuscript at the University of Buffalo and published it as a chapbook. In his poem "A Few Days" Schuyler wrote, "The Platonic Blow gives me hives. Funny porn / I guess is a gift, / like any other."

thing like: "Mr Kelso is out of town this week. He's at The Mills," can mysteriously break us up for a good deal of our writing time.

I like your and Joe's [Brainard] machine collaboration in the *Many Penises of Joe Gould* issue of *Mother*.[464]

I hope you're seeing all the sights in Paris, including all the Delacroix frescoes I missed. Well, not quite all, I did make it to the nifties in St Sulpice, one of my favorite churches. In France, anyhow.

Friday

Dear Ron and Pat,

Suddenly it was Supper—I guess I write letters on the same style as anything else, a little here, a little there. Now a big bookcase is being built in my room, and the route to desk, typewriter, unfinished letters and so on is as effectively blocked as a thru-way that's getting its soft shoulders asphaltized.

Unfortunately there is news now. Ruth Yorck[465] died quite suddenly the day before yesterday of heart failure. She went with a friend to a matinee of *Marat / Sade*,[466] felt sick before it began, started to leave but collapsed in the lobby. It was very quick and, I hope, relatively painless.

Kenward and Joe were going to Vermont this weekend and since Ruth had wanted to be cremated without any funeral or other ceremonials, it will be done there. Perhaps Joe has already written this to you? Anyway, I know Kenward would welcome a letter or letters from you all: all the address that's needed is, Calais, Vermont. But I forgot. You have been there of course.

I'm awfully glad they are going, which will give a couple weeks respite from the telephone. When Fairfield and his car became entangled with an LIRR engine last spring, I was more than staggered by the avidity for detail I got every time I went uptown, and mostly from people I wasn't aware I knew or heartily wished I didn't. It made going to Maine doubly wonderful.

My next letter won't be so many months aborning. Thanks for the many marvelous cards, which are now fighting it out with the California Wild Flower Wallpaper in my room.

love,

Jimmy

464. The little magazine *Mother*, edited by poet Peter Schjeldahl, published painter Alice Neel's (1900–1984) portrait of the Greenwich Village bohemian and author of *An Oral History of the World*, Joe Gould, in which Gould hças three penises.
465. Ruth Yorck (1904–1966), German-born writer and actress.
466. Hit Broadway play written by Peter Weiss.

TO JOE BRAINARD

[Southampton, New York]

March 23, 1966

Dear Joe,

I'm sorry I forgot to send these sooner.

Thanks for all the pretties!

John and the Hazans were out last weekend—well, Saturday night & Sunday, rather a short weekend. JA & I wrote some of *A Nest*, and went to antique shops: only one of them was cute, you might like to visit it sometime. John bought a very brown pitcher and a spattered brown pottery plate, called Benningtonware. Next time he comes out the woman who owns the shop is going to produce a Benningtonware spittoon for him to consider.

I saw a terrible movie, *The Heroes of Telemark*.[467] Tonight there's something with Sean Connery. Will it be better?

It's funny early spring weather, very pale and washy, sort of the color of a mild head cold.

Guess I'll see you soon, I hope. Love to KGE,

love,

Jimmy

P.S. Why don't you add a critique of Fairfield's show?

TO JOHN ASHBERY

[Great Spruce Head Island]

July 9, 1966

Dear Grinling Gibbons,[468]

Well, it was sure nice to have your letter and enclosure come scudding across the bay: do get your tasks done so you can visit. Unless we hear differently, we will expect to meet you in Camden at the Camden Yacht Club on Monday, July 18 *at noon*. A bite in Camden, then off to the islands. I assume you'll be coming from the Katz's . . . ? (and not Edwin's . . .). And that they will get you there, since, though mere driving minutes away, you would find it rather a jolly hike.

---

467. *The Heroes of Telemark* (1965), directed by Anthony Mann and set in "war-torn" Norway, starred Kirk Douglas.

468. Grinling Gibbons (1648–1721), British decorative wood-carver and architect.

If you can write, right away (once the mail arrives Sat. noon a 48 hour communication cut-off begins), it would be an easement.

I would love to add some items of the Ashbery Americana to my present holdings: I am particularly weak in the authors you mention (and in any others you might think of, for that matter). I wonder if there's a Samantha[469] at the Buffalo Exposition? That ought to be rich. In return I'll send you a record—but only if you really want it: Tauber singing an excerpt from Kreisler's *Sissy* (Eterna 723).

Do you think that in *A Nest* it might suddenly be summer? We could do another of our wonderful seasonal evocations, of course, but what I really want to get in is a reference to "cut-and-come-again" lettuce in the home garden. I had some other ideas the other day in a sphagnum bog, but seem to have left them there.

I don't think there is such a thing as a Collected Ade (it would weight as much as Nakian's[470] "Rape of Lucrece"). What I probably had was *The Fables in Slang (I and II)*—Dover, T533, $1.00. I'm sure I saw it lately in some of your paperback book stores. I'd be happy to send it whizzing to you but Dover, to judge by the time it takes them to send anything, is strictly a one-man operation. Under the General Editorship of Saul Bellow (snore), the U. of Chi. has been publishing a series of minor works by members of the Chicago School: a project as chilling in achievement as conception. From them one can get Ade's once-popular, now seldom-read *Pink Marsh*. Pink Marsh is not a kind of sundae or another sobriquet for the Windy City but the wise-cracker in the office who spends most of his time telling about his afterwork adventures and misadventures. On the whole, you'll be happier sticking to *Sketches by Boz*. (*The Fables*, on the other hand, are truly great.)

Gee, it just occurred to me that Anna & Lizzie are going to mass in Stonington tomorrow morning, and if they mail these there you may get it before you return from Maine.

The tide is high and it's time for a chastening dip in the melted (but just) ice-cubes. I'll try to find a couple of columns from last Sunday's Portland paper that are among my favorite summer reading. "A shower of cards" for a shut-in might go into *A Nest*, too.

I'll put the Ohio Shakers' Lemon Pie on a separate sheet, so you won't get egg all over my letter, in case you ever want to sell it to City College.

469. A series of Samantha books were published early in the twentieth century.
470. Reuben Nakian (1897–1986), sculptor whose monumental *Rape of Lucrece* is in the Museum of Modern Art's collection.

Later. My apologies to the cove, G.S.H.I., where the water, thanks to a south-west wind, was delicious. I swam for over an hour, and feel quite faint—just the condition in which to finish *Martin Chuzzlewit*. Have you ever . . . ? The famous American episodes are rather like being strapped into one of Mark Twain's after-dinner speeches and pointed out to sea, but, still: "don't ask me whether I won't take none or whether I will, but leave the bottle on the chimney-piece and let me put my lips to it when I am so disposed." Come to think of it, there are a couple of limes awastin' in the fruit boat right now.

love,

Jimmy
Theodore Besterman[471]

PS: An Ade opus I want to read sometime is his comedy hit, *The College Widow*. The branch library on 58th 'tween Park & Lex. has a lot of plays, and one could no doubt easily read it, if they have it (and they used to have the complete publishings of Samuel French)[472] during a lunch hour; particularly if Tom [Hess] were in Europe.

Have you noted Angel's new hot release, the Elgar violin concerto[473] with Yehudi at the fiddle? Gets a "first" for my autumn orderings list.

TO JOHN ASHBERY

[Great Spruce Head Island]

July 22, 1966

Dear Lad of Sunnybrook Farm,

Thanks for your chuckleful latest. I read the Story of Spike[474] aloud and it won plaudits of glee. Though I'm not *sure* Anne thinks you're doing your mother any great favor. Do keep me abreast of the developments—I can't wait for "Spike and Sunny Visit Grandma on the Farm."

As you will see in the enclosed,[475] my addition to what we wrote is not what usually passes for a page. But (if you find it acceptable) it seems a natural end-

---

471. Theodore Besterman (1904–1976), biographer of Voltaire and editor of *The Complete Works of Voltaire*.

472. Publishing house founded in 1830, specializing in plays.

473. Edward Elgar (1857–1934), British composer whose "Violin Concerto in B Minor op. 61 was first recorded by Yehudi Menuhin (1916–1999).

474. Ashbery's adopted stray cat.

475. Two pages from *A Nest of Ninnies*.

ing for the episode. Though it occurs to me that we have not given space to any shopping sprees—surely, along with movies, hooch and food, a subject on which we could authoritatively spread ourselves? But as Mayor Lindsay[476] lately said, "The ball and the burden are in your hands and on your shoulders."

What date do you return from P-ville [Pultneyville, New York]? I suppose you've had your fill of this song and dance, but my mother fondly thinks I'm going to visit her in September (so does Kenward—oops), and perhaps we could write it up in a club car some Sat. or Sun. afternoon? Hmm? Lemme know. The 29th is the latest I'll be here, and I'll be there round the first or second. (A. & F. are having their annual wrangle about driving on or in the vicinity of Labor Day weekend. Since we once proved that everybody then leaves Boston and nobody leaves Maine, I guess its purpose is more ritualistic than fact-finding). By "be there" I mean Southampton, of course, not East Aurora or Calais or . . .

What a day this is—though it may be a shame you didn't have one like it while here: it's loaded with nostalgia for an unheated Paris apartment in the depths of winter. You could also satisfy your curiosity about many unmet Porters. They've been arriving in Kittiwake-loads[477] to spend their *ferragosto* on this happy chunk of the Porter realty. It seems rather crowded, though perhaps *I* am not the one who should say it.

On the way back we're going to stop at Anne's brother's at Wareham, though I don't know if plans are for one or two nights. If two, it seems a golden opportunity to visit Boston & catch up on the holdings of the Boston Art Institute. But I suppose Boston would stage a race riot in honor of my visit, so it's probably safer all round to pile into the packed Channing compound.[478]

Did you note in the paper that the NYCentral has plans of suspending all "runs" of over 200 miles, come the new year? Does that mean, do you think, that this pair of York State Clarie Tootsies will have to hoof it from Albany? Sigh. I can't decide which is worst: the bus, flying or learning to drive a driveyourself car. On this island, the latter seems to have a certain charm—in a year or so of trans-state driving one could winkle out many a half-forgotten mansard. On the other hand, I believe an extension of the N.Y. Thru-Way is soon to brush

476. John Lindsay (1921–2000), mayor of New York City who served two consecutive terms from 1965 to 1973.

477. The Kittiwake was Fairfield Porter's brother John's powerboat moored at Great Spruce Head Island.

478. Anne Porter's maiden name was Channing. Her family home was in Sherborn, outside Boston.

past East Aurora. But the Greyhound people would probably give me a choice of getting out at Wales Center or going on to Buffalo. (If you'll learn to drive, I'll learn to drive—we could take turns at the wheel in the event our mothers should remove, say, to Santa Barbara. I feel quite safe about making this offer. Safe from learning to drive I mean.)

As you see, I have no news. The light is still not leaping, to say the least, so guess I'll go curl up with the *Penguin History of Scotland*, which it turns out, is one long bicker—not unlike, I'm afraid, an off evening with McLeaf and the Laird of Droll. Did you know that "the reckoning eight oxgangs = one plough-gate, and four ploughgates = one davach was never universal"? Since a davach was a measure of arable land of no particular size, I can see how it might not have caught on. Perhaps I'd better go back to *The Gardener's Companion*, an anthology aimed at those of us who can't stomach the rough stuff in *The Saturday Book*.

Give my love to Michael and tell him I hope his way is rich in Davachs—love,

Fran Hagood, Ye Ed
Jimmy

PS Guess what the mailboat brought *me* today! *The Reger Variations*[479] I ordered at Discophile last February. Now I know what the august clerk meant by, "You realize it will take a month or so." Dumb kraut—mutter curse. I assume you dug the Busoni / Reger reviews in last Sun.'s *Times*? I especially enjoyed the bit about J. Gruen.

TO JOHN ASHBERY

[Great Spruce Head Island]

July 28, 1966

Dear John,

I still feel stunned by Frank's death.[480] If you feel equal to it, I would like to know a little more than is in today's *Times*: who was he staying with? Or any

---

479. Max Reger (1873–1916), German composer.
480. Frank O'Hara suffered fatal injuries after being struck by a beach buggy on Fire Island and died two days later, July 25, in a Long Island hospital. Janice Koch sent a telegram with the news to the Porters and Schuyler on Great Spruce Head Island.

thing you think I might want to know. But if you would rather not write about it don't.

I finished copying the enclosed. Please go over it carefully for spelling, pointing, accents and anything else. If you want to change or add anything, do so. Camellia does have two ll's and Sally Lunn is singular—anything else that looks like a mistake is a mistake.

It was like a dream come true to have you here, and unfortunately as quickly passed. Joe [Brainard] writes that "you got some dishes"—what are they like? Also, how long does the bus trip from Vermont (Burlington?) take?

I'll send the parts of what we wrote here that you don't have soon.

I'm sorry my typewriter and I are such bum copyists.

Let me hear from you soon. My love to M.

love,

Jimmy

PS: I've been sending things to your office because in my day there were two deliveries a day in midtown and only one in residential uptown. If you prefer that I write to 95th Street, say so and I will. I enclose the draft in case you want to check anything.

The postcards are ones I thought you might want to send to Pierre sometime (including the one you mentioned). I haven't found your missing nut. Any hints on where to look? Where did you find the rod? I'm sure you can get one to replace it—measure the diameter of the rod & ask for a nut to fit it—if it's iron, you can easily rust it on your fire-escape. Oops. Balcony!

TO JOHN ASHBERY

[Great Spruce Head Island]

Aug 7, 1966

Caro Amico Fritz,[481]

It was very good to get your letter. What with it, and Janice's [Koch] arrival, Frank's accident now exists in a more credible context than that provided by the N.Y. *Times* obituary. But I'll spare us both any extended comment.

I'm just as pleased you put back the first page of "At Mrs K's." It seemed a loss to lose Fabia's, "'it's base,' she said, 'is tea.'" Anyway, even if it is a little slow, it

481. *L'Amico Fritz* (1891), opera by Pietro Mascagni.

may, when the grand design is revealed in hard binding, make an agreeable *lento ma non marcato* (though those who go in for *piu presto possibile* will no doubt just have to look elsewhere). By the way, I agree with you that to finish by Christmas is desirable—but just how are you planning to implement this? One way I thought of was: between sessions, we might write a page each; or rather one write a page, send it to the other, and so on. I don't know that it's a very good idea, or that in practice it wouldn't break down almost instantly, but, well, what do *you* think? In the next day or two I'll try to copy the pages you haven't got, add a bit of my own, and send all to you.

Did you, by the way, succeed in finishing the review and the article? I suppose so, since you seem able to write with stunning and sustained speed once the deadline has put a tiger on your tail . . .

By the way, have you made a will? I haven't, but from what Janice tells me about the involvements in the O'Hara family I think I will—if only to save your letters from my mother's pyromania. Not to speak of my sister-in-law (when I was home she passionately allowed that the police ought to "do something" about the town beatnik. His crimes against society seem to consist of long hair, tight pants and a Honda—I'm not sure which she minds most).

Before I started this I was going to tell you that someone or something was my "pet noire" but I can't remember who or what it was.

When we met Janice at the Rockland airport I couldn't help wishing I could get over my "claim" (as the C.S's call it)[482] of air-terror. They left New York at 10:30, had an expensive lunch at the Boston airport, and arrived in Rockland at 1:30, in a Northeast airliner that inspired no confidence (it looked sort of like the kind Larry [Rivers] used to buy). I guess I'll stay grounded.

My visit to Kenward is up in the air again: it seems Katie will get back on Sept. 4 and leave for Manhattanville on Sept. 8—or more likely, the day before, come to think of it, since a trip of over 100 miles by way of New York seems to require for Fairfield an overnight stay at the Chelsea, New York's answer to a youth hostel I once saw in Venice. I want to see her while she's in Southampton. I may go to Calais from say, the 27th of Aug. to Sept. 3—how would that fit in with your schemes? Isn't that the period you've promised to go to Pultneyville wise? Or could you subtract some? I think if you could be there, the simplest way to broach it to Kenward would be to call him up and say you have some unexpected free days and that your idea of heaven would be etc. etc. blah blah and so on. They both like you very much and certainly would welcome you any

482. Schuyler's mother was a Christian Scientist.

time there was bed room (at the moment they have the Padgetts and Claibe Richardson,[483] who I rather picture as the heir to the Clabber Girl millions;[484] but I don't suppose they're staying all summer, and I may well be wrong). If you can go, I will. Even though it involves getting to Camden at 7 a.m. so I can spend several hours waiting in Portland for the bus to Montpelier, which arrives at 6:10 in the evening sigh. I just hope I don't get arrested in Portland for vagrancy. Let me know: and *do tell me how long the bus trip to NYC took.*

next day

Well, Mizz' Jan is up and I type again, before taking the little girls on another mystery canoe trip. The only object is to provide them with a different setting for their reading. What they really need is an outboard motor and an automatic pilot.

Say, I see by the current N.Y. *Review* that two books of Constable-iana are out here—or rather, one is out & the other will be out in the fall: a collection of his oil sketches, and a book about him by Carlos somebody—can it be Peacock? A stinker, I suspect. I'll have them soon in their Inglese editions, and would like to review them (along with 3 vols. of his letters already published in England—there will be 6 in all) for Heart Snooze. But perhaps you needn't mention this to Tom [Hess] until the Brainard piece[485] is in hand—your hand, that is—unless the matter comes up.

Would you send me some of that plastic glop for pressing flowers? The address is on the back of that pickaniney card . . .

Do you know who the author is of some "printed books"—as it said on the envelope—I've just received? *Sunlight in Jungleland, What's Cooking* and *Letters from Narvik.* Needless to say, I haven't read them yet.

Let me know right away if the visit to Calais, Vt., is a possibility for you. I may stay here otherwise (but keep it under your hat) since I like Maine better than Vermont, and so on and so forth.

Love,

la Muette de Portici[486]

J.

483. Claibe Richardson (1929–2003), composer and Kenward Elmslie's collaborator on the musical adaptation of Truman Capote's short story *The Grass Harp.*
484. Clabber Girl Baking Powder was advertised during the 1930s by signs painted on the sides of barns throughout rural America.
485. Schuyler's "Joe Brainard: Quotes and Notes" appeared in the April 1967 *Art News.*
486. French opera by Daniel Francois Esprit Auber (1782–1871).

TO KENWARD ELMSLIE

[Great Spruce Head Island]

Aug. 24, 1966

Dear Kenward,

I'm afraid I can't, after all, come when I said I would. Katie is getting back on the 4th and going right off on the 7th or 8th to college. I don't want to miss seeing her and hearing about her trip, which I don't suppose will be what she talks about when she comes home at Thanksgiving. She wrote me that she hoped I would be there, and though I would have been anyway, that really clinched it. Finally I'm in the middle of my piece for Paul,[487] which stopped with a thump when I heard about Frank, and that will occupy me until we pack the black trunk. Since, I want very much to visit you there, I've been a climax of indecision for the past few weeks. Well, either it's kismet or else my dharma needs a new set of spark-plugs. Or do I mean my kharma?

Janice [Koch] and Koko (Only Child of Only Child—oops) came for the better part of a week—in case you've ever wondered, "the better part" is six days. It was a great relief to talk to her about Frank, and be able to ask questions. She was somehow the best person to talk to, and hearing it all while coming out across the bay—a setting more real than claustrophobic NYC apartments or telephones—did finally make it seem credible, and not merely horribly improbable. We did quite a bit of canoeing while she was here, of the slow and stately sort which I prefer. This was mostly at Lizzie and KoKo's behest, because they found it a comfortable way to read. We also ate lobster: end of the Koch saga.

What do you think of the enclosed? Rose and Liz asked me what they could write stories about, so, from the shallow depths of my unconscious I said, "Write about a lobster who falls in love with a clam." Lizzie's was very descriptive and poetic. Rose's I enclose. Maybe I'll invite *you* up to my house sometime and we can "have some 'Fresca'." Hmm?

Tell Joe that when Fairfield had finished reading the piece about him, he *glowed*.

How long are you going to stay in Vermont? I'll be back in Southampton around the end of next week.

Give my love to Pat and Ron and Joe, to whom I will write by this mail, or by

---

487. This might be Schuyler's *The Fireproof Floors of Witley Court*, originally intended to be set to music by Paul Bowles.

the next mail (right now Fairfield is waiting for me to join him in a nice freeze at Landing Beach).

love,

Jimmy

PS Have you heard anything of a new *Art & Lit*? I just got a check from them (for a piece about Jane) which usually comes after it's out. Not that it matters. I'm afraid Jane is going to find it rather lacking (in length, for one thing)—the dear girl sets a high standard for her critics, you know.

TO JOHN ASHBERY

Great Spruce Head Island

Aug 27, 1966

Dear John,

I suppose you're just back from "going into Rochester for the day" with the Hummel[488] *Fantasy for Viola* tucked under your arm. Is there a phonograph there, or do you spend your time hunting the curlew with Kodak and stealth? The burden of this letter—which could easily have gotten onto a mini card—is, don't feel you have to hold yourself to a *page*, should Ninny-spiration hit you. I also meant to tell you that on anything I send you may feel free to use the larding needle (and the marrow scoop, for all of that). Of course you may not wish to channel all of your afflatus in a Nest—I would give a genuine silver dollar, in the form of a money clip, to read act II of your sequel to *The Bat*, nor does your public want to wait too long for *Glaciers and Greeks*.

While strolling about the Double Beaches Janice asked me, "And when is *Son of May 24th or so* coming out?" A conversation which was interrupted by my picking up and dropping a small dented pewter-colored box. "What was it," Janice said, "part of a sink?" "As a matter of fact, it was a container for condoms." "???" "Because it said in raised letters on the lid, *Merry Widows*." I always thought that was a byword, not a trade-mark. I'll bet there were plenty of sniggers and winks the day that one rolled into the copyright works—do you think they have locked files for unsuitable suggestions?

The John Porters have a guest at the moment who is yet more Island-devoted

488. Johann Nepomuk Hummel (1778–1837), German composer.

than even I. He's a Dane named something like Paer Johansen and when his vacation comes round he flies as directly as the airlines allow to Great Spruce Head—or rather, to its tennis court. When Paer and John aren't on this island, they go to other islands that have tennis courts. I suppose for him it combines the charms of a trip to Norway with tropic heat and the fact that he is here "*quelque chose d'exotique*," to quote you.

I just had a horrid encounter with a wasp,[489] a glass and a piece of cardboard. I won.

How did you and Spike make out on your trip? Has he turned all Pultneyville into an armed camp?

I'm waiting for Ebbie Porter to come up and discuss a limited edition of some poems of mine he projects. He has a press and a degree in graphics—perhaps his style has changed since his Yale days, when I recollect it as being a blend of Eric Gill and Lynd Ward.[490] Another choice item for that rarest of birds, the amateur of Schuyleriana.

I'll be looking for a letter from you in Southampton where—goodness gracious—I will be in five days.

Please remember me to your mother, and thanks for sending the books, which I value.

love,

Jimmy
H. V. Kaltenborn[491]

489. This may be the encounter Schuyler records in his elegy for Frank O'Hara "Buried at Springs," "There is a hornet in the room / and one of us will have to go / out into the late / August midafternoon sun. I / won."

490. Eric Gill (1882–1940), British sculptor and typographer. Lynd Ward (1905–1985), American illustrator and wood engraver of the 1930s and '40s. Best known for "novels in wood-cuts."

491. H. V. Kaltenborn (1878–1965), American radio commentator who is recognized as the father of his profession.

TO JOE BRAINARD

[Great Spruce Head Island]

August 28, 1966

Dear Joe,

Right after I wrote to Kenward the *Paris Review* he sent me came—I love the "Power Plant Sestina," it's so funny and great. It couldn't be in a better place for best effect than erupting out of the pale pages of the *Paris Review*, lightly shaded by that anemic type-face. It's so wonderful to see and read something that's terribly funny and not at all mean. It's wonderfully black to look at and wonderfully un-black to read. You're a pair of champs.

Thanks for the cards you sent. I've decided to use the post-card album you gave me only for plants and flowers (I guess that's a hint) of which I have a number already. But I can't decide whether to make it a rule that they all have to have messages on them or if it's OK to put in "blanks." What do you suggest, Dr. Brothers?[492]

John wrote that Tom Hess wants to use a "Pepsi-Flora" for the cover of the December *Art News*. He seems somewhat mysteriously to have written before calling you, so this is probably already settled, but if you would like Tom to see the one you gave me, write me in good old Southampton, where I'll arrive the evening of September 1st or a.m. of the 2nd. Write me in Southampton anyway for all of that.

Fairfield and Anne and the girls may go to Europe next summer, in which case I'll have the house in Southampton. It would be very nice, if this comes about, if you and Kenward would like to stay there with me, for all summer or part of the summer. Vermont or Maine it isn't—oh well I guess I don't have to explain the difference between the Hamptons, GSH and Calais to you. My acein-the-hole—in attempting to entice you that is—is Fairfield's studio which is so very BIG and delightful and private. As a matter of fact, being in town is much more private than being, say, on Flying Point Road[493] where if you go to one house you always seem to bump into someone from another house and get a look from dark questioning eyes. As much as I like Maine, I wouldn't mind

---

492. Dr. Joyce Brothers, psychologist who then dispensed advice through a newspaper column.

493. Road between Southampton and Water Mill, Long Island, on which Gold and Fizdale, the Hazans, and the Gruens lived.

staying there for a change—I'm sick of coming back to an acre of crab grass and dying roses.

Anyway, this is something you and Kenward might like to mull over—nobody's bought any steamer tickets yet.

I love what you wrote about Fairfield, and I think about what you said about there being a lot of talent around and that being a good painter is a matter of intention (and I'm glad you say it the way you say it and not "matter of intention").

Do you know when you're leaving Vermont?

The "cleaning up the house" movement has just started today—I can hear Fairfield tossing stretchers around on his porch. So I guess I'd better go dump some of my junk in a box.

Everybody here is fine: give my love to Kenward and Ron and Pat, or rather, as I read in the Portland paper society column, "warm smiles to all my friends."

Do you suppose people with Warm Smiles spend a lot of time practicing? Like Marlene Dietrich eating in front of a big mirror so she could practice crossing her legs?

love,

Jimmy

TO KENWARD ELMSLIE

Une visite à Montreal
I'm not missing at all
But the dam! And the beaver!

(fill in superfluous last line in *rime riche* & win free
ride of Staten Island ferry. Only one ride to a family)

[Southampton, New York]

Sept. 18, 1966

Dear Kenward,

It's very distressing to have you up there writing whole operas while I'm down here still pecking away at my mini-tata over a hot bottle of low calorie lemon. Oh well, somebody somewhere said that Waller is immortal because he linked

172

three words together so perfectly that . . . ahchooh! The words are: lovely, rose and go. No, it is not, Rose Golovely.

Your card came just as I was reaching for the phone to see if you weren't at one of your more southerly numbers. Well, for *your* sake I am glad you're still there, but don't stay all winter.

Southampton is very nice since the sudden chill, which drove all the soft stuff back to the city. Last night we bridged with the Hazans: one rubber which lasted from 8.30 to 11. Joe was determined, it seemed, to play as many hands as possible, with spectacular results for our opponents. Earlier in the week there was a nice dinner party with (guess) the Hazans, and Elaine de K [Kooning]. and Bob Corliss.[494] Elaine got too drunk to drive home to the house she just bought on Shelter Island so it became a house party. Donald Droll is said to be going to buy a house on Shelter Island, too, and what do you think of that for a bit of red hot gossip.

Fairfield and I are going up to Maine to fetch his pictures around the 1st of Oct., but we won't be away long. Although I guess we'll be here that weekend, since the Kochs are said to be coming out here. Katie ran into Kenneth on the street in London (yes, it *is* a small place) and visited the National Gallery with him, where she learned the 3 best painters are Titian, Giovanni Bellini and Larry Rivers. Little does Kenneth know that in far away Water Mill a dark-haired, blue-eyed paintrix is brooding over that remark this very moment. Well, he'll find out in due course . . .

Katie had a marvelous time in Europe, stayed here long enough to buy a portable typewriter and now is in Purchase, New York, studying French, Greek, English, Theology, and botany. The last she says is easy. Although come to think of it today she is in New York City showing the Metropolitan Museum to her Peruvian room-mate Carmen East.

Did you see the enclosed clipping about you? I'll also throw in the *Times'* total coverage of the new Met. Opening. The boys say the acoustics are very good . . .

Well, back to the nameless nothing I'm writing. I seem to have just written a song called "Under Blue Freeway Lights" that would give Petula Clark[495] a good chill. I don't think it's going to get much further than the cutting room

---

494. Bob Corliss, painter, and a protégé of Elaine de Kooning. He died of a heroin overdose.

495. Petula Clark, pop singer. "Downtown" was one of her hits.

floor. What I would really like is to have some fat girls get up and sing. Can't help it, Jest can't help it, while Pigmeat[496] tells a few good ones.

Give my love to Pat and Ron and Joe—perhaps I'll see you sooner than it seems like—

love,

Jimmy

TO JOHN ASHBERY

[Southampton, New York]

Oct. 30, 1966

Dear Prinny,[497]

Now about that Tolmiea (toll-mi-EE-a—perennial herb named for Dr. William Fraser Tolmie (d. 1886), surgeon to the Hudson's Bay Company, Puget Sound) Menziesii (men-ZEE-si-eye, the specific name of Arbutus, from Archibald Menzies (1754–1842), British naval surgeon and botanist who accompanied Vancouver on his voyage of Northwest Pacific exploration, 1790–95. So I take the name to mean Menzie's Tolmiea, which seems strange, because if Menzies found it, then this monotypic genus should be named for him) popularly Mother-of-thousands or Pickaback plant, according to Andree Vilas Grabe, the rather sleepy author of the painfully thin *Complete Book of House Plants*, though L. H. Bailey[498] prefers Thousand Mothers, Youth-on-Age (not to be confused with Youth and Age, our old friend zinnia elegans) and Piggy back plant. Well, after the "adventitious buds have occurred in the sinuses of the leafblades," one author says you wait till the leafdrops, then root it (the plantlets) in an average rooting mixture. Miss Grabe wakes up long enough to disagree: "Plant leaf cuttings with plantlets attached in any rooting medium" (dirt is a typical rooting medium—though a better one is sand, sand and peatmoss, or vermiculite) but she says to "select healthy, firm, not quite full-grown leaves."

---

496. Dewey "Pigmeat" Markham (1904–1981), African American cabaret performer and comic.

497. Nickname of George III's son Prince Rupert.

498. Liberty Hyde Bailey (1858–1954), noted horticulturalist.

I'm not sure whether you lightly bury the parent leaf, or merely anchor it with toothpicks. I should think either would work. And I'm sure if you pop into Goldfarb's or Max Schling's they can sell you some "rooting medium" and a plastic pot to hold same.

I note, by the way, that gardenia cuttings will root in a glass of water. Just think, your bedroom a bower of home-grown gardenias. You can also root cuttings from your rose geranium. Yours can be a full and happy winter.

Say, I don't suppose you took in much at the Uptown Velvet Underground — but if you call Richard Miller at the Tiber Press and remind him, he'll send your set of The Books to you. He did say it's more convenient if people picked them up, but he guessed sending them was the least he can do. However, now that I've signed, he intends to put them in cases and store them, so if I were you I'd call him right away — once they're stored I'm sure he'll never get them out again.

Can't wait to find out whether we're all going to Wash. D.C. next weekend.

Did you know Bill Weaver is coming for a few weeks in Dec.? Around the first, I think. No doubt you'll want to give a choice little affair for him — hmm? See you soon — love Cynthia Westcott, the Rose Doctor

TO KENWARD ELMSLIE

[Southampton, New York]

Nov. 16, 1966

Dear Kenward,

I had a note lately from Don Allen (enclosing the annual royalty check for his anthology — this year I hit $14.36 — for mere minutes of typing) and he's making an enlarged *New American Poets.* I assume he's adding new poets as well as new poems by the old or rear guard, so perhaps you would like to send him a few of your recent yummies? I told him I like them, but I doubt that my say-so counts for much (in fact, without Frank, I rather wonder who is now his gray eminence; not that he isn't gray enough himself — help — I must stop that).

His address is: Donald Allen
                1815 Jones Street
                San Francisco 94109
But he doesn't say what state.

If you are going to be in town next Monday or Tuesday, perhaps we could have dinner before the Snow Queen tows little Kay away on his sled. Give me a ring if you can.

175

Fairfield's looking very rested and full of piss and vinegar. I told Anne his room at his hospital (which he got out of four days early) was quite nice, but he says it was like the prison of the future. He seems quite devoted to an exchange nurse from Japan, named Miss Chara. Anne & Liz are getting over in-depth colds. Otherwise, all is well.

We're having the Hazans for the weekend—not so much from their love of travel, as because of the new room their (*sic*) they're building at The Open Arms of F'ing Point Road.

FP and family are sailing on June fifth and coming home on August 17th. It would be better than very nice if you and Joe would like to come here. But if you don't want to decide at this rather hectic point, that's OK. Though I may take the liberty of saying I *think* you're going to—some people are quite outspoken in their requests, while I'm fond of Them, ten weeks of solid-state living might be another matter. I may have a reputation for liking children, but it's not necessarily total infatuation . . .

Now I must go plant Prince Camille de Rohan, who has very dark red petals. love,

Jimmy

TO RON PADGETT

> DEAR DR. MOLNAR: Is it harmful to eat frost that gathers in a refrigerator? I have been doing it for some time. —B.J.
> IT'S just moisture that has condensed. I can't see how it could harm you. But you don't tempt my palate, particularly.

Southampton, New York

May 23, [1967]
[misdated as 1966 by JS]

Dear Ron,

Did you say thirty pages? in diamond type on India paper? Are you sure this isn't a put-on? or a send up? or a put-down? or an old-fashioned leg pull? Your letter was enough to get my nose out of Harriet Beecher Stowe's *Old Town Folks* and out into the yard, uprooting the pig-weed.

Still, in case you're not kidding—I like the four poems of mine in Donald Allen's the New Victorians; and I guess anything in *May 24th or so*,[499] except "Dorabella's Hat," which seems rather "old game" to me. There are a half dozen or so newer poems I'd like you to see, which I'll try to send within the week.

This doesn't mean, as it may sound, that I expect you to do my typing (are you and David[500] averse to Xeroxed copies? I hope not). But I'm a rather poky inaccurate typist, and assembling a pseudo-mass. For Paris Review Editions at the swift command of Maxine (The Cutie Who Dwells in the East) rather took it out of me, energy-wise. But I *will* do it.

I hope, by the way, you aren't going to bear down too hard on The New York School (or use that term). It sounds, uh, insular, and somehow isn't altogether true. But for Barbara G and me, the group in the Don Anthology might just as well be called The Harvard Wits . . . oh well, it's your book.

Yes, it *seems* some of my poems are to be published by Doubleday in the Paris Review Editions Series[501] (which sounds like being caught trying things on in one of Macy's Better Shops); I'll believe it when I've signed something—possibly to my undying regret, since, between you and me and the lamp post, I've always regarded Doubleday as the worst publisher. They are, in the trade, notorious for dumping—which you may take in any sense you please. Still, humble pie tastes pretty good when it's a matter of boards and crushed morocco. (Actually, all publishers are beasts so it makes no difference after all.)

I hope you & Pat go near the Guggenheim before the Cornell show is over; one can scarcely get too close to it. And that the three of you will come out for a visit during the summer—tell Pat the town sports a good baby doctor, whose name Jane Hazan will divulge—reveal for a token sum. love,

Jimmy

---

499. Schuyler's first book of poems, published by Tibor de Nagy Editions.
500. Poet David Shapiro (b. 1947), with whom Padgett edited *An Anthology of New York Poets*. Random House published the book in 1970.
501. Freely Espousing appeared in 1969

TO ANNE AND FAIRFIELD PORTER

[Southampton, New York]

June 9, 1967

Dear Anne and Fairfield,

The weather here has been as beautiful as the news has been dismal (though if there had to be a war,[502] I'm glad it went as it did). Too cool for some, but I still call it balmy and love it.

Kenward and Joe moved in Sunday evening. On Monday Joe went into the studio and hasn't been seen since, not much anyway. He's painting in oil which he says is impossible, but I thought a couple of them already were very pretty. Last evening we were looking at all the swelling buds and he said, "I hope I get *good* in time!" I rather think he will.

Kenward came complete with an IBM electric typewriter, about the size and weight of a Volkswagen, which promptly acted funny and had to be carried to Dunkerley's. (K: "I can't understand instruction manuals." Me: "Sometimes I can. Let me see it." K: "Well, actually it was so confusing I didn't bother to bring it.") It was easily fixed and can sometimes be heard humming swiftly in the distance like the Tokyo Express.

I spent the last four days typing from dawn until dusk so Doubleday can have (or see?) a whole lot more poems. Since these were of the third-pressing in quality I didn't enjoy it a bit. I wish they could have been buried among the first group, where they might at least have had the effect of making a background . . . oh well.

Last night we saw a Western, the night before we had dinner at Bobby and Arthur's, which is all open and white downstairs now, and the night before that, we went to the Hazan's and watched the Security Council on TV. In many ways stupefying, and I'm afraid our representative earned the Horace Horsecollar award when he assured one and all that the United States would never dream of meddling in the internal affairs of another country. Abba Eban,[503] however, made a very reasonable, intelligent and moving speech, despite the invidious-ness of Israel's position. The tide seems to be coming in under the UN with the speed of a whippet.

---

502. Israeli Six-Day War.
503. Israeli chief delegate to the United Nations.

Of which there is only one here, since Whipporwill has gone on a visit to Stockbridge, Mass. Rossignol is thought to be in heat. She's very well behaved and no trouble, in fact she's quite a lot of fun, and hasn't dug up the flowers yet. I enclose the personal mail. Otherwise, bills have been more in evidence than dividends, and the former I pay with FPesque rapidity. The telephone went all but dead as soon as you left—I guess the word flashed round. There has been only one call for you, a Mrs Wade who asked if I thought Mr Porter would like to have his house sheathed in Du Pont aluminum siding? I said, yes, especially the windows.

And now to see if the Osborne Agency will divulge the Naples address of American Express . . .

I miss all of you very much.

Love to Katie and Liz,

love,

Jimmy

I hope no one is planning to save up *all* his or her travel impressions until he, she or they gets/get home. I'm also very fond, as you know, of postcards of all sorts—views of buildings and streets come first, panoramas featuring chair-lifts come last.

TO FAIRFIELD PORTER

[Southampton, New York]

June 16, 1967

Dear Fairfield,

This isn't a letter, it's a note to go with the enclosed. (Which, by the way, *is* the copy; I've kept the original.) Some hundreds of dollars worth of shares of Southold Royalty arrived in a plain envelope, the result of a 3 for 1 stock split. I'll put them in the strong box on Monday. Meantime I have them chained to my ankle like a giant egg.

It was wonderful hearing from you both—I couldn't believe mail came so quickly from Naples; nor did it. I'd forgotten the pleasures and beauties of shipboard; and I'm glad you got a look at the fortunate isles.

The big sycamore gave me a turn. All over it, leaves were curling up, turning gray and dying. T. Anthony told me, however, that it is the result of the big storm a month or so ago and that I ought to see *his* maple. "You got nothing to worry

179

about," he said. Such is not the case. The barn has settled so much that the drop-lock won't work, so I have to take the door off and plant it. "Which I hasten to do," to quote JA.

Who is coming out tonight with JJ Mitchell[504] (do you think that stands for Jorrick Johns?). It's monstrous hot in New York, and he said dinners had better be good. I told him no such allurements were provided this time of year, when would-be guests are a dime a dozen. Mr Crust (I mean Kenneth) called up and asked to borrow a car *before* he came out. I cut off a piece of shrift and gave him that instead. He guessed he would have had to ask you, which was too true for comment. (Please don't offer to lend him one—he is, for the moment, at peace. He didn't need it for anything anyway—he said, "It's always nice to have one in the summer.")

I got a gardenia at the fancy house-plant place in Easthampton, and intend to give it the old Ruth Stout.[505]

The yardman, of whom I'd despaired, just appeared. He's going to come beginning next Wednesday, and welcome he will be.

Maybe this *is* a letter, after all, though abrupt.

Love to Anne and Katie and Liz and you,

Jimmy

ps Please tell Katie that Kathy Achtellick (sp?) called up and she has Katie's yearbook and does Katie have hers? I looked in Katie's bookshelf and I didn't see it.

The letter for "Shmizo!" was in with a gift-wrapped book which I did not unwrap, please tell Liz . . .

Please keep me up to date on your schedule as it evolves. On the sheet of addresses, it says Rome til July 18: is that right?

---

504. John Joseph Mitchell (1940–1986), poet who was with Frank O'Hara on Fire Island the night of the beach buggy accident that caused O'Hara's death.

505. Author of *How to Have a Green Thumb Without an Aching Back* (1955).

TO JOHN ASHBERY

[Southampton, New York]

Nov. 5, 1967

Dear Purvis,

I made a lightning descent on Cornelia Street[506] for a recent 48 hour period—it was fascinating to see how folks live south of East 95th Street, quite
nicely it would seem, though I still think in deep Village it's scary—well, un-
settling—of a Friday evening. And why I bother to mention it I have no idea,
except perhaps a lurking fear that you might on impulse rent a garden apartment under the Minetta Tavern.[507]

Guess you've heard from Jane that she and Joe are tendering me a small dinner (small but choice, that is) on Thursday, Nov. 9th [Schuyler's birthday]. I'll
come in & stay with you if that's OK? (A rhetorical question, I guess.) Maybe
we can make the De Kooning opening the next day—though since even I got
an invite, I imagine attending it will consist of walking on the far side of 5th
and staring in wonder at the hordes . . .

Joe B and I went out to Brooklyn and saw the Triumph of Realism show. The
utter horror of a roomful of Duvenecks[508] had never crashed over my head before. And the Ashcan School[509] was looking more than usually seedy. There
are some nice Homers and such, and Courbets, a Degas portrait and a big
Manet still life that was new to me. But I can't endorse a visit, unless made
on Company Time. Their shop though is very nice, and I laid in a supply of
stocking stuffers which include an elephant hair bracelet that I'm not sure I
can bring myself to part with.

We had dinner on Friday night at the Jamaican restaurant on 6th Avenue I
think we have sometimes discussed as a dining possibility. It isn't. Joe found the
spareribs tough, Kenward voted the special pork ("roasted in a sauce of Island

---

506. Kenward Elmslie's home.

507. A tavern on Minetta Lane in New York's Greenwich Village.

508. Frank Duveneck (1848–1919), painter known for his realistic portraits, genre scenes,
and landscapes.

509. American painters of realistic scenes of contemporary urban life active mostly in New
York City during the first decades of the twentieth century. Robert Henri, John Sloan, and
George Bellows were chief among them.

spices") nothing much, and the curried mutton with Montego chutney left me with a rich glaze of sweat. At the approach of a table hopping calypso singer, we fled.

I haven't typed up our recent additions to *Nest*, pending the return of my Olivetti from the Dunkerly Typewriter hospital. Fairfield's is impossible for anyone less muscular than Joe Namath.

I dipped into Sam Goody's[510] and am now the proud and happy owner of two Reger sonatas for unaccompanied viola. They're quite lovely and all that one might expect from the great man, though of course not without a certain ribtickling quality. On the flip side there is quite a nice Hindemith[511] opus for the same instrument.

Bill [Berkson] writes me that John [Bernard Myers] did put him back into the anthology, but in such a way that Bill fired back a refusal.[512] There doesn't seem much point in withdrawing our work because he isn't in a book he doesn't want to be in, so I guess we're stuck with it. Oh well, perhaps it will be a runaway bestseller and head everybody's Lenten reading list next year.

One thing I did lately was finish a for me quite long poem, which I think I like (by quite long I mean seven pages). It is about Vermont, was "for Kenward." If you're very good I may force you to read it in the not too distant future.[513]

Charles Heilemann, who was also in Goody's (clatching with Mona Rose, natch), would like us to come to dinner "sometime soon." But we can discuss that later . . .

I hope your mother and her friend and you are all getting the most out of Funny Farm City. Can't wait to hear all about it.

Love,

the Hookers of Kew[514]

---

510. Chain of New York City record stores.
511. Paul Hindemith (1895–1963), German composer.
512. John Bernard Myers edited an anthology, *The Poets of the New York School* (1969).
513. "Now and Then" appeared in *Freely Espousing*.
514. William Jackson Hooker (1785–1865) and Joseph Dalton Hooker (1817–1911), British botanists.

TO RON PADGETT

Southampton, New York

Jan. 11, 1968

Dear Ron,

I just remembered (perhaps because — oh thrill — I'm listening to Marguerite Long[515] explain Fauré's 2nd piano quartet, while waiting for the furnace to go out) something I meant to mention the other evening — to wit — Joe says you're waiting for the shops on a stereo? recommended? and it costs about $150 & is made in Japan? Very mysterious. The one I have is a KLH model 11, & is made in Cambridge, Mass. & costs — I think — about $199.99. John Ashbery has a model 22 — *si je me souvien bien* — which costs not much more & only one of us thinks is better. Then there's one that includes FM & costs about 299.99 & worth it if you live in the city & have the "it" to pay for it. KLH is usually said to be "best in price range" in audiophile reports — which seem to have a funny idea of what peanuts cost.

On the other hand, this may be all a mare's nest, since in Vermont Joe told me that the chanteuse Hildegarde[516] had died in abject indigence & now I see she's singing in some swanky supper club in N.Y.C. — causing my white hairs to turn dowager blue.

By the way, I hope it was clear that my Russian postcard was a thank you note for the Ukrainian picture. It's beautiful & I admire the artist for making the leaves identifiable. I've hung it in the bathroom but turned to the wall, because of the salacious caption.

Don't forget you're going to send me a poem. Do you think *Adventures in Poetry* is the place for "Within the Dome"?[517] Should I send it or will you, or is it some place else? Did you see a poem about Vermont I sent Kenward a while ago? If not I'll send it to you. I changed it some, though very little & not enough. The fine art of polishing the midnight oil (or whatever it is called) is a closed book to me.

515. Marguerite Long (1874–1966), pianist and teacher who championed the music of Fauré. Over twenty years later Schuyler wrote his poem "Fauré's Second Piano Quartet."

516. Hildegarde (1906–2005), credited with being the first American singer with one name.

517. Padgett / Schuyler collaboration written on Great Spruce Head Island.

Who'd've guessed that Fauré's first piano quartet is even more thrilling than the second? It's like an excited whisper.

Give my love to Pat & Wayne.

love,

Jimmy

(This may well be the only letter I write with a Pentel on a book in my lap in '68)

TO JOHN ASHBERY

[East Aurora, New York]

Jan. 27, 1968

Dear Carolyn Court,

My mother is better, and my message for you is, just be glad you can get yours to see a doctor, when needful. I think she was a little bit torn between getting better quick and making a good demonstration, and not doing so and keeping me here longer. Oof—that sentence puts me in a pretty light—it never occurred to me to cut out while she was sick, on the other hand, I'm not geared to watching someone get sicker while enjoying the benefits of a Boston-based Conjure Woman.[518]

I'm sorry you're not handy so we could have a quick one at the Roycroft Inn, followed by a Prime Steal at "The Block and Cleaver," which also offers an all-you-can-eat smorgasbord for a dollar extra. I haven't been inside, but the outside is alarming enough, featuring three giant flambeaux, from which flaming gas streams 24 hours a day. My three year old niece can't be driven past it, since the sight of same brings on hysterics. After dinner we could go for a drive on Girdle Road and admire the Country Club.

The local Loblaw's also has the first semi-automated checkout: a kind of

518. This could refer either to Mary Baker Eddy or to a generic Christian Scientist based in Boston (where the mother church is located).

toothed treadmill grabs the basket on your cart and empties it, then an arm reaches out and hurls the cart at you while the girl at the checkout hollers, "Watch out! Watch out!" The first time it nearly got me. It's my impression that Loblaw's is soon going to be pelted to death with cracked eggs by enraged East Aurora housewives.

Did you know: that until the 1870s East Aurora was known as Willink? (No, there is no adjacent town of Barkie). Or that Elbert Hubbard[519] had a grand-child named Elberta Hubbard? Or that Buffalo has a sinister little street called Ashbury Alley? (Another spelling, perhaps?)

I enclose a few gleanings from the *Courier Express* and *Buffalo Evening News*. After reading William P. Mulhall's column, I'm sure you'll redo your apartment in aqua, old gold and toast. I especially like the sub-head, "Fringed Draperies a Brightener."

There's about a foot of snow on the ground and a steady drizzle is falling. I have a wondrous sinus pain, but all the same I guess it's time to drag down to Dunk Hill's and see if I'm neither too early or too late to get a *Sunday Times*
 . . . love,

Jimmy
Connie Marie Talluto Paa

PS My sister-in-law's cooking (duck with bread stuffing, whipped potatoes, but-tered succotash, choice of pie) is playing old Ned with my diet; that is when my mother's freezer-full of butter-rich coffee cakes isn't playing hob with it. Although advised by me to climb into her Castro Convertible and watch television, I believe she is out in the kitchen this minute, adding chopped maraschino cherries to some coconut frosting. Help!

Oh: The sleeper coach was tested and found perfectly acceptable, once the ini-tial claustrophobia wore off. The difference is that the bed *completely* fills the compartment (except for a teeny space by the door, where one stands while low-ering the bed). The WC *is* completely sealed, but, I had an Edison-like break-through, and discovered that if the washbasin is placed in a partially open po-

---

519. Elbert Hubbard (1856–1915), writer who in 1893 founded the Roycrofters, a commu-nity of craftsmen in East Aurora, New York, the town where Schuyler grew up. Schuyler described Hubbard's ideas as "A lot of bullshit . . . [but] there was a certain romance in my life from living in a place associated with him . . . "

sition *before* lowering the bed, it can then be kept open. Otherwise, of course, it won't open at all. Since you are addicted to wee-hours facials as I am, I know you'll value the hint from Heloise . . .

TO RON PADGETT

Southampton, New York

Feb. 23, 1968

Dear Ron,

I'm rather a new hand at this "How Lava Soap solved my complexion problems" endorsement writing, so perhaps you'd best cast a weather eye over it. Or one of the others if you prefer. In fact a spell might not be a bad idea. If it's too far off track, let me know and I'll change it. I hope nothing in it causes you to suffer mental anguish or a burning sensation. I put the "his generation" in the last sentence not because I know a lot of dark horses in some other group, but because it sounded a little too much without it . . .

By the way, I hope you have asked Kenneth for a letter. Not so long ago, one evening when we had gazed upon the wine when it was red, we let down Janice's hair and agreed that you had the most IT in your—awk—that word again! peer group. Yes, that's better. I'm sure his opinion carries weight, even with people who may not be all that crazy about him. He is rather a nice old Bozo.

Who is putting whom on in the Michael B sweepstakes? And how many poets are there who'll answer to those call letters? You're very mistaken if you think I'd lie around reading M [Michael] Benedikt when I could be floating face down in a pond. On the other hand, I can't share your enthusiasm for M. Brownstein's[520] *Locus Solus* poems—remarkable though they are for a thirteen year old. His later things however, I like a lot, and can only wonder why both you and David [Shapiro] are so set against him. Still, it's none of *my* business.

Say, now that you've doubled your bump investment, why don't you take them to your friendly local clinic and let some conjure woman have a peek? (I'm a great believer in my friends seeing as many doctors as often as possible. For myself, I prefer a blend of Watchful Waiting, It Can't Happen Here, and This, Too, Will Pass.)

---

520. Michael Brownstein (b. 1943), poet. Schuyler dedicated the poem "Bleeding Gums" to Brownstein. It appeared in *Hymn to Life* (1974).

I'll do something about the poems right away, which doesn't mean right now. First I have to finish explaining to the panting readers of April *Art News* why Nell Blaine[521] is the greatest painter who resides at 210 Riverside Drive. Or at 200 or 220 for that matter. Love to Pat and Wayne.

Love,

Jimmy

TO RON PADGETT

[Southampton, New York]

March 17, 1968

Dear Ron,

Don't you think it's rather odd of the Irish to choose green for their favorite color? It's like living in Death Valley and only liking beige, ecru and bone-white.

So you accuse me of pulling a Ted Berrigan, eh. Well, you can unbend your knee and get up now, here's the carbon of the mss., which I'm going to re-entitle, *Total Impact* (with a credit for you). I'm sorry about the Xerox, every time I went to Dunkerley's, Tiny Wilson (guess how much *he* weighs? Well, not quite that much, but close) said they, or it, were/was booked for the day. To be truthful, that happened both times I went. You see, it was rather a touchy situation, since we've been feuding about a 2-drawer file. Last November I bought one at mark-down, a "floor sample," which seems to involve quite a bit of kicking and gashing, on the understanding that an exchange of drawers "in the next week or two" would convert it into a lockable file. To make it short, on Friday, to my great surprise, I finally won, and now have a new 2-drawer that locks and without paying the difference. I don't know how this came about, and it is just the sort of seeming good luck that makes one feel suspicious.

You have to admit that's a pretty exciting story I just told you.

Back to poetry. Mine, I mean. I've marked in the contents which poems are published, and where. Oh: I intend to take out "A Head" and put in "Now and Then." And maybe "Milk". Otherwise . . . I'm very glad you like "December," me too. I always have a fond spot for a poem that I'm surprised to have written,

---

521. Schuyler's article "Nell Blaine: The View from 210 Riverside Drive" appeared in the May 1968 *Art News* and is reprinted in *Selected Art Writings*.

or almost didn't, or that so to speak wrote itself. Hmmm. Oh well. Pick what you like (though I'd much prefer you didn't pick "A Head," "Dorabella's Hat" or "Grand Duo," which was in a *Locus Solus* you probably have). It probably makes no difference, but the only poems of mine which could be said to have had a wide circulation are the four in Don Allen's *New A. P.* (Now I have to stop and take Bruno out in the rain, so he can put his big muddy feet on my cream colored pants.)

Walking in the rain wasn't as inspiring as I thought it would be.

Say, what do you think of the title *Freely Espousing*? For the book, that is? No one I have asked (Kenneth, John, Arthur Chen) likes it. Any suggestions? I think *Poems* would be nice myself, but I suppose it's not stylish enough.

Guess I'll pop in three unpublished duds for you to look at. The one called "Couplets" is a collage (as are "Walter Scott" and "A New Yorker"). I don't know anything about the one called "Say," except that I may have meant it to sound like a collage. I don't think it does though. "3:30" I wrote in 1956, and it may be a little *too* self-explanatory.

If you send the mss back as soon as you can, it would be nice. I finally got tired of not hearing from Doubleday and wrote to Lynn Nesbit to find out who it was I wasn't hearing from and learned that it is George P.[522] who hasn't been hearing from me. Perhaps I should have written him a cringing thank-you note. On the other hand, perhaps he would like to go fuck himself with his triangle. But don't tell Maggie Paley[523] (or anyone else on *The Paris Review* for that matter).

That paragraph slightly reveals that I have been in a foul mood for the last couple of weeks and will continue so until I get caught up on some stuff of no interest to anyone, me least of all. I'm also very angry* with John Ashbery for the first time since 1954 (no, '58), although he is not aware of it. Yet.

You're quite right about "the last band on side two" and I also like "End of the Season," which is the way *all* popular music used to sound. At high school dances anyway. What's the status of your new phonograph? Does that mean you have it?

I've been enjoying the Busoni piano concerto,[524] one of the few in five move-

---

522. Nesbit was literary agent for Ashbery and Schuyler's *A Nest of Ninnies*. George Plimpton (1927–2003) was editor of *The Paris Review*. *Freely Espousing* was published by Doubleday as a Paris Review Edition.

523. Editorial assistant on the *Paris Review*.

524. Busoni's Concerto in C Major, op. 39, which Schuyler once described as "a runaway train."

ments, and with a male chorus (" . . . the poem dies away" they thunder).
Fewer piano concertos still have so much to offer the tympanist, particularly in
the kettle drum area. The best part is when Tashkent swims into view, to the
rejoicing of the Smyrna fig dealers.

I was extra sorry to miss Joe's party, since he wrote me from Jamaica that this
time he was getting tan "on my back side too." Can't wait for the viewing.

love to Pat and Wayne,

love,

Jimmy
*(Perhaps "chilled" is the word)

TO JOHN ASHBERY

Southampton, New York

Mothering Sunday, 1968

Dear Regencey Rake,

I trust the Squire gave you and the other 'prentices the day off so you could
take your mums the traditional simmel cake (for further details, see my *More
Other Days and Ways*, Country Life Press, 1903).

I thought I'd better tell you a couple of proof changes which will certainly
not be fresh in my mind by Wednesday. For one, you did say, didn't you, that
you've made the Saint Francois, in English, I mean, of course? Anyway, it's
Francis de Sales–all pronounced as in English, including the duh. I believe
only a choice few rate this accolade: Joan, the other, or, big Francis . . . in fact,
I even looked it up to make sure it wasn't "of" rather than "de," but it isn't. This
caused me some hard thinking until I remembered the precedent of St Philip
Neri and relaxed. I guess America isn't quite ready for a Saint Phil Black—
though now I see it in type I see it's what we need most.

The other change is that I did take out the italics you said you liked (Marshall: . . . it say in *this*.") Before you reach for the can of Mace, let me explain.
But first, a word from Bruno. Blap blap. What I'd forgotten on the phone was
that it's a repeat of *your* much funnier line on the previous page (Alice: . . . I was
rewarded with *this*.) So . . .

I had quite a bit of fun with the Italian . . . for instance, while climbing
through the jungle gym of Hoare's Shorter I fell afoul of "fru, fru," which I

always thought was the name of somebody mentioned in *The Merry Widow*. Not on your OED: "the dull murmuring of a crowd, e.g. at the beginning of a seditious rising; rustling of silk dresses; *far fru fru*, to dash at a thing; *donna fru fru*, woman who wants to do everything at once." Exciting? I also wanted to reassure myself that Barye[525] wasn't in the creche when "Ile Bourbon," was last used (1848 for safety, 1850 in the broader view). Well, we can all relax. It's true that his "Jaguar devouring a Hare" dates from 1852, but as early as 1831 he was causing a stir with his "Tiger devouring a Crocodile." Always some new thrill in the 11th Edition.

The goodies gave me quite a surprise: when I opened your letter there was a shower of tiny somethings. I was relieved to find it wasn't a lot of costly cannabis seed. (Which reminds me: a 30 year old male, described in the *Southampton Press* as an author-playwright, was lately hauled in for growing pot in his bedroom. Wonder who squealed?)

Ron writes me that in their (his and David's) anthology, one Guest[526] won't be among those star-scattered on the grass. I guess it's time to head for the hills.

Some people we might think about (you doubtless have) as *A Nest* winds towards its final can-can are Giorgio's relatives in this country and Memmo's married sister in Elizabeth. I also thought that if we should decide it needs some beefing up, *I* wouldn't mind a visit to the—help—I've forgotten their names: the French consul from Honolulu and his wife.

On second thought, I realize it's a case of "more would be less."

love,

Jimmy
Petunia Think Petunia

(One of the "Entrancing New Flowers Developed For You on Our 100th Anniversary" along with Dianthus Zing, Zinnia Zipasee and Impatiens A-Go-Go.)

---

525. Antoine-Louise Bayre (1796–1875), French *animalier* sculptor.
526. Editors Ron Padgett and David Shapiro left Barbara Guest out of *An Anthology of New York Poets* published by Random House in 1970.

TO JOHN ASHBERY

[Great Spruce Head Island]

June 26, 1968[527]

Dear Hosty with the Mosty,

And a very happy Arthur Cohen's[528] birthday to you too, dear.

Well here I be, and just as happy as an unsteamed clam. The sky is a rather dense gray, of a shade that in Southampton would have me humming "Gloomy Sunday" but here seems just another of Maine's little miracles. Of course it helps to have it reflected on the bosom of the bay (which would place its cunt somewhere down around Vinalhaven) where for some reason it picks up a faint purplish flush. Oh well, I won't lay it on too thick . . .

We made it here, which is about as much as I can say for the trip. I'm afraid FP is emotionally unable to think of a drive as anything but another Dunkirk. In New London I did manage, by dint of taking Bruno for a quick trot, to peek into an antique shop window where I spotted two student lamps, one of them desirable at 70 simoleons — much nicer than the smaller one Inez [MacWhin-nie] recently rid herself of for a cool 65. Bruno, contrary to my expectations, turned out to be the best traveler of all, and we did not arrive covered with hair and dog vomit. He was, however, quite a sketch at the Camden Yacht Club. It was an unusually mean low tide, and he took one look at the abyss that divided the almost vertical gangplank from the seawall and refused to budge. F and I must have made quite a sight as he pulled in front and I attempted to pour his hindquarters after — judging, at least, by the chuckles lavished on us by the local tars. Then we went through it all again getting him off the float and onto the Kittiwake. Fortunately I was by then in such a state that I more or less picked him up and hurled him aboard, rather like wee Geordie tossing the caber. The arrival was quite easy, since I had become a stone.

I hope Aline Porter (wife of Eliot, the painter who "shows" at Betty Parson's) is still here when you come. She's very *Nest*. She came up to help yesterday afternoon, and decided to make beds. She vanished for a long time, her little velvet bow bobbing behind her, then reappeared murmuring in her couth Boston tones, "Anne, where is the linen closet?" There, a good deal later, I found her

---

527. On this day Schuyler wrote in his diary, "Delicately and thoroughly overcast, cool above and the water with a rosy cast, and the more distant island a blue with a low hum to it."
528. Arthur Cohen, novelist and publisher who published *A Nest of Ninnies*.

sighing that there were no double sheets. So I dug some out of last year's clean laundry (it winters in a basket, don't ask why). Then she slowly made three beds and returned to the kitchen to announce, "Well, there doesn't seem to be anything else I can do . . . " as she eyed with evident horror the chaos and filth, and faded from our sight. She has a remarkably silly, though good natured, scottie, and at one point when I was out in the front inspecting the weeds with Mousie or whatever it's called, Aline's head popped out of an upstairs window long enough to coo, "Sweetheart didn't know I was up here did she?" and popped back in again. As a matter of fact, she makes a rather refreshing change from the nautical know-it-alls who usually clutter the float at mail call. Yesterday she had been to Camden to do some "shopping," which appeared to consist of a dozen eggs, a large brown bag that went clink clink and a pair of scales with charming early Atlantic & Pacific Tea Company Designs. So you see . . .

Say, how would you like to do a girl a favor? I refer to Anna. I promised to pick up a paperback Italian cookbook for her at Bob Keene's, but all he had was one that seemed to have been written by the chef at the Minetta Tavern. So, if you're ankling by your local paperback outlet, and have a mind to . . . and if you haven't, no one will be the wiser.

If these pangs speak true, it's lunch time. More later.

Two days later and a few hours earlier

What a lovely surprise the floating postman brought me yesterday—I can't wait to follow Bonita[529] on her adventures among the sinister spruces. Do you think the author is really Nancy Straus? Thanks oodles.

In case you're sweltering—*pace* Wednesday's *Times*—we're enjoying a mighty cool 49 degrees and what appears to be the beginning of at least a three day blow. Another of Maine's little gifts that I won't look into the mouth of. Have you heard anything from *Harper's Bazaar*? I ask, to be lucid, because I'm feeling decidedly broke, and not without reason. Heaven be praised for thrifty islands.

If this is to make today's mail, I'd best interrupt myself. I have some thoughts on the final chapter, but they'll keep a few days. Besides, I ran a huge spruce

---

529. Schuyler was reading *Bonita Granville and the Mystery of Star Island.*

splinter (beastly tree) into my thumb, which makes anything but eating, reading and sleeping rather hell. (Last night I went in before dark and, despite a 10 minute period of wakefulness, managed to sleep until 7:30. Bliss.)

We're presently (and hopefully) expecting the arrival of Laurence with a party of seven—there *will* be a lot of milling about the larder! In fact, I'm thinking of stashing a box of prunes or two under my bed.

love,

(Mrs) Birdsey Youngs

> Mrs Birdsey Youngs recently gave her tenth Book Report on the book, "Those Who Love" by Irving Stone. The book deals with the life and times of John and Abigail Adams and Mrs Youngs gave her report in period costume complete with cap. She has given it to the Sound Avenue Grange, the Sound Avenue Women's Fellowship, the Mattituck Historical Society and recently at a Fellowship meeting at the Riverhead Congregational Church which honored Miss Eva Terry. These are among other places and word has gone out how very well she does Abigail Adams.

TO JOE BRAINARD

[Great Spruce Head Island]

July 6, 1968

Dear Joe,

It was wonderful to get your long letter today: because it was from you, because it was today, and because it was my first piece of "real" mail. John A. did send me a book—*Bonita Granville and the Mystery of Star Island*—which I've been reading a drop at a time (a sample: "Bonita opened her lips to say, 'Yes,' but no sound came. She coughed and then said the word, 'Yes.'") And an envelope addressed by Ron came but it was just a Xerox letter about the anthology. So you see, I was very ripe for a great letter. Especially since the fog came in and filled the house with restless noisy people which made work this morning futile (which of course I don't mind quite as much as you would—except it wouldn't make work futile for you). The fog is lifting some now and I can see as far as the boats but dimly.

First, small practicalities: yes, please do snip off the heads of flowers that have bloomed, the rose and pansies I mean, the others won't bloom again no how. But only if you're cutting some anyway. It should give you more blooms in August.

Maybe John would water the plants since you do the stove, and I sometimes watered his. Most of them don't need much, though the big begonia in the white pot can take almost as much water as one gives it. I usually use a white enamel tea pot—big, fat and kitcheny looking—that is probably somewhere in the pantry. The spout makes it easy to pour water into the saucers. Most of the ratty looking things in the living room are geraniums, and do best if let get a bit dry between times.

No books should have come for me (the dopes—at the post office I mean) so if you would forward them, I would appreciate it. Just cross out that address and put on this one and drop them in the box at the corner. Did any magazines for me come there? If so I'll write to the postmaster and straighten it out. I did mark the card to forward everything. Oh well, the mail service gets worse and worse. It counts as one of my Pet Peeves. In fact, perhaps it's my *very* pet ("For pity sake don't get him started on junk mail . . ." the more serious things, like pollution, I let Fairfield worry about).

Glad to hear the stove is perking along all right. It really is just about fool proof, as I've often proved to myself—but F. always speaks of it in such a passionate way that I think people sometimes get a slightly doomed feeling about it, like the one door Fatima couldn't unlock in *Bluebeard*. It's much better for most meats (roasted or baked covered) than the electric stove. And so much for that.

Since I've been here I've mostly written one poem,[530] which I'm afraid to look at (it's about the fire, and I think what I like in it is something about a couple of dogs pissing on a hot oil drum incinerator) and some of my diary, though not much. I think I told you that people never get into it—perhaps because I'm secretly afraid others might keep Roremish diaries and put things about me in them, and if I don't, they won't—like knocking on wood.[531] And I've been typ-

---

530. The first section of "Cenotaph," which appeared in *The Crystal Lithium*.
531. Roremish—resembling Ned Rorem's diary.

ing up some poems to send to the man who published *The Champ*,[532] who wants to see something of mine. And so he shall.

That doesn't sound quite so lazy as I thought it would. Actually, I haven't been lazy, and jump out of bed at 7:30 at the very latest. It doesn't make the day seem very long. But somehow it's mostly only here that I get to sleep early enough to do it—partly because here is about the only place I know where I can get out and exercise, like swimming (brrr) or walking without destroying the continuity of my thought, so I do it more, and sleep better. That's my theory anyway.

Laurence Porter, and wife Betsy and son Leon and friends the Berchands with their daughters, Monica and Juana, all leave on Monday, the day after tomorrow. Because of Betsy, who is a strain, I would be utterly glad except that Anne is so happy to have them here. This morning Betsy almost succeeded in picking a fight with Fairfield, and the subject was wonderfully typical: steel mixing bowls. As near as I can make out, she would like to fill the house with them (she is an architect, along with her other faults). F. of course likes the old-fashioned, or real, earthenware kind.

Betsy: "They break!"

FP (on a rising note): "Not for twenty years they don't."

Betsy: (rising a note higher) "There's a big broken bowl *in there right now!*"

FP: "Some of these bowls have been there for fifty years!"

Betsy: "The other morning when I wanted to fix *Leon* his breakfast . . . " Needless to say, babies always have the last word, so F. went to walk it off in the fog and came back and offered her—or rather Laurence and Betsy—the choice of any painting of his they'd like to have. The terrible thing about the provoker is that one always has to remember that it does take two to make a fight, and since she is apparently helpless the decision lies with oneself. The closest she comes to getting my goat is at meals, when she pops Leon into his playpen by the table and then decides that this is the time to discipline him. "I'll put him to bed if he doesn't stop crying in five minutes or so." Since Bruno is right beyond the screen barking his head off to be let in (he can't be on the porch while we eat because "he takes Leon's toys"—I nearly split when I heard that one—Bruno is really terribly funny when he grabs a Creative Plaything out of the playpen and gallops off—the poor mutt seems to think life is all fun and games), anyway, meals get to be pandemoniumsville. I spend as much time as

532. Elmslie/Brainard collaboration, published by John Martin's Black Sparrow Press and reprinted by Geoffrey Young's The Figures Press (see glossary).

I can in the kitchen making coffee, and with a wood burning stove to abet me, that can take quite a healthy while.

Actually, this fiend has many admirable qualities—I have a feeling that if one stayed at her own house, she'd be sweet as pie—do you know the type? Or have you been luckier than I?

The kids are quite cute—Leon is about the age Wayne [Padgett] was last September in Vermont, and looks rather like him, but with a good dose of Winston Churchill mixed in, especially from the back. Juana (pronounced *Hhhh-wanna*), who is three, is very dark, Latin looking and full of beans. She gave me quite a turn when she spilled her milk the other afternoon and said in a small gentle voice, "Oh. Shit." She also likes to pummel me quite a lot, and to be "read" to out [of] a dreary book about a little girl who went West without any shoes on. The reading consists of me describing what's in the picture we're looking at—"There's the grandma on the porch, see? And there's the well, and the fox . . . " until she finally points at the little girl's feet and says, "No shoes." Then on to the next.

Now I'm going to go make some more coffee (the kids drank all my Fresca—no more till Monday).

Later. When I went downstairs, Mary Berchand was sitting with Juana on her lap, and Betsy with Leon on hers, while the mothers played chess, like a couple of highbrow madonnas. I felt quite guilty about bitching B in this letter, and toyed with the idea of tearing it up and writing something more High Minded to you. However, while I was fixing my iced coffee (to match the weather) she came in and got off a Couple of Good Ones ("This *Kitchen!*" which was indeed a mess, since Anne has been cooking steadily since 7 a.m.) so I regained my equanimity.

What's turning me on lately, in a pleasanter way, is grasses, which are in bloom right now. I'll bet there are some nice ones in the field there right now. Up here anyway, they're blooming, and while the flowers don't amount to much, without a magnifying glass anyway, the way they open up, and the subtle colors, are quite something. Especially one which I think is called Quaking Grass, and which makes the best 18th century trembler I ever saw look clunky. (Have you ever seen a trembler in motion? A piece of jewelry with some of the stones mounted on fine wires, so they quiver all the time.)

Now it's about supper time, or will be very soon, so I'll go socialize. It seems to me that I had a lot of interesting things to tell you, some of which are in here. Well, that will be an excuse to write another letter.

If it's nice tomorrow morning I'll go into Stonington when Anne and Lizzie go to church and mail this there. It's an awfully cute town.

Love to the folks at your house.

Love,

J.

TO ALEX KATZ

Great Spruce Head Island

July 9, 1968

Dear Alex,

I just had a letter from Doubleday—well, not from Doubleday *himself*, but from one of the minions—from which I gather that they thought you would be getting in touch with them, *pace* George Plimpton, and that you were in New York, and so on. I imagine (vividly) that George P. said he would give you some message or other then skedaddled off to Indiana. Anyway, Walter Bradbury writes, ". . . but if our information means that he is going to be in Maine all summer, perhaps you would be seeing him (I have no idea where Lincolnville is in relation to Sunset) and would have him call our art director collect, to plan the mechanics of the jacket design. Our art director is Mr Alex Gotfryd." And his telephone number is: 212 TA 6-2000.

Don't you think *Our Art Director* sounds like a novel by Trollope? And I'm all for some Mechanics on the jacket, wearing gray twill work shirts, snap-on bow ties and jaunty caps . . .

Here are the poems that are going to be in it.[533] Most of them you've seen before. This is the only copy I have up here, so could you send it back in a week or so . . . (Having it Xeroxed turned out to be beyond my powers.)

We began the summer with ten days of seven guests (Laurence Porter, wife and babe, and another French professor with wife and two babes). They were all very nice, but somehow it's *not* the way to begin. I feel as though I'm still moving beds, and there's something extra maddening about an army of people all trying to do the dishes. It consists mostly of a chorus of, "Where does *this* go?" while various enormous and rusty objects you've never seen before are

533. *Freely Espousing*, for which Alex Katz provided a collage for the cover.

thrust under your nose. But things have subsided now, and Fairfield immediately painted a terrific gray picture (early morning sunlight on the side of the house with a couple of windows. Or rather, a triangle of sunlight on a gray wall).

Have you and Ada discovered the great new old book store in Camden yet? It's on the street to the Yacht Club, a few doors beyond the one that goes down to the Public Landing (on which is quite a nice antique shop I don't remember being there two years ago). I was able to snap up Walter Scott's Journals, two vols., a book of Mendelssohn's letters and an especially minor novel of Harriet Beecher Stowe's for $7—. Lots and lots of 19 centuryana.

A fresh sheet and I think I hear the mailboat.

Love to Ada (thanks for the great card) and Vincent (thanks for the great thank you letter).

Anne and Fairfield and Liz are all dandy; so is Bruno, the dog, and me too.
love,

Jimmy

P.S. "The photograph of the author" was put in by Ron Padgett.

TO JOHN ASHBERY

Great Spruce Head Island

July 13, 1968

Dear Joseph Hergesheimer,[534]
First things first: I'm afraid I can't help you with your Sherwood Anderson query, since I spend a good deal of time sedulously avoiding his works. This is not because I dislike them, but because I don't know much about them and prefer to keep it that way. When I was a child, back in the days of flagpole sitters, Billie Dove, the Golddust Twins and Knee-Hi Grape, a baby sitter once treated me to a read from what I've always fondly imagined was a novel of his, which concerned the thoughts of a man while hopping the midnight freight to get away from his wife. So I've always imagined that true maturity would be to read, enjoy and understand a Sherwood Anderson novel. A day I hope to postpone as long as possible.

---

534. Joseph Hergesheimer (1880–1954), American novelist who wrote best-sellers in the 1910s and 1920s.

(Liz says I promised to go swimming *right now*. Well, I wouldn't want to keep Rose Anne Shepherd waiting . . .)

July 14th. Good grief, it's almost time to go swimming again. Though I may just skip it. Even if it is mighty warm for Maine, it's still damn cold.

Well, since breaking off yesterday, life has been more than usually exciting. First there was a dip in the cove, with the exciting Haskell children from Stonington. Then Bruno and I took a long walk. True to his character, the great gunshy duck retriever refuses to learn to swim. I spent quite a long time at Fisherman's Beach throwing sticks just out of his depth, and a couple of times actually got him to be briefly water-born. But he eluded my attempts to grab him by the collar and drag him in (these trys can only be made when Liz is not around). Then I found a thrilling new (to me) sort of cranesbill growing on the Double Beaches, *and* gooseberries. So home to supper, a few games of solitaire while Fairfield read some more of *Middlemarch* aloud (a marvelous book—how odious that Leavis[535] should be right about anything) and so to bed and up before the larks (5:30) and to Stonington, where I visited Bartlett's Market in search of local newspapers (rather dull today) and yearned through the closed antique shop window while Anne and Liz were at mass. And so the days wear away.

Apropos George Eliot: I don't remember *Silas Marner* as very funny-on-purpose, do you? *Middlemarch* is—it's sort of a highbrow *Barchester Towers*,[536] or so I conclude at this point. We've only decimated its thousand pages. Do you, by the way, have any inside info on how to pronounce Mr Casaubon? I suppose it's anglicized . . .

I'm sorry you missed the visit to the island of Mike Straus's Parisian cousins, minus any English at all. Well, the couple didn't have any, but their postcollege son, who works for a farm-machinery branch of Sperry-Rand in Lancaster, Pa., had a little, so I cottoned on to him—though without ulterior motive, since the person he most resembled is David Sachs. He seemed quite startled when I suggested that Lancaster is a rather pretty city. It would have pleasured your ears to hear him pronounce Ottawa. I had my usual *fleuve-riviere-ruisseau* French conversation, and learned to distinguish a *crique* from a — I forget what—an *ance*, perhaps? I'm sorry I've forgotten their last name, which was nice and plain, but Mama's first name was Monique. I wish they had stayed longer. It's nice that the French have such an instructive bent. I'm sure one

535. F. R. Leavis (1895–1978), British literary critic of the mid-twentieth century whose forcefully expressed opinions were influential.

536. Novel by British novelist Anthony Trollope (1815–1882).

could sustain a lengthy cocktail party simply by asking the names of the Departments of France. (Hmmm — it just occurred to me that that may be my own one Gallic quality.)

I loved your ad. in the *New York Review of Books*, and have been dining at home for a week on the story that you are on tour with Bobby and Arthur in the two piano reduction of *Façade* . . . [537]

Tee-hee.

The Portland paper of a few days back got used to start a fire before I could cut out a recipe for you, Golfball Dessert. However I doubt that you would have wished to make it: chocolate sludge containing angel food cake torn into pieces the size of golfballs. Mold and chill.

If you've a mind to try Irma's[538] fool-proof popovers, you may do so with this caution: if you use individual custard cups do not, as she suggests, try to line them up on a whippy cookie sheet. When you pick up the sheet, you will see why. The survivors were delicious. As was my Swedish tea ring, for which I invented a memorable currant-cardamom filling (and how). It brought gasps from the Laurence Porters and friends, so I didn't risk any squeals until they had left. The meat pie, for which I preferred CHICKEN POT PIE TOPPING (pg 421) however . . . Irma says it will soak up a lot of gravy. But only, I find, if contact is intimately established between gravy and topping. Otherwise all you get is Beef Stew Under a Cloud, and a cloud which is rather like biting into a motel pillow.

There is a phonograph here, but it is not of an epoch you could do much for. The records that go with it have grooves on only one side. In fact, I played one for you (the trio from *I Lombardi*, I believe) but it seemed to suggest to you that your presence was required at the crowning of the Miss Maine Broiler Queen in Bangor, so I turned it off.

Now I can't find your letter before last, 'case it contained any queries. Shucks. But the "tawny hockey pucks" are unforgettable.

Guess I will pull on my impeccably tailored Lastex trunks that have lost their stretch and my dyed-to-match pearlized Keds and go for a dip. Marian Christy[539] to the contrary, I wouldn't mind a bit having a gray mink boa over my shoulders on this heavily air-conditioned island.

---

537. *Façade* (1922), music and spoken word collaboration by British composer William Walton and British poet Edith Sitwell.

538. Irma S. Rombauer, author of *Joy of Cooking*.

539. Newspaper columnist.

Keep me posted as plans mature for your projected swing through the New England States. And don't forget to leave time for a bite at Wildwood Park.

love,

Starling F. Scruggs

TO JANE FREILICHER AND JOE HAZAN

[Great Spruce Head Island]

July 17, 1968

Dear Jane & Joe,

It's three in the morning—I can't believe it, but I was woken up by the *heat*. To think that the land of the frosted firs should become the hot squat of the north. This afternoon—well, yesterday afternoon—at lunch time in the shady porch the thermometer hit an unprecedented 94 and even Fairfield downed brushes and went & threw himself in the cove. (Anne was truer to her New England rearing and elected to sweep their broiling hot room, then cook a pot-roast for the Eliot Porters.) At the cove we found Nancy Strauss, whose memory is one-up's-manship personified—Fairfield made the mistake of saying it was the hottest it's ever been on the island—"Oh-I don't know—(which is Nancy's version of, I know for a fact-it was really *much hotter* the summer the Browns came and brought the summer flu. There were *four cots* out on the porch and it was so hot father took everyone off in the Hippocampus[540] during the day. Everyone who could go, that is.") Then she chuckled a lot—perhaps at the last sentence as an instance of the Porters' passion for accuracy, perhaps at the thought of four summer flu victims abandoned in their cots while the others went yachting. So I left the cove's tepid delights (actually put down by a visitor as "like swimming in baked Alaska") and went to truly frigid Landing Beach and *sat* in the water.

The Porter family saga, especially when Nancy has the podium, is cluttered with people like "the Browns" who suddenly erupt, waving madly, and are never heard from again. Others are more persistent, in their small way—rather on the order of the butler Yasha in (Anton Chekov's) *The Cherry Orchard*. Two such families just sailed away on the North Star—the last schooner built at the

540. Fairfield Porter's father, James's, motorboat, which the family sold after James died in 1939.

Camden shipyard—Mr and Mrs Foote and the Bob Sawdecks. The latter Lizzie described as "a man who looks like he smoked a pipe and with a rather wide wife. They have a euphonious name that begins with S." All I know about the Footes is that Mike Strauss always refers to them as—of course—the feet.

What are you reading these dawnings? F. and I are reading *Middlemarch* aloud—I suppose everybody else has read it already—I had no idea it would be so funny—and, to myself, another Theodore Fontane, *Beyond Recall*. It, too, is very funny; and very, very beautiful; and very, very, very sad, already (I'm about a quarter of the way through). He has an eerie way of making the story he's telling you seem the necessary background to the story's he's leading up to, which, however he will never get to tell. And the novel begins by the sea during an Indian summer that last and lasts—like all good novels that start warming up the tear ducts before you know what you're going to cry about.

How are your Skowhegan plans coming? A word to the wise—we got to the Orient Point Ferry a half-hour before time and had to wait for the next ferry, and they don't run all that often. Perhaps if you phoned them they would suggest a safe margin—the day of the week seems to make a difference. (Monday morning, when we went, counts as bad.) Let me know when you're coming, and I'll reserve space for you in the mailboat—by law he can only carry six and is often booked up. If you can get to Sunset by 10 a.m. you can come out on the mail run in time for lunch (steamed scrod). Otherwise you have to come after 1 p.m.—Sunset is about 65 miles from the Katz area (allow for twisty roads) and about three hours from Skowhegan. That's how long it took us (me & the Padgetts, that is) last September in the dark, which has a noticeable effect on the speed at which Ron drives. Yes, he really likes to barrelass along. Shudder.

I do believe Morpheus is trying to tell me something—should I listen? He's so seldom counted on—

How is your Elizabeth? Our Liz (say, that's quite a nifty title) is nubile.

Guess I'll wake up everybody & see if they want to send their love: they do—and Bruno says to give Elizabeth a special "Woof."

It'll be great to see you—

love,

Jimmy

TO TREVOR WINKFIELD [541]

Great Spruce Head Island

July 19, 1968

Dear Trevor Winkfield,

It was very cheering to get your kind letter yesterday, when I was recovering from a case of Bum Back, brought on by carrying a box of groceries which contained nothing I much wanted to eat, and feeling distinctly put upon and neglected. I'm sorry it took so long for *May (24th Or So)*, etc. to get to you; though if you ordered it from the Tibor de Nagy Gallery, I'm surprised you got it at all. I'll send you a copy of the *Paris Review* book when it's ready, next January.

Thanks very much for the copy of *JUILLIARD* [542] — I threw away the envelope it came in with some others, so when I wanted to find out who had sent it, I decided it must be Kenward Elmslie, on internal evidence. So much for scholarship. I liked the issue by the way, though not having it here, I can't be more specific.

I'll send you something very soon for the fall issue.

I would take it as a kindness if in your copy of *May 24th* you would strike out the date that appears at the end of (I think) "Penobscot" and write it in below and to the right of the title "Today." The pleasures of pedantry apart, it actually forms—good grief, what a word—*is* the dedication to a Catholic friend (Anne Porter) whose name day it is. So you see . . .

Do you see, or have you seen, a couple of mimeographed magazines, *The World* [543] and *Adventures in Poetry*? [544] They have quite a range of people in them, and if you would like them, I'll try to get copies sent to you. I have an extra issue of *Adventures in Poetry #2* (an all prose issue) and would be glad to send it to you. Though it might well end up burnt at the dock, since it contains some rather heady passages, particularly in the Padgett/Berrigan novel in progress. Hmmm. Perhaps I could unstaple it and send the offending pages as a letter. An invitation to deviousness is always a welcome challenge.

I don't know anything about Leeds, though I wish I did, but I seem to recall

541. See glossary.

542. Magazine edited by Winkfield.

543. Magazine edited by Anne Waldman of The Poetry Project at St. Mark's Church in-the-Bowery in New York City.

544. Publisher of mimeographed books and a magazine, all edited by poet Larry Fagin.

that one can, or could, go by Aire, by Humber and canal to Goole, a place where I should very much like to spend a few hours between trains.

The mailboat is tooting in the fog. With my best,

Jimmy Schuyler

TO RON PADGETT

[Great Spruce Head Island]

July 21, 1968

Dear Ron,

So you're back to tending oil-wells, eh, and with all your wampum on no doubt. I can see that those big hats "cowpokes" wear might be cool, but how can you walk in heels? My ankles always give way.

It's 8 a.m., I've been up for an hour and 32 minutes (ping, 33 minutes) and it's one of those mornings when it seems the First principle may not have been all thumbs after all—It certainly had some pretty nifty ideas about what constitutes a nice day—sun, no clouds, a little breeze, a sky fading out into peach in the south and green in the west, a few white boats dozing in the deep cerulean and a crow for laughs. On the other hand, it is quite a tease and we may be having storms of liquid shit by noon. Variety is indeed the spice of life but who wants to live on curried ice cream?

I like your strolling to hug loneliness poem. I've written one poem since I've been here that I'm not afraid to turn over and see the typing on. But I don't do that too much. Mostly I just let it lie there, in the mold. Sometimes the island is too inspiring. I rushed up here to the Green machine, ready to shoot, so to speak, but all that popped out was a wrinkled pea on which was stamped in meat-mauve the word, blue. Maybe I should get over the idea that the way to write a poem is to look out the window and put it all down. But I don't see why. And I also at the moment don't see how—

> *blue day*
> *turn back half an hour*

(hmmm rather Padgettesque; or perhaps more Padgettusk)

or
> *blue bay*
> *into which I cast myself*

> chatteringly
> as far as the chin

(or how about, Chattertoningly?)

or   *The sea is old.*
                          It has a blue rinse.

or   *in a cold sweat*
                          the bosom of the bay
                          heaved and out popped
                          a stone tit with
                          a cormorant on it

or   *roll on*
                          deodorant
                          in the salt pits
                          and clammy parts
                          not forgetting
                          behind the knees

or   *I can't swim in those spruce*

And that's enough of that. Oh good. There's a cloud over the sun. There's nothing more boring than unending blue.

I still don't know who, what, where, when, why or how many Kochs are coming. The thought of Kenneth the Menneth (as Kenward lately called him) here is faintly alarming. He fills up the house so with his Henry VIII impersonations and mad German Scientist impersonations and cries for meals between meals, and types so fast and long (I especially resent that), and never helps with the dishes, and that's very annoying, since really you don't want him to help, as, dish-wise, he's strictly a bull in a hoop-skirt. Still, it would be fun to see him. From my point of view he has rather more conversation than Koko (as she's called) — the latter always teams up with Lizzie in a giggling rhapsody for Sousaphones.

What are you doing with yourself la-bas? I bet if you searched all the junk and antique shops and seedy magazine stands you would find one postcard worth all your efforts. Let's see, here's what I imagine you doing: calling Dick Gallup[545] to tell him that a movie you saw with him in 1959 is on the late late show. Walk-

---

545. Dick Gallup (1941–2021), poet and Padgett's friend from their hometown of Tulsa, Oklahoma.

ing the dog. Answering the phone. It is Dick Gallup. He wants to read you an item from page 41 of yesterday's *Sooner* but you have already cut it out, altered a few words and sent it to Trevor Winkfield (loved your two stories; honest). Having a picnic on the grounds of the Normal School: chili with beans, prepared by Carol[546] and Pat. It's a big day for Wayne who 1) spits between his teeth without getting any on his chin and 2) finds his first four-leaf clover. Unfortunately he can't find another and is reduced to tears, and so dump him on Mrs. Mitchell[547] and go to the double bill: *Prudence and the Pill* and *Don't Raise the Bridge, Lower the River*[548] (or is it lower the water?). But what is this? The leaves are tuning. It must be Vermont. We are still around, eating Mrs. Kent's lace cookies and cutting up magazines in the dark while the gibbering farmer lurks in the canebrake with his .22 . . .

It's high tide and I'm going for a swim that will last exactly as long as it takes to get out. Which is sometimes quite long: it's hard to find your footing when crazed with fear. Let me get out of your icy clutch, please Thalassa.

A hearty "Howdy" to Wayne and love to Pat and to you,

Harry Frigg[549]

Later. The water wasn't warm but the sun was so I lay on the stones and felt at one with the fish and the seals until something gave me a tiny nip and sent me scuttling home.

Here's the latest antho-Xerox back, with a suggested order for the poems i.e. that in which they were written.

If you need more copyright material, lemme know and I'll see what I can drag up.

I will also hoke up my bibliography (isn't that something better left to Theodore Besterman and lessermen of his sort?) and bio. note—though I assure you that for artful brevity the latter will make your favorite epitaph in the Greek Anthology look like the works of Theodore Dreiser—unless I can do it all my own way, all lies. "Petit, thick-waisted JS, after earning his living caber-tossing . . ."

546. Carol Gallup, wife of poet Dick Gallup.
547. Pat Padgett's mother.
548. Fielder Cook directed *Prudence and the Pill* (1968), starring David Niven and Deborah Kerr. Jerry Paris directed *Don't Raise the Bridge, Lower the Water* (1968), starring Jerry Lewis.
549. *The Secret War of Harry Frigg* (1968) starred Paul Newman.

What by the way is slowing up the anthology? I think the public should get the beauty of it *hot*.

love,

Jimmy

P.S. "Buckie" Fuller,[550] as I don't call him, is building a new dome on Little Spruce Head! So on to *Within a Little Dome*.

TO ALEX KATZ

[Great Spruce Head Island]

July 23, 1968

Dear Alex,

The maquette — as *Art News* reviewers insist on saying, even when put out to grass — is absolutely beautiful. You certainly know what my poems aspire to; to which is not so much the condition of music (as Mallarme said — I *think* it was Mallarme) as a Katz-eye view. In fact, just the other day I found in a pocket notebook a note (what else?) and a scribble that seemed, and was, a drawing, made early last April on the Long Island train, of an overturned rowboat with some reeds bent over it by the wind: "among the rushes / brown gold after winter / a blue boat / the color of spring." Which left me feeling, I vividly remember that it was one of those sudden views of which only you could get the goods. To be brief, you're terrific.

Happy birthday. Is it today, or is today party day? Ada's card came yesterday on the non mailboat, and the Camden-trip-boat (LSD on the high seas) had left at ten, or one or more of us might well have decided to descend on you. We all hope to, before you pack the mattress in the Conestoga wagon and follow the sun. But your description of your social life — wow. Have you ever thought of trying an unlisted number? No wonder you want to stake a claim in the West.

Fairfield has painted a 7/8ths figure of Lizzie, which he describes as "Weak"; a picture of Anne, which he painted the face out of; a beautiful Harbor View, which he says, "Anybody could have painted"; the boathouses, which he says, "is always on the verge of dropping into an abyss of sentimentality, and probab-

550. Buckminster Fuller (1895–1983), architect, poet, and inventor of the geodesic dome His family summered on Little Spruce Head Island, visible from Great Spruce Head.

ly already has," (you know how given he is to gooey excess); he further states that, "I'm not getting anything done." So you see, all is well with the Master of the Maroger Medium.[551]

Also with Anne, with Lizzie, with Bruno and with me. We don't have any news here—that tide sets from your direction.

Love to Ada and Vincent,

love,

Jimmy

TO KENWARD ELMSLIE

Great Spruce Head Island

July 29, 1968

Dear Kenward,

It's 7:30 (a.m., I mean) and I've been up since five, by choice, that is. I've decided the early part is the best part, though it makes the rest of the day rather a let down.

The Hazans and peti' JA were here on their New England swing for a 40 hour layover—we only had time to show them the looms, the bottle museum and the place where they used to scutch the flax. Still, it was nice to see them and hear the Jane version of the Hampton Summer Story, with John's febrile footnotes. Goodness, the things that can happen under a bayberry bush . . .

For the island, it was rather a whirl—drinks at Mike-and-Nancy's, *and* after dinner at the Eliot Porters'. Wow. The next evening Joe conceded that he would play hearts since John won't play bridge, so we played what John wanted to play: Parchesi. Fairfield, Joe and I (Jane, who would rather read than compromise, having gone to bed) were keeling over with sleepiness, while John, who was rigid with boredom, forced us on to the long-postponed finish. Some folks sure find it hard to believe that they would ever, ever, ever be cast as a Loser. No, not even at Parchesi.

The weather has, by and large, been quite superb. In fact glorious—our one

---

551. The medium used by Porter was developed by Jacques Maroger, director of the conservation department at the Louvre, who claimed to have reconstructed Reubens's "black oil" medium. This made for paint that was slow to dry, enabling the painter to rework his painting with ease.

day heat-wave merely adding a tang to the cool nights—and what would Maine be without a dab of fog ever and anon? Joe got so overheated on an FP-type stroll-to-the-precipice that he stripped to the buff and plunged in, then pronounced the water eminently swimmable. A triumph, I feel. I always find it very touching when John turns out to be the energetic one—our walk was on a rather humid afternoon, and when others would have turned back (me, most of all) John persisted because he wanted "to see the seals again." Somehow, I never think of him as having that particular sort of ambition. I can hardly wait for his "The Indefatigable Traveler Visits Provo."

I hope your case of Athlete's Mind isn't interfering with the growth of the Orchid Stories?[552] I think the enclosed clipping might introduce a wonderful new character—Cap'n Jem Perry . . .

Oops, the Elizabeth A. is revving up, about to take me, Eliot and Aline Porter on another exciting visit to the fleshpots of Camden. Maybe this time Aline will let me have a peek at her "secret" antiques-&-junkyard shop in the environs of Owl's Head. Sure do hope so.

What, if any, are your September, or, festival of the leaves, plans? Hmm? That's not a hint, it's a plea.

Love to Joe—love & xxx's Jimmy

TO JOE BRAINARD

[Great Spruce Head Island]

July 31, 1968

Dear Joe,

Gosh, I forgot all about the horseshit. Well, no, we don't usually invite the horses over—did it happen more than once? I imagine they got loose by mistake, since they're always tethered, except when being ridden. But if it does happen again, just call up the Diefenbachs (they're in the book) and say, "Hi! I'm your summer next door neighbor—Joe Brainard, the famous artist. Well, I just called up to introduce myself and tell you that your cuntchewers are over here and if it happens again Jimmy Schuyler is personally going to cut their applesnatching throats with an onyx knife which he bought in Mexico just for that purpose. OK?" That ought to do the trick.

---

552. *The Orchid Stories* (1973), a novel by Elmslie published by Paris Review Editions.

Actually, the Diefenbachs are very nice and would be embarrassingly apologetic. Still, last year one of the horses did eat an apple tree.

A couple of other things I forgot: in the living room is, or was, a small wicker wastebasket about 1/4 full of "fingernail shells." They are yours for the carting. Also, I meant to take down some of the California wildflower wallpaper for you. Well, as you go toward the back of the house, near the back (my) bathroom, a lot of it is loose. Take all you want.

Cenneth and Catherine Cock are coming on Saturday (how funny—I was going to ask if you were aware that in your last letter you spelt his name "Kock" once—I just did more or less the same thing—I had meant to write, Coch; because I thought it would look funny, that's why). Which somehow makes the present—which is like the trough of a wave—seem even more fragile and precious, like a piece of very rare, beautiful old glass, the kind that seems to be always quivering. I'm also trying to get myself in the mood of feeling bored and starved for company. Well, he does like to talk about Literature with a capital L and so do I. Very few of the writers "we" like do. They prefer movies. Although Jane when she was here said she prefers to read the classics: "I've never known a classic to let me down." Then she did manage to think of one, but I can't remember what it was. Maybe *Our Mutual Friend*?

Gosh all hemlock, something else I forgot: the magazines finally began to come. It took some of them five weeks from NYC here, just being forwarded from Southampton. I got six copies of the *Times Literary Supplement* in three days—which is horribly like taking the Webster's Unabridged to read on the subway. Did you say that a book, or books, came for me there? And did you forward it if so? Nothing's come here, and I like to keep track, so I can reorder it if it gets lost in the mail. Is why I ask. Not to carp & criticize.

Well, I guess I'll see if I can get to the mailboat before it gets me. Oh I thought you might like to see the tracing of Alex's "rough" for my book jacket—I love it. Would you send it back when you and the Champ have gazed your fill? I like to take it out now and then and finger it (whoops—where did *that* sentence come from—).

Were our guys as moved as I by the Adamant P.O. story in the *Times*? Just bet you were. Tears came to my eyes when I got to the words, "Maple Corners."
love,

Jimmy
Leroy Blood
(a name I found in a local paper)

TO JOHN ASHBERY

[Great Spruce Head Island]

August 7, 1968

Dear Bouvardine,[553]

Kenneth is up, so it's all right for me to use my typewriter, which I hasten to do.

I loved your last from the Mecca of Minor Music — is the Clementi Concerto[554] the same as the one I have on a European label? — which seems to be a concerto only in some extremely general sense. It seems to be more of a Divagation, or perhaps a Meander. I'm beginning rather to miss my electrified Victrola . . . oh dear, I hope Sam Goody won't have any over-stimulating sales on when I come back with my *Ninny* advance in my hot little hand, to borrow an Arthur Goldism. There are so many other things I want! No doubt however when I see my share spelled out on a check I will cool down considerably.

I would have answered you more promptly, but the arrival of your letter co-incided with that of the Visitors from Porlock[555] — need I say things have been rather a whirl? Or perhaps a tizzy. K is very much, I must say, on his good behavior. Which, as you know, is none too . . . oops. No, he really is being quite saintly, judged by his own standards. Judged by more ordinary, everyday human standards, it is another story, and one which would scarcely be news to you. So far I haven't had to hand him any Tart Tongue, though he seemed to think otherwise when he gave me his weighty "base mss" (as he calls it) for his Forthcoming and I suggested he call it *Trilogy*. I get to read the equally voluminous alternate choices soon. In fact, he asked me last night as I toddled to my cot whether I would be free to begin discussing it this morning. I assured him all my mornings are bespoke and he said, "Oh is *that* when you write." Grrrr. Anne this morning said, or rather whispered since the very walls are paper, "*Please* give a terrible cry if the mailboat should come early. Kenneth says if the beer runs out he will lie on the floor and kick his heels and scream. And," she

---

553. Alludes to Bouvard of Gustave Flaubert's last, and unfinished, novel, *Bouvard and Pecuchet*.

554. Muzio Clementi (1752–1832), Italian composer.

555. "A person from Porlock" interrupted Samuel Taylor Coleridge while he was writing "Kubla Khan," the poem that came to him in a dream. When Coleridge returned to the poem, he had lost his train of thought and had to leave the poem as fragment.

added, turning a whiter shade of pale, "I wouldn't want *that* to happen." Oh well, he and KoKo are meeting MooMoo at the Rockland airport next Monday, then off on an Isle-au-Haut, Nova Scotian whirl. He has already "sounded" me on the possibility of our fetching Janice, bringing her here then providing transport to the distant reaches of Isle au Haut—the ferry from Stonington leaves at an inconveniently early hour, it seems. I have scotched this idea but I doubt that I've killed it. Oh well, Fairfield will have no trouble doing that.

I just went downstairs to get my Fresca (it's hotter than hinges) and greet the morning boy, who turned on me a face like a Pompeian potato. We didn't sleep so well, it seems, and are full of aches and pains from playing too much tennis and, "I'm allergic to *something on this island*," though not, it would seem, the food. Needless to say, any and all suggestions were rejected with scorn and contumely. So I find myself once more at one with your Elmira connections, long past caring.

Of course I heartily concur with your nixing a "cast of characters" (if that wouldn't be pulling our punches . . . ! I think it's most important that the reader should greet each fresh arrival on the scene with another gasp of incredulity) and by all means let's have Joe B. for cover artist. What I would like very much is if he used Roycroft type—there is a stunning example of it on the (I think) highboy in my room, *Elbert Hubbard's Scrapbook*. The colors are nice too. Do you think there's some good research material in your Bungalow book, perhaps? Why not let him (and KGE too, of course read Moira Manuscript and see what he comes up with? Needless to say, I look to you for a little inspiration too . . . (that's supposed to be a compliment, not an exhortation to get in there and pitch).

Any word from *Harper's B*? If they don't use the penultimate chapter (Say, how about "A Penultimate Chapter," as a title for it, if published apart?) why don't we let Maxine have a gander at it? I had a sweet note from Arthur G [Gold] in answer to a sweet note from me, in which he said, "and I've had some chats with John about minor points. He boffed me on all of them." Well, my message for you is, Keep Boffing.

As you no doubt are. And I only regret that the details of your visit to Skowhegan aren't such as can be confided to paper. Can't wait to hear all.

I got the contacts of the pictures taken while you were here and conclude that I am not the one who is going to rub any of the silver-gilt off Cecil Beaton's laurels. Oof. The few acceptable ones of you (and Jane) you will get to see in slow due course. Some I am committing to the flames . . .

I'm glad you took up the New York Society Library. I suspected it was rather one.

Have you mapped out your September tour yet? Do keep a feller up to date—

love,

Pecuchette

TO JOE BRAINARD

[Great Spruce Head Island]

August 13, 1968

Dear Joe,

Guess where I'm going tomorrow. Can't? Well, I'll tell you, at the end of this letter—maybe. Or maybe I'd rather surprise you with a postcard.

I loved your latest bushel o'letter. The desserts sound formidable and very good. Last Saturday I made three coffee cakes, a Rome apple cake (beloved by all "mankind," Irma Rombauer says—it is very yummy—just some brown sugar and butter held together by a little flour) and a bucket of apple sauce. Baking is much easier than people think, and the things you make that way (with yeast, I mean) are so impressively *real*.

Kenneth and Katherine left yesterday. He was really not bad (though if Clarice[556] thinks he fills a house up, she ought to try him in this cardboard chateau) but it is very tiring to have some one around all the time whom you expect to have a tantrum at any moment, or who will say something offensive, most likely in the guise of a joke. He made a big hit with the other islanders, especially the tennis players, of which there are a number right now. "My brother John thinks you're a *card*," Fairfield told him with a slightly malicious twinkle. And everytime he came near Trudi Porter would begin to laugh her funny Danish laugh: "Hew. Hew. Hew." Like some sort of seabird that sits around talking to itself. Now the house is strangely hushed, though I rather expect to hear a jolly yodel, "Anne, did you remember to bring in my green shirt off the line?" As Jane (Freilicher) sometimes says, what a guy.

Of course I think it's OK to be babyish sometimes, everyone is about something. Fairfield, for instance, about the stove—as I recently pointed out to him, in my bossiest "kindly" style, he is completely wrong to think it has to be on all summer, since if it's properly oiled it would be just as OK as the stove here, which goes for ten months without being used. I think he has seen the light.

---

556. Clarice Rivers, wife of painter Larry Rivers.

Don't bother to write him about it, in fact, let us all never mention or think of it again! I hope he didn't say anything in his letter that made you mad at him — he isn't at you, I know. If he took a testy Grand-dad tone, as he sometimes does with most of his friends and family, it's a little because he *is* in his sixties, and even more because he's of a generation which takes for granted a whole series of skills, like chopping kindling, we don't know much about. And skills of course become values — cold rooms and hot stoves — so if one lacks the skill, one sometimes feels judged and found wanting, which is irritating.

It's funny, Anne I know much prefers the wood stove here to any of those in Southampton, and yet she has only the most general, and often mistaken, ideas of how to use it. I wouldn't be at all surprised to walk in the kitchen one day and find her with a match in one hand and a log in the other, in hopes of boiling some water.

Anne, by the way, greatly admires your writing. She says the best modern prose writers are you and Gertrude Stein. I read your Jamaica diary out loud, to many laughs, and she said Joe's writing is clear because he really wants to tell you something, he isn't trying to conceal anything, like most writers. It's true. There's never any fuzz about what you write.

I love the cards you sent me, especially the mysterious man in the snow, who does look a lot like Larry [Rivers]. I got some cards in Camden recently, and a beautiful album, and a few little "hidden hand" cards, or love tokens. I enclose one for you (cheap is cheap), but the very best I can't bear to part with — it shows the hand holding a long stemmed rose perfectly horizontally, with four white doves perched on it. The background flowers are all roses, too. I tried to find one for you with pansies, but no soap.

Are you and Kenward going to Vermont? And what's happening with his play — *The Grass Harp*, I mean. I was going to ask him when I last wrote, but then I thought he might not be thinking about it, and so why remind him? John says that Kenward told them he wouldn't do anymore rewriting? Good, if so. I suppose he feels responsible to the other people involved. Which would be very understandable and like his good character, but I wish he would tell them all to go jump in the lake.

Guess I'd better start to pack.

lots of love,

Jimmy

ps Where I'm going is to Nova Scotia with the Kochs.

214

TO JOHN ASHBERY

August 21, 1968

Dear Painless Parker,[557]

After a week in the Kochs' skyblue compact I am slowly recovering the use of my legs. I put our mileage at something well over 1200 miles, accomplished by a good deal of dangerous driving on twisty roads. There was a moment going down-mountain on Cape Smoky when I thought of re-enacting a famous Spanish scene starring Jane vs. Larry . . . However, I can't really blame Kenneth, since I pointed out how even the most resolute member of the "Not over 50" club would cast all caution to the winds (of which there are plenty in Nova Scotia) to get in an hour's shopping in Yarmouth. And mighty glad I am we did, since I picked up for 25 crisp ones a Jaeger sweater I'm quite smitten with. It's a medium heavy fisherman-knit (bas-relief stripes, raglan sleeves) in a color Kenneth describes as Florentine green but which seems to me in sunlight olive drab and in electric light a pleasing shade of mud. I also picked up a *very* Canadian plaid shirt (the MacDour tartan, I think it must be), a soft wool scarf in Reinhardt colors (banker's gray and maroon until you look closely), and an English shaped felt cap in off-camel which Janice pronounced cute and very becoming and Kenneth said made me look like a tourist from Transylvania. Hah. Wait till you see him in *his* cap— which, as Janice understated, "makes your hair bush out a little at the sides."

We all got along very well, and the closest K and I came to a fight never got past having "words," as he put it, when it turned out that we had each silently assumed we were going to make the circuit of Cape Breton's Cabot Trail in opposite directions. We went his way, which proved a big mistake—a somewhat rancid satisfaction, since I too was a loser. There was quite a rich scene when he discovered that all liquor stores are closed from Sat. noon until Monday at 1pm—about which I had different feelings, since he had already suggested I drink from my own quart of vodka rather than have a snort from his pint of scotch, which was by then empty. My manner I regret to say was rather, "I sold for cash."

One reason for the lack of abrasions is that Nova Scotia is cheap enough for *anyone*. And the opportunities for that great human need, to fritter money, are notable for their absence. In a week I spent about 175, and that includes

557. Joke name for a dentist, c. 1900s.

my wardrobe trifles and six bottles of Moosehead ale which presently grace the bottled-gas frigidaire. Gourmet-wise, I endorse only the fried Digby clams. It is very hard to find a place to eat in, or on, Cape Breton — it usually turns out to be a tiny eatery contained in an Irving filling station. For the landscape, it's a must for all New England States lovers, but rather hard to describe — unless you can take the word "empty" as the high praise I mean it to be. There are lots of lovely place-names, though for the moment I've forgotten most of them, except, north of Bridgewater, Larry's River and Ecum Secum (pronounced Eecum Seekum) . . .

It was a fair treat to come back and find your latest from the environs of Pig Lane. Apropos the *Nest*: before Lynn[558] went for her well-earned month at the Vineyard she wrote me (July 31st) that "Anita Gross has the full details of the contract and will forward it to you after she has checked it over." Surely it's taking rather a time? Anyway, if you haven't heard anything more, would you give the Lovely a ring and find out what's going on? I'm utterly broke (I had to borrow the money to go to N.S. and I do mean borrow) and while it doesn't matter here, I shan't be able to leave the lot in Southampton until they come across. I take it you haven't heard further from friendly *Harper's B.*?

Your suggestion of a nibble trip through the by-ways of Ben-Lux is intriguing, though the thought of Iceland Airways is somewhat chilling. However, I loathe ships and a plane couldn't help but be safer that some of the drivers to whom I regularly entrust myself . . . As for when I'll be back from Vermont, Kenward hints at an October visit. We will see.

Did you know by the way that K has (Kenneth I mean) has a 4,000 Merrill grant? He's going to Paris for 8 months, beginning in Feb.

Guess that's all for now. I slept twelve hours last night and could still use another baker's dozen. Give my love to Pierre —

love,

J.
Cyrus S. Ching

558. Literary agent Lynn Nesbit.

TO RON PADGETT

[Southampton, New York]

Friday
[September] 7, 1968
[misdated as August by JS]

Dear Ron—

Joe writes that you have a kind of sickness that's called a "hole." And that you have to stay in the hospital for several weeks until your "hole" heals. I'm mighty sorry to hear it—have you thought of trying a cork? (And perhaps I'm not so funny as I think I am)—

We got back last night—well, 4:24 p.m. to be precise, and it was sure nice to have the 4:30 whistle jump me out of my skin. I rushed off to have dinner with the Hazans (they're fine & so is Elizabeth) & then saw my first movie in several months, *The Legend of Lylah Clair*,[559] a sluggish tale of demonic dyke possession, dedicated to the dubious proposition that what Hollywood needs is to kid itself a little. If I were you, I wouldn't break training to see it. And though it was fairly pleasant to experience again the mild narcosis Kim Novak dishes out. She certainly is the original dumb Polack of the ethnic jokes (did you know they're not allowed to swim in Lake Superior? They leave a ring—)

I spent my last week in Maine postponing finishing an article about Franz Kline,[560] so when I walked in the door here & picked up the ringing phone & found it was Tom Hess, I was very glad indeed that I'd sent it special del. the morning before from Camden. The big bozo even said he liked it—now why did I launch into this pointless story? Perhaps I'm distracted yes, I am, that's it. For one thing I keep thinking I hear the mailman, despite Fauré's first piano quartet—whose lugubrious third movement we have just reached—but it never is, and Lizzie is telling her mother about her first day at school, while Katie & friend are upstairs with their recorders—and here comes roly-poly Pamela Diefenbach. Besides Fauré, the living room is full of tremendous gifts from the world's most desirable tenants. Among my loot is a beautiful album by Mister Guess Who called *Brown Things in the Yard, August 1968* of dead leaves, grass and other elegant natural discards. The drawings are really great—it's sort of like having Durer for a pal. He—or they—also left a gorgeous paisley shawl on the table & a note about "the pasley (I think there's an i somewhere in pasley . . .)"

---

559. *The Legend of Lylah Clair* (1968), directed by Robert Aldrich and starring Peter Finch and Kim Novak.

560. "As American as Franz Kline" appeared in the October 1968 *Art News*.

I've reached the point in this non-letter where I'd like to start asking questions—not that anybody ever answers questions in letters, but they make a nice bulky kind of filler—but maybe you're not supposed to write letters? Just rest? So do so.

Perhaps in the next day or so something will happen (I *hope not*) and I'll have something entertaining to write about. Or do you prefer abstract letters? Oops, don't answer that, just rest.

And try to keep your hands outside the covers. Because—well—you've seen those old men around town whose hands tremble all the time haven't you? And you've heard of hairy palms? Don't bother to answer that—*rest*.

Give Patty my love and tell her a postcard progress report would be truly welcome.

Thanks for the engraved fragment & the Padgett Original Productions card—

love,

Jimmy

TO JOHN ASHBERY

Southampton, New York

Sept. 11, 1968

Dear Prince of Fiddlers,[561]

To your surprise, and even more to mine, I've finished with the copy-edited mss. You may be further stunned to hear that I've acceded to all your "p.e.s" (the audio area of the living room is now a Sargossa Sea of eraser crumbs), yes, even the sunflowers, though it wasn't until rather late in the night that I "got" the joke. Now for a few terse comments—

The date in the Bush family kitchen fireplace is too early. I think Southampton and Southold are at daggers drawn over which got here fustest with the leastest, and Southampton, as you know, is 1640. Perhaps I'll stroll down South Main and see what date is on The Hollyhocks (though why I feel the Bush-date need be motivated, I couldn't say . . .)

561. Allusion to *A Nest of Ninnies*.

At first I thought of changing Polaris splashdown to Sputnik I, Sputnik II, or Laika. Unfortunately the *World Almanac* implies that all three perished in space, so I settled for: "he concluded, like Walter M. Schirra, Jr.,[562] plunging toward a successful splashdown . . . " OK?

pg 26: I cut "in the cup" out of this: "Leave a little room for the cream," Alice said. "It tastes vile without it."

pg 15: I took out the two speeches (Henry won't need your help, etc.) but didn't add "her face beginning to glow" to Fabia's previous speech, since the phrase, or variations thereof, is used several times elsewhere (though usually of Victor).

pg 159: I cut: "Mrs Kelso took a spoonful of broth and began to choke." This comes quite soon after Alice began to choke on her Rabarbaro Zucca, and leaving it out seems to make the passage funnier (to me, anyway).

pg 160: "Well, dear, aren't we to be treated to a little announcement on the festive occasion?" she leered coquettishly at Alice. I cut "coquettishly," which is used of Mrs Bridgewater in the Posting the Banns scene in Palermo to more telling effect.

pg 188: "Haugtussa is how I spell my name in the *Schwann Artist's* catalog" (which is how they and L. L. Bean spell that—do you still prefer ogue? I mean, since it's specifically the L. L. Bean one—but this I've left between you and your Editor).

I caught a few minor bloopers, most of which I can't remember except that the song is "*Ihr* glocken von Marling . . . "

Needless to say, if you don't dig any of my emendations, speak up. I'll listen to reason, up to a point. (I even left, "I'm so hungry I could eat a wolf." What more can you ask?)

I'd be delighted to play guest Huneker[563] at the *New Republic* for a few turns. In fact, I guess I'll have to, since I mentioned the possibility to the Water Mill Morisot, who expressed her pleasure by asking if I'd mind signing myself "Hilton Kramer" and pointed out that the *New Republic* does not exactly have the circulation of the *Daily News*. I don't know why I find this kind of sauce acceptable from *her*—perhaps because it's the kind I like to dish out myself . . .

---

562. Walter M. Schirra, Jr., American astronaut.
563. James Huneker (1860–1921), biographer, novelist, memoirist, and *New Republic* music critic.

("By the way, shouldn't "palois" have a small p? I queried this to ye ed . . .)

I just thought of making the date in the hearth "1652"—get it? Three hundred years before we started this opus—to the day.

I stopped this to leaf through Melissina Manuscript, preparatory to sending it off to the stamperia this afternoon, and have come across one or two other items—Webster II gives pet cock and petcock so I came down hard in favor of the latter. On a more serious note, I cut "in Palermo" from the last paragraph of our "Twilight in Sicily" chapter, so the sentence now reads: "Dusk had long since set in by the time they drew up before the Albergo delle Palme." It's said earlier that they have to get back to Palermo, and the sentence somehow reminded me of a famous WNYC panel exchange—Larry: "I was reading Tolstoi's *War and Peace* . . . Frank: "Whose *War and Peace?*"

After all, surely *our* readers will know where the Albergo Delle Palme is . . . ? I left it "jazz" on pg 210, with this note on the query: "ProfScott is affecting to be mixed up." I also put some stets in where she had put question marks where it seemed to me questions weren't intended . . . *E basta con quella porcherria.*

The contracts were here just long enough for Anne to attest my signature and, whisk. I suppose they will now try to set some tortoise record in getting checks out.

Joe and Kenward drove down on Monday so Joe could teach Tuesday, then presumably drove back last night. They're coming back next week, "for good." Did you know that Ron is out of the hospital? He had a "blat (t?)" on his lung, a hole which allows air to leak into the body cavity, which is all wrong. They say he'll be OK, though Kenward says Ron was rather startled when, due to lack of equipment, they had to deflate his lung with a stomach pump. Good grief.

I'm afraid I'll have to count poor dear Dale Harris[564] as one of my failures—not that I ever counted him as anything else (see enclosed). Now to struggle into "that great something else"; culottes! and go oublier Palermo in the Hazans' plunge.

love, Mr Calandro[565]

love to your mother & to Pierre.

564. Dance critic who taught at Sarah Lawrence College.
565. Character in *A Nest of Ninnies.*

TO JOHN ASHBERY

[Southampton, New York]

Oct. 3, 1968

Dear Tempest Storm,[566]

Just back from Pleasure Island, a return most brightened by a check from Kimberly Sue Dutton and a note from Mr Ennis,[567] the Friendly Family Lawyer, inviting me to serve as a Trustee with Kenny Koch and pick winners. Do I detect your shapely paw in this? Even if it isn't your doing, you might as well take the credit. I've already thought up quite a list of poets whose work deserves no further encouragement. However, the power thrill is wearing off, and I wish I could have discussed this with you—if only to pick up a few hints on how to deal with the big Woof. I wish I could figure out what it is he's going to want me to do that I won't want to do, so I could forestall him.

Goodness gracious, guess who just called up. That's right, my Mother. I guess she wanted to spare herself not getting a phone call from me on her 78th birthday, tomorrow. Oh dear, I wish I were more of a model son along your lines, Skeezix. But I promised a visit "within the month or so." Well, there's November shot to hell.

While in Maine I did quite a bit of reveling among the pots and pans—the level of quality was pretty high, though in detail a bit spotty. The apple slices poached in honey—"Sounds even better than it tastes!"—and I'm not sure the garden-fresh broccoli was helped much by a hollandaise into which I put enough lemon juice to prevent an entire den of Cub Scouts from getting scurvy. On the other hand, the dumplings with the sauerbraten were as feather light as Bob Dash's head, while it turns out that the lemon meringue pie Grandad used to like is the one on the corn starch package. The filling certainly does hold its shape, yet can manage a quiver, and I'm afraid I much prefer it to Irma's l.m.p. "de luxe" which is so very runny. Naturally I find that I'm able to manage quite a quiver myself, and am now trying to subsist on Fresca and celery curls.

I've been trying to call Kenward—all I get of course is his @!!# answering service. "That's S-K-..." "No, no "S-c-h-" "Oh. S-k-c-h-u-" Wonder if I'll ever hear from him in this life? I'm quite anxious to get them to go on our long

566. Striptease dancer.
567. Trustee of the Poets Foundation.

planned Vermont trek, while the leaves are on the turn. And I want to feel them out about a party Morris [Golde] is giving for Ned's [Rorem] latest (snore) tomorrow night. I'm tempted to go, but I wish someone would guarantee a lower temperature — today in big town it's a muggy 86.

Did I tell you that Don Schrader is back and planning to live out here, while taking some courses in education at Southampton U? I hope he's gotten over his little way of dropping in just as the cap is coming off the gin bottle. The first thing he ever said to me was, "I'm Don Schrader, I read your book out loud to my mother." I *think* he went on to say that he liked it and she didn't, but I may be imagining that. Anyway, it's been down hill ever since.

I read *The Pearl of Orr's Island* [568] with great pleasure — you're a dear to have given it to me. She seems to have lifted the plot (if that's the word) from some forgotten opus of Bellini's or Donizetti's — in Chapter one, a lovely young woman and a grizzled salt drive up to the banks of Kennebeck and watch a sloop dash to pieces on some rocks. Her husband is on board so in chapter II she dies, giving birth to the Pearl. Quite soon thereafter, bigger ship is dashed to pieces one stormy night. In the morning a drowned foreign lady is found on the beach. She is holding a live baby boy and wears a bracelet of curious design, a glimpse of which causes the local reverend to turn pale and bug his eyes. Seems that as a student at Harvard he had gone to tutor in a Cuban family in Florida . . . Things settle down then for a long time, with lots of nice descriptions of mending, cooking and house-cleaning (her strong suit), until a third of the way from the end the Pearl develops a hectic flush while her fiancee — who is also adoptive brother — is on a slow boat to China, and we get a hundred and some pages of making a Good Death. This part I read at a very merry clip. The brother comes home and, having inherited a large Cuban sugar fortune, marries their best friend, a hearty girl from up the cove. It's hard to imagine what Mrs S. thought she was doing when she wrote it, besides bringing home the bacon, which may well have seemed to her sufficient. Here's a bit which is typical of the parts I like —

"'Captain Kittridge, you ought to be ashamed of yourself, at your age, talking as you do.'

'Why, laws, mother, I don't feel my age,' said the frisky Captain, giving a sort of skip."

568. This novel by Harriet Beecher Stowe appears in Schuyler's poem "Now and Then." "Have you read *The Pearl of Orr's Island* / That's a book, I'd want to read myself."

Now to see if I cannot render a little fat unto Caesar by having another Fresca.

Love to Pierre, and write real soon —

love,

Norma Vincent Peel

TO JOHN ASHBERY

[Southampton, New York]

Oct 14, 1968

Dear Isham Jones,[569]

Now that's what I call a letter, and if anything could have made it more welcome, it was finding it waiting when I emerged from the dank dark last evening before a stint — I choose the word with care — in NYC. It's nice that Paris fits you like an old shoe, though it alarms me a little for your return. I'm so afraid *U.S. News & World Report* will snap you up for their Ghent office. Don't forget New York too has its charms, few though they be.

I saw quite a bit of art last week, but will spare you a rundown of what's current and choice at the Met, Whitney, Kornblee, Emmerich and what have you Except that a panoply of Kenneth Snelson's[570] in Bryant Park (solemnly listed as, Sculpture of the Month) should offer a prime time to any playful vandals — if one of the tension wires snaps, the whole city will be filled with riccocheting metal bars; all a part of the artist's plan, no doubt. I still haven't figured out how I'm to convince the readers of *The New Republic* that what appears to be an unusually ugly and perilous playground is in fact a wonderful thing (perhaps the wonder is in the brevity of its stay?) but doubtless inspiration will come.

(I wish I could find a way to keep the Fresca off the typewriter keys.)

(I just stopped and gave them — the keys — a swipe with a hankie soaked in Gasma. Now if I hold my breath for an hour or two, all would be well.)

Kenward's house is slowly shaping up — the total eclectic look seems the aim. Numerous small unpainted parsons tables are vying with six new inlaid art-nouveau tables (small, tall and wobbly) from Lilian Nassau. There is also an enor-

---

569. Jazz-band leader of the 1920s.
570. American sculptor known for his use of polished steel rods and wire.

mous chair, along the lines of a Chesterfield; in fact, there seems to be just as much of it as there could possibly be in a full sized one, the only difference being that it seats one. Kenward found it in a "Home" issue of the *Sunday Times Mag.*, and I seem to recall a price tag in the $1,600 area—so I was relieved when Joe asked him if he wasn't getting the matching (aubergine) sofa to hear him say, "Well, Joe it *does* cost ten arms and ten legs . . . ", the only time I've heard him make that objection to anything. There seem to be all sorts of possibilities to the things they're amassing, but I do wish you'd come and push them around —the unconscious thinking behind the present arrangement seems to be that since it's a long room everything should be oblong and go with the length. Oh well, I had some swell ideas but decided to keep them to myself, on the grounds that getting too deep into other people's slipcovers can only end badly.

Kenward has also just gotten some beds for the top floor, so I guess in the future his guest (ahem) won't have to sleep with one ear to the subway grill. The other yawning some navvies were testing for metal fatigue with sledge hammers—I never heard anything like it, not even in the concert hall.

I went into town resolved to see Godard's *Weekend*, so instead I saw, and don't recommend in descending order, *Flesh*, *The Fireman's Ball* and *Les Biches*.[571] Oh well, I guess compared to the others I do recommend *Flesh*, since it would be hypocritical to pretend that I'm bored with big screen, full color lascivious nudity. In fact some of it is even a little bit funny—quite a bit of it may be, but with those home cooked sound tracks it's hard to tell. I still can't quite believe that I saw *Les Biches*, whose triangular plot seems based on some rejected episodes from "The Edge of Night" (my mother's favorite daytime serial) and high life at St.Tropez in December to offer a choice of a hideous comic riding on another comic and yelling "*Mon royaume pour un cheval!*" or interminable poker games—which may well be true. The evils of dyke-life are put across with demands for a "cold bottle of beer—*right now.*" Is it possible that Chabrol ever made a good movie?

I did, on the other hand, rather enjoy Morris's party. Perhaps because it is so early in the season, everyone seemed in a jolly mood and I even got a big hellow from Aaron [Copland]. Unfortunately Morris's demon crew of party helpers are still mixing atom smashers instead of drinks—more than one guest was heard sobbing "I can't drink this!" though most did. Before the mists closed

571. *Weekend*, Jean-Luc Godard's (1930–2022) movie released in 1968. *Flesh* (1968), directed by Andy Warhol (1927–1987); *The Fireman's Ball* (1967), directed by Milos Forman (1932–2018); and *Les Biches* (1968), directed by Claude Chabrol (1930–2010).

in I had a nice chat with Saphronis[572] (is that how its spelt?) who tells me that Arthur has gone back to Elaine. Bill has the apartment (recently featured in the *Sunday Times*). Saphronis seemed quite pleased when I said, "You mean Bill got custody of the day-glo beams?" He also seems ready, willing and anxious to cast Bill in the home-wrecker role, and says that Arthur and Elaine are being terribly kind and patient with him—a situation which surpasses even my expectations of what modern life is likely to offer. Richard[573] was looking very gorgeous—I don't know why I didn't notice this about him before—and made rather a hit with Joe Brainard, je pense. The evening wore on as it will, and so did I, and have a not-too-vivid memory of getting in some heavy public petting with Janice which Father Koch came and broke up. I was musing aloud about the tackiness of this episode next day to Kenward who remarked that he thought it was about time and that KK has it coming and then some. True, no doubt—but I wish I could remember exactly what I *said*. (Words speak much louder than actions.) I also have a feeling I haven't quite heard the last of it—tactful silence not being Kenneth's strong suit. Oh well, I suppose he really can't afford to do much stone casting at that . . .

Another memory that glimmers out of the late night fuming mists is of a well-informed lady taxi driver asking in a motherly way, "Are you sure it's Sixth Avenue and twenty-*seventh* you want?"[574] It seemed simpler to say yes than try to figure out just what was wrong. Though I sensed that something was. Needless to say, I did not wander the streets until dawn, since the feet can reason even when the head can't. But over the rest of that scene I will let the great simulated gold curtain fall. Suffice it that I have no complaints—and let's hope nothing else, for that matter.

Before the party Kenward and Joe gave a small dinner—me, Clarice—making her return appearance—and the Ryans,[575] who showed up well after nine for the eight o'clock spread, which was quite tasty, though I've swung round to your view and I'd just as soon have the caviar without the potato. Clarice tells me that during Larry's absence Joe* and Stevie looted the apartment (Larry caught them in the act, when they returned for some lesser items) including a bulging portfolio of drawings which Stevie sold to "a man from the Mafia." Everyone then agreed that the Mafia puts lots of their money into art, for in-

572. Sophronus Mundy, social worker and chef.
573. Richard Hennessey, painter, and lover of Sophronus Mundy.
574. The Everard Baths were at West 28th Street.
575. John and D. D. Ryan, New York socialites.

come tax purposes (remember, this isn't my story). Larry and a D.A. prevailed on Stephen to go chat with the man about the possibilities of supplying some stolen goods while carrying a concealed tape-recorder. He did this twice but failed to show up for the third appointment, and hasn't been seen since. "Perhaps the Mafia caught on," I ventured. "Don't be silly," said the toothsome stepmother, "*Stephen's* allright." She seemed to feel a good deal of contempt for anyone so benighted as to imagine that anything so devoutly to be wished could ever come to pass. Yes, all in all it was quite an evening.

I just went downstairs for more of this deadly drink (the Fresca, I mean) and Anne told me that Tom Clyde[576] is in the hospital, having had a massive stroke and been unconscious for several days. I don't know why I tell you this—perhaps because it happened? Which reminds me—as long as I'm on the cheerless note—that Joe Hazan's mother is in the hospital too. Complications with her diabetes.

But this is beginning to seem as though I thought a letter to you had to cover as many aspects of life as a *Sunday Times*. Since it's too late for this to get out this evening, I'll put it aside and see if memory has any fresh offerings in the morning.

* Clarice seemed especially pleased that Joe should've been caught red-handed & proved as bad as—I take it—she's told Larry he is—.

Oct. 15

The morning began about one p.m., after a night tossing and turning with *The First Four Georges* and it's now an extra lovely afternoon. I'm rather tempted to scoot off to the beach, if I weren't so certain of what I'd find when I got there: the neighborhood husbands surf-casting for sea bass. Most of those caught will doubtless find their way into our ice-box, where I just found the first of the parade lounging. There is nothing like the sight of a fresh caught sea bass to set me hankering for a smoking joint. There was one great year when the surplus foods took the form of wild duck—but that was only once.

I haven't bought any records since you left, and by ignoring Sam Goody's continuing blandishments managed to make it into Brooks where I bought a suit. I tried on one with their daringly modified nipped-in waist, but after observing the conflict of curves, settled for one stamped out of their traditional cookie cutter. It's either whipcord or cavalry twill, or some hybrid of the two, and the color I think is called "natural"—meaning it's closer to dirty gray sand

576. Husband of painter Mary Abbott Clyde.

than to dirty brown sand. As much as I like new clothes, I hate the whole process of getting them. Kenward says he doesn't like the obsequiousness and buddy-buddying of the clerks and tailors: my experience is rather the opposite. And though, as you know, not usually chary of parting with a buck, I do mind when it comes to suits—a rather mysterious and self-defeating point of view. Still, I have one and hope it fits.

The contact prints came of the last batch of author photos, and I think we can find one among them that will be OK. Anyway I'll have some enlargements made and send them to you. Now I am going to the beach.

On second thought, maybe I'll rustle up a batch of Chewy Noels, as featured in Fanny Farmer. Love to your house from my house,

Darby Bannard[577]

PS What is the book you'd like me to send? Mentioned in the lovely An-nemasse[578] card but not in your letter . . .

love, J.

I *love* creamed oyster plant, as we indeed used to call it (but I've never actually *heard* anyone call rhubarb "pie plant," have you?). It was one of my mother's better specialties, before she gave up cooking food freezing it—

You must get the Chabrier VoxBox piano music when you come back–it's become my favorite listening thanks to your putting me on to the " ." There's a "Habeñera" that brings out all the Jenny Touial in me.—

TO JOHN ASHBERY

[Southampton, New York]

Nov. 15, 1968[579]

Dear Beany Bacon Dip,

Fust things fust: of course I'll be delighted to run through my wardrobe with a razor blade, a thing I have long wanted to do, nor will it take all that much time. I may, in fact, join you at the customs barrier—I'm curious to observe the

577. Walter Darby Bannard (1934–2016), painter and art critic who showed at Tibor de Nagy Gallery.

578. A village in France.

579. Schuyler's diary entry for this date reads, "The hateful street with the handsome houses."

man on the pier when he discovers what a nifty line of goods the Sweet-Orr[580] folks are turning out these days. When I got your letter yesterday afternoon, I had the good idea of bustling up to the corner and inviting our mutual friend, Little Peter, to help carry the ball. Unfortunately, he was nowhere in sight, though both the Schleps were there in force. Nothing so vividly brings home to me the true state of my Dow-Jones rating as the lackluster tones in which the Missus asks, "Can I help you in any way?" The sheer improbability of parting me from more than a necktie's worth seems to send her spiritually into hibernation.

But are you sure you want the labels from your old suits? Seems to me they all come from Les Socurs Old MacDonald, 17 bis rue Jupien . . . [581] or are you planning some sort of double agent ploy?

And just as surely—isn't the "ay" sound in Italian after e always ie? Igei would be Idjeea, and Igia would be Idja; but I don't know why either of those happens. Let's see what the dictionary has to say—yes, there is only one entry for IG followed by a vowel: *Igienico*. It comes right in between *Iettatura*: malign influence, ill-luck, evil eye; and *Igname*, yam. (Which reminds me of a sequence currently offered by the Southampton phone book: Lynn Clutterbuck—Tom Clyde's girl friend, though she looks more like a mistress—Mary Clyde, and Tom. The latter was whisked away in a coma to NY where he is now on the mend, you'll be happy to hear.) Look what it says under "il": " . . . optional with islands except three near Leghorn which always take it, Capri, Procida and Ischia." Oh to be in Leghorn, now that no one's there . . . I knew I should never have opened Hoare's Shorter.

As for your birthday offering, as Mrs Kelso might say, "Mmmm." I've played it front, back and sideways, and only wish I had a second turntable so I could play both versions of the Mozart variations simultaneously. In a word, I love it (I was going to say "You're a sweetie," but that sounds rather Arthur Goldish, don't you think?) Fairfield also likes it—much preferring the piano version. I never know what's going to pique his musical appetite: "What," he recently asked, "was that mournful music? I like it." It was, of course, Bruch's Scottish, the "I'm a-Down for lack of Johnnie" moment, another happy choice of your recommending. What with that, the Reger and the Tchaikovsky Trio, my listening pleasure has been optimum (in the last, I especially love the part just before the waltz where the piano does a dance while the strings imitate bagpipes).

580. Makers of workingmen's clothes, including overalls.
581. The tailor who becomes valet to Baron Charlus in Proust's *Remembrance of Things Past*.

I don't believe I wrote you about my whirlwind and lightning trip to Vermont—exhausting is one word that comes to mind; another is hellish. But don't tell Kenward. Would you have guessed that what the stylish Mrs Ryan Three wanted most for her birthday was a Hoover? The house had, in fact, been abandoned by KGE, Joe and the Padgetts in rather a state, and early the first morning Dee Dee [Ryan] had me making a list, while she sanitized the 'fridge, which began with Copper Glo and ended with, vacuum cleaner. Nor did we fail to get any on our visit to Montpelier, so I was awakened on the second morning by the motherly hum of a Hoover. As Dee Dee remarked in an aside to me, "What was really monkey was the dead flies." Where do those Nightingale-Bamford girls get their vile language? Case your wondering, yes she does put on her face—the constituents of which went with us in two Vuitton footlockers—before she begins dusting; all of it. About D.D. (how does she spell it, do you know?) I just don't know. Either I really like her, wish that I did or feel that I ought to. It might help if she'd lay off such gambits as, "James," (she likes to have her own little name for folks—Bill Berkson is always Billy, just as you emerged as Johnny) "Tell me, what is a poem?" Nothing so very witty came to mind, and the effect was to make me feel even more than usually like a Buffalo moth.

About her driving, however, there can be no two opinions, and Larry [Rivers] and Harry [Mathews] will have to look to their laurels if one or the other does-n't want to surrender the And Sudden Death Trophy. "I hate to do this," she said, "so I *always* give them five minutes," pulling into the right hand or no-pass-ing lane while the speedometer clocked a hilarious ninety plus. The car we passed had a visible attack of the shakes, nor was it the only one. "*On ne voit point deux fois le rivage des morts*, D.D.," I replied, but my words were lost in the whistling wind and the yammering of her two charming but rather fiendish little boys, Beau Barry Ryan, aged ten, and Drew Dixon, going on seven.[582] It was from one of them that I caught a stunning cold—I prefer to call it, the 'flu—from which I recovered only in time to get the good of this Tuesday's storm, which qualified in every way as a hurricane, except that of originating in the tropics. Rather fun but scary, and not unlike D.D.'s driving, with the creaking trees replacing other hazards.

The autumn leaves in Vermont, however, were ginger peachy.

[Letter ends here]

---

582. Schuyler retells this story in "The Morning of the Poem."

TO JOHN ASHBERY

[Southampton, New York]

Dec. 3, 1968

Dear Warren Galjour,[583]

I'm back from some extended play in NYC, extended not so much by my wish as that of the LIRR, whose soi-disant employees celebrated Thanksgiving week with a couple of complimentary wild-cat strikes—the conductors were in a pet because of a new schedule which they seem to feel might cut into their elevenses, while the engineers were outraged by a button, whose location implied that it perhaps does not require a separate adult in each car to open and close the doors (this may well be true, considering what goes on in self-service elevators). So far I haven't taken sides, but I imagine Fairfield has. During a deceptive lull between strikes he took a morning train to the city and then had to return by subway, bus and an Avis car, which he was grudgingly allowed to rent in Patchogue. Perhaps the best thing is to think of it as delightfully French, and let it go at that.

This enabled me to join the Kochs at their Thanksgiving blockbuster—we sat down seventeen, and the food was plentiful, traditional and tasty. The company was more mixed—on the plus side, Jane and Joe, Ada and Alex, Kenward and Joe, and so on; then there were Bill and Janice Boretree,[584] who gained luster when seen with her sister and brother-in-law, whose big career selling school supplies of the gym chair sort seemed to entitle him to act like an H. V. Kaltenborn substitute—oh well, I can't really do justice to his sardonic witlessness so we'll just drop him back in the pond. As soon as dinner was over all left (the kiddies had a separate dinner above decks in the Boretrees) except for Kenward and myself who were nailed to the bridge table until three a.m. It's a shame you won't play, if only to enjoy the wonder of Kenward winning while sound asleep.

Kenneth and I finally had our summit or Nobel Prize meeting—not very taxing since there is only $2,500 in the kitty at the moment (over and above our stipends, that is)—both Ron (who has had a blat recurrence) and Frank Lima[585] have had special dispensations already. (Did you know that the latter got back on horse last summer and is now away, taking a cure? As I got the story from

---

583. A singer of Cajun origin who recorded Francois Poulenc songs in the 1950s.
584. Friends of Kenneth and Janice Koch.
585. Frank Lima (1929–2013), poet whose book *Inventory* was published by Tibor de Nagy Editions.

Ada, it was grimly depressing and I'll spare us both.) At the moment the decision is to divide a thousand between Anne Waldman (and Lewis Warsh), and to give another thousand to Michael Brownstein (I successfully concealed from Pooh Bear that I find him—M.B.—not only talented but distinctly cute). The other five hundred we're to decide about this week; mostly because, I think, it seemed to Kenneth that I was getting off too easy, and he would somehow lose face if we decided it all in the course of an hour's chat. Well, be Kenneth Mc-Koch as he may, I still doubt that this is going to be the winter of Mary Ferrara or any of several other of his ex-students; though I'm rather tempted to get something for John Giorno,[586] largely because Kenneth began by announcing that no matter what, he just wasn't going to give anything to *him*. Up until that moment I had, I imagine, pretty much shared his view of John's work; since then, I have really liked it more—if the virtues are a bit on the bleak, simplistic side, it at least lacks the faults of the modish East Village manner. Besides, as Kenneth rightly suspected I do think he's cute (he came to Lita Hornick's[587] annual bash in Wellington boots and red sash, looking remarkably like a high-school crush of mine as he appeared one starry night in the *Pirates of Penzance*). Oh well . . . still, Kenneth *is* funny, and though he agreed with me about Michael Brownstein, the moment he realized I was deathly set on getting that poor dog a bone—and as a breadwinner, I've seldom seen anyone less likely to bring home the bacon—he became a ferment of ways to cut down his share so that we could invent a series of postage stamp awards, the object being, I guess, to encourage with faint cash.

On the other hand, I think he is even sicker than I am of acting a lie, or rather, maintaining a pretense. For several weeks he got quite a bit of mileage out of Mr. Ennis, with luscious hints that I would soon be hearing *more* from *him*, which alternated with late night party statements that he was, actually, quite au fait himself and would tell me all, soon . . . it took him no time at all to get his feet well entangled in his train, and I had my work cut out pretending not to notice the mounting inconsistencies. It finally seemed obvious that he was torn by a desire to make a clean breast, to remain loyal to his Oath, and a truly rending wish to find out exactly what I knew or suspected (my line has been strictly, gentlemen don't ask questions, which at least offers no handle). In fact, I'd feel

586. Poets Mary Ferrara and John Giorno (1935–2019).
587. Lita and Morton Hornick were generous patrons who hosted lavish annual parties for the New York poets at their 888 Park Avenue apartment. Lita edited Kulchur, a small press and journal.

a certain sympathy for him, *except for one thing*. After I spent two weeks trying to date him up, he finally made the date in his most preemptory way—"Now Jimmy, do you think *you* could make it tomorrow? etc." I was amused by his manner and only after agreeing realized that Kenward had come silently into the room behind me. That really sizzled me. Especially as Kenward instantly left, before I could loudly complain of his persistent date avoidance. But I have to hand it to him—it was a trick worthy of Marshall Bush[588] himself.

But I didn't mean to run on about that. Though just for the record he did say that you had acted as a trustee for the foundation last year; perhaps he said for the past two years. You were, by the way, absolutely right about the play he made of "next year," plus the fact that some had had a little something in the past (his memory seemed to glaze over when I said "How much and how recently?").

Jane's opening day was very nice, and her show, you won't be surprised to hear, is lovely. It's the first time, I think, that the whole effect is as strong as the best pictures—it's like strolling into the Vale of Sunshine (which is, I believe, in Sussex). Kenward, Joe and I had dinner with them, but first we all went for a drink with the Riverses—Larry was wearing something expensive and unbecoming which brought out the bear-grease in his hair while Clarice was styled as only she knows how—ankle length brocade topped by a weary horsehide coat, and she was carrying the kind of cloth satchel from which one might expect a *flute* and a bunch of leeks to protrude but instead featured mysterious packages done up in Reynolds wrap—cookies in which all the ingredients were organic, including the wheat germ and the pot. I'm sorry you weren't there to take in the maitre d' of the King Cole Room taking us in—"*Pas de cravate!*" he cried with evident relief at such an easy out. Larry got in a few good ones, plus almost having a fistfight with some uptight out-of-towner, who was heard to opine that along with a necktie he might as well get a haircut. Most of this I have to take on faith, since I was out waiting at the corner in record time. The Gotham, which was empty, proved more tolerant. We ate at a place called, I think, La Poulliadaire (is that possible?)[589] near Lincoln Center, which we all enjoyed—partly because of a head waiter of wonderfully transparent professional charm, partly because of the food, and mostly because we were all, and Jane in particular, in exceptionally good spirits. Then we went on to what I guess was a nice party given by Judy and Mauro [Calamandrei]—though it fea-

588. Character in *A Nest of Ninnies*.
589. Le Poulailler (The Chicken Coop).

tured an awful lot of Herbert . . . Jane's birthday, a week later, was done in quieter style; in fact, as far as guests go, I was it. After champagne, chicken and some Reuben's cheese cake, Joe took us to see 2001, which was just the thing for the night after Thanksgiving. I liked it while it was going on but haven't thought about it much since, perhaps because the soundtrack in the part [about] how beyond infinity lie the bright lights of Wilshire Boulevard gave me a splitting headache. The first time Zarathustra began to Sprach Jane said, "Quick, Henry, the Flints!"[590] So much for the big town . . .

Or is there more news of the big town? Let me see . . . Scott Burton[591] is in New York Hospital with hepatitis, where he intends to read Proust, Alex tells me. Things seem to be coming to a perk in the new artists co-op[592]—John Button got tired of standing on one foot and complained to the contractor (whose name I forget—no I don't—Manuel, the one who runs a bar for Puerto Rican teeny-bopper dykes) that he didn't see why Donald's bookshelves couldn't wait until he, John Button, at least had some plumbing put in; to which Manuel replied that he was in no rush, since Donald had told him that John couldn't pay him anyway. This was told me by a perfectly delighted Alvin, with whom I had dinner chez his friend, Sid Talisman, a social worker with a remarkably green thumb. He's gotten his *ficus* to do things I never dreamt of. Alvin [Novak] is now head of the piano department in a performing arts school Dorothy Maynard started in Harlem. He likes it, which is quite a change.

The jacket copy seems OK to me. All is quiet on that front, except that I've had a siege of conflicting phone calls from Anita Gross, Peggy Brooks and Miss Bueno (P. B.'s secretary), having to do with previously printed portions and copyright. As of yesterday, all was straightened out. Peggy Brooks seems kind of a pleasant folksy soul.[593] Oh. Kenneth, who has a set of our galleys, says they come with what he called "quite a letter" from Arthur Cohen, which began something like, "Begun twelve years ago on a crazy automobile ride to a party . . . " I didn't see the letter so I can't vouch for that as a true quote, but even if there's a germ of truth in it, it is dismaying enough. Just as long as you're back in time to keep a steady hand on him in the trying review copies period . . .

---

590. "Quick, Henry, the Flit!", slogan for Flit, an insect spray of the 1930s and the title of a poem in *Freely Espousing*.

591. Scott Burton (1939–1989), sculptor known for his granite chairs.

592. Soho loft building at 435 West Broadway, purchased by artists organized by Donald Droll, then director of the Fischbach Gallery.

593. Gross, Brooks (the editor of *A Nest of Ninnies*), and Bueno were working on the details of the publication of *A Nest of Ninnies*.

Jane says, by the by, the Cohen-Ridenour re-alignment has made all concerned miserable . . . for further details, consult your Sybil.

Is your mother still there? I was quite dumbfounded by the news. I can't wait to hear all about it—bet Pierre is having a lot of fun.

Thanks for the "in series" postals—though the French post office has suddenly taken to mural-sized postmarks which certainly put the recipient on his mettle.

love, xxx
Ozzie Nelson[594] J.

TO JOHN ASHBERY

[Southampton, New York]

Nov 4 (oops)—
Dec 4 1968

Dear Edwin Way Teale,[595]

It's 3:30 and already too dark to see at my desk, without some elaborate re-arrangement of defunct lamps. Some chill rain is falling all over itself, & the elms are gesticulating in the gloom like the catalpas. It's all a bit too *une si jolie petite plage*,[596] & it wouldn't take much to get me down to the beach for a good stare, if it weren't so much pleasanter to be within earshot of Baby KLH— the latest disc of solace is the Paganini *Caprices*, all 25 of them. It turns out to be that record for which we've all been waiting—"The Heart of the Cadenza." I don't suppose anyone but Paganini has ever been able to make them in some sense musically acceptable—but it is probably better [Ruggiero] Ricci's way— without any pretense that they're in anyway agreeable—half Kilkenny cat & half barbwire; listening to them straight through is as shattering as a box of chocolates with stone centers. Can't wait to play it for you.

Now about your friend with this strange interest in American literature of the gray nineties, I suppose he's as aware as I that most "minor masterpieces" that are also "little known" don't get that way by accident—how—some ever—.

---

594. Ozzie Nelson, father on the *Ozzie and Harriet* television sitcom.
595. Edwin Way Teale (1899–1980), American writer and naturalist.
596. Title of a 1950s French film noir.

234

There is one book I know that probably qualifies, Andy Adams' *The Log of a Cowboy* (first published in 1903). It's about cattledriving. The narrative part is fairly flat & straightforward, while the dialogue is a bit more stylized & often very funny—there's a lot of swapping of tales around the camp fire.

"Calling bear sign doughnuts," interrupted Quince Forrest, "reminds me what . . . "

"Will you kindly hobble your lip," said Officer.

It is, by the way, really quite a famous book, particularly among those who'll pay thousands for a Remington or a Charles M. Russell or would if they could. Happily, Adams' had none of their sinister expertness—in fact, what probably makes him good is that his literary equipment was just sufficient to his needs, & he didn't try for the big one (would that could be said of Howells or Cable).

Anyway, if you think your friend might like to see for himself, it's available as a "Bison" paperback (the series that includes *The Home Place*) from the U. of Nebraska for $1.50. I'd be happy to get & send a copy. Let me know.

How far on either side of 1900 is your friend casting his net? And how much emphasis is on minor & how much on masterpiece? If it's in some sense *document* too, that might open the door for Hamlin Garland's *Boy Life on the Prairie*, which I think is much better—except for the title—than *Son of the Middle Border* (or *Daughter* or *Brother-in-Law* for the matter of that). What you might not guess from the title is the horror with which such backward glances filled him—he's very good at the "me & my pony" parts, but what really comes across is the way the life destroyed all values—not just values but plain humanity & almost any family feeling. What's scary is that with all the energy in the world, & what seems like a most marvelous opportunity, they suffer such a strangely Golovlyov-like[597] fate.

To turn to a higher mesa—what about Walt Whitman's letters? Particularly those to Peter Doyle. One might assume that all Whitman is available in French, & one might be quite wrong if the situation is anything like that here. Anyway, even if they have been translated, they'd be more than worth reprinting.

And what about Henry James' last collection of stories? I think it's called *The Finer Grain*. "The Bench of Desolation" is one of the ones in it, though "minor" is perhaps not the operative word, except alongside *The Golden Bowl*.

Then there's Kate Chopin's *The Awakening* (1899) which claims to have a niche of its own. I bought it a while ago, but whenever I pick it up something

597. *The Golovlyov Family* (1875), by Shchedrin (Mikhail Evgrafovich Saltykov).

intervenes (could it be common sense?) the same thing, I guess, that keeps me from roistering through the works of Katherine Mansfield. But hasn't she always been rather big in France? Perhaps Kate Chopin is what they pine for.

I really haven't read Henry B. Fuller. Kenneth says *The Chevalier of Pensione Vani* (or is it Vanni?) is the best. He also likes H. Garland's early novel *Rose of Dutcher's Cooley* which I haven't read.

I liked Cable's *The Grandissime* when I read it (unlike some books, which I liked before I read them) but surely that's been translated? *The Story of Bras Coupé*, which is part of it, is quite great. Then there are the *Creole Sketches*, which are quite interesting, & I wish the translator joy of the subtly varied Creole & other dialects. But most of Cable is only for buffs (like me)—he had his family to support & the notoriety of Richard Watson Gilder[598] seems to have been well earned.

Here life intervened, & if I had any thoughts they're now gone. Let me know if I can send any books. I'd be happy to.

Jane & Joe came out last weekend to view the latest ell they're throwing out & guess who they ran into first on Flying Point? That's right, les Boys, who called up a bit ago to invite me to dinner. Bobby [Fizdale] says he saw Maxine [Groffsky] at a dinner party in Paris, which you missed because you were on a seven hour train trip to join Harry at a 3 star restaurant. Is that true or is it a Maxine cover story?

What is new austerity Paris like? The papers are maddeningly undetailed. I was very taken with the general's glamour when we all knew—yes, even I—that he had to devalue the franc, & he said, "I won't." I think one should take a page out of his book—the one on which he says No to Life—

love, Tania Grossman[599]

PS I read every last—almost every last—word of *The Custom of the Country*. Well, she [Edith Wharton] didn't look like Margaret Dumont[600] for nothing. It seems strange though that *all* had to be sacrificed because she could never forget that she was a New York Jones. There are some very funny bits in it, but they're not more frequent than the raisins in a Raggedy Ann salad, alackaday.

598. Richard Watson Gilder (1844–1909), American poet who dubbed himself "a squire of poesy."
599. Director of ULAE Graphics Workshop.
600. Margaret Dumont (1889–1965), actress. She played the grand dame in seven Marx Brothers movies including *A Night at the Opera* (1935).

Are the *Fables in Slang* unthinkable in French? I suppose it would take a Boileau to translate them.

Then there's Howells' *Indian Summer*, one of his less ambitious & better novels. The scene is Florence & Jamesian in effect. Caspar Goodwood meets Isabel Archer years later &, after a bit of finagling [?] gets her. "Cute" — Edmund Wilson. "Proustian" — Newton Arvin.

love to Pierre,
ton ami

Boardman Robinson[601]

Fairfield just came in & said, "Do the French know about Frank Stockton?" Who knows? Perhaps *Rudder Grange* is proto-surrealist. It's certainly much more entertaining than *Penrod and Sam*, *Peck's Bad Boy* or *The Story of a Bad Boy*. *Rudder Grange* — like all his books — is entirely about house & apartment hunting —.

TO JOHN ASHBERY

[Southampton, New York]

A Friday in December '68
(never mind which)

Dear "paysage choisi" —

Now where was I? There's been many a phone call from Dutton this week, so I'll tell you their trivialities before I forget them, & perhaps finish this tomorrow when hopefully I will have a letter from you. If Peg Brooks, why not me? (Yes I know she sent you a cable, & your letter got there in the nick.)

(I'm back in the living room — or rather, still there — *Die Winterreise* is on the great turntable — it suits my mood best in this season of grim cheer.)

Arthur Cohen called Monday afternoon & said he'd had great success selling *Nest* to the Dutton salesmen (later confirmed by Peg who said, "He did a wonderful presentation — of which I feel I am perhaps a better judge than he" — surely it's jealousy that makes the world go round?). He had also seen the photographs which P.B. received that morning. In my letter to her, I had said I wished Arthur could see them — partly [?] to make "compliment;" & because he

601. Boardman Robinson (1876–1952), book reviewer and critic.

at least knows what we look like. He was quite pleased to have been invoked, & chose the same as I. Peg said, "But Jimmy looks *hefty*!" I said, "Peg, Jimmy *is* hefty." "No, you can't fight nature," I said with a wry simper. But from his pause I gathered that he thinks one can, and should. It was then decided that next time I'll put on a frayed work shirt & turn myself over to Walker Evans.[602] Or is Karsh of Ottawa[603] the answer?

Arthur then said, "You know we were saying, we don't have to wait until John comes back to have Jimmy to supper." I suppressed an impulse to say "define 'we,'" but at the end of our badinage (Marivaudage it wasn't) I took my courage in both hands and said, "Give my love to Bill," which seemed the right thing.

Then yesterday Peg called all of a fuss because both you & I had written her about page proofs (If I *did* promise them to him, I *shouldn't* have, because we *never* show page proofs). She was concerned at not having had an answer available to her ("I know poets are particular about having things just right. They're so word-minded"). So I spent plenty time hunting up your last, in which you mentioned some of the mistakes—I could find every letter you'd written me except that, which turned out to be marking my place in Kate Chopin's *The Awakening*—which though short I doubt that I'll finish (it's better than I thought but, well, adultery is perhaps the dullest subject, especially if it ends with the tarnished one swimming out into the Gulf). Of course when I called her, *your* letter had arrived. To your corrections I added "cassoulet toulousain" and "giardiniera." I believe you wrote her about that some time ago, but it seemed wise to insist. I wonder what we'll discover in the printed product? Maybe the English edition will be the one to get, except it's the edition with the misprints that collectors covet isn't it? Have we been too scrupulous?

Peg was thrilled with the news I'd passed on to her from Kenneth that "Fred" Dupee[604] once called *Nest* "the funniest novel since *Lolita*" (1955), & in despair that all the bound galleys had been sent out, she's writing him, & I think I'll ask K to pass on his copy. I've heard not one word from him this week, despite his promise to put the awards business "at the top of my list"—his *very words*.

[letter ends here]

---

602. Walker Evans (1903–1975), American photographer.
603. Yousuf Karsh (1908–2002), Canadian portrait photographer.
604. F. W. Dupee (1904–1979), professor at Columbia University and literary critic.

TO MISS BATIE [605]

March 25, 1969

Dear Miss Batie,

Thank you for your letter. It is always pleasant to learn that someone takes an interest in a work which one enjoyed writing. In the past I have declined to comment on my own work: because, it seems to me, a poem is what it is; because a poem is itself a definition, and to try to redefine it is to be apt to falsify it; and because the author is the person least able to consider his own work objectively. Though as for the last, one certainly has to try. However, I liked your letter, and I have a great curiosity about Vancouver, so I'll see if I can think of anything that may be of use to you.

Of the ideas you suggest, the one that seems closest to what I might think is that of "an art where everything is ambiguous until superimposed into an entity." To change your phrase somewhat, I know that I like an art where disparate elements form an entity. De Kooning's work, which I greatly admire, has less to do with it than that of Kurt Schwitters', whose collages are made of commercial bits and "found" pieces but which always compose a whole striking for its completeness.

I had no religious intention, though I can see why a poem whose "idea," if [we may] call it such, is that of an essential harmony, or perhaps congruity is a better word, might suggest one. However, intention needn't enter in, and if a reader sees things in a religious way, and the work is dogmatically acceptable, then I don't see why it should not be interpreted in that way, as well as in others. In this case, though, I really can't see that purification comes into it at all. Part of the point would seem to be that junk like the trucks and the lions, and things that matter, like flowers, the sea, a mother and her baby (in an ascending scale of value) have each its place, and that it is the world in its impurity which is so very beautiful and acceptable, if only because one has so little choice.

As for evocation/communication, I don't find the first separate from the second, though subsidiary to it. The aim of any poet, or other artist, is first to make something; and it's impossible to make something out of words and *not* communicate. However, if a poem can be reduced to a prose sentence, there can't be much to it. (Someone, I believe, has said that "what a poem communicates is itself." This seems to me true.)

605. See glossary.

I am not quite sure what you mean by the "development" of the poem. If you mean it in the sense it's used in music, I hope it's there in the poem; anyway I have nothing to add to it. If you mean how I came to write it, well, let's see.

It was late February and I had very recently returned from Europe, where for the first time I had visited Palermo, and made an excursion to see the temples a Agrigento (where there were also wild snap-dragons in blooms among the lion colored drums of fallen columns), a rather dusty and disappointing affair at the time, but on which it was a pleasure to recollect. The day on which I wrote the poem I had been trying to write a poem in a regular form about (I think) Palermo, the Palazzo Abatelli, which has splendid carved stone ropes around its doors and windows, and the chapels decorated by Serpotta[606] with clouds of plaster cherubs; the poem turned out laborious and flat, and looking out the window I saw that something marvelous was happening to the light, transforming everything. It then occurred to me that this happened more often than not (a beautiful sunset I mean) and that it was "a day like any other," which I put down as a title. The rest of the poem popped out of its own accord. Or so it seems now.

I do not usually revise much, though I often cut, particularly the end or to-ward the end of a poem. One tends to write beyond what's needed.

It seems to me that readers sometimes make the genesis of a poem more mys-terious than it is (by that I perhaps mean, think of it as something outside their own experience). Often a poem "happens" to the writer in exactly the same way that it "happens" to someone who reads it.

As for stimuli, I hope you won't "perceive a similar response" in this instance, since what stimulated me to write was the apathy following on the disappoint-ment of a wasted day. However, what seemed like waste then may have been a warming up. Who knows? Not me.

[letter ends here]

TO KENNETH KOCH

[East Aurora, New York]

April 1, 1969

Dear Cap'n Kenny,

I enclose the heart of EVO's [*East Village Other*] latest offering *Jive Comics*, which I felt you needed. It ought to look lovely over the *causeuase* in your new

606. Giacomo Serpotta (1656–1732), recognized as the greatest Sicilian sculptor to work in stucco. He decorated numerous churches in Palermo.

apartment. I thought of sending you the whole issue of *Jive*, but the rest of the comix didn't'seem worth the postage (none are by our Crumb).

I'm visiting mother in East Aurora, N.Y.—the sometime home of Millard Fillmore and Elbert Hubbard, presently known for Fisher-Price Toys and Moos Electronics. It's quite pretty here, in a sullen sort of a way. Saturday I'm joining little J. A. at Pultneyville, where Harry [Mathews] also may materialize. That should be fun, though whether Mrs Ashbery will feel she's getting all the good she might of her boy's visit, I couldn't say.

Guess you know by now that Michael B [Brownstein] is this year's O'Hara poet. John and I did a lot of buck passing to no avail, since we both felt that somehow Tony [Towle] ought—or needed—to get it. But John finally confessed to finding a certain monotony in Tony's mss. and that tore it. Michael is now revising his, whatever that means, and has changed the title from *Shining Vistas* to *Waves of Freedom* but says he doesn't like either and expects to find another. At a lunch with the "Phil" O'Haras and Harry Seggersman, John told Michael he liked the first title, *Smiling Vistas*. Michael said that was a good one, too.

J.A. also had a letter from John Cheever[607] telling him he's to receive an award from the Academy of Arts and Letters "for making a contribution"—5,000 simoleons. This is perhaps still a secret—at least John says it is, each time he announces it to another full table.

Wystan's review of *A Nest* still hasn't come out in the *Times* Book Review. Grrrr—we must have a terrible enemy there. Jack Kroll told John that "*Newsweek* might even review it." Instead they will probably run some new photographs of Philip Roth, Malcolm Muggeridge and Tom Clark. (The Tom Clarks now have a girl—a baby girl. Bet that sends a surge of blood through the old ticker.)

Another not-yet-publicly-announced secret is that Eliot and Fairfield Porter are to be made honorary doctors of something or other by Colby College (which is in Maine, of course) at some sort of double ring ceremony. For no good reason this strikes me as very cute.

I've gotten copies of my poems from Doubleday—the book really looks very good—and I'll send you a copy of the paperback edition when I get back to the South Fork (the deluxe hand-bound Koch family copy has already gone off to Janice, to whom I trust it came as a surprise that the jacket photo is credited to "Janice Koch"—taken at Neil's Harbor, N[ova] S[cotia]). If you think of anyone to whom Lickspittle here should fawningly offer a copy, let me know.

Let's see—can I possibly have run dry? Larry Fagin[608] is back in town, and

607. John Cheever (1912–1982), novelist and short-story writer.
608. See glossary.

Ted [Berrigan] paid an Easter visit looking a good bit like Mr Bunny himself. He and Sandy are splitsville—not divorcing necessarily but separating as the curds from the whey. John thinks the O'Hara benefit will clear $6,000+ after expenses—there might have been more but Barrett N. sent out some hundreds of free tickets. Still, it's enough to keep the project going a little longer.

It would certainly be grand if that unlikely event—a letter from Kenneth— came to pass. Look at Byron—Byron found time to write lots of lovely letters and Byron was a very busy poet. Or is it your theory that it was the letters that killed him? I wouldn't want you to run any unnecessary risks.

Good grief, here comes my mother with that plate of brownies again. Scream. I agree with Philip Roth's mother, as lately quoted in the *Times*, "Every mother is a Jewish mother."

By the way during the recent poetry judging at the County Fair, I got quite a bit of static from John about Allen Kaplan,[609] "Kenneth thinks he's very good; and so do I." This formula, expressed in reverse order, was also used as a second telling argument. Sometime I'd like to look at some of his poems with you. There must be something I'm missing; it all seems very pallid to me—but not right now.

Is it true that you already have an apartment with a view of the Ile de la Cite? *Vous avez le derrière dans la beurre*—which I believe means some folks sure do land on their feet.

Love,

The Swan of Litchfield

The *East Aurora Advertiser* in which my book is described as by "Former East Auroran" . . .—announces that a shower is being tendered a couple brides-to-be: Maxine Puffer and Betty Huff.

TO JOE BRAINARD

[Great Spruce Head Island]

June 26, 1969

Dear Joe,

Two letters *and* a photograph (which I love)!—yes, you certainly got the first letter.

---

609. Allen Kaplan, poet.

Not that I have a thing to write about. The rip here was the usual chore, especially so this year, since we had also to pack for Amherst next winter. But that I'm rather looking forward to: visions of book shops dance in my head. We stopped at Kensington, in New Hampshire, to visit Anne's (Porter) sister Barbara Birch and her husband, Francis. I'm sure I've told you about their house—it's an 18th century farmhouse of a not at all fancy kind, painted brick red (or barn red) with white trim, up on the side of a high hill. Francis spends all the time he can treasuring and nurturing it. I walked up to a meadow he had just mowed. Here and there in the further part he had left clumps of daisies, also some tall bushes of high bush cranberry, which made it like the most marvelous garden—with the swaths of mowed hay and the flowers it was a little like that pebble garden in Japan which is kept carefully raked with a few boulders jutting up in it; though scarcely so unpleasantly contrived. Right around their house is like that too, with granite sticking out here and there, and all the flowers growing in clumps right in the grass. I would like to grow things that way in Southampton (or anywhere else for the matter of that) but a rose bush in the grass would last for exactly one mowing. Anyway, it is a place I like to visit—except for the bed. I'm always given Young Frank's room, which is on the ground floor with a view out a screen door of fields and woods, very pretty in the morning—but the bed! It not only has a mattress —if that isn't too fancy a word for it—that ties me in knots, but also a brass bedstead (don't ever get one) which is like something in the orchestration of Mahler's Symphony of One Thousand—in some positions just breathing makes it jingle like a wind-chime. Then when you shift in hopes of silence the whole thing goes off like the gong at the beginning of a J. Arthur Rank production. So I'm glad to be here and have my own mattress, stuffed with silent stone hair.

Our first three days were cold and drizzly, but today—gorgeous. If you think of the island at the best you saw it that's how it is. Laurence and Betsy and Leon were already here when we arrived. Leon is really great, about the same age as Wayne and just as terrific, which you may find hard to believe, but it's true. He's also very beautiful in the blonde, blue-eyed, pink chubby cheeked style. And so good natured! Almost as good natured as Bruno [the Porters' dog], who is rather jealous, and tries to get him alone so he can frig on him. Luckily, Betsy has not seen him try this. As a matter of fact, I find it impossible not to like her more since she produced this paragon. She also is easier to get on with; perhaps because she's pregnant or perhaps looking after a toddler burns up some of her excess energy, of which she has a good deal. (One of Leon's treats I saw in the larder is a jar of tiny Wienies called Toddler Finger Food. That's almost as bad as the English treat called Fish Fingers.)

The day we got here Fairfield told off his brother John (the dumb bossy Porter brother who plays tennis. Since he's rather apt to look down his nose at people it pleases me that, now he's retired from teaching, he can accurately be called a Tennis Bum). Anyway, John told Katie and me that the big house used too much electricity and we should all be more careful about turning off the lights, and that he was going to tell Fairfield about this, though he didn't. Needless to say others passed on the news. Fairfield leapt up, counted the number of lights on (three), marched down to John's and counted the number on there (also three) and put a bee in his kid brother's ear. John is louder but Fairfield is much more effective in that kind of exchange. One reason I was pleased about this is that last year he acted very put upon because the caretaker's boat was out of commission, so all Camden trips (mainly for food supplies) had to be on the Kittiwake — which, since it *is* his boat, one couldn't do anything about.

Katie, who is a really good person, felt badly about having passed on the electricity story; but I didn't, unh-unh.

And now that I've disclosed the depths of my wicked nature, let's talk about fattening you up. I have heard of someone who had to gain weight and did it by having a tablespoon of heavy cream every hour; but that sounds rather cholesterolly to me. I think what would do most is if you could form the habit of eating lunch. I know you hate to stop working for more food, but it really takes almost no time at all to choke down a peanut butter and jam sandwich and a glass of milk (with Hershey's chocolate syrup stirred in, if you can bear it). Otherwise, you may lose any weight you gain when you go back to New York. Be that as it may, I'm sending you a calorie book (I find I'm getting plenty already) which you can use in a backwards way — who would have guessed that a porterhouse steak was so rich? Or from butterbeans? (Though the name rather gives them away.) All kinds of nuts are very rich, so are avocados, and Sara Lee pound cake — toasted and buttered, perhaps? (In a minute I'm going to be dripping saliva on the typewriter keys) — but this is beginning to sound a little hard on Kenward, so I won't extol the pleasures and virtues of thickly buttered mashed potatoes, or candied sweets . . .

I think I'll stop for a moment and have a snack . . .

Actually, all I did was get a can of icy cold Fresca, since as far as I can see there isn't anything to snack on. I guess that's one way to lose weight.

I haven't written anything yet, except a very lousy poem, but I've taken a mess of snapshots, mostly of Leon but some of flowers, bunchberry and twinflower.

Yes, I really have no news, but keep the letters coming anyway. Give Kenward a big kiss for me,

love,

Jimmy

PS If you go to Hardwick antiquing[610]—the drawing I wanted was (I think) on the second floor of the main house. It shows—as near as I can remember—a farmhouse and trees, it's in pencil and looks as though a ruler had been used to get the lines of the house straight. It cost $15, framed. I can't imagine why I think I want it—perhaps because it exists in some borderland between instinctive art and more conscious art, an area of which I am very fond. But if you don't go to Hardwick antiquing, that's all right too . . .

TO JOHN ASHBERY

[Great Spruce Head Island]

June 29, 1969

Dear Rich Freeze-Dried Coffee Chunks,

Thanks a mil' for the forbidden comix. As a matter of fact, a pair of young eyes did glimpse their gaily colored covers when I did open the envelope. However, I assured her that it was merely some underground little magazines gotten up to look like comic books, then twitched my mantle blue and headed for the privacy of my room with same. As a matter of fact, the raciest reading I've had since arriving la-bas (can that possibly pass as a translation of "downeast"? I spose not) was an entry in *A Gardener's Book of Plant Names*: "Cliteria: Butterfly pea. From L. *clitoris*; an anatomical term; an allusion to a characteristic of the flower." Reading that vividly brought back the thrills and dissatisfactions of Webster's Unabridged in fifth grade—"whore" had been all but obliterated by sticky fingers.

Here is very nice, though we're enjoying a spell of the kind of weather I always claim doesn't happen in Penobscot Bay: hot and sultry. Unfortunately this is combined with what F. calls an off-shore wind, which means that all the warm surface water is being carried down to Flying Point Road for the boys' use, so, though swimming seems a delicious resort, to actually do it is rather like tak-

---

610. Hardwick is a small town in Vermont's Northeast Kingdom where Schuyler went antiquing, as recorded in his poem "Now and Then."

ing a cold shower in your bathroom when Giorgio's gone away for Christmas. Still, it is — it being the Island — gorgeous, as that wouldn't be after Southampton, since Job's Lane changed its name to Anna Capri: there are now six bars on it, and the last two weekends I was driven up the wall and across the ceiling by an electronic folk singer — the kind who makes up his own words to one of those nameless laments you can't quite put your foot on. And you know how I feel about having anything like that intrude on my 2 a.m. read-feed.

Laurence, Betsy, and Baby Leon were already here when we arrived, and saintly Laurence had swept and garnished the whole enormous place. I find I'm less up-tight with Betsy, perhaps because she is not quite so strung-out. This may be due to the fact that Leon is a paragon — blond, blue-eyed and chubby-cheeked all over; his figure, indeed, is not unlike mine, though more suited to his years. But I won't elaborate on the little tyke, since I feel sure you're about as interested in the wonderful doings of toddlers as you are in getting a nice wet hairy kiss from Bruno. Which reminds me — the larder is full of jars of something called Toddler Finger Food, small blunt ended frankfurters which look alarmingly like pickled Toddler Fingers.

Thanks for telling me about D. Barthelme's new mag[611] — naturally, I have recently sent away the few poems I had that did not induce a sharp case of cringe, the best one to Bull (oops — or sic?) Berkson for his no doubt never to appear *Best & Co*[612] and some others to T. Winkfield. Maybe I should stop hiding my light under berry-baskets. Anyway, I will certainly try 'n run something up for him, and for you to comment on (provided you promise not to say "Yes Kenneth" when I offer them to you).

It's funny that even here Sunday is distinctly Sundayish, I can't imagine why. Maybe it's because there's no mail delivery. Even the most tranquil life needs some sort of focus, other than When do we eat next? I haven't done anything kitchen-wise yet, though I have plans . . . And now, even though I die the death of some arctic explorer, I must go swim; or dip. The sweat is running off me in freshets — ill-smelling ones, that is.

Tues July 1, 1969
Dominion Day (in Canada)

It got much sultrier on Sunday I couldn't face coming back up here where the typewriter lives (yesterday it was too cold) — anyway, here it is Tuesday. My

611. The novelist Donald Barthelme's magazine, *Location*.

612. A single issue did appear, and it included two Schuyler poems, "Empathy and New Year" and "Walking to the Edge with a Cup of Coffee," an early version of "The Cenotaph."

letter writing career has gotten off to a bum start—and I've already had four from Joe! They're both well. He's trying to gain the weight that Kenward is trying to lose—does that remind you of an old old poem?

Last night we went to Trudie and John's to see Nancy's [Straus] slides of My Trip to Greece, Crete and Turkey, which was all one might expect or hope. As a matter of fact, I enjoy slides at least as much as any issue of the *National Geographic*, and this occasion had the plus of commentary. John Porter seems to think it's funny the Greeks haven't tidied up the Acropolis yet—"Same old columns still lying around where they fell—just like they were in 1923" while Mike explained to us that it was Lord Elgin who blew up the Parthenon. You would have enjoyed the part where Nancy flashed on something like an unfinished Motherwell Elegy[613] and said, "This is the cave where Zeus was born" then switched to one of Mike Strauss in front of same, "And this is Zeus." Another exchange: Nancy: "This is asphodel growing in the theater at (someplace)." Aline: "Asphodel grows absolutely everywhere in Greece." Nancy: "I love it." Eliot got quite a lot of mileage out of the fact that she didn't bother taking her camera to Ephesus because "I didn't think it would be so very different from all the others." Yes, it was a fun evening.

Good night, nurse, Laurence has gotten out his guitar and struck up the nameless tune I thought I left behind on Job's Lane. Trumbull Higgins[614] is right, the Eastern seaboard is one continuous urban area.

I can't wait for you to go to Indiana and come back, so I could hear all about it. Are you planning a Little Journey to the birthplace of George Ade?[615]

Last night I thought of lots of things to tell you, while waiting for Morpheus, who had once again missed the mailboat. Now I can't remember a one. So will close now in hopes of hearing from you soon.

love,

J.
Stubborn Stains

Guess I'll stroll down to the South Meadow and see if any kickias are in bloom.

---

613. Robert Motherwell painted a series, *Elegies to the Spanish Republic.*
614. Trumbull Higgins, military historian and husband of Barbara Guest.
615. George Ade (1866–1940), newspaperman, fabulist, and playwright born in Kentland, Indiana.

TO JOE BRAINARD

Great Spruce Head Island

July 1 maybe? 1969
anyway it's Tuesday

Dear Joe,

I'm off to a poor start in the letters sweepstakes—I've had four from you, counting today's and my first one just left. Actually, I wrote it last week and stood it in a kind of box where we put mail to go down to the dockhouse. But it fell over and yesterday I found it still lying in the bottom of the box. Which among other things shows that nobody has been writing many letters.

Last night we went to John and Trudie's to see slides Nancy took in Greece, Crete and Turkey. They weren't bad (though somehow I can never seem to *see* anything in a slide) and in fact would have been very nice if the uninteresting ones had been left out. I've never seen slides that there wasn't a lot of "You can't see it very clearly here because the light wasn't right but on the left . . ." To my regret, the ones that were most that way were of flowers: "The asphodels grow everywhere and were *perfectly lovely* . . . " picture of dim fuzz balls. There was also some vintage chat: "This is the cave where Zeus was born" picture of black area. Next picture, Mike Strauss in front of same "And this is Zeus."

Bruno and Leon did their bit to enliven the occasion. Leon kept escaping from one parent or the other and heading for the projector so he could walk up the beam of light and try to get a clear look at the picture inside (smart kid). He also kicked up quite a fuss every time "boats," which is a word in his vocabulary, gave way to a friendly girl, known to me as "Annie's Mommy," who kept sliding him cookies in the dark. Bruno was less fortunate, and all his efforts to raid Trudie's kitchen were foiled. He still managed to do a lot of noisy marching around and snorting and trying to pick unidentifiable objects off of low tables. I finally collared him and by dint of scratching his belly till my arm was ready to drop off kept him in one place for the rest of the show. This was quite a sacrifice, since that afternoon he had been rolling in dead seal. If you poured a pint of rancid cod liver oil over yourself you would approach, though not achieve, the same effect. Poor Trudie was seated on his other side, but managed to contain herself, except to remark that the atmosphere was a bit rich (when their children bring dogs to the house, the dogs aren't allowed indoors). I did think I heard a stifled gasp when Bruno went and spread himself on the braided hearthrug. I'll bet there was a great deal of airing and scrubbing down there today. All the same, a good time was had by all, not least by me.

Fairfield's gorgeous nephew, Stephen Porter, is said to be arriving today with his second wife (he's about twenty-four, I guess—what's come over our young folks?). I have nothing to add to that; guess it was just in my mind.

Fairfield has already painted an interior (about as big as the drawing board you left here). It's of a bit of the living room with a mulberry juice floor and the walls much yellower than they really are. He thinks the walls are maybe too yellow, but if he repaints them all the other colors will look wrong (I think) but he probably will anyway. He painted it very quickly and it has that look of there not being much there, as though there were barely enough paint to get from one edge to the other, a look some might call thin and which seems to me marvelously so. He also did a portrait of Katie, quite a bit bigger though not "big." She's seated at the dining table on the porch and the view is down one side of the table to the door to the pantry—so there's a lot of white, gray and black in the background. It's in his rather blunt stiff style of figure painting where things are kept generalized (it is not at all like last year's small very green picture of Katie—did I tell you that that one, which he had given to Anne, was stolen from a show at Southampton College? From something he said to his sister Nancy, I think he's transferring his anger with the thieves to people who laughingly tell him it's a compliment and shows what a success he is—and I can see why he would). Now he has started a portrait commission, which is big (though not the "biggest"). It's to be of a young man named, maybe, Harry Streibel, who has built a house in the woods near East Hampton and become interested in art through knowing Ted Dragon, Alfonso Ossorio's friend.[616] (His collection at present I believe consists of an Ossorio, a John MacWhinnie and a John Little—a mediocre East Hampton artist said to be very good at selling out of his studio.) Before we came here I went with F. to Harry S.'s and took photographs while he sketched. Then F. paid to have 14" x 17" enlargements made of the ones he wanted (it's six dollars a shot). This was very satisfying—there is absolutely no reason—for me, that is—to have enlargements that big, but very satisfying to see the snippy little contacts turn out looking so professional and *Town & Country*ish. There really isn't anything to photography except point and snap (I'm not sure that's true) but I often wondered how successful fashion photographers I've met could be such successes, since they're such dopes. Now I see it isn't a mysterious talent, it's largely gall.

616. Ted Dragon, dancer, and Alfonso Ossorio (1916–1990), collagist and art collector who owned Jackson Pollock's *Lavender Mist*.

On the other hand, perhaps there isn't much more to poetry than point and snap.

Now maybe I'll go swimming. I've only been once this year—fiendishly cold. I'll try to remember to put in the calorie book this time. Glad to hear you're waxing beefy.

Love to KGE and a good pat to Whip'erwill (a word I don't know how to spell).

love, Jimmy

PS I'm thinking of C Comics.[617] Maybe we should try it all ways. If and when you have something to send, send it. Unfilled in or incomplete or as you will . . .

TO JOHN ASHBERY

[Great Spruce Head Island]

July 8, 1969

Dear Piccolo Pete,[618]

It's the sleepy time of day (3:10 pm) when Inspiration sinks downward to darkness on leaden wing. How better to pass it than writing to ask a lot of favors of you?

First, the lead casket favor: I think I left a book at your house, called something like *Intellectual Life in Gay Colonial New England*, by Samuel Eliot Morrison. If I did, and seeing as it's quite a slim light weight paperback which could easily be fed to the *Art News* postage franking machine, would you pop it in a manila envelope and do the gallant needful? I'm laboring under a delusion that I want to go on reading it, but a delusion is probably what it is, so if you can't really lay your hand on it, don't hunt.

Next, the silver casket favor: enclosed please find our check for ten dollars. I can't get the kind of film I like best up here in, or on, the Styx. It's called, Kodak Panatomic-X, FX 135-35. Or in other words, it's black and white 35 mm film, 35 frames to a role, slow emulsion, or Pan-X. Would you ask your neighborhood camera store to send as many rolls to me as ten skins will buy, inclusive of

617. Brainard collaborated with various poets to produce the mimeographed *C Comics*.
618. "Piccolo Pete" was a popular song of the 1920s.

250

postage? It seems to me that I've seen such a shop in the vicinity of Tart News: or there is a Peerless-Willoby (sp?) on the corner of Lex and 43rd, should your steps go dawdling Goodyward.

And now, the brass ring. I think I'll apply for a Guggenheim this fall: to whom do you write for an application blank? What's a reasonable amount to ask for? How many sponsors does one need? Can you think of a good project, other than going to London to get some clothes? I thought of asking Kenneth (not him—the hairdresser) and Jimmy Merrill for letters—don't you think it might look a little nepotismish if I had a letter from you? Or don't you? (I already feel quite depressed, as I look forward to being turned down.) Any hints or advice will be appreciated.

As a matter of fact, I had a project in mind, a sort of a travel book—Nova Scotia, perhaps? I don't really feel up to *all* of Canada, especially the French speaking parts—the kind that is of no use to anyone, a sort of pastiche of *Now and Then, Letters from High Latitudes, Eothen,* and *Dere Mabel. Que pense-tu?* I would rather like to write such a book, though I would not, of course, feel constrained to do so, should I get a grant.

Can't say as anything much has happened since I wrote to you yesterday. Yes, nothing has. Last night John and Trudie came to dinner, along with Jean (Mrs David Porter—David is the nicest of their children. He specializes in slime molds) and daughter Anne Marie aged two. A quiet time was had by all. John P seems easier to get on with this year. Last year he was very up-tight, particularly about taking anyone to Camden, which, as you know, is our major entertainment recourse. I suppose being the dumb Porter brother is not such an easy role to fill—

Tomorrow I'll start looking for Indiana postcards[619]—can't wait to get the full playback. (I hope, by the way, that you received a long letter I sent to you there.) Love to Pierre—how long is he staying? For the matter of that, is he still here?

love,

J.
Sam, the old accordion man

Tomorrow (good grief) the crabby Porter brother, Edward,[620] is coming to stay—with Nancy, thank God—for several weeks. So is his astonishingly plain

619. Ashbery had taught a poetry workshop at Indiana University.
620. Fairfield Porter had three brothers, Eliot, Edward, and John, and one sister, Nancy.

wife. Unfortunately, when she opens her malocclusion, which is quite like a pair of cowcatchers off some old-time choo-choos one is not so much conscious of the beauty of the Inner Audrey as of her rasp-like tongue. Oh well, maybe she's just plain spoken, like Queen Victoria, but Edward really makes a specialty of the put-on and the send up. They once spent a few days in Southampton and by the time they left I was feeling like Marsyas towards the end of his career. (It was during that visit that Lizzie remarked to me — she was four or five at the time — "Uncle Edward is shorter and thicker than Dad, but he has those same little squinty eyes.")

PS Guess you're right about zip codes. My mother sent me a letter addressed here but with the Southampton zip on it. Needless to say, it did not go to Southampton first.

TO JOE BRAINARD

[Great Spruce Head Island]

July 16, 1969

Dear Joe,

Every time I start to write to you it seems the mailboat is about due, so I put it off until I have more time to write a *real* letter, and none gets written. Well, the mailboat is due quite soon, so if this isn't a letter, at least it will be a message, and I can enclose the requested autograph, attached to something for you. The something may not be finished: perhaps I will change "faded" at the end to "weathered"; and cut out "Woodpile Paper."[621] And maybe I won't. I was going to type it again because of the typing mistakes; but anything from me that didn't have some, would scarcely seem authentic.

"Pair of scales" because: (here I will try to draw the kind of scales Justice holds)

Something like a stone,* of an accepted weight, was put in one side, then whatever you wanted to weigh was put in the other, until they balanced. All good scales, such as doctors use, are variations of this principle; though it's not always apparent. Bathroom scales, however, work by a spring: so much weight pushes it so far down. Obviously, something which easily gets out of order sooner or

---

621. The poem referred to is "After Joe Was at the Island." Schuyler did not change "faded" but did cut "Woodpile Paper."

later, usually sooner. Perhaps one should get a new pair every year, along with one's Topsiders and suntan oil. It seemed to me that I don't say "pair of scales" for bathroom scales; but after trying to take my mind by surprise, I finally succeed and find that I do.

I *love* the tintypes and photographs you sent me, and look at them a lot.

Have you done any C-3 Comix with anybody yet? I've been cutting stuff out in preparation.

Fairfield made a great picture, it's evening primroses (some grow around the studio—the Calais studio I mean—and along the road, rather tall, pale clear light yellow flowers in a bunch at the top, some of the lower narrow leaves usually turning red). It has a wonderful blue sky, for which he used cerulean rather than cobalt blue—more a Katz-Freilicher blue than he usually uses, though it doesn't *look* like he got it from them in the picture (Jane told him about it).

Nothing much is going on here—the Katzes may come to visit this week. Friday, day after tomorrow, there's a trip to Camden. Haven't been on one yet this summer, so I'm looking forward to it with all the delirium of a crazed shophound.

Keep writing! I love your letters. Give Kenward a love-pinch.

love,

Jimmy

*So in England weight is still given in "stones" (1 stone—14 pounds); if you weigh 140 pounds here you would weigh 10 stone (*not* 10 stones) there. So the English are much more stoned than we. Now if you're a good boy & don't run away with the potato masher, some day Uncle Wiggily will tell you all about rods and poods, though it may not be for a score of years.

TO JOE BRAINARD

[Great Spruce Head Island]

July 17, 1969

Dear Joe,

Wow, what a couple of wonderful letters—I sure was glad when the first one and the postcards came that the mailboat was taking away a letter and a magazine to you. There isn't much in the magazine of interest but I didn't want to tear out what I was sending it for; oh well, *any* magazine is worth leafing through once.

I love the postcards, especially "Bird's Eye View, Franklin, N. H." which I rate class one A. I forgot to thank you for the *Womens Circles*, too; I read every single word—no, not quite; "Teensville" is too boring. My only regret is the fever for refunding—I can't get very excited about S&H Green Stamps. Though I have a lurking feeling that Balzac would have made something great out of it— little old granny absolutely destroying the family as she amasses more and more and more Betty Crocker and Raleigh Cigarette coupons. But I liked the severe put-down the lady who explains how it all works gave to the "this coupon plus one dollar brings Colonial cheesecake server." This is *not* funding. (But it is collecting.) I'm tempted—but haven't fallen yet—to get a couple of cookbooks put out by the churches and such; but that kind of book is cheaper in used bookstores, and you can see if it's really any good. Nowadays too many of them turn out to be Cake-Mix and mushroom soup concoctions; instead of thrilling old heirloom recipes.

I'm being bad at the moment—there is some kind of an ice cream do at John and Trudie's (it's only 4 in the afternoon for pity's sake) but I said sternly I was going to work and shut myself up here (in Kenward's room). Tonight there's no escape though, the Edward Porters & the Mike Strausses are coming for dinner; I really can hardly bear to be in the same room with Uncle Mike, who tells horrible endless boring anecdotes—I don't so much dislike him as hate the feeling of waves of claustrophobia I get when I realize that instead of going home he's launched into another story which will last quite possibly for a half an hour. A typical one has for the clincher his saying to Gary Cooper, "Sir, my wife once slept in your bed." (At some hunting lodge or something which Gary Cooper had previously visited)—I can just see the poor guy looking around for help. Which reminds me, Audrey Porter (Edward's wife) has for a sister-in-law a lady named Leatrice Fountain, who is the daughter of the great silent-movie film stars, Leatrice Joy and John Gilbert.[622] As a matter of fact, their marriage was one of the great Hollywood publicity production numbers of about 1928. I've heard that John Gilbert (he's in lots of movies with Garbo, such as the one where she falls through the ice and just her sable coat floats up to the surface, leaving Gilbert and Nils Asther to happily bugger each other forever after) was

622. Leatrice Joy (1893–1985), silent movie actress and actor John Gilbert's (1899–1936) second wife. Gilbert and Greta Garbo, who co-starred in *Queen Christiana*, are said to have had a love affair.

queer. But since one's source for that kind of story is usually someone like John Button . . . Anyway it always thrills me and fills me with wonder that there should be this fine thread connecting Fairfield with Grauman's Chinese.[623] (I can never get it through my head that Leatrice Fountain—who had a novel published by Doubleday a year or so ago—is younger than I am. Somehow the name Leatrice instantly invokes a lady dressed all in one pale shade of silk, with a nose and tiny teeth peeking and twinkling out from under a gauze cloche.) Now about quickly fading wild flowers: well, they do, there's no doubt about it. One thing you might do, is get at the florists in Montpelier any of the products that you put in water to make cut flowers last longer, It's especially good with bushy kinds of things, I read. (One of them is called, I think, FloraLife—but they are all more or less the same.) It's best to cut flowers early in the morning or in the evening, when the sun isn't hot on them. If you're getting a bunch, carry a can of water with you, and pop them in as you pick them. I find flowers—wild flowers last a good deal longer if picked only in the bud, and then let open in the house in the water. The buds should be fairly far along; you get so you can tell about this. Also, always have the water as deep as you can on the stems.

Why don't you line up a battery of cream jars and bottles, then when you're doing a bouquet, you could have a number of whatever you're painting in the bud, so they would be opening as the ones on stage fade. Hmm? By the way, your method of not having them all in the bouquet at once (that are going to be in the painting) is the way the old master flower painters worked, so often there are lots of things in one bunch that in nature never are in bloom at the same time. Naturally, by the 19th century this came to be regarded as "cheating"; there is, it seems, nothing in the whole world that someone can't manage to be moral about; which strikes me as both funny and dreary.

And now, Dear Tortured Tootsies: yes, I believe the nails are the same substance all the way through. Mine are, anyway (chomp, chew). I *really* wish you would go to a nice foot-doctor in Montpelier—there's bound to be one—and have him deal with it. Go on, do it for me. (I can see you with that slightly far-away smile which means . . . well, "unh-unh.") Or maybe Kenward could deal with it: he gives Whippy perfectly lovely pedicures. (Did you know that if you cut your nails after a shower or a bath, they're much softer and easier to deal with?) If you're determined to go on wearing Chinese Lady Torture shoes next fall, at least go and get a pair custom made. They're expensive, but nothing is

623. Grauman's Chinese Theater in Hollywood, site of numerous movie premieres.

expensive that will prevent you from ruining your feet. Anyway they're not all that expensive, and you're famous! A success! Do it!

Thank you for telling me about Mrs. Kent,[624] and I will write to her. We're going to Camden tomorrow morning (if there isn't a typhoon) and I'll find a suitable nice card there. There are some pretty ones of Maine nowadays, all printed in Ireland.

Well, the folks are back from the ice cream revel, guess I'd better think about what to wear—maybe the plum organza and the see-through pants.

love to Kenward,

love,

Jimmy

TO BILL BERKSON

Great Spruce Head Island

July 24, 1969[625]

Dear Smoky Stover,[626]

So you're going to Vermont! Travel tip: seal your stash in tampons; that way it will be safe from light-fingered valets-de-chambres, etc.

Just before I left Southampton I unearthed the Frankobilia[627] I mentioned to you one fragrant evening last spring. They were in an envelope on which, the previous year, I had written LETTERS TO TAKE TO MAINE. There were no letters, however—wonder what I did with them? For the matter of that, I wonder what they were. Anyway, such as they are, here they are. I don't know what I think of them, not much I guess. But you be the judge, and *please* be frank (if you can't be frank, be john and kenneth).

Say, maybe our friend's names would make good verbs: to kenneth: emit a loud red noise; to ashbery: cast a sidewise salacious glance while holding a champagne glass by the stem; to kenward: glide from the room and not make waves; to brainard: give a broad and silent chuckle; to machiz, shower with con-

624. Louise Andrews Kent, owner of a house at Kent Corners in Calais, Vermont, and author of the Mrs. Appleyard cookbooks, among other books.

625. On this date Schuyler wrote in his diary, "The fog burned off but there are still bits of mist drifting around in the distance like dust kitties."

626. Comic strip about a fireman.

627. Berkson was a protégé of Frank O'Hara's. He edited *In Memory of My Feelings* (Museum of Modern Art, 1967) and, with Joe LeSueur, *Homage to Frank O'Hara* (1978; 1988).

versational spit drops—but I said friends, didn't I—cancel the last. To berkson and schuyler I leave to you.

I'm also sending a passage from G. T. Strong's diary[628] to amaze and amuse (or bemuse) you—but to really get the amazement you would have to read a good some of four volumes to know how unlikely this entry is from such a pillar of Trinity Church, Columbia College, The Philharmonic and the Sanitary Commission. Though as a youth he did turn on a few times with chloroform (feh) and ether (pah) in a spirit of scientific inquiry. The only other reference to grass is when he is dying, and it was given to him as an anodyne.

The three little Katzes are coming to visit the "end of this week"—today, or tomorrow, or the next day; or some other time. I hope it's not today, since there's a lot of fog leaning on the window and the last time they came, a few years ago, there was fog for their entire stay, the big wet drippy kind that makes your clothes feel like balls of clay. Then when they were on the go away boat the sun came out. But it was too late to see View****, as they were already in it.

Is it true that Joe has gained so much weight he has to be hoisted through a window like a Steinway? And Kenward, what's he been up to down in that little house? tell them I llok t (awk) look to hear from them both, and from you too. Any new news of *Best & Co*? What I saw of it looked really great.

Love,

Fanny's First Ball
Jimmy

I've been writing quite a bit (for me anyway) *et toi?*

TO JOE BRAINARD

[Great Spruce Head Island]

July 28, 1969

Dear Joe,

And a happy John Ashbery's birthday to you and yours. Or a happy John Ashbery's birthday . . . you see it's a red letter day.

It rained so hard last night it woke me up and 4 a.m. found me in the kitchen

---

628. George Templeton Strong (1820–1875), lawyer and nineteenth-century New York diarist.

stirring up a batch of French breakfast puffs (don't bother) and while they baked I copied down the enclosed recipe for Butterscotch brownies (do bother). They are no bother at all — very quick — and uhmmmm. The first time I made them I kept waiting for the sugar to melt and get liquid looking. It doesn't, when it gets sort of slippery and amalgamated, that's enough. The only thing that could improve them might be a hearty helping of grass, along with the walnuts or whatever. And speaking of that — yes, I would like a couple of joints, in fact, I would love it. I think if it was inside one of your folded up thick letters it would be undetectable. (But if you have any second thoughts about risk, don't do it.) It was a very kind offer.

When I was in Camden a week ago I tried to get you some Exacto blades — but every package had a different code number on it and no way of telling what kind you might like. Why don't you send $10 or whatever (check or money order do not send cash) to an art supply store in NYC and tell them to send as many as that will buy plus postage? Or have you been to Burlington?

Does that come under the heading of advice? It isn't, it's a suggestion. And here is another, get some gold stars and put them next to any questions you *really* want answered. That way, I'll know. Now, Joe, about that foot. I can see it as plainly as if it were right here on this typewriter, and what I want you to do is . . . what you please.

Tell Kenward I hope he caught the last article in the N Y *State Conservationist*, on wild rice. I'm certain it could be introduced into Veronica and may already be there. Your very own home grown wild rice — that's *class*. You could design a pretty label, put it in small bags, tie it with a ribbon and give it away at Christmas. D. D. [Ryan] would plotz. I can hear her telling Truman [Capote] about it now. Or you could throw it at people in opulent moments.

Yes, you bet I still do intend to visit Apple Hill. But I don't know quite when or how long yet. I have to go to Southampton with Fairfield and help him move stuff to Amherst — hope this can wait until Pat and Ron are there; but that depends on F's teaching schedule, somewhat, and other things. One way or another I will come, you bet.

My copy of the flower guide just came, so you should get yours soon. And I just ordered another book for you which I'm curious about. Its subject is . . . guess I won't tell you but I'll give you a hint: it's not about flowers or tattooing. Though it *might* be said to have some connection with them, at least, as a gift to you. Yes, I think I can go that far.

Now I had more things to tell you — what were they — I even made a couple of notes on a scrap of paper which must be somewhere in this room. Oh well,

I'll blame it on the weather, which is suddenly like November. The weather in general though, if it hasn't been consistently great, has been better than good, so can't complain.

Do you remember the clipping I sent you about the beach glass lady at Prout's Neck [Maine]? Well. Hold onto your chair. The day I mailed it to you I went down to Landing Beach and found a piece of *red beach glass*. Like so many precious things, it's very small. I suppose I should send it to the good woman but I'm not going to. It's mine and I'm going to keep it.

Started a couple of comix, tentative titles, *Storm* and *Steel Penis Farming*. Will follow soon. *Storm* is mostly composed of cameo appearances by some greats, but stars N*A*C oh shit NANCY (by special arrangement with Ernie Bushmiller)[629] (I am going to take typing lessons I am I am.)

I sent something to Bill c/o you, so hope he did or does come (I trust he'll show them to you—plural you). Give Kenward a group grope for me. And if you feel Bill might be slighted, give him same too.

love,

Jimmy

One art supply address: New York Central Supply, 62 3rd Avenue, New York, N.Y. 10003. Tell them to send it (if you order anything) special handling or you'll be standing around on one foot all summer waiting.

TO JOHN ASHBERY

[Great Spruce Head Island]

August 5, 1969

BLUEBERRY
QUEEN
WANTED

Dear Cullen Landis,[630]

Well, this is a thrill. So you're going to bring Pierre to see the *real America* I couldn't be pleaseder. First, practicalities.

---

629. Ernie Bushmiller (1905–1982), comic-strip artist who invented the character Nancy. Joe Brainard drew her in a series of adventures never imagined by Bushmiller.

630. Cullen Landis (1895–1975), leading man in over one hundred silent movies.

Fairfield wrote yesterday about how to get to Sunset, and I suppose the mailboat. Did he tell you it's now possible to get telephonic messages, not calls, messages) to the island? Reynald Hardie, the new strapping young caretaker (he's married) has a ship-to-shore device and he listens in at 6 a.m. and 8 p.m. and receives any messages for the island. You can send us same by telephoning either Woolcot Hardie (Reynald's father), Deer Isle or James Quinn, same address. However, if you're coming on Monday afternoon (the 11th), don't bother to phone, just come.

It seems to me it took us about five hours to drive from Kensington, N. H.— just north of Boston—to Camden. Sylvester's Cove, or Sunset, is two hours further. So I should think you could do it easily in 8 hours from Boston or less, with Pierre rather than Fairfield at the wheel (not that Fairfield is always the slowpoke I could wish). Of course much depends on antique shops and lunch rests. I recommend the Stowe House in Brunswick for lunch—mostly for the delicious Gibsons—which you would want to visit in any case (wonder what Hattie[631] would think of it all?) and the Hawthorne haunted campus of Bowdoin is right around the corner. If you want to see some Wyeths,[632] you can pop into the Farnsworth in Rockland: visiting time, $3\frac{1}{2}$ minutes—even so, you might feel you had wasted it. You will note on the map that, somewhere north of Bath and the Bath Ironworks, it's possible to get to Camden without going through such coastal towns (on US 1) as Thomaston. Fairfield takes this route, but you don't gain much in time, and you do get to see a lot of scrub with an occasional sign inviting you to turn off and visit The Yankee Whittler (I've always had an extra pine for your company at this point so I could say, "There's the Yankee Whittler; and there's his Mother.") The Prison Shop at the Pen. in Thomaston is, or rather was, the home of one of my favorite American diarists, Hezakiah Prince,[633] which I'll be happy to lend you after you've driven through it; all 800 pages. He's most illuminating on early 19th century weather conditions.

It just occurred to me that there's an all day trip to Camden on Thursday— what could be simpler than to phone youse? So I will. Talking to you would be piquant enough, even without the fact that my favorite telephone is nailed next

631. Harriet Beecher Stowe was inspired to write *Uncle Tom's Cabin* while living in Brunswick, Maine.

632. Paintings and drawings by Andrew Wyeth (1917–2009) and his father Newell Convers Wyeth (1882–1945), summer residents of Maine from 1920.

633. Hezekiah Prince, Sr. (1789–1839). *Remarks of My Life* was drawn from the diaries and journals of this prominent Thomaston, Maine, resident.

to the Camden Yacht Club men's room. Nothing ever happens (well, once Mike Straus went in to take a shower) but it *might*.

The place in Maine that I have always most wanted to visit (and therefore have never been allowed to) is the old Shaker settlement at Sabbathday Lake—an inland detour somewhere between the southern border and Brunswick. Easy to find on a map—but then, not everyone feels as I do about the austere, not to say bleak beauty of their craftings. There are even a couple of senile Shakers in residence, I believe.

I was just going to warn you about the Rockingham in Portsmouth—but then I remembered: you *know*. And don't waste any time on Kittery. On the other hand, if you have time for a detour (you haven't) Castine is charming, and sports a maritime academy.

Oh no—the sun came out 20 minutes ago, but now the sky is sludging up again. As I wrote Jane this morning, I'm beginning to feel like something you find in the woods with an elf sitting on it.

Thanks, by the way, for all your efforts to get the *Times* to print a review of my book [*Freely Espousing*]. When, by the way, do you think we'll be paid for the *Nest* excerpt that was in *Adventures*? And speaking of that, did you ever broach the possibility of me becoming a trustee of a triumvirate Poet's Foundation? I don't mind if Kenward said no (if Kenneth said no, I'd mind plenty); nor am I so much trying to extend the range of my good works by giving away some money as trying to get a little more for me. (The nice Guggenheim people sent me a form, and I now see I needn't trouble myself with the agonizing inward battle between greed and fear involved in deciding what the traffic will bear.)

Eds. I mean, Weds.

Ecco domani, Giovanni.

Guess I'll send this spec. del., in faint hopes that you'll have it before I telephone tomorrow—who knows? It might stir some essential query out of its lair.

Lessee. Well, if you would like anything more choice than 7 Cellars Vino Fino or near beer with your meals, perhaps you would pop off a couple of bottles into the tonneau. I'll roust out the daiquiri makings tomorrow, and set some Fresca to stale, in case you want to set your hair . . .

love to Pierre

xx Ekin Wallick
(author of *The Small House For a Moderate Income* (Hearst, 1915))

I got those "House for a 40' Lot Blues"—wait till you see my "Book of 100 Homes" (1906)

Dear Gentleman's Relish,[634]

It emerges that the all day trip to Camden tomorrow begins in an hour. Thrilling as the prospect of a whole day in Camden's two shops is, I can't quite overcome my reluctance to spend a lovely evening alone at the Green Gables—even the one movie theater in town, which used to run a sort of perpetual Saturday matinee, has become a 5 and dime—very peculiar, like a Shopping Cellar, with meager paper pennants high overhead.

So don't work late waiting for my call. As I said earlier, we'll expect you Monday if we don't hear differently.

I think I can count on Trudie for a couple of bottles of rum, but do bring a bottle of after dinner hard stuff, for which I'll pay you. I insist. Scotch might be nice; it would certainly be nicer than Fernet-Branca or Pink Rum. And if you have any grass, bring that too. But you needn't feel obliged to offer it around. I've long wished to blow a little towards the seals (my desperation hasn't reached the point of wanting to blow a little seal, however).

Have a nice tripsky-pipsky.

love

J.

Military Pickle

TO JOE BRAINARD

[Great Spruce Head Island]

August 10, 1969

Dear Joe,

I decided to tear a leaf off your pad & write to you *like this*.[635] Actually I was going to write to you on one of my orange pads, but I like them so much to type on it seems a waste to use them for a long-hand letter, though I don't feel that way about a typed letter. Do you think there is something funny about me, doctor?

---

634. An anchovy paste made in England.

635. Joe Brainard printed his letters in distinctive capitals on cheap ruled paper that Schuyler mimics here.

Of course I wouldn't think it a waste, really, to write you on hand-beaten sheets of gold, which this is, artfully disguised. And it occurs to me that I'm writing on this because I prefer lined paper for long-hand, and somehow feel that the orange pads "belong" with the Olivetti portable. I especially like the rare occasions that call for the red half of the ribbon on it. Then, too, I got quite a shock when I went into the Camden Village Shop, the only orange pad contact I have, and they said they didn't have any in stock—although they—the saleslady—was *scribbling on one*. She'll never know how close she came—but thanks to you, Doctor, I let this one go. Here's your $50—you've made a difference in my life.

Not that I ever paid any of my analysts $50 an hour—and that may explain a lot, too.

On the other hand I'm not imitating you to the extent of trying to sunbathe. For one thing it's cloudy—which wouldn't stop you. It's sort of raining which doesn't always stop you. And it's six in the evening and we're about to have dinner. Still, maybe I should go out and try—I don't have any color, and high summer is winding to a close.

I'm glad you liked *Storm*—I do too. I don't think I'll *really* find anything more to add to it, so if you should want to start drawing it now, do. I guess I got into the habit of collecting rain-squares and don't want to stop. *Cicero's Cat*[636] which I've sort of tried saving, isn't much of a substitute. Although I'm also trying to save another better kind—two other kinds—no, maybe, three other kinds (but they all go together): 1) face frames without any dialogue; 2) sudden violence frames, such as fist & chin, or a car going off a cliff with the tires saying SCREE!; 3) way-back dolly shots, say of a city street with balloons coming out of an incinerator or something. Ideally, these would all be silents, but I don't mind an occasional "No, Greasy, No!" or a "Do you plan to spend the winter in Sun City, doctor?" "Not if the patient lives, I don't, nurse." Yes, the world of comix is a rich, rewarding, wonderful one, especially on this island where you can't get them.

Monday, Aug. 11, 1969 (still)

The sun came out—hooray hooray—and the mailboat brought me three Vodoo Darkskin Love Beans, which I ordered from *Womens's Circle*. Just know they'll do the trick and I'll go down in history as the Sweetheart of the Boston Red Sox.

636. Comic-strip spin-off of *Mutt and Jeff*.

I'd really rather be typing at this point, but somewhere nearby Koko [Katherine Koch] is taking a nap, so it seems mean to climb on to my thunder machine. Still, there is something very "Koch" about this situation. I'm not complaining—just observing a fact.

Liz and Koko are *said* to be camping out on the other side of the island. Fairfield took them & their 300 pounds of equipment around there yesterday & set up a tent for them. But they appeared this noon, rather wan and announced they had spent all yesterday afternoon and evening trying to start a fire. All wood on the island is sopping sponge wet but they are—or rather Liz is—determined to make a wood fire without newspaper or house-store kindling, which is cheating. Matches are not cheating, however—I think something great could be written about which things give them the feeling of "cheating." (Is "faking it" cheating?)

Shortly I'm to go off and give a lesson in firebuilding—who knows? maybe even build a fire. But this shortly is getting to be too damned long; in fact, it has been going on now for 31/2 hours. It's amazing how two little girls camping out can ruin your life. Fairfield waited all Saturday afternoon before they decided "not to go today," then he spent almost all yesterday on them. So it seems only fair that I should be today's living sacrifice. It will probably be fun—especially if I get the fire to burn. I have quite a lot of masculine vanity up my sleeve—as well as in my britches.

Remind me when I see you that I have a small plan. But if I tell you about it now it might spoil it. How's *that* for mysterious? Now don't forget. (This isn't a secret from Kenward—feel free to tell him all you know about it.)

I know *exactly* how you feel about "joint" mail. The sight of an envelope addressed to "the Porters and Jimmy Schuyler" is enough to set me racing around the yard frothing and snapping at the postman's ankles. Some people even begin letters to Anne and Fairfield "Dear Porters," which gives me goose-bumps. It's like people who put up signs by their driveway that say "the Caseys." But I like houses with Ha-Ha names. "D'un roamin'" and all the rest.

[letter ends here]

TO JOE BRAINARD

[Great Spruce Head Island]

Aug 17, 69

Dear Joe,

Guess you can tell by the size of the sheet that this is one of my not real letters. John and Pierre just left this morning (it's afternoon now)—they left in a dense fog made spooky by blue flashes and distant thunder. And that at six in the morning they went with Anne & Lizzie who go to early mass on Sunday in Stonington. I got up to see them off but only went as far as the laundry porch. It was very nice to have them here. I like Pierre very much and, of course, love my "inconsiderate little bastard," who wasn't that at all this time. I think his analyst must be very good—John was a much easier guest than ever before. Sometimes I get irritable with him (in the past, I mean) when he gets worked up about crowding every second with pleasure and plans, conflicting plans, at that. This time he did quite a bit of cooking, as usual, but he let me off mussel picking and fixing, the last part you may remember is quite a chore. I gathered they had a very good time in Calais. I didn't "gather" it (here, have some good time leaves I just gathered)—they said it.

John is right in thinking he's not as handsome when hefty (I like his looks very much) but he has a different look, more relaxed and less preoccupied with himself and his looks, and I think I like it better. Maybe he's headed for a stunning middle road. I mean, looking handsome *and* relaxed.

However, the big rich blueberry pie I made and the delicious rich lentil soup John made haven't done much for my own looks. Or rather, they did plenty. At the moment I'm deep in a can of Fresca.

We'll be leaving a week from the day you'll probably get this! Aug 26; or maybe the 27th. I think I'll want to spend a day or so in Amherst, then I intend to come to see you, or go see you. John says I'm expected—good—and you're staying until about the 15th? One thing about Amherst, I have this feeling that I'm getting a terrific bonus because I can come to Calais without having first to go to New York, plus missing all the bad part of the bus trip—after Springfield I enjoy it, even by Greyhound. In fact, there was one section of the drive somewhere north of White River Junction, I'm quite anxious to re-experience.

Can't wait to see all the improvements.

I hope you'll forgive me if my letters should sort of tail off about now—I want to type up what I've written, which takes forever (not because of the bulk). Every time I think I've finally gotten a poem right I decide something should be a little different, and it means typing the whole thing over again. I was doing it this morning and my desk has eraser crumbs rolling and bounding all over it like tumbleweed in the . . . well wherever it is tumbleweed does its thing. Then there's packing. WHY did I bring so much stuff? because I like having it with me, that's why. And I don't regret one single bit of it. No, not even the garters.

Now I'm just back from a swim (am I ever sleepy)—Are Rn and Pt and Wn [Ron, Pat and Wayne Padgett] there now? Hope so. My love to them if they are.

Give Kenward my love and tell him I was glad to hear from *Bill* that *he* liked my poem. Maybe you'd better tell him that first, then give my love. That will take the curse off the reproach. (It is not a *serious* reproach, anyway. But the love I send, that is serious.)

love,

Jimmy

PS I love the picture you took of Anne [Waldman]—our Anne said, "It's *so* beautifully timeless." and it is.

I've been meaning to send you this for that drawing you bought me—really, I was waiting to send handier cash, but the last time I was in Camden and got cash I then proceeded to Lillian Brailowsky: Costly Books, Inc. and spent it. I'm glad to say I don't regret it—but I've already claimed not to regret something else in this letter: do you think I'm fighting the truth, and that way down deep inside, $1/2$ an inch below the dandruff, I regret the books *and* the garters? It's true they don't match. In fact, if you force me to, I'll admit it, they clash. Oh well I can always throw the stupid things out. Or better yet burn them. Haven't had a good book and garter burning in I don't know how long. Yahoo.

I don't remember the Vermont sales tax so I'm guessing at 4%.

I have some photos for you but may bring them rather than risk them getting mashed in the mail.

PS2 Finished my goodies. Sure did enjoy it! Most of it I ate.

Personal

PS Your two letters before his last one sounded as though you had something on your mind. I even thought of writing to say that if you wanted to talk to me (by letter) about whatever it was I wished you would. But even that sounded a little like offering advice (that's not an allusion to the kind of advice we talked about earlier this summer) so I'm glad now I didn't. If you would like to go for a walk some afternoon and talk about it a little more, fine; and if you find while I'm there you never do feel like it, *that's* fine too. Sometimes talking—but I'm not going to finish that sentence. It wasn't interesting. Whatever decisions you make, though, they won't be wrong ones.

TO JOE BRAINARD

[Great Spruce Head Island]

Aug 20 69

Dear Joe,

You sure do hustle a fellow (hope you're a little bit impressed—I whisked these together between a late swim and supper—fried chicken; without bananas, however).[637]

What a day—if this one doesn't win the Academy Award it will prove the whole thing is fixed.

I was thrilled a while back when you told me you'd found those blue berries in the woods (not "blueberries" the kind you eat, but the ones you picked to maybe paint). It's one of my all-time Tops. In fact six stems of them are gracing my desk at the moment—and believe me, it could do with a little gracing. They're called "blue bead," and sometimes "bear's tongue," from the shape of the leaf. Bears must have very funny tongues.

Pretty busy these days—time seems to fly by—don't know where it goes—and I've looked everywhere.

love to all,

Jimmy

637. Joe Brainard had sent out a call for anything in writing about or prominently mentioning bananas. He eventually put all that he gathered into *The Banana Book*. In this letter, and for several that follow, Schuyler enclosed banana recipies and all manner of quotations in which bananas appeared, from the writing of Edward Everett Hale through excerpts from gardening books to the *Encyclopedia Britannica* and this, which he must have plucked from his memory: "Josephine Baker made her Paris debut in the *Revue Négre* wearing just a string, or frill, of bananas (in 1928, I think)."

TO BILL BERKSON

[Great Spruce Head Island]

August 21, 1969

Dear Master of the Shining Leaves,[638]

Enclosed please find tribute. Your book is beautiful.

By when do you need the art stuff? I *knew* if I were to stay away from South H. for a year and a day there would be all sorts of things there I'd be dying to consult—this time Fairfield's complete run of *Art News* (so handy when stuck and Tom [Hess] is snarling down the phone). I expect to go there for a day or few, Padgetts[639]permitting, in September or at latest, early Oct. My original reason was to prevent the gardener—sic—read yardman or Grim reaper—from pruning a lot of things and thus preventing future bloom. It's his prime objective and he often achieves it, so it's safe to say that his is a happy life.

Would I like any of my Conte crayon renderings reproduced? Not on your aspidistra. It's sweet of you to ask; but I would as soon send Canaday, Kramer, Greenberg & Lynch[640] my secret love diary, the one I keep in mauve on dove paper, with red for the extra hot parts.

The only artists I've collaborated with, that I can think of at the moment, are Brainard, Freilicher and Dash. The one with Jane didn't come to anything and the ones with Bob, well, they're pretty awful. I'm not being modest—John Ashbery once saw one, against my best efforts, and talk about *schadenfreude*— which I *think* means, malicious pleasure at another's discomfort. The ones with Joe of course are a great joy (to me I mean)—some I especially like are the Hilton (the Swan) Kramer ones, one of which shows a swan saying "I got my job at the *New York Times.*"

Of the articles: I know I like the ones about Fairfield, Kline, Joe B, and I think the one on Nell Blaine (though if you were to use it, it might be wise not to reproduce the large painting so rapturously evoked). Also one on Jane Freilicher in *Art & L.* I don't think the paintsapix on Alex and on Lee Bell are anything much. Nor the Edwin Dickinson in an *Art News Annual* nor something about Al Leslie in B. H. Friedman's NY School book[641]—at this

---

638. *Shining Leaves*, Bill Berkson's book referred to in this letter.

639. The Padgetts were renting Fairfied Porter's Southampton home.

640. Art critics John Canaday, Hilton Kramer, and Clement Greenberg. Lynch is probably a pun on the New York brokerage firm, Merrill, Lynch, Pierce, Fenner, and Smith.

641. Schuyler's essay on painter Alfred Leslie first appeared in B. H. Friedman's book published by Grove Press. This eassy is reprinted in Schuyler's *Selected Art Writings*.

moment in time I don't feel much like throwing nosegays at the ineffable Alfredo.

You get double thanks for what you say about *Shriners Last Stand*: I haven't heard boo from Kenward since I sent it, while Joe says it's over his head he guesses and anyway it isn't poetry he likes it's poets. As Jean Harlow remarked in *Bombshell*,[642] "Now I ask you, what kind of a dish of class is that to hand a lady?" I'm still planning to go there end of next week, however, or my name isn't Caligula. On the other hand I hear Cuba is *divine* in September — they even let you help harvest the sugar cane.

A week from today I'll be in a house I've never seen before, waiting for the Home Sweet Home Movers to deliver the trunks, Amherst! Emily Dickinson! Hope I'm not going to get any guff from her.

Give New York a big hug for me — it gets so great in Sept. and Oct. — as what place doesn't.

love, Jimmy
Vielia (da veetch of da vood)[643]

Just thought of a nice title for a very contemp. novel — *The Mattachine Society Dropout*)[644] a sequel to, *Myron Manlius, Gay Marriage Counsellor*).

TO BILL BERKSON

[Calais, Vermont]

September 8, 1969

Dear Bill,

It was raining in Vermont and Kenward and I are about to light out for the Mrs. J. Watson Webb bequest, Sheburne. Oops. She*l*burne. It must be kinda nice to be able to bequest a village, and one called together by oneself at that. "What this street needs is some fanlights, and an amusing bit of gingerbread to glimpse through the smokebush hedge." I hope it's not going to be all neo-colonial soap balls and hairy neckties.

642. Jean Harlow was in Victor Fleming's *Bombshell* (1933).
643. "Vilia, Witch of the Wood," aria from Franz Lehar's *The Merry Widow*.
644. Mattachine Society, one of the earliest organizations of gay men. It began in Los Angeles in 1950 or 1951.

Ummm, Kenward's Lettera 22 has a tasty line in accessory keys—I especially like "is it a cedilla, or a tilde" (awk where do they hide a whiteman's question mark hunt hunt? why there you are).

Your letter of Awg 25 trudged around after me until we finally met at the Coop on Sept 8 (yes the Grim Greetings I sent you were a Gratuitous Act, in the worst Gidean tradition). Since you don't say what the Fog Tribute has to offer in way of character analysis (yours) I can't, I guess, say you're mistaken: but you are, surely? It's all character analysis (mine). The day *Shining Leaves* arrived it filled me with glittering flux, off which I meant to skim what I hoped would turn out to be a Berkson-inspired flight. The intention remained but some days galloped by and when I went to write it (write what I never knew) the time for skimming was past and I had to get out the cold chisel and the drill. And along with outer fog some inner miasma brought on, or up, by Don Allen sending his total notes for Frank's poems, which brought back, just reading the titles in sequence, well, a Marcellian trip, not depressing, but sad—there's a difference, I finally find. (24 hours just passed. No, 26). Anyway, when I sent it to you I thought of explaining that the tribute was in fact that your poems caused me to write one, which I always count as a *good thing*. And that any faces found reflected in the oil slick were strictly the proprietor's.

Your poems go from strength to strength—the untitled poem "the hand . . . " is a kind I've often tried to write. That I wind up with a limp-celery epigram is no doubt simply because I do "try": such a mistake. Those three lines have a quality in common with all your shining leaves, as though you took a beautiful fresh piece of wire and gave it a twist, and it stays. Your poems keep the quality of your thought, to blast through to something true, right now. Or also, to keep "right now" because it is true. In your homage to Bill de K. strip, the Frank page, about seeing through his eyes, is so great—because "20/20 All the way"[645] is true, and much more because "to try to see the world through his eyes" is a terrific thing to do, and to have *thought* of doing. And of course it's something one does without thinking about it (one can't go out in the sun without getting a bit of color) but it helps to have it put in words and made conscious—not "helps": it illuminates and inspires and changes the way I feel. More I don't ask of art.

It's still raining in Vermont. No, it isn't, but it's the color, or colors—the sky is anyway—shades of smoke. Shades of shades, tones of mercury poisoning

645. The complete quote is "some sunny days it's great to try to see the world through Frank O'Hara's eyes 20/20 all the way." It is from the Bill Berkson and Joe Brainard collaboration, *I Love You, de Kooning.*

(and do you think there's something unpleasant about the turn of my mind? Me neither). Shelburne was a hoot, nice American pix—I had never seen a pretty Bierstadt[646] before—and a terribly funny Greek revival fake which houses the first floor rooms of Electra and J. Watson's triplex[647]—including a hearty helping of the Havemeyer holdings in Rembrandt (2), Monet-Manet-Degas; but there's something funny about a Courbet still-life of (apples) painted, as the D.A.R.-ish lady in charge of that room said, "when he was a political prisoner." I had a feeling she thought of him as a friend of Mrs. Webb's who had been entrapped by the reds—. At the end Kenward and I lingered a bit too long among the quilts and got some good natured, I guess, guff from one of the other ladies. "You boys interior decorators?" Kenward the Kool gave no sign that she existed, but I favored her with a tolerant "No," meant to imply that my endeavors were at some further extreme. "Had a fellow in here last week—was from Canada. He said he'd made two quilts himself. *He was an interior decorator.*" Then they locked the Village and we went to Stowe for broiled, toughened native pork chops and maple cream pie. So today I'm living on radishes and cucumber slices.

We're staying until the 17th, about then to Amherst—and maybe New York (no maybe for KGE, of course), depending on when Fairfield wants to go back to the Island and close the house. I'll do the review-gleaning as soon as I can. Maybe the Jones Library at Amherst has the bound volumes of *Art News*. When do you start at Yale? Are you going to be a sleep-in or a New Haven R.R. griper. Oh—if you want to use the Al Leslie piece, do. I suppose what I don't like is that I feel I made him out to be a better painter than he is (or was then). However, I haven't looked at it since it was published (1960?) so it may be merely a feeling without too much basis in fact. *You* be the judge.

Hope I'll see you soon.

love,

Jimmy

646. Albert Bierstadt (1830–1902), German-born painter of billboard-size landscapes of the American West.

647. Electra Havemeyer and J. Watson Webb, patrons of the Shelburne Museum in Shelburne, Vermont.

TO RON PADGETT

104 Greenwich Ave.

[New York, New York]   *Nov 9 1969*

Dear Ron,

Let *me* wish you many happy returns of my birthday. Forty-six seems slightly unreal—partly because that's how old I've thought I was for the past year, & partly because it's the age people are in newspapers. Forty-six hasn't much of a swing to it, unlike forty-seven which is definitely an Age of Distinction—but it's better than forty-five which is much too abstract (Oh he must be about forty-five) and it does have sort of a soft roll to it, like the farmlands of eastern Pennsylvania—a district now crowned by a thin coppice.

So you want to harvest in mid-May. Contrary to some, I think it can be done, if you concentrate on salad truck-lettuces, green onions, radishes (there are white ones & black ones as well as red). Also beet greens & maybe small carrots —*nantes*. Early forcing. Also French turnips. Very tiny—young turnip greens are delicious. You would probably have to start the seeds indoors in February— at the foot of the cellar stairs there is a hole where they used to store ferns which would be a good place for them. Use little peat cubes—called something like Fer-Til Cubes—to start them in. The whole cube is eventually planted in the ground so they (the seedlings) never have to be transplanted. Transplanting seedlings out of a seed flat is a good way to learn how to climb walls.

One thing that isn't there you might need is a cold frame in which to harden off the seedlings. If they receive a check from the cold it may soon be mate. A carpenter of your caliber could easily knock one together out of boards & plastic. Look in Bailey's *Cyclopedia of Horticulture* (3 vol. in my room) under cold frames, & vegetable gardens. There are also some U.S. Printing Office bulletins stuck in the shelves in that area. Also an interesting book called *Intensive Gardening*. There are some seed catalogues on the top shelf in my room. Harris is the best for vegetables in this country while Thompson & Morgan in Ipswich, England, is the best, period. Somewhere in the shelves in "Laurence's Room" (the one next to mine) there are a couple of French seed catalogues—Vilmorin & some other company. These are priceless, & list salad greens unobtainable in this country. So just cut the Harrumphs & set to.

One thing you can find out from catalogues is how long seeds take to germinate, & to mature. Leaf crops of course one can begin to harvest as soon as the true leaves appear (what the first two leaves are called, I don't know—

phoney-balonies, perhaps), but it takes a heap of seedlings to make a salad at the 4-leaf stage.

(Another book that should be there is *The Vegetable Garden Displayed*—although like most RHS it is no doubt dishearteningly filled with councils of perfection.)

You also might look into the making of a hot frame, a hot bed. The *Organic Gardening Encyclopedia* ought to have something on that. They used to be made by burying horse dung under the frame, which as it decays gives off heat. The early vegetables are still grown outside Paris on this plan, I believe. Nowadays it's done with electric wires. It is not complicated, expensive or scary.

You also might write to—but I don't know the *right* name—Agricultural Extension at Cornell, which puts out a lot of bulletins for farmers & home gardeners. Maybe the library could help you track down the address. One thing Cornell knows is when the last heavy frost is apt to be in a specific area.

I seem to have run out for a moment—not really, but I can see book length looming. By the way, Bob Dash is a terrific gardener, and may have some good ideas & practical info.

It was a lot of fun visiting you & Pat & Wayne. Fairfield is very pleased that you're there. "People like the Epsteins," he said, "like the house as an *idea*." He also said, "Sometimes when Ron is talking he reminds me just a little of Kenneth. But of course Ron is *much* more mature than Kenneth."

At a party honoring Kenneth on Friday at Morris's I saw . . . Harry Mathews. Joe likes his new place, Anne is going to pose for him, Kenward is writing poems & I'm going to go out and buy pomegranates and persimmons.

love,

Jimmy

TO RON PADGETT

Amherst, Massachusetts

Dec. 3, 1969
or is it 1869?
How the years whiz by

Dear Ron,

Oh well if they pay money (". . . his selfless and unswerving devotion to the almighty buck . . ."). Feel free to close up the lines—the double spacing is just the way I type. And the reason for that is I usually find I've left out a few words here and there. If this should turn out to be too big for your oven, write us for our mocha-filled cupcakes — "A crumb to remember."

Your book is beautiful. I read it all the time, and sometime I may tell you what I like the best and why; though maybe I won't too: one thinks of too many things to say when poetry is that good. Thank you for causing it to be sent to me.

Everybody here is fine. Fairfield is off telling the youngsters how to do it ("Where you see blue, put blue," as Franz Kline once said). Lizzie is tooling a leather notebook cover—sorry—sketchbook cover—for Koko Koch's Xmas. Bruno is lying on a rug, waiting for Anne to leave the kitchen so he can give the garbage can a good rummage. A truck just went by—clop, clop, clop (chains, not hooves) and in the distance some jet planes are drag racing; or playing chicken. In the intervals of depressing these keys I am admiring the garage on whose black roof someone has spread a tattered linen tea cloth. Someone being Mr Snow, of course—it's a cozy 25 degrees in Amherst, Mass., and the silver radiator gives an agreeable hiss.

But why do you think Richard Jeffreys'[648] Hodge is a silly book? It isn't cut, so you too have not read it. He had an obstinate wish to write in an imaginative form which didn't suit his gift; but he had a wonderfully detailed knowledge of landscape and the creatures and men who live and work in it and even his clumsiest books are full of a kind of truth that is very rare in literature— since booklearning usually precludes having the time to get other, though inarticulate, kinds of knowledge. Almost anything written about the life of, say, a plain or dirt farmer before the 19th century is surmise. You might like to take a peek sometime into Peter Laslett's A World We Have Lost.[649] On the other hand Jeffreys has no cause to complain at being sent to join Leopardi and Wallace Stevens in the august company of Ron's Rejects.

Good grief, what came over me? It must be the collegiate air—"You may return to your classroom, but remember: no more spitting in the inkwells."

By the way, are all the rooms at your inn booked solid for 'tween Christmas and New Year spell? The reason I ask is that Liz has been invited to visit Pamela Diefenbach during the holidays, but the trip is a bit much for her to make alone.

648. Richard Jeffries (1848–1887), writer on British countryside and rural life. Schuyler refers to his book *Hodge and His Masters*.

649. Peter Laslett (1916–2001), British historian. *A World We Have Lost* was published in 1965.

So I thought that if I were visiting you . . . but I don't yet know what her true feelings are about this; but let me know if it's possible, and I'll find out.

Now I must get back to my snowflake meeting. I'm sending the damaged ones to the Jumble Shop.

love to Pat and Wayne,
love, Jimmy

What is the kind of pen you use called? I want one too (Monkey see . . . .).

TO KENNETH KOCH

[Southampton, New York]

Dec 9, 1969

Dear Kenneth,

You are very inspiring, and I would much rather be writing my own Swan of Bees[650] (a case of scotch and a dozen hags, please) than anything else; even this. However, here we go.

The essay falls roughly into three parts: poor, good and brilliant. If you read from page 33 to the end, then read the first 14 pages, you will see what I mean. Although I have done some drastic editing in the first part (brackets enclose what I think should be cut—these cuts of course are merely suggestions), the best solution would be to rewrite it. The big trouble is that when you wrote it you had not yet found your tone; you don't speak in your own voice, which results in all kinds of clumsinesses: recapitulating the previous sentence as a clause; a hesitant qualifying—"I think/thought," "it seemed to me that . . . " perhaps and maybe—which isn't like you; conversational crudities, such as beginning sentences with "Also,"; tired words—"The sestina, with its set system of repetitions . . . " (pg 12): is set redundant, or system, or both? Or is it not the kind of cliché that keeps one reading while switching off thought?—; not using the simple past and present—"I did think" and "I had thought" which land one in grammatical bogs of "had had" and so on. Now to be more detailed.

---

650. Schuyler refers to Koch's manuscript, *Wishes, Lies and Dreams: Teaching Children to Write Poetry*, which Koch has sent for his comments. Published in 1970, Koch's book quickly became influential.

Most of the first three pages, and some of the fourth, are acknowledgments and outside the essay, which is about teaching children how to write poetry. The tone is too official and stately: "My entry into the New York public school system . . ." is reminiscent of the stage direction in the last act of *Faust*: "The Mater Gloriosa soars into space." How you came to take up this kind of teaching, and where you did it, should be said in a page, and set off from the text proper by a simple device, such as heading the first part of the essay with a numeral (1 would be a good choice). In this section, don't deal with ideas. Cut out all sentences like: "The children I taught wrote a great many remarkably good poems." It's too Beverly Boys,[651] and, more important, you prove this, which is the way to do it.

A word which bothered me a lot, though most the first time I read the essay, was assignment. On page three, there is a bad effect of anti-climax when, having promised to tell us your secret, we read: "The method of teaching I used was based on writing assignments." It's as though one were told the secret of the new math: homework. The trouble here goes beyond the word, however: you have fallen into the "expository prose trap" (don't use quotes or inverted commas or whatever they are): trying to encapsulate all you have to say in one sentence or paragraph. You don't have to, and it rarely works.

pg 5 The entry of the principal ("What's this?") strikes me as too cozy.

pg 6 "hearing their words read out loud, with respect, by a poet . . ." I wonder if kids are that conscious of distinctions among adult roles? It's OK, but that you were an adult and a teacher entered in too, surely.

"One thing I told my students right away was not to use rhyme." Would this be better: At the beginning, I asked them not to use rhyme. The latter avoids "telling," where your real intent was to get them to feel free and not constrained, and it avoids "my students," which has a school marm flavor. The rest of the paragraph is great: "Rhyme is wonderful but children aren't able to use it skillfully enough to make good poetry with it." Now *you're* talking. (On third thought, I prefer your sentence.)

pg 8 It "turned on" their imaginations. You use turned on later, and, getting high. I would drop the drug talk—which here is facetious, which is bad—and will certainly fall on chilly ears, if grade school teachers are among your readers.

'I WANTED TO GET THE CHILDREN HIGH'
AVERS HIPPY POET PROF

651. Refers to Koch's short story *The Beverly Boys' Summer Vacation.*

Margaret Mead[652] slated to head
bail drive

pg 10 "The Lie assignment . . . " " . . . The Dawn of Me was written for this assignment . . . " If you count how many times assignment has been used by page 10, you'll be horrified. But it is not the repetition that's bad: somehow it becomes the operative word, everything flows into and out of it. I'm sorry I haven't a synonym to offer, but the problem is more serious than that (though often "poem" or "form" can be substituted). The name of a category is being substituted for the thing done. (Lizzie lately said to me that she likes the school here, partly because there is less *homework*, said with a shudder. "What is that you're doing then?" "Oh this is my *project* for social studies: I'm doing it on Soul Food." very tasty too. But I think the reader will quickly get to feel that way about ass-gnm-nt.)

pg 12 "rather beautiful" a thing is either beautiful or it's something else. Don't qualify unless truth demands it.

pg 13 "who succeeded me as poetry teacher at PS 61" sounds stuffy; I don't think it's important enough to bother saying.

pg 19 "the combined first and second graders" elsewhere they are called primary class (or grades) I think; it sounds better.

pg 19 & elsewhere: wilder, wild: not everyone will know, as I do, that this is the ultimate kudo. Since wild is very much your own word, I think that somewhere you should define it, as used by you.

pg 21 "Her poem showed other children how to write about such emotions without feeling bad about them and so it opened up a lot of new things for them to say." I like this, and like it so much more than when you talk about "subject matter." One trouble with ready-mades like "subject matter" is that they provoke a ready-made response.

pg 22, last 3 lines: the tone sounds teachery to me, but what you are saying is too interesting for me to want to fool with it. (I especially dislike, "the presentation of the assignment," educator's cant).

pg 23 a minor point: need the student-poet's name be in quotes after a quotation? And I think titles of lyric poems are usually given in quotes & not italics. Others nearer home know more about this than I.

pg 24 sentence beginning "In presenting" too abstract and flavorless. And we don't say "absolutely clear" when we mean clear.

652. Margaret Mead (1901–1978), anthropologist and noted social activist who advocated extreme permissiveness.

pg 24–25 "Color poem assignment," etc. This gets to be like saying "the drinking cup of coffee experience." In this kind of writing, I don't think contractions like "I'd" sound right; the context is insufficiently idiomatic. Or colloquial. (Choose one).

Watch out for "and so on." Somewhere you use this of the sense, whose number is not large enough to warrant it. In a series, it can be taken for granted, or begin by saying something like, "such things as"

pg 26 para. beginning: "The procedure, then . . . " A recap here seems a good idea, but can't you say it more briefly and pungently? Maybe beginning, "What I did, then, was . . . "

pg 28 "*more* regularly" tsk tsk tsk tsk, and so on

pg 29 "taught a particular class" you overdo this use of particular; also forms of "specific"

pg 32 I like "champion sestina writers" better than "impressive formal control"—is it the control that impresses, or the successful use of an existing form?

pg 33 et seq Everything about teaching the N.E. kids is inspired, inspiring, beautiful, moving to tears. And it zooms along with passion because you're speaking from deep inner feelings yourself.

page 39 short para. about Muse: This says nothing new about teaching; or else say it even more simply: "The way of teaching also worked well as Muse, with children of five to twelve." Pretty flat, but it gets away from the (too often used) nothing-prop of "very fine poems too." A number of sentences lead me to some such conclusion; the effect is always one of a letdown.

pg 39 2nd para: you suddenly drop quotes around illiterate & semi-literate (I think that's one word without a dash)—do you mean literally illiterate? Page 40 O radiant page . . .

However, I wonder if the strictures about teachers' attitudes toward Poetry (that low and universal art) are not too securely attached to the living, breathing actual people you worked with at PS 61? I think their feelings will be hurt; and they will certainly read the book. Maybe you could cushion the bad news with a generalization about teaching in grade schools everywhere, even Cincinnati . . . [653]

But, really, for the last ten pages I'm willing to be born along on the racing tide.

---

653. Koch's hometown.

*Dec. 11 (yesterday was
actually the 10th)*

At this point, night having long since fallen like a shade, I broke off and headed for a tasty glass of Charmes-Chambertin—mmmm—those S.S. Pierce folks sure know their onions.

I think you should divide the essay into four sections: preface-acknowledgments (a page); the summary of the forms that worked best; commentary on, and expansion of, the summary; how it worked with NE students & on to the end. Repetitions that can be cut, or things that can be talked about more fully in one place, may show up plainly if read in this way.

If you decide to divide it, I would number the main sections 1,2,3 and not number the first part, which will plainly show that it is outside the text proper.

I had the feeling that more could be said at the point where you mention the sestina—perhaps about the kind of poem you have given older students but think would be unsuitable for kids in grade school.

Watch out for Instruction Manual jargon—in Instruction Manuals one is told how to Disassemble a gun, rather than how to take it apart.

By itself, a phrase like "good classroom atmosphere" conveys little and that little is self-evident. If you use it, or others like it, immediately say what you mean by it (and having done so, you may find you don't need the opaque phrase at all).

I think it would be worth spelling out that you aimed to get the children freer, wilder, more open; but that you never said so in so many words to them. I've met the kind of teacher who wants to make anything a command: "Be free! Soar, damn it, soar!"

You might want to point out the advantage of having The Creative Situation come in the afternoon after the Learning Situation (I used to hate it when art came first thing in the morning; it made the rest of the day such a drag. But when it was from one to two. One could zip through the last period on the leftover elan).

A few words or terms I had doubts about—sometimes merely because of frequency of use:

subject matter
theme
by example, for example
just (as in, I just wanted; a little of that goes a long way)
the point being, the point of which was
very fine things; fine

I hope there's something here you can use. I've been so critical and carping in order to give you wider choice—unlikely as it may sound.

Let me know what you think. My emotional cart has become hitched to a horse of grade-school poets; assuage my involvement.

love,

Jimmy

TO JOHN ASHBERY

> "Just bring me the *Low Down Review*, dear. There's something about Lois Van Schuyler in it and that Moroccan guide of hers."

[Southampton, New York]

Dec. 12, 1969

Dear Blue Eyed Winner,

I'm still bemused by the fact that your Quiz Kid[654] story came out in the Rochester paper on my 18th birthday—it's had a reverse Proustian effect, since I find I remember nothing of the occasion, at all. I can remember vividly wanting to be 18; and had to spend my 17th summer working for pennies at the Silver Dairy because you had to be 18 to get the big cabbage working at Bell Aircraft. Perhaps as a freshman in college I thought it was uncool to make a big thing out of it? I wonder who I had a crush on—Robb Henry, no doubt, though I probably had a third eye out for Bill Stophel . . .

The other day while trying to find a magazine to fritter away some money on, I leafed through *Harper's*, the first time I'd touched a copy in years. Imagine my surprise—The poem is lovely, and I can't image why I ever demurred at your puzzled goddess. As usual, you were right. And now here is the new issue of *World*, with Cravan-Ashbery.[655] It's so funny, and weirdly insightful (the latter word a favorite of my analyst), do you think he's the French Emily Dickinson?

654. Because of his ability to answer general knowledge questions, Ashbery was chosen as a Quiz Kid at age fourteen in a contest sponsored by a Rochester, New York, department store.

655. Arthur Cravan (1887–1918), poet and boxer who once fought the great heavyweight Jack Johnson. Cravan disappeared while traveling in Mexico. There were reports of his being seen in Paris and New York, but his disappearance remains a mystery. Ashbery translated into English several of the poems that Cravan wrote in French.

And if he isn't, who is? Have you caught my prose patches, or mauve meanderings, in same? Since they both mention friends by name, you may not want to give them too much time—a thing it is nearly impossible to do. After buzzing through the issue, I don't think the Committee on Awards overlooked any major figure in the New York School. (Say have you received a copy of that Strand anthology? or been paid? Not that $10 is going to make all that much difference in my life.)

And I've never properly thanked you for my birthday discs. I love them. I think the Bocklin sweet would make a lovely dance, provided the choreographer would forget about the isle of the dead.[656] I see it as more about washing dishes. The Medtner is purely great (the Glinka is purely hell)—what mysterious harmonies; if only Reynaldo Hahn[657] were a bit more like him one would be less inclined to keep those ribbons in a tightly knotted bunch. As for the Offenbach[658]—it's true I have not yet worn it out, but what composer so thoroughly realizes the role of the Tune in the music? In fact, I'm planning to use them, a la Kismet-Song of Norway,[659] for a one woman show. It's to be called "Hortense!" and will star Taylor Mead.[660] In the first act finale I expect to get a lot of mileage out of the Guerlaine cologne works, and the fabrication of Imperial as a tribute to Louis Napoleon's goatee. The trio, in which Taylor impersonates Eugénie, Hortense Schneider and la Castiglione,[661] simultaneously, ought to be something.

I don't suppose you've been staying home nights to read the January issue of *Esquire*, but it has a curious article on Wystan. Most of it is moderately dull reporting of his conversation, but the setting, a description of a day in Their Life in Austria, makes Rex Reed[662] seem like "The Little Catholic's First Book of Saints." But why describe when a quote from the first paragraph gives the flavor:

656. Arnold Bocklin (1827–1901), Swiss painter known for *The Isle of the Dead. Bocklin Suite* is by German composer Max Reger (1873–1916).

657. Nicholas Medtner (1880–1951), Russian composer who lived abroad after 1921. He was famously anti-modernist. Mikhael Ivanovich Glinka (1804–1857), Russian composer. Reynaldo Hahn (1874–1947), French composer of art songs and a friend of Marcel Proust.

658. Jacques Offenbach (1819–1880), French composer of operettas.

659. Robert Wright (1914–2005) and George Forrest (1915–1999) wrote the Broadway musicals *Kismet* (1953) and *Song of Norway* (1944), which was their first Broadway show and a hit.

660. Taylor Mead (1924–2013), poet and actor who appeared in several Andy Warhol movies.

661. Schuyler's fantasy involves Napoleon III, emperor of France, his wife, Eugénie, and Hortense Schneider, famous nineteenth-century courtesan.

662. Rex Reed (b. 1938), movie critic who gained notoriety by asking movie stars he interviewed, "Do you sleep in the nude?"

"Now Chester has pushed his place aside; surrounded by scraps of paper and dictionaries, he toys with Sunday's crossword puzzles. He wears pajamas and a dressing gown. A gross, ungainly man, with dull and knobby eyes, he has the look of one too old to play the naughty cherub anymore." Arhg. I've never heard of the author, Jon Bradshaw, before. But he'll be well advised steer clear of Wystan.

I quite like Amherst, and would like it quite a bit more if the sun would come out. It rained on all our nice snow and now the view is, frankly, terribly reminiscent of Southampton in the winter. Guess I'll have to light out for Winnipeg. Are you planning to make the Pultneyville-Elmira scene over Christmas? Watcha doin' for New Year's? Is Kenward going to give his 12th Night Party? What will the new year bring? More Bach on the Moog synthesizer, doubtless.

Which reminds me — I hope you've gotten your very own copy of the new Melodyia release, Scriabin's 1st symphony. Lovely, though the last movement with voices is strangely like a suppressed scene from some forgotten opera of the *Come le foglie* epoch — A *Quiet Game of Caroms*, perhaps.

> This is all the room I have for this time. It is getting dark much earlier these days—and earlier each day, so drive carefully always, watching for pedestrians and cyclists. Stay well and keep happy.......... Aunt Evelyn

love,

J.

By the way, your passing reference to how you "could fly to Mexico and spend two weeks there" was not lost on me, for all its casualness. I can't tell if you've become that debonair, or if you'd rather just not talk or think about it, or all three. Be that as it may, that you even entertain the idea causes me to take my hat off to Carlos (and as it happens, I am wearing one, my Panama. I hunted and hunted for your letter which turned out to be underneath it, so I decided the best place for it was on my head. Since I now have the letter anyway, and there was nothing else under it, my reasoning is no more flawless than usual).

Something I wrote above, you can easily figure out what, causes me to ask the following, which just occurred to me this second. Are you in any position to lend me five hundred dollars until next February, at the latest? Which is when I'll next collect my, uh, allowance. F. was very nice about giving me a bonus while I was staying in NY and taking the cure last spring, but my, it was expensive (not the cure the stay). If you can't, or the idea makes you feel at all constrained and constricted, don't give it a second thought. Or even a first one. I'll ask Kenward; which might seem the logical thing to do anyway, but I did borrow a hunk from him the last time I was broke (summer of '67, I make it), and while he was in no way unpleasant about it, I can't say he was much the opposite either. It's a subject on which he rather scares me. But then, one would rather not try to imagine how many times he's had cause to think, "Oh so that's why X was suddenly so pleasant . . . " Anyway, I'm not flat yet, quite. But some one seems to be paddling toward me across the bay.

And now for a change of pace, we take you to the Highlands, home of haggis and fling: Canon Young[663] says the Burns' line, "Ca' the yowes to the knowes" seems to miss something in the French translation, "*Appelle les brebis sur les hauteurs*" as does "Sing hey, my braw John Highlandman" in Italian, "*Cantate, oh! il mio bravo Giovanni il Montanaro!*" And *that* reminds me that I'm trying to run down a cookbook put out by the English Folk Cooking Assoc. so I can learn how to make Lardy John and Spotted Dick.[664]

Love,

The Fag at Bay[665]

TO RON PADGETT

Amherst, Massachusetts

Jan. 4, 1970

Dear Zinnia Hot Buttons,

(I'm suddenly overcome by the 1970ness of today— all those 60s that seemed once to stretch on and on, infinite as sand or leaves are as gone as . . . as . . .)

I love my flat presents. Flatness is beautiful, especially in The Works of Wayne, who seems to have snapshot us all just as we are into immortality. Could anything be more life-like than the picture of Ted [Berrigan]? Oops. And the one about me seemed strangely prescient, since yesterday I spent the morning just as described, including deciding in the bath that I had *not* had enough sleep, and so back to bed.

---

663. Andrew Young (1885–1971), British nature poet and clergyman.
664. Two popular British desserts.
665. Play on *The Stag at Bay*, title of a painting by Sir Edwin Henry Landseer (1802–1873).

I'll have a couple of puffy New Year thoughts for you and Patty, which I'll bring when I come to eat my other present.

Elstir—word wise—is I believe an anagram, sort of, on Whistler, whose nocturnes the little anglophile no doubt admired. I think Monet may be one of the models, also Vuillard—the works though are by still more various hands. For instance, when Marcel keeps everybody waiting for dinner while he admires the Guermantes' Impressionists, one of the pictures is a Manet, a bunch of asparagus, which is now in the Met., where we can all re-experience the passage, minus the eats. Is Bergotte the great writer who somehow never quite makes it?[666] I think the main model was Anatole France, although his deathbed visit to see—but I won't tell you what in case you haven't read that part yet—is surely autobiographical, in essence if not in fact. But as the book progresses the artists tend to vanish in favor of their works, not a bad idea. I rather envy the point Patty has reached, where the squalor, nausea and despair become unendurable, until the final party, when the reader realizes that the cork-lined room in which Marcel has held him prisoner (say, maybe that's who Albertine is: the reader) is in fact, a freight elevator from which he is disgorged onto a small platform atop Mont Blanc. The sun is rising or setting and all about him the frosted peaks flame in rainbow tints and . . . But I don't want to give the story away. There is nothing more beautiful than the ending in all art or nature or more horrible than the dawning realization that you have accomplished the unachievable and "finished Proust."

If you wonder who some of the characters are, and you do, there is a handy book in the Fenelon area of your study, called A Reader's Handbook to Proust. In the back section, he—the author of same—gives some of the people who sat to him (Proust). The one on the little musical motif is quite funny as I recall, since it seems to have been formulated out of bits of everything, from a tinkle of Saint-Saens to the Good Friday Spell in Parsifal.[667] If you just look at those back pages, the book won't interfere with your reading pleasure.

Those Poets Foundation Garment handouts come in very handy, when they do come. One year a little bird told me I was getting one. That little bird is now a dead duck—if there's anything I hate it's a lying hen. Still, it's a thoughtful foundation that sends its checks by way of Santa.

---

666. Elstir is a painter and Bergotte a writer in Marcel Proust's *Remembrance of Things Past*, which the Padgetts were reading at the time.

667. Ethereal climax in Richard Wagner's (1813–1883) opera *Parsifal* (1882).

Lob-the-Louse put too many words in your Pen Portrait, so I asked the Tooth Fairy to extract a few. Ouch. "Shorter is better," our motto at the skirt works.

A member of the English faculty said to Anne, "I wonder why I seem to associate James Schuyler's name with John Ashbery's?" This place is not so much Squaresville as Dimsdale.

Well, if you think it would be wise to give the Rogers Memorial Library, Southampton, my poems, I guess I won't try to prevent you. Now that they have a *Nest* I can't go on kidding them with my impersonation of an Absentee Landlord. But perhaps you could get Wayne to take it out a few times — I don't want to relive the experience I once had in the Donnell Branch,[668] where I took down a copy of *Alfred & Guinevere* and found it *had never been taken out ever by anybody.*

(Those last paragraphs are an attractive flight — I keep forgetting my New Year injunction to myself — Walk on the Sunny Side in Seventy Sonny.)

Having finished Proust myself, for the time being, I continue to munch my way through Walter Scott. I'm now midway in *Waverly, Or Tis Sixty Years Since* I started it. I just got to, "Your honour sall get ane o' the Colonel's ain ruffled sarks, but this maun gang in the baggage cart" when I thought I might prefer writing a letter to you to going on. (The two spellings of "ane" is an especially nifty touch).

Love to Wayne and his Ma,

Love, J.

Tushy Nixon

Here's one I heard down to the Convention. You may want to tell it to Wayne, when he's older. 1st Traveling Salesman: Pow-pow. 2nd Traveling Salesman: Pie-pie. Farmer's Daughter: God damn foreigners.

"Nothing in that drawer"[669] is a wonderful poem for reading on long car trips.

---

668. Branch of the New York Public Library located across from the Museum of Modern Art.

669. Poem by Ron Padgett that appeared in his book *Great Balls of Fire*.

TO RON PADGETT

New York, New York

Feb. 28, 1970

Dear Ron,

Visiting you and Patty was totally great, in the fullest sense of the term. Now about the New York art world. FYI, or rather, For Harry Mathews' Information, John [Ashbery] describes the Findlay Gallery as "a perfectly terrible place" and you know how rare perfection is on a plant with built-in obsolescence. I gather it's a kind of high-class "schlock" art gallery, foisting the dregs of ecole de Paris painting on the expense account rich. He seems to think the question of its being reputable in any way does not arise. But a lot of other questions arose, such as why Harry could possibly be interested in it, how come he hadn't asked John about it, and wasn't he up to his old deliberate mystification tricks? Quien sabe.

Of more personal interest to you, perhaps: John sold his Warhol for $1200, through Larry Rubin of the eponymous gallery. He was first going to do it through Robert Elkon, who got $750 for a look-alike for Saphronis Mundy. When he (John) told Elkon how much he had gotten elsewhere, he — Elkon — said *he* would have gotten $1500 for it. John says you "certainly can" sell the box, should you wish: and suggests doing it through Larry Rubin, as the more reputable in money matters. Knock twice and tell them Ashbery sent you.

It was nice at the Whitney to have a distant glimpse of the tall young poets — you, Tom [Clark], Ted [Berrigan], Clark [Coolidge][670] — above the heads of the art lovers, the long haired Watusis of American letters. Perhaps Larry Fagin should take Gro-Mor pills.

By the way — I don't think you need to start radishes indoors — they go very fast outdoors, and like coolness. Or if you were going to start some inside, you can also plant some in vacant areas of the garden, such as among the sage, in the round bed near the pear tree, at the north of the peonies behind the house or the front part of the bed that runs along the east side of the barn. Constance Spry[671] says that the radish called Icicle is "a most seductive root." If you see seeds of something called roquette, it's the same thing as that lubricious leaf used in Italian salads, rugola (also arugola). (I think it's also called rocket: but sweet rocket or dame's rocket is something else.)

670. See glossary.
671. Constance Spry (1886–1960), British florist and writer.

I'm not sure that remark about Watusis is quite the compliment or has the esprit I intended (and certainly I should have said "above the heads *and* art lovers"). But I was struck by how much ease and natural elegance you all had, and the pleasantness of the expressions sported—qualities in rather short supply otherwise at such events. I'm still trying to pick some rather gluey conversational threads off my mind left there by Trumbull Higgins—why should he think I care whether John buys a co-op in a falling money market? Oh well, I rather like his conversation, which is memorable in that it's unforgettable— the words "falling money market" have become another windmill of my mind. I see it as a Japanese print, hundreds of little figures fleeing before the driving yen; then, as Breughel might paint it . . .

I owe you pots of money for phone calls, of which I kept a list, and will send you a check from Hampherst. At the moment I'm down to my last check, the blank secret one I always carry, mostly as a talisman against the enigmas of a sometimes uneasily anticipated tomorrow. "Will you take a check?" is the caption of the blank cartoon.

Love to Patty and Wayne.

What color did the freesias turn out?

love,

Jimmy

TO RON PADGETT

Amherst, Massachusetts

March 17, 1970

Dear Ron,

Thanks for the great letters, which took the curse, or Kiss of Death, off the rest of the mail waiting for me, which was mostly eleven copies of the *Ellsworth* (Maine) *American* and a letter from the Guggenheim foundation beginning, "We regret . . . " They are, however, at some future date going to send me a little printed brochure listing the names of all who successfully applied. As Florence Nightingale once said, "Too kind, too kind." There was also a gift book, one in which my interest is vibrantly moderate, and a postcard from the gifter demanding I acknowledge receipt of same. It's not just monkies who're the cwaziest people. Also a bunch of books from Bromyard, Herts., England, which Boob McNutt must have ordered—*Social Life in Scotland in the Eighteenth*

Century ("Why, don't mind if I do" about tells the story), *The Victorian Fern Craze: A History of Pteridomania*, *The Truth About Cottages* (grim) and, *The Hungry Future*. So it won't surprise you that I'm just finishing *Swann's Way* — I remembered a lot, but forgot a lot too, such as the cruise the Verdurins managed to prolong a year. But I can already see I'm going to do a lot of skipping in *The Captive*; even some of the Odette episode makes me want to take up table tennis or some other active sport.

Guess you know that Tony Towle is It[672] for 1970. There was a Grass Roots movement from the floor to force John Koethe, but it didn't quite work, Native Son or no Native Son. But he's gotten very good. Ditto Keith Abbott, Frank Lima's new poems and — I've blanked out on a Columbia poet's name; not Allen Senauke, another one, very sweet. Kenneth and John claimed to like the *penseur* in prose (from Iowa? or Idaho?) but it seemed to me that while it's nice that he's after something a little different, it turns out on closer examination not to be all that different; in fact, he may become the Norman Rockwell of the prose poem, whose real name is John Updike. The only mss I was disappointed in was Carter's [Ratcliff]. Harry Seggessman (that can't be right) called up and asked me to write 200 words about Tony for the catalogue — I said yes, but might not have had I known it was Kenneth who put him up to it. Of all the crust — the big ape won't sneeze for less than $500. Yes, I know he's a saint. Perhaps I'll begin the little note. These paranoid and drunken maunderings . . .

I drove up here with Kenneth and as we were entering Connecticut he said, "There seems to be a roadblock or car check up ahead." Since I was transporting a little gift from Kenward — about an ounce of his latest purchase — my heart did "shunts and double shunts, and/all tricks known to common cunts" to quote Mother Goose. Turned out it was just a detour (we got lost) but my that was a long, long couple of minutes, and I thought of reforming and giving up Contemporaneity, but then I realized that Kenneth was unaware that I had been feeling anything — he was unaware of what I had, since I was both unwilling to share it with him and apprehensive as to what effect the news might have on his driving — and, filled with admiration for my own cool, decided to continue as a Swinger, at least until I've finished the ounce.

After avoiding the January crush here, I now find that the Laurence Porters and kids, Leon and Sarah, plus Katie, are coming here day after tomorrow. Let's

672. Winner of the Frank O'Hara Award whose book, *After Dinner We Take a Drive into the Night*, was published by Columbia University Press. John Koethe (b. 1945) won the award in 1972 for *Domes* (1973).

see, nine people go into five bedrooms . . . but as far as I'm concerned, they don't, so guess I'll make my annual pilgrimage to East Aurora and Mum. Getting there from here seems to take a good deal of bus schedule reading ingenuity, so don't be surprised if you hear from me from Montreal.

Are you really going to grow ferns? What courage. I think there's a very moving passage on how to in one of Gertrude Jekyll's books, *Wood & Garden* or else *House and Garden*. I always like a second authority; but maybe you just find it confusing.

Give my love to Pat and Wayne. I'll only be away a few days—my linger potential doesn't apply in Western New York—so write soon.

love,

Jimmy

Now I'm going to buy food for my Rapidograph.

TO RON PADGETT

> If you haven't heard of the creaky, scarping sound of the common grackle within the past few days, you probably live well up in Maine or are not observant

Amherst, Massachusetts

April 9, 1970

Dear Larry O'Dendron,

You think you and Patty and Wayne have had colds. Well. Let me tell you about mine.

It's better.

It seems like about a million years since I last wrote to you, but that's because I've been to East Aurora; and back. I hardly know what not to tell you about first—that my sister-in-law was elected Most Worthy Matron of the local Eastern Star? Or maybe it was more Brainard that that: Most Really Worthy Matron of the Eastern Star. Or the hypnotic and brain mangling sessions with the TV set. I got hooked, totally, on the daytime serials, channel 4 from 2 to 4. I especially enjoyed one ("Guiding Light," maybe?) in which Rachel, who never appeared, had capped a lifetime of double dealing by renting an apartment, which her husband had never seen, for $325 a month—and got one month's security and the first month's rent out of—hang on—the baby's trust fund! This news was broken to about thirty different people in five days, and the art of staggering speechlessness, as though struck by an unseen force, scaled new depths. Joe says he likes daytime serials because the actors are so good and the stories so strangely true to life. Uhm. Maybe the attraction is that they are what one fears life may be like—a lot of decorous people sitting around TVless living rooms telling lies on demand. "Did you see Helen today?" Commence sneaky music. "Why—why—" close up of quivering wrinkle "No!" Asthma attack begins as Wurlitzer explodes into fragments through which we see a woman buy a beauty shop so she can give herself a decent home permanent— "I like lots of body—not much curl." Where is my Build-a-Bomb kit.

As for the folks. They *seemed* well.

At that point Bruno came to tell me it was 70 degrees—in the shade—and why not go for a wallow in the swamp? So we did. Skunk cabbage shoots rioting out of the muck like students. Also a lot of students lying around like limp skunk cabbage leaves. It's a nice little nature preserve but somehow measly. Just when you think you're getting into it you realize that flick of blue is a Corvair bound for nearby Belchertown (Massachusetts) and no jay. Civilization is all right, but I prefer to be one of its discontents. Except that's getting to be a bit modish, isn't it.

I hear you have conquered New Jersey and plan to use it as a launching pad when you storm England. Or that was the word at Kenward's smoke-in (or booze-up—dealer's choice) after Joe [Brainard] and Anne's [Waldman] reading. It was a nice party notable for the absence of anyone named Padgett, Mitchell, [George and Katie] Schneeman or [Tom] Veitch.[673] I liked Tom's poems in *World* 18, especially the "Hello Nose" one.

Yes, New York Poetry (*An Anthology of New York Poets*) came and so did a check. I like them both.

The little flowers by the rhododendron are species crocuses, they're much nicer than the big kinds I think. Although this time of year anything that will bloom is jake with me—yesterday I found a stray Siberian squill doing its dark blue thing, but they have gone the way of garden plants by now. How, by the

673. Tom Veitch (1941–2022), poet.

way, is your earliest (last fall) planted crop doing, and what did you do with it when the in-laws came to visit?

Speaking of coming to visit—why, I'd love to. But not before May. I absolutely can't think about travel at the moment—the trip back from Rochester in the Easter blizzard was even worse than the trip to Buffalo in a cloudburst. At least the cloudburst trip only took eleven hours.

Fairfield and Anne were in town—oops, NYC—over the past weekend— Fairfield's show is up at Tibor's, and I hope you'll get to see it. There is a biggish picture of the living room in Maine which I rate tops.

Lessee. I thought I had something real to tell you. No. Guess not. Nothing real has happened to me.

Proust gets better and better—have you crashed yet?

love to Patty and Wayne

> All this week, all day, every day, stay
> well and keep happy ... —Aunt Evelyn

TO KENWARD ELMSLIE

[Amherst, Massachusetts]

April 20 1970

Dear Upcoming Birthday Boy,

Oh dear he's growing up—pretty soon he'll be wanting to wear tight pants to school—I've just been busily trying to encase your birthday present in a Plain Brown Wrapper—don't get excited, it's just another book—in hopes it will reach you in time for the Birthday honors, which caused me to be overcome by a desire to communicate. I thought of telephoning (say, that's kind of a good title) but as it's about 8:30 a.m. . . . News? In *Amherst*? Which is looking quite cute, now the red-flowered maples are in bloom. Other flowers I've seen, aside from the ever-popular daffs, croci, and bon-bon colored hyacinths, are: Quaker Ladies (or bluets—a favorite),[674] a bank of white violets (unfortunately the bank also included enough gum wrappers to print the *Sunday Times* on), a few purple violets (mysteriously known as blue violets), and a field with a band of periwinkles down it (*pervenche* Rousseau's favorite flower). Amherst is not unchic,

---

674. Schuyler's poem "The Bluet" appeared in *Hymn to Life*.

too: the folks tap the sugar maples that line the streets and on many a tree I saw hanging the familiar red and green Medaglio d'Oro can.

Hmm. I just opened Harrap's French-English (to check *pervenche*) to *fagotage*: ridiculous manner of dressing, ridiculous get-up, dowdy get-up. Too right. While under *Les Pervers* we find: The evil-doers, the froward. So that's what froward means. My latest mystery adventure: the other night I was reading in bed rather late, rather late for here, say one a.m., when in the Great White Way of my mind all the signs began flashing HAVE A SMOKE. So I got the strainer and so on and, by dint of using my elbows and knees, managed to hammer out something like Br'er Rabbit's penis which would (maybe) burn, and, in my tattersall flannelette pajamas and L.L. Bean fleece-side-in slippers, went out into the yard. It was a lovely night. The moon had set, the stars flamed and I lit up. From the other side of the blackberry tangle came something, which combined features of a whisper, a giggle and a snort of jealousy and/or rage. I didn't know whether to down it or eat it, flame and all. I settled for smoking it up as fast as I could, with the result that I soon felt the Pleiades had become entangled in my hair. "But who cares, once the evidence had gone down in smoke?" I thought as I wandered back to the house, all unmindful of the mole tunnels in the lawn which are more like battlements, and over one of which I tripped and fell. Not that it seemed to matter—at worst Bruno could bring me in when he went out for his morning run. But a few minutes later, needless to say, found me back in bed, and a few minutes later than that found me in the kitchen getting out the Maple Corner Syrup to put on the French Toast I had just made. (Did you know that in England French Toast is called Poor Knights on Horseback?) The next day I looked out the window in the front door and saw a frat boy and his chick sitting on a protuberance on Snell Common, as the empty spot across the street is called, sharing a joint. It's different for *them*.

I've been admiring our accomplishments in the New York Poets anthology, and Joe's especially, at least until Ron let me know all the things Joe wanted Random House to do that they didn't. The schmucks. Maybe we could get lots of bright red ink and have Joe draw in the end papers in *our* copies . . . I love reading the index of first lines, and note with joy that I have U all to myself.

My travel plans are to stay put until sometime in May, then go to Southampton and thence to NYC. I would love to salute you in the flesh on your b.day, but somehow my two days in bigtown have a way of turning into two months. What are your travel plenz? When are you going to have your Calais seed-in? Or does the last frost not come until the 4th? The weather has been so gorgeous for the past week (though it's raining right now—I don't care, so long as it isn't snow)—I hope you got a good Westhampton burn last weekend—it's too bad you can't look away from the ocean and see the Vermont mountains. The Holyoke hills here are the most incredible pinks, mauves, blues, all scratched and flashed with silver. It's wonderful what effects can be gotten with the inconspicuous flowers of hardwood trees.

Love to Joe. How is John Bennett coming?[675]

love,

Jimmy

PS: Anne, Fairfield and Katie each told me what a good time they had at your dinner. "The food of course was simply mar-r-r-velous, the way it always is at Kenward's," said Fairfield. In fact the only thing that got a bad, well, temperate review is John's eye-boggling shirt. Poor dear. But plainly, it makes him feel dressed up, and *that's* what counts.

Lizzie to Katie: "Mom seems dumb but she has flashes of genius." And driving slowly through the UMass campus the other day Anne heard a co-ed say, "Look, there's an old lady in granny glasses."

TO RON PADGETT

Amherst, Massachusetts

April 29 1970

Dear Ron,

I'm relieved to hear that Landsman's[676] sent the right dictionary. A doom shaped cloud rose over the golden oak desk as I was ordering it: it seemed totally unlikely that one could order one volume of two and not receive the other and that, compelled by obscure forces, I would begin by asking for the wrong one. In that state of mind it quickly becomes impossible to feel at all certain you know what English-French means: "Here is the English for the French you are looking up." So I foresaw endless returns of books to England from which you would emerge the owner of *Harrap's Conversational Serbo-Croat* and with a severe case of Anglophobia. Glad to be disappointed. Again.

675. John Bennett, artist and carpenter doing work on Elsmlie's house.
676. Landsman Booksellers of Buckenhill, Bromyard, Herefordshire, England, specialists in "publications dealing with Farming, Gardening and Allied Subjects."

I'm equally relieved to hear the Clam Broth House[677] is still there — after I spoke to you I began to wonder if I hadn't heard that it was torn down. I think I was last in it about 1947. But perhaps what I heard was that they sold their Remington bronzes for an Undisclosed Sum (and perhaps la vida is being just a bit more *sueno* than usual). Isn't there a great Remington[678] collection in Tulsa? Anyway, *revenon a nos* clams, believe on my first visit I had a similarly clamless and brothless meal, and vaguely assumed the name was just one of those things, like calling a restaurant The Trading Post or the Villa d'Este. You have no doubt found the clams, but (or at least so it used to be) the broth is on a help-yourself basis, in a tea urn thing surrounded by little white cups. Many think the broth is the best part. And I hope you realize no obligation attaches to eating the little shriveled penis thing on the clam — they *are* called piss clams — no, it's just one of those things, they squirt sea water out of it, or maybe they use it to sing with. There's no harm in eating it of course, it's just rather rubbery. Help. Get me out of this.

I have fixed my mind on arriving at Orient Point on Monday, May 11th: afternoon, of course. Would that suit? I haven't yet puzzled out the complexities of when the ferry gets there, but a telephone call will fix that. I'll let you know. If this isn't such a good day, say so; it's picked in quite an arbitrary spirit.

I asked Fairfield about the car. He said, and I quote, "Yes." (Yes, keep it for a while after you've left Southampton. Not, "Yes, he can't have it," or "Yes, I'd mind.")

The spring persists, and I realized yesterday while looking at a lackluster tulip, that I was beginning to take it for granted. So I trotted out to the corner of Woodside and Walnut where a cherry tree higher than a house top is in full pale pink bloom, right down to the ground. The tree is completely covered with blossoms, and yet it looks completely naked. An inspiring sight, though of what, I'm not sure.

Here is a short vision for your collection, from William Allingham's diary.[679] (Do you know his poems, "The Fairies?" "Up the airy mountain, down the rushy glen . . . ") The drug seems to have been given him as an anodyne during an illness.

677. A restaurant in Hoboken, New Jersey, mentioned by Schuyler in his poem "Dining Out with Doug and Frank."
678. Frederic Remington (1861–1909), painter and sculptor of the American West.
679. *William Allingham's Diary 1847–1889*, with an introduction by Geoffrey Grigson.

Eastbourne, March 14, 1889. I had a very curious dream whose floating imagery evades every cast of the net of language. I thought I found myself somehow, by merely looking aside, aware of some of the main secrets of Nature's material workshop. There was no tinge of aesthetic feeling. Merely, I saw a little below the superficial appearance of things, and found the methods by which forms are innumerably varied and sent on their courses to be so simple and obvious that I smiled at myself with a sort of impatience at not having seen all this before. A pleasurable satisfaction remained after I had awakened and said to myself, "This is the haschisch."

I notice all the Government ads against pot ("When your child points out that you smoke, drink and wear cheap perfume . . . ") make a big thing out of its not being in the pharmacopoeia. It certainly used to be. We should start an agitation, Get Pot Back in the USP [United States Pharmacopeia].

Now I wonder, if I take a nap, will I wake up before the creamy rice pudding has to come out of the oven? Probably, it has three hours to go. "Lady Bernard, wife of Sir Charles Bernard, Chief Commissioner of Burma, used to make a rice pudding as follows every day for her husband's tiffin. He said no one could make it as well as she did. The secret is slow, very slow and prolonged baking." From "Good Things in England" which might better be called, 101 Things to do with Suet.

Love to Patty and Wayne. See you all soon,
love,

Jimmy

TO KENWARD ELMSLIE

Great Spruce Head Island

June 19, 1970

Dear Kenward,

One trouble with cigars is that you can't light them and lay them in an ashtray. Well, you can, of course, but they immediately go out. Which makes writing very, very difficult, since the only way I know how to write is to light something, take a puff, and put it in an ashtray.

A pause, while I get a cigar.

Uhhhm. That was nasty.

We made it! Unlikely as it seemed, moment by moment, especially the one when the car made a funny noise on the freeway of somebody else's choice ("Unequal air pressure in the tires," said the kindly redhead at the Ford agency). The sun is shining on the sea, the yellow hawkweed is shining in the grass, and I feel as though yesterday I was sitting at this desk writing to Joe. As Lizzie said on the Kittiwake, "Going to the island makes me feel schizophrenic." Because it really seems as though no time had passed—there's a person who only lives here, and there's somebody else who lives in the inferior places. Scary and beautiful.

I'm joining Joe in making 1970 the biggest and best summer of deprivation yet. I'm giving up food. It's that, or Fatties Anonymous will start building elephant traps for me. One thing that helps, in a sense, is that I brought no booze, no not even curdled grape juice. Then too once the stove has gone out for the night there's not such a temptation to start running up bacon and peanut butter samadges—yes dieting's going to be real easy; but I'd better stop talking about it or I will have to go finish off the cold boiled potatoes.

No, I guess one does forget each winter the utter sameness of here as a place. It's not enough to be here and see it, I want to be it.

Not smoking dope will make dieting a good deal easier, I think. (One thing pinned up near my desk is the anonymously addressed envelope that brought me joints—it's as unmistakably by You Know Who as certain great dust jackets; I'm naming no names).

And thinking about the myriad charms of Calais there rose in my mind a vision—the A&W Root Beer Stand—those French fries. You don't think ten ay em is too early for lunch do you? I'm doing the low carbohydrate one, so I can have all the butter I want. But I can't have it *on* anything . . .

Love to Joe, who owes me a letter, though I'm far too noble to let that keep me from writing to him. It was a very marvelous stay at Apple Hill.

love,

Jimmy

TO JOE BRAINARD

[Great Spruce Head Island]

Monday morning
June 28th (perhaps?) 1970

Dear Joe,

Jimmy Quinn, Cap'n of the (Penobscot Bay) mail boat, is usually a little late on Monday morning, so perhaps I can write a letter and still have it leave today. If not, manana . . .

It's a bright pale blue morning and what I think is called a spanking breeze is blowing. Wait a minute while I put my ass out the window. Yes, it *is* a spanking breeze. I wouldn't mind if the air were a touch warmer, and yet, I'm quite fond of the well chilled martini effect of hot sun pouring on iced air. And as soon as one steps into the woods there's no wind at all, always startling, as though one had stepped into another country.

I don't know whether I'm used to being here yet or not—sometimes I think Why, I've been here more than a week, which seems to stretch endlessly into the past; then I realize we often arrive here as late or later than this, and, well, it's confusing.

Not smoking cigs in Amherst was far from easy. But they had a very good tobacco store there which I patronized enough to discover that if cigarettes are an irritating expense, cigars can be downright ruinous. Yes, the 3 for 50¢ are better than the 5 for 30¢, and so I suspect it goes, up and up the great gold toppling ladder. Except I don't think I can ever "make it," really, with those super Corona-Coronas. Sometimes I get the feeling after lighting a real cigar that whole years will go by before I get to the end of it. It's like being on the Long Island railroad and realizing that the most boring person is bearing down on you and the empty seat by your side. So I let them go out, but they don't taste as good when relit. But not smoking cigs in Amherst was far from easy, I tell you. It's in the back of my mind that sometimes I might quit, or drastically cut down on, cigars; but first, I want to lose some weight. I think I've lost the seven pounds I gained in Calais (no criticism intended, I don't regret a bite), which no cigs plus dope and heavy heavenly cream made inevitable. Ah well there's a whole summer before us and the low carbohydrate diet is easier than some. And one can drink (though I haven't had one, not even a sipski wine, since Amherst) on it; and have all the butter and cream you wish—but you can't put the butter on anything, and you can't put any sugar in the cream, so what's the good?

And Jimmy Quinn is not late after all. Nothing from you, I'll warrant.

Later. After lunch (one boiled onion, chopped cabbage with butter—*cooked* chopped cabbage that is—unlimited amounts of roast lamb; no potato and sigh, no chocolate cream tapioca). And I got a lovely letter from Kenward, which I will answer soonliest.

Fairfield has started painting, a landscape I don't think he's going to finish, and a so-so still life, and a portrait of the caretaker and his wife which, so far, is brilliant. Liz is downstairs banging around cleaning, making the house worthy of the presence of KoKo Koch, who arrives this week. To be followed in ten days or so—by—her—Dad. Yes. We won the raffle. But I forgot, I've decided that, since I'm really very fond of the monster, I'm just going to anticipate pleasure from his company and console myself for any non-pleasure with the fact that the silence is never lovelier than when noisy guests depart. Katherine is, though, staying for *all* of July—surely Kenneth is too restless to?—. . . And when I think of all the people on Eastern Long Island who must have said no, or "No!", to his eager bid to come live [with] them and be their love. . . . But, no, I mustn't think these thoughts . . .

"Every day in every way Kenneth gets better and better . . ."

As soon as I got here I started to make you a trash book out of an address book I had never used. I thought it would take about an hour, but who would guess that an address book, such a little itty bitty address book, could have so many pages? Or that one's trash runs out so soon? A trash book, in case you're wondering, is something like a scrap book, only, well, you put trash in it. Which is not the same as garbage. That you put in boxes, like a candy box, and call it a Garbage Box. Garbage Boxes are not quite so nice as Trash Books.

Didn't I have a lot more things to tell you? Didn't I have anything to tell you, for the matter of that? If I did it's quite gone out of my head. So I'll go for a walk. Write soon.

love to K,

love,

Jimmy

You once asked me for the birthday list in my address book. Here it is.

Jan. 19	Elizabeth Hazan
Feb. 14	Harry Mathews (also, Valentine's Day)
Feb. 27	Kenneth Koch
March 11	JOE BRAINARD
April 1	Lizzie Porter
April 17	Joe Hazan
April 27	Guess Who?
May 20	Katie Porter
June 4	Vincent Katz
June 10	Fairfield Porter
June 13	Katherine Koch
June 17	Ron Padgett (I *think* it's the 17th)
July 12	Rachel Towle
July 2	John Ashbery
Aug 30	Bill Berson (oops—here—have a k)
Nov 6	Anne Porter
Nov 9	Yours Truly and, Lewis Warsh, My Birthday Twin
Nov. 29	Jane Hazan and, Wayne Padgett, Her Birthday Twin

—That's it, except a few I don't think you want to know (W. H. Auden, Feb 21)—Got any to swap? Pat's true birthday, or Maxine's, or the Fagins? This year I'm sending everyone a roll of pennies.

TO KENWARD ELMSLIE

[Great Spruce Head Island]

July 2, 1970

Dear Kenward,

Ever since the *Vermont Life* with those great photographs in it came I've been meaning to send for one of their Bargain Bundles—and here it is. I'm saving them to read at breakfast (to replace the *Times*, which here goes with lunch). So 10 breakfasts are now all set. I've tried the oldest issue, Fall 1958—cover story, "The Fabulous Machine Tool Industry"—which contained an article about the

Vermont photographer Clara Sipprell,[680] whose nephew "Puss" was the first great love of my life, when I was a senior in high school. The name Sipprell still gives me a turn. What a terrible boy.

We're having a funny overcast day, with total clouds very low but underneath it very clear so that Isle au Haute, which is often barely visible, emerges a sharp vivid dull cold blue. The tide is running quickly away and there go Laurence and Betsy in a green canoe. So the babies—Leon and Sarah—are babbling happily in the dragon-haunted living room. Though a bit ago Sarah got in some good shrieking and I heard Leon say, contentedly, "I made Baby cry."

Whoops. Fairfield wants to go for a walk. See you later.

Well. That was fun. I saw a withered moccasin flower and I don't know what all. Here comes Nancy Straus, casting an amused eye on my weed-choked flower tubs, in her well-faded Levis and Fair Isle sweater—to invite us for a drink, I hope I hope I hope? I've had *one* since reaching here. Drink, not bottle. Why am I punishing myself this way? Gonna go to Camden, smoke Camels, eat French fries and drink bottled Still—which is what you can get in Maine—until it's coming out of my ears. I awoke the other night and found myself musing on what death I was electing rather than that by lung cancer. So I hastily put on the light and read *The Hand Reared Boy*,[681] which, as you might guess, is a novel about masturbation. It's England's answer to *Portnoy's Complaint* and Philip Roth is still the Winner and Holder of the Title.

Our social life is shaping up—next week, the Katzes (I'll believe it when I see them), then Kenneth (I hear he's changed terribly and his friends call him "Lovable Old Mr Manners")—I loved the San Fran photo of him you sent: Edna Mae Oliver in *Well of Loneliness*),[682] and now Big Little John Ashberger writers that he and Aladar Marbary[683] plan to drop by, end of July, possibly bringing swinging Elaine de Kooning with them. We'll see. He also says they are looking for an apartment—they being he and Aladar, minus Elaine, I guess. He found a lovely one at W 23rd and 10th Avenue which he has turned down. Myself, I believe in *long* engagements. However I'm not the one who's signing

680. Clara Estelle Sipprell (1885–1975), photographer. Paul Sipprell, who appears in "The Morning of the Poem," was her nephew. The Sipprell family also appears in "A Few Days."

681. *The Hand Reared Boy* by Brian W. Aldiss (1970).

682. Edna May Oliver (1883–1942), Hollywood character actress who appeared in *Little Women* (1933). Radclyffe Hall's lesbian novel, *The Well of Loneliness*, was not made into a movie.

683. Aladar Marberger (1947–1988), director of New York's Fischbach Gallery.

the lease . . . Let's just hope it doesn't all end as a feature story in Vitamin G. (I just fantasy-spasmed writing JA the truth—for a change—as to what I think about the whole brouhaha in a few, a very few, words. Heaven forbid and besides there's no point since I wouldn't be there to see his face as he read it. Do you think one's ego remains intact—in so far as it does—largely through the courtesy of one's friends? Well no scare—though the Pultneyville Plover does have a way of demanding answers to questions where courtesy forbids the truth. Though I notice he's rather selective about the people he makes the demands of . . .)

I also note that tenants of 49 South (you and Joe are the shining exceptions to this rule of thumb) tend to hate each other. Ron wrote that the Bigelows had rearranged everything so that it was the kind of house where he wouldn't want to live, so he could leave it with less regret (he was out returning the Volkswagen after the Bs moved in). Mr B, on the other hand, writes that now that his wife has washed the windows they can *see* the yard; and, casting implication aside, that they came on a cache of *good dishes*, all broken by the Padgetts (on the contrary, we broke them and they have been there for years). From which I conclude that Ron, who took an instant dislike to the Bigelows, was his best or worst Testy Tulsa self with them . . . la di da di dum dum dum—monkies is the cwaziest people . . .

I lately caused Walnut Acres to send you-all (I told them to send it) to Joe B Elmslie so you'll know it's for both of you—ho ho—that's a good one—some insecticide-free yummies—I had Joe most in mind while selecting the Nut Butters, while the Apricot Kernel oil is to see if you can think of anything to do with it . . .

A thought for the week: Joe hates group-addressed letters, while Joe Hazan is bitterly offended if one writes just to Jane. Yes, there are no sure-fire rules of conduct.

lotsalove,

Jimmy
love to Joe, too

PS among the obits the *Times-Argus* didn't carry while I was *chez toi* were those of Ungaretti and E. M. Forster.

TO KENWARD ELMSLIE

[Great Spruce Head Island]

July 21, 1970

Dear Kenward,

You're probably wondering what Kenneth [Koch] does about helping out with the dishes. It's funny you should ask, since I was just chuckling to myself about that this very moment. When he first got here—my, *that* was a long long time ago—he pulled a fast one. After his traditional, "I'd offer to dry but I don't know where things go—" (quick fade to the living room), he actually *did* dry some plates, two nights in a row, with many a merry quip and clanking couplet. Then his after dinner Havana came into play—he would forget and light it, just before the willing workers began to head for the sinks, and, as we all know, once a good cigar is lit, you can't let it go out, or it's ruined. Well, that's a good excuse but it's not one that can be used, convincingly, very often. As luck would have it, his doctor has prescribed a daily scalding bath for his prostatitis. At first this was taken after tennis and before dinner, with loud injunctions to let him know five minutes before serving time so he could get out of the tub and to the table without missing anything. Then the great realization: by a little fancy footwork between the courts and his typewriter, he could pop out of the room and say, "I guess there isn't time for a bath—I'll have to take it after dinner." A clever ploy, and rather a blessing, since when trying to do something in the kitchen—even dishes—the last thing one wants is the chorus line from the Latin Quarter prancing around.

Then there's the chapter called, "Getting Him the Root Beer," (finally achieved yesterday—"The trouble is," he confided to me in a stage whisper, "this kind of root beer isn't any good." Well, no it isn't. But it's what they sell), and the one called, "Oh! My Aching Shoulder" (Kenneth thinks he strained it playing tennis, but I think he's mistaken since tennis is not among the things it prevents him from doing. This morning he offered it as a reason not to carry the insulated milk box—admittedly a mite heavy—down to the dock. I suggested he carry it in the *other* hand), and the interlude, "What John Porter said at the Camden Yacht Club" ("We're all ready to leave but we've got a trouble maker with us: Karl Koch." Edward Porter: "Kenneth Koch." John P: "Yes that's right: Kenneth Koch." Kenneth says he doesn't think much of Camden, but I pointed out that any town where you spend all your time in a phone booth trying to make collect long distance calls to people you know are out is not going to seem like much); and "Getting Stoned (which we did one moonflooded night on the float and was thoroughly enjoyed. The famous pot purchase written up in Vitamin G was for _ ounce—as a debauchee, he reminds me of[Ezra] Pound's roue who threw himself "into a sea of three women"). Then there's the chapter called, "Bitching to Kenward," which one shouldn't, not about a departing guest, only: *is* he? He was to have gone last Saturday, now it's to be this Friday—only Jimmy Quinn[684] isn't at all sure he can drive him to Bangor—

You may see me sooner than you think.

I have decided all guests can be divided into two sorts, You and Joe, and, The Others. Kenneth is definitely a "The Others." Ada, Alex, Vincent and Sunny Katz are a "You and Joe." The deciding factor is whether the hosuehold must be wrenched all out of shape to fit the (possibly warped) personality of the guest, or if it is allowed to potter on in its own accustomed quotidian way.

But one would think I had nothing else to write about! Let me tell you about the sea, and how wet it is. And the blueberries, how ripe they're getting. And the chanterelles, and the huge mess of them I picked yesterday, and how quickly they were eaten. Yum.

For some reason I have been shaving every other day, and today is it and here I go. Give Joe a big affectionate apologetic kiss—I'm sorry I'm not being a more frequent letter writer, and will try to mend my ways for the rest of the summer. Smooch,

love,

Jimmy

TO JOE BRAINARD

[Great Spruce Head Island]

July 23 '70

Dear Joe—

Maybe if I write you while your letter is still hot from the reading, I can break through my non-letter-writing barrier. I'm writing on this kind of paper because

---

684. Captain of mailboat that serviced Great Spruce Head Island.

it's too *hot* in my writing room, a once-a-summer happening on the island. I mean, it's hot enough so it would be noticed as such somewhere else. (I hate this kind of "poor people" paper—my meaning here could be easily misunderstood—I hate "poor people" anything.)

Kenneth is also here (on the dining porch) eating lunch. Liz and KoKo have eaten theirs—I have eaten mine, well, not lunch, breakfast (got up real late)— Anne & Fairfield have gone to Bangor to meet Katie, who is flying up for a long weekend & rest from studying organic chemistry. Here comes Bruno—he will soon settle down in a big noisy heap—and "Sigh!" there he goes.

Nope, I have not smoked one single cigarette. I do of course go merrily on with cigars—Kenneth brought me some good ones, Brazilian and a few Havanas, smuggled in from Switzerland. They are very good *and* a bit much—they last too long and by the end make me feel faintly queasy. But I like having them. Giving up cigs, or maybe giving up inhaling, has had much more effect on me than I thought at first. Some kind of shock? Easily depressed, & often gloomy, listless with bursts of aimless energy. And *very* irritable. So I stopped dieting! Seriously, it was too much on top of the way I felt—if a meal was 5 minutes late (& an hour late is more like it) I was ready to tear the house apart. But I think I'm leveling off. Besides I just realized that if I can get along without cigarettes while Kenneth is here, I've got it licked. I'm a winner! (Kenneth asked me what I was going to have for breakfast the other day & I said, "Special K, the breakfast of losers.")

Here comes Liz who says "Anybody want to go swimming in about 20 minutes?" You bet—it's the day perfect for the swimming chilly.

I'm glad you like the peanut butter. I think it's tops—including other organic kinds—be sure to tell me how the other nut butters are—I've never tried them & really want to know, so be candid.

Kenward sent me a postcard—the picture is a map of the Camden—Deer Isle area, with a black line drawn on it ending at the island (here). Written on it (the front) was a word I took to be "August." So I assumed it meant you & Kenward were coming to visit us in August. But Lizzie says the word is Augusta (Maine's state capital). So now I think it's a card Fairfield once sent in a letter to Kenward, showing how to get here. But now that my hopes are aroused, I feel you should come—so do—But I know how binding the chains of a vegetable garden are. Besides, it's hard to leave one's summer behind, even if it's nice in some other place too.

Yesterday I finished your little trash book. I'm rather pleased with it. Partly because of its nothingness, partly because I didn't think anybody else would think of making one for you. You'll get it soon.

Now I'm going to put on my swimmin' trunks. More later.

It's a swimming and cucumber sandwich later. It was cold—the swim I mean; but so was the cucumber come to think of it—it's my current favorite—salt, pepper & sweet butter—yummy-yums.

I'm glad—very glad—you finally got the proofs of I Remember[685] (but it bores me that it took so long: off-Broadway publishers apparently have their tiresome side too). Hope you didn't cut much? It's wonderful to think that something which is so fresh is also so enduring.

When I was reading your letter earlier Kenneth came up behind me so I folded it shut. "Ha ha" he said "You're so funny: you think I'm going to read Joe Brainard's letter over your shoulder." "How did you know it's from Joe Brainard?" I mildly queried. Then when he left I went on reading it, & it was the page on which you said something about people he (Kenneth) makes climb walls! Don't worry he didn't see it—or he and I would still be thrashing it out.

Here I had just written his name when he came out again. But my real reason for crossing it out is that I resolved to make this letter not all about Kenneth. But I did tell you he—No! not today.

Guess that's all. But I'll leave this open until tomorrow ayem.

Friday

Well, he's gone. Sailed away on the mailboat—I can hardly believe it. Now it's safe to reflect that I like him quite a lot, always enjoy our chats about literature, even find him quite amusing (though not half so funny as he bills himself to be). It's a shame I can't bear to stay in the same house with him, but, well, guess I don't have to do any explaining to you about *that*, however. Today is another hot one, broiling. The tide unfortunately isn't right for swimming until late in the afternoon. Can hardly wait—Love to Kenward—love,

Jimmy

685. Joe Brainard's *I Remember*, first published by Anne Waldman and Lewis Warsh's Angel Hair press.

TO TREVOR WINKFIELD

[Great Spruce Head Island]

July 27, 1970

Dear Trevor,

Venice it is, you lucky Loiner. I'm so glad you're going in October—though it's worth going there in August to see what the light becomes by then, and the way the water changes after it rains in September. In the summer the water is hard and glassy and the light so bright that its pleasure is in the way it lights up the shadows. But in October the light turns to the color of sunlight and the canals become green, as though laced with snow. All walks in Venice are nice— the main thing about the city is that, unlike many beautiful cities, the big things are very much not to be missed. I mean, you may not rush to Notre Dame or to St. Peter's, but in Venice, the Palazzo Ducale is what one should rush to. And the Academia, and the Scuolas. If you are there for only a week or so, some per- haps secondary things I would hope for you not to miss are: the Ca Rezonico, the 18th century museum on the Grand Canal, with the Longhis and the Tiepolo (one of the sons) called "The New World," and his punchinello fres- coes; another small museum on the Piazza, up over Florian's (I think), with a very beautiful almost destroyed Antonello da Messina; the Bellini in Saint Zachary's (I forgot the Italian—San Zacaria, maybe?), very big and calm on which, sometime during the afternoon, the sunlight directly falls with exhila- rating effect; the Veronese's in the Plazzo Ducale (though I don't know why I should think you would miss them); the interior of any church on which Mauro Coducci worked—there's one in the same square with Verocchio's Colleoni sculpture, and the trompe l'oeil marble panels on the scuola toward which his horse is pointed are quite something too; and, which I love the most, Santa Maria dei Miracoli. But see a lot of big Venice first, it means more, I think, if one knows its setting first. Do go up the steps to the altar, and look at and feel the small sculptures emerging from the balustrade. And there is or used to be a small café in back of it, where you can sit and wonder why one man's right an- gles and circles mean so much more than another's. Or don't wonder anything, but don't miss it. Now I'm going to go eat dinner.

July 28 1970

I wonder if I'm vaguely right about the date? The last Tuesday in July—nine- teen seventy, I *think*. It's after dinner (roast beef, cold, with pickles and gar- denfresh green beans), and after washing dishes (Ivory Liquid), and solitaire (a kind where you put out all the cards face up), and going to bed with Norman Douglas (*Looking Back*—I like it),[686] and falling asleep and waking up in the small hours (sandwich of peanut butter made from organically grown peanuts), and breakfast (blackest coffee), and a cigar ("Swagger" by "Gold Label"—bleh) and, in a word, it is tomorrow.

But you were saying something about Venice. Well, at the risk of repeating myself—I think one could have a marvelous time in Paris without setting foot (or head) inside the Louvre or a theater or a church, though rather a fool not to. But in Venice? Not unless one had unlimited funds to spend on silk suits, hideous Murano glass and rather fatigued gondoliers and even more fatigued would-be gondoliers (but don't misunderstand—this is based on observation). The restaurants are nothing—the strolling has not the mad enchantment of Naples—but the sights, oh my! Where are you planning to stay? When I get back to Southampton I'll look in an old guide book and see if I can roust out a couple of names of places to eat or sleep; but all that changes so fast.

Here is a pretty snow scene by Thomas Bewick for you—rather like a Winkfield oil. Orderly, white and mysterious.

> *From my sheep thus drawing into shelter, gave rise to an opinion I formed, and which has been confirmed by long reflection, that must yet be done to protect the larger flocks from being overblown and lost on the bleak moors, in great snowstorms. Were long avenues made by double rows of whin hedges, planted parallel to each other at about six feet asunder, and continued in the form of two sides of a square, with the whins of each side drawn together, and to grow interplanted at the tops, so as to form an arched kind of relief, the sheep would, on instinctively seeing the coming storm, immediately avail themselves of such asylums, and particularly in the lambing season. In the corner of the angle of the square, the shepherd might have his hovel, thatched with heather and ling, and his beds for himself and his dogs, made of the same materials; and the whole of his "field" might be rendered so snug as greatly to defy the severity of the winter's drifting blasts and wreaths of snow.*
> —Memoir of Thomas Bewick pg 11[687]

I meant to say above—about gondoliers—they don't seem to allow women to prostitute themselves in Venice, just men. I think it's a way of honoring Lord Byron. And as for Venetian food treats—well, *fegato a la Veneziana* is liver and

686. *Looking Back: An Autobiographical Excursion* (1933)
687. Thomas Bewick (1753–1828), British wood engraver

onions. Then there's *risi-bisi* (rice and peas), and *baiccoli*, a hard biscuit with all the charm of a testy bus conductor.

I think I had better trot down to the dockhouse and mail this, if I'm to make an apple pie in time for dinner. Bet none of the other fellows on Wesley Road get a letter on this stationary today. I will send something for the paper soon — I mean magazine.[688] I said paper, I guess, because I would love it if you sent me a few copies of local newspapers — Leeds and round about. The localer and scruffier the better. How I would love to go to Venice with you! Curse the Guggenheim foundation for preferring Louis Simpson's[689] verse to mine. Write soon. love,

Jimmy

TO LARRY FAGIN

Great Spruce Head Island

Aug 2 1970

Dear Larry,

I can't believe I am where I was — Yesterday was the foggiest day I've ever seen, and today is, well, it isn't the clearest, but then, yesterday wasn't the foggiest. Two days as unalike as two peas in a pod when examined by a professional eye, and linked by a midnight thunderclap. What a downpour, and lets hope some fell on Vermont, where Kenward's beaver pond has shrunk to a stinking puddle.

What, by the way, is so "yetch" about reading at Edinburgh? The city's an architectural wonderland. Don't you groove on the 18th century?

News. There isn't any. Even I have never written less. My soma, or maybe it was my psyche, started kicking up a fuss about all the nicotine it wasn't getting, so I instantly stopped dieting, gained 800 pounds and now look like something you find glowering in a back alley of Naples (I now take a 36 in a kilt, in case you care).

Since I was feeling quite grouchy in July it was, mebbe, not the ideal moment for Kenny Koch to come bustling up for a visit. "Ideal moment?" He stayed two weeks. I'm very fond of the old goat, but I hate staying in the same house with

688. Winkfield's mimeographed magazine *Juilliard*.
689. Louis Simpson (1923–2012), poet and Guggenheim fellow for 1970.

him. I guess the trouble is that his personality only has two settings: Ecstatic and Peevish, and both are set at Loud. Oh well it was fun having him here. Bye bye Kenneth.

Day after tomorrow I expect to see little John Ashbery and his friend—whoa, I mean, His Friend—Aladar Marberger stepping off the mailboat in their city shoes. John writes me that he finally socked down a payment on a new apartment, a three bedroom duplex on Van Dam Street next to or near Paul Taylor's.[690] Since it still has linoleum on the floor, costs $485 a month and will require a couple of thou's worth of attention from John Bennett (creator of the Elmslie Image on Greenwich Ave), I incline to think she's gone off her—oops. Sorry. Oh well old Mr. Ashbery did pretty well in the prune business. While he's here John and I are going to start another novel. I would tell you the last line he has thought of except 1) I can't remember it and 2) Every time John sniffs a martini olive pit this fall he will confide it to you anew. And why spoil his good time?

Your summer sounds absolutely terrific, and so different from mine—there goes another sea gull—that I can hardly believe we're occupying the same time span. Say, maybe I'm stuck in 1870, while you and Joan are happy in an ever present future.

Love to you both

Jimmy

P.S. I may get to Vermont for a visit—and I may not—so keep the postcards coming here. When are you veering state side?

TO KENWARD ELMSLIE

Great Spruce Head Island

August 17, 1970

Dear Kenward,

We were ten at lunch today—visitors from nearby Beach Island, which I have often stared at and wondered about. (Uh-oh-more Eliot Porter fans—a big sailing vessel of some sort—a yawl? A ketch? A sloop? A schooner?—just tied up at the float, and I heard a loud Westchestrian voice say, "Thought maybe you

690. Paul Taylor (1930–2018), dancer and choreographer with his own dance company.

wouldn't mind if we took a look at *Summer Island*—"Place is getting to be like Coney Island).[691] Seems it's quite different from here—no flush toilets, and kerosene instead of electricity. No vegetable garden. But they have a shrine— Mrs Rhoades and some of the children are Catholic. The Porter family story; the F. Porter family, I mean. They brought with them a cute lady etcher from Boston and an even cuter black half from Alabama, with a smile as broad as his shoulders, on one of which I thought of asking permission to curl up for a nap. The Rhodes children have permissive eating habits—Carrington Rhoades, aged 11 maybe?, chose to eat his spaghetti without sauce, scooped onto white bread with a liberal smear of Dijon mustard over it. Watching him was a wonderful appetite inhibitor.

John and Aladar's visit was pleasant, but I can't seem to remember much about it. I didn't find Aladar as hysterical as I did in Vermont—but perhaps here he lacked places to want to rush off to. He and John have evolved a kind of Maggie and Jiggs style—Aladar has picked up John's trick of pretending in a very convincing way to be terribly angry (with John, that is, not with other people)— he takes to it like a duck to water. When alone with me they also do quite a bit of Hubby and Wifey billing-and-cooing—I'm not a bit sure that I prefer the dish-throwing act—they make me feel just a little bit like Frances Waldman not seeing what Scott Burton is up to with that boy on the bed.[692] Perhaps I'm a little jealous at not having John's full attention—but I do prefer Pierre's Parisian style. However, I don't mean to make it sound as though their visit was unpleasant—it wasn't. It was *nice*.

But I'm projecting for some other summer a series of lunches consisting of things like jellied consomme served in the can with wooden spoon. Grouch. Bitch. Snarl. (I've used up half a lifetime jar of Lubriderm trying to restore the natural oils leached out by Liquid Ivory.)

I don't think I told Joe when I wrote him last that Mike Straus had died. He and Nancy had gone to visit friends in Damariscotta, where he had an attack and died in the hospital there. It happened very quickly, although he had had several attacks before, and seemed this summer very aged, slow and not attentive and dozing off all the time. If I may say it without sounding callous, it seemed a natural time for him to die, and preferable to a prolonged decline into

691. Eliot Porter, photographer brother of Fairfield. *Summer Island* is a book of his photographs of the Porter family island, accompanied by various texts, some of which are by Schuyler.

692. Frances Waldman (1909–1982), poet, translator, and mother of poet Anne.

senility—preferable to him, I guess, and to Nancy, were it a choice. Nancy is very strong, and so the small ways in which one sees how much she misses him are all the more moving.

I'm sorry the recession has caused postponements—does that change your return to New York plans? We're going to Southampton by way of New Hampshire—Anne's sister's—on the 8th of September, a week later than usual (Lizzie's school starts late). I look forward to the roses; I missed seeing them this spring.

Love to Joe. And to Harry (Mathews) and Maxine (Groffsky), if they are there. love,

Jimmy

PS Fairfield said, "Kenneth is right about Aladar—he does look like a toothbrush."

TO TREVOR WINKFIELD

[Great Spruce Head Island]

Aug 28 '70

Dear Trevor,
you certainly
write a mean let-
ter (which in Ameri-
can is a great compli-
ment) (I'm not sure I'm
going to like Shaped Let-
ters any better that I do s-
haped poems.) I was suffering
yesterday bad Mail Withdrawal sy-
mptoms. And now I'm all better.
even though you mention two dangerous
topics: rich food and cigarettes. Yes,
I have stanuch (good grief) staunchly re
fused to touch a fag since June 4
I think it was though I did switch to ci
gars (no inhaling). This had had the ef

311

fect of ruining my summer, more or less.
All July I was so irritable I don't know
how anyone could bear to be near me and
they probably couldn't: on an island lik
e this they just couldn't get away. It
has almost bankrupted me, since a halfway bearable
cigar, well, they don't give them away. Then the
thing that is supposed to happen to one's appetite
did happen to mine, and I got fatter and fatter and fatter until I stopped getting on the scales. So now I am on a
diet and how I hate it (At the moment I'm smoking a Ben Franklin which I would never have bought if I had noticed their m
otto: A Penny Saved is a Penny Earned. Blgh). I dripped saliva
as well as some spit all over the part of your letter a-
bout patisserie parisienne taste treats (my typing gets worse
and worse—that nearly came out: tax teats). Actually one d
rop fell on the V in Venice.
  Yup I think I do have a Venice Guide Book. More anent same
when I get back to Southampton. And I'll send you a copy of
S'ing and W'ing,[693] but let me think until then about publishing
it again. If you don't mind? (Though I sneeze and sneeze
and sneeze—I mean, though I sense the answer will be go a-
head if you really want to. "Publish *that* old thing? But my
dear I've had it for ages").
That clipping you sent about old Southampton
through jaundiced Limey eyes made me think it was maligned
—I especially hated the little anti-Semitic touch about
Finkelstein, Stein. Then the enclosed came out in the *Time*
s and I see it's all much worse—millionaires in many costumes! But the time is coming and the local negro ghetto
will soon be singing Burn Baby Burn if they don't watch
out. The Southampton rich are, as Jane Freilicher
  once put it, real sewage material.

693. Schuyler's play *Shopping and Waiting*, which Winkfield published in his mimeographed magazine *Juilliard*.

No, I haven't seen the latest *Paris Review*, but may
be you'll like the next issue better: Ashbery, Elmsli
e and maybe Schuyler, if Maxine could s
queeze it in at the last minute. But,
in Tom Clark's defense, I do know
that there's pressure
from George Plimp
ton that it
not be
done
(thank God that's over) the exclusive stamping ground of the New York
School—and without *us*, what is there? The Bolinas school,[694] I guess. Which
has now enrolled Bill Berkson and Jim Carroll. Yes, they're all out there
puffing away and grooving on the San Andreas Fault.

More
Late
r

I liked the "Children' Story," but wondered about the end. I don't think
I like so much texture leading up to a baldly melodramatic event; though I
realize a bullet doesn't necessarily come out of a gun. Or else it shouldn't stop
there? But continue on about life, so it doesn't all seem to lead up to a negative
and incidental event. (You needn't agree).

It *is* later—five days. I wonder what I'm doing? Besides hobbling on over fell
and dale after William and Dorothy Wordsworth. Twelve hundred pages of it—I
have only fifty to go. Then I went for some walks. Wrote quite a lot—snooze,
snore. I seem to have run out of things to say. !

I look to hear from you soon, and I'll keep my eye cocked for anything about
mazes. It's about 5 pm on a Wednesday; in exactly one week to the minute we
should be pulling into the drive at 49 South Main, cross, tired and dying for
a drink.

Well, toodley-odeley,

love,

Jimmy

694. Berkson and Carroll had moved from New York to Bolinas, north of San Francisco.
Poets Joanne Kyger, Robert Creeley, and Lewis Macadams lived there at the time, and other
poets visited from San Francisco and New York. City Lights published the anthology of Bolinas poets, *On the Mesa*, in 1970.

TO JOE BRAINARD

[Great Spruce Head Island]

August 30, 1970
Bill Berkson's Birthday Eve

Dear Joe,

And let's hope he doesn't celebrate *too* hard—I wouldn't want him to turn
into a vision.

Here it is the end of the weekend, just before Sunday supper, thrilling words.
It is in reality merely, just before supper. Don't you think it's funny the way
"Weekend" hangs on, long after one has escaped from school? On Sunday I always feel I ought to put on my good shoes and sit on the sofa looking at the fun-
nies while I wait for a stupefying meal to be served at some hellishly irregular
time. Whereas on Saturday I always feel I ought to do something special, such
as go downtown and see two first-run movies; which was great when I could do
it, and a drag when I couldn't. Then there was a sort of a Sunday evening letdown from Friday's unfulfilled anticipation—it always seemed as though the
weekend would be great. This time. But all that was a good long time ago and
still the feeling somewhat persists—in Southampton I hate the empty streets
and the cars full of people looking into Clorox ads and in New York I hate the
way everything is closed that you want to have be open (Sam Goody's) and the
crowds in the museums. Even here, I get a Sunday supper feeling. What do you
suggest, Dr. Franzblau?[695] Actually, it's not all that bad.

And now you've heard your Summer Sermonette.

I made a Mark Trail Birthday Ode to send to Bill; now I can't find the letter
from you with his *full* address; but if Bolinas is as small as I think, I guess just
Bolinas will reach him.

Chow time. Finish this tomorrow.

It's Monday! No School! Hooray! I feel like a million.

Your worries about cig resisting in Bigtown seemed pretty scary, until I realized that one doesn't have to face *all* the different temptations at the same
time—I don't mean I think it's going to be easy (for either of us) but each time
one doesn't take a cig, it gets easier. We seem to have become a kind of Smokers
Anonymous. Now let me tell you about how I was tempted, threw the demon
cig and made him say uncle. The other day I was in a nearby house, alone in
the living room, and there, right on the mantle, was an open pack of Camels.

---

695. Dr. Rose Franzblau, advice columnist in the *New York Post*.

Well, it wasn't the first pack of Camels I've ever seen—in fact I've seen a good few—what was tempting was the thought that if I took one and went and enjoyed it in the woods, why, I couldn't relapse because I just wouldn't *have* any cigarettes to relapse with! Joe, when you get to my age you don't arguefy with the devil, you leave him to be, and I want you to know that I walked out of that room so fast that . . . Actually, I didn't, I went to the bookcase and admired John and Trudy's nautical novels—admirable, perhaps, because so very much of a temptation. Actually, I don't think either one of us is in much danger, for the slightly sinister reason that, because of our churchified upbringing, we rather enjoy giving things up—"I'm bein' good! I'm bein' good! Gonna go to Heaven when I die. HOT DOG." But this is getting awfully close to "Sunday Supper" so I'll shut up.

Please tell Kenward—no no, please *tell* Kenward—oh forget it I'll do it myself. But do give him my love. That's an order.

Jimmy

TO KENWARD ELMSLIE

[Great Spruce Head Island]

August 31, 1970

Deark
that's a good start

Dear Kenward,

I just finished a letter to Joe and have the childish feeling that if I write you, it has to be exactly as long a letter, word for word. Well, dear, life isn't like that. This is the real world, in which my view of the mountains would be a lovely one; if the valleys weren't all full of water. (I just had the chilling realization that the ocean is full of islands—*that didn't quite make it*. Yes, they failed. We don't know why and we don't like to talk about it much, but . . .)

Lizzie is busy packing: she wants to mail some of her luggage, so there will be room in the car for Katie and her friend, Ruth Morales, who are coming on Friday. We will be six, plus Bruno, who really needs a horse van of his own. (Ruth, at the risk of unkindness, I may as well tell you, has been ordered by her doctor to lose one hundred pounds. As of Katie's last letter, she had lost 18.) I asked Liz where Bruno was going to ride. "That's easy," said the juvenile mad woman, "he's going to ride under my feet." I suggested that some might just leak

315

out on either side ofher feet (the idea that anyone who has met Bruno could imagine he would spend one split second in the pit in between seats is, well . . .). However, if we lash enough onto the roof of the car—yes, when we travel we are the pitiful family you glide by on the freeway, the one with the playpen and mattress on the roof and a tarpaulin dragging in the road behind. Then when we get to Southampton there is one very large, very light box which, when opened, discloses an old hat, some coat hangers, a hymnal wedged in sideways and some loose postage. The hat has been brought back to give to the Paulist Fathers, a kind of Catholic Salvation army. They, however, have no use for it. As a matter of fact, I always enjoy the trip back. I just wish we could stay overnight at a nice motel instead of visiting Anne's—whoops.

Joe says something like: you are going to stay way into September; or else you are going back to New York. It's nice to have a Plan. Have you formulated any Leaf Thoughts yet? Last year I know they were at their dressiest roundabout October 10th. Anyway, sometime in September I'll be coming back here with F for a week and am just kind of wondering . . . No, I don't have to know right this minute (tomorrow will do) and yes, if you change your mind about going back when you see smogcity glittering in what was once sunlight, that's all right too.

love,

Jimmy

TO PAT AND RON PADGETT

Calais, Vermont

Nov 5 1970

Dear Pat and Ron,

I hope, Kenward hopes, Joe hopes you both and Wayne will come to dinner at Kenward's on Monday November 9th, to honor Lewis [Warsh] and me![696] On our birthdays.

It's wonderful here, and very strange, strange for anyone at least like me who expected snow. While you were having rain this week we were having it blue beyond bearing. "*Real* Indian summer," Marian Anderson says. Seems it only

---

696. This is the party referred to at the end of Schuyler's poem "A Vermont Diary": "To morrow we return to New York, a long drive, and the next night, a big birthday party (mine)."

counts if the warm spell comes after the leaves are down, and down they are indeed. Crunch crunch they go in the woods which are carpeted with them, trunk to trunk, in epithet-defying shades of brown, varying with the tree sort. And here and there set on top of them is a "Boston" fern. The other kinds are frosted off. The woods are great for walking in now since you can see so far. The leaves don't all close in with that great "I gotcha!" And if you like paper birch, *well*, it's quite astonishing to see a whole mountainside colored by them. And with the leaves down they have a kind of frill of twigs at top, rather sooty, but against an intensely blue afternoon sky they change to a deep lowing violet-red and the trunks turn pink. We drove over to and through Smuggler's Notch the other day, where thick-trunked silver birch are the *spécialité de la maison*. All the trees at the top of the pass are very contorted and strange from the weight of the snow, I surmise. (I'm liking birch better that I did for awhile. Sometimes in Maine they seem a bit, well, flashy. Then in Amherst every house of an at all recent vintage has a "foundation planting" (about as attractive as a foundation garment) of taxis (short i) & juniper and one clump of clump birch. Disenchanting.)

But I only meant to invite you to dinner.

Joe has written more great installments of *I Remember*. The *Times-Argus* was full of fears about "Kill a cop tonight—Hallowe'en!" when we got here, so I said in the interests of good feeling we ought to change it to, "Ball your local sheriff."

"Why?" Joe said, "Is he cute?"[697] The paper was forced to report the quietest Hallowe'en ever—but they still don't trust Goddard.[698]

See you Monday (I hope)

love,

Jimmy

P.S. "Jimmmy" is even funnier than I remembered.

---

697. Schuyler made use of this exchange in his poem "A Vermont Diary":
November 4
Antiquing: Hardwicke.

me—"We ought to change 'Kill a cop tonight: Hallowe'en,' to 'Ball your local sheriff.'"
Joe—"Why? Is he cute?"

Thinking about Larry Fagin—"Then I went home and had this wonderful dream."
698. Schuyler is writing from Kenward Elmslie's house in Calais, Vermont. Goddard College, a center of radical politics and hippie life, was in nearby Plainfield.

TO HARRY MATHEWS

[Southampton, New York]

November 15, 1970
(Pat Padgett's birthday;
it's also her birthday).

Dear Harry,

Is the day chilly and dark? And how, nor is it brightened any by my knowing that Trumbull Higgins is downstairs, paying a call at 11:30 on a Sunday morning. Oh well it might be worse — he might have caught me downstairs listening to an Ashbery-Marberger birthday gift, Busoni's *Doctor Fuss*.[699] Somehow any call [by] Trumbull (and he's quite fond of paying them) becomes a call of condolence. For his having been there, that is. But why am I being such a sourpuss? T., as Babs [Barbara Guest] calls him, has many fine qualities — over-weening pride in his forebears, for instance — but let's not get into that right *now*.

I'm just back from the Grand Tour, which in America means Maple Corner and return. On the way up we (Joe, Kenward, Whippoorwill)[700] stopped at the Shaker museum in Chatham, NY — lots of beautiful things, but sadly unevocative in its lumber-room clutter. If you ever have the chance, you must take in the Shaker meeting house at Sabbathday Lake, in Maine (not far from Portland and Poland Springs), which contains almost nothing but scruples. There are a few old Shaker ladies there, too, making rather unfortunate potholders out of the kind of fabric people we don't know buy. On the way back from Calais we stopped at Olana, the painter Church's 1880 dream of Araby, on a marvelous height above the Hudson.[701] We ran into Robert Rosenblum on a porch who said, "Don't you love it?" Well, no. It's almost indescribably meager and gimcrack, home made in the worst way, a kind of kitsch fantasy Alhambra. But it makes one appreciate the reality of what Henry James found insupportable. And, of course, lots of people like it, so I suppose it's wonderful.

We got back to NY in time for a nice party at 104 Greenwich,[702] for me and my birthday twin, Lewis Warsh. I thought Lewis looked sad as he unwrapped Anne's [Waldman] present (skintight velvet Levis), and noticed that as he did

---

699. Busoni's opera, *Doctor Faust*, left unfinished at his death and completed by his student and friend Philip Jarnach, was first staged in 1925.

700. Elmslie's whippet dog, who appears in Schuyler's "The Morning of the Poem" and was often painted by Joe Brainard.

701. Frederic Edwin Church (1826–1900), painter of the Hudson River School. His house and studio, Olana, is open to visitors.

so Michael [Brownstein] had suddenly vanished. Which somehow exhausts my interest in the party, of which I can, to my surprise, remember a great deal, though nothing worth retailing. I think I prefer parties at which I am not "featured."

John has, actually, moved. It's a splendid apartment, very roomy in a nice brick house with brownstone details and cast-iron railings to the steps—the works, short of a penthouse on upper Fifth Avenoo. John claims to like the colors it has been painted, but this is not actually possible. The smoldering red bedroom gives on a library painted a dark and lifeless brown not found in nature ("Nor shit not chocolate was the scene . . ." as somebody or other might have put it), and has matching drapes (curtains they aren't) of an economical corduroy which, by a 20 watt bulb, might be mistaken for velvet. And on the floor below, I'm afraid, there is more and worse. (I told sweetmeats I thought the Pompeian john would be nice for small pizza parties). It's all distinctly middlebrow queer, and I don't doubt will soon pall on his nibs, and the painters and paperhangers will be swarming about the place. You must, of course, *never* let John know I said an unkind word about it . . . he only claims not to mind that sort of thing.

As for Aladar—why do I suddenly feel as tired as the Lady of Shalott after a hard day at the loom? First, we all (i.e. Jane [Freilicher] and myself) decided he's not so black as he's painted (by us). Now we are considering revising our opinion. He seems not so bad when I see him with John and people his (Aladar's) age, who treat him as if he were just silly but not unlikable, which he then becomes. But at other times the childish lying and brattishness and talebearing get awfully wearing—he obviously doesn't care what one thinks of him, providing one *is* thinking about him, as exclusively as possible. Still, all agree that though as a troublemaker he takes the cake, he isn't malicious. I suspect the time may come when this seems rather an academic distinction, but, for the nonce, it will have to console us for our gains.

I sent the G. Thomas book,[703] as a matter of fact, because you asked about hostas the morning you and Maxine [Groffsky] stopped by. I have only lately overcome my prejudice towards what used to be called funkia—it's used an awful lot for edging walks around houses where the more ominous sorts of marigolds are all the go. And the flowers don't look well in the sun, just dinky,

702. Kenward Elmslie's New York home.
703. Graham Stuart Thomas (1909–2003), British rose and garden expert mentioned in the poem "Horse-Chestnut Trees and Roses."

but in the shade they make sense, and the light violet kinds have a nice elu-
siveness. I should think that if you got a couple of sorts, roughed them up a
little, they could look quite terrific. By the way, let me recommend, if you
haven't read them, *all* of Graham Thomas's books—I'm sure he's the best
garden writer since Gertrude Jekyll. Here is a pleasantly typical passage
from *Colour in the Winter Garden*:

If I were making a winter garden I would always try to have a nut in
it somewhere. There is nothing quite like the charm of a catkin in the early
year, and, if neither the cob nor filbert, nor their copper-leaved variants be
needed, and the Turkish hazel be too large, then we can turn to that strange
Gloucestershire foundling, *Corylus availana contorta*. The spiral twists and
tortuous turns of every twig are amusing to contemplate in their nullity in
winter, but when February comes the perpendicular line of the yellow catkins
gives a subtle quietness to the huddle of branches. Careful gardeners may like
to train the main branches on canes for a few years to give their plants grace
and balance.

As you see, he isn't *spairsta*. I hate garden writers who are such good plants-
men they can only speak Latin.

Later. It's the same day but it's not Pat Padgett's birthday anymore—it's Ted
Berrigan's. Joe once told me today is Pat's, he having switched them around,
and I've never gotten them straight since (hers, in reality, is the 12th). I just got
this news from Ted, our new neighbor over at the Rivers's ex-garage guesthouse.
I feel rather discombobulated by it, since I've been waiting for it to be safely
post-Padgett get up time (3 p.m.; well, 2 p.m.) so I could call Patty and wish her
a happy birthday. You may well take it for granted any "fact" that comes from
me is apt to contain a large area of fuzz.

Sunday Calls. One would think that this far into the 20th century they would
be done with. I had an ungenerous thought while listening to Ted run on that
he may be the thinking man's Trumbull Higgins. I like him, but I wish he
wouldn't shoot speed, or eat hash as though it were candied ants. After a while
I begin feeling there's a faucet somewhere that urgently needs shutting off.

In fact the call lasted so long that if I'm going to have a drink before going to
see *Goodbye, Columbus*,[704] I'll have to hitch up my britches and get cracking.

Give my love to Maxine, and please let me hear from you very soon.

love,

Jimmy

704. The 1969 movie adaptation, directed by Larry Peerce, of Philip Roth's 1959 novella.

Let me know what you've been reading. I've been reading St-Simon[705] in English which even the translator seems to think is like reading "Brer Rabbit" in French. Are you acquainted with Charles Cotton's[706] poems? ("Muses Library"). His "Winter Quatrains," or his "Clepsydra"? hmmmm . . .

TO HARRY MATHEWS

[Southampton, New York]

Feb 28, 1971

And now I seem to be breaking one of Lewis Carroll's other rules, one of my own inventing: ". . . if more than two months have passed since you began your letter, begin again . . ." but two months haven't passed, so I hasten on.

Where was I? Well, in New York a good bit, where I went to some nice parties and saw some lousy movies, of which I particularly disliked *The Music Lovers*.[707] "You didn't think it was beyond *Beyond the Valley of the Dolls?*"[708] said Joe LeSueur or Peter Kemeny or Robert Rosenblum at a party Alex and Ada gave to honor Rodrigo [Moynihan] (no doubt Anne will be here soon and we can all get in another round of honoring). Probably it is, way beyond; but wherever it is it's no place I want to go. On the other hand, the Japanese screens at Asia House were to kiss the fingers; ditto the 18th century Italian drawings and prints at the Metropolitan—ninety-five drawings by *babo* Tiepolo for starters, which is a little like beginning a meal with all the oysters you can eat. But do you ever find you have *doubts* about Piranesi? Particularly the prison whimsies, which up close were looking quite blowsy and in need of a great Florestan and an extra brilliant Lenora. But Pevsner[709] seems to imply I should see it differently—perhaps as an essential tread in the great escalator of aesthetic Time. It must be wonderful to be an art historian and get way away from liking things. And at the other end of the building—up near 105th Street, it seems

705. Louis de Rouvroy, Duc de Saint-Simon (1675–1755), memoirist of the court of Louis XIV.

706. Charles Cotton (1630–1687), British poet and translator.

707. Director Ken Russell's movie on Tchaikovsky's life and times, starring Richard Chamberlin and Glenda Jackson.

708. Director Russ Meyer's 1970 cult movie.

709. Nicholas Pevsner (1903–1983), German art historian who moved to England and became a great authority on English architecture.

there was a small room of Joseph Cornell collages, most of them not unlike the back panel from some one of his boxes; and as seductive and evocative as I hope that suggests; the Verlaine of the workbench, the jigsaw and the glue.

I don't think I have much news of the Personalities on Parade sort—I've been back from the city for nearly two weeks so any I had would be either stale or no longer true. If the Hazans haven't left for some warm, not unhandy island, then they're about to. Their various dramas—"Whatever Happened to Real Estate?", "Bonded Servants," and, "Here Comes Lizzie with an Axe"—continue to play to full houses and in modes with which you are familiar. Jane's show was very beautiful—the individual pictures and also as making an ensemble (in a way her work doesn't always do—giving a false impression to some of inconsistency, or rather, uncertainty). So she has been rewarded by receiving not one inch of notice in the NY Times, which today gave a friend of ours, Alvin Ross,[710] a nice guy but a meager and rather academic painter—a dizzyingly good review comparing him to Chardin. Poor Jane, and it goes on show after show. I don't understand it—her work seems to be so filled with appeal; but I guess that's what Kramer and Canaday don't like in art.

Tom Hess did let Peter Schjeldahl[711] write an article about her in Art News. She saw the page proofs when her show opened and I asked her what it was like. "He ran out of ideas right at the start," said grateful Jane, "so he gushed."

Kenward raves about his trip, and most particularly the company. I have nothing to add to what he's no doubt already told you both, except a tiny liqueur glass of jealousy; and not much of that, for if I envy him your (plural) company, I am on the other hand not a bit sure that Desert Sands are my dish. He's written, or rather finished a very funny 3 act play, which has for its point of departure le Douanier's' "A Visit to the Exhibition of 1889" (right title? Not sure). He once published a version of act 1—in, could it have been Juilliard? somewhere anyhow—(the postal strike must be driving Trevor right up all the walls of Leeds, and I hear they've got plenty)—but he's rewritten that and the whole thing has moved much further off from France and deeper into mysterious Kenwardland.[712] Larry Fagin is going to publish it, so you'll get to do your own perusing of it in the not too distant future.

But. Ah, but. Things seem very much over between Joe and Kenward. They

710. Alvin Ross (1920–1975), American painter.

711. Peter Schjeldahl (1942–2022), poet and art critic.

712. Elmslie's play City Junket, first published in Larry Fagin's Adventures in Poetry. It was based on a play by Henri Rousseau (known as the Douanier.)

didn't see each other at all for a week or more while I was in town, though we did all three have dinner together the night before I left. They have had their difficulties before, but this time Joe thinks it's done. I'm very surprised—a year ago I thought Kenward was very down, and that it was the half living together arrangement that was making him so, and wondered if he would want to go on sustaining it, or even could. But then in the fall it seemed to have settled into some acceptable (to them, I mean) pattern. I thought of feeling sad, but, on second thought, if people don't want to live together, then it seems unpleasantly and vicariously lachrymose to permit oneself to do so, however attractive a picture the words "Kenward and Joe" may paint for one. I think they will continue on closely friendly terms, which, right now is what matters: I would hate for that relationship to end by producing any bitterness; which for a moment seemed not impossible. (Perhaps I shouldn't go into this at all, if only because there's quite an element of supposition; and the rest is a few dark statements thrown out to me by Joe. Which wouldn't have happened except that I got sick of the stories Aladar kept trotting around with, all of them said to have come straight from Joe that very morning. And none, of course, true.)

On which note we may turn our attention from Mme de Lafayette to the earlier works of Feydeau.[713] I'm repeatedly told that John has given Aladar his walking papers—perhaps he has. The language of love is all encompassing, and particularly delights in saying the opposite of what is meant. In some cases anyway. John, by the way, has never looked better—his moustache has shaped into a most becoming accessory, he's thin, his hair of a sexy length, he's mostly not drinking, and, when he is, not necessarily everything in sight—he's never appeared more in control—though I sometimes think he's the captain of a rather leaky kayak in very high seas. As for Aladar—I'll say this for him, he's consistent and has done nothing to change whatever opinion I held of him when last we met (you and I met, I mean). If he tells lies out of mind, it's largely because he doesn't listen but can't shut up. Larry Fagin, Peter Schjeldahl and one other agreed (again, at the Katzes) that Aladar is the next Henry Geldzahler[714] (spelling?)—it's a fact, he's made his presence felt. But HG had an education,

713. Madame de Lafayette (1634–1692), seventeenth-century French novelist known for *The Princess of Cleves*. Feydeau (1862–1921), French playwright, master of the well-made farce.

714. Henry Geldzahler (1935–1994), art critic who, as curator of twentieth-century art at New York's Metropolitan Museum of Art, assembled the exhibition *New York Painting and Sculpture, 1940–1970*.

quite a lot of one I gather. But then John Myers didn't, and dear knows he's made himself felt all right. Ah well, I keep reminding myself to try to be more like Fairfield who, when taxed for an opinion of Aladar said, "he's callow; but he has a good heart." I don't think I ever heard anyone use the word callow in conversation before. It was a thrilling day.

And when I incline to resent the degree to which Aladar has come between John and me, I'm stuck with the fact that if it weren't this one, it would have been that. I'm afraid I'm just one of those Dads there's no pleasing, no matter how nice a boy his boy decided to marry.

Everyone this winter is particularly taken with Joan Fagin.[715] Jane seems to have rather a crush on her; or so I would say, if I weren't afraid of being misunderstood . . . I had a pleasant dinner at home with the Padgett family, on whom I dote; giggling Tessie (Mitchell) was there to make it complete. And that's enough social life; for one letter, anyway.

Your note on the female ginko, or, garbage tree, reminded me of my earliest schooldays in Washington, D.C., where the street home from school had been rather carelessly planted with both sorts. We used to delight, in the fruiting or ookie-gookie season, to run down it stomping on the fruits and yelling P-U! It is an incredible putrid stink, though a tiny distant whiff might be not unsexy; at any rate, to a male ginko. We called it, if memory serves, the stinkbomb tree.

I wish I could help you with the name of the Cleveland pitcher in whom the restless soul of Arthur Cravan has taken refuge, but, our local library doesn't keep weeklies more than a month or so. I too liked *Ball Four*[716] though I can't say I know much more about baseball than I did before; but I accomplished my aim, which was to find out a lot more about locker rooms, beaver shooting and all the rest . . .

My own reading has been even less shaped than usual. I'm finishing the new Ross Macdonald, *The Underground Man* — chapter XV begins, "The Star Motel stood with its rear end on pilings . . ." a lovely use of the word "stood." Have you read him? I don't recommend him, and I don't not recommend him. He's one of those California thriller writers who see a two car redwood garage as a pretty grave symptom of moral rot, and reads best in paperback. Then I've been reading a book on Clematis — "Alba luxurians is rather a pet, though; its pure white flowers shade to green at the tips. This may sound a bit fey, but when carefully placed against a dark background it is a sweetie." Aren't we all. And I've

---

715. Joan Fagin (b. 1948), fashion designer and wife of Larry Fagin.
716. Former New York Yankee pitcher Jim Bouton's 1971 baseball memoir.

been dipping into Sydney Smith's[717] letters, which I've read before. What a wonderfully sensible funny likeable man—writing to Jeffrey on Dec 26, 1809, about the latest issue of the *Edinburgh Review*: "Brougham's review is not in good taste; he should have put on an air of serious concern, not raillery and ridicule; things are too serious for that. But it is very able. It is long yet vigorous like the penis of a jackass."

And now it is March first, and I think the only way I'll ever finish and send this letter is by halting right here. At which point I grasp your hand and felicita you on your coming grandfatherhood and urge you to enter our Most Youthful Gramps contest we'll be holding at Tampa Springs next New Years. You're bound to win.

When does spring come to your mountain? It *seems* to be here today—but many a blizzard has blown between now and the first of May.

love,

Jimmy

TO HARRY MATHEWS

[Southampton, New York]

March 16, 1971

Dear Harry,

I know I was forgetting something, and something pretty important, when I kept driving on in my last. Your birthday, of course. Many happy returns. The enclosed is a small birthday ahum birthday thought not a gift. Thoughts are aberrant, they set no precedent, imply no reciprocity. Gifts, well, about them I'm not so sure.

Our sandy quiet was broken last week by something called a Poetry Explosion. The Hampton Day School decided they should have Ron, Dick G [Gallup], Ted B, Anne W [Waldman], Michael Brownstein, David Ignatow[718] (David who?) and some others come and tell it to the kids like Kenneth thinks it is. It was quite a dopey idea, to have them all at once, instead of spreading

717. Sidney Smith (1771–1845), British clergyman, wit, and writer. The quote here appears in Schuyler's "The Fauré Ballade."

718. David Ignatow (1914–1997), American poet not commonly associated with the second-generation New York School.

them over a semester, an idea which became yet dopier when (Ron tells me) it turned out that Poetry Explosion conflicted with African Cooking week, and all the kids old enough to pass as literate were off in various Bridgehampton kitchens and well into cous-cous. But I think they (the poets) enjoyed themselves and Ted, who likes to keep alive the tradition of the poet as Oaf, managed to give the sponsors a few kicks and some Irish lip in return for his stipend ($100). Pat, Ron and Wayne stayed with us which was fun. Ron is so bright and witty, Patty so pretty and nice, and fun, and Wayne is great, so . . .

No sooner had they enbused than ting-a-ling the telephone and it was John, wanting to know in mournful tones if he might come and spend a night or two. I asked him what was wrong and he said Aladar had moved out and the house was "filled with deafening silence." As soon as he arrived the phone rang: Aladar (it kept ringing for the rest of John's visit, too). When he finally got off I asked him where Aladar was. "At home," was the succinct reply. However, I think it is working toward a close. I hope so. John told me a story which has given me a few more white hairs about A. trailing him to a turkish bath (new ones spring up like crocuses lately) where he hit John in the face, very hard. I suggested this was grounds for getting out the elephant gun but John mildly said, "He hits me quite a lot but usually it doesn't hurt." Oh chill. On the other hand, when John talks about A and the things he likes about him, such as his mama-propisms (oops—or perhaps sic)—he recently referred to my book as Freeley Exposing—I find that I imagine I like him. But now John has hustled back to the city to keep a tryst with one of his other heart-throbs, one David Kermani,[719] a Columbia graduate student of Iranian extraction with eyes like pools.

John has also finished a new long poem in, or mostly in, prose, not unlike his last, I believe. He says he intends to write another, perhaps not quite so long, so that he can call his next book, *Three Poems*. He wants to use that title because he thinks it will sound especially well in German. Fairfield said he thought *Two Poems* would also sound well in German, but John did not agree.

Let's see. A week ago Monday Kenward gave a reading-cum-song recital, including some songs with words by him and music by Lee Crabtree,[720] who officiated at the Bechstein. It got raves from everybody—John, Fairfield, Ron—and even I might have gone, had I been in Cityville. I think I may have implied that Kenward &/or Joe are unhappy or unhappier than is the case (all I really

719. David Kermani, director of the Tibor de Nagy Gallery in the late 1970s and early 1980s.

720. Lee Crabtree (d. 1973), musician and member of The Fugs rock group.

meant was that I hoped they wouldn't be on the angry outs). Joan Fagin spoke of having met "Joe's new friend," somebody I don't know named Bill Katz,[721] whom she described as "tall and sort of smooth looking." He used to be Robert Indiana's friend (who in turn used to be Bob Dash's friend—can you hear "The Windmills of My Mind" whispering in the background?). Joe has a certain weakness, I've noticed, for the suave and stupid; but really, I guess it's another aspect of his wonderful gift for seeing things as they are, and no more. I doubt that he ever thinks "He's handsome—but dumb" or "Pansies are beautiful— but short." How nice, not to be a critic. I vowed to make this a 1 pager, so must stop. Anyway, that's all I got to say. love, Jimmy

TO TREVOR WINKFIELD

[Southampton, New York]

March 22, 1971

Dear Trevor,

I trust you're having a wonderful, wonderful spring; though Reginald Farrer's book about his rock garden—which seemed to occupy most of non-urban Yorkshire—implies that March may well be the worst thing. Oh well, gardeners who insist on hating snowdrops . . .

Your card of Jan.15thish didn't, quite, beat the postal strike, and arrived last week. Were you able to stick out the strike, or did you flee to some other continent? It's hard to think of you with your mail supply cut off—"I faint, hmm I fail . . ." The winter here was dull and largely snowless (on Long Island that is—extra heavy snow elsewhere). I tried to write some snow poems but, well, I enclose the least worst one.

Have you come across a magazine called *Antaeus?*[722] It seems to be centered in Morocco, and the first issue (summer, '70) has some beautiful excerpts from an unfinished novel by Jane Bowles. I don't have a copy, but Kenward did: it's available from: Villiers Publications, Ltd, Ingestre Road, London NW 5 (which I surmise is London, England rather than London, South Dakota). Since you

721. Bill Katz, designer frequently employed by the Merce Cunningham Dance Company.

722. American literary magazine founded in Tangiers by Daniel Halpern and the writer Paul Bowles.

asked me once about Jane's health:[723] I'm told it is as bad as it can be; she is paralyzed, and whether there is any hope of a recovery, I don't know. None of her friends have mentioned any.

Difficult to go onto cheerfuller things after that note. Things in New York are much as you would imagine them to be. Ted Berrigan has spent the winter out here. A couple of blocks away, but I have been without planning it, very rude and seen as little of him as possible. For one thing, he never shuts up and at the same time seems to say very little that I want to hear. Perhaps the Irish in me is hostile to the phoney-baloney Irishman in him . . . at dishing out the malarkey, he's a whizz. He's also one of Ron's best friends, and one of Joe's oldest friends, which somehow enters into things, so I guess that view of him is just between you, me and the gatepost.

The Padgett family was out here for a visit not so long ago, which was fun. They haven't changed, except, if possible, for the better. Well, Wayne of course *has* changed. For one thing, there's more of him; he's less hostile to girls and women; and he can count and recite things like the alphabet. Ron was here for something called A Poetry Explosion at the Hampton Day School (a sort of blitzed and brainwashed would-be replica of Summerhill).[724] I'll see if I still have a stupefying clipping about it to send you.

I have a cold. Enough of one to have spent all yesterday drowing—ho hum—drowsing in bed, which, since it was Sunday, seemed a sensible plan. But having escaped all winter, it seems a silly thing to greet the spring with. My ears go pop and squish and I'm force feeding some rather yummy acerola vitamin C tablets.

There is a book published by Dover you might like—I think the correct title is *Mazes and Labyrinths*. I haven't found it in stock in the Elmslie neighborhood, or I would have sent it. Dover takes a lifetime filling orders, but their books are distributed in England by, I think, Constable.

Are you still interested in log cabins, their how and why? I looked in *Books in Print* at Bob Keene's [Bookshop], and there are several, all priced in the $8 area, but I couldn't figure out any way to tell which is any good—If you're still in the market I'll try to remember and "check out" some of them at the NY Public Library. (I had meant to send you one my stepfather had, but when I was last home I discovered it had migrated from my mother's house to my brother's . . .)

723. She had suffered a stroke.
724. Experimental British school, progressive, coeducational and residential, founded in 1921 by educator A. S. Neill (1883–1973).

Let's see. John Ashbery has moved from East 95th Street to West 25th (or, Chelsea), a luxurious duplex pad with self-spiral stairway. I believe he is beginning to regret the vastly increased rent. His hair is now down to here and he has a modified Mark Twain moustache which on him looks good. And he's written another long poem in prose, to go with the one that was in the *Paris Review*. I believe he projects a third, so that his next book can be called, *Three Poems*, which he thinks will sound very well when and if it's translated into German. Kenward has finished a very funny play — it takes off from le Douanier's *A Visit to the Exposition* of 1889 — oops — but I believe act one was published by you?[725] Or am I mixing things up again? At any rate, the first act has been rewritten and is both simpler and further out . . . whatever I may mean by that. Joe Brainard is readying (a word I'm fond of) his first show at Fischbach — cut-outs of things like grass, in layers, say three lace-like layers separated by sheets of glass (or whatever plastic is used instead of glass these days). Wonderfully subtle and beautiful and Brainard like. Ron says 1) he hasn't been writing any poems and 2) that he will type up some of his new poems and send them to me. To date, the first appears truer than the second.

And here is the postman with, hmm, a bill from the Blue Cross Medical or Scalp'em Plan, no TLS which should have come today, and a very short letter from Harry which says he'll be in NYC in about six days. Well, that is nice, nicer than the *Genealogy of the Rev. W. H. Van Dusen Family* and "many related families dating back to the Caesars" which Cherry Laura Van Dusen Pratt of Fort Recovery, Ohio, is willing to sell me for $7.50. Gosh, Cherry, not during this recession.

Well, Trevor, as they say in Italy, Many Beautiful Things,

Jimmy

TO TREVOR WINKFIELD

[Southampton, New York]

March 31, '71

Dear Trevor,

Somehow, just when I'm off on one of my N.Y.C. ventures, I always seem to feel an impulse to write — scribble — a note to you. You must represent stability to me. *Yes*, that's it.

725. *City Junket.*

329

My other reason for writing, however, is: before all the hiatuses—strikes, Xmas, what-have-yous, you said something about a feeling of death as far as a next issue of *Juilliard* goes. And of course *Juilliard* must not die; nor you feel bored. It's an ill-kept secret that I'm one of the judges for the O'Hara award competish, & I've just finished reading—acute indigestion—what seemed like a century's subscription to *World*; with a few lifetimes of *Mother & Fuck You* tossed in. While not at liberty to say who this year's Mick Jagger of the N.Y. School is (Kenneth K., O'Hara Foundation top-kick is away 'til next week), there were some very good poets among the mss's and I thought you might like to ask some of them for works—? Yes? No?

Have you ever exchanged magazines with Keith Abbott? His is, or was, *Blue Suede Shoes*. I like a lot of his poems—sort of West Coast Padgett, with a lot of the dilution that might imply—also someone he's published named Pat Nolan, who's a little closer to being a West Coast Larry Fagin; or perhaps is to Abbott what Fagin is to Padgett? Only different—(I have the feeling you just decided never to publish any more American writers). Then there was somebody in Providence, Rhode Island named Randy Blasing. And I forget whether you've ever published anything by John A's friend (not friend in—oh help—a friend, not a boyfriend) John Koethe? (pronounced, K-T & not like Goethe). The one I most particularly liked is Charles North,[726] who studied (at St. Mark's Church, maybe?, or the New School) with Tony Towle. I think he has quite a gift.

I was disappointed with some of the ex-Koch Columbia poets. He seems to turn people on, but it doesn't always last when they graduate & come unplugged. However, just to have had Ron for a pupil assures him of Teacher immortality—*je pense*—

Katie Porter, F & A's elder daughter (22) is taking pre-Med at Columbia & a course with Kenneth, who, at the beginning of the term, told her her poems were "too thinking." Katie called her mother up and said Kenneth is a *great* teacher, but she finds she *much* prefers John Ashbery's poetry. Ta-tum. (But she's gone on to write some poems they both like—& me too.)

Kind friends at *Angel Hair* published a poem of mine as a giant, handsome, totally impractical broadside.[727] Part of the impracticality comes out in the rarity—& expense—of suitable mailing tubes. I'm sending one to you, & also one

726. See glossary.
727. "Verge," published by Angel Hair.

to a friend in Italy: would you be so kind as to extract one (I suggest you not take the one signed, Kisses to Edith — but as Don Giovanni says — Liberty Hall) and then send the other one to:

Edith Schloss
18, via Vetrina
Roma, Italy

(and who might she be? Why the first Mrs. Rudi Burckhardt, of course: & do look her up if Rome should fall across your path).

Rudi's latest movie: subject: dope has gotten *very* mixed reviews from friends. But all agree Joan Fagin & Tessie Mitchell on speed (with speeded up camera) are great while Jim Carroll,[728] who does, at times, have a scary H-problem struck some as in spooky taste.

There is a new place in N.Y.C., by the way, where they show all Cornell's own movies — all the collage ones & hand-tinted ones — so you'd better come visit us. But this is just a note so here are the addresses of poets (& I certainly won't mind if you don't want to use them — & do use my name if you wish, minus the O'Hara context) —

Charles North 251 W. 92nd St. NYC
Randy Blasing 302 Hope St. Providence, R.I.
Keith Abbott 724 Lottie Monterey, Calif. 93940
John Koethe 18 Upland Rd. Cambridge, Mass. 02140
Pat Nolan 1531 12th Ave. Oakland, Calif. 94606

Now *you* write *me*. I'm going to NY partly to see Harry M., who is here because his friend, ex-Ambassador to Laos, is getting married enroute to becoming "our" Ambassador to Tokyo. "Just tell the Ambassador it's a friend of Harry Mathews's calling, & come get me out of here—!" love, Jimmy

And thank you for the stupefying, great, incredible local English newspapers —.

---

728. Tessie Mitchell, sister of Pat Mitchell Padgett; Jim Carroll, poet and rock singer.

TO HARRY MATHEWS

104 Greenwich Ave[729]

[New York, New York]   *April 16 1971*

Dear Harry,

Perhaps this paper will remind you of days, and nights, at Happy House, with its Pleyel and views of sunsets down Jane Street. And keep me from writing a book-letter, rather than the thank you note I intend. (There's all this typing to do—for one a chronology of Fairfield's days at Knoedler[730]—did you know that in '27 he flew from Berlin to Moscow, 1500 miles at 100 mph, and attended an interview with Trotsky? *Well . . .*)

Gage and Tollner[731] night was one of the great evenings. Jane wants her life to be like that all the time and keeps comparing each event to it and minding the lack, Joe smiles broadly when the evening is mentioned, and Kenward makes Kenward noises, and I burble silently. You have even inspired two of the most reluctant people in NY—Jane and myself—to talk of going to *Company*[732] before the cast changes. Can these bones get up and move? It would seem; at least, "When Harry's in Town." But that evening was only a—I was going to say, "a part of it, though the crown"—which surely does not make sense?

But you take my drift.

JA and I had a good drive to P'ville with Saphronis,[733] where the pharmaco-paeia meets the Cordon Bleu. In winter, dried tarragon is to be preferred to fresh; if you wish to ball for 7 consecutive hours on the planet Moo, take a squirt of booze, one-half "line" of meth, some blue-streak, or opiated hash, and—make sure the guy ropes for the nets have been secured, Mrs A was in better shape than at Thanksgiving—"John wouldn't you like to borrow one of my hair-nets?" "Have you got one with you?" I strolled by the leaden waters of blue On-tario and bought a 1918 *Fannie Farmer* and a copy (some foxing) of *The Adventures of Mr Verdant Green* a 19th century (as you no doubt know) laffnovel about Oxford. JA went into his head and shut the little door. It, the head, contained, at my surmise, some illusory young men, semi-illusory tax worries, and two real

---

729. Kenward Elmslie's New York home.

730. Commissioned by Manhattan's Knoedler Gallery for the catalog of a 1971 show at the gallery.

731. Landmark Brooklyn restaurant.

732. Stephen Sondheim musical starring Elaine Stritch.

733. Sophronus Mundy's family lived near Rochester, and he sometimes gave John Ash-bery a ride to Pultneyville en route there.

poems, parts of which the genius read me. He is. The bus trip by way of Paramus, NJ, and the Holland Tunnel at rush hour . . .

You once in a letter asked, *"Whose* Irish eyebrows?" anent a poem of mine. *My* Irish eyebrows, that's whose. Why else was my mother's maiden name Margaret ("Don't call me Maggie") Daisy Connor? We must meet sometime for a quiet talk on an Alp; or perhaps in a lea by the river Usk. love, Jimmy

P.S. I squired Jane to *Company* (KE and JB came along to groove on us grooving) Act II, great. Jane says Elaine Stritch "is just like Garbo in *Camille."*

TO KENNETH KOCH

[Southampton, New York]

May 27, 1971

Dear Kenneth,

Here is a typed up, cleaner version of THE CRYSTAL LITHIUM. (I got the name off a post card: an old-timey spa, somewhere in the south Kaintuck, I think.) When I showed this poem to JA in Pultneyville, he unbent and did not give me the old "One of your loveliest efforts, dear." The day he last said that — and *Nest* had at least two or three climatic — climactic, also — chapters to go — I decided, well, I won't show him any more until he asks. After a long time, he did ask. After another long time, I showed him some. Well, he did not give me the kind of Constructive Criticism you can, and do. (You are as good a Teach' as you think you are — no, I can put that in a better way: you are as good as Ron Padgett says you are, and talk about grudging praise: Ron vanishes with sheaf, years pass, he returns with sheaf: "Totally great.") But John had doubts about the title. A few weeks later he called me up specifically to say, "I've been thinking it over and you must NOT change that title." "Actually, I wasn't going to." "I didn't imagine you were." So much for the title mystery: I like the sound of it; and, for me, the 'crystal' connects directly with the snow imagery (Imagery, hunn-ee, what you doin' in my sentence? I tol' you nebber, nebber . . .). Lithium; well, I thought everybody knew what Lithia Water was, or is. At my house, they used to guzzle it like Perrier water. Or club soda. Yes, I have convinced myself that I am not going to change the label on that poem. I could call it, Poem; or, The Grand Orison; or, Ode in the form of a Rhapsody; well, no.

I know there isn't much I'm going to change about this, so, your close reading will be all the more important. You wondered about "briefly in the cold with his eyes as one might hug oneself for warmth for love" I mean, you wondered about "for warmth for love": well, people do hug themselves for other reasons: it can be a sign of uptightness; it can also be a symptom of aenemia: a lack of iron makes the sufferer feel tired and chilled; somewhat clammy, or so Lizzie said (how old was she? Well, it was when I read her the Laura Ingalls Wilder books:[734] Koko could hazard a good guess. And what a great girl she is: talk about witty long-haired blossoms. And that smile). Anyway he is hugging himself (I was thinking of the manager of the Southampton Gristede's—oh never mind) with love of his car, with *amour propre*, the warmth of its heater: *it* loves *him* (here, life interrupted, in the form of John Bennett with a crowbar: he is redoing the floor beneath this: which means, at the moment, destroying the walls. I find it hard to believe that you will be unable to *hear* the hideous racket when you open this letter. What? *You did?*)

Anyway, what I care about is the ending. I have chopped off the last two lines (a little trick I picked up from Bill Coleridge: see "Frost at Midnight," versions 1 & 2. Oh. You already have. Sorry, Doc.) I know the ending is abrupt: well, meeting Bob Jordan[735] was pretty abrupt—and great—too. I feel pretty sure it's right now: but, what do you think? I enclose the first, and second, endings. Those I guess I would like back.

The other new poems: I'd rather wait and show you, in the country, my mss., plus a folder of "maybes" "should Is?" "Are these really as bad as I think?" etc. Half of it is typed, and the rest will be soon.

Now, a business matter. Sit down. Be cool. When you first asked me if I would look over the intro. to *Wishes* [*Lies and Dreams*], you said you might be able to get some money for me for doing it. Well, the publisher went bankrupt, no problem there. But, I put more work into that introduction than I ever put into any *Art News* article. I did it because you're a friend, I was interested, and I became involved. I loved doing it. But it *was* work. Had the book not been a success, that would have been the end of it. It is a success: the book, the lectures, the *Times* (that was wonderful) all of it. So, I now would like you to pay me for the "work," part of it. *Art News'* top is $250., and that is what I would like, no more, no less. Have I anything to add to that? Yes, one thing. You're much more business-like than I, and I admire you for it. The August when you stayed with me—and you were *my* guest, not Anne and Fairfield's or anybody else's—Larry [Rivers] asked

734. Laura Ingalls Wilder (1867–1957), novelist who wrote the *Little House on the Prairie* series.

735. Schuyler had recently met Robert Jordan, his lover for the next couple of years. See glossary.

334

you for ideas for his African movie. You first made it plain to him that you expected to be paid. You later told me a very funny story about Larry, his checkbook, his pen—he wanted to fill it in, he couldn't stand filling it in, you told him to forget it! tear it up!—but you were paid. I would like to be, too.

Should I have made this two different letters, and not mixed art and business? No. Because that is precisely what I did last year in Amherst—only I left the business part a bit messy. One shouldn't. I await your answer—to all the questions. Love as ever, Jimmy

TO TREVOR WINKFIELD

[Southampton, New York]

May 29, 1971

Dear Trevor,

I have been in New York since I last wrote. Came back this noon (now 6:30pm & I am hungry). How come I stayed so long? T'was Palm Sunday eve, and I met someone I like, very much indeed. His name is Bob Jordan,* I hope you will meet him sometime. At the moment he is in either Frankfurt, Paris, London or Scotland. He will be back in a week or so; i.e. about ten years.

Your 4 pager: wow. I loved & lived every word. Yes, I would like to take a bleeding footsteps tour with you within, oh, how about Iran, during their spring? (Among my new acquaintances is someone named Sina, who looks like someone designed to play the part of a lithe, decadent, good-hearted, aristocratic Persian, a cousin of the Empress; which he is.

He is a friend of John Ashbery's new friend, David Kermani, a truly wonderful man (Columbia grad school: studying Iranian). His father left there for Political Reasons (the father of the present Shah was rather a Hitler in his own right). John & David are going there in the fall. I want to go for strictly non-snob reasons (help: they are not going in order to meet royalty either!). Am I serious? Never more so. Please read: Robert Byron: THE ROAD TO OXIANA, and, Christopher Sykes: FOUR STUDIES IN TEMPERAMENT. I don't think either is in print. (The first was published before the war, and reissued twice since—once by John Lehmann.) I would give an eye tooth for a copy ("reading copy, heavily foxed, spine broken")—though not one of my own eye teeth, of course. But do read them (in the Sykes, the chapter about Byron). Can't get them? Surely Leeds runs to a public liberry, or the U of Leeds? Perhaps the Duchess of Leeds would lend you one of her copies?

Oh well, if you don't *want* to go to Persia with me . . .

"Lilac" is one of the few words in English which comes directly from Persian, to us, smelling so sweetly.

Please reprint *Shopping and Waiting*.[736] Say that it has been previously published, but please, *do not say*, in *Folder*. Why? Because on the cover of that issue it is called, A Playlet. I hated that then and I hate it now. If you ever want to meet a meathead, I will introduce you to Richard Miller. If crass stupidity is what you would prefer, then I will present you to Daisy Aldan.[737] They both Mean Well. (*Shopping* is a play—PERIOD.)

I will send you something choice— [or] as choice as I can rake up—for *Juilliard* o. (Hunh? 9). I'm staying at 49 South Main street this summer—with la famille Padgett. Dinner is ready. Je m'en vais go eat grub. Kenward is in Brazil, visiting Mary Martin. love, Jimmy

Kenward's *MOTOR DISTURBANCE* is 1971 O'Hara Award book. (I *am* one of the judges, by the way).

———————

which title do you prefer for my next book of poems—simply as a book label:

THE CRYSTAL LITHIUM

or

THE EDGE IN THE MORNING

(both are titles of poems in the to-be book).

and there is

CLOSED GENTIAN DISTANCES

but, well, no. not the latter. (uh, not the last)

Do you still want logcabin book, o man of mystery? I liked *Juilliard* 8, [Glen] Baxter[738] very much—. So do others.

Have you seen [Robert] Bresson's *Une Femme Douce*?[739] I put Bresson first; then, the others.

*he is not in the arts, oh happy day.

736. Schuyler play, first printed in the magazine *Folder*.
737. Richard Miller and poet Daisy Aldan edited Tiber Press and *Folder*.
738. Glen Baxter (b. 1944), British artist and cartoonist who, like Winkfield, was born in Leeds.
739. French director Robert Bresson's (1907–1999) 1969 movie starring Dominique Sanda.

TO RON PADGETT

Southampton, New York

Saturday, May 29, 1971

Dear Ron,

I came out on the 8:25 with D. Droll. We gave the art scene a good shake
and some mealey bugs fell out in our laps. I arrived (DDroll is at the other or
Paul Waldmans), admired 1) my wallflowers, and 2) F's [Porter] city lithos (I
chose the not-pink sky one for myself) and 3) your vegetable patch. Nize, I
started to say something to F about unsuitability of sycamore (or plane tree)
leaves as mulch, but, "Well," chuckled he, "it *is* Ron's vegetable garden." Hush
ma —lunch, a few prayers to the rain gods and a nap. The rain gods are not
cooperating. Haul, port, slosh—with care. Somewhere, I know, the rosette off
that watering can is hiding. I saw it once and thought, "Oh that's where it is."
But where. Come Tuesday, F and I are going to go rather thoroughly into the
questions of needed hose lengths. (Dear Thunderclap: let it come down! the
rain, I mean.)

Now about my unnecessary taking-on about homegrown pot. I see no harm
in saying what I think; it would be better said face to face, or on the phone. What
I don't like is the tone I took (in each of us—in this one anyway—there lurks a
Kenneth Koch), and I particularly don't like people who tell other people what
they can or can't do. So, you know how I feel, but if you want to plow up the
field and plant it with the cannabis of your preference, and I throw myself in
front of the harrow, it is only because, for the first time in ten years, I am in love
with someone other than myself, and it would be, therefore, on reluctant feet
that I followed you, Wayne and Patty to the pen. However, suit yourself.

By the way, I brought out on the train a lid or two (or was it a key or two? this
technical jargon is so confusing), and $50. worth of Mundy's Blue Streak hash.
A couple of tokes of that is all that's needed to go right up Hilarity Hill and down
the other side to Lake Laughing Water. It is not something one would care to
smoke every day; or even every week for that matter. But it is *nice*. (On the train
coming out I didn't give a thought to it. Not until—Westhamptonish—a loud
voice some ways behind me said, "What is that you are smoking?" I did not give
a start, nor did I drop the scalpel with which, at the moment, I was operating
on John Bernard Myers. After a while I looked around and saw it was just a man,
addressing another just a man, who had a briar pipe. "Suture, nurse.") And
I plan to score rather more grass—soon. One gets a little spoiled, living in the

Elmslie Home. Besides, allers like to have sumpin' Nice in the larder, in case of callers dropping in.

Knowing what a lot can go unsaid here, at No. 49: Lizzie would like to stay with us until July 1, with Katie, who is escorting her to Montana on that date. Lizzie's sidekick, Koko Koch, will probably come visit her. They (the two young'uns) for giggling teenage reasons, sleep in the attic, with Bruno, books, and plenty of drawing materials. I had thought I might go stay at JA's in NYC, while he and David Kermani are in Europe, after the 17th of June. Now that I am here, and can see and smell the lilacs, it does not seem all that likely to me. Besides, Bob Jordan has that van, and, well. Anyway, he is in Europe, and won't be back for ten years. I mean, another week or so. In a word, I don't know what I'm doing, so long as I keep doing something.

I mention all this, because of the Schneemans. (me: How did you like George? F: I like him very much.) I intend to use the studio to work in this summer — and, if the Men are going to be digging under my bedroom at some hellish hour, to sleep out there too. Which frees one double bed. Then there's the room next to mine, and Lizzie's and Johnny's. It might be fun — like a commune; but with Klass.

Anne was surprised, when you met Katie, by the thought that you and Katie are close in age (in your 20s). "I think of Ron as a patriarch."

me: Hunh?

Anne: Patty, Wayne, the vegetable garden.

me: I am sometimes surprised when I realize that I am quite close in age to Ron's father, i.e., Wayne's grandfather.

Anne paled, and hastened to reassure: Oh, but one doesn't think of *Wayne* as being any particular *age* . . .

Which is, of course, true. I think of Wayne as a friend; not my oldest friend, but? — prattle prattle, on I go. Hmmm. House seems quiet. Guess I'll try to roll one of those thin thin jobs you do so well — how the hell do you get them so even? (I wish Joe wouldn't — it's his only flaw — roll those bombers. After a third or even a third of one I can't focus on the big type on the cover of *Woman's Circle*.)

Guess what I have. Joe's [Brainard] show? The White Wall? Two with color? Birches (now M. Fischbach Collection, big deal) and under it, the grass stems in the snow? Mine mine mine it's all mine. But I want to pay for it. (Not the gallery their $125. — but Joe his). He says, "We'll work something out . . ." twinkle twinkle. The problem: how to convince him I would *enjoy* buying a picture of his, the first serious picture I ever bought in my life? Send a check. That might really be sort of a downer for him. I Must Formulate a Plan. I will give him a lot of things he doesn't want.

Something—Curmudgeonly yours,

Jimmy
The Idiot Savant

TO DON ALLEN

[Southampton, New York]

May 30, 1971

Dear Don,

I came back from New York yesterday, and was delighted to find your letter, asking me if I would be interested in doing something I would love to do. In a word, yes. It has been in my mind to write something about Frank and the Museum, partly because of something John A wrote (very much *en passant*) about Frank having given, perhaps, too much to the Museum. Perhaps he did. But I now and then run into, in conversation, a semi-myth, in which Frank plays Fair White Maiden to the Museum's Bela Lugosi. It was not like that, as you know, at all. The Museum, of course, is only part of the story.

How long would it take me? Not long. I think I could make a draft, at any rate, in the space of a week. That would be after seeing a Xerox of the mss., and, well, dropping the idea into the pit of my mind. However, let's say it would take me a month.

If Knopf takes the book, have you any idea of what they would pay, or of what would be a reasonable price to ask? Or is this best left to Lynn Nesbitt and good old "Famous?" I will ask John what he got for the intro. to the *Collected Poems*; however, I intend to put more work, and thought, into this than John did into that. On the other hand, I also realize that Knopf is unlikely to dig down real deep for an introduction to a volume of art criticism, even though one by Frank has (I think) a definite "Sales potential"—what a way one comes to think, and to talk, about art, and writing. (I recently felt decidedly stung by a Noted Firm, because I was a bit vague at the beginning of a task as to exactly what I was to be paid).

Let me see. I am not going to Maine this year, but am staying here at 49 South with my rather special roses (*variegata di Bologna* is indeed something else striped, raspberry and cream, and smells much the same) and la famille Padgett. Fairfield and Anne are going to the Island. Anyway, should I want to ask, say, Joe LeS. a question, or pop into the NY Library, in connection with this, it would be easy. In the middle of Penobscot Bay, it would not.

At the moment, I am writing a—prose work. Perhaps it is a novel; a damn short one if it is. I hope no one calls it a novella, or a prose poem. But it is something I write on first thing in the morning, not for very long and then turn my attention to other things. Towards the middle of August, I may go to Vermont for two or three weeks; I want to keep those free.

So, when you know something definite, let me know, and I will schedule my time accordingly. (Did I write that sentence? Good Grief. Well, it's late, but there will be only one mail going out of town tomorrow, and it's early, and I want this to be in it.)

In going through *Art News*, did you pick up on any of Frank's short reviews?[740] It seems to me he was a staff reviewer, if memory serves, from the fall of '53 until sometime in the fall of '55. I remember a very pretty one of Dali, with something about ". . . the sea purrs at your fingers . . ." and one of Edward Lanning, in which the word "friends" was misprinted "fiends,"[741] giving Frank occasion to write a very amusing, very Frank, letter of correction, printed in the subsequent issue.

If it is possible, I would like a Xerox of the contents, as it now stands. If I'm getting ahead of myself, say so, and I'll cool down.

Thank you for asking me. There are many people who could write it, and many who know more about Frank in the years after '61 (when I moved out here, after leaving the Museum not under a cloud, but encased in one). However, I really think that I am the person best qualified to do it—and I want to.

In the middle of that sentence, John A returned my call to Pultneyville, NY. Knopfpaid him $500; but "Lynn had to put the screws on a bit—*they* wanted to pay me something like $150." So one question is already answered: Let Lynn Do It.

With my best,

Jimmy

740. O'Hara wrote short reviews for *Art News* from December 1953 until December 1955. They have been published by Skanky Possum Press with an afterword by Bill Berkson.
741. The sentence read "His fiends are really ugly . . ."

I always enjoy your annual check,[742] and the mental arithmetic that goes with it. My, how it does add up over the years, and each year a little bigger than the last. This year, I also enjoyed the witty brevity of your explanation of why the checks were not mailed out, as usual, in December.

J. J. Mitchell tells me, "Joan [Mitchell] is in town, and *dying* to see you." Ah, dear Joan, our very own Florence Nightingale — that kindly meant, that ministering, zonked-out glance —! Do you know who made life a living hell for Ron & David, because they wouldn't put Barbara in that anthology (the dopes)? Kenneth Koch. Yes, he has his moments.

But Joan! what a lot of corns I will have to avoid treading on! That should be easy — "Frank had so many friends — so many, many friends, that, in the present context. . . ."

TO HARRY MATHEWS

[Southampton, New York]

June 2, 1971

Dear Harry,

It's 11pm, my eyes are closing like swamps — why did I choose that image? I have no idea: it's the way they, and I, and various other parts of me feel — I suppose that low bussing — buzzing — sensation is my mind, there somewhere, or what's left of it after reading, re-reading, devouring, savoring and so on your letter. No, I can't fold, fall out, tumble in or pull off my sneakers by stepping on the heels, thus obviating unlaceage, without (perhaps that word would look better thus: wih tout) at least beginning a letter to you. (At some point I am — this is to me a vivid certainty — going to arise and go to a nearby drawer and have one (oh well two) tokes of some of Saphronis Mundy's Best. I won't tell you where it hit until tomorrow; most likely, that won't be necessary. My that was good, too good not to share with you, even though merely in a letter. Here, have a lung-toke: HUH.

That I was reading to the tune of *Follies*, nice 'n loud, helped; so did certain numbers from *Company*.[743] Mostly the recurrent motif, (Motif?), well, words:

---

742. Royalty check from the Allen anthology *The New American Poetry*. At this time checks were well under $100.

743. *Follies* and *Company* are musicals by lyricist/composer Stephen Sondheim.

"Bobby, Bobby Baby, Robert, Robert Darling . . ." Yup. That first weekend, the one when you went (uh-oh — wooze) to Georgica, ten or so years locked in a turkish bath came to a, for me, glorious finale in the person of Mr Robert Jordan, gentleman buyer for Brooks Bros. (sport coats, slacks, bermuda shorts: the foto I am contemplating beyond this page shows HIM in a nifty turtleneck, recumbent against some unlikely rocks: why it's Bermuda), partner in a firm that imports Anglo-Scots-Irish Free State sweaters. Bob, yes, that's what I call him, has now been in Europe 2½ weeks. He *may* (excuse me — something I thought of to say several pages beyond this just caused a great snort of chuckle to come out of my nose.) be back this Sunday, June 6. Problem, how to *kill* the intervening time. He's 6'2", eyes of hazel, a man in the midst of life 3½ years younger than yours truly, and, Kenward, Joe and he took to one another — on quite separate occasions, and with a lot of easy enthusiasm. More of him anon. I'm not sure there's more to tell (there is). Next to last things first (but that's how I meant to begin this letter — years ago, when I was downstairs). The [Henry] James question. 1) "The Beach of Desolation," late story in (I think this is the title) *The Finer Grain*; 2) *The Europeans*, early and very funny; 3) *The Ambassadors* which I prefer to, or enjoyed more than, *Wings of D.** 4) *The Middle Years*, which is last only because, once having read it, one never ceases to read it, the one in which The Master steps forward, all in white with a stethoscope, à la Sir Thomas Browne,[744] and says:

Dencombe lay taking this in; then he gathered strength to speak once more. "A second chance — *that's* the delusion. There never was to be but one. We work in the dark — we do what we can — we give what we have. Our doubt is our passion and our passion is our task. The rest is the madness of art."

No, it is not the hash that makes me feel what I feel. I will not comment. Oh I won't won't I. I know of no more beautiful use of underscoring than: *"that's the delusion."* The rest of course are simple sentences, ordered by punctuation. The three tied together so floatingly, like rowboats on an outhaul. The nitty, linked to the gritty by a bronze "and." The coda, a 'plain' simple sentence, whose simplicity repeats the form of the gentle, elegiac, factual: "There never was to be but one." The tone, the key, has changed: "The rest is the madness of art." It's quiet all right, a quiet charged with all the passion, the art, the conviction of a lifetime.

744. Sir Thomas Browne (1605–1682), British physician and philosopher and author of *Religio Medici* (1643).

I realize I needn't explicate for you—It may be the hash, but it was what I felt and I felt like saying it; and perhaps would have anyway, stoned sober. Why Harry, I think I'm going to say nighty-night now. Nighty-night now, Harry.

And what's wrong with that? Plenty. For one thing, trying to write after hashing gave me a less than lovely white night—one of the (pretty) dingey gray, do I wake—snore—or—start—kind. Needless to say, it was not *just* the hash. There was a dinner timing mix-up and the Dyke-ries (usually pronounced DAK rees) I bestirred were ready along with the lamb. I only make them because FP thinks he likes them; nobody wanted any: save one body, mine. Harry, I know you are enough of a gourmet that I need not disrecommend a pitcherful of iced light rum and hand-squeezed lime juice (easy on the sugar: real diet drink) as the "thing" with lamb; not even with American 'lamb'; the leg in question was about the size of a zebra haunch. Tasted OK though.

Now quick, before you scoot up to Paris and John tells you to ignore anything I may have said about HJ: because, *"The Golden Bowl* is *the* supreme work, period."* I have not read it. In my little list I managed to leave out my favorite of all his novels: *The Bostonians.* (Or was that on your list. *Where* have I so carefully put Harry's beautiful letter? "Yes," Fairfield said, "that *is* a very beautiful letter," which from the Great Spruce Head is something. No. That is a checkbook. That is an issue of *Gum* (cute: for once, not the size of a bedsheet: 5½" [times-sign] 4¼"); and that—). If you haven't read it, do. Now I am told it is lunch time—Bob [Jordan] came back. Spent an aircondition bliss night chez JA [John Ashbery], looking forward to one next week out here. He is, by the way, married; they live on 17 acres (sounds very nice—old farmhouse, with ells, no fixin' up, sort of place); he did not get married until he was 36, so I surmise they knew what they were doing. That, as far as I am concerned, is their business.

Now, should John neglect to instantly confide this confidence to you (and he might, he is that wrapped up in David Kermani: as is only fit; one of the most terrific guys I have ever met) you can perhaps lure him into doing same. You then might like to frown (a little)—a faint shock? distaste? surprise?—"You mean . . . ." In other words, if you feel like teasing Our Boy a little, *I* see no harm in it. And I suspect neither will you. I much admired the Firm Line you took with him when, at the last moment, he decided he would rather sit and stare at a telephone than join his Dearest Friends, as your Guest, at Gage & Tollners (yes, Jane and I are still yearning for more, more). Oh well, do it your own great way. Please give Maxine [Groffsky] something special in the way of a hug and a kiss for me, and tell her that—alas—I am not above reading Kenward's postcards, especially when he is in Brazil, and that I too am a poppy freak. Hell. I forgot to order seeds of *papaver commutatum*—heavily endorsed by I forget which English garden book grinder outer. You do, I hope, get Thompson & Morgan's catalogue? It's said to be the most comprehensive; except, maybe, for one in Germany; but I lost that address. T & M's is: Ipswich, England. Cheap, service swift.

With love, in haste,

Jimmy

Thanks for getting me over my Christ-how-I-hate-all-religions block, as applied to the *Commedia*. I find its structure loathesome. Which is, of course, silly. I mean it: thanks. Good grief (it's my head they'll be having for lunch): the Degas monotypes! How did you know? Oh well, I am rather transparent, in some ways, I guess. Larry Fagin is consumed with envy (not that that is all that unusual). Fairfield flipped: i.e., studied it with care; I have loaned it, for a few days, to Bob Dash—in hope that this may, just possibly, be the way to do *something* about his color. More soon.

*I have never read *The Golden Bowl*, which JA rates supreme.

Jimmy

TO JOE BRAINARD

[Southampton, New York]

June 4 1971

Dear Joe—

Wow, what a mail I got today—the greatest. (And if you throw in yesterday's *long* letter from Ron—Patty got her hair cut short at Henri Bendel—Ron is about to faint—card from Kenward, flying over a jungle, & incredible 3 pager, typed, single spaced from Harry at his best, & you know what that's like!) Today, well, you are top—and yet—no, *one* was top, my first letter from Bob. Even the envelope looks beautiful,

and it *is* beautiful: thin gold letters you would like, as on some Italian wine bottles, but *very* raised, so you want to feel it, making the letters look gold & bronzy
at the same time. Envelope the color "of an old egg" with the BY AIR MAIL
/ PAR AVION / PER VIA AEREA left *pure* white—postmark & machine
stamp very bold in great red—oh, and thin line oblong for address (takes up
most of envelope)—in same gold, but *printed*, not engraved, so it looks brown
golden. Then, in ordinary blue ball point ink—fast, nervous energy printing
(thinks his handwriting is "messy"— maybe it is—I can read it) *my* name & address. As for letter—he is like you, Joe, in more ways than one. Bob says *now* he
thinks he will be back "Monday week"=a week from next Monday. *Which* next
Monday?—there is *no date on the letter.* But that red postmark was nice & clear:
he will be back a week from next Monday (today is a nice sunny Friday), which
is fine. I need another week to unwind, get good color (long walks—1-1/2
hours—on beach with Fairfield) finish up Knoedlers (in mail today, nice check:
"an advance"—makes it easier to get that off my back)—garden (fuck gardening)—going to New York for *one* night—to see movie I loved with Fairfield,
BRESSON'S *UNE FEMME DOUCE* (A GENTLE SOUL—) among
passionate fans: the Fagins; Rudi & Yvonne [Jacquette]; Ron; Jim Bishop[745]
loves [Robert] Bresson but, about this one, he *wonders*: which is very like his
painting, I think. A favorite shot: feet in shoes on oriental rug; feet go away; you
go on looking at rug—like one here, right now, in living room—a long time,
in color. Nice National Geographic color, not wishy-washy Swede tits-in-the-
rushes-with-Mozart color.[746] Then, dinner with J.A., David & Sina (cousin of
Empress of Persia who wants to see me again. I like him too: the one who is
going to get me a Sasanian onyx seal)—then, zap, back to rosebudbing here—
lilacs terrific this year—one rainy day then two very sunshiny—it's not just me,
everybody says, "Why, I can't remember *when* we've had such a spring—even
if it is *so late*." Other mail—sweet note from Kenneth (I had asked, nicely, to be
paid for two weeks work on *Wishes Lies & Dreams* at *Art News* top rate: $250).
K.K.: "*Art News* does not pay you enough, and neither am I (bad grammar)"—
check: $300. A gent. Also delightful letter from Rudi, telling me how much to

745. James Bishop, American painter based in Paris.
746. *Elvira Madigan* (1967).

sock M. Knoedler & Co for photos: $6.00 for first print of foto of painting; for foto of Fairfield painting—& I was careful, good shots, getting F., canvas, & subject, when possible—$25., at least, for first print.[747] I've got *lots* of those, & I'm going to handle it, with care. Finish garbage they want. Donald [Droll] is invited here for F.P. opening at Parrish museum (that weird dump around the corner). Then, maybe, I'll show him a few good prints, and, maybe, look at contacts with him. It will work out.

(Have I gone money-mad? You bet I have. I intend to spend much time in NYC, near Bob—and my friends—*and*, well, he never knows until the last moment when he is going off for 2 or 3 weeks to Europe. I want some money in the bank so—well, dump some things in my pigskin case & *go*.)

Your letter is so beautiful—it tells me everything nobody else ever did: what it's *like* in Bolinas. Lot of rocks, Pacific Ocean: so what? A voice: "It's nice— foggy, warm, dank—in the spring it *really* gets very nice." You—"*tons* of forget-me-nots"—I *see*: flowers! the marvelous dangle-ear-ring kind are fuschias (FEW-shas—& not FUCK-sias, as some, mistakenly, say). The white wrap-arounds with the yellow dicks are calla lilies—. It's midnight & I have 1,000 things to say but am going to fold (yes, I *am* unwinding). Reading Bob's letter I got a hard-on—& it (the letter) wasn't "personal"—others were in the room so, I crossed my legs & kept reading. TAKE CARE yourself. I'm fed up with that & would rather take chances. Be happy (you are). *love* to Bill [Berkson].

love, Jimmy

TO JOE BRAINARD

[Southampton, New York]

> *June 19 no, June 20, 1971*
> *and a foggy-ish Sunday at*
> *that*

Dear Joe,

Small pad paper always—almost always—means, Haven't got time for a letter so will just dash off a quick note, Joe.

---

747. Schuyler's photographs of Porter at work and of various views of Great Spruce Head Island show that he had a photographer's sense of composition and did not take just snapshots.

The beautiful leaves are a kind of eucalyptus (there are *many* kinds of EWEka-lip-ts; too many, in fact), a tree native to Australia (and, maybe, New Zealand and Tasmania — not sure) now widely grown all over the globe, where the climate suits it (none here: winters too cold). Branches of one kind are sold in New York in the winter — a lot — because they are thought decorative (not by me — they are nothing like the beautiful scimitar-shaped leaves you sent). They also make a room smell like a "Vicks Menthol-Eucalyptus Dual Action" cough drop. Whether that is a good ida, *or* a good idea, is a matter of taste.

Isn't "Take care" one of the great Anne Waldman's great ways of saying good-bye? Anyway, that's how I took it in your letter. I just used it as a way to say something I meant: really meant, up to a point. There are limits, though; night before last, Bob came out (arrived Bridgehampton after 9) and we stayed in Bob Dash's quiet, peaceful, very private guest wing. (Does it irk me, just a little, that Mr Dash and Mr Jordan have the same first name? YOU BET. There is one Bob as far as I'm concerned; and I've noted that I now often address B. Dash — and I do like him — by various Italian-type nicknames: Roberto; Robertino; even Bobolino. He likes it; and I can keep that name that means so much to me attached to the one person I "feel" it belongs to.)

Ah: Lorraine Ellison is singing my top fave of all her numbers on *Stay With Me*, "Heart Be Still." "HOW! CAN ah FO-get you! How Can Ah Go to SLEEP — oh heart be still — When AH KNOW that AH love YOU?"[748] Great. Sort of Motown only more so — screaming, yelling, backup group, draggy drums — "maybe maybe maybe he'll come back sum day — " backup: "heart. heart. heart. be still." And she utterly throws her voice around: *but slow* and screaming. Think you'd like it. Gave a copy to Bob. He thinks it's great (he took a cassette and the [Janis] Joplins to Europe with him).

Where was I. Oh yes. Anyway, I said I was utterly zonked for this and that reason, and how about, come bedtime, getting *some* sleep? "Terrific," said Mr Terrific, and so we did. Not that we turned into monks exactly. I have never really much liked doing it with the lights on: (I don't mean *very dim* lights, of course) it always seemed to interfere with the wonderful mysteriousness of touching someone else, so that even your fingertips become erogenous zones. With Bob, I find a blazing near-the-beach Long Island total sunlight morning is, perhaps, light enough. In some ways, I *have* changed.

There has *got* to be someone to make it with in big bold Bolinas. If not, how

748. Lorraine Ellison (1931–1983), rhythm and blues singer. Schuyler's poem "Like Lorraine Ellison" first appeared in *The Crystal Lithium* (1972).

about a day or 2 in San Fran? They say there are great Turk' Baths. Ask Don Allen. I never have made out what, if anything, or who, if anyone, he "likes." But he loves to *tell*. I think it makes him feel a little bit devilish. No, I think he really likes the fact that someone might ask him that sort of "personal" question, and it gives him a feeling of intimacy. He is (or used to be) in some ways very uptight, like a scholar, which he is.

("AH'M so HAP PY! Take GOOD care A'ME!" I really think you would like this record (*STAY WITH ME*). It is the one I heard a cut from on a taxi radio, and tried to find on 8th Street. Finally got it through Rick's on Job's Lane. Great guy Rick, ditto his dopey rock-'n-roll assistant.)

But he—Don Allen—used to light up like Manhattan at sundown when Frank knocked back a swig, opened his yap, and *cut loose*.

Bob, by the way, is Irish in a number of Frank-like ways: such as regarding sleep as some sort of nuisance and waste of time. Maybe. Personally, I tend to think of it as more (like a Brooks Brothers shirt) of a necessity. And is *that* some kind of a problem? Quit yo' kiddin'. It's just another way of getting to know each other—not quarreling, and not "working things out together" either—I don't know: you know: another part of being *personal*. (Now it's *Kosmic Blues*. Was it her greatest of all? Who cares. It's more Pearl, or pearls, as far as I'm concerned.)[749]

I keep thinking about all those roses, forget-me-nots, callas etc.

They—flowers—are a reason why I'd like to visit Calif. *and* Oregon and Washington. Some time. Rite now, I'd rather visit N Y C & See Bob. JA *is* in London. I *do* have the keys. . . .

love,

Jimmy

P.S. The name of the wallpaper in my bedroom—& the rest of the upstairs back—*is* "California Wild Flowers—"

---

749. *Kosmic Blues* is a Janis Joplin record album, and Pearl was her nickname.

TO ROBERT JORDAN

[New York, New York]

Sunday June 27

Dear Bob,[750]

Eight a.m.—21 hours since you left in the Saks blue. I seriously think there was time to consider the dark red—it might have been just the thing with the black tie with the red figure. And had we done it my way, i.e. thinned my hair, *then* thought of what to do next to Jimmy's cock—the thought of the two finest minds of our generation concentrating on this problem, utterly engrossed in it, to the exclusion of the most urgent problems of our time, quite broke me up as I showered and Fitched this evening. After casing I don't know how many drug stores I found a bottle in the top floor bathroom. It is and was mine: it was moved here from the 95th street apartment with what was a fabulous collection of colognes. John [Ashbery] is not so interested in colognes (or soon won't be), now that he is coming to grips with reality: David [Kermani], taking an airplane trip, and doing it ok, etc. Me neither. I'm glad I didn't ask you to get me any Trumper's cologne—beautiful as is the *small* bottle—I've had the Caswell-Massey trip. I could afford it. Now I feel differently about the money. Yup, I'm looking forward to the Jaeger sweater. There is no hurry—it is summer—relax—are you sure tan? Or a very particular dark gray or perhaps dull silvery (not pewter) shade of gray? You decide. Or is it possible that we might look at them together, have a hideous fight, and never speak to each other again? I have, by the way, a cashmere cardigan—tan—from Bill's: of course: I got it because I had one in 1941, when lithe young uptight pervert that I was—remind me to tell you about my college adventures, a hoot: going into the Librarian's house at night, total dark, not knowing which bedroom was his, which his sister's (also a maiden lady), finding the right one, tiptoeing out to his car, drive to the woods, suckage. His Name: E. Hugh Behymer; and he was, or is, oh never mind. There is more to that another time. Now, a cardigan gives me a portly look, like a man of 47 with a piss distended gut. Good or bad? You can see it Wednesday night. Or Thursday at 1:31 pm; if you prefer, me Lord and master (I mean it). By the way, you said lately that I had "fought you every step of the way." Not literally true: as in the silver chain removal scene: I have not felt

---

750. The only letter to Robert Jordan uncovered to date. It is among Schuyler's papers at the Mandeville Special Collections Library at the University of California, San Diego. Since the letter ends in mid-sentence, the likelihood is that it was neither finished nor mailed.

closer, more yours, more at one with you. I have told you, plainly, I needed, that night, all your affection. Right after the chain I said, I had to piss, and instead of lately

TO KENWARD ELMSLIE

[Southampton, New York]

July 13 1971

Dear Kenward,

I be here, at 49 South. About to attempt Calais phonage. The Plan: Kenneth and I will drive up, leaving here a week from tomorrow, Bastille Day (i.e. leaving on July 21st and I guess arriving at The Snuggery, Apple Hill,[751] that night or the next day. Kenneth will stay a bit; I will stay until booted out or Bob [Jordan] sends for me. The Saint (thank God he ain't).

I'm gonna bring my phonograph and a bunch of discs—do you hate *Follies* already? Unless you tell me that you've gotten a terrific new phonograph there . . . OK? Hunh? I'm sleepy.

It's 11 a.m. ish.

Jane [Freilicher] and Barbara Guest came and took me away yesterday. I came home to find a bill for one ambulance ride (not my idea): $105.00 simoleons, including an item "$20." For "Special handling." I beg their pardon . . .

What happened was a religious experience in the guise of a psychotic—or as far as I'm concerned—psychic—episode.[752] I was very open about it with Ron and Pat, but it did get pretty hairy. Ron panicked, the police came—now I ask

751. Kenward Elmslie's Calais, Vermont, home.
752. Schuyler refers to the events of July 2 at the Porter house in Southampton. The Porters had gone to Maine for the summer on June 23, leaving their home in the care of the Padgetts. For three years the Porters had been asking Schuyler to move out of their house into a place of his own. He had been told that he could not accompany the Porters to Maine, but that he was welcome to stay in his room at their Southampton home for the summer. When the Padgetts arrived, Schuyler was in New York City with Robert Jordan. He returned the next day in a very good mood. His behavior quickly deteriorated and he threw his money in the trash because, he said, "Money is shit," took to walking around the house naked, turned on all the faucets, and opened the windows. Disturbed by this but loyal to their friend and uncertain of what was happening, the Padgetts were at a loss. On the morning of July 2 Ron Padgett heard Schuyler declare, "Harm may befall the infant." Interpreting this as a threat to their son Wayne, the Padgetts immediately left the house. After speaking with Kenneth Koch and a neighbor of the Porters, Ron Padgett reluctantly went to the Southampton police. They re-

you, dear, if a friend wigged out, would you gallop off to the hospital and speak to a strange—"horribly hostile": K Koch—shrink and the fuzz? Well, hysteria *is* contagious. And I'm not in any sense mad at Ron, who was very shaken by it all; especially the part where I landed in Suffolk County Psychiatric Hospital, an experience I loved.* Still, Ron is *awfully* young; he managed to speak to Fairfield by phone—twice—which he didn't bother to tell me until three days ago. So Fairfield and Anne are in a dither—well, worried, and, really, unnecessarily. Oh well. Live and learn—at least I trust he has learned something about what not to do when the roof doesn't fall in. I see what Joe means about Ron being an only child; he is very innocent and inexperienced, too protected, so far. Well, I've done all I plan about that. Now he's on his own; luckily, with Wayne and Pat to keep him pointed in the right direction.

Here are some seedlets you might like to try an X-tra row of.

Will I be glad to get out of this burg. But first, a heavy Fri-Sat. date with you-know-who. He sent me his Astro-Flash chart by special delivery this morning, arriving as I was about to hit the Special K and sending me into planetary Ecstasy. Already with thee, Heddy.

love,

Jimmy
The Witch of The Wild Wood

*no sarcasm

TO ANNE AND FAIRFIELD PORTER

Calais, Vermont

[postmarked July 22 1971]

Dear Anne & Fairfield—I arrived this evening after a beautiful ride on a half empty bus. Joe, KGE & Whippoorwill are all great, the silence rippled by the

---

turned with him to the Porter house where they encountered a now seemingly rational, albeit naked, Schuyler. But the police accepted Padgett's word and drove Schuyler and Padgett to Southampton Hospital. There the examining psychiatrist asked Schuyler just a few questions before diagnosing him as schizophrenic and committing him to the State Mental Hospital in Islip. An ambulance took Schuyler there, and he spent nine and one-half days under sedation until his release on July 12. Within days of Schuyler's release Kenward Elmslie invited him to come to his summer home in Calais, Vermont.

waterfall; the pond is now a lake; the views are blue & it was lovely to find letters from you both (forwarded from 49 S.) waiting. Now to bed—love, Jimmy
PS The man who passed out digging is OK.

TO ROBERT DASH

[Calais, Vermont]

July 29 1971

Dear Bob—

I'm sorry—I should have flashed you a postcard the moment I got here—instead thought, I'll wait a day or two—type up those poems—write a *great* letter etc. I was more, much more tired, than I knew. As you said I've been incandescent since April 3rd (night Bob & I connected—& now, have to—not face myself—but, relax, unwind, get back to my normal tempo (whatever that is!)

The diaries—3 years of them, much better than I realized—will be typed up by Mac McGinnes in September when he gets back from Crete, & I return to:

c/o Elmslie

104 Greenwich Ave

New York, N.Y. 10011

(round Sept 1). I'll be in Southampton some but not much—not being in the city where Bob Jordan works is not to be born & I'm not about to bear it.

I'll send the calendar poems—soon. I simply have to tell myself: NO PRESSURE—so, if not for this year, then next.

You are so wonderful—I do love. There were plenty of people in Southampton who *would* see me—gladly—*if* I called; one person didn't stand on ceremony & called *me*: you. Typical, just as you came & dug me out when I was holed up on Avenue A. Some people don't understand you: I do. You know how good you are, & much better your work is going to be, so sometimes you drive yourself a little ragged. Try not to: it makes it rough for yourself, & when you feel that way, then people you like—casual Hampton friends—begin to grate on your nerves. Of course not drinking/smoking when surrounded by boozers & nicotine clouds isn't easy; but I can see that after a year on the wagon, it's getting easier to take.

And (very big with advice) leave a little room for casual romance. I know it's your nature to be monogamous—mine, too, in a way—but I had to wait until I was 47 to find Bob, & in a filthy wonderful dump—The Everard—at that. So—! Come into New York more—there are nice people there—Bob & I will always like to see you. Perhaps take you to a clean ill-lighted bath, put you in a room, & send in something nice. Or perhaps those are things you would rather do on your own? Truthfully, I have never been any good at all at fixing people up— but—in NYC there *are* more opportunities in the winter than in Sagaponack— that I know. Your pied-a-terre idea was sound—you just picked the wrong roomie.

More soon—it's after dinner—KE in NYC on show big gig—mauve pink mist over beaver pond—trees lean heavily on the air after a day of rain—you are indeed—dear dear friend.

love,

Jimmy

TO FAIRFIELD PORTER

Calais, Vermont

7/3/71[753]

Dear F. Please write me as often & as freely as you like: you barked at me & I barked back. And you know it, Daddy Longlegs. I *will* write you a letter soon— love to Anne. Keep your pecker up. Love, Jimmy

TO ANNE AND FAIRFIELD PORTER

7/7/71

Vermont General Hospital
Waterbury, Vt.[754]

Dear Anne and Fairfield,

I lost my (cosmic) temper & Kenward, who does not hesitate when duty calls & fetched a doc & here I am where I can do most good & have most fun, a thing

753. The actual date is August 3 but, beginning with this postcard, Schuyler gave many of the postcards and letters he wrote during the month July dates.

754. From this letter until the September 13 letter to Harry Mathews, Schuyler was in the Vermont General Hospital in Waterbury, Vermont. At the beginning of August, a breakdown at Kenward Elmslie's house landed Schuyler in the hospital's psychiatric ward, where he spent three and a half weeks. This episode began on a night that Schuyler locked himself in a bathroom and proceeded to wash his money. In the morning Elmslie and Joe Brainard and John Ashbery, who were also staying in the house, realized that Schuyler was not going to

for which I have developed a positive genius. If it isn't fun fuck it and if that isn't fun I don't know what is.

I'm out on the grass under a giant Audrey Fountain elm ("get that pun"?) with Gary Greene, my son adopted for life last night. I popped the question and he did not say no. He is 17, you will see what he looks like, he can do anything in the world from Zen to yoga to build a harp. I tried to give him $10 & he shuddered and asked for something smaller so I forced $5 on him. Guess he will spend it some year or other—he is a monster of extravagance. He is also, of course, my buddy friend, kid brother, troop leader, health & exercise instructor, dietician & you name it. This is what our radiance is like: he is born on Nixon's birthday, January 9th and I on life-enhancing (I love him) Spiro T. Agnew's (Nov. 9—my birthday—hint, hint—love birthday presents especially if on time, but always welcome). Any way we toasted the administration in milk and two wall lamps, which previously wouldn't work, sprang alight, which is either a miracle or heap big magic, you choose, Mr "Fate" Reader, or you, Anne of Great Faith.

When is Johnny [Porter] coming back to Vermont? We go to NYC Sept. 1 where we house sit while Kenward goes to Ann Arbor for production of *The Grass Harp*.

Please write to me at Calais. Oh, Fairfield I've decided to forgive your rude letter and you may send me a cheque for the $125 I paid Eddie, the heaven-sent gardener. M. Knoedler sent me some pollution ($250) in an envelope so I boxed its ears and sent it to the Bishop's Fund, Burlington. One way to clean the shit off bread is to slice it away: no I will not lend you a dollar I will give you one. Here. Later "No I won't give you anymore. Why? Because I don't feel like it." Love to whoever is there. Did you catch my act in July 2nd *New Yorker*?[755] Hope the Kittiwake hits another rock *real soon*. Love,

Yours in Christ,

Jimmy

---

snap out of it. Elmslie called the state police, who came with a doctor. Not wanting to be institutionalized again, Schuyler refused to go until Ashbery agreed to accompany him in the police car.

755. Schuyler's poem "Light from Canada" actually appeared in the July 31 issue of *The New Yorker*.

TO RON PADGETT

Friday Aug 7 (?) 1971

Dear Ron—

Guess where I *am*. Mental Hospital in Waterbury, VT. Believe. Baby Sweet-
ness blew his cool—*again*—and at *Kenward* at that. "Kenward! *Twice* yesterday made me miss *that* call (from Bob Jordan, *senze dubio*).[756] Now COME!"
There are necessary acts; losing one's temper is *not* one of them. Nuff said.
Guess I'll be out soon—back at Beaver Pond—Apple Hill—no worries—

Let's see if I have any more hellish errands for you & thine to run—. This
may be fun; get a few flats of chrysanthemums—mixed soft brown, pink
tones—& have Eddy plant in empty part of round mint & roses bed by pear
tree. At the end of the house where peonies are, please (if in mood) transplant
or buy, mix & mulch a few herbs & in the north (Dr Mary) side of said peonies.
Which here stand accused of being almost too beauteous. A likely tale.

Ron, remember Patty was born a Catholic, & you know how I feel. *But*: you
are *Ron Padgett*, & if you want to worship the Great Horn Spoon—*that* is your
right.

Love Wayne. "Wayne, *where* the effing Kiss Kiss are some super watercolors
(or other) for you buddy, Uncle Bimbo Limbo?" Love to Patty, you & w—

Yours in Christ, Jimmy

TO RON PADGETT

7/14/71

Dear Ron—
Here's another.

Can you get & send to me Jim Brodey's Trib. Address?[757] Nothing's easy—or
everything is—communicating wise.

The goods on the enclosed check is for tax purposes. U keep $150—(you will
earn it, *je t'assure*) & please send *me* 10 $10s in a short letter and long envelope.

---

756. Elmslie's home did not have a telephone. He and guests used the public phone at the
nearby Maple Corner store. This necessitated sometimes complicated arrangements to make
and receive phone calls.

757. Jim Brodey (1942–1993), poet then working at a short-lived The New York newspaper
called the *Tribune*.

Saturday, waiting (hopefully—!) for Kenward—and—one—*promised*—"I'll really come" visit from his nibs, JOE. (We will see.)

Think of McNiven Tate like Sou Hampton Gristede's—full of "sun" gear—decorations for sale—a wall (I think pale sky blue—what could be better with flowers? The right gray like 49 South dining room, Dieffenbach house, light with rage in it)—a wall of what Schnemann nudies; 100 Brainard tattoo drawings (accepts commissions—gay—bi—hetero—menage a trois), big big *unsold* great Alex Katz's from last year (we split take with Marilyn (Fischbach) and Aladar, the language mangler—"Freely Exposing"—"I axe you"—) lots of Pat Padgett letter—Katy S. sitting D. D. Ryan's crowd $$$ straight—D. D. I hope will be "in" as partner—her costumes for *Company*—anemone colors—so beautiful!

Sorry you have to put off Europe—so glad you'll be here to help & earn bread—read "free" time capitalist enterprise—store closed Sat. Sunday. Monday—open, oh 1 p.m.–6–7 p.m. Have a drink—want to see new book? *LARRY RIVERS' PENIS*, a Schuyler Doerfner production—

love,

Jimmy

Hi Pat! (Keep painting) Hi Wayne!

TO RON PADGETT

Sunday Aug. 15, 1971

Dear Crumbling Manse,

If I start to copy out anything for you to type I hope somebody grabs me and makes me look over my shoulder at the T.B.[758] It's about 8 pm (all the hospital's clocks are 15 minutes off, per Burlington radio) on a dull gray uninspired Sunday.

Please take some black ink, my poem ROXY ROSE, and eliminate, ROSE, thus restoring the original title, ROXY. There is a reason & I will write about it some time (in '43 Sid Catlett[759] entrusted his cute sailor found-object to a

---

758. Wayne Padgett called T.V. "T.B."
759. "Big" Sid Catlett (1910–1951), jazz drummer.

"friend" who took me to meet a lady lush in a "Volunteer" uniform who once starred in a flop musical: her big number, Rosy Rose—she, we, got bad drunk & she did her number. Hubby came home to his STAR looking pissed, friend took me to the Everard Baths—& me still "19" well, just 20, maybe—yes, 20— where I grooved with a nifty soldier &, Ron, I can feel those dogtags this minute. Wonder where he is tonight—middle years & all—hot damn—"Sonny & Cher" more later.

9:20 p.m.

Sonny & C very funny—called Bob Dash—then mother—Jim Westland so *good* (to me among others) has died, so I wrote Kathryn.[760] Life goes on, and so does death.

Please send ROXY to Jim Brodey (with enclosed note) at that paper (*Tribune, Herald*). I will, on second thought, save up the big religious poems, and give Howard Moss at *The New Yorker* first look see. Jim is O.K.—but what the hell Ron—Howard, 20 years ago this November, accepted "Salute" for a new mag, and—.

More tomorrow.

August 16, 1971

I see I have dated all my poems the "7" of the month—please change to "8" where applicable (sigh). This 3 day Battle of Bennington holiday weekend[761] is something else—not even any *mail*. No way to cash a check—money will come (from you, from Bob Dash, from J.A.)—someday. Oh. Well. It is a gorgeous evening in a gorgeous place & I am one, pissed-off poet.

I *could* copy some more poems to put in this—hmm—maybe I will. Ron, what the fuck else is there to do? Chinese Checkers? Guess I'll go yell up at Barbara Strezelec the-poet-with-the-funny-last-name on her locked ward (thought to have once been maybe suicidal, hence, maybe she was—they'll let her out some day—J. More later, Mr Patience

---

760. Jim Westland and his wife, Kathryn, were an East Aurora, New York, couple who befriended the young Schuyler.

761. The Revolutionary War Battle of Bennington, fought in Bennington, Vermont, August 16, 1777, is commemorated by is a state holiday.

I hate to waste any paper—finally woke up & called "Mom" & said wire me twenty—not a *nickel* for 3 days (not true—squeezed a buck out of a guy who owes me $105—2 packs multifilter—all filter—no tobacco—2 plays juke box— "Green Green Grass of Home" and "Overture" special trip-out recording of overture to *Jesus Christ Superstar.*

Say, Ron, don't you think you & yours & I in the month of Sept., early Oct., can find a store (Brainard says Soho—I wonder—Upper East Side—where the bread lives?)—paint it an interesting tone, move in some gear, pictures (Patty's [Padgett], George [Schneeman], Joe tattoos, Mary Abbott watercolors), mad genius I know here—oh—you saw an Xmas card by him—lots of lithos & multiples by friends—high class clothes from Mc Niven Tate) & start rolling? *And*—*you* will be *paid* for your *time*, while STUDYING AT HOME!

Wayne can be manager. If Mc Niven Tate doesn't turn out to be fun, I'm a bean bag. Flash Harry Segessman[762] address, please—love, Jimmy

TO JIM BRODEY

August 16, 1971

Vermont State Hospital
Waterbury, Vermont 05676

Dear Jim—

Here is a poem: "ROXY." I wrote it; Ron Padgett typed it—you may publish it should that be your wish. However, if it is not going to be *soon*, please send it back. I see no point in publishing in newspapers if the weeks are going to drift into months, as they do in magazines. I'm disappointed—to put it mildly—that my Jim Morrison poem was not zapped out, instantly.

All the best to you, and love to Tandy—

Peace,

Jimmy

762. Editor at Columbia University Press who edited the Frank O'Hara Poetry Prize series.

TO RON PADGETT

Aug 13 '71
A lucky day

Dear Ron & all,

I'm in the circular TV freak-out lounge—Ward 5—I wish you all could groove on up here and see this brick beauty bath, embowered in hills (hunh?) "Still don't trust me—after 20 years—" "We don't have a nickel—not a penny" Something behind me about Joe Calico. Great pool shark, amputated hand: can he make it with a falsie?!?!?

Please type enclosed, one final page, 2 or 3 carbons, and send (except Gary Greene's) to Jim Brodey, the *Tribune* (or is it the *Herald*?) They're printing what Shelley (Lustig)[763] calls my "tribute" to Jim Morrison—ends—"We're on/Jim's dong") as part of a group, POEMS FROM VERMONT STATE HOSPITAL.

More soon—as Dante said, my rest is thy piss—xxx, Jimmy
Hi WAYNE!

P.S. Please send one set of carbons to me, "HERE," another to Robert Jordan, McNiven Tate/17 East 37th NYC 10016 (O.K.? You keep 3rd carbon?)
P.S. Please keep all wiggy punctuation & caps.

BEFORE

The men's
room a
large room
with a
fountain
and chairs
and one
man,
crying. "Would
you like to
talk
with me/
or be
left
alone?"

763. Shelley Lustig, poet and a friend of Schuyler to whom he wrote while in the hospital.

His
hands
cover
his face.
He
is
sobbing.
"Alone,"
he says.
The privilege
to weep
and wash
no matter
what
away.
When
I piss,
I pray.

7/13/71

AT

THE
HORSE
SHOE
PITCH
SPAR-
ROWS
DUST
BATH

7/13/71

BARBARA

"Comes from
    California"
        Tree
says. Juke

360

plays: I'm
free: you
"in locked
ward." Juke
box sings
"My Sweet
Lord." We
both are free!
Barbara.

7/12/71

PEOPLE

better bury
her in prayers —

—GARY GREENE
7/12/71

TO HARRY MATHEWS

August 16 1971

Dear Harry —

Your noble letter! Like my dream of writing a great true travel beauty, like Virgil & (I imagine) Pausanius, N. Douglas (he's terrific [get *Southwind*] — *Sea & Sardinia*), Lady Mary Wortley Montague letters, Patrick Leigh Fermor's (1915–2011) books on Greece, *Mani* & the other one[764] — I read your letter, I sip it like your wines, out of just the right glasses — *You* are something else.

My address: VERMONT STATE HOSPITAL / WATERBURY, VT. 05676. Why am I here? Ask Kenward — he's *your* friend. And, in a sense, I mean that. My doctor here (a groovy babe in flame red pants suit — "Dr Colette" her

---

764. Norman Douglas (1868–1952), Scottish novelist and travel writer. Lady Mary Wortley Montague (1689–1762), British writer. She wrote letters home while journeying with her husband to Turkey. Patrick Leigh Fermor (1915–2011), British writer, scholar, and soldier.

moniker, her hubby, "Dr Garcia," seems a swinger) agrees I do not need to be here: some thorazine & freedom—Southampton, *Chez Ma Mère*: but, here I am, friend KGE having appeared with a doctor & the deputy sheriff, & I was *committed*, because said doctor did not have time to drive me down here so I could sign in voluntarily. Hence, my sanity will be discussed in Montpelier Court on August 26th—in solemn convocation. I have the option of being present or absent—opted for absent. Yawn. (I can, should I feel like it, get in a cab, go to Burlington, and, away, by plane or by bus.) Kenward is behaving like a shit—although he doesn't—I think—know it. For further details, ask John Ashbery. He was there.

"My beautiful friendship with" J. Pulitzer's crazy grandson will survive; or it won't.[765] When someone behaves badly toward me, I like to think it over before the make-up kisses get *too* sticky. This paper was decorated for me, for you, by Ed Demar, a favorite genius crazy of mine. It is "Lone Star"—his name "Lone Star has usurped God's power"—I give the theological horselaugh & he loves it. His home-baked Kandinsky-Malevich's are *great*!

How is Maxine? I think about her & you—oodles. Hope to get to Europe— oh—soon—spring? Can I tempt you with spring in Iran—(February, I think —) a week or two? Decided *Miss* Ashbery can fly, then this pup is going to sprout wings. Think about it. I'm *serious*. And David K's friend, Simma, is the cousin of the Empress—and I like him & he likes me—and—oh Harry (& Maxine) what fun!—we could collaborate on a "Letter from Isfahan" book—hmm? (No one but you & me has a *speck* of adventure in their soul—& Bob Jordan and my newly adopted son Gary Greene. Met him here (Gee, thanx, Kenward! You're swell—you dolt). He is 17, very outdoorsy soul brother from Newport, R.I.—mother dead—dad a machinist in Oregon hasn't written in three years—so, without any double ring ceremony, he's my boy & I'm his dad. As father of Philip, you can understand how I feel (Kenward & John both met & liked him—big deal if they hadn't)—you'll be hearing more about My Boy, a Brainard-type "natural"—chosen field, music, a la Bob Dylan. We will see, we will hear.

Always wanted a kid of my own, just never got around to spring planting— and now. Gary is Mormon by background ("MORMON BY BACK-GROUND"—Harry, my *prose*—) & plans for 40 kids. So you'll be calling me granddad soon. Say—speaking of granddad—what news from the East—huh?

I've written up a storm of poems—meeting Bob Jordan last April 3rd un-

---

765. Kenward Elmslie's grandfather was Joseph Pulitzer.

leashed a rain of creativity hysteria—it all hung up—I mean, out. Hence the wiggery—never enjoyed myself more: except life keeps me from Bob Jordan, now vacationing with his wife, Jane, on island off the Carolinas. Suddenly I feel sad. I'll write more—no—yes—in the morning. Oh. We swingers here are publishing a VSH magazine THE DAILY PLANET—I want works by real conscious, live out crazies—so, would you send, please, some thing *short*—poem or *page choisi?*

I haven't received the further part of *Stadium*,[766] but my mail has been wandering from Southampton to Calais to here—and—

Flash a postcard. Loads a' love—always—xxx

Jimmy

I'm not *really* mad at Kenward: bemused as usual, by life & "My God, people *really* are like that"—as in Balzac.

TO KENWARD ELMSLIE

August 16, '71

Dear K—

Where *Is* you? NYC is my guess, & all to do with the G. [Grass] Harp.

Please take books and records to 104, & I think I can *face* Martha [Macon][767] without fainting. Tell her where you put them—& I'll gather them up circa Sept. 1, assuming I'm sprung by then. In New York State a commitment can be quietly set aside (patient signed "Voluntary" & other is torn up—or lost in the shuffle)—Vermont, no surprise, is more literal, so I'll sit it (sweat it, freeze it) out until Aug 26th, when, I trust, I'll be free to go.

The telephone number here in the ward is 802 (area) 244-8970—say when you're coming. If I am not in plain sight, ask them to try "Research" where the Brains are putting out a mag., *The Daily Planet*. Contributions (short) by you & Joe welcome, if possible (time wise).

Your letter, like you, was altogether truthful. I would not have taken on so over Fairfield's letter if it had not enclosed the final version of the fatal Knoedler's chronology—no matter what I *said* that evening; all I ever intended

---

766. Harry Mathews's novel *The Sinking of the Odrodek Stadium*.
767. Kenward Elmslie's housekeeper in New York.

was to ask might I stay, the coming winter, chez you & visit Southampton, rather than vice versa? That this was something you might like, I got directly from a letter of Joe's. It also annoyed me *very much* in Suffolk County that well meaning friends (Kenneth abetted by others) "arranged" for me to rest at Calais, instead of letting me make my own plans i.e., write or phone you and *ask*.

I think my McNiven Tate idea is a good one, but I won't take you up on any loan (not giant, anyway) until I've talked to Bob J. & looked into things a bit.

Talked to Ron, who is typing for me. He's a bit blue — Europe travel plans off, but hope he will want to help & have fun with me in "boutique" scheme. Anything with Tessie Mitchell as floorwalker is bound to swing. *Tell Joe to write or call.*

Love, Big North

TO BILL BERKSON

August 17, 1971

Dear Bill,

Here I am in another one. Vermont State Hospital, Waterbury, Vermont 05676. We crazies here are mimeoing our own little mag — THE DAILY PLANET[768] & I want to include work by live-out freaks: you, & selected Bolinas. Would you send something, (we're limited to 10 pages an issue) and ask Tom Clark, Philip Whalen, Joanne K. [Kyger] — to send too? Postcards always cheer the incarcerated.

If you want to know how I landed in a second hospital, ask Kenward. It is a *fact* that I need not, for any health or head reason, be here, but K. thought otherwise & so here I am, sitting out a commitment. I am feeling chilly (it *is* Vermont) toward Kenward, whose head holds more than its fair share of bent.

Write me a missive & send it by mail. I should be released after August 26th, which seems, after nearly 2 weeks, rather far off. This too will pass, I hope.

I really feel great. Last April 3rd I met a Mr Terrific, Bob Jordan, and the Cre-

768. Schuyler and his fellow editors published two issues of *The Daily Planet*, in which appeared poems, stories, and news items about the hospital drug rehab program and softball team. Issue number two began with a quote from Thomas Lovell Beddoes, "Dreaming a dream to prize/Were to ask a ghost to rise."

ative Gates flew open—been on a writing bender ever since. Can't wait to get out & back at ½ finished (short) novel, *Death, Life & Other Dreams*.[769]

Haven't seen much of your poetry lately. I love it, & want to see some—OK?

Joe gave good [qua?] about you on the West Coast. His *Bolinas Journal* is GREAT ☐ A FLOP ☐ INSCRUTABLE.

As you know—let's hear—

Love,

Jimmy

TO ANNE AND FAIRFIELD PORTER

August 19, 1971

Dear Anne & Fairfield—

My young friend, Gary Greene, is coming—probably—to the Island to visit you with a friend of his, "J.B." (Jim I forget what) It's possible he will have arrived before this letter, or that some other plan will develop (in which case, I'll let you know).

Gary is of Mormon background and, brought up in Newport, R.I., by a young aunt, since his mother died when he was 10. His father is a machinist in Oregon, & has not troubled to write his son for 3 years. Him, I view dimly. I am very fond of Gary—I think he has genius of some sort—he is a "natural," like Joe Brainard, as you will see. He will not be 18 until January 9, and I want to be sure that in the meantime, his uncle by marriage—with whom, I gather he now "gets along" (Gary beat him up at 14, and then hit the road)—does not unnecessarily put him in a hospital. I want, in general, to stand in relation to him as Fairfield has to me, someone on whom he can unquestionably rely.

I hope you will both like him, & want him to stay, for awhile, at Southampton. Right now, I have to assure Dr Colette (she is also my doctor) that you are respectable folk, &, more important (respectability gets no special nod here), that at the Island he can earn some money doing work (he *likes* to do work, & is very woodsy/outdoorsy). I don't care if the money comes out of the island funds or F.'s pocket—the latter may be better, so there will not be a production number with John P. (Island Boss).

---

769. Published in *The Paris Review* No. 55 (Fall 1972) under the title "Life, Death and Other Dreams: An Eclogue for Gerrit Henry."

I hope—well, I hope you will like him. Period. If he grates, I'll find a place for him to stay in New York.

I am sorry that you both cannot visit me here, since that is the only thing that would make clear to you, despite the chatter you are in receipt of, that I am sane, healthy & in a productive therapeutic situation. I am making *my own* decisions about my future, with expert help. I intend to continue doing so. Yesterday I had a gratuitous letter from John A. (which I have dealt with summarily), saying that "my friends"—Fairfield, Jane, Bob (Dash—not Jordan), & he, are "acting in concert" about my future. If there is any truth in this, I had best scorch & kill it right now. If there is to be any attempt to meddle with my plans—which depend entirely on Bob Jordan & no one else—then I will have to acquire new ones, an easy thing, I find, for me to do.

I cannot speak plainer than that; but if I must, I will try.

Fairfield, I wish that you would write to Peter Schjeldahl directly & invite him out to 49 South in early September. I have had a letter from Donald [Droll] dated August 5th, saying he is "a little hysterical" (no news to me) & Peter needs this, & Peter needs that. I have spoken to Donald's secretary, & find you don't want the January date (*good* stick to your guns!) so it is not so urgent. I could write to Peter, but I think it is better that you do so, and let me get out of the middle of this. Peter's address is

Mr Peter Schjeldahl
113 Sullivan St
New York, N.Y. 10012[770]

I am sorry to speak so sternly, but I think it is better to be forthright than to find myself in a situation similar to that last June.

Love,

Jimmy

---

770. Schuyler knew Schjeldahl on the poetry scene and admired his art writing. Porter contacted Schjeldahl about writing a catalogue essay for his 1972 Hirschl & Adler show. Schjeldahl produced an essay that has not been reprinted in any of his collections of art writing.

TO FAIRFIELD PORTER

August 20, 1971

Dear Fairfield,

Kenward and Joe brought me my typewriter and papers last night, a week later than promised. Oh well. In a hospital one's friends' quirky little ways—and at keeping appointments and so on Kenward is a fuzz head—become more noticeable than usual. One has to depend on people who aren't quite equal to simply running an errand for someone who is confined and can't do it for himself. Item: I asked Bob Dash by phone to send me twenty dollars in a letter, in cash, because neither the hospital nor the bank will cash checks. Next day on the phone he gave me his The Royal Governess tones, "It seemed unwise to send cash in an envelope . . ." so he sent a bank money order. This precipitated a comedy of horrors that went on for 36 hours, when an aide was finally released to accompany me to the bank, which reluctantly cashed it. So I sent Bob a postcard blessing him for promptness. As anyone who has been at his mercy knows, he does not wield power with a kindly hand. He can't help it; so, frankly, I keep a tight rein. The moment he gives the Missing Dauphin number, I stop calling, or tell him, it's time for me to go home now. That usually does the trick. As for John A: but I've already apologized, by card, for my "venomous note," making it clear that I did not regret sending it. In the past year I have had a bellyful of John's bad manners, and I plan not to see so much of him for a while. It is not so much his manners—he is as witty and as John as ever, when he bothers—as that he bores me to tears. I don't want to hear any more about his problems, his apartments, his phobia this, his hangup about antibuse (which alcoholics take) and belting down three double martinis. He doesn't even try. Someone else can carry the load.

My letter about Gary and his friend J.B. is a false alarm. They are going instead to visit J.B's sister, in (someplace—New Hampshire, I think), then to what Gary calls, "Manhattan, New York," to see—NYC (GG has never been there) and the latter's girl friend, Dee. I like J.B. a lot; he is much more sensible—on top—than Gary, who is a clown (a wonderful one). But I'm glad Gary is independent and I won't have to spend *too* much time auditing teen age conversation. It's great; but I have read more than they have, and, frankly, I often yearn for a nice chinwag on solar pollution or Thought Waves behind the iron curtain (haven't gotten to read that yet) with someone of my own mental age. I'm glad they changed their plans. I know that all would have welcomed them, but also that the week before leaving is not the time ideal for guests.

I thought I would make this a "real" letter, but life has again intervened—medication time, lunch—& I want to post this so beds won't be made for nonarrivers. Please bear with this testiness on my part—I miss Bob Jordan so much that I can hardly stand to be around me myself.

Love, Jimmy

TO KENWARD ELMSLIE

Aug 20 1971

Dear Kenward,

Just a line

To say I'm fine

And hope that thine—etc.

It was great seeing you two. "*My*" aide was most distressed by "Mr Will's" bad temper ("I told you boys . . .")—it was the first & (I hope) last I've seen of the tiger of the South office—gather he's an old line hard hat and—well, the hospital has all these rules on the book, but one simply doesn't keep them, not anymore.

I spoke to Bob today. (Jordan that is—Miss Dash is simply going to have to change her name—how about [   ] Rainer? *She* never uses it. The plan is this. I am 99% certain of being discharged, Saturday, the 29th. Bob will fly up, rent a car, get me. We will flash by the Eyrie, pick up my things (I do need—or want—the clothes) and then drive halfway to Southampton. *Please* don't invite us to stay over—Bob might accept & TROOTH-FULLY I am dying for what I've never had: a big wicked motel shack up scene. You know—like Lizbeth Scott or Ida Lupino[771]—only heftier. Perhaps there will be lightning behind the broken blind, rain on the tin roof & a big-name swing band on the radio. "Bob, we've got to take this thing out—I mean, *talk* this thing up—oh! Dear—"

And there I go, jumping the gun again?

Don't bother calling—a week isn't long & I know you're probably writing & "doing" [   ] or whatever—brush cutting—before Vermont time runs out. If you're near, visiting hours are 2–4:30; 6–8 p.m.

771. Lizabeth Scott (1922–2015) and Ida Lupino (1918–1995), movie actresses often cast in films noir of the 1940s and 1950s.

I think we'll come by early afternoonish—so soon, so far away! I'll write Mr "No Joint" *real* soon. I *love* the Roycroft cards.

xxx love,

the Blurb

TO FAIRFIELD PORTER

[August 1971]

Dear Anne and Fairfield—

May I borrow $5,000 from you? What happened was this—Bob Jordan is so kind, that, though I knew something was on his mind, he did not tell me that McNiven Tate[772] was bankrupt: the phone was being turned off: at the same time, Brooks Bros. (owned by Garfinkels—Washington, D.C. department store) has been hit hard by not being "with it." Many were fired—not Bob—his work is too good. (His problem: he does not know how good he is: a literary genius & he is just waking up, you'll see) (Edwin DeMar[773] is sitting writing a poem "I can't spell" and at this table—all hell is breaking loose on TV & I love it.)

Anyway I flashed them a check for $500 as a no interest business loan—& they think I am a saint. I am not. As Sister Claire said this evening (not to *me*, of course)—"Oh I'm not a saint. God has free will and he has given it to us. That distinguishes us from the animals. We are sinners: becoming a saint consists in trying to be one." Sister C. is terrific—has taught 4th graders for 30 years & is now summering as an "aide" & is she ever.

It is plain to me that McNiven Tate needs a partner—me—as idea man and financial adviser, honed in the school of hard knocks. (Here is Larry. Ah ha! He would like to go to the canteen & play the great juke box. Baby, you're on.) So I'm going to buy in as partner.

I could go on & on—tomorrow I'll (Larry offers giant gum drops—I am trying to diet—"Oh! Thank you very much—I'll take a red one!") flash you a copy of *our* local paper.

Thanks Anne for Arthur B[ullowa]'s[774] address—I do indeed need a good

---

772. New York men's clothing store where Bob Jordan worked.
773. Edwin DeMar, fellow resident in the hospital and an editor of *The Daily Planet*.
774. Lawyer who collected Fairfield Porter's and Alice Neel's work.

lawyer (does not one have the right to freak out *at home*—49 South? Yes one does. Forget it).

God Bless us all,

love, Jimmy

The check the sooner the better!
PS. Here is Ed Demar's poem (good not top.) I told him I'm going to frame it— "You are? Why?" *Why not?* Keep it safe. xxJ

TO FAIRFIELD PORTER

August 23 1971

Dear Fairfield—

Thanks for not lending me the $5,000. After I mailed the letter I realized I had jumped the gun, which is [ ], because you [have] to go back to "go."

I'm 99% certain I'll leave here next Saturday the 28th. Bob Jordan is going to fly up to Burlington, then we'll rent a car and drive to Southampton. So I'll probably be there when you get back, unless I'm in NYC for the day. Knowing there is a terminal date does not make it seem soon, but far away—But sometimes I think, "Well, a week from now—"then it seems sooner. If I were at the Island (Great Spruce Head) I would feel I didn't have time enough left to do anything, or not most of the things I wanted to do anyway.

I'm dying to see your new pictures—

The muzak is on instead of the TV—casting an infernal spell. It's more [ ], more abstract; hearing TV without seeing it, you soon wouldn't mind it if you *had* to be around it. But please don't buy one for *my* sake—

Love to Anne & Liz & Bruno & all, Love, Jimmy

TO BARBARA GUEST

from Waterbury, VT
to Toylesome Lane,
Southampton, NY 11968

August 25, 1971

Dear Barbara,

Kenward said the other day you're coming to visit people in Vermont—or so I understood him? I'm getting out this Saturday (the 28th), when my friend Bob Jordan is flying up to Burlington, then we will Hertz together to Southampton, getting there most likely late Sunday. Then I may go into the city for a few days—depending on heat waves, typhoons, and the 'feel' of Southampton (I have no doubt I'll prefer that in post Labor Day, coming fall days; or haze). I think Anne and Fairfield are coming back the 3rd, a settling down date. Fairfield will march march march into the studio and paint paint (his first Knoedler show is this winter, and, I think, faintly inhibits him—an odd concept); and Anne will do her thing, which is, I believe, denominated 'housekeeping'—whatever it is, it is lovely and inimitable.

Can't wait to see how the roses do. There are usually September surprises.

I put your Ovid poem into a stencil for THE DAILY PLANET: then took it out. I want very much for Howard Moss to have first look-see at your new poems—and that is one I seriously think he—or the New Yorker—might take. He tells me that he can't get long poems in (groups of poems, sometimes, yes; longies, no), but I know he would like reading 'Swan,' so, why don't you send the group I saw, to reach him right after Labor Day? At the New Yorker (don't have the address on me—). Please say I suggested it: editors, too, are human, and so are we poets, and I think Howard would like the idea of 'the shock of recognition' that—does whatever Melville said it does—flashes and hooks up, and that a friend recommends poems I truly like (read, love).

If any other friends of yours hit the Thorazine (and Stelazine) trail, tell them JS recommends they cool it with the Pot until they are certain sure that their vibes are tuned down to normal. Mine weren't, to be brief. It's odd to think of Kenward, Joe and (most of all) John Ashbery, as dangerous *liaisons*, but, for Mr Suggestible here, such was the case. A trance estate is not that subjectively unpleasant for me, but, it is open to misinterpretation, and I would as soon not be misinterpreted into another hospital (this one *is* great—and so beautiful—Milanese Sforza brick in Vermont hills) when all I need is a change of company and some soothing contemporary medication: gripe; bitch.

371

The NYer is very nice in being quick in saying, "We like them, but no"; then on to Tom Clark [Poetry Editor, *The Paris Review*]. There is plenty of time, as I believe the next issue going to press now is full. However, if you want to be ahead of the game, you could send him Swan [ ] now, and let the unwritten proviso in mind be, that if the NYer should bite, all offers are off. His address (of course) is Bolinas, Cal. 94924

love,

Jimmy

TO HARRY MATHEWS

[Southampton, New York]

Sept. 13, 1971

Dear Harry,

Ahh, so you're back from Isolde-land.

I would love to tell you all about my "spells" as Ron calls them — 9-1/2 days in Suffolk Co. Psychiatric, with a further Maine Chance type rest (24 days) in Vermont State Hospital. I had a ball, though I got good and bored before the end. Sleeping with 32 pair of feet not all that clean, I'm simply not used to. But it will all emerge when I get the poems I scribbled in both places typed and ready for viewing.

Right now I'm absorbed in the mss. of THE CRYSTAL LITHIUM. I'm offering it to Dial, because that's where the editor (Robert Cornfield) of my choice would hang his hat if he had one. Today I have to collate 5 or 6 sets of xeroxes, O Noia, thy name is of-ten in my thoughts.

Listen Harry, I had an idea. All ready? I want to do a foto-offset magazine, one with contributions kept pretty much to one poem, or a couple of pages of prose. And with as many drawings as there are lit. contributors. Fairfield, Jane, Joe B, John Button, Jim Bishop, Larry Rivers — it could look quite nifty. Please send a poem — I guarantee the editor will not go crass and offer any money. Now the problem.

What to call it? I thought of several rejectables, CHAPPED LIPS, WHITE PAPER, THE MULE EARED GORGON, but I want something plain, and, what I would like to call it is Locus Solus 6. My objection to it is that I associate the name with the way the volumes look. I could get that done locally at Bob Keene's — but hand set type! All winter. No. Besides, then, no drawings.

Does it give you bad vibes if I use it? (There are other title contenders: LONE STAR and 49 SOUTH.) I like Locus best, but if [you] don't like the idea of an exhumation, say so. It won't bug me.

John Button bopped by today, in beard, which makes him look like he's about to appear in something, dear knows what. I asked him for a drawing—india ink on a sheet of typing paper. "Can it be of a *boy*?" demanded the gay libertarian. "Yes, child," allowed this middle aged member of the demi-establishment. And Fairfield has promised his. And so on.

As you can see, this isn't a letter. It's just a big messy question. Lemme hear, hunh? love, Jimmy　　　　　　　　　　　　　　　　P.T.O.

JA and I are on the outs, for what that's worth. I rather like it.

September 14, 1971

Dear Harry,

This is a ps to the letter I wrote yesterday. I got the impression from your long glorious letter that you thought I would have seen a further installment of your novel? Well, I haven't. Did you send me something, or do you mean an issue of the *Paris Review* which I have not seen? Write. Tell all.

I dined, just we two, at Kenneth's. He has become—a cook. A correctly sliced tomato with a personable vinaigret sauced over (manners constrained me from speaking my mind about *chilled*tomatos [sic]); a delicious onion soup, straight from the pages of *Tante Marie*—K called it Paris Tourist food, with a merry manic laugh—cold roast lamb (I refuse to call it gigot)—locally grown corn on the cob served American style. Choice of fruit and black coffee, served in cups of an appropriate size. Nor did he ask me to do the dishes—I did help clear. My only criticism was of the pre-dinner nick-nack: shoving a pimento up her and slapping her into brine is no way to treat a nice girl like Olive. A minor point, and doubtless just an eccentricity of mine. No wonder men do call me Doctor Fuss.

Sometime I wish you would send me a list of your top favorite classical records. I am a musical ignoramus who loves music. Can't carry a tune, and a piece of printed music to me might just as well be so many crows sitting on a fence. For instance: my recording of *Fidelio* has *actors* speaking the melodrama instead of the singers! You can imagine the hideousness of the effect! Right now I'm "into" rock, country and western, and heavy on Carly Simon, Carole King,

Kris Kristofferson, Cat Stevens, and various groups. And *oh yes* Rod Stewart singing "Reason to Believe," not to be believed. By the way, a very good record is *Women of the Blues* from Victor on their Vintage label. Two cuts have Fats Waller at the *organ*, Mazie, quick, bring my fan.

John A wrote me a nice letter, so I wrote a nice one back. So we're over the hump. Not, to be truthful, that I cared during our lull. John has been a terrible love-life, apartment hunting bore, and I was well content to put him in the ice chest of my heart—for a while.

love   Jimmy

TO RON PADGETT

Southampton, New York

September 15, 1971

Dear Ron,

I love the Schubert poems. It is the greatest cycle since Heine's North Sea Cycle, which was the greatest thing since Erasmus Darwin's Loves of the Plants.[775] One of the pleasures it gives me (Cat Stevens says he's lookin' for a hard-headed woman; should be easy to find) is that I can feel the joy with which Schubert—what a great guy: I love artists who have good characters, like Keats and William Constable—would have set them. Why haven't we lieder lovers got more of a choice than [Lee] Crabtree or [Ned] Rorem? Please answer. You are one terrific poet, Mr Padgett sir. And if it was partly my record collection that turned you on for this set, well, groovy: it would make me feel like Big Uncle, a nice way to feel.

Cat Stevens says, Oh baby baby it's a wild world. Cat is a fount of wisdom.

Looks like Dial will publish my poems, editor, Bob "Tennis Champ" Cornfield. Couldn't be pleaseder. And to think, mere weeks ago I didn't even know if he particularly liked my stuff. Seems he does, and so does a biggie editor, a Mr Hutter. We're to meet sometime. I wish offices didn't give me bad vibes, Oh well, I'll pop a Stelazine, and perhaps $1/2$ a five grain Valium and shuffle on in. I'm really pleased about this. All my previous doings with commercial publishers have been along the lines of the shit you got from Random

---

775. Erasmus Darwin (1731–1802), British poet, physician, and botanist.

House over the anthology. "Piss on it/ shit on it" as Ed Sanders[776] lyricized. A poem I like; it expresses my transcendental sense of life.

By the way, I wouldn't have had my Vermont relapse if I had not done what, really, I knew I should have not: start in on the pot (those bombers of Joe's!) so soon after Suffolk Co. Psych. Believe me, I'm off it now, so long as I'm on medication, which will be several months. Then we will see. The cosmic humor of my best friends being forced to go off and get the cops because Mr Religious Nut has twigged out again. (Rod Stewart says Every picture tells a story. Oh it's so true, Rod. And so is anything else you sing; especially the ones I can't understand.)

I've decided to go into Off set publishing myself, to be called *Locus Solus* 6, if Harry gives the big OK. Otherwise maybe 49 South, or White Paper. But not Chapped Lips or the Mule Eared Gorgon; though I like them as titles. Anyway, I want there to be as many drawings as pages of lit (more or less—I don't intend to be uptight about it). And one work from each writer—I mean like a page or so. Really, I will publish whatever anybody I ask sends. It's going to be pretty and it's going to be fun. I want kids in it too, as in The Daily Planet. I am a deep Celia Coolidge[777] fan, though we haven't met. So: would you send what you feel like, if you feel like playing? Maybe Patty (Padgett) would make a black and white drawing on a sheet of typing paper—or an excerpt from her novel? And I definitely want some writing from Wayne. A drawing too if he feels like it—but he seems to be "into" color, which is not the idea. I hope to have the stuff within a month—say end of October. OK?

Is Ted still sitting on Sugared Turd 13? That pisses me off. There is a poet who needs a kick in the ass that would land him on some poor slob of an analyst's couch. There is a kind of self-pitying deliberateness about the way he is killing himself with speed and whatever else that elicits no kindly feeling from ice heart here. He knows what he's doing and goes on doing it, so: it's his trip. His whining after money utterly turns me off. And yet really he is such a terrific guy. And what does the world "really" mean in that sentence?

Peter Schjeldahl came out for a weekend and was fine. He sure can rap can't he? Love to have a tape of him and Larry F [Fagin] telling it like it isn't about some dumb movie. Not that I would play it all that often. It would be nice to know it existed, potential bonfire stuff. Don't get me wrong. I've always felt an

776. Ed Sanders (b. 1939), poet, writer, editor, and lead singer of The Fugs.
777. Daughter of Clark and Susan Coolidge.

affinity for Peter and like him very much. Rod says he's gunna ress in his bed agin. Good for you Rod. I love Carole King by the way, also Susan Raye singing L.A. International Airport. It is lovely.

Now that I can see Bob Jordan sort of regularly I am as happy as the King of Norway. See enclosed latest opus.

Love to Patty: we had a feast when we heard it was not hepatitis. You and yours are very much loved out here. Hodge sends a wail and Danny a fur-TIVE Glance.

love Jimmy

TO HARRY MATHEWS [778]

Southampton, New York

Jan. 15, 1972

Dear Harry,

I've decided to recycle my anomalous mail, hence the striking letter paper. I'm very glad you've decided to make a stab at the O'Hara Foundation, and trust your claymore will come out with many a victorious gout dripping from it (can a gout drip? and am I right to imagine a claymore is a sort of sword, and not a cousin german to a sporran?). The competition *is* stiff, and it's a shame there isn't enough money to publish more than one mss. But I don't mean to divulge anything that goes on when the judges don their togas—wrangle, wrangle, wrangle. The year the coin had Tony Towle's head on one side and Michael B's (Brownstein) tail on the other, the judges nearly went out the window. Tony took it very bad, indeed, I tell you. But I don't mean to hand you a downer, and you have the advantage of having waited, so that your work is both more mature and more selective than most. Some of the most talented work doesn't seem quite to add up, owing to the youth of the submitters. However, there are at least five touchy poets who have the say about who is going to get the bay, so I guess we'll just wait and see.

I rather hate things that have to be applied for, myself, and am just coming

778. See glossary.

out of a fit of mss. submitting blues. I have signed up with Random House[779] which takes the curse off of first being accepted, then turned down, by Dial (I wanted the latter to do it because my friend Bob Cornfield is an editor there). For some reason, I don't get any pleasure out of publication business—there's bound to be a nut designer in the works who will want to use all lower case, or set all the titles hard left because that's the way we're doing it this year, baby. Then there's dust jacket copy, which I would rather not think about, but I had better anyway, or it will come out all wrong and asinine, as it did last time. Still, it is a more distinguished house than Alan Swallow,[780] so I'll shut up and stop complaining.

A large gray lid is clamped over Long Island, and I'm trying to type by a lamp which casts a large shadow over the typewriter—perhaps if I held a light bulb in my teeth. . . . I'm just back from a two-dayer in NYC: dinner one night at John A's, who on my arriving with Gerrit[781] announced we were going to eat in, and produced a very raw, very cold duck. Some hours later it was cooked. And tasty, but I do have country or 6.30 dining habits. John's sexual activities proceed apace. It's like some oriental game where you toss counters around and see what combo's you get: David, a Brooklyn layer (I mean, lawyer) named Sal, a 23 year old English poet from Yale [Peter Ackroyd], and his friend, Christopher [Lethbridge], who graduated from Deerfield (that other side of this had to do with a pigskin business case which was abstracted from my room) exactly a quarter of a century after John himself. Ah youth, youth. It's all like a blue movie version of *The Wings of the Dove*. Gerrit (I'm very fond of him) was fine, except that he'd been smoking pot in the afternoon and every now and then seemed about to swoon. The next night I spent with MY BOB, which I consider an ideal way to pass the time. John and I, after the martinis which preceded the duck, let down some hair and I raved about the sheer beauty of Bob's penis. It is funny that a flap of skin can so brighten up the world. (Which reminds me, that in *The Story of My Life* by Augustus J.C. Hare[782] with which I've been tormenting myself, he alludes to a M. et Mme. Pinus—surely even in France an unusual name?) And now I'm back here, eagerly awaiting my next date on

779. Random House published *The Crystal Lithium* and *Hymn to Life*. Both books had covers by Fairfield Porter.

780. Alan Swallow (1915–1966), poet and small press publisher. Swallow books were known for their non-descript covers.

781. Gerrit Henry (1951–2003), poet and art critic.

782. Augustus J. C. Hare (1834–1903), British painter and travel writer.

Friday. While loving a married man has marked disadvantages—I didn't get to see him at all over the holidays—it does place star-like dates like ever fixed marks in one's private firmament.

I cannot see one word I am typing, so I'm going to let this "lay over" in the machine until tomorrow in hopes of sun or an improved lighting arrangement. Yes, the sun *is* an improved lighting arrangement. It's Sunday, there are 20 degrees of frost, not to speak of the wind chill factor or whatever it's called. I have on my country-check Duafolds (from L. L. Bean, natch) and at some point will probably go for a beach walk with Fairfield and Bruno, the golden retriever. Or I may just lie on the bed reading Augustus J. C. Hare and using the stone paper cutter Kenward gave me.

Thank you so much for sending my very own copy of THE RING.[783] I'd read it before, and loved your mysterious combos, and now I'll read it again. Among other things, I love the sound of your poetry: no drizzling off into thump thump iambics—so many people do it, and seem unaware that they are. Your phrases glisten like the links in a silver chain (such as the one I'm wearing—very fetching with a red flannel shirt) so that the sound flashes like your glinting intelligence.

I decided to reciprocate with a little gift. One of my favorite organizations is soliciting for new members, so you will soon be, a, Fellow of the Royal Horticultural Society; and if you wish can sport FRHS after your John Hancock. Perhaps some might even mistake it for FRS, though I gather the latter requires a little more than a small fee to get into. Or am I wrong? The Journal is short and crammed and larded with lore—I'm 99% sure you'll get a charge out of it. At least I hope so. The annual Masters lecture is always a treat—unforgettable the year it was devoted to a proposed series of museums of wheat. Ditto the history of the potato.

My typewriter is suddenly acting funny: the carriage goes whizzing off on its own. Nothing makes me more certain I want to write than a busted machine. Oh. Dear.

I saw our Joe B [Brainard] in town—we went to the Metropolitan to see the [John Singer] Sargeant water colors, which had just been taken down. He said he had just been allowed to start his post hepatitis drinking again: "I got completely drunk on a half bottle of wine. (pause). Well, not *completely* . . ." He seemed peppier too, though he can't seem to figure out why he doesn't feel like

783. Harry Mathews's first book of poems.

378

doing anything much in the evenings—it's funny how people with hepatitis depression don't seem to realize what it is. Utni (utni is a pretty word) until it's over, that is.

This typewriter is giving me the feebs. I don't really mind writing in long hand—provided the typewriter is in good tone and ready to go.

Hmmm. There's a strong north wind blowing which at the beach means sand in your face, or my eyes. Yes, I think I'll consecrate this afternoon to reading. I always feel very up and free right after I've seen Bob Jordan, but then the days pass and I sink slowly into a slump, like a stock market or a fever chart. I wish I had a little more coolth. Have you any hints on how to stabilize one's emotional life, Mr World Traveler? One thing, I'm seeing a lot more of the Long Island railroad than I ever wished to. But that is truly a boring story—yesterday's unheated car, plus changing engines in unlikely Speonk.

Let me hear from you soon. Your beautiful letters are wonderful shots in the arm (somebody says Larry R [Rivers] is back on speed—foolish middle aged boy). Blessings on you and your snow views—

love,

Jimmy

TO HARRY MATHEWS

Southampton, New York

March 8, 1972

Dear Harry,

I'm suddenly struck, as by a sledge hammer, how far we are into what I still think of as 'the new year.' Moth eaten and dank around the edges already. There must be some better way of measuring time—or *not* measuring it—but before I get too far into corn planting festivals and burying virgins alive on 12th night, I'm reminded of what Harris Schiff [784] once said to me at a Kenward affair. We had been discussing Life—the hour, she was late—when Harris said, "I guess the only answer is, stay stoned." It's a pretty dusty answer (especially after the contribution pot made to my over-dramatic summer) but—well—it's just that kind of day. I enclose some mud and a spattered snowdrop.

I love your novel [*The Sinking of the Odradek Stadium*]—it goes from

784. Harris Schiff (b. 1944), poet.

379

hilarity to further heights of profoundness (a profound height? hmmm . . .). I particularly broke up over Twang's letter explaining how she had not enclosed the rosemary. Where will this madness end? I can't wait to see how it all comes, or doesn't, come together. As for your query: I don't see anything wrong with the paragraph you ask about. I'm very fond of the name, sidecar, for a drink, so I may be prejudiced. But there it is—I think it would be a mistake if it were wilder, considering what it's leading into. I do wish you had a carbon of the rest I could read. Not since the crowds stood on the New York docks, waiting for the installment which would disclose the death of Little Nell, has there been such suspense.

I'm listening to a lovely song by Brook (Mr Soul) Benton—'Big Mable Murphey' 'she loved little Melvin' but bathtub gin used to cause him to sass big Mable who would black both his eyes. Alas, it's very sad: someone shoots little Melvin, so big Mable—'they say that Scarface had died of a good whipping'. Big Mable's place / went on until she dahd . . . ! I'd give anything, if once more I could black little Melvin's eyes . . . He's very good. And so is the hit song of the year, 'American Pie' (Don McClean); but that you will have to hear sometime.

I sent Maxine, the other day, a 45 page prose work I hope you'll get to see. It's called 'Life, Death and Other Dreams' and . . . tell me what you think. My reading lately has been nothing much, the novels of Anthony Powell.[785] Somehow this time of year I crave the frothier, attention holding kind of books.

My good news—and I do have some—is that the National Council on the Arts has given me a $5,000 creative writing grant. Kenneth was my sponsor, the dear galoot. Needless to say, Proust's law was in full effect when the news came—that nothing good ever happens without some redeeming ill—and I received the news in the midst of a hideous attack of piles: I would much have preferred a lifetime supply of opium suppositories, such as I enjoyed in Rome in 1948 (December was the month, I believe). I have Mr Jordan to thank for this, though he was more than abetted by me, so I'm not exactly complaining. I then decided I should keep my movements loose, and took to eating stewed prunes, which gave me the runs, or trots, and had the obverse effect of proving an irritant. Sigh. I'm on the mend, however, as the fact that I can sit here and type this letter proves. Such was not the case for some days.

Suspense at the moment is provided by the question of whether Joe will let Kenward give a "do" for him this Saturday, his—Joe's—birthday. Kenward can-

---

785. Anthony Powell (1905–2002), British novelist. Schuyler was probaby reading in the twelve-volume A *Dance to the Music of Time* (1951–75).

celled his annual 12th night party at the last moment this year, so, as John Ashbery says, "he owes us *something*." John tells me he woke up this morning in one of his easy chairs wearing his overcoat. He seems to take this to mean that he did not make out. A nice English boy, Peter Ackroyd[786] (a Mellon fellow at Yale) told him that he gave Peter a terrible tongue-lashing in some bar for drinking too much! John said, "Consider the source." Now I'm going to take my sitz bath, all uncertain whether to send this to Paris or the country.

love, dear Harry,

Jimmy

TO CLARK COOLIDGE

[Southampton, New York]

June 21, 1971 (oops) 72

Dear Clark,

Happy longest day of the year when, I've read, the greatest variety of wild flowers are in bloom in the Northeastern states. Wonder if that's true of California, too, in case you're there?

But the weather we're having—rain, fog, mist, mugginess. And just when the roses are coming on. The weather causes them to 'ball,' not so enjoyable as it sounds. The outer petals sort of mold (mould?) and the flower doesn't open properly, or looks a mess if it does. In many ways, gardening is a big mistake. In the country at least it's all just nature. Not that I'm much of a gardener—for a couple of years I had a fit and planted quite a few hardy shrub roses; and there the tale ends. Except for my peonies, which, if possible, look worse than the roses.

Remember my magazine (*49 South*), from way back when? Well, it's finally going to happen. Trevor Winkfield, for a sum, typed it for me and got it to a printer in Brooklyn, before he returned to Leeds. It seems to me I should have heard from the printer by now (the same one Larry F uses) but doubtless I will, in the fullness of time. I sometimes wonder why I undertook it, or invited so many contributors. Anyone who is as bad a typist as I am, and as lazy, should

786. Peter Ackroyd (b. 1949), this Mellon Fellow went on to become a major British writer and the biographer of William Blake, Charles Dickens, and the city of London.

think before he acts! I guess I was inspired by the little issue I did last summer in Vermont State Hospital—but there messiness seemed the order of the day, and besides, there were others to run it off and help with the collating.

If I've read any interesting books, their names escape me (I don't really recommend Simenon's journal, 'When I was Old'). Sacher-Masoch's 'Venus in Furs' has just arrived, prefaced by a long and ground-breaking introduction by someone named Gilles DeLeuze.[787] I've only dipped into the novel part so far; it's hard to take a book seriously when the heroine's name is Wanda.

The house is all mild chaos—Fairfield and Anne are leaving for Maine on Saturday, which causes a lot of putting away and misplacing of things. And Katie and Lizzie are leaving for Milwaukee, where K. is in medical school and Liz (who is just 16) will work as a Casa Maria, a kind of Catholic Worker set-up. I think I'm going to be sharing the house with Donald Droll, an art dealer you may or may not know.

I've reached page 17 of a novel (I'm writing, not reading). The working title is, *What's for Dinner?* So far it seems to me rather like a sequel to a *Nest of Ninnies*. Which I didn't want to do; but I guess I, like John A., am indelibly stamped by the outer suburbs. Certain things about his mother and her house, and my mother and *her* house are strangely (?) alike—as a glance in their respective china cupboards would plainly show. At the moment he—John—is in London, where he's taking part in that big international read-in they have every June. Kenneth Koch, who only got invited to Rotterdam, was *green* with envy. I mean it.

I saw Harry Mathews and Maxine out here the other weekend. I have nothing to add to that. Except they were both in dandy shape. Maxine is taking a crash course in movie making at NYU—12 hours a day, 10 to 10. And have you followed Harry's novel in the *Paris Review*? I think it's terribly funny myself.

And now, if I have any further news, it all escapes me. Love to the family.
love,

Jimmy

787. Gilles Deleuze (1925–1996), French philosopher.

TO FAIRFIELD PORTER

Southampton, New York

August 9, 1972

Dear Fairfield,

I'm glad to see its the 9th and not the 8th, as I'd thought. That means you will all be home that much sooner. Good.

In case you've been wondering about the stove—it has conducted itself, to date, with the dignity that becomes a Swede. It did go out a couple of times when I went to New York to see Bob, but that was soon put right with a little denatured alcohol. And the clocks have all been wound, though I often remember about six Sunday evening with a start. Last evening, having no invite out, I read through what I've written of my novel. I'm afraid I never like my own writing as it goes along—afterwards I sometimes do—but the whole thing seemed pawkey to me. I'm not sure what 'pawkey' means, but it's the word that comes to mind. At least I discovered that I'd given a Mr Mulwin (rather a bear) a different first name in an early chapter than the one I used later. I've opted for Greg over Frank. I also discovered two passages that more or less duplicate each other, so I suppose I'll have to re-write one of them. I do, by the way, like writing it while I *am* writing it. I think I wish it were funnier, or deeper, but I guess a work of art turns out as it turns out, and once it's launched one has to go with it, without controlling or trying to control it more than it will allow. We'll see.

The press in Brooklyn which is printing my magazine, 49 SOUTH, wrote me several weeks ago that they had had mechanical trouble, but would be sending it parcel post in a few days. Now I receive a letter saying they have misplaced the table of contents, and could I supply another? Which with a lot of muttering I did. I suppose some day it will come out!

Kenneth came over the other night, and we read each others poems. He's embarked on a racy masterwork, 'The Art of Love,' and praised my 'Hymn to Life' highly. Did I tell you *Poetry* is going to publish it? I think I did—despite what the editor calls its 'intimidating' length.

My social life is going to take a turn for the hyper-active. Peter Ackroyd and his friend Bryan (blank) are coming tomorrow for a few days. Then on the 17th the Rasmussen family are coming out until your return—Waldo, Gary, and, for part of the time, their college age kids, Mark David and Lisa. Mark David (second year Harvard) is a fan of my work and of John's. Bright boy.

Hodge finally came back, much the worse for wear. He's still very scrawny, and for a while seemed to have an eye infection, but it's cleared up. All he seems to want to eat is milk, and an occasional dab of hamburger. Danny Rex, I discovered, sometimes uses the tub in the front bathroom as a cat box. I think it's because Hodge hangs around the laundry and she's afraid to go in there. The obvious solution, to shut the bathroom door, seems dangerous, since where would she choose next? And a tub is at least very easy to clean. I had resolved to keep them outdoors during the summer, but both have discovered where to loiter for a dash inside—such as when I'm taking out the ashes. I think Hodge misses you. He comes and sits in my lap and asks to be patted and scratched.

John says it's 99% certain that *Art News* is being sold, and that almost all the staff will get the ax, including John and Tom and Henry (the latter doesn't know about it yet, so JA says this is a "secret" to everyone he tells). I think he feels both relieved and hopeful—he does a lot of readings now, and also has a chance to teach a seminar at Yale, at least for a semester (maybe). He's also trying to get an apartment in Westbeth, so he won't be burdened by such an enormous rent. But he's having second thoughts about going to Iran—the ticket they supplied is economy class, which John thinks is too uncomfortable all the way from here to Tehran. This was to have been the beginning of a long vacation, through Sept. 24th, so in the light of new events I don't think he knows what his next step will be. No doubt he will, as the French say, land with his ass in the butter. (Which counts as a good, not a bad, thing.)

It was so nice of Anne to call me from Bangor airport. It made me feel very glad.

I am, as always, dying to see your new pictures. Keep swinging. love,

Jimmy

TO TREVOR WINKFIELD

[Southampton, New York]

Labor Day
Sept 4, 1972

Dear Trevor,

First off, I finally received 49 *South* from the printers about a week ago, and a sea-born copy wends toward you. They did a good job, but were mysterious. First weeks turned into months, then they wrote they had mechanical difficulties but I would have the mag in a week. A couple of weeks passed and they wrote that the table of contents was misplaced and would I supply a new one? Which I did, from the material you gave Kenward and he gave me. Unfortunately, not all the drawings were included, so some of the artists go uncredited. Do you think the print shop would have them? Or did Kenward have a second envelope which he forgot (he's a great forgetter) to give me? Anyway, a major tragedy it's not. The mag looks good, the blacks nice and *black*. You'll see.

Thanks for your communiqués—I envy you Scotland, a country about which I have a curious fixation. I mean, I would rather go there than, say, Dublin. I don't know why.

I had a good summer, right here in dak (read: dank) old Southampton. I've written 120+ pages of a novel—*What's For Dinner*. It's about family life and written in a very flat style. My philosophy of novel writing is that if one person says something, then somebody else is apt to say something, too. This is really a very limiting approach to writing and I'm sweating b-l-o-o-d over it. Though once I get launched on my daily stint (two or three pages) it seems to go quite swimmingly. I think I wish it were funnier; but it isn't.

July I spent alone, which was grim on the evenings when I wasn't asked out or didn't ask anyone in. My acquaintance out here isn't all that wide. (Oops— dinner time. See you in the morning.)

* * * * * * * * * * * *

Sept 6

Yesterday and today I spent posing for Fairfield, who is painting a series of heads. I came out looking in a way that reminded me that Larry Rivers once said I looked like an English boxer. Pugilist, not dog.

August I had a houseful—Peter Ackroyd (an English poet with a fellowship at Yale: do you know him?), his friend, Bryan Kuhn, and the Rasmussen family: Waldo, Gary and their college age kids, Mark David and Lisa. Gary turned out to be a sensational cook, and took over in the kitchen, while the kids officiated at the dishwasher. We all got along very well, and in general had fun.

My book, *The Crystal Lithium*, will be officially published the day after to-morrow. I think the *Sunday Times* intends to feature it with a favorable review by someone named, I think, David Kalstone. I'll send you a copy of the book (not the review) soon. I'm sorry it will have to be a paperback copy, which doesn't acknowledge Fairfield's beautiful cover, or have the jacket copy, which makes it plain that on the inside the reader will find love poems by someone as queer as an owl. Oh well, it's true, so I can't complain about that. I did receive ten author's copies of the hard-bound edition, but I ran through those like a dose of salts. I'm pleased with the way it looks, except for some little fleurons that flank the page numbers in a rather pointless way. But the type and the page lay-out is good. You'll see.

John Ashbery and David Kermani are in Iran, and I've been receiving a small flow of views of Isfahan and the Shah Abbas hotel. End of that story. Except that *Art News* was sold, and the old staff fired, so John is part of the army of the unemployed. I think he has a few leads, but where they will take him, I don't know.

This is a dopey sort of a letter—don't let it stop you from writing to me soon. Rootle-rootle, and love,

Jimmy

TO CLARK COOLIDGE

[Southampton, New York]

Dec 14 1972

Dear Clark,

What a long time I've owed you a letter! I think I secretly hoped that sending you the magazine would trick you into writing me one, hors concours. See it doesn't work. Nor do I blame you—when I write a letter, I want a whole one in return.

The trouble with putting off letters is that it's hard to know where to pick up. Perhaps with the you issue of *Big Sky*—a mind blower.[788] I think I've told you before that you're the only 'abstract' poet who turns me on—you seem to have some insight into language, or English, or American, or poetry, that eludes all others who try to write in a pure, inventive way. Oh dear, it's hard to say what I mean: I only know I'm happy to go along with you, phrase by phrase (or letter by letter) where with others I just think, unh-huh. Your poems seem carved and in relief, not something applied to a surface. And their sound to me is like finding a new record I really love, whether it's Sviatoslav Richter, or the Kinks.

Speaking of the Kinks, I like their new double album[789] very much—have you hard (sic) it?

I spent the end of October and early November in Vermont, visiting Kenward. Lowering skys, sunny days, and finally snow. Which I imagine you have now. I always hope that on the drive back from Vermont we can stop and see

788. *Big Sky* 3, edited by Bill Berkson, was devoted to Coolidge's work.
789. *Everyone's in Showbiz* (1972).

you—but the thru-way is off track, and our driver (and John Ashbery) had to get back that day to vote. To small effect.

Did you get a copy of THE CRYSTAL LITHIUM? You were on the list I gave Random House, so you should have. If you didn't, I'll send you one.

My novel progresses like a sleepy worm. Most days I write some on it. Truthfully, it's reached a poijt (yes, a poijt) where I don't know what next, and inspiration seems out to lunch. But I've sent a new mss. of poems off to Random House, where my editor assures me it's much too soon for me to have another book out. I suppose I could burn the poems, write some new ones and thus get into proper time-synch. This is a terrible letter, really just a plea to have one of your marvelous epistles.

love,

Jimmy

TO KENWARD ELMSLIE

[Southampton, New York]

August 4, 1973

Dear Kenward,

I'm sorry I got my wires crossed about who owes who a letter. I've been meaning to write you a letter for days, but we have had this incredible heat wave. My room has no attic over it, and in the afternoon it's like a sauna bath. I sit out on the lawn reading Kenneth's novel, the *Red Robins*. Parts are very beautiful, but, really, I think Harry does it better.

Dame Rumour (Ron) has it that you're going to Kansas City for the rehearsals and production of MISS JULIE.[790] Great. Ned threatened to come out for three days all summer, but kept putting it off (he has a fistula in his ass. No fun). He's setting three poems of mine = none of them top faves.

I haven't talked to Joe yet—I assume he's deep in the paint box.

This has been the summer of Ruth [Kligman].[791] I like her very much, despite her occasional tantrums. When she heard that Sheila Isham was giving a big party, and we weren't invited, I thought she was going to roll on the floor

790. Elmslie's opera adaptation of August Strindberg's play *Miss Julie*, with music by Ned Rorem.

791. Ruth Kligman was in the car with Jackson Pollock in 1956 when he was killed. A painter herself, she later wrote a book called *Love Affair: A Memoir of Jackson Pollock* (1974).

and foam. Actually, we were invited, at 5 for a 7 o'clock party. Nice party. Jane and Joe, and the Dash household (John A, David K, Darragh Park,[792] and, of course, Bob). Plenty of others.

It's been a rather disasters summer. A number of people have died, including Linda Cavallon and Robert Smithson (close friend of Ruth's). Ellen Oppenheim (drunk) totaled her car, but got off with a black eye and bruises. Lucky lass. Some people you probably know, Jackie Rogers' employs, were in a smash, one of them still on the critical list. I could go on in this vein for quite a while, but won't.[793]

John has stayed at Bob Dash's quite a lot (one of my keys just got caught in my chains and flew off God knows where. It was the 6, so I won't worry about it too much.) Bob was very rude to John and Darragh this past weekend—I think I'll be able to keep Neil Welliver's apartment, which is cozy and cheap. My shrink thinks this is a good idea—I'm not sure I do. After twelve years I'm attached to my room here, and what to do with all my books and records? There just isn't room on 35th street.

Did I tell you I got an Ingram Merrill grant? $500, due to arrive soon, bless its heart.

I'm still stuck on the last two chapters of my novel, but I have written quite a few poems, some of which I sent to Richard Howard at the *New American Review*. We'll see. And my book is coming out in March.

Yes, I like Ruth, but I won't be sorry not to see the little bottle of nail polish standing on the dining room table.

Dull letter, but it's late and I'm going to fall out.

Dr [Hyman] Weitzen[794] is very good about pills, and has announced that he intends to get me off them altogether. Coming off Thorazine was no easy trip, I tell you!

Stay in Vermont as long as you can—the heat waves, even [ ] have been something else.

love,

Jimmy

792. See glossary.
793. Robert Smithson (1938–1973), sculptor who created *The Spiral Jetty* in Utah, died in an airplane crash. Ellen Adler Oppenheim (1927–2019), painter living in New York City and on Long Island. Jackie Rogers ran a trendy men's clothing store on Madison Ave.
794. Schuyler's psychiatrist.

TO KENWARD ELMSLIE

[New York, New York]

June 9, 1974

Dear Kenward,

You slipped out of town
quiet and easy! Didn't
even get to say goodbye.
Here, it's Sunday: I've
"done" *The Times*, and it's
only 1pm: poached eggs
at the corner, a shower, a
shave—now what? Every-
body's out of town, ex-
cept Mr Joe, with whom I
dine tonight. But he joins
you in Vermont tomorrow:
you'll see him before you see
this. The radio predicts 90
for tomorrow; bet it's cooler
there. Are the seeds in? Is
anything up? (Maxine
last week called John rather
late to cancel a dinner date:
"Something's come up," she
said. "I hope it stays up,"
replied our John, presently
weekending in Stonington,
Conn.). How's Trevor?
But no, by now—the now
when you read this—he'll
be gone, home to Leeds,
his mind relieved about the
doctor's terrifying health
prediction. I hope. I
tried to see Jane last week
on one of their last two

389

days in town. "We can't
see *anybody*!" and she gave
a friendly little scream.
Their Memorial Day week-
end was, I gather, much
like what the Hamptons so
often hold in store: rain,
fog, their furnace blew up,
an over-heated car. Jane,
of course, somehow made it
all sound funny. But,
" . . . can't see anybody!"
Anybody: that's me, I feel,
in summery, simmery New
York. John keeps threatening Europe: Scandinavia,
perhaps. He also wants
to stay here and finish
his play. Barbara (I
think) is in England,
giving readings. Darragh
natch is in Sagaponack:
yesterday was Bob's birthday. Wonder how old he
is? *He*'ll never tell! My
only gift, a long distance
phone chat. I'm going out
the weekend after next.
Strange to be weekending in
the Hamptons, where folks
used to visit me. (Kiss
the waterfall for me, and
wind it round your finger.)
Did you know that Lottie
Louise Carrington (b.
1889) married one R. C.
Elmslie? Well, she did.

I could explain about
Carrington, a book Anne
Dunn gave me, but guess
it will keep. Now, I
rather wish I'd gone with
Anne to France. But at
the time it seemed too
complicated. And so it
was. Diagonally across
Second Avenue young men
in shorts are playing ball.
I go them one better, and
am typing naked (dis-
counting my silver chains
that break my heart). And
cars that come from the
mid-town tunnel go
Toot! to hurry one another
up. What's the rush?
Are you writing? I'm
not much. When shall we
finish our living room
play? Some day: no sweat.
I was at Darragh's the
other night: outside his
rear or garden window
on a fence there flared and
toppled rose red
roses, so huge, so red
I wanted to plunge into
them in the soda and
vodka hour. There is,
you see, no news. Write
soon. I long to hear
about Calais, the Co-Op,
Apple Hill, Whipperwill,
and you know, all, how

ever small corn it may
seem to you. My love, J.

love, Jimmy

TO KENWARD ELMSLIE

[New York, New York]

Nov. 23, 1974

Dear KGE,

November twenty-third! Can I slip a letter in under the line before your return? Locally rumored to be about December first. Since I note you're giving
a reading at Barnard on the 5th, I guess the rumor is not without basis.

I don't know why I turned into such a terrible letter writer; non-letter writer,
I should say. Perhaps because everything in NYC is so all alike? Anyway, the
whole summer, I only wrote two letters: one to you, one to Anne Porter.

My summer. A weekend at Bob D's, a weekend at the Hazan's, three weeks
at Mary Abbott's, with and without Mary, broken by visits to town to see Dr
Shrink, and six weeks with my mother in East Aurora, home of Elbert Hubbard,
the Roycroft and the limp leather binding. JA drove over for a night from not
too distant Pultneyville and turned on the charm for Moms; which worked.
The first week I was there I thought, "What have I done?" and my mother and
I had a couple of set-tos, mostly about my hour of arisal. "You can sleep as late
as you like dear," she said when I arrived: "Well, don't let me sleep past 12," I
said. But the idea of anyone getting up later than eight really goes morally
against the grain—morally? I think it was more the idea of what the neighbors
must think when they saw the front bedroom blinds *still drawn at noon*! My
mother has always been very big for the look of things . . . But we settled down,
and I did enjoy my brother's children very much, especially Michael, aged
eleven, who likes to take long walks, play paper games and practical jokes. And
God knows it was cooler than NYC!

Since I've returned—I don't really know where the time has gone. I've been
out to Bob's [Dash] again (where I'm going for Xmas through New Year's: I
think he intends to put me on the midnight train, 12:01, Jan. 1, 1975: can you *believe* 1975?) and to the Portes'. Who were in fine shape and all Great Spruce
Headed up. And I've written a few poems, nothing great, though I guess not
too shaming.

Night before last was the [Lita] Hornick's annual—need I describe it? There were few changes, though a few absent faces: the Padgetts (Ron has vowed never to go again, because of Lita's light switch flicking ways), and Anne W [Waldman], who's in Minnesota, and so on. I first asked Trevor to be my guest, who rather grumpily accepted, then called me the next day and said, "I think I'd rather not go. I don't really like her and I hate him." So I squired Ms Kligman instead. We got there early (i.e. on time) and Morton's greeting to Ruth was, "Hello, Ruth. I only seem to see you here. And a few other places." Several other people gave her some lip, but, mercifully, I forget the details. Did I hear any news? Well, John Myers says we must all read the short stories of someone named Guy Davenport (it suddenly comes back to me that that's the schmuk who gave *Freely Espousing* a bad review in the Times. So fuck him and his short stories). And Joe LeS is winging his way to France Dec 3rd to spend the holidays with Joan [Mitchell] and Jane (oops) J. J. Mitchell. The latter has been there since May. J. J. and Joan are taking care of each other, per Joe L [LeSueur], which in one case involved "getting him off speed" (news to me, though not altogether surprising after the way J. J. acted a couple of times last spring—you know, terribly sparkling, and as though about to say something very witty, only no words came out). While on the other hand he is said to be limiting her booze intake. I wouldn't have thought that was quite the work he was cut out for; but live and learn.

Trevor and I are thinking of sharing an apartment, since he intends to try to get a resident visa and live here full time. I don't really like living alone, and neither does he, and we always seem to get along, so . . . we'll see.

Harry's [Mathews] here and Betsy's[795] got him. Anyway she did at Jane's last Wednesday, where most (not me) got marvellously stoned on some potent grass Mr Marberger was rolling. I've always found him a teeny bit talkative, but I had no idea of how high fast and far he could fly until the other night. Talk about a duck's ass . . .

And on that note, I'll say goodbye, only in hopes of giving you a big kiss in ten days or so.

love,

Jimmy

---

795. Elizabeth Baker, editor of *Art in America*.

TO KENWARD ELMSLIE

[New York, New York]

June 12, 1975

Dear Kenward dear,

Did you say it's raining in Vermont? I'm just back from my shrink, soaked to the skin and cross as two sticks. The rain has caused me to break a lunch date with Donald Droll which would have been fun and tasty. But a hot shower and a change right down to the skin puts me in a slightly better mood.

I am utterly thrilled that you are doing A NEST OF NINNIES.[796] It will be elegant, and it will be back in print. I feel very grateful to you that you want to do it, and are doing it. The fact that Z is a "small press" doesn't matter: those who want it, will be able to get it, and that's what counts. When a book as special as NEST bombs commercially, no big time publisher is going to touch it with a ten foot pole. Actually, John and I made a surprising amount of money out of it. Arthur Cohen, Mr Sharp Cookie, got us a very good advance out of Dutton. Then a German publisher signed it up, reneged, but had to pay to get out of the contract. Heh heh. I think the Auden quote on the cover is a good idea, and I'll talk to John about the photo when I see him Saturday (right now he's at Miami U, Ohio, reading his heart out). All I've got to say to you sweets is "thanks."

Did you get the chapters of WHAT'S FOR DINNER? I saw Trevor mail them Tuesday eve. He had to take over, because the clean copy is at Random House and Maxine has the only Xerox. She tells me that Charlotte Mayerson has read it and wants to do it (Charlotte was my editor for my last two books) and now it's being read by some other biggie. Waiting is very anxious-making: I'd like to have it signed up and jacket settled before I go to France July 3rd (with D Droll to stay with the Moynihans for a month).

I had a pleasant dinner with Trevor and Mr Joe (who was only an hour late) at Duff's t'other night. While waiting, I suddenly heard the woman behind me say, "He's afraid he's got this homosexual streak . . ." "This I've got to hear," I decided, only I couldn't. Too maddening. But then I tuned in again and, alas, heard the words "Big Daddy" and realized she was just recapping the plot of *Cat on a Hot Tin Roof*. What a downer. I was very pleased to learn that Joe is off speed. "Did you crash?" "Unh-huh. Mostly slept for a week." Why such a fiendish worker thinks he needs further energy I'll never understand.

796. Elmslie's Z Press reprinted *A Nest of Ninnies* with a cover by Joe Brainard.

394

I saw *Chicago* and liked it some, a little less than you and Darragh did. Talk about book trouble! I'm not much of a Bob Fosse fan: I'm bored with seeing how many things a dancer can do with a kitchen chair. But I did like Jerry Orbach's big-fan dance number, and I'd never seen Gwen Verdon and Chita Rivera do their stuff before.[797] They do it very nicely. D.D. Ryan told me I simply must not miss *A Chorus Line*.[798] It sounded rather my dish, so I called up about tickets: sold out until July 25th, when it moves to the Schubert: and that was before the reviews came out! Maybe some time next winter. . . .

I'm on a joint economy-weight loss drive. The price of the *Post* went up to a quarter. I actually sat down and figured out how much that comes to in a year and decided the *Times* is ample. More to the point, I've cut out cabs where possible and walk. From 250 East 35th to 104 Greenwich[799] takes 45 minutes and is very healthful. My main problem is restaurants: I really would like not to drop fifteen dollars at Duff's; but I do want to see my friends. Well, well — when I visit my mother in August I won't spend a nickle, except on cigarettes. And lately a few people have said, "Haven't you lost some weight?" which makes me feel that finally it's all beginning to work . . .

The night I saw D.D., after John had rushed off to bed, she said, out of the blue, "You *do* realize that Kenward and I are *not* on the outs. It's merely a hiatus. Which I think is sometimes *good* for a friendship." I looked dumb (very easy since I hadn't a glimmer of what she was talking about) and she passed on to Truman Capote's private life. Was that something you wanted to hear? I like D. D. but she is a silly billy.

Keep those sprouts a-growin, and let me hear from you.

love,

Jimmy

---

797. Jerry Orhbach, Gwen Verdon, and Chita Rivera appeared in choreographer and director Bob Fosse's (1927–1987) musical, *Chicago* (1975).

798. Musical directed and choreographed by Michael Kidd; it opened in 1975 and ran for fifteen years.

799. Elmslie's New York home.

TO ANNE DUNN[800]

Decoration Day, 1976

348 West 20th St., NY NY 10011

July & August: c/o Ridenour
784 Chestnut Hill Road
East Aurora, NY

Dearest Anne,

May without you is very hell.

No one seems to know your news, although Barbara [Guest] gave a hint. First she knew nothing, but when I wondered if Rodrigo's[801] operation was over, she said yes, it was and you were probably taking him off to France for sun and rest. True, I hope. Oh yes, she'd also heard that in London you "were going out a lot." Good, dear, hope you liked it.

That sick I had the last time we met got much worse, enough to scare me into the office of Dr. Murray Rogers (Dr. in waiting to Robin Green, Bob Dash and Darragh Park).[802] Lots of punching and squeezing, "Is that sensitive? Hurt?" then off to another costly Park Avenue doc for X-rays. No ulcer, which had been the general fear. Diagnosis, a heavy virus. And what was odd is that it ceased to

---

800. Between leaving the Porter house in 1973 for painter Neil Welliver's apartment on 35th Street and his move to the Chelsea Hotel in May 1979, Schuyler wrote fewer letters than at any other period in his writing life. The reasons for this are many. He suffered numerous nervous breakdowns that led to stays in New York's Payne Whitney Hospital and in Bloomingdale Psychiatric Hospital in Westchester County, and he moved several times, staying in a West 20th Street rooming house, a nursing home at Broadway and 74th Street, and the Allerton Hotel on West 22nd Street in Chelsea, where he caused a fire by smoking in bed. Some of his old friends, unable to recognize the man they knew in the 1950s and 1960s, grew estranged. Others, like John Ashbery, saw Schuyler infrequently but lived in Manhattan and so were not at letter-writing distance. In the mid-1970s, the painter Anne Dunn, who first met Schuyler in the 1960s, and the painter Darragh Park, who got to know Schuyler on Long Island in the summers of 1972 and 1973, drew closer to him. Since Dunn lived abroad much of the year she became one of Schuyler's chief correspondents. Park, by the end of the decade Schuyler's closest friend, assumed a role of caretaker. Because he and Schuyler talked frequently on the phone they did not exchange many letters. For all that Schuyler endured in the 1970s, he published four books *and* wrote "The Morning of the Poem." It appeared in 1980 in the book *The Morning of the Poem* — Schuyler dedicated poem and book to Darragh Park — and was awarded the Pulitzer Prize in 1981.

801. Anne Dunn's husband, the British painter Rodrigo Moynihan (1910–1990).

802. Dr. Murray Rogers was an Uptown general practitioner, and Robin Green assisted Thomas Messer, director of the Guggenheim Museum.

trouble me the morning of the day I saw Dr. Rogers, nor have I had a twinge since. I eat everything in sight, as my figure will attest. Shall I tell you about the oral surgeon? No, this is getting too grim, enough to say it was brief, painful enough to satisfy John Richardson, and costly.

I'm all moved and happy to be a Chelsea-ite, embowered in friends. I'm two blocks from John and David and David Kallstone and Darragh, four blocks from Doug Crase and Frank Polach, a stroll from Ruth (which may be a bit too near), a walk from Kenward (only he's in Vermont) but Trevor will shortly replace him. Then there's Julie Whittiker[803] and Janice Koch, handy in the West Village. Such a saving on cabs! Except Dr. Weitzen. And Barbara's penthouse, which is still a five dollar run. That aged aunt of hers in California is sick again (well, as a Christian Scientist she isn't "sick," but she may pass on) and Barbara will probably have to go out there. She sounds quite strong about it (good), but I remember the last spell and after a time it really began to get to her. Say a prayer. (I live next door to St. Peter's, the church John claims to attend.) No luck with her novel. Maxine was nice, and, despite its literary quality, was afraid she could not "place" it. Kenward was nice, but Z Press is not going to publish it. Now where? I haven't a clue.

This cheerless letter has caused me to put on a disc of Damia's[804] more cheerless songs — *La amuvaise prière, Sombre dimanche* — very cheering up.

But this apartment. It's a little strange, I guess. It's in an old brownstone, and is what Kenward accurately calls a pensione. I share a large bath, in which there is a small refrigerator. The first time I looked inside it there were huge cucumbers. To which I have added an equal number of bottles of Perrier. (Dr. Weitzen: Isn't that rather expensive? Me: When you give up booze, you can afford anything.) What's really great about this place is that it faces south, utterly quiet and flooded with sunshine (well, not today, but when there is sunshine). That was what I really hated about 35th Street: never a ray of daylight. And I have a marble fireplace. Leaning on the mantel is George Schneeman's naked portrait of Bill Berkson. It looked OK in the other apartment, but here it's the wrong height, so all you see is the penis, no special treat. I'll sell it to you cheap — just the thing to brighten up the south of France.

Damia is a bit much. Fauré's second piano quartet[805] — ah, that goes better with a breezy day that has at last become sunny.

---

803. A friend of Kenneth Koch's.

804. Damia, the stage name of French chanteuse Marie-Louise Damien.

805. Gabriel Fauré (1845–1924), French composer. Schuyler's poem "Fauré's Second Piano Quartet" appeared in *A Few Days*.

I'm sorry you missed Fairfield's last show, just ending.[806] It's a shame (other considerations aside) that he didn't have at least another ten years as a painter. Everything became easier, freer, and the color truly stunning. In his early paintings there were none that existed entirely as color, but among the last paintings there are. Anne Porter bought back four, so there would be one for each of the children (she has already given me a very nice portrait of me in '61). And Darragh bought a small one, but one of the best. Then he went out to Bridgehampton and from the Benson Gallery bought a watercolor of me with a glass of wine. Sigh. That's what I'd like, a tall glass of wine and soda and ice. Easy on the soda.

I'm reading, and enjoying, Acton's memoir of Nancy Mitford. Perhaps her letters are her best thing? I recently encountered what has got to be her worst thing, Wigs on the Green, a lark about Nazism in an English village. At the time, I suppose, the point was to show Unity and a few others how silly they were. But it makes pretty chilly reading. I much prefer her in her Mme. de Pompadour mood.[807]

After saying how quiet it is here, someone out there is murdering someone; and I'm not going to look.

Then there's the matter of the Poiret dresses.[808] There are eighty of them nearby at the Fashion Institute of Technology (you explain what that means; I can't). John told me this was going to happen, and that he intended to go every day. Last Wednesday I was allowed to have dinner with John and David. John mixed himself a martini of a depth and clarity that impressed even me. "I see you intend to get good and drunk." "But David, it's my last day of teaching. You don't know what I go through out there in Brooklyn." I let them wrangle while I studied, and liked even more, your drawing. That red line is magical. Finally it was nine, time to leave for our eight-thirty reservation at Duff's. To my surprise John did not have another martini. They did have two bottles of wine— David tried to order a half bottle when he thought John wasn't listening. Hah. In changing the order, John managed to give Vito a good grope. But, like any

806. Fairfield Porter died suddenly in 1975. The show was at Manhattan's Hirschl and Adler Gallery.

807. Harold Acton's Nancy Mitford: A Memoir (1975). Nancy Mitford's Wigs on the Green appeared in 1935, and her biography of Mme. de Pompadour in 1954. Her sister Unity Valkyrie Mitford (1914–1948) was a notorious Nazi sympathizer.

808. Paul Poiret (1879–1944), French fashion designer. In "The Morning of the Poem," Schuyler writes, "rich / as those Poiret robes / and dresses I went to see in the cellar of the / Fashion Institute of Technology."

nice Italian, he took it as a compliment. Then they had a real wrangle. A completely ungay student of John's was coming over the next evening for advice on what to see in Europe. David had a fit, since the student's ex-wife is his secretary, and student and -ex still make out and tell each other everything, especially about what goes on in John's class (David is under the illusion that there's something about John nobody knows: John having told all years ago). John's gripe was that David not come home before 8 and then to telephone first. "Under every straight, there's a layer of gay." Mostly to change the subject I asked him if he'd like to go see the dresses the next afternoon. "What dresses?" I realized that even if I got an answer, he wouldn't remember it, so I walked home rather than share a cab and hear more about the un-gay student. The next day at noon I called the little rascal. "Do you want to go see the dresses?" "What dresses? I'm still asleep." "I'm going out to lunch. Call me when you get up." "OK." "Will you remember?" "Yes." So I hung around the apartment, memorizing the newspapers. About three I realized something hadn't taken. Call him? Never. At six I went out for my lonely supper, and ran into John. He was not precisely asleep at noon: the night before he had gone home and to sleep, but David, who has more staying power, had gotten out his little black book and summoned a cutie. In the morning, David went off to work, and John woke up to find a nice surprise in bed with him. Then at three, while I was sitting by the phone, he was picking up a number in front of my house (I'm going to put up a sign, no cruising). The crust. So I left him and a bunch of Sweet William off to keep the tryst with the un-gay student. I'd love to know how it turned out, but call him? I'll ask Darragh. Maybe Darragh knows.

Next day. Somewhere above Ruth [Kligman] called. Deep depression, as well she might, her beautiful white boxer is dying of kidney failure. The Sunday night I spent with them in a ritzy animal hospital (it costs more than Payne Whitney) I won't soon forget. Anyway, I stopped writing to you and trotted down to 14th Street. Hard to say which looked more wasted, Ruth or the dog (Ruth had decided not to have her put down, but to bring her home and let her pass out naturally). After I'd heard a good deal more than I care for about reincarnation, I decided Ruth needed to get out of the house and I needed my dinner. First I had to read something she'd written, then she did her make up for several days, while I pulled the dog's tits, which we both enjoy (and Ruth thinks is a "little bit funny"), but I finally got her into Duff's. Wonderful what a couple of cocktails, some wine and pasta and veal chops and chocolate mousse will do for a girl. She was quite perky when she hit the street—we went hunting for blue sneakers for me, no luck, and luckily Discophile was closed so I did not arrive home totally broke. Now I've just had a chat with the little lady and I'd like to kill her. Never mind why. It makes no sense; it never does.

Tonight, a birthday dinner for Bob Dash at Darragh's. Next Tuesday Aladar and Marilyn[809] are giving a fiesta for John (you can't imagine the fuss that's being made over the little dear, but he's being sweet about it, only a little anxious about being drummed into the establishment). Oh dear, what a drag it is going to a bash and not drinking or even smoking grass. The grass I don't miss, but the booze. But I don't have to spell that out for you! I hope you told Rodrigo how much I liked his painting. They stay very vividly in my mind. Are you working? What's your plan—France, and then New B. in August?[810] I'm spending July and August with my mother. I don't want a New York summer, and, when my mother dies, I don't want to feel that I treated her like an utter shit. John is a much better son than I am. Now, Dr. Weitzen is whistling in the wind. I love you and miss you. Come back some day soon.

Jimmy

TO VINCENT KATZ

New York, New York

Oct. 17 77

Dear Vincent,

If you are still in the market for a poem of mine, see enclosure. One favor: if you're not going to use it, would you let me know?

It was very good of you to come visit me in that odious hospital: it was a real surprise and I enjoyed it.

My new address and phone number are

> J.S.
> 1106
> 201 West 74th St
> NY, NY 10023
> phone: 799 7214

809. Marilyn Fishbach, Fishbach Gallery owner.
810. Anne Dunn had homes in the south of France and New Brunswick, Canada.

You might divulge that to Ada, while telling Alex that I think what he's done at that 42nd Street corner is a fucking sensation.

All the best,

Jimmy

FOR VINCENT KATZ

I sometimes think that I
live surrounded by boors
and ill-mannered clods
who, when you try to
help them—'The word
is pronounced Kam-ELL-ia'
or, 'No, I do not want a
SIGH-kl-mn: I want a
SICK-l-mn' go 'Hnhn?'
and scratch their rump
and pick their nose. Yes,
I have definitely given
up on them. And so it
was a most particular
joy when you, a young
man of seventeen, came
to visit me in St Vincent's,
(that makes him your
patron saint, but don't
let it go to your head)
and I made contact
for the first time
with the young young
guys and they like my
poetry and want it for
your magazine. I accept
with rapture: look, here
is a poem you may have
but there is a catch
to it (there almost

always is as you will
shortly learn) which is
I have misspelt Sir
Leslie's name: cut off
the s and make Stephans
into Stephan and all will
be hunky dory. And yet, and yet . . . .
You notice that the
poem I am sending you-ward
is called Labor Day. Nothing wrong
with that except there
is: I have already written
and published a poem of
that name and I like to
think that I don't chew
my cookies twice, ma as
they say in bella Italia
a new name is needed for
the poem. I would like it
(if this is agreeable to
you) that you think up
some other titles and
let me chew one (how's
that again?) and I will
decide which one to use.
No cop outs: 'Poem' will
not do. Vincent you are
totally great (as Larry
Fagin would say) and I
look forward to hearing
from you soon. Love
to Ada and Alex. Ciao.

JIMMY SCHUYLER
NOV 7 77

TO [ ]⁸¹¹

September 25, 1978

We are going to do a one-shot magazine, and would like very much to have something by you in it. Our plan is to have one poem (drawing) per poet (artist) so send your best poem (drawing) to either address below.

Sincerely,

James Schuyler
Charles North

James Schuyler   Charles North
2120 Broadway   251 W. 92 St.
New York, NY 10023   New York, NY 10025

TO ANNE DUNN

[East Aurora, New York]

August 16, 1979

Dearest Anne,

Thank you for your letters. I'm sorry I've been such a correspondent, but there hasn't been anything. Did you know that John bought a house? It's up the Hudson in a town called Hudson, and, from photographs is a Victorian bijou. David spends more time there than John does. I haven't been there yet but doubtless I will when he gets some furniture.

I'm in East Aurora (NY) visiting my family. My mother now lives with my brother and his folks. She is very depressing. She is eighty-nine, almost blind and her memory is gone. She asks the same questions over and over: "Where is Michael? Is he at work?" "He's traveling." I've contracted to stay here another week but I don't know if I can take it. Boredom reaches new depths.

---

811. This letter solicited poems and drawings for the magazine *Broadway*. Although Charles North was, as he has said, "the junior partner," he did all of the production work. The perfect-bound, glossy magazine appeared with a cover by North's wife, Paula, in 1979. Ten years later *Broadway* 2 appeared. This issue carried poems by Schuyler and North, who had thought it classier to leave themselves out of the first issue.

You aren't the only one who has had a work block. I've been shameful, but there doesn't seem to be any way out of it. Since I've been here, a few days, I've been writing, which is the desperation of my setting. As a matter of fact I'm writing a poem called, "A Few Days." Anything to get away from the family. My brother [Fred Ridenour], whom I like, is one of the grouchiest men alive. Nothing suits him; everything is going from bad to worse, just as he expects it to.

Will you come to New York after Bathurst? I hope so. I miss you something awful.

My sitter, Eileen Myles,[812] worked out very well. I have her trained to bring me the *Times* and make French toast for my breakfast. Unfortunately, she went to Colorado, and I have a less simpatico girl with the euphonious name, Shelley Kraus.[813] But Eileen will be back next month.

Is Francis [Wishart] there? I hope he can work out his visa, he would be a real addition to the New York social scene. I see him at little dinners at the Hazans (who *never* invite me to Water Mill).

This is dull stuff, and no substitute for the real thing, seeing you.

All my love, Jimmy

TO JOE BRAINARD

[Hotel Chelsea, New York][814]

Labor Day, 1979

Dear Joe,

Thanks for your lovely letter: we should never let our summer letter exchange lapse. Our letters are the stuff classics are made of! I would still like to make a book of them — your letters and mine. What do you think? I could do the editorial part, so it wouldn't be much of a chore for you. The only catch is that when Anne Porter sent my books and records to me everything is in unmarked cartons. Now the other question is: did she unpack the filing cabinet in my

---

812. Eileen Myles (b. 1949), poet and short-story writer who worked as his assistant for a period during his stay in the Chelsea Hotel.

813. Rochelle Kraus, poet.

814. On May 24 Schuyler's friends Ruth Kligman and Anne Dunn moved him into room 625 of the Hotel Chelsea, where he spent the rest of his life. Today a plaque is affixed to the front of the Chelsea commemorating Schuyler's residence there. Unless otherwise noted, all future letters were written from the Chelsea.

room? I think it's locked. And if so that's where your letters . . . I'm going out to Southampton soon and will look into this. I have a funny feeling that you're already in New York, recalling your resolve not to get caught in the Labor Day turmoil.

Did you get the book of Fairfield's art criticism. *Art In Its Own Terms*?[815] I always liked his writing, but I had no idea of what the cumulative effect would be. His essay on Joseph Cornell makes me ache to see a show of his boxes.

I saw a very funny movie: *Cage aux Folles*.[816] Here I rest: it's dinner time. Down to the Spanish restaurant for melon and clams "Quixote," which means a red sauce.

Now it's tomorrow. Almost time for lunch! Melon and a slice of quiche. So the days go by.

Have you read the Benson "Lucia" novels?[817] They're very funny and frothy light. I wish he had lived longer and written more. Trollope is going to be my next project. He lived forever and wrote endless novels. When I read a book I really like I want there to be another book by the same author: reading Henry James is like that: always more to come.

Call me when you get back: my number is: 243-4700 (the Hotel Chelsea), ext 625.

My love to Kenward,

love, Jimmy

TO GEOFFREY YOUNG [818]

Aug. 19, 1981

Dear Geof [sic],

If you *really* want to publish something by me, how about making a small chapbook of the enclosed? They—these pages—just came to light among some books and papers I got out of storage. I like them: they relate closely, and are very like the poems I wrote at that time, published in *The Crystal Lithium* and

---

815. *Art in its Own Terms—Selected Criticism, 1939–1975*, edited and with an introduction by Rackstraw Downes.

816. *La Cage aux Folles* (1978), French farce directed by Edouard Molinaro.

817. Edward Frederick (E. F.) Benson (1867–1940), British novelist who published six Lucia novels between 1920 and 1939, spoofing polite English society.

818. See glossary.

Hymn to Life. At one point in the 6os I dried up hopelessly about writing one summer in Maine. I decided that I would force myself to write *something* every-day, and that would be a weather diary. A few pages from it—the Maine diary—are in my book, *The Home Book* (I think I sent you a copy? If I didn't, say so, and I will. Do you have *Freely Espousing* and *The Crystal Lithium*? Yes, you have *Freely*, I remember, but what about *Crystal*? If you don't have it, again, say so and I'll send. I don't have any spare copies of *Hymn*) under the title of "For Joe Brainard." There is more, I think, but still in storage. I have room for next to nothing here, except a giant nude painting of Bill Berkson. If you want to do it, I suggest a plain sky blue cover, without design, just type. The rest I leave up to your fertile imagination, assuming you want to publish this. You said you wanted to publish only top Schuyler, and I think some of these scribbles are that (all my works are scribbles).

I just had a lovely experience: someone I loved and trusted and who worked for me a few hours a day got on heroin and ripped me off, but good. Forged checks on his sister-in-law's account, which he cashed here at the hotel, which bounced and for which I'm now responsible, stole mss. and letters from poet friends, like Frank O'Hara and W. H. Auden, and sold them to rare book deal-ers. Most of those are now recovered, except the O'Hara letters, especially dear to me: I really loved Frank, and I can only recover the letters by buying them back from the collectors who have already bought them. I'm by no means the only friend he victimized. "He" is now in California, kicking the habit; I hope, for his sake. "You must feel vandalized and raped," my shrink said. Precisely. Never trust blondes from Sherman Oaks.

While you were sporting in Wisconsin (Why Wisconsin? Are you from there?)[819] I was doing same in Marion, Mass., on Cape Cod. Fun, except the first night I was there I rolled out of bed in my sleep and sprained my toe! August '81 is definitely not my month.

What are you reading? Writing? Publishing? Are you surfing?

I don't think in my last I really expressed my gratitude for your supportive-ness of me as expressed in $$$$. You're quite a guy; and I am grateful.

Love to your wife and chilluns, and my best to you—

Jimmy

PS Please don't lose the mss. enclosed: they are the originals, which I like to keep (I do have a Xerox, however, in case you're moved to burn these).

819. Geoffrey Young's in-laws had a house in Wisconsin.

TO GEOFFREY YOUNG

Sunday

Dear Geoff,

Help! Two more pages of the '71 diary have turned up among quite inappropriate papers. I enclose them. Insert wherever fancy moves you. If you do decide to publish these, please take off "Pages from a Diary" from the title. That that is what is what it is will, I trust, be self-evident.[820]

No news, which, the way things have been going for me lately, is indeed good news. And you?

A while ago I got hooked — no, not on junk, on a cultured milk product you may know called kefir, sort of a cross between buttermilk and yogurt and comes in delicious fruit flavors. I got so that was what I was living on, and did I put on the pounds! While I was up on Cape Cod I got a good look at myself, naked, in a full-length mirror! Oiks! I have now kicked kefir and subsist on two slices of toast (breakfast) and a honeydew melon (dinner). I've already shed a little, but am not yet Slim Jim. Oh well, why not level with you? Yesterday I broke down and had some bacon.

My friend (Tom Carey)[821] who ripped me off called from L.A. He's getting a job out there, living with his folks (his dad is the actor Harry Carey, much employed by John Ford),[822] kicking the habit and going to see a therapist. He has already gone that road once before, when he was heavily into speed. Since I am hopelessly in love with him (though not him with me) I am, of course, glad. So everything turns out well in the end!

Now I'll go cultivate my window box — or would if I had one.

My best to the folks.

and to you,

Jimmy

---

820. In 1982, Young's press, The Figures, published the diary *Early in '71* with a sky-blue cover.

821. See glossary.

822. Harry Carey, Jr. (1921–2012), was a member of the John Ford stock company. He appeared in many of Ford's movies, including *She Wore a Yellow Ribbon, Rio Grande*, and *Cheyenne Autumn*. His memoir about working with Ford is titled *Company of Heroes* (1994).

TO TOM CAREY

July 28, 1938
(oops: well, the depression seems
about over but things don't look too
good in Europe)

Dear Boychick,

As the song says, I'm going to sit right down and write myself a letter
And make believe it came from you . . .

Nearly two weeks, and you've written me one teeny-weeny, itty-bitty letter! I was talking about you with Dr. Newman[823] yesterday and he said, "I'm afraid, Jim, that in the orchard of life you've picked a lemon." "No no doc: Tom's a good boy." "Jim," he said with stern Jewish rectitude, "I can spot a BAD BOY a mile off . . ." So you see.

Speaking of the Doc: my blood sugar number is down from 500 plus to 297, and my sight is pretty much normal. Now and then things look a little funny, like the building across the street, which looks pretty funny anyway.

John's [Ashbery] getting out of the hospital today, and it's his birthday! He's 108. Why don't you send him a belated birthday card? 440 W 22nd, as though you could forget, since you enjoyed working for him so much more than you did working for me. Sniff. They put him in a new invention, which he says was like being shot from guns like puffed wheat, and it turns out his spine is OK. The abscess in his shoulder was dissolved by being fed anti-biotics intravenously. So next week she's off to Ireland and the Gorey festival. But we're going to see each other before she goes.

And Darragh's birthday was last Sunday. *She's* 44.

Helena's back—but I told you that. She went to see Alice [Notley], and was very upset: as she said, "Ted [Berrigan] was always there." Her Lama friends were thrilled by *Return of the Jedi*:[824] it seems one of the little creatures speaks Tibetan!

I've gotten very, very bored with the tube, and scarcely watch it. Nothing but re-runs and movies too dopey to think about. I do watch the news (the divine

---

823. Dr. Daniel Newman (1947–1994), Schuyler's physician from 1983 until Schuyler's death. Newman's skill in diagnosing and prescribing treatment made the poet's final years among of his happiest and most productive. Schuyler's *Selected Poems* is dedicated to Newman, in gratitude.

824. First of the *Star Wars Trilogy* (1983), directed by George Lucas.

Chuck Scarborough), and *Hill Street Blues*, of course, but that's about it. Like to buy a nice TV set? And there's nothing on HBO.

Here's a joke from junior high: A traveling salesman asked a farmer to put him up for the night. "Sure, but you'll have to sleep with my daughter: she's blind." So he got in bed and began to screw her. The girl felt around and found his balls and said, "Aren't you going to put these in?" "No: this goes in, but not those." The girl said, "You wouldn't kid a poor little blind girl, would you, mister?"

Now get some ink. Take the cap off. Get a clean sheet of paper. Dip your dick in the ink and make a print. When it's dry send the print to me. You know how I dote on ink dipped dick. Just like Oscar and Andre and Jean.

It's much harder to fill up the page with this close spacing, so I won't try. You haven't called me no not even once: what a terrible fellow! All the same, I miss you and love you,

all the best,

Jimmy
The Old Coot

TO JOE BRAINARD

July 29, 1985

Dear Joe,

I often think of writing to you, but the letter writing impulse seems to have left me. A lot of it is due to not going to the Island anymore: somehow it was a wonderful place to receive mail, your marvelous letters most of all. And there's something especially enchanting about letters that have to come by mailboat, their arrival announced by the toot of a nautical horn.

Tom and I lately spent a few days out at Darragh's which was, of course, delightful. Although my hope of escaping the heat and especially the humidity of this rather awful NY summer was not altogether realized: it was a shock to get off the train into the same 90 degrees from which we had fled! But it was better at D's, and better still at night. Darragh painted, Tom went to the beach and sun tanned, and I sat under the butternut tree and wrote and read (a very funny 1890's novel I think you'd like, *The Diary of a Nobody*, by George and Weedon Grossmith. It's sometimes around in Penguin). And ate so well: Darragh is one of the few who can make me like vegetarian cooking.

Helena [Hughes][825] is in Ireland, vacationing and visiting her family: visits which sometimes turn out very, very badly. But I spoke to her yesterday and this year seems to be going better than usual. She promised to bring me the newly discovered Barbara Pym,[826] which you no doubt have already read three times. I can never remember its name: Crompton Shitfuck, or something.

I called on Anne Porter, who was embedded in small blonde grandmothers—help!—that should be grandchildren. And I was put into a tantrum by the way the new owner of Fairfield's house has cut down trees and uprooted *my* roses and put in the tackiest suburban "foundation planting" one could imagine. It inspired me to write a poem called "Horse Chestnut Trees, Roses, and Hate,"[827] in which I put a curse on him. I expect him to keel over any day now.

I also saw Alvin Novak and Syd Talisman at the pretty house Syd designed. Alvin showed me a brochure which had reproductions of John Button's drawings of the male (need I say?) nude. What they most disclosed was John's intense involvement with BIG DICK. I decided I prefer his study of the Pan Am Building.

I'll bet you are brown as a nut! And is it true that la Hornick has commissioned a colab. between you and K. [Kenward] for which you must produce 70 drawings?[828] I think it had better rain up there so you can go inside and get busy. . . .

The radio just said that the humidity is 100%—but why do I keep bitching about it? I have an excellent air conditioner: in fact at the moment I am not wearing one stitch: not really a very appetizing sight.

I know you don't "do" TV in NYC, but what about Apple Hill? If you do, I hope you catch *Miami Vice* and the divine Don Johnson. Did you know that Daniel Travanti of *Hill Street Blues* is gay, and very promiscuous? This is said—*on the best authority*—to make Veronica Hammil (Hamill?) who gets to kiss him quite a lot, feel rather itsy-itsy.

A great deal of love to KGE from Big North—what an age since I played a nice game of bridge! I don't think I could add up a hand.

825. Helena Hughes (b. 1951), poet. She worked as Schuyler's assistant from late 1979 until 1986. During this time she and Schuyler collaborated on the unpublished novel *In County Wexford* and together wrote the poems in their book, *Collabs with Helena Hughes* (Misty Terrace Press, 1980). Schuyler dedicated the poems "Lilacs," "Tomorrow," and "November" to her.

826. Barbara Pym (1913–1980), British novelist whose *Crampton Hadnot* was published posthumously in 1985.

827. When he published the poem Schuyler dropped "and Hate."

Do write, if art and sunbathing permit.

love,

Jimmy

PS Which is your favorite B. Pym? Mine is *Some Tame Gazelle*: I love stout but stunning Belinda in her chic uncomfortable shoes; and everybody else. The only one I feel so-so about is *Excellent Women*: I can't abide that artsy-tartsy couple who are on stage much too much.

Johnny Carson says killer bees are so mean they sting you without any foreplay!

I recently re-read *The Champ*,[829] taking equal pleasure in text & pix.

Just spoke to Tom who sends love—is he looking great!

TO DAVID TRINIDAD [830]

some fuckin' date in Sept.
a Monday, for sure [831]

Dear David,

I think you should know that during an all too recent visit at St. Vincent's Psychiatric someone disguised as a black nurse entered and said to my visitor, "This old man has one dirty mouth," perhaps referring to some totally unremembered wipe-out event—surely I didn't make a pass at a lady? After all, my faithless friend, Tom Carey, never seems to notice my unsought advances, except to reject them: which is fine with me, so long as he give up his plan of spending a month in Venice next spring. What an ugly dump. As for St V's, I highly recommend the therapy as the best in NYC or vicinity (and I *know*), provided your insurance or medicaide or secret bank account can cover $600 a day . . . for say, a minimum of 3 weeks, rising to a possible 3 months. It is a short term hospital. And that is enough.

Please, would you for possible self-benefit, send copies of—help, sudden

828. Lita Hornick of Kulchur Press commissioned the collaboration, published under the title *Sung Sex*.

829. A collaboration by Kenward Elmslie (poem) and Joe Brainard (drawings), published by Black Sparrow Press and reprinted by Geoffrey Young's The Figures press.

830. See glossary.

831. September 2, 1985.

411

blank on title of second book, somehow hidden from me in distracting mountains of LPs sorted into Classic, Pierre Fourier in unaccompanied cello pieces by Bach, Soul, White Soul, Garden Variety Soul (I am a Brook Benton freakout)—Duke Ellington's Greatest Hits is on the turnable (hunh?)—turntable— so send 1 copy of book, with brief card or note, "sent at suggestion of JS," to: (editor and translator of poems of mine published by Gallimard in Paris in 20 *American Poets*—along with Ashbery Stein etc. *not* O'Hara, how odd):

> Dominique Fourcade
> 17 rue de Rochefoucauld
> 75009 Paris, France

(don't ask questions, do it)
To my editor at Random House, who is also poetry editor of the *Paris Review*:

> Jonathan Galassi
> Random House
> 201 East 50th St
> NY NY 10022

(I cannot find my reading glasses so I hope the above is correct. It is.)

When submitting to the New Yorker address same to Howard Moss, say "sending at suggestion of JS", sit back and wait for nothing to happen. When it does, John Ashbery and I find it not unenjoyable to relax over our Lipton's while reviewing the bank balance and leap to stardom (Miss JA recently received a MacArthur grant of $300,000 causing me no pain until I learnt it was all tax exempt upon which I emitted a loud yelp).

I trust you can make some sense of this mish-mash. I sure envy you living in gay L.A., where, if the TLS is to be believed, the current architectural fashion is: the Drop Dead effect and Hairdresser's Baroque. How quaint.

I have written a poem for your delectation which I will send as soon as A) I learn to type, and B) find my frigging glasses. They are probably, as usual, up my butt, as they usually are. Or up Tom's. Would they were. (I should warn you that during a hospital stay a black nurse, said of me to a visitor. "This old man has one dirty mouth." OOPS!

As Miss Master (W. H. Auden) used to say, "The cheek!"

Thank you for writing the poems you do. I feel sincerely privileged to read them.

love,

Jimmy

PS (Good grief: more letter! More stamps! There are none. Who around here is supposed to buy the stamps? Oh. You is it. Well strip while I put on there—perhaps these—knuckle-dusters etc. In case you're wondering how knuckles taste, fried, well I can't tell you as a recent convert to—what? Deism? Oh yes—vegetarianism. You don't believe me? Wait until some far distant date when you read the poem composed early this a.m. before proceeding to shrink and so on: "Some Half-Forgotten Cookbook by the Sea." The poem is utterly delightful and begins, "That sea urchin you just stepped on:" "An exercise in my New Manner which resembles the Old Guff . . . " Hope you enjoy "exercise" good grief . . . one of my Roomies during recent Sequestration (Angel: real name) remarked: "When I saw you naked last night I thought of an old goat." Talk about fresh!

To be secret—oops—serious, I am in secret devising with Random House an anthology of—younger? Little known? Must age always be a criteria? criterion? You choose. I'm tired. In strictest confidence, I would like your personal choices. Certain people you can skip, having already decided—a confidence—about Dennis Cooper, Bill Berkson (could 666 oh my god . . . I mean) forget paren: what was I going to say? During your delightful blow j—no no not you some other unskilled . . . Ahem. Included will be: yourself, Eileen Piles, your greatest admirer outside self and Tom, who doubtless has a base motive, Harry Mathews (who he? well he lives in France and looked a lot more stunning before all that hair fell out: forget it) Fairfield Porter (Hunh? Yes) . . . Perhaps Geoff Young and wife Charlotte[832] . . . hold on, perhaps I have enough already—no send suggestions: then there's Barbara Guest. Yes I know she's old as the hills but she is little known in proportion to *my* estimate. Now I must cut and run to the fridge and get out and heat up the leftovers from last night's rosemary-scented white beans: take beans forget it. You probably wish you'd never heard of me. Well up yours, Kate. Perhaps that nurse was right. Yours truly & sincere & so on regards, I beg to remain, myself when possible, as ever,

Jimmy

P.S. Found book could not remember title of and am once again enjoying "Wednesday" etc. madly—alas
P.S. Tom C reluctantly discloses he's not going [to] Venice but [to] Tuscany. Which could take *years*! My dear!

832. Geoffrey Young was then married to the novelist and poet Laura Chester.

TO DARRAGH PARK

Tuesday Sept 17 1985

Mistake try to write letter in semi-dark! Regret inferior Xeroxes; cause, Jewish holy day

Dear Johnathan, (oops—typing error)

My antique Olivetti gives often me a hard time.

Dear Darragh,

As you can see (I can see a good deal better now I have solved the eternal question of, where are me effin' glasses: they were of course, like the Purloined Letter in plain sight playing cache-cache in their own wicked way) etc.

I am sending you a bundle containing (not the poem enclosed) new poems: Tuscany* (3 pages of verse addresses ever-youthful (to) cointing (obviously I cannot type so forget it) advice of what to look it when there; "Mood Indigo"; One of my Favorite Gardens; David Trinidad's address in LA for letter given me by TC; a recent diary (2 pages) entry from which you can deduce anything you please including my wish to stage a certain scene in *The Duchess of* Malfi[833] (Helena saw a now already famous current production of same in Lodon (a.k.a. London) *basta*, what else? Oh yes a recently discovered by me, in this dwelling, 4 page article on me (Freely & short poems from you—dedicated book with pointless (unh-huh) reference to long poem (I am not and never was in a Master relationship with Frank O'Hara—but read it and think of whatever you please and learn, as I did, such an idea of the importance of shit oh I remember (hunh) "Salute" and where it stands in relation to my subsequent poems; etc. also project in form of letter to Anne Porter for Fairfield study (does your name appear? Am I planning to come out of retirement and review your show in Exquisite review-trek for Betsy Baker's eyes only if she has not moved on from present post: it will appear somewhere believe me or my name isn't [Ruth] Felicity Kligman; what else oh see all enclosed and make up your mind. I'm tired.

Read enclosed and know sincerely I love you and am now a convinced vegetarian who discovered at cheese shop the hideous fact that they vend Gourmandize a calorie—I wonder what I was saying: oh yes said shop offers 2 buck all evening snacks and have been ordered by giddy Doc Newman while enjoying protein richness while enjoying new-you oriented vegetarian regime; Hy Weitzen also approves. What else, why nothing except correct Xerox from *New Yorker* then send me not them for any small alterations so on to be sent in page

833. John Webster's (1580–1635) classic Jacobean tragedy.

proofs of the poem no doubt soon to be published (now I must stop listening to Brook Benton in favor of late, great Duke Ellington conducting his own Greatest Hits. Well, have to split now and go out and buy garlic for supper of pasta with garlic and oil-sauce style Miss Jimmy. I *loved* the Fairfield review in the *Times* so very much, as perhaps only you can understand. Love thee madly (ho ho), you'll be hearing more soon. Read enclosed. I meanwhile am patiently tapping my foot until next Tuesday at 9:30 a.m. when I will be in Daniel's examination room. Can hardly wait. Meantime am recovering rusty cooking skills. You are indeed my best friend; no other way.

    kisses to you and Mme O,

Jimmy

found enclosed postcards addressed you & never mailed—who forgot to mail them? Not me—. Enjoy and forget—I prefer the Daumier wash drawing to rabbit: Oriane[834] and I have *seen* a rabbit. Perhaps you were too busy to notice—?
   *later

TO ANNE PORTER

Sept. 17, 1985

Dear Anne,

Believe it or not this is a *business* letter enclosing an encoded second letter which you will understand.

My publisher, Random House, is willing to consider my proposal of a work, by me, concerning Fairfield and his paintings. It would take the form of: my recollections of strictly painterly matters: remembered conversations and remarks, posing, reading aloud while posing (everything from Marc Bloch[835] to *Richard II*); etc. possibly other similar pieces by Jane, Darragh, Joe Brainard, John A., Elaine (de Kooning) if available, possibly others (much depends on available space); black-and-white photos by me of Fairfield in numerous action

834. Park's dog. "My name is Oriane / the lurcher: / half whippet, half border collie," from Schuyler's poem "Oriane."

835. Marc Bloch (1886–1944), French historian and authority on medieval feudalism. He fought in the French Resistance and was executed by the Nazis. Schuyler may have read aloud his book on wartime France, *Strange Defeat*.

painting specific paintings which will then be reproduced in color in back of book (the number of color plates vastly effects the cost of the volume: I imagine nothing in the Skira line, or so-called cocktail-table book, but one which can be held in the hand and read); also uncollected articles and reviews located in *Art News* and elsewhere by: myself (who else), Whitney Balliett's brilliant, tender *New Yorker* piece[836] (a star performance: *if* available for publication before publication in a collection of his own), Hilton Kramer's exclamation of surprise upon discovering what everybody else knew already: that Fairfield is a great colorist (somewhere in said tome I would like to spell out, if possible, this development over the years: at the moment this seems quite impossible) John Ashbery's *Newsweek* review of the retrospective, the review in last Friday's *Times* of the current show at Hirschl & Adler (which I plan to see next week) — this part will be highly selective.

You can see the problem of production cost etc. Therefore I am sending Xerox copies of this letter to: Maxine Groffsky, my agent and former editor: Jonathan Galassi, my editor*: and Mr. Balliett.

*at Random House

I expect to hear from you when I do: no rush. Or when I see you, which may be within a month or next spring. I still enjoy my annual present: *The New Yorker.*

love,

Jimmy

All biographical matter I [ ] to sort & assembled in 1971 in curriculum vitae, plus necessary new material up to '75. Already collected criticism. [ ] Also letters which were underway.

TO ANNE PORTER

Saturday

Dear Anne,

I will say this as simply as possible: in a recent "visionary episode," which occurred since I saw you last, I felt I was protected by the wind of the wings of your

836. Whitney Balliet's review of the Fairfield Porter retrospective at Boston's Museum of Fine Arts, "An Akimbo Quality," appeared in the March 14, 1983 *New Yorker.*

prayers: they came like angels to me: I went back of beyond, further and further and saw that there was nothing to see: does God have a face like a human being? How silly: what I saw was the creation of the world out of fiery whirling gases which gradually formed a crust and I was privileged to see the ultimate mystery: the seed out of which sprang everything. And where did it come from, who created it? Who but God? Who is He? Need anyone ask, has anyone the presumption to interfere? The infinite mercy, the uncorruptible love, for everyone, anyone everywhere. And there was so much more. I cannot help but thank you that I was allowed a vision of which I am so utterly unworthy. Thank you, dearest Anne. I owe everything to you: and to God and the Catholic church to which I have never felt closer, that there is hope for me yet, that it is not too late: it is never too late: there is an infinity of time.

I hope to see you soon, when I may be visiting Darragh's with Helena.

I do not regard personal letters as literature: do what you feel best.

love,

Jimmy

TO DAVID TRINIDAD

Oct 5, 1985

Dear Cutie Pie,

(Sorry: I couldn't resist. Actually, I'm not like that at all . . . I mean—oh well ask Tom and Eileen [Myles]: they can tell you the full hideous truth.)

Help! Am in receipt yr latest stop did I really and truly never send you the enclosed *poem* written with dedication to you in mind describing actual happening to me trip in D.C. theatre circa me 10 years old . . . can you believe it? Can you believe you were so far from being born that . . . well, I'll be 62 on upcoming November 9th: I adore picture postcards, with greetings. Your friend Tom Carey (I want no part of him except the part I can't have: can you imagine six years of single minded devoted (oops) I mean devotion without getting laid once? Frankly in the age of AIDS I *like* it that way: no way have *I* got *it*. And in plague ridden NYC that's something to count your blessings about. Shudder) anyway Mr Undesirable usually manages to send me one postcard, say of the Villa Getty, with message: "House where I was born Ha! Ha! Joke." I mean I love the child-like in Tom but there are limits. Tom of course was conceived in

417

Eve Arden's[837] house and his first memory is of nearly drowning in Gregory Peck's swimming pool (we Anglophiles call it a swimming bath) — I mean you would scarcely look for *class* in Sherman Oaks but it's true, the Careys are covered with it. And if Mistress Mine TC thinks he's going to LA for one of those endless (to me) ten day stays and is going "in the spring" for God knows how long on a visit to Tuscany where I once lingered for a year: believe me, there is absolutely nothing to look at, as I keep telling Tom.

Meanwhile "hush" about the vaguest possibility of that anthology. But thanks for suggestions: can you cause me — but I see you have already answered my plea and I will, in time, receive poems by Amy Gerstler. I do not share your enthusiasm for [Tim] Dlugos or [Dennis] Cooper, am ready to try Cooper again because of your liking, but as for Tim, oh well, will try him too, grouch grouch. Where in world can I read poems by [Jack] Skelly, [Bob] Flanagan, [Maxine] Chernoff (have heard of) [Elaine] Equi (read some but no opinion), [Jerome] Sala, Harris[838] and "etc." meaning what? I should say my intention, should unlikely come about, not to make a survey of any sort "young" or other, but to offer generous helpings of insufficiently heard voices: you most of all, Fairfield Porter's little known because largely unpublished poetic delights; Barbara Guest — published by uptown publishers yes, but well enough known, no; ditto for Charles North; Eileen but yes, [Alice] Notley maybe well known because frequently published slim books perhaps keep happy few up-to-date; great wildly funny novelist Harry Mathews insanely experimental verse and how! etc. (as you say). Is a picture forming? Would like to include Tom's poems *and* song lyrics *and* collaborative verse written with "I," but the bizarre one refuses.

I quite understand tearful outbursts — I had several when death of Rock Hudson[839] was announced. To say I loved Rock, considered him a great actor (have you ever *seen Written on the Wind?*[840] Or fascinating *Darling Lili*, where Rock runs around in World War I type long undershorts while lovable Julie Andrews

---

837. Eve Arden (1912–1990), comedienne who had a long career on the stage and radio, in movies, and on television, where she is remembered for the title role in the sit-com *Our Miss Brooks*.

838. Poets of Trinidad's generation, several of whom — Gerstler, Cooper, Skelley, and Flanagan — were living in Los Angeles.

839. Rock Hudson (1925–1985), leading man in movies for over thirty years. Hudson was the first prominent gay man to announce having AIDS. His quest for a cure focused national attention on the disease.

840. *Written on the Wind* (1956), highly stylized melodrama directed by Douglas Sirk.

gets, as usual, to sing some more of the World's Worst Music. She has lovely pipes but why sing *that*? Why am I perpetually opening parens I then forget to close. Acute Anxiety Neurosis doubtless. Do I suffer from same? Well Myrtle if that's your idea of *fun*. . . .

If you do not have these books by your devoted admirer, moi, lemme know and will send: *Freely Espousing, Crystal Lithium* (surely I sent already, if not, tough toenails, hardly any left); *Hymn to Life* (maybe), *The Home Book* (when and if I can: contains highly secret rarities), *Early in 71* (tiny weather Diary, will send or maybe not). Novels out of print except *Nest of Ninnies*, will eventually send if I can remember that long.

Am preparing *Selected Poems* (publication indefinite future), and would like your thoughts re must keep forever. Those that must go, I don't want to hear about. So ends my song . . . is it too early to call Tom? Oh what the hell . . .

love,

Jimmy

add to "will send" books below *Morning of the Poem* — of course new A *Few Days* coming to you when ready? Savvy?
PS At moment cannot find any copy poem "Mood Indigo" will send "soon" Regrets (bitter). Found it. New Xerox!!

Next Day, Same Place
Same gay, Same

PS: There is simply nothing wrong with a PS if you keep your mind on the Piss and avoid the Shit. No wonder that black nurse's aide abrupted into my room at Beekman Hospital, jerked her thumb at me and said to Helena, "This old man has one dirty mouth." True and so what? By my time of life you really have to learn how to take it!

(I wish the soprano murderess who is this moment being ruthless with Verdi's "Pace, pace mio dio" — a supreme moment from the last act of incredible *La forza del destino*: oh good here comes the Curse; soprano now retreats to holy cave, enter her brother and quondam suitor, dueling, and Abbot being ineffectual, (Good grief soprano was my well loved Leontyne Price! Look, dearest, some roles just don't suit thee) I forget what happens next: forgiveness, of course, one at least of duelers dies as monks come trooping in (maybe), Abbot gets to reveal his excellent bass, Leonora di Calatravo is not about to marry anybody having sworn a Vow; well it all ends that evening in the Rome Opera House where this one made an ass of himself yelling Brava Brava for the Leonora de C. that night was none other than — are you holding your breath?—Renata Tebaldi.[841] (I can keep this up forever so no swanking about established fact you know every groupette in recent history. Me: "Are any of these made up?" Tom, "No no they're all as real as roses." "Good grief!"

Some things I like about your poems: crystal clarity of language and "diction"; that you understand the vital importance of "enjambment"—where the line turns, that something has to happen there or else nothing happens on purpose (I sometimes leave a dangling "the," proof of the extent to which I don't give a damn); I picked this up with speed of light from Frank O'Hara: I had read *one* poem of his, "Three Penny Opera,"[842] and retreated to elegant sanatorium called Bloomingdale in nearby White Plains (endless tree studded grounds) and wrote a bale of junk out of which *New Yorker* poetry editor (and poet)* fished my all-important "Salute" ("I salute / that various field") which will appear as first or last poem in my *Selected*; your utter denunciation of San Fran sexual perversions—some of which many years ago I thought I enjoyed shudder, a strong, courageous forthright statement of, The Truth: and admire Truth in your work? Baby it's all I care about. Do not think the title *Pavane* a happy choice: calls up for me perhaps wrong image of what's inside; however not important since titles are merely labels that help one find things more easily than say *Poems*; *More Poems*; *Another Helping of Poems*; etc.

Hope you can read monstrous Xerox of "Mood Indigo." I love this poem and am happy it was dedicated to you before I started writing it. Sometime we must have a good cry together. Tom says that's OK with him, so

love,

Miss Monster
Lilian del Gado

*Howard Moss (a sweetheart)

What? Another page. Maybe yes maybe yes. You see, David, I went to the (for me) endless pain of typing, by hand, a "clean" copy of The Poem: which since it's—as you see it's scattered all over the page. Counting spaces is my idea of nothing to do when I could be doing—it matters not, I'll only mention pullin' my Pud', fixing delicious iced Taster's Choice instant iced coffee; listening to Peggy Lee which I am doing: it seems Peggy doesn't want to "Leave Me

841. Giuseppe Verdi's *La Forza del Destino* was first performed in 1862. The American soprano Leontyne Price (b. 1927) is famous for her performances of Verdi, and the Italian soprano Renata Tebaldi (1922–2004) is renowned for singing the role of Leonora di Calatravo.

842. Schuyler read this poem in the issue of *Accent* magazine in which he too had some poems.

Now."[843] In that case, why did she get out of her stretch limo after lastest (hunh?) NYC gig and head back to her California roses? "The bigger the better," quoth she. Anyway, the good Xerox place is closed until Monday and it's Saturday so I send exclusive handtyped version. Try not to get mustard or chili or whatever on it.

I'm going to leave this in the Olivetti until manana; now I'm around the corner to Onini where I'll join best friend, Mr. Elegance, Darragh Park, and long time chum J. J. Mitchell, uhm-hmmm, Frank O'Hara's one time, yes yes. Adios muchchacha. For now.

Here it is pre-dawn again. Delicious meal at Onini's: stuffed baby eggplant and vegetable something, not gnocchi, oh, lasagna. My friend J.J. you would have met with, were you in NY (where you belong) at Meetings of the Program, wit mutual friends Tom or Eileen. I was in quite a turmoil in the head already at St. Vincent's when Tom broke the news to me that J.J. was in Beth Israel dying of AIDS. I found consolation when a gay psychiatric aide (male) told me, "My very, very best friend died of AIDS a year ago." J.J. is in remission, looks still very like his startling handsomeness of so long ago; his only reference (direct) to his fatal condition was, "It's like something you read about that's happening to somebody else." And they say gallantry is dead! Now, my main aim in life is get this detritus into the mail box and off to you. Do write! Do come here for a non-alcoholic visit!

love,

Jimmy

TO DARRAGH PARK

Tuesday Oct 8, 85

Dear Infinite Generosity,

On running across this I thought: why persist in misplacing same and possibility of not conveying it to DAP III when Helena and I arrive unexpectedly (planning to stay until day after New Year; or at least until Boxing Day)? Why indeed? All I know about it is turned up in a "box" containing other treasures: the original of "How about an oak life / if you had to be a leaf?"[844] which I picked

---

843. Peggy Lee (1920–2002), jazz-oriented American pop singer.
844. The opening lines of "Poem" "How about an oak leaf," which appears in *Freely Espousing*.

up in Bill de K [Kooning]'s driveway! Ah, memories, memories: anyway here it is for thy collection of Schyleriana/Katzomania. Looked at under a "raking light" reveals there is a pelci (oops) pencil intention as well as the intention color collage, of a famous book jacket[845] of which, no doubt, you are already tiring . . .

Oof, Clea-el d'Alferez[846] says I must call the pregnancy hot line. Here goes nothing.

As termination day for my DIARY nears (Oct 19, I believe) I am filled with longing, good and hot, not to go on to the next step: editing down and selecting (no, she never revises anything, ever and never: it—everything—flows out of the non-electric "hot and hot" (C. Dickens): well, I do seem always to refer to Daniel [Newman] (sigh) as darling Daniel and guess who as Lovely Tom (that is when I don't dub him Phoebus-Apollo: I mean he's good looking but). Then I'm going to cut all references to illness, doctor visits etc. Well I will keep some of utterly adorable Daniel's (will you ever see him? Better believe it) one-liners: "My mother wanted me to be a surgeon but I don't like to cut" and "I'm gay but I'm not promiscuous" Perhaps simly (simply) strung across the page, as though found in a fortune cookie . . . look, cookie I'll finish painting for the show (which is not until next *April* . . . I mean even Fairfield at his most persistent had time for a game of bridge. Talk about lousy: there was the time when I was his partner and F. was about to play to hand when his brother flashes his hand at me and lo and behold Edward [Porter] had *all* the court cards in lovable huggable Furl's bid . . . and we were playing for a sawbuck a point: what is a sawbuck?)

Why have I started a second page? Maybe to tell that yesterday, in a one-to-one confrontation with ol' Doc Weitzen "call me Hy" I said I valued your good opinion and advice more than anyone's "except of course *your's*, Hy" (lick lick, suck suck). Well, if I were you I would go on swimming at the Pitti-Palace-like-only-bigger Racket Club no matter what Joe Hazan thinks: and do I admire your style, your elegance? Yes, and I don't care about head shapes, you are too much like yourself to resemble even J. J.—then there are the sandals and a (to me) famous train ride with Dads when nobody heading home to Stumpy Mountains was at all taken aback. I think they always knew somehow that one day DAP

845. Schuyler refers to an early version of the Alex Katz cover of his book *Freely Espousing*.
846. Clayelle Dalferes, classical music radio announcer.

(Darragh Park) III was going to show up one day in sandals accompanied by a Negress (unlovely word) and little mulatto (more unlovely yet) DAP IV?

With that thought I depart, because I truly prefer my disc called Heliotrope Rag to anything by JS Bach, surely this is that worst thing, a mirror fugue: oh the news " . . . digging through mud and rubble . . . Little Richard. . . . Good God! Hotel fire . . . oh in Prince George on 28th Street . . ."

farewell beloved

Gloria Vanderbilt Schuyler

TO CARL LITTLE [847]

Oct 8, 1985

Dear Mr. Little

My name is James Schuyler, and if you are still living on West 17th, an ad-dress given me by Robert Wilson) then we are indeed neighbors, for I live at the historic (and far from fireproof) Hotel Chelsea on far from glamorous West 23rd. I am fascinated by an article you published in the *Downtown Review* — uh — some time ago: I always knew there was something special about my poem "Salute" and I had no idea what it was until I read your straightforward state-ment. (That you do not use critical jargon is only one of the pleasures of read-ing you: said pleasures being not unegomaniacal.)

I would have read your article sooner than this summer! had not some of the reviews *and* critical articles been so personally offensive that I stopped reading any and all (I hate anything that may interfere with whatever work is or isn't in progress, including re-reading my own poems). Anyway, before I could write earlier on I had another "visionary episode" which landed me first in Beekman Downtown etc hospital, where I dreamt a dream so beautiful I won't bore you by trying to describe it, then removed to St Vincent's Psychiatric where I spent a mere three weeks, a record for the course.

Despite this, and the non-pleasures of Older Persons Diabetes — to say that I have memorized all the views from pricey Beekman Hospital! my favorite last year this time was a view from the convenience right up Willow Street to treeembedded City Hall and beyond that, the Gothic-enhanced wizardry of the Woolworth Building.

847. See glossary.

Despite anything, I am determined to get to the point. I would like to meet you and talk. How about the possibility of an interview, or better, perhaps, a conversation, about my writing—it could originate in your article, with comments by both of us: or whatever seems mutually suitable. This would be aimed directly at the *Paris Review* where it would form another link in the chain of well-known series on writers about their own writing.

I certainly hope this morsel will tempt you!

May I point out that the "Payne Whitney Poems" were scarcely written "from a hospital bed"! In any decent psychiatric hospital bed may be where the patient wishes to languish the daylight hours away, but he's no way going to be permitted to do so. The poems were written at a desk (whether in longhand or on a portable Olivetti much like this antique I no longer recall), on which were friends' floral tributes including heather, a view to the right through the grill on a window which caught much (it seemed) of the snow from a blizzard, cars moving below like fat dancers, etc.

I hope to hear from you,

with gratitude,

James Schuyler

P.S. I have a new book, *A Few Days* due out from Random House, more or less new. I look forward to presenting you with your OWN HAND SIGNED copy—

TO DAVID TRINIDAD

The first day of spring, 1986

Dear David,

I'm so sorry I haven't written—around Xmas I went into a writing slump, which reached out and engulfed even letters, and it went on and on. So. But here I am again, and I'm sure you'll understand and forgive my lapse.

I *love* your diary poem, "November." And I'm very glad [Raymond] Foye[848] is going to publish it—it's ideal to make a small book. For about a year ('84–'85) I kept a short-entry prose diary—it was kept with intent to publish: a collabora-

---

848. Raymond Foye (b. 1957), writer, editor, and publisher. Schuyler refers to Hanuman Books, a small press established in India by Foye and the painter Francesco Clemente in the 1980s and 1990s. Hanuman published nothing by Schuyler.

tion with my friend Darragh Park, who did the cover for A *Few Days*: he's to keep a diary of drawings, but he's taking his time about getting around to it. Some people are even worse than I am . . . but someday it will shape up, then we hope for luxurious publication. My part, as it stands, is rather repetitive, but when I've made needed cuts, I'll make a Xerox and send it to you.

I'm glad you sent something to the *New Yorker*. Believe me, the fact that Howard Moss wrote a note is a very good sign; they're deluged with submissions—although I sometimes wonder why I give a damn about publishing there, when I see another Amy Clampshit entry. Still, they publish a lot of Auden, Bishop, Ashbery, so, why not? And a lot of people see it, and they pay better than anybody else: for two poems I wrote last summer I was paid $700.

And what have you been up to, and writing? I hope you won't punish me by abstaining from writing to me . . .

Tom has gotten over a bad case of influenza, and was seen at a Whitney Museum preview of an Alex Katz retrospective looking "very handsome" in a tux. Eileen was there, too, in *leather*: perhaps she was making a point? Do you know about Tom's PLAN? He's going to go to Columbia and get a degree, and then go to the Theological Seminary and become a priest. So there. But don't say anything [about] the priest part: I don't know if that is a semi-secret or not, and Tom's always complaining about my big mouth.

Are you grumpy in the morning? I'm not. In fact I'm rarely grumpy at all. But I sometimes explode, if provoked. . . .

love,

Jimmy

TO ANNE DUNN

April 20, 1987 6 A.M.

Dear Anne,

Up and shaved and showered and full of beans and coffee and V8 Juice, Easter behind us and another sweltering summer in front: good morning, good morning.

Lovely to hear from you, though I've known you to be in better cheer—I don't think I really understood how you feel about St. Esteve,[849] but when you say, "a family house without a family," I think I do. Plus, "cripplingly expensive!"

---

849. Anne Dunn's house in Lambesc, France.

425

And the leaks that don't get fixed. . . . I asked Raymond Foye (the nice Young Man who is cataloging my "Archives," with sale in view) about studios here in the Chelsea. They do change hands sometimes: the one Raymond knows best belongs to a photographer, is roughly three times the size of mine, twice as high, big, big, north windows, bath and kitchen (kitchenette, more likely): but, he thinks the rent is "probably" about $3,000.00 per month! Sounds a fortune to me, but I don't know what studios and lofts cost in New York. Or what your top figure would be. Still, it seems more suitable to your needs than moving from one apartment to another apartment in a building like the Hazans. But I probably have mistaken notions about things like "north light" in the age of la feé electricité.

Speaking of real estate, John has already managed to sell his mother's house in Pultneyville: $135,000, and he did it without recourse to an agent, which saves a bundle. Talk about landing on your feet! Or having *"la derrière dans le beurre."* I saw him at a dinner party the other night, given by a pair of young poets named Susan Baran and Marc Cohen,[850] and how the young people did hang upon his lip as he held forth, and did he hold! I'm afraid I've never really adapted to what my John has evolved into over the years, and I find I'm not crazy about the role of straight man, my irritation—well, no: more impatience— mounting as the evening wears on. Gerrit [Henry] was there, already chock- ablock with diet pills and booze and clamoring for pot, which was provided, and Darragh, and Ellen [Oppenheim], always nice to see but rather frazzled with concern about her son who (as you no doubt know) is in de-tox, and John Ash,[851] who wrangled an invitation when he found out what was afoot. When he came in our John made one of his monster faces, and John Ash said, "what a hideous face," to which John said, "I am hideously glad, but not surprised, to see you." When the afterdinner entertainment turned out to be an old movie called, "Killer Bats," I slipped away. The lasagna was nice. So was their cat.

If I told you about my financial situation you might faint. I've sent three Fairfield Porters (two small landscapes and a portrait of me) up to Tibor with the message, "I'll take anything." Tibor recently sold two small—tiny, like mine—landscapes for Edith Schloss, Rudy Burckhardt's first wife, and got $10,000 each, which he thinks is very poor, but I think mine are probably con- siderably better than hers, and hope springs. . . . Of course I don't like to part

850. Susan Baran (b. 1947) and Marc Cohen (b. 1951), poets, husband-and-wife, and or- ganizers of the Intuflo reading series in New York, in which Schuyler read.

851. John Ash (1948–2019), British poet who lived in New York City during the 1980s and 1990s.

with them (except the portrait, I don't really want a portrait of myself around the house), but then, Fairfield sold his deKoonings to put his son Laurence through Harvard, so I have a good example.

This letter seems to be rather squalidly all about money. Perhaps it is on both our minds?

I'm sorry to think you ever thought my life was all that filled with Helena. Yes, I used to like her, but she was here so much (and not, really all that much: two or three hours a day, never in the evening) because Dr. Weitzen thought I was alone too much. It was all for a price and the price was money. At the moment Miss H is tramping over the Himalayas, en route to Tibet (this is a fact, not a fancy). Perhaps Big Foot will get her. As for Tom, yes, I do have a particular feeling for him—just as you, I imagine, have for Jane. Which Jane? I'm not saying. Just don't vanish again, for you are indeed my favorite person, and have been for a long time.

Here are my newest poems, let me know what you think. Making the Gilbert White was taxing, but fun.[852]

Love,

Pabrille

TO ANNE DUNN

June 5, 1987

Dear Anne,

I trust that your silence means your brush is working overtime, and not that some new disaster has struck. . . .

But not being here you missed the worst weather episode ever known to May and June: the temperature in the 90s day after day, with the sinus-stuffing humidity trotting right along. Now it has cooled off, but remains muggy. However tomorrow, they say, may be better, with even a trace of blue. I'm hastily planting petunias (pink ones, that come already in flower) in my window box, and trying to track down a packet of blue morning glory seed: not, exactly, esoteric gardening.

The Senate investigation of the Contra Money Mystery (Where Did it Go?) like "a wounded snake, drags its slow length along." Yesterdays disclosure was

---

852. The Gilbert White poem is "Under the Hanger." The other two enclosed with the letter were "On the Dresser" and "The Light Within."

that a General Secord probably spent a $100,000 on himself, for a sports car and — a visit to a fat farm! Lucky General Secord: he's looking much better.

Speaking of money, Tibor sold one of my little Fairfield's for me, for $10,000, of which he kindly took only 10%. So I paid my rent, Dr. Weitzen and ordered shaving soap from London, though not in that order. The shaving soap came second. Now I'm going to order Andrew Young's *A Prospect of Flowers*, and Redcliffe Soloman's *The History and Social Influence of the Potato*, which Jane Grigson, in *Country Life*, says is the cat's meow. I think I also want her late husband's[853] *The New Flora*, but do I want it 25 pounds worth? I'm not sure.

Like you, when there's a pause in my reading I reach for Evelyn [Waugh]. So having finished Thomas Jefferson's garden notebook, I grabbed *Put Out More Flags*, a gem of gems. Jefferson (what a wonderful man) really liked to get his teeth into a problem and shake it: a mill that continually got flooded out, but determined not to move it; equally determined that the rice planters of South Carolina switch from the Carolina long grain that made them famous to the Italian aborrio, more acceptable to the French market, where it was preferred (with good reason); determined to *make* the olive grow on the Eastern seaboard; and other quirks, most of them utterly sound. Now I am either reading Captain Clark's field notes of the Lewis and Clark expedition, or a book about the Carthusians (loaned by Tom), but am *really* reading the *Oxford Book of Oxford*, with many a funny anecdote. I also read *Dutch Houses in the Hudson Valley before 1176*. Meet Madam Schuyler: "Shortly after Colonel Schuyler's death (supposedly in the summer of 1759) the house on *The Flatts* took fire and the roof and the interior were destroyed. Mrs. Grant in the *Memoirs* draws a graphic picture of the scene of the fire. The "American Lady" (Madam Schuyler) was seated out of doors one warm summer day in the driveway, lined with cherry trees, that led to the house. General John Bradstreet (commander of the British troops stationed at Albany) came riding down the *King's Highway* to call on Madam. He saw smoke issuing from the house and gave the alarm. Madam retained her composure and from her chair under the cherry trees directed the work of rescue."

I'll show you a picture of The Flatts when next you are here. In the meantime,

Much love,

Jimmy

853. Jane Grigson, cookbook writer, and her husband, Geoffrey Grigson (1905–1985), British poet, literary critic, and naturalist.

P.S. anent the enclosed clipping: but where are Bruce, Keith and Kevin? And I think the rage for naming girls Tiffany dates from the days of Audrey Hepburn's hit, Breakfast at Tiffany's. Lisa and Shirley seem quite to have evaporated.

Write! (Please)

Michael and Jessica, You Have Company

Jessica, after six years of finishing second, finally made it to the top. Robert disappeared from the top 10 entirely. And Jonathan was third, with a bullet.

Those were among the results announced yesterday by the City Health Department in the annual compilation of the 10 most popular names for newborn girls and boys. The list, derived from birth records, showed that in 1986 Jessica surpassed Jennifer as the most popular name for baby girls. Jennifer had reigned for the previous six years.

Among boys, Michael led the list for the 23rd consecutive year. Jonathan, which first made it to the top 10 in 1983 and which was seventh in 1985, jumped to third last year. Robert, the No. 10 choice in 1985, was replaced in that spot by Andrew.

One female name also disappeared from the list: Lauren. It was replaced in the 1986 top 10 by Tiffany, which finished in eighth place.

The top 10 male newborn names last year, in descending order were: Michael, Christopher, Jonathan, Anthony, David, Daniel, Joseph, John, Jason and Andrew.

The top 10 female names were: Jessica, Jennifer, Stephanie, Nicole, Christina, Amanda, Melissa, Tiffany and, tied for ninth place, Danielle and Elizabeth.

TO DAVID TRINIDAD

June 12, '87

Dear David—

This was going to be my first letter on my new, new, new ELECTRONIC typewriter. The cheapest Smith-Coronas, without spelling memory—so I can't spell—so what? But the damn thing is too responsive. It suffers from premature ejaculation—touch it, and BANG! I'm used to a typewriter that puts up some fight. Well, time will tell.

What a charming letter your last was. (Tom thinks so too.) I'm glad that

Jonathan [Galassi][854] took the poem for *Paris Review*, and that you're letting him see the mss. Try hard not to be down if it isn't accepted—well, I won't spell out the story of hardcover poetry & hard nose publishers. When I see Jonathan he always asks about you & what you're writing. He *cares*! So don't expect anything & don't give up hope . . .

Very good news about the hike in pay. Personally, I've always liked ties, and used to collect them. Keep your eye peeled in "Nostalgia" shops, and you'll find some beauties.

And don't worry about job/poetry conflicts—spaces will open up. Frank O'Hara wrote his *Lunch Poems* at the Museum of Modern Art & he didn't write them *during* his lunch hour; he wrote them when he got back from lunch. I wrote poems when I worked there too—"December" & "Faberge," for instance. Wallace Stevens used to walk to work in Hartford, making up poems, and then dictate them to his secretary; do you have a secretary? If not, get one.

By the way, after Labor Day send something new to Howard Moss at *The New Yorker*, and remind him that he asked to see more. Howard has been very sick, but is, I believe, on the mend. And why not *Poetry*, the one in Chicago? I think that's a good place to publish, & they pay—you'll need it, for all those neckties!

Raymond is through cataloging the archives and it's now on the market—it may end up in Japan! OK with me: I only care about the top dollar, or top yen, in this case. The *Selected Poems* are scheduled for next spring, we'll see. Darragh Park, who did the jacket for *A Few Days*, will do it again for this.

I can get it together, I'll enclosed a xerox of a poem that was in last week's *New Yorker*.[855] By the way, I liked what you said about the poems I sent you. I would always like to know what you think—.

love,

Jimmy

854. Jonathan Galassi (b. 1949), writer, translator, and editor in chief at Farrar, Straus, and Giroux, publisher of Schuyler's *Collected Poems*.
855. "Horse Chestnut Trees and Roses."

TO ANNE DUNN

Jan. 16, 1988

Dear Anne,

1988 got off to a not too bad start: first, a mysterious something called The Fund for Poetry sent me a check for $5,000, as they — or it — did last January. No idea who finances it. Then the Ingram Merrill Foundation wrote that they would, on consideration, grant me $10,000 provided I would agree to send them a half-yearly *detailed* report of my expenses connected with my project (huh? Writing poetry? "Bought some more paper: $3.29"). Well, I thought about that for a long, long time (they also wanted me to divulge my Social Security number), and then reluctantly agreed.

If every month were like this life would be a piece of cake. Financially.

The weather here has been a bitch: record breaking lows and searing wind-chill-factors. Snow. Freezing rain. Icy sidewalks. Nearly broke my neck. But I don't want to talk about it and you don't want to hear about it.

At the end of January Tom is going to L.A. to see his folks for two weeks, then he's coming back and starting his — I've forgotten the word: postulancy? — out at Little Portion Friary in Port Jefferson, where Leonid [Berman] used to paint. I always think of the Friary as Small Comfort, but he seems to like it. I'm quite calm about it all, to my surprise; even you might say *noble*: like a mother sending her boy off to the trenches. Well, he will be coming in to town two or three days a month, so I guess I haven't got all that much to get worked up about.

Darragh gave a nice dinner party the other evening: the Hazan-Freilichers, the Ashbery-Martory's, the Carey-Schuylers, and — STARRING — Aladar Marberger. He talked and talked and talked and it was altogether a telling impersonation of the Ancient Mariner, especially his lengthy explication of roulette. On the other hand, he was very sweet, and he is certainly most courageous. I wish I could remember some of JA's bon mots for you; but, actually, they were mostly bounced off Aladar's soliloquy, and only a tape recorder could capture them.

Meantime (right now, I mean) your chum Jonathan Leake[856] has come in and gone out to get my lunch (black bean soup and corn bread), so will close.

---

856. Friend of Anne Dunn's who, for a brief period, served as Schuyler's caretaker/assistant.

I don't expect a letter, but a p.c. would be nice. Got any gray view of Lambesc? I live in terror that you won't come in February, or you will and then you'll hide! Don't: I have found a nice new restaurant.

Love,

Jimmy

August T. Baden
Toothpick Producer, 93

INDEPENDENCE, Kan., Jan., 13 (AP)— August T. Baden, a drugstore owner who founded cinnamon-flavored Baden's Hot Toothpicks almost 40 years ago, died Sunday. He was 93 years old.

What began as a treat for neighborhood children in 1949 turned into a big business, with Mr. Baden shipping millions of cinnamon toothpicks around the world.

Mr. Baden closed his drugstore, the Cozy Corner, in 1962 but continued producing cinnamon toothpicks at a plant in Independence until his retirement eight years ago.

TO TOM CAREY

Sunday Feb. 21, 1988

Dear Tom,

I was thinking I couldn't write you today, because I wrote to you yesterday, but if I start it today and finish it tomorrow, that would be OK, wouldn't it? I don't want to give any brothers the wrong idea. Be sure to let me know what day and date I'll see you. I don't know why, just do. (You did let me know.) Daniel [Newman] was sweet yesterday, perhaps because I lost a few. And I finally found out: no, he doesn't have lover! Well. Then I went to Jason's new place in the Village (corner of West 4th & Bank), and got my haircut. I told him about discovering my bald spot, and he said, "What bald spot? You haven't got a bald spot." So I showed him. "*That's* not a bald spot, that's thinning hair. But don't worry, if we ever need to, there are a lot of little things I can do about it. You know, Darragh has a 'highlight' up there we're always contriving about." "Ooohhh?" "You'd better not tell Darragh I told you that." "Never fear . . ." By the way, if you'd ever like to visit Jason yourself, I'd love to treat.

432

I didn't tell you about the quim friend of Bob Dash's who came to interview me for some book she's writing (for Simon & Schuster, I think), on the subject of The New York School, to be told in terms of Frank O'Hara's life. I've about had it with both those subjects, in every aspect. One of her more lively remarks was, "Now, your novel *What's for Dinner?* that's about the Porters, right?" "Good God. no! Where did you get that idea?" "Bob Dash told me. I mean he knew you and the Porters and . . ." "Darragh Park. Wasn't he Bob's lover and now they don't speak and Bob makes those wild accusations against him?" "What wild accusations?" "Oh, that he stole Bob's painting style from him . . ." She was pretty ditzy, and after claiming she knew my work well, asked, "What was the name of that novel you say you wrote with John Ashbery?" I'm tempted to send a scorching missive winging Miss Dash-ward, but first I'll unload these gems on Darragh. That may do the trick.

I saw a mess of movies last night and this yawning: A *Night at the Opera* which Evelyn W (Waugh) thought was so funny, but not me (I hate Groucho); *Gold Diggers of 1937* which First National financed with a plugged nickel. I knew it was no good, but I wanted to see it because I first saw it in Buffalo in 1937 (on New Year's Day) with my chum Bernie Oshei. We were given a lift downtown by a rich cousin of Bernie's, in his silver wraith Rolls-Royce convertible. I was wearing my pork pie hat. It has a truly weird finale, with the dancers on giant white rocking chairs! Then the delightful "Going Hollywood," well worth waiting 54 years to see. It may have been Bing's first starring vehicle: at least Marion Davies had top billing. Hearst must have had some incredible fantasy about her as a dear young thing, or maybe she really always looked 18 to him. She would have been perfectly acceptable as—I don't know what, provided the role was in the vicinity of her real age. There was an incredible shot, the first time she appears in frilly old-time costume, next to Bing: like some aging queen in drag. I had hysterics. But the picture was good, not just a camp, because Bing never stopped singing, one classic after another. Near the end he goes on a bender, rendered by a lot of shots of signs like Joe's Saloon in light bulbs with rows of martini glasses being filled from a silver shaker (everything tilted). Marion finally corners him, rather the worse for wear, South of the Border in a seedy dive. She says her piece and exits. Then he turns on Fifi d'Orsay and sings (my favorite film song), "Temptation! Leading me on! I should have known! You were Temp(warble warble)tation!" Once, during the war, at Virginia Beach, I encountered a rare kind of jukebox, that had film clips, including that. To say that I played it more than once. . . .

At the moment I'm quite sated with entertainment. More tomorrow. Maybe. We'll see.

Horrible Michael Jackson is on the tube, the wind chill factor is o, Barbara is belly up by the radiator, now it's equally appalling Carly Simon (to say that she does not have the moves!) and yesterday you called up. Wasn't that nice: you bet.

Raymond couldn't movie on the weekend, which is OK by me: it seems a dumb time to go, if your life permits otherwise. I saw another great movie, *The Outfit*, with Robert Duvall and Jo Don Baker, to me one of Hollywood's most desirable couples. I'll spare you a reprise, since it was all, "Don't try anything and nobody'll get hurt." Need I say quite a few people got hurt? Even mortally? Including poor Karen Black, but that was because Duvall loved her, even if he did slap her quite hard.

"Don't . . . ever . . . touch . . . that . . . gun . . . again." I also saw 20 minutes of Warren Beatty's *Reds*; too Magnificent-Ambersons-stately. Guess *she* thinks *she's* Orson Welles! Well, pooh. Now Patrick Swayze is singing his song, She's like the Wind ("Blowin' thru my trees" . . . I beg your pardon). What channel *is* this?

I need something good to read, though a new Ed McBain[857] would do. Any suggestions? I keep flirting with that Larry McMurtry[858] you gave me, but it's so thick. Maybe I'll wait and see the flick. I find the flick is almost always better than the book.

"Barbara, have you a message for Tom?" "I'm *sleeping*!" But we're counting the days.

love,

Jimmy

TO TOM CAREY

March 16, 1988

Dear Sticky Buns,

I waited and waited and waited at Dr. Scheers: ears much, much better, I can stop the nuisance ear drops, and don't have to see him again until May 19th!

---

857. "Ed McBain—pseudonym for Evan Hunter—(1926–2005) wrote a series of crime novels-set in New York City. Schuyler probably refers to *The Last Best Hope*.

858. Larry McMurtry (1936–2021), novelist who often writes of Texas and the American West. Schuyler probably refers to McMurtry's novel *Lonesome Dove*.

Boy, does that seem far away. Then I came back and found your delightful letter, and a cost sheet from the Friary for retreats (some of them are rather pricey, no?) ate lunch and now I'm waiting for it to be time to call Dan'l. So. It wasn't until I'd read your letter several times that I realized it was written before I saw you on Monday, not after!

Who is all that bread for? Do you eat it all, or do you sell some? (Darragh and Raymond both want to know the answer to this, too.) As for shit: mine doesn't always look so odious to me, in fact, in corn on the cob season I rather *like* seeing a brown hunk studded with golden kernels. The smell, however, I can do without. It should—and can—be disposed of in such a way as to turn into nontoxic manure. That's what Nancy Straus (Fairfield's sister) manures her lawn with, as her husband Mike used to love to tell everybody, to her great annoyance. Don't you think it's industrial wastes that are the major pollutants of our rills, creeks, streams, rivers, lakes, and oceans? And ponds and meres? A man in Delaware Park in Buffalo once asked young Bernie Oshei to do something really nasty for him. Bernie said no, but he couldn't resist asking what it tastes like. "Fruitcake," the pervert said. A likely story.

Barbara will rarely get out of her chair and come get on the bed, simply because I call her. But if I say, "Bar-r-r-r-ba-r-r-r-a," while slowly opening the drawer in the bedstead under me, she comes a "runnin." Cute? I tell you. Well, maybe I'll add a little to this tomorrow.

St Patrick's Day

And I bet you're gnashing your teeth because you're not in town to see the big parade. Barbara and I are going to be in it. I bought her a green leash and collar and a little green pixie hat I'm going to glue to her head. She'll love it, after the first twenty blocks or so. I'm grooming her for Grand Marshaldom.

It's fiendishly early, but I've already been out for the *Times*, and Ollie's obituary[859] is in it. Since you asked about it last Monday, I send it, though I'm sure someone out there will point it out to you. It's not long, but I think it's remarkably well done, and I'm especially pleased by the first paragraph: it really catches the spirit, and Dobe[860] could easily have been relegated to the role of an also-ran by some dopey re-write man. Practically every fact in the story is news to

859. Olive Carey (1895–1988), actress, actor Harry Carey's wife, and Tom Carey's grandmother.

860. Tom Carey's father, Harry Carey, Jr., was given the nickname Dobe by his father because his hair was adobe colored.

me: why are you such a button lip? Have you ever seen *The Sorrowful Shore*? I yearn to. And *seven* great grandchildren? You mean Cappy has four? I didn't even know she's married. Perhaps she isn't.

During the Requiem out at Little Portion yesterday, I read in the Book of Common Prayer you gave me.

Dinner last night with Barbara G [Guest] at Union SC. Next time I have dinner with her it's going to be on condition that she has done ordering before (goodness, Barbara Carey just rubbed her nose on my bare butt: *quelle surprise!*) I arrive. At one point she told Mr. Kewtie, the waiter, "Goodness I'm behaving just like my mother. I mean my grandmother!" We had a long cat people talk. She said, "Oh your Barbara is a *silver* tabby; or she would be, except for the white. Silver tabbies are very special and rare." Well, I prefer her with the white: don't you? And I got a lecture on how you must never feed a house-bound cat on dry food. I'm supposed to call Beastie Feastie's rival and order something in cans called Optimum (maybe), which they will "deliver right to your door!" Where else? She thinks it's very important I put Barbara on a diet, although her cat is the size of a Rolls Royce Roadster. I can hear Barbara now when I put out the yukky tinned stuff: "So where's ma fuckin' food?" That cat's got a filthy mouth. In the March 21 *New Yorker* in "Talk of the Town," read "Dog Park": Darragh's dog park! I miss you, but your life makes me happy,

your

Jim

TO ANNE DUNN

April 21, 1988

Dear Anne,

Yesterday I went uptown to see Jane's [Freilicher] show again, and Alex's [Katz] which I had not seen. If you'll tell me your sincere thoughts about the latter, I'll tell you mine. He certainly wields a dexterous brush; but not always. Do you remember the one called (I think) "The Meeting"? Two guys against a river background, the whole shown twice, one strip above the other, in slightly different perspective? It probably did not escape your searching eye that the left forearm of the gent on the right is terribly out of drawing—I mean the foreshortening is all wrong. Alex! Alex! What's *happening*? Jane's show looked even better than it did at the opening, as almost any show does, unless, of course, it looks even worse. I particularly love the country views, most of all the gray sky one, with a sun seen through the clouds. The way she paints all the rummage in the middle distance is marvelous. But I wonder why J. [John] Russell[861] found the fish so particularly dead? What did he expect them to be? They certainly look fresh enough. Perhaps he thinks fish should be painted in a kitchen, or swimming around in a bowl, ala Matisse. While I was at Marlborough I took in, but was not taken in by, their sculpture terrace. Good grief! It makes one yearn for a nice Despiau[862] retrospective.

I meant to see the show you recommended at R. [Robert] Miller, but when I got to 41 W. 57 and found myself confronted by a tacky fur store in the kind of building no art gallery has been in since 1952, I realized I should have gone east to the Fuller Building. So I bent my steps further west to the Coliseum bookstore, where I found the new, new ELMORE LEONARD, *Freaky Deaky*, which I think is a kind of dance. The first 30 pages give promise of pneumatic bliss.

The other night I went to a delightful dinner for 8 at 8 at Ellen's [Oppenheim], painters and poets, including Gerrit. I'm fond of Gerrit but before the festivities were over I decided he had a lot of ill-suppressed rage. But when I was home tucked up in bed with faithful Barbara by my side, I decided, no, ill-suppressed petulance.

Love as always,

Jimmy

TO TOM CAREY

April 28, 1988

Dear Tom,

I had a session with Hy on Tuesday, devoted entirely to—unh hunh—that Dia Foundation reading. When I was about to leave he said, "So, when you give that reading, Tom will be with you every step of the way; and so will I." I was feeling quite good when I hit the street and decided, "Yes, I'll do it! I am going to buy a pack of cigarettes when I get downtown, and smoke them." I didn't, but not until I had popped into various shops that sell Benson & Hedges de Luxe— when will the curse be lifted? I even had a dream in which I was God knows where with you: I left, hoping that if you looked out the window you wouldn't

861. John Russell, senior art critic at *The New York Times*.
862. Twentieth-century French neoclassical sculptor.

notice I was swigging on a bottle and lighting up! I guess it was you Wordsworth had in mind when he wrote, "Stern daughter of the voice of God . . ."[863]

Is the reason you haven't written or sent the poem(s) you said you would that you've been so busy writing new poems? I certainly hope so; I can't think of any other acceptable excuse, no I can't, not even writing to David Trinidad (who has been accepted by Brooklyn College) . . .

Barbara has a new trick: sitting in my lap! She would never do it before, but she has for the past three days—and why does she always wait until I have a sandwich in one hand and *Country Life* in the other? She's such a big girl; but slimming.

After saying I wasn't going to eat at Chelsea Central anymore I had lunch there Monday with Trevor Winkfield! I thought our date was for Wednesday, but he showed up Monday and said I was mistaken (I wasn't) so I didn't have time to make a reservation at Union SC, as I intended. But I rather like eating lunch there (oysters and a hamburger) so, what the hell. But dinner, I hope not!

Did I tell you I lost 4 pounds?

The police kicked in the door of a black guy down the hall and around the corner from me—spooky—and evicted him and his two cute little kids. The place was solid cat shit, which is odd, since the room opens on the balcony. What a great place to live.

I told Hy that at the end of my reading, I want you to rush up with a bucket of Gatorade and dump it over my head!

I love you even if you don't write to me; perhaps just a *little* less.

oh well, *all* my love, Jim

TO ANNE DUNN

June 29, 1988

Dear Anne,

If only you were here! For no particular reason—I just wish you were. Jane [Kitselman][864]—yours—called to thank me for my book, and said you would be

---

863. From William Wordsworth's "Ode to Duty"—"Stern Daughter of the Voice of God! / O duty! If that name thou love, / Who art a light to guide, a rod /To check the erring, and reprove."

864. Jane Kitselman, painter, art collector, and friend of Anne Dunn.

here, briefly, end of July. Sure hope you can fit me in, if only for a cup of tea and a Peake Freane.

Jonathan Galassi—my editor—gave a highly select lunch for me last week at the Union Square Cafe (which is much nicer than it must have seemed to you that noisy evening): Darragh, Eileen Myles, Raymond Foye, Jonathan G., Maxine, me, Roger Straus, and John, who forgot to come, but phoned in mid-lunch. When Jonathan came back from taking his call, I said, "You should have told him we were waiting to order," which Roger appeared to find the funniest thing he had ever heard. Perhaps it is. John's absence only brightened the party: a guest who doesn't show usually makes the others try a little harder, even me. I was quite gay (better believe it) myself, once I got over such hurdles as: (Roger): "What are you called, James?" Frankly, I don't know: sometimes Jim, sometimes Jimmy—I can be quite tedious on this point; also, "What have you been reading?" "I'll tell you when I'm ready." John was so mortified that I'm letting him take me to dinner tonight.

Living at the friary with the Brothers has had a marvelous effect on Tom. He has blossomed and it has broadened his allure—I cannot put it more neatly than that! He speaks so much more freely about the things he cares most about. Here, I looked at my watch, rushed off to Greenmarket in Union Square, wandered about sneering at the rip-offs (by no means everything), almost bought Barbara (mine) a pot of catnip, but, well, she already has dried catnip and there's no place to put it, and finally found what was well worth $4.00: a bunch of daisies (field type) with some yellow ones mixed in, a big bunch with long stems and they look great in whatever that I put them in.

I feel I had many more things to tell you, but my head is empty as a copper cauldron hanging on a hook, and I want Jonathan [Leake] to mail this before—or rather, when—he goes.

love,

Jimmy

P.S. I thought of a Waughish name for John's house: Spendthrift. "I dreamt last night I went back to Spendthrift . . ." And, Carcanet is going to publish my selected poems in England; but not right this minute. I don't mind. I've got enough on my hands without having a lot of needle jobs done on my back. The heat wave last week! 104° heat index—God. I go to church alone (alas) a lot. Beautiful St. Paul's chapel down by City Hall, where George Washington used to worship—8 a.m. low mass—no hymns, no sermon—if only at the altar rail I could stop feeling I'm having a light snack! Tom says I will—

TO ANNE DUNN

Dear Anne,

Back, nice and early, from the supermarket, before all Chelsea queus (that doesn't look right) up at the checkout, with the blueberries and grapefruit juice I wanted, and the purported blackberries which I do not. A delightful, delicious, delovely morning: the breeze brisk, the sky clear, and the thermometer has soared to 62°.

I take pen in hand to add to yesterday's, the fact that next November I have agreed to, or consented to, give my first public reading, at the Dia Foundation (one of the de Menil girls).[865] Why? $3000.00 worth of why—which might not have seemed reason enough, had the date been nearer at hand. Hy Weitzen says he will be there, in the front row, which is not as supportive as he imagines. Tom says he will be with me, every step of the way, and if you will stand behind me and massage my neck, I think I'll make it. Don't know yet when in November: I said, "Any day except Thanksgiving," to the Dodo who is arranging this, and he gave me a keen, waiting look, as though I might explain why this should be.

Dinner with John last night, which was in many ways so agreeable that I will not mention any of the ways in which it was, well, less. But—I do *not* like to be taken up sharply, least of all, over light-hearted quips. I need scarcely stretch this out! But it reminds me of an eerie moment in Hudson—we were driving about and the subject turned to his staying with Danny,[866] and London and he began speaking in that improbable English accent he sometimes assumes. To say that I had a thought for you! I thought it only happened when he was in his cups.

I never did get to see *The Unbearable Lightness of Being*. It was showing down the street, but when I finally set out, it had been replaced by family fare. So instead I saw *Bull Durham* again, a sexy, hilarious Baseball comedy which I take to the way cotton candy used to take to me. John: "I hate baseball." So I rejected his *Roger the Rabbit*, which involves a three dimensional Bob Hoskins with a one dimensional rabbit. I said, "Perhaps you like cartoons a good deal more than I do." "Perhaps so," John averred.

865. Phillippa de Menil and her husband, Heiner Friedrich, were founders of the DIA Foundation, with an art and performance space then located on Mercer Street.
866. Danny Moynihan, Anne Dunn's youngest son.

I love getting mail from you, and you as well.

Jimmy

P.S. I had to tear up the first envelope, addressed to—Larubesc, Paris, France.

TO TOM CAREY

Nov. 4, 1988

Dear Tom,

I love your poem about Ted[867]—it's so clear and strong, and moves so firmly from point to point, and the language—your choice of words—is perfect; the poem hasn't an ounce of superfluous fat on it (but then, that's not *your* department, is it, dear?). It's really something to write a poem that is so wrenching because of the one word it ends with: the double meaning of "ashes" makes my heart skip a beat.

Is the fragment of a song something you're quoting, or something you invented for the poem? Well, sugar, all I can say is:

> My oh my
> What a guy

And who, by the way, is the James Schuyler to whom the envelope was addressed? Mere luck that I happened to get it.

I think today is Helena's birthday. Chew on that for a while.

This evening I'm giving the first of two warm-up readings at Raymond's (9th Street, that is). Joe Brainard just called, wheezing and coughing so much that I could barely understand what he was saying: which was, of course, that he thought he *might* not be able to come tonight! I urged him to go to bed, and to come on the 10th, when it's all going to happen again; which I hope he does, for all our sakes. (His most of all, of course!) I don't seem to be feeling particularly nervous, although it's all going to happen in six or so hours. And if that's true, why am I so sweaty? Because, although it's a lovely, lovely—almost perfect—day, the humidity is about one zillion percent. Rain by midnight and going on all day tomorrow is guaranteed by Al Roker, Pat Harper, Sue Simmons

---

867. Tom Carey's elegy "Ted" to the poet Ted Berrigan, dead of a heart attack on July 4, 1983. "Ashes" refers to both the cigarette ashes in Ted's beard and his ashes after cremation.

and Jack Cafferty[868]—the last said something really crass the other day (on Halloween) about . . ."there're plenty of weirdoes in the Village already." Quick as a flash Sue said, "Oh, *Jack*."

If your armpits are very sweaty, it helps to strip down to your shorts. I find. The enclosed map was in the *Times* today because Bryan Miller (the restaurant critic) thinks this stretch of 8th Avenue is in danger of turning into a second Restaurant Row; and why that should be a bad thing I don't know; but I never go to any of them. They must be gnashing their teeth at Onini's, since they saw 20th Street as the cut-off!

But, do you remember: your birthday dinner with Darragh at Chelsea Trattoria? The agreeable time when we went to Miss Ruby's Cafe and had South-Western cookin'? Or how you grew to like Man Ray less and less until—to my astonishment—you suddenly dug in your heels? Ah, memories.

I didn't take a second sheet of paper, by the by, because I didn't feel like tangling with Big Furry, who is passed out on top of the stack of typing paper. And now, Mr. Schuyler will read your beautiful poem once more and then—oh, maybe do my nails.

All my love,

Jimmy

TO ANNE DUNN

Nov. 7, 1988

Dear Anne,

I know the enclosed won't be news to you, but I thought you might not have seen the actual obituary—Aladar would have wanted a good review in the *Times*! I think this would have pleased him. Someone described it as "highly selective"—perhaps so, but at least there are no hard-nosed "facts" such as the *Times* lately sometimes likes to slip in.

I didn't go to the funeral, but Darragh did, and he said there was, at Aladar's insistence, a black gospel singer who sang "Swing Low, Sweet Chariot." Darragh said it was the most real, the most affecting thing he ever heard at any funeral; it was such a voice from the heart.

868. Local news, weather, and sports broadcasters on New York's television channel 4 (NBC).

John read a poem, and said beforehand that Aladar had once gone to a funeral where John had read a poem. Afterward Aladar told him he thought it was a wonderful thing to do, and he wanted John to read a poem at his—"But don't you *dare* read *that* poem at mine!"

Writing you about this is making me even more depressed than I already was! Depressed because I woke up much earlier than I meant to; because no elevators were working when I wanted to get the *Times* (at 5); because the weather was so beautiful yesterday and is so gloomy today; because that reading is yet to happen; and maybe a little because I'll turn 65 day after tomorrow. I haven't been minding that, but somehow this morning I've been glooming about the aspect of "only five years to 70: if I make it." They call me Little Mary Sunshine. . . .

As for the reading: I'm giving a couple of trial runs at Raymond Foye's on West 9th Street. The first was last Friday, and went extremely well: partly because I do (ahem) read very well, and much because of a wonderful beta blocker pill called *Inderol*. It's counter-stage fright, and stops the blood from getting that fizzy feeling and the other accelerations. There were about a dozen people, and there will be another dozen or more (depending on how la famille Hazan decides to play their cards) next Thursday, which will be the "you" crowd: Jane, John, Darragh, Joe Brainard, Barbara G . . . Now if the *Inderol* will just get me through that evening in that intimidatingly vast space on (155) Mercer Street! I don't doubt it will, but with it (the reading) there, blocking my view, I can't seem to write or do anything but run goofily around and fritter, and what I like least, I keep having this "closed in" feeling. I suppose it's a form of self-consciousness, of being aware all the time of how one seems (and sounds!) to others. Like having to listen to a recording of one's own voice! Christ! I don't envy them, but people who are in love with the sound of their own voice do have it easy.

Now can I think of anything cheerful to tell you? Why yes: Tom had (for the first time) that AIDS test and passed with flying colors. He said he didn't tell me beforehand (you have to wait two weeks for the result), because he was afraid I'd worry. What a sweetie.

And so are you, and how I wish I saw you much, much, much oftener than I do. I hope you're going to give New York a bumper crop of yourself this winter.

Love, as always,

xxxxxoooo

Jimmy

TO ANNE DUNN

Nov 17, 1988

Dearest Anne,

Well, dearie, having had my day, here it is yours. I wish I knew where you're staying, so I could call, or send a wire. My thoughts, and a prayer, are all for success, and lots of it! Your pictures deserve it. And so do you, for the matter of that.

As for my moment in the spotlight—well, truth to tell, I was a fucking sensation. I can't think of any other way to put it. When Darragh and Raymond Foye and I came down Mercer Street half an hour early, and saw this line stretching off into infinity . . . all I could think was, "This too will pass," and of the fact that my 40 mgs of *Inderol* would soon be working at maximum effect: when about to enter a tumbrel, *always* take a beta blocker! John read a two-page introduction which was sweet, generous, and amusing as only he can be: and for me, a big relaxing pause. But once I was started, I enjoyed it. I don't read badly, the amplification (I'm told) was excellent; and the audience attentive in the hear-a-pin-drop way—except when they laughed or clapped, both welcome sounds. At the end there was an "ovation—", then I climbed down. Whew.

I learned two things: if you have to do it under videotaping lights, wear something summery, and not a sweater under a jacket, as I did. And when you're done, keep moving, don't sit down, as I did, waiting for the hall to clear, because if you do, people with books they want to have signed ("May I have your autograph, Sir?") will quickly surround you, making life moderately intolerable. Eventually, we went off to a Soho restaurant (the Dia Foundation's treat), The Manhattan Bistro, where we were one of those A Long Narrow Table for 13 parties. In other words I could talk to left, right, and straight ahead. Instead of a naked girl springing out of a huge cake, as at some celebrations, we had John come dancing out of a bottle, on his way to a cab, and so to bed.

The check is safely in the bank, I'm quite ready to do it again, for a suitable fee . . . ah well, it's the usual sordid story: greed and vanity, vanity and greed . . . But I did enjoy it.

Here is a rather pointless clipping, which I send mostly because I always find this kind of item about any neighborhood of my own endlessly fascinating.

I long to hear about your show.

A less egocentric letter soon. Do write! And I hope you're coming here in December . . . ? (The question mark is not about my hope!)

love,

Jimmy

444

TO TOM CAREY

Feb 19 1989

Dear Tom,

Well, lambink (that was supposed to be "lambkin," but lambink will do just as well), I *had* rather hoped that by now (Sunday) you might have availed yourself of the wonderful collect-calling facilities I bet they have in Utah, but never mind. It was much too wonderful seeing you — but it's growing a little unreal — for me to start getting seriously cross. Not yet, anyway.

I had a wonderful smooth flight back, an hour and a half early as we prepared to go into the ritual landing dance at JFK. So of course "they" put us on hold for forty minutes; then we landed, and sat out on the tarmac for another 40 minutes. But somehow I was still 10 minutes ahead of schedule as my taxi pulled out into the sluggish rainy traffic. After the charms of S.F. airport, landing at JFK is like finding yourself at Sing Sing. As soon as I got in, I called you at your office, but he'd left early. "Perhaps *I* could help you . . . ???" But I allowed I'd call you later at the Friary. *By* the time later rolled around, the novelty of getting home safe and sound had worn off, so . . .

Barbara was more than glad to see me! Never did anyone get such a burst of affection and cuddling; plus a few good nips, in case she wasn't making her point clear. But she's a sweet girl, and it's very nice to be back in her furry embrace. The missing wasn't all on one side, no indeed.

I haven't been up to much so far, since I was very worn out when I got back, and took some masterful naps. Last night I had dinner with Darragh, then we went to a party for the publication of Kenward & Joe's book, *Sung Sex*, at Annie Lauterbach's[869] on Duane Street. The driver tried very hard to find the address — on Reade Street. But we were only a block away, so it all worked out, and we arrived to find that her party, lavishly financed by Kenward, *was* for dinner. But since nobody got anything before 10:30 I'm just as glad we did eat before-

869. Ann Lauterbach (b. 1942), poet.

hand. I talked to a lot of people, but all I can remember today is Lorna Smedman: pushy is the word, I believe. Tim Dlugos[870] was there, and today Darragh says he "meant" to bring us together; I had said at dinner I would like him to, if Tim was there. Humph. But I'm told he looked well, rather elegant in a way becoming a seminarian, hair very short, and with his young blonde curly haired chum alongside. But I haven't heard of his having said anything memorable to report. A lot of people asked after you (but *not* Lorna Smedman).

The weather, which was rather awful and raw, then got cold and bitingly windy, but now is almost forty degrees and deliciously sunny, and not windy. So. Hard to believe a week ago yesterday we were at Bolinas! Now and then I take out the snapshots to remind myself. And there's the mimosa in full bloom, and there you are, and there's the Pacific, and there we are, and there's Bill (goodness! he *is* good looking) and—what—is—that—dog—doing!!!

The enclosed is for the IRS (surprise) and a little for fags, so you won't spend all your birthday shoe money that way.

Try to be a good boy and remember to have a clean handkerchief pinned to your habit when you go to church.

I love you so much, and it was wonderful to see you, and to stay at the Friary. I especially love to share in religious ceremonies with you, whether at the Friary, or at St John's, or the Franciscan meditation evening. And I want to hear about your mission. For me, it's onward and upward in the Episcopal world: on Wednesday, Father Ousley is taking me to lunch at his club.

All my love, and more, and some from Barbara—

J.

The terrible Episcopal clergyman who was so difficult about Darragh's friend David Collins' funeral is named Cupit. He's a noted alcoholic, was one of *two* clergymen who went to Boston for Barbara Harris' ordination as Bishop, in order to protest! Which he did, although no one who might have a reason to be concerned did; his parish all long to get rid of him, but how, without doing something unbecoming? That news does come from Tim . . .

870. Tim Dlugos (1950–1990), poet. During the two years before his death from AIDS, Dlugos studied for the Episcopalian priesthood at the Yale Divinity School.

TO BILL BERKSON

Feb. 24, 1989

Dear Bill,

Had a fast, smooth and sunny return flight: that is, until we went into "hold" over rain-swept JFK, the Alcatraz of aerodromes. San Francisco is but a dream, one in which Bolinas is the brightest star. As we drove away Tom said, "Now that's what I call civilized conversation"; which I take to be a compliment to the family Berkson, though it may also be a comment on the dinner chat at the Friary, at least as I found it. But Bolinas is so beautiful, and so cozy, in a way I like. And I was converted to the beauty of the Pacific, which, as an ardent admirer of the Atlantic and its severities, I'd secretly hoped to have reservations about! The various East-West Coast bigotries, or perhaps I mean prejudices, are really very funny.

I spent a nice day with Bob Gluck,[871] including the Dim Sum lunch and visit to Christian Science church in Berkeley. Also a call on Don Allen, of which I can only say it went well as an act of Lenten abasement. What a malevolent old asp! Or wasp. But what a view from his apartment. The roller coaster hills of S.F. fill me with terror—how does anyone get used to driving on them?

If I come up with anything for the Bill de K issue,[872] I'll send it. But I doubt I will. When I think about him, my mind veers round to Elaine, and the sadness of her dying at only 68. I won't pretend that we were close, but I was fond of her, and admired her wit and spunk. And when I try to put Bill into the picture, what I remember is a night years ago at Joan's [Mitchell] studio, when they were both there. Elaine was talking and laughing a mile a minute, her only competition coming from Frank. Bill was in such a total black and glowering humor he could hardly choke down another drink. "Listen to her," he kept saying, "listen to her: she laughs just like a goat." Astute Elaine once said, "Bill likes Jimmy because he thinks he's a gentleman." Hmmm.

Nothing much doing in Big Burg—a party at Annie Lauterbach's last Saturday for Kenward and Joe and their book *Sung Sex*; and next week, Darragh Park has an opening, a show I have agreed to review for *Art in America*. My first art writing for 15 years! As I recall, there's a certain knack to it, but I can't seem to remember what it is. . . .

871. Robert Gluck (b. 1947), fiction writer and poet.
872. *Art Journal* issue celebrating de Kooning's seventy-fifth birthday, edited by Berkson and the painter Rackstraw Downes. Schuyler did not contribute.

I trust I'll see you both when you next come to NYC, which will *probably* be before my next trip to San Francisco. And yet, who knows?

Love to Lynn,[873]

love,

Jimmy

TO BILL BERKSON

March 9, 1989

Dear Bill,

When you want to summon up Simon Pettet's[874] address, think Ginsberg, think Fagin, think Scholnick, think: Apt 6, 437 East 12th St, NYC 10009 (212) 260-3050.

If you were coming to see me, and at the corner of 7th Ave and 23rd, two improbable black men came up and engaged you in a fast chat about one of the unlikelier African countries (but produced no passport), flashed a lot of bucks and claimed to know nothing about American Banks, would you lead them to your nearest cash machine (and all on a Saturday afternoon) and teach them how to work it? Then sincerely believe a phone call was coming, after they picked up some luggage at JFK, when they would return your $200? No? I didn't think so. Simon did. I saw him in the midst of this for a moment and tried to explain the ways of the world, at least as lived on that particularly horrid corner, but there is no getting through to someone when he wants to believe the truly unbelievable. "He trusts me!" Simon cried, and left. Poor dear.

But if I can see through this everyday scam, I wonder which are the scams I'm not prepared for? I was offered some tempting stock in the Brooklyn Bridge the other day . . .

I thought hard about Bill de K. but nothing came of it, beyond recalling going to the Cedar Bar once after—what? the Club? a John Myers play?—with Kenneth and some nice (not really very Cedar Bar type) young people, including a very pretty girl. Bill was at the bar, wearing a determined fedora. "Ha ha ha Bill," Kenneth said, "you look so funny! Why are you wearing a business man's hat?" Bill didn't stoop to comment, but his glower spoke volumes. So we sat at one of the round tables up front and ordered. After a while Bill came over

873. Berkson's then wife, painter Lynn O'Hare.

874. Simon Pettet (b. 1953), British-born poet resident in New York City. He edited Schuyler's *Selected Art Writings*.

448

and said, "You! You think you're so funny. Why don't you publish your funny poems in *The New Yorker*? Where they belong." And he threw his drink straight in the face of the pretty girl. Later, at the bar, when I could see it was safe, I pointed out that the girl hadn't really done anything to offend Bill (I'm afraid a drink in KK's kisser would not have been an unwelcome sight). "Ah," Bill said, "it's good for them." He was in quite a good humor.

(*The New Yorker* never published Kenneth's poems because—can you guess?—Howard Moss didn't like them.)

Otherwise, I've been busy writing 600 words about Darragh Park's show for *Art in America* one I really like, and the first "Art Criticism" I've written since the early 70s. Rusty indeed was I. Perhaps I'll dedicate my sunset years to de-professionalizing Art Writing, and turning it back into the scullery securing it always was.

Very glad you finally got that rain—I was worried about your garden! (Your toilet, I felt, could take care of itself.) What I liked most about my visit was our trip to Bolinas, and the view of the city from the Oakland Bridge coming back in the late afternoon. I love the way it looks so uncorsetted, spread out over all those hills.

So, I trust you'll both be careful when strolling about on foggy nights not to have any edgescapades (always a hazard).

Love,

Jimmy

TO PETER GIZZI

April 10, 1989

Dear Peter,

or, may I call you Honeybunch? But I'll be serious. I'm in a good mood because I think I just got a poem right, one I've been fiddling with since March 24th, all 29—what the hell—let's throw in the title, all 30 lines of it. But I wouldn't feel any better if it was 30 pages, that's for sure.

I liked getting your letter so much, I wanted to answer it right away. But I thought, he'll think I'm answering too soon, he'll wonder this and he'll wonder that. So I waited. But now I don't feel like waiting anymore. But I must feel like doing something, to judge by the way my typing suddenly flew apart!

875. See glossary.

Did you write that letter to your father? I keep wondering about it.[876]

I'm glad you think we were all "young and beautiful with great haircuts!" The haircut part was very easy, I used to go to the cheapest barber I could find and say, "Thin it and cut it just long enough to comb." I didn't want to look feminine, you see! Now that I no longer care, I go to the most expensive hairstylist I can find, and tell him to give me a finger wave and spit curls.

As to your reading (what you've been reading, that is): I love Frank's poetry (a lot of it, anyway: towards the end I think he may have written too much when he was smashed), Weiners I like a lot, and what do you think of Spicer? When he was in New York in the early 50s he hung out at a Village bar, the San Remo,[877] which went through a gay phase, and I never met anyone else quite so morose and grouchy. And that's what I find when I try to read him. But my friend the painter John Button said the poetry was very good, when you stopped reading it *that* way. After reading a lot of [Philip] Whalen,[878] a lot of it with real pleasure, I've been enjoying Wm Corbett's[879] books. He sent me a collected which is full of wonderful things: Que pense-tu, beau Sphinx?[880]

You must have a very sexy typewriter, that you can put it in sidewise. I can only put it in this way, you see!

I was planning to come visit John [Ashbery] about now, and dragoon him into driving to dinner in Stockbridge, but his friend Pierre Martory has just come on a visit from France, and since John only has (in that mansion) one serious guestroom, I will have to be patient. Or you must live up to your promises of coming to New York so we can get together here. I wish you would.

I'll write a sensible letter soon: don't take so long to write this time.

love,

xoxxxoooxxo

Jimmy

876. Gizzi's father died in a plane crash when the poet was twelve. The idea of writing a letter to him came from either Gizzi's therapist, his AA sponsor, or Schuyler himself. Gizzi remembers bonding with Schuyler over their mutual sobriety.

877. Popular bar in the 1950s on the northwest corner of Bleecker and MacDougal in Greenwich Village.

878. Philip Whalen (1923–2002), poet.

879. William Corbett (1942–2018), poet and editor of this book. Schuyler was reading *City Nature* and *Runaway Pond*.

880. A line from the movie *Les Enfants du Paradis*.

TO ANNE DUNN

August 21, 1989

Dear Anne,

Having just spilled water on some freshly typed pages, *and* onto a roll of stamps, all in the interest of watering a small pot of ivy, writing a letter to you is the one thing I can think of that might restore my humor. Why, it already has. If I haven't written, it's because of a total lack of subject—how about the weather? It has been merely seasonable, which is to say dreadful. So I stay home in my air conditioned (heavily) cave, along with Artie.[881] When we don't watch baseball games we watch horse races (his choice), the broadcasts of which are divinely brief. So it goes. And I like it a lot more than the un-air-conditioned guestrooms of X, Y, and Z. Especially Z.

Otherwise, I struggle on, or try to, with my commissioned opus about Andrew Lord's ceramics.[882] At least the deadline is not all that way off, though needs must it can probably be pushed on a way. And it would certainly be better if it couldn't.

This will be an exciting week socially: dinner tomorrow with that rare visitor, Darragh, and on Thursday with a new pal, young(ish) poet Marc Cohen, when John may even join us! Exciting. The poor lamb told me a story about himself which he vowed me not to repeat, but if you think, "falling down in the rain," I don't really think you would need total elaboration. I had asked him if his new anti-depressant pills had begun to work, and he said one of their side effects is to accelerate the intoxicating effect of alcohol, and the proof that they were working was simply that he did not feel depressed about this incident when he woke up and thought of it the next morning. A pill the whole world could use, no doubt.

And that, I think, is just the kind of little story that makes John wish that all his own, as well as his friends, letters would be burned, at least as soon as they're profitably sold to some University library. You know what a whited sepulchre he would like to leave behind—fat chance, with the merry life he's led and the friends he has. On the other hand, I don't see why he shouldn't have one if he wants one. I wonder what I can do to help?

881. Artie Growich (b. 1956), employee at the Chelsea Hotel and Schuyler's lover from 1989 until his death.
882. Andrew Lord, British-born sculptor. Schuyler's poem "Andrew Lord Poems" appears in his *Collected Poems*.

451

I've been reading a collection of just-published prose works by Harry M [Mathews].—I'll lend it to you, if you like—tee-hee. On Darragh's recommendation I tried the autobiography, and found it more and more a less than tasty dish of self-pity and self-praise, liberally laced with dashes of worldly cultivation. It oozes something—I don't know what. I liked his novels, up until the last one, anyway. Perhaps I won't lend it to you.

Barbara—my puss, that is—has posed a problem. She's supposed to have a powdery vitamin supplement added to her food. But at the slightest whiff, she won't eat. I've tried numerous tricks of disguise, but none work, what with a cat's nose being that much more sensitive than mine. People say, Leave the food: she will eat when she gets hungry enough. But she doesn't. What she does is come sit at my feet and stare up with big, round, hungry eyes. I tend to agree with her, that there's more to life than vitamins.

My love to Jane, and send, if not a letter, then a card. Does your grandmother's house still stand? I hope so.

love—xoxox

Jimmy

TO JOE BRAINARD

June 25 90

Dear Joe—

You beat me to it! And I *was* going to write to you today—to send you your annual antique basketball card (a tradition fast drawing to a close), & this clipping—I can't find scissors to trim it up, & I'm too "all thumbs" to do the razor blade bit—so—Here you are, lucky fellow!

Your reading always sound so much more clear-cut than mine—I fritter away a lot of reading time on assorted periodicals, like the English *Country Life*, with wonderful real estate ads, and—well, like that. Right now I'm reading a book about monastery gardens—lots of names of herbs, & lists of what to plant, & how to make a wattle fence (weave it in the spring, out of willow, or anything else that will bend). Not much use on 23rd St., but when I finish it I'll pass it on to a gardening friar/friend, who will use it. Then I have the new Dave Bradstetter mystery, *The Boy Who Was Buried This Morning*.[883] And I keep planning to read all of Jane Austen again, but TV gets in the way.

883. Dave Bradstetter is a gay private detective in mystery novels by Joseph Hansen.

Artie is fine. Right now he's off at the laundromat doing his favorite thing, making sure he has the cleanest jeans in town. For his birthday I gave him what he wanted: a flat iron! He thinks jeans should have a sharp crease, which goes against every tradition I've ever heard of—but what the hell—he's from Queens.

Tom goes off today on his annual 3 week vacation: 1 week in San Francisco, 1 week with his folks in Durango, 1 week on retreat in a monastery in the desert of New Mexico, where he plans to quit smoking. Oh oh—step back folks—he rather turned into a fiend last time. But I miss him, fiend or not.

I talked to Anne D. [Dunn] the other day—she was full of giggles & complaints, the latter mostly about the ankle she hurt when she was last here (this bit of news seems rather a dead end). Pierre Martory is (or was) here—now he & John have gone off to San Fran. & then to someplace in Western Canada, where John's friend Richard Thomas is making a movie. But perhaps he's a friend, of yours, too?[884]

I just turned on the "set" to see what's cooking, & it seems to be Paulette Goddard, or soon will be, when the Indians' pot comes to a boil. I'm not worried—Randolph Scott is climbing up the waterfall in a 3-cornered hat—&—

love

Jimmy

TO NATHAN KERNAN[885]

Jan 31, 91

Dear Nathan—

When it comes down to it, I find I have so few things to say about your poems, in detail that is, and really only want to say, please keep writing, write more!

To begin with one I meant to end with & my favorite, your Sonnet, "XXXX",[886] this seems to me your most concentrated, & unlike anyone else of

884. Actor and poet Richard Thomas starred as John Boy in the popular television series *The Waltons*. He was a friend of Brainard's.

885. See glossary.

886. Anne Dunn told Schuyler that Nathan Kernan had been writing poems, and Schuyler asked to see some of his work. "XXXX" appears in the anthology *Gents, Bad Boys and Barbarians*, edited by Rudy Kikel and published by Alyson Publications in 1995.

all the poems. The language is truly majestic in its movement and the image of love, into pearl & images of possible love, develop with a convincing reality: usually I would object to both "nacre" & to incindered, but here they sound right, & fit into the almost Baroque weight of the language—which is by no means over done.

In "Souvenir d'Antan," more is sometimes said than need be—is the first sentence necessary? And throughout the poem there are perhaps too many specific dates—you now the age yr parents were (40)—it doesn't matter—or that your earliest memories (you were five)—I won't go on, but I think this poem could be tighter—but the switch in subject to Danny, is sharp & beautiful—"milkweed from a / summer twenty years ago." Lovely and *no* objection to "20"! But compare the harsh truth of "He / used to sell his blood on / Mission Street every few weeks" to the somewhat randomness of the first few pages—But this is really a very strange & moving poem—

"Almost afraid . . ." needs no comment from me—you seem to know exactly where you're going. From the word go—(the penultimate stanza is certainly an eye-catcher!). But do you really never cry? I hope you do—when you have to—

"Between Errors" seems to have things I like and things I don't get in it—the ambiguity of Lee K's "Don't go *limp*."—doesn't seem clear enough—who was Parsla?[887] The poem seems to go from subject to subject, without really ever coming to light—

And now, I don't seem to have said a thing—and your poems are so clear & strong, so admirable!

love

Jimmy

p.s. I thought of offering to trade apartments, but decided I'd best stick with my perilous elevators—

---

887. Parsla Berzins is an old friend of Kernan's prone to malapropisms.

Epilogue

On April 5, 1991, at about 3:00 in the afternoon, Tom Carey called on Schuyler in his room at the Chelsea Hotel and found him conscious but unresponsive. He had had a stroke. Carey and Raymond Foye, a fellow resident of the Chelsea, accompanied him in an ambulance to the intensive care unit at Saint Vincent's Hospital. For a week many of Schuyler's friends, including John Ashbery, Anne Dunn, Ron Padgett, Darragh Park, Charles North, Simon Pettet, David Trinidad, and Nathan Kernan, visited Schuyler. Though alert and seemingly responsive he could not speak. Anne Porter visited Schuyler on April 11, and on the twelfth he died.

Appendix: Postcards

Throughout his corresponding life James Schuyler sent thousands of postcards. In a few instances, the most notable being the close friend and confidant of his last years, Raymond Foye, who also resided in the Chelsea Hotel in the 1980s, Schuyler corresponded only in this way. Foye received upwards of two hundred postcards, slipped in his mailbox behind the hotel's front desk by Schuyler himself.

The earliest piece of Schuyler's correspondence to turn up so far is a postcard sent from Montreal in July 1945 addressed to the poet Chester Kallman. Schuyler and his lover Bill Aalto were visiting the city as tourists. "Montreal succeeds," wrote Schuyler, "being what Pittsburgh only *tries* to be—but it's *infested* with *Beauty*. That light in the North isn't Aurora Borealis— its Montreal. Come north (*much more* my town than Bill's) we're going to Quebec tonight—Beauty is not enough—" He signed himself "Jim R," R for Ridenour because in 1945 he had yet to return to his birth name.

The image on the postcard's face is of fourteen Canadian doughboy-helmeted soldiers astride the barrel of a long siege cannon. The caption under them reads: "Smile! Smile! Smile! Stalwart coastal defense troops."

The postcard's image is almost always part of Schuyler's message or the reason for him sending the card in the first place. Most often this image provides Schuyler the opportunity for a joke. The volume and frequency with which he sent postcards underlines what is evident in the number of poems he wrote to friends—Schuyler thought constantly about his friends, and he liked to be in touch whenever an occasion occurred to him.

Glossary of Names

ALLEN, DONALD (1912–2004)

Editor. After working briefly at New Directions, Allen joined Grove Press and there made his mark as an editor. His anthology *The New American Poetry* is arguably the most significant anthology of American poetry published since World War II. By identifying the Black Mountain and New York Schools Allen redrew the map of American poetry. While at Grove he edited Charles Olson's book of poems *The Distances* and Frank O'Hara's *Meditations in an Emergency*. His work on Grove's magazine, *Evergreen Review*, helped make it one of the liveliest and most influential literary magazines of the 1950s and 1960s. Allen went on to edit *The Collected Poems of Frank O'Hara* (1971) and to publish work by Philip Whalen, Lew Welch, and Michael Rumaker, among others, under the imprints Four Seasons Foundation and Grey Fox Press.

ASHBERY, JOHN (1927–2017)

Poet, art critic, playwright, and translator. Ashbery and Schuyler met in 1951, became friends the following year, but did not begin what became the most intense correspondence of Schuyler's life until Ashbery moved to Paris in 1955. Earlier letters seem to have been lost, and it is odd that the first surviving letter comes from 1957, the year Ashbery returned for a few months to live in Manhattan as Schuyler's roommate at 346 East 49th Street. By this time Ashbery had published his first book of poems, *Some Trees*. Throughout their correspondence Ashbery and Schuyler address one another by names other than their own, some of which have resisted identification. After Schuyler's very difficult time in the 1970s, both men lived in Chelsea, and while their correspondence stopped, they saw one another frequently for meals. Of Schuyler's close friends Ashbery appears most often in his poems. On the dust jacket of Schuyler's *Collected Poems* is a single sentence by Ashbery that reads, "Schuyler is simply the best we have."

BATIE, NANCY

Miss Batie resided in Vancouver, British Columbia, and was a serious enough reader of Schuyler's poetry to write him a letter in response to his poem "February." Nothing else is known about her. The letter Schuyler wrote to her was discovered among John Ashbery's papers. Ashbery does not remember having seen it. That it is without Schuyler's signature suggests that it was never sent.

BERKSON, BILL (1939-2016)

Poet, art critic, editor, and native New Yorker who dropped out of Brown University in 1959 to become part of the downtown New York art and poetry scene. Berkson met Schuyler either in the spring or fall of that year, but they did not get to know one another well until the late 1960s. Berkson's book of poems, *Blue Is the Hero*, takes its title from a line in a Schuyler art review. Schuyler dedicated his poem "Gray, intermittently blue, eyed hero" to Berkson. By the end of the 1960s Berkson had relocated to Bolinas, north of San Francisco, where he edited the magazine *Big Sky*. In the 1980s he began to teach at the San Francisco Art Institute, and he brought Schuyler to read there in 1989.

BRAINARD, JOE (1942-1994)

Painter and writer Brainard arrived in New York City in the early 1960s. There he joined Ron Padgett, a childhood friend from Tulsa, Oklahoma, and Ted Berrigan in producing *C magazine*. Brainard soon became a fixture on the downtown painting and poetry scene. He collaborated with and/or made book covers for Frank O'Hara, Schuyler, John Ashbery, Ron Padgett, Kenward Elmslie, Anne Waldman, and a host of other poets. He and Elmslie became lovers, a relationship that lasted until Brainard's death. In his poem "Dear Joe" Schuyler gives an account of first meeting Brainard:

> I remember
> how young you seemed (and were)
> the first time I met you
> when Kenward invited a few
> of the younger poets
> (Ted, Tony) to meet me and
> you came too. You didn't say
> much (you said nothing) but
> looked at books in that little
> house on Cornelia Street, not
> aware of what would come to pass
> for you there: why, you came
> to live there.

In time Brainard became one of Schuyler's two "great correspondents"—John Ashbery was the other—and they remained steadfast friends until Schuyler's death.

BUTTON, JOHN (1929-1982)

Painter. Button came to New York from his native San Francisco in 1953 to study at Hans Hofmann's School of Fine Arts. He worked briefly at the Museum of Modern Art's Information Desk, where Frank O'Hara had worked before him, and he met Fairfield Porter and Schuyler, who fell head over heels in love with him. In 1975, long after their friendship had ended, Schuyler reviewed Button's show at the Kornblee Gallery. He wrote, "Button is a master cloud painter . . . a brilliant draftsman . . . how he loves New York, his adopted city and constant theme. These pictures radiate love: there is no satire, no cartooning, no pity. So brick and stone crumble. Let them crumble. They are the perishable monuments of our daily life."

CAREY, TOM (B. 1951)

Poet, actor, musician. Carey's brother, the poet Steve (1945–1989), worked briefly in 1979 as Schuyler's assistant. Unable to deliver medicine to Schuyler at the Chelsea Hotel, Steve asked Tom to do it for him. Shortly after this Tom became Schuyler's assistant, employment that lasted from late in 1979 until mid-March 1980. Schuyler's obsessive love for Carey contributed to Carey's leaving, but they remained close and either saw each other or spoke by phone most days until Schuyler's death. A *Few Days* contains Schuyler's love poems to Carey, whose own book is *Desire: Poems, 1986–1996*. Carey became a Franciscan brother in the Society of St. Francis and an Episcopal priest.

COOLIDGE, CLARK (B. 1939)

Poet. Coolidge met Schuyler in the early summer of 1970 on a visit to Fairfield Porter's home in Southampton where the Padgetts were housesitting. Schuyler dedicated the poem "The Dog Wants His Dinner," which appears in *The Crystal Lithium*, to Coolidge. Coolidge in turn dedicated several poems he wrote during the 1970s, including "The Grin Steeps," to Schuyler. The Susan Coolidge quoted in Schuyler's poem "Crocus Night" is not Coolidge's wife, Susan, but the nineteenth-century author of the "Katy Did" series of children's books. After long residence in the Berkshires, the Coolidges now live in Petaluma, California.

DASH, ROBERT (1931-2013)

Painter. During the 1950s Dash shared a Manhattan studio with Fairfield Porter, who introduced Dash to Schuyler. They were friendly—"An East Window on Elizabeth

Street," dedicated to Dash, appeared in Schuyler's fourth book, *The Crystal Lithium* (1972)—but became close friends after Dash moved to Sagaponack, Long Island. Schuyler visited him often while living in the Porters' house. Schuyler set numerous poems in Dash's home and garden, Madoo, including "Korean Mums." In his last book, *A Few Days* (1985), "A Belated Birthday Poem" is dedicated to Dash. The two collaborated on *Garden* (1972), a portfolio of lithographs with lines from Schuyler's diary.

DUNN, ANNE (B. 1929)

British painter. Dunn, her second husband the painter Rodrigo Moynihan (1910–1990), and Sonia Orwell, and John Ashbery edited and published in Paris the important journal *Art and Literature* (1964–1967). She first met Schuyler on a visit to New York in 1961 and got to know him when she visited the Porters in Southampton in 1968. They became close friends in the 1970s when she and Moynihan frequently stayed in the city. Incorporated into Schuyler's "The Morning of the Poem" is a long letter from Dunn, and her drawing is used on the cover of that book. The poem "A Name Day" is dedicated to her. In a review of her 1975 exhibition of drawings at the Fischbach Gallery, Schuyler wrote, "Dunn has the courage and strength of her femininity. Her strength is achieved by delicate, persistent means."

ELMSLIE, KENWARD (1929-2022)

Elmslie and Schuyler knew one another for some years before they began to correspond. It was at the apartment Elmslie shared with his lover John Latouche that Schuyler heard John Ashbery, Frank O'Hara, and Barbara Guest read in 1952. Elmslie remembers meeting Schuyler at the Periscope-Holliday Bookshop where Schuyler worked, visiting Alex Katz's studio with him, and playing bridge with Schuyler and Kenneth and Janice Koch. In the mid-1960s Schuyler began to visit Elmslie at his summer home in Calais, Vermont. Schuyler set many poems there, including the diary poems "Now and Then" and "Vermont Diary" and the sequence "Evenings in Vermont." Schuyler wrote more often about Elmslie and his Vermont home than about any other places he loved, even Great Spruce Head Island. After Schuyler's breakdown in the early 1970s, Elmslie helped support him, and his Z Press published *The Home Book* in 1977.

FAGIN, LARRY (1937-2017)

Poet and publisher. As editor of the mimeo magazine *Adventures in Poetry* he published an excerpt from Ashbery and Schuyler's *A Nest of Ninnies* in 1969, and Adventures in Poetry Books published Schuyler's collection *A Sun Cab* (1972), with cover and illustrations by Fairfield Porter. In his diary entry for "February 15, 1971" Schuyler notes having dinner with Fagin and asks, "Why can't I remember for sure and for certain whether it's Fagin or Fagen?" Later—"It's Fagin."

FREILICHER, JANE (1924–2014)

Painter. Born in Brooklyn, Freilicher became the friend, and sometime muse, of Frank O'Hara, John Ashbery, and Kenneth Koch in 1951. A year later she met Schuyler, and soon after he wrote *Presenting Jane* (originally *Presenting Jane Freilicher*), a play now lost. In 1957 she married the painter Joe Hazan. Freilicher kept studios in downtown Manhattan and in Water Mill on Long Island, drawing the subject matter of her paintings from both places. Schuyler's poem "June 30, 1974" recounts a weekend visit to the Hazans' Long Island home. In his November 1961 review of a Freilicher show, Schuyler wrote, "Jane Freilicher has abandoned motif and taken beauty for subject matter, a brave and winning choice; and a rare one in New York."

GIZZI, PETER (1924–2014)

Poet. As co-editor of the magazine *O.blek*, Gizzi solicited poems from Schuyler initiating their correspondence. At the time he lived in the Berkshires, not far from where he now teaches at the University of Massachusetts Amherst. His brother Michael (1949–2010), also a poet, organized Schuyler's November 1989 reading in the barn at Herman Melville's Pittsfield, Massachusetts, home, Arrowhead. Schuyler describes the reading and lists the poems he read in his diary entry "Tuesday, November 14, 1989."

GUEST, BARBARA (1920–2006)

Poet, novelist, and biographer. Guest met Schuyler on a night in the early 1950s when she and Frank O'Hara read at a party given by librettist and songwriter John Latouche. "Barbara read first: she read rather short poems," Schuyler remembered, "There was one that was rather like a still life of tropical fruit that reminded me very much of a [Kurt] Schwitters collage." Guest's reading stayed with Schuyler so much that in a 1977 interview with Peter Schjeldahl he said, "The impression her poems made on me still excites and makes me want to get out the pencil or typewriter."

HOHNSBEEN, JOHN (1926–2007)

Art dealer, met Schuyler in the late 1940s in the circle of Chester Kallman and W. H. Auden. In the summer of 1950 Hohnsbeen and Schuyler rented a beach house in Sagaponack, Long Island. Through contacts developed while working for the art dealer Curt Valentin, Hohnsbeen arranged a job for Schuyler with the art dealer Henry Kleemann. Hohnsbeen moved to Paris in 1960, losing touch with Schuyler.

JORDAN, ROBERT

Little is known of Robert Jordan beyond what Schuyler reveals in his poems, diary, and letters. When they met at Manhattan's Everard Baths on April 3, 1971, Jordan was a salesman at Brooks Brothers, married, and living in New Jersey. Their affair lasted from the spring of 1971 until some time in 1973. Schuyler dedicated his books *The Crystal Lithium* and *Hymn to Life* to Jordan, and Jordan is the object of the love poems headed "Loving You" in the latter book. Jordan did not make any friends in Schuyler's set and seems to have had no other literary friendships. Several of Schuyler's friends who met Jordan failed to see what Schuyler saw in him.

KATZ, ADA (DEL MORO) (B. 1928)

Wife of painter Alex Katz. At the time of her marriage to Katz in 1958 she worked as a research biologist. In 1962 *Art News* published Schuyler's essay "Alex Katz Paints a Picture." The picture Katz painted was variously titled *Ada, Jimmy, Rudy*—Rudy being Rudy Burckhardt, whose photographs of Katz in action illustrated the essay—or *The Incident*. The painting is now lost.

KATZ, ALEX (B. 1927)

Painter. Schuyler met Katz and his wife, Ada, in the late 1950s. He reviewed Katz's January 1959 show at Manhattan's Tanager Gallery and wrote, "The image is always specific: at its simplest, a canvas all sunny cream is banded at the horizon by a canted Maine landscape. In the figures he risks banality: the prettiness of a pretty woman is as factual, and as simply achieved, as in an ad. It is taste that wins, and the existence of the picture as a resolution of color tensions. The mat surround counts for a lot. There is a gradual taking out of detail that leaves their force behind." Katz's painting of an overturned rowboat in sea grass adorned the cover of Schuyler's book of poems *Freely Espousing*.

KATZ, VINCENT (B. 1960)

Poet and translator. The son of Alex and Ada Katz, whom Schuyler knew from infancy. When Schuyler posed with Ada Katz and Rudy Burckhardt for the painting recorded in his "Alex Katz Paints a Picture," the baby Vincent crawled around at their feet. He has curated major shows of the work of Rudy Burckhardt and the artists who taught at and attended Black Mountain College.

KERNAN, NATHAN (B. 1950)

Poet, art critic, and the editor of *The Diary of James Schuyler* (1997). Kernan remembers, "I first met, or rather, was introduced to Jimmy on Valentine's Day, 1987 at a party at John Ashbery's. Jimmy was sitting in a chair by the door, heavy and sweaty, and unforthcoming. Our real friendship dates from March 1990, when Anne Dunn invited us both to dinner at a restaurant. That time he was funny and wonderful. All of a sudden we were seeing each other once a week or so. I took him to his last reading, when he read with Barbara Guest at New York University on February 6, 1991." Kernan has signed a contract with the publisher of Schuyler's poetry, Farrar, Straus and Giroux, to write his biography.

KOCH, JANICE (ELWOOD) (1931–1981)

First wife of Kenneth Koch.

KOCH, KENNETH (1925–2002)

Schuyler met Kenneth Koch after meeting John Ashbery and Frank O'Hara. He told interviewer Carl Little, "I had the feeling that he (Koch) wasn't too crazy about what the cuckoo had laid in his nest, and he perhaps was a bit snubbing. But later, we relaxed and became friends. I was very fond of his wife, Janice." Ashbery, Koch, O'Hara, Schuyler, and Barbara Guest made up what came to be called the New York School of poets. Only Koch had a lifetime career as a teacher. At Columbia University his popular courses inspired another generation of New York poets that included Ron Padgett, Gerrit Henry, and David Shapiro. Koch was a prolific poet who wrote plays, fiction, and several how-to books aimed at teaching poetry writing to children and the elderly. Schuyler dedicated his poem "The Cenotaph" to Koch and wrote of him in the poem "I sit down to type," "Kenneth Koch / could teach a golfball / to write pantoums." Schuyler dedicated his poem "Money Musk" to Janice Koch.

LITTLE, CARL (B. 1954)

Art critic. In the fall of 1980 Little reviewed the Sun Press reissue of *Freely Espousing* and the newly published *The Morning of the Poem* for the New York magazine *Downtown Review*. Four years later Little, now living in Paris, heard from Schuyler, who praised the review and asked if Little would like to interview him for *The Paris Review*. Little did so at the Chelsea, but after holding the interview for four years *The Paris Review* did not publish it. In 1993 the interview appeared in the Boston-based magazine *Agni*. Little lives in Mt. Desert, Maine, where he works for the Maine Community Foundation and publishes books on Maine and New England arts.

MATHEWS, HARRY (1930–2017)

Novelist and poet. Mathews is a native New Yorker who graduated from Harvard a few years after Ashbery, Koch, and O'Hara and went to live in Paris. He studied music with thoughts of becoming a composer but instead became a novelist and member of Oulipo, the French-based group of writers and scientists dedicated to the invention of new literary forms. The magazine *Locus Solus* was Mathews's brainchild. Schuyler, Ashbery, Koch, and O'Hara were its co-editors through five issues. Mathews's first novel, *The Conversions*, was serialized in the pages of *Locus Solus*.

NORTH, CHARLES (B. 1941)

Poet. North and his wife, the painter Paula, became friends with Schuyler in the 1970s. The poem "Light from Canada" that appears in *The Crystal Lithium* is dedicated to North. At some point in 1978 North said how much he liked the one-shot mimeo magazine Schuyler had edited, *49 South*. Out of this grew *Broadway*, which became, in North's words, "something between a mag and an anthology" of poems and drawings. North remembers, "We met to hash out the (sometimes thorny!) issue of contributors. He was plenty tough, and had no use for some of those I suggested—at least originally." *Broadway* appeared in 1978, followed ten years later by the anthology *Broadway II*, with a cover by Trevor Winkfield.

PADGETT, RON (B. 1942), PATRICIA (B. 1937), AND WAYNE (B. 1966)

Poet, translator, and editor Ron Padgett came to New York City from Tulsa, Oklahoma, in 1960 to attend Columbia University, from which he graduated in 1964. In Tulsa he had known the artist Joe Brainard since grade school, and while in high school he met poet Ted Berrigan. Before coming to New York Padgett edited the poetry magazine *The White Dove Review*, which put him in touch with Allen Ginsberg, Frank O'Hara, and other poets in New York. Together with Brainard, Berrigan, and poet Dick Gallup, another friend from Tulsa, Padgett became active on the New York poetry and art scene editing and publishing the mimeographed *C* magazine. He does not remember where or when he first met Schuyler, but it was most likely in 1964 or 1965. A fictitious Ron Padgett appears in Schuyler's short story "At Home with Ron and Pat Padgett" published in *The Home Book*. Of Padgett's poems Schuyler wrote, "Ron Padgett's poems are remarkably clear, almost invisibly so, like a refreshing glass of water."

PARK, DARRAGH (1939-2009)

Painter. Park grew up in New Jersey but spent summers in Easten, Long Island. He got to know Schuyler during the last years Schuyler spent at the Porter home in Southampton. Their friendship deepened when Schuyler moved into Park's Chelsea, Manhattan, neighborhood after leaving the Porters' in 1973. From then until Schuyler's death Park was his most devoted friend. They talked on the phone frequently, and Schuyler often visited Park's Bridgehampton home. Schuyler dedicated both the poem "The Morning of the Poem" and the book of the same title to Park. In 1981 it won the Pulitzer Prize. Several poems collected in *A Few Days* are dedicated to Park and his dog Oriane or are set at Park's Long Island home. Park provided the cover illustrations for Schuyler's *The Home Book* (1977), *A Few Days* (1985), *Selected Poems* and *Collected Poems*, the New York Review of Books reissue of Schuyler's novel *Alfred and Guinevere* (2001), *The Diary of James Schuyler* (1997), *Art Writings* (1998), and for the first edition of this book. In reviewing Park's 1979 Tibor de Nagy Gallery show, Schuyler wrote, "These paintings, so apparently purely visual, are also strong matters of comment, about what is, and what is not, worthwhile."

PORTER, ANNE (CHANNING) (1911-2011)

Poet, mother, and housewife whose Maine home Schuyler came to in 1961, in her words, "for a weekend and stayed eleven years."

PORTER, FAIRFIELD (1907-1975)

Painter and art critic. Schuyler met the Porters in 1952. He met Fairfield Porter first at an "after-dinner thing" at the apartment of photographer Rudy Burckhardt and his first wife, Edith. At the time Porter commuted to a studio in Manhattan from the family home at 49 South Main Street in Southampton. Schuyler first visited the Porters there in June of 1954 when he and Arthur Gold were in the midst of their affair. In July 1955 Schuyler made his first visit to the Porter's summer home on Great Spruce Head Island, in Penobscot Bay, Maine. During this visit Porter painted a portrait of Schuyler wearing a yellow button-down shirt, the first of Schuyler's many appearances in Porter's paintings. Schuyler developed an intense friendship with Porter for which "best friend"— Schuyler's description of their relationship—seems inadequate. Following Schuyler's breakdown in March 1961 and subsequent stay in Connecticut's Grace–New Haven Community Hospital, Porter brought him to Maine. Schuyler lived with the Porters until 1973. In September 1975 Porter died suddenly at the age of 68. Schuyler often referred to Porter as the one person in his life who never let him down.

Schuyler wrote his elegy for Frank O'Hara, "Buried at Springs," on Great Spruce Head Island, and references to the island, Southampton, the Porters, and their children abound in his poems. In the late poem "A Cardinal," Schuyler hears the bird whistle its song but wonders, "or is it that mimic/ Fairfield / saluting the day." Although Porter wrote only a few sentences about Schuyler's poetry, every one of them is illuminating. "He (Schuyler) tends," Porter wrote in reviewing Schuyler's *Salute* with prints by Grace Hartigan, "toward a deceptively simple Chinese visibility, like transparent windows on a complex view." Of Porter's paintings Schuyler wrote in a 1967 *Art News* review, "Its art is one that values the everyday as the ultimate, the most varied and desirable knowledge."

RIDENOUR, MARGARET DAISY CONNOR SCHUYLER (1890-1981)

Schuyler's mother, Margaret Connor, grew up in Albert Lea, Minnesota, and graduated from Albert Lea College with a BA in 1913. She worked at several secretarial jobs before marrying Marcus James Schuyler in 1922. He had his own newspaper in Downers Grove, Illinois, for which his wife also wrote. Their son, James, was born in Chicago in 1923. The family moved to Washington, D.C., in 1926 or 1927 where the couple divorced in 1929. Two years later Margaret Connor Schuyler married F. Berton Ridenour, a building contractor. James Schuyler took his stepfather's name and used it into his early twenties. Fredric Ridenour, half-brother to James, was born in 1933, and in 1935 the Ridenour family moved to Buffalo, New York, where James began junior high school. Two years later they moved to the suburb of East Aurora, New York. Margaret Ridenour F. Berton died in 1964 and in 1981 in East Aurora. Schuyler's poem "A Few Days" is, in effect, an elegy for his mother.

TRINIDAD, DAVID (B. 1953)

Poet. In 1982, on his first visit to New York City, Trinidad's Los Angeles friend Tom Carey arranged for him to meet Schuyler at the Chelsea Hotel. Delayed, Trinidad called to say he'd be late. A peeved Schuyler told him via Carey not to bother. Devastated at blowing the chance to meet his favorite poet, Trinidad did not contact Schuyler again until 1985 when he sent him a copy of his new book *Monday, Monday*. Schuyler liked the book, and a correspondence ensued. They met in person in New York in May 1988. Schuyler wrote a blurb for Trinidad's book *Hand Over Heart* (1991) praising Trinidad for "turning the paste jewels of pop art into the real thing." Schuyler dedicated the poem "Mood Indigo" to him.

WALDMAN, ANNE (B. 1945)

Poet and troubadour. A native New Yorker Waldman is a former Director of The Poetry Project at St. Mark's Church-in-the-Bowery and of the Department of Writing and Poetics at Naropa University in Boulder, Colorado. She has published a shelf of books and travels the world reading and singing her poetry. In the late 1960s Waldman and her first husband the poet Lewis Warsh kept an open house at the St. Mark's Place apartment for the poets and artists of their generation. During this time she got to know Schuyler who dedicated the poem "Wonderful World" to her.

WICKENDEN, DAN (1913–1989)

Edited Schuyler's novel *Alfred and Guinevere* for Harcourt, Brace. The two did not work together again.

WINKFIELD, TREVOR (B. 1944)

Painter. Educated in London, Winkfield returned to his hometown of Leeds while editing the mimeograph magazine *Juilliard*. He wrote Schuyler a fan letter; Schuyler's reply began their friendship. They met on October 10, 1969, when Winkfield, having moved permanently to New York City, drove north to visit Kenward Elmslie in Vermont, stopping on the way to see Schuyler who was then living with the Porters in Amherst, Massachusetts. At that meeting Schuyler slipped into a second-hand bookstore and came out with a book of Emily Dickinson's poems that he gave Winkfield as a welcome-to-America gift. Schuyler dedicated his poem "The wind tears up the sun" to Winkfield, and Winkfield edited the miscellany of Schuyler's writings, *The Home Book*, published by Z Press in 1977.

YOUNG, GEOFFREY (B. 1944)

Poet and publisher. His press, The Figures, published *Early in '71* (1982), an excerpt from Schuyler's diaries. Young remembers that early in their correspondence about the chapbook Schuyler wrote on an envelope, "Are you gay?" Schuyler dedicated the poem "Sleep-Gummed Eyes" to Young. In 1991 Young and William Corbett edited the volume of memorial tributes to Schuyler published by The Figures, *That Various Field*. Located in the Berkshires for over twenty years, Young can lay claim to being one of the most prolific small-press publishers of poetry in his generation.

Acknowledgments

When James Schuyler's literary executor, Darragh Park, asked if I might be interested in editing Schuyler's letters I leapt to say yes. Although I had edited nothing grander than little magazines, I had long loved Schuyler's work and did not pause to think for a second. Had I looked first I could not have seen how many people it would take to make good on my lightening yes. About halfway through the thirteen years necessary to complete *Just the Thing* it dawned on me that no one makes a book like this alone. My name on the title page would not be there without the help of those who follow. I am grateful for what they gave to this book and hope that I have served them well. Errors and omissions are, of course, my own.

Darragh Park sustained me from first to last. All who love Schuyler's work owe him gratitude not the least for the beautiful cover art that graces this and many other of Schuyler's books. His fellow executors Raymond Foye, whose sharp eye led to numerous last-minute corrections, and Tom Carey were quick to help when needed. John Ashbery graciously put his exceptional memory at my service. Kenneth Koch and Barbara Guest knew the answers to my questions, and they too were gracious. Anne Porter, Jane Freilicher, Bill Berkson, John Hohnsbeen, the late Morris Golde (whose "Anything for Jimmy!" attitude is shared by many) for his contributions to Schuyler's books, Charles North, David Trinidad, Larry Fagin, and Alex and Ada Katz responded with alacrity and in great detail to my calls for information.

Nathan Kernan, the editor of *The Diary of James Schuyler* now at work on Schuyler's biography, and Simon Pettet, the editor of Schuyler's *Selected Art Writings*, are in a category of their own. Without them no book. Both Nathan and Simon gave me full access to their research and provided valuable advice when I was in need of it. Most significant was their help with the footnotes, at which Simon was and is a demon. I think of them as my silent partners.

And a special thanks to Rene Ricard for his help with the footnotes, and to Raymond Foye, who taught me that footnotes are best terse.

Kenward Elmslie and Ron Padgett also deserve special mention. During the summer they are neighbors of mine in Vermont, where I did much of the work on this book. They answered my letters and telephone calls with no-nonsense directness and good humor. *Just the Thing* is lucky to have them as friends.

I thank the Rex Foundation for a generous grant that allowed me to do the first stages of work on this book.

When I began this book most of the letters it contains were in private hands. Only those to John Ashbery, Bill Berkson, and Larry Fagin were in university collections. This means that Harry Mathews, Trevor Winkfield, Donald Allen, Anne Waldman, Robert Dash, Peter Gizzi, Tom Carey, David Trinidad, Anne Dunn, and all the other correspondents Xeroxed their Schuyler letters and postcards and sent them to me. The late Joe Brainard was exemplary in this connection. A few years after Schuyler's death Brainard decided that his letters from Schuyler would make a great Christmas present. He had them typed, and he bound copies as gifts for his friends. The copy he gave me provided a base on which to build this book.

Harvard University's Houghton Library, where Ashbery's papers are; the University of Connecticut, which holds Bill Berkson's and Larry Fagin's papers; and the University of California at San Diego's Mandeville Department of Special Collections, where Schuyler's papers are housed, have my gratitude. Thanks especially to Richard Fyffe at UCONN, Lynda Clausson and Bradley Westbrook of UCSD, and to Rodney Phillips of the New York Public Library.

For various and sundry acts of friendship to me and to this book I thank Z Press, Clark Coolidge, Jonathan Galassi, Charles Bernstein, David Lehman, C. W. Swets, Jim Behrle, Richard Hennessey, Ange Mlinko, Roland Pease, Jr., Carl Little, Pat Padgett, David Kermani, Donald Windham, Claude Peck, Harry Carey, Jr., Ned Rorem, Alice Notley, Vincent Katz, Patrick Merla, Alvin Novak, Carl Morse, Edward Mendelsson, Duncan Hannah, Mark Hillringhouse, Douglas Crase, Michael Davidson, Fanny Howe, Nick Lawrence, Michael Gizzi, Angelo Toricini, Gerald Coble, Robert Nunnelley, Nicholas Altenbernd, John Gruen, Olivier Brossard, Susan Baran, Ed Barrett, Marni Corbett, Arden Corbett, Jane Gunther, the late Lawrence Campbell, and the late Joe LeSueur.

For the love of doing it, Connie Deanovich typed all of the letters Schuyler wrote in the 1980s. She deserves a paragraph to herself.

I made use, good use I hope, of Brad Gooch's biography of Frank O'Hara; John Spike's biography of Fairfield Porter; Justin Spring's biography of Porter; Porter's own art writing in *Art in its Own Terms*, edited by Rackstraw Downs; John Gruen's *The Party's Over Now*; John Bernard Myers's *Tracking the Marvelous*, *Tibor de Nagy Gallery: The First Fifty Years* (thanks also to Andy Arnott and Eric Brown of Tibor de Nagy); Joe LeSueur's *Digressions on Some Poems by Frank O'Hara*; Nathan Kernan's *The Diary of James Schuyler*; and Simon Pettet's *Selected Art Writings of James Schuyler*. A tip of the hat to Ephraim Katz's *The Film Encyclopedia*, fourth edition, revised by Fred Klein and Ronald Dean Nolen.

Five editors published selections from this book. My thanks to J. D. McClatchy of the *Yale Review*, Mark Rudman of *Tri-Quarterly*, Larry Fagin of *Sal Mimeo*, and Linda Norton and Jamie Robles of the *Five Fingers Review*.

Thirty-four years ago in San Francisco Michael Palmer pulled from his bookshelf a copy of *Freely Espousing* and handed it to me, saying, "I think you'll like this." Michael knew his man, knew both men, and that is where this book really began.

There is, alas, one hole in *Just the Thing*. Frank O'Hara's Estate repeatedly promised to send me Schuyler's letters to O'Hara but never delivered. The Estate did not explain itself to me nor did it tell me how many letters exist. Even if there are but a handful of letters, their absence is a loss to all who love the work of O'Hara and Schuyler.

I am fortunate to have been married to Beverly Corbett for forty years. She has the gift of never taking me too seriously, which, most of the time, cuts through my darker moments when the tasks I've set myself seem insurmountable. She has been a steadfast and wise friend of this book, and I am a grateful husband.

A NOTE ON THE INDEX

In creating the index, indexer Judith Watkins and I faced one big problem—how to index the countless references to Schuyler's intimate friends John Ashbery, Fairfield and Anne Porter, Joe Brainard, Ron Padgett, Kenward Elmslie, and a few others. These names came up so often that unless we added subheadings the index would be an unsorted jumble of page numbers. We looked at more than two dozen books where we found dizzyingly complicated ways of solving this problem—Elizabeth Bishop's *One Art* with its cumbersome and confusing subheadings—and bare bones solutions—Dawn Powell's letters. We decided on the simpler alternative. Thus Ashbery and company are listed only when there is a whole letter to them. We have, on the other hand included all references to important figures in Schuyler's life such as Arthur Gold, Darragh Park, and Frank O'Hara, who are referred to far less often.

—William Corbett

Index